THIS SCEPTRED ISLE: TWENTIETH CENTURY

THIS SCEPTRED ISLE: TWENTIETH CENTURY

CHRISTOPHER LEE

BBC WORLDWIDE IN ASSOCIATION WITH
PENGUIN BOOKS

This book accompanies the series *This Sceptred Isle: Twentieth Century*,
produced by Martin Weitz Associates for BBC Radio 4
and first broadcast in 1999.

Producer: Pete Atkin

First published 1999
Reprinted 1999 (three times), 2000

ISBN 0 563 38472 7

Published by BBC Worldwide Limited, Woodlands, 80 Wood Lane,
London W12 0TT and by the Penguin Group, Penguin Books Limited,
27 Wrights Lane, London W8 5TZ, England
Penguin Putnam Inc., 375 Hudson Street, New York 10014, USA
Penguin Books Australia Ltd, Ringwood, Victoria, Australia
Penguin Books Canada Ltd, 10 Alcorn Avenue, Toronto,
Ontario, Canada M4V 3B2
Penguin Books (NZ) Ltd, 182–190 Wairau Road, Auckland 10,
New Zealand
Penguin Books Ltd, Registered Offices: Harmondsworth,
Middlesex, England

Commissioning Editor: Sue Kerr
Text Editor: Lydia Darbyshire
Cover Artwork: Town Group Creative

Typeset in Bembo by Keystroke, Jacaranda Lodge, Wolverhampton
Printed and bound by Butler & Tanner Ltd, Frome, Somerset
Jacket printed by Lawrence Allen Ltd, Weston-super-Mare

CONTENTS

Preface vii

Introduction ix

Chapter One The New Century 1901–1909 1

Chapter Two The Road to Wars 1910–1919 60

Chapter Three The Roaring Twenties 1920–1929 120

Chapter Four The Coalition Decade 1930–1939 164

Chapter Five The Iron Curtain Falls 1940–1949 207

Chapter Six The End of Power 1950–1959 251

Chapter Seven The 1960s and Freedom 1960–1969 293

Chapter Eight The Winters of Discontent 1970–1979 335

Chapter Nine Thatcherism 1980–1989 380

Chapter Ten The End of Party Politics 1990–1999 421

Appendices:
First World War Diary 469
Second World War Diary 480

Index 487

For Alexandra and Victoria
who will span the centuries

PREFACE

As a child, I was in awe of my great-aunts and -uncles and of two of my grandparents, who had been born in the nineteenth century and had seen Disraeli and Gladstone. One had even curtsied before the 'Old Queen'. One of the great-uncles had been told by his grandfather what it was like at the Battle of Waterloo. Just imagine – there I was, sitting in front of the fire, being retold stories of Wellington and Napoleon and never tiring of hearing my Uncle Eliot say: 'And that's when Grandfather got a musket ball through his leg.'

Today, some of us will be the great-uncles and great-aunts for a new generation in the twenty-first century. If they want to hear, we will have our own stories to tell. When the century began, Britain was at war – the Second Boer War – and politicians were grappling with that war, with the future of Ireland, whether to enter fully into a European alliance, with the future of the education and social security systems, and with the reform of the House of Lords. Which is precisely how we are ending the century. We will remember Winston Churchill fighting them on the beaches; the first newsreel of the great nuclear mushroom rising into the sky; the bleep of the first sputnik in space; Margaret Thatcher rejoicing and rejoicing; and the moment when the front-room curtains were drawn and the television (always in the corner by the fire) was switched on for the first time.

But will the twentieth century be thought as exciting as the last? It is certainly the fastest-moving century ever. In the past hundred years more changes have come than during any equivalent period. Within the first decade we were caught up in the scientific whirlwind that was to blow through the next ninety years – communications. For this has been the century of communications. We have devised the science and implemented its technology so that today the whole world is in 'real-time' communication. We bounce signals from space to talk to friends in the next town, and we walk in the Somerset countryside while we talk to a back-packing cousin in Queensland. We are learning to live with never being alone. Yet, the advances seem to have outstripped our ability to put them to the best use.

The two major events of the twentieth century are obvious: the development of the nuclear bomb and penicillin. Nuclear weaponry may – perhaps inevitably will – decide our children's futures, but it is penicillin that is the greatest single discovery of the century. To give one illustration of its importance: penicillin was not available until the 1940s, but if doctors had had it in 1914, the losses sustained during the Great War might have been halved, at least. If we had not had it during the Second World War, the losses might have been doubled, at least. Today, penicillin and nuclear warheads are accepted as parts of our everyday lives, and perhaps that is the real – and sad – story of this century. Scientific and technological developments have been so rapid that most of us now take for granted discoveries and new technologies. We remain amazed (although not for long), but we are rarely surprised.

The great-uncle gap between the middle of the nineteenth century and the middle of this one is not nearly as wide as the gap between the 1950s and the 1990s, and it was to explain the changes of this century that this book came to be written. It is the natural sequel to *This Sceptred Isle*, which covered the period between the Romans in Britain and the death of Queen Victoria. As with *This Sceptred Isle*, this book is not written for academics. It is a simple chronology and explanation of the events seen in Britain during the past one hundred years. It is a book for people who want to put into perspective the transformation of Britain in the 1900s into the Britain of the 1990s. Many of us, for example, are confused about which prime minister did what and when; how we got into two world wars; what Churchill did apart from being a wartime leader. And there are many more such instances. The book is not, therefore, a series of themes. Each year is described individually, and it is easy to look up, say, 1926, and see the reasons for, and importance of, the General Strike, or even, for instance, to see what was happening in the year you were born!

We have not included lengthy passages, chronicling the details of the huge events. There are, for example, no battle-by-battle accounts of the two world wars (although there are two World War diaries beginning on page 469), but there are explanations of why those wars broke out and how and why the victors of 1918 caused the Second World War.

Above all, this is a simply told story of a century that we can all touch. It is the first century to have been recorded and filmed, and we have all lived through part of it. Nearly all of us will have known those who can tell what happened during each of its decades. This book is, therefore, a companion volume to the tales of our grandfathers, great-uncles and -aunts and our parents.

The style of the book follows the pattern of the BBC Radio 4 programmes and, while the content is mine, the book has been improved by the attentions given it by three important people: Sally Potter of BBC Worldwide, whose chasing kept it on course; Lydia Darbyshire, whose demanding and uncompromising copy-editing has made this a better book than the manuscript she first saw; and Ellen Parker, whose imaginative jackets on this, on *This Sceptred Isle* and on the tapes made the whole a handsome book, not to be hidden on the shelf but kept at hand, ready to dip into whenever there's the urge to see if twentieth-century great-uncles really do know what they're talking about.

Christopher Lee
May 1999

INTRODUCTION

On New Year's Day 1900 the British were still Victorians, and if we are to understand the nation at the start of the twentieth century, it is worth reflecting on the lifetime of the last Hanoverian.

Victoria, Queen of Great Britain and Ireland and in 1877 proclaimed Empress of India, had come to the throne in 1837. During her reign she had been counselled by, and had counselled, some of the greatest men in British political history: Lord Palmerston, 1st Earl Russell, Benjamin Disraeli, Sir Robert Peel and William Ewart Gladstone. She had survived them all. She had witnessed the Chartists, the repeal of the Corn Laws, the Rochdale Pioneers and the opening of the first Co-op. In her time the Public Records Office had been set up; William Fox Talbot had produced photographs; James Joule had propounded the laws of the conservation of energy; Charles Darwin had written *On the Origin of Species by Means of Natural Selection*; the first bicycle had been made; the clipper *Cutty Sark* had been launched; the *Daily Telegraph*, the *Daily Mail* and the *Daily Express* had appeared for the first time; Dr Barnardo's first home had opened; and Bank Holidays had been inaugurated. In Victoria's reign Charles Dickens, Thomas Hardy, Robert Louis Stevenson, the Brontës, Lord Macaulay, Gilbert and Sullivan, George Eliot and Anthony Trollope had produced the works that still epitomize the word 'Victorian' for many of us.

At the beginning of the new century about 41 million people lived in the British Isles,[1] of whom some 32 million were English or Welsh. There were about 4.5 million Irish and about the same number of Scots. In addition, two centuries[2] of empire building had given Victoria rule over about 6 million square miles, in which lived a further 300 million or so people all over the globe. There was hardly a port in the world that was not dominated by British freight. Fifty per cent of all merchant ships were registered in the United Kingdom.[3] Some 30 per cent of manufacturing imports abroad came from British factories, although this percentage was falling as the industrial capability of Germany and the United States increased.

---

1 W. Page (ed.), *Commerce and Industry*, Table of Statistics, Constable (1919).

2 By the Treaty of Utrecht (1713) Britain had gained control over Gibraltar, Minorca, Hudson Bay, Nova Scotia and Newfoundland. Although Britain had been longer in other countries – India, for example – these were the first places over which Britain achieved formal control by treaty.

3 British Chamber of Shipping.

The world's banks and trading institutions followed the pound sterling, one of which would buy almost five American dollars. Global trading was carried out in sterling. Domestic, commercial and trading goods and chattels throughout the world were covered by British insurance markets.

Although great progress had been made during the previous century in social and constitutional equality, the nation was still riddled with prejudices, which from the point of view of a century later seem bizarre. Only a member of the Church of England could be a professor at Oxford or Cambridge.[4] Educational restrictions on Roman Catholics in Ireland were so severe that it was proposed that a special university for Catholics should be established. Women did not have the right to vote. Access to education was limited, although Forster's Education Act of 1870 had laid the foundations for an efficient system of elementary schooling, and this was reinforced in 1880. However, schooling was compulsory only for children under the age of ten, and the Church of England strenuously resisted attempts at reform that would remove its right to be the one religion taught in any school.

The people living in Britain were relatively well off. The average wage in England was £40 a year, much to the annoyance of some MPs, who did not receive a salary. Most of the population lived on a cereal-based diet and, although better off than their parents' generation, were poorly nourished. Between 1893 and 1902, nearly 35 per cent of army recruits were rejected on medical grounds, even though standards were the lowest since 1815.[5] Eight out of ten people lived in towns and cities, and migration from countryside to urban living was a trend that had been well documented since the 1851 census. Twenty per cent of the nation lived in and around London (a percentage that would remain more or less steady throughout the century), and there were more than seventy towns and cities with populations of more than 50,000.

Farm production had dropped dramatically during the previous two decades, largely because prices had fallen. There was no single reason for lower prices. They came about because of free trade (trading without tariffs and import quotas) and the success of British engineering. British systems and engineers had opened up the great North American prairies, which were there because of the climate – ideal for cornfields. That same engineering flair had developed the high-pressure boilers that made the steam shipping industry viable, thus cutting freight rates, thus cutting prices, so making it cheaper to import than to grow.

Furthermore, Britain had long moved from an agriculture-based economy to an industrial manufacturing society that, combined with its financial services, especially the so-called international invisible earnings division (banking, insurance and so on), had meant that Britain was the globe's foremost international trader, although this position was threatened.

4 For more on this see Hansard parliamentary debates, 4th series, 1900, cols. 202–225.
5 Report of Army Medical Corps Director-General to Parliament, 1903; Cmd. Paper 1501.

At the coasts you would have still seen more sailing ships than steamers, although this was about to change in terms of tonnage. On the beaches, many trippers and holidaymakers dressed formally. It was common for men to wear hats and three-piece suits and the women long and full frocks, although the Rational Dress League announced that bustles and laced corsets were being abandoned. When they wanted to get to the coast, people travelled by train. Travelling further afield might cost a week's wages or more. Germany was still a popular destination, and a first class return to Hamburg on the 8.40 p.m. from Liverpool Street cost 56s 3d (about £2.81), while a second class return cost 38s 9d (about £1.94).

At home and in the towns, public transport was well established and privately run. London had had an underground railway system since 1863, and Birkenhead had trams as early as 1860. But in 1900 these vehicles were still horse drawn, and it was not until 1910 that steam, and then electric, trams replaced drays.

Motor cars were a luxury and would remain so until the 1930s, yet in 1900 the car was not an unusual sight. Automobile engineering had arrived. Karl Friedrich Benz had built the first petrol-driven car in 1885, and Gottlieb Daimler's first 'horseless carriage' had been produced in 1886 and by the turn of the century he was building a new vehicle that could travel at more than 50 mph. It was designed for a man called Emil Jellinek, the Austro-Hungarian consul-general in Nice. When Jellinek took delivery of the vehicle in April 1901, he liked it so much that he named it after his daughter, Mercedes.

Aircraft showed by the end of 1918 that the British could no longer rely on being an island for their protection. For the first time since 1066, British civilians were slaughtered by an invader, whereas continental Europeans had always been criss-crossed by armies. But in 1900 all this was yet to be found out, although the imaginations were fired when H.G. Wells published *The War of the Worlds* in 1898.

There were three main political parties: the Liberals, the Conservatives (who were Unionists) and the so-called Liberal Unionists. These were the men who had broken from the main Liberal Party during the closing years of the nineteenth century because the then Liberal prime minister, William Ewart Gladstone, had wanted Home Rule for Ireland. The rebels wanted to preserve the Irish union with Britain – hence they were known as Unionists. The Independent Labour Party (ILP) had been formed in 1893 to champion trade union parliamentary representation. In 1900 the ILP was about to join with like-minded organizations, including the Fabians, to form the Labour Representation Committee. Six years later, after the 1906 general election, this group would become the Labour Party.

The 1900 government was a coalition of the Conservatives and Liberal-Unionists led by a High Tory, the seventy-year-old Robert Cecil, 3rd Marquess of Salisbury. Salisbury had been prime minister since 1895, but now the government's popularity was failing, although its majority was safe enough. In October 1900 Salisbury called an election because his advisers judged that successes in the Boer War would give an increased majority and reinforce its mandate.

While British troops were perspiring and expiring in the heat of the 'dark continent',[6] many of those left behind were freezing and succumbing to a quite different epidemic. January 1900 was a bitterly cold month across the British Isles. The temperature fell as low as –3°F (–19°C), and the whole nation seemed to be sneezing. In London the death rate from influenza had reached fifty people a day.[7]

Within an average man's lifetime, every household would take for granted complex electronics, engineering and technologies, barely imaginable by the previous generation. The 1900s would be more complicated than any previous century. Technology, engineering and science made such advances that for many the new society became a more complex rather than a simpler place in which to live. The most obvious changes occurred in communications, both physical and electronic. Twentieth centurions would hear of events so quickly that sometimes they would have to cope with demands for answers before the questions themselves were understood or even before the right questions had been asked.

Since the late eighteenth century every moderate sized town in Britain had had its own newspaper. Many carried national and international news, although almost all of it was fed from the London newspapers and there was little independent reporting. By the start of the twentieth century newspapers had passed through two revolutions: money and technology. Apart from the printing processes, it was now possible to 'wire' copy from one city to another and therefore to produce the same newspaper in more than one centre. In addition, newspapers were now big business. In the 1880s they were all privately run. By about 1910 there were more than ten newspaper holdings quoted on the Stock Exchange. The *Daily Mail* was the leader in finding new ways of increasing circulation and advertising revenue, expanding into the regions with editions of its two London papers, the *Mail* itself and the *Evening News*. The *Daily Express*, which was launched by C. Arthur Pearson in 1900, was an attempt to copy the *Daily Mail*. Pearson failed, but the *Express* did not.

Public and political instincts could quickly identify with newspapers. Conservatives read *The Times*, the *Daily Telegraph*, the *London Standard* and the *Morning Post*. Liberals tended to read the *Manchester Guardian* and, after 1937, the weekly *Tribune*. The *Daily Mirror* was launched in November 1903 to cater for a new market, women, but within a few years it had changed tack and become a more generalist newspaper.

The most profitable papers were in the regions, and there were many of them. By the 1820s, for example, Scotland already had more than twenty newspapers. The major provincial cities produced long-lasting examples of good journalism and reasonable profits, and *The Scotsman* (first published in 1817), the *Manchester Guardian* (1821), the *Birmingham Post* (1857), the *Western Daily Press* (1858) and the *Yorkshire Post* (1866) were all flourishing by the start of the twentieth century.

---

6 More than two-thirds perished from disease rather than from their wounds.

7 *Illustrated London News*, News Round-up.

Little wonder that the British, at the start of the twentieth century, believed in themselves so much.

CHAPTER ONE

THE NEW CENTURY 1901–1909

1901

THE YEAR 1901 saw the end of the Victorian era: the Queen, who would have been eighty-two in May, died at half past six in the evening of Tuesday, 22 January. With the exception of physical catastrophes, it is usually difficult to be objective about the importance of a single event in a nation's year, but certainly the Queen's death should be recorded as the most notable occurrence in 1901.

Her passing, at Osborne on the Isle of Wight, took time but was apparently not agonizingly drawn out, as recorded by one of her biographers, Giles St Aubyn:

> Early that afternoon [22 January] she had another relapse. . . . Most of the family kept coming and going, but the Kaiser[1] never left, kneeling for hours by her bed and helping Reid[2] to support her. At four p.m. a bulletin was issued warning the world 'The Queen is sinking'. Shortly before she died, she held out her hand to the Prince of Wales and murmured 'Bertie'. Meanwhile Davidson[3] read her one of her favourite hymns, 'Lead Kindly Light'. At first she did not appear to be listening, but when he came to the lines:
>
> And with the morn those Angel faces smile,
> Which I have loved long since and lost awhile
>
> it was clear she had grasped their meaning. In the silence that followed, her children and grandchildren called out their names as if to arouse her from the eternal sleep into which she was peacefully drifting.
>
> While the Queen's life slowly drew to its close, Balfour[4] sat waiting in the equerries' room, contemplating the mountain of despatch boxes which had

---

1 Kaiser Wilhelm II of Germany, Victoria's grandson.

2 Sir James Reid, Victoria's physician.

3 Randall Davidson (1848–1930), Bishop of Winchester, sometime Dean of Windsor and a confidant of Victoria; in 1902 he succeeded Frederick Temple as Archbishop of Canterbury.

4 Arthur Balfour, who was standing in for his uncle, Lord Salisbury; he became prime minister the following year (see page 14).

> piled up over the past few days: impressive testimony to a lifetime of hard labour. Just before the end, the Queen suddenly raised herself and gazed towards the window. There was a look of sudden joy and recognition in her eyes. 'Oh Albert,' she cried, and sank back on her pillow.[5]

The funeral, which took place on 2 February, had been planned by Victoria herself. The ceremony was full of military pomp, which is not surprising, but what might intrigue is the image of the dead Queen. Victoria's black widow's weeds became a symbol of Victorian Britain, but now that she believed she was to be reunited with Albert, her mourning was done. Perhaps inspired by a thought given her by Alfred, Lord Tennyson, the Poet Laureate, who had once told her that funerals were moments for white purity, she had decreed that she should be buried in white. Her wedding veil was in place, and by her side was a cast of Albert's hand. In her hand was a photograph of John Brown, placed there, as she had asked him, by her physician, Sir James Reid; the family was apparently unaware of Victoria's request.

The coffin was taken aboard a small ship, the *Alberta*, which sailed between two flotillas of warships from Cowes across the Solent to Portsmouth. The next morning the coffin was taken to London by train and then to Windsor, where it was placed on a horse-drawn gun carriage. At that point came the only hitch in the proceedings: the horses kicked and broke their traces. Much to the army's fury, Royal Navy ratings rescued the carriage and dragged it along the line of procession to St George's Chapel. The navy has not given up this right.

The following day, a bitterly cold one but warm enough for snow, the coffin began its last journey to Frogmore, where Victoria was laid to rest beside the remains of her husband. Newspapers across the globe published long farewells, not simply to a monarch but to one who had become the most influential and, perhaps, the most powerful in the world. The novelist Henry James wrote that she had been a 'sustaining symbol', and the Tsarina said that she could not imagine England without her. But could her subjects contemplate life without her?

Certainly the national mourning was genuine and prolonged, but we should remember that the British did not suddenly step from being Victorians into the long hot summer of the Edwardian age. Indeed, the Queen's death did not change the lives of anyone outside government and royal family. With Victoria died the House of Hanover, the line of German Kings and one Queen, which had ruled these islands since George I, the Elector of Hanover, came to the throne in 1714. Queen Victoria's son became Edward VII, but he was not a Hanoverian because the line had to come through the father. Edward VII's father, Prince Albert, was Albert of Saxe-Coburg and Gotha, so the House of Saxe-Coburg was now on the throne.

---

5 Giles St Aubyn, *Queen Victoria*, Sinclair-Stevenson (1991).

The first child of Victoria and Albert had been born in 1841 in Buckingham Palace, and in that same year he became Prince of Wales. He had been baptized Albert Edward and was known to the family as Bertie. In the great tradition of Hanoverian Princes of Wales, Edward was a problem heir apparent. During the sixty years he waited to be King, he was considered frivolous and not at all suited to the heavy responsibilities of monarchy – that most certainly appears to have been his mother's view – but unlike previous Princes of Wales he did not plot against the crown.

The young Prince of Wales's education had been rounded. He was taught to some extent or another in the then three great universities – Edinburgh, Oxford and Cambridge – but apart from his devotion to horse racing, yachting, dancing, theatre, music halls and a series of celebrated mistresses, his interests were said to be largely directed towards foreign affairs, although this was more a reflection of his overseas travels than a deep understanding of his country's international interests. In 1860 he had been the first Prince of Wales to tour Canada. He also went to India, and there was a notable and long visit to Egypt in 1869.

Three weeks after Victoria's death, on a crisp and sunny St Valentine's Day, the new monarch opened the first Parliament of his reign. Although the crowds may have lined the streets of London to cheer on their King and Queen as they drove to the state opening of Parliament in February 1901, there was a less spontaneous response to news that was emerging from South Africa, where British troops had been engaged in the Second Boer War since 1899. Following the relief of Mafeking in May 1900 after a 217-day siege, the media had made Baden-Powell into a national hero, which was just as well because the high command in Africa was not conspicuously successful. Moreover, in its determination to overcome the Boers, the British army committed the most appalling atrocities – as, indeed, did Baden-Powell. He decided that he had to choose between feeding the people of Mafeking and feeding the Europeans, so he starved the natives, partly in a belief that they would choose to escape rather than stay, although he must have full known what the Boers would do to them if they fled. Certainly the native population understood the odds. They stayed. Emerson Neilly sent a despatch to his paper, the *Pall Mall Gazette*, describing the conditions and the tactics of Baden-Powell. The report was spiked, but a copy survived:

> I saw them fall down on the veldt and lie where they had fallen, too weak to go on their way . . . five or six hundred human frameworks of both sexes and all ages, from tender infant upwards . . . they fed like outcast curs. . . . Day after day I heard outside my door continuous thumping sounds. They were caused by the living skeletons who, having eaten all that was outside the bones smashed them up with stones and devoured what marrow they could find.[6]

---

6 Emerson Neilly, quoted by Philip Knightly in Raymond Sibbald, *The Boer War*, Alan Sutton (1993).

None of this reached the columns of the British press, although it most certainly reached both the newsrooms and the editors' offices. It was considered terribly important to maintain morale at home and, of course, the political stability without which it was impossible to prosecute a war – especially when it was going badly.

Lord Kitchener, the hero of Khartoum, had been appointed commander-in-chief in 1900 and had tried to negotiate some form of peace, but the Boers would not give in, hoping that the British would give them full independence. They carried on a guerrilla campaign against often ineptly commanded troops. In January 1901 Kitchener began what later tacticians described as a scorched earth policy – burning farms and clearing the veldt to destroy anything that could sustain an army. This tactic produced thousands of refugees, who were put into camps. These camps had few medical or sanitary facilities. Food was poor and in short supply. Sometimes a dozen refugees were put in small bell tents to escape the heat, the cold and the dust. There was not enough water, no bedding and, in some areas, rations were below starvation levels. The result was almost uncontainable disease and very high death rates.

The truth of these conditions was slow to emerge, and newspapers like *The Times* attempted to cover up the existence of the camps. The Germans, who had tacitly and sometimes physically supported the Boers, saw an opportunity to make mischief and criticized the British. Relations between the two countries were made worse when in a speech in April the Secretary for the Colonies, Joseph Chamberlain, declared that Britain's conduct was no worse than German behaviour at other times. Nevertheless, eyewitness reports began to touch the national conscience, and in June the Liberal leader, Sir Henry Campbell-Bannerman, publicly denounced the camps: 'When is a war not a war? When it is carried on by methods of barbarism in South Africa.'

By November 1901 almost 100,000 white and black families had been interned in camps spread across Natal, the Transvaal and the Orange River, and it is possible that as many as one in three Boers died in the camps. The conditions in the camps were appalling and inexcusable, but we should try to remember that the British commanders believed that the camps would be shelters from Kitchener's scorched earth policy. Like so many of Kitchener's ideas, however, the staff work had not been done. No one had thought through the way in which the camps should be run, and no one had considered how the Boers would be cared for – if at all. It is probable that no one understood that these were farmers who lived in open areas and were, therefore, even more vulnerable to the dangers of closely confined living.

Kitchener believed there was little room for any emotion that might get in the path of winning, but if he thought that the camps and his tactics would quickly bring the Boers to their knees, he was wrong. He was right in his belief that even if the war raised questions in the minds of political philosophers and economists, it raised few in the minds of the people. On the whole, the British believed the

Boer War was a just cause because the Boers had started it. But right and might failed to bring about a swift conclusion and the fighting went on until May the following year.

Britain was changing, but only slowly. A new set of statistics showed what Britons did for a living, and ten years later about the same number of people were doing the same sort of things. There were 229,000 coachmen, grooms, cabmen and drivers in the omnibus service, while 163,000 men worked on the seas, the rivers and the canals. There were 221 messengers, porters and watchmen. As many as 2,300,000 people worked on the land, many fewer than ten years previously, but the number of shepherds had grown to 40,651. In houses both modest and great there were nearly 2 million indoor domestic servants, 127,000 charwomen and 236,000 washerwomen, ironers and manglers. Their employers included 52,000 clergymen, 27,000 lawyers, 28,000 physicians and surgeons, and 276,000 schoolmasters, professors and lecturers.

If the numbers engaged in various occupations changed only slowly, Britain was about to witness a huge expansion in another area. In 1901 there were only 703 drivers, including cab and van drivers, on the nation's roads. By 1911 this number had risen to 48,000.

Britain had for some time been a relatively gentle place and, according to the statistics available, there had even been a decline in the crime rate. The Criminal Registrar's Report of 1901 observed that during the last half of the nineteenth century, the nation's manners had improved: 'the substitution of words without blows for blows with or without words; and approximation in the manners of different classes; a decline in the spirit of lawlessness'. This might seem odd when we consider the industrial changes in society and the migration of rural populations to the towns. Industrial conurbations were growing in England at a faster rate than anywhere in the world, and 20 per cent of the population lived in London.

Britain was not, however, a religious society, certainly not a church-going one. Less than 20 per cent of the capital's population went to church and those who did tended to be higher in the social scale. The rural labourer did not take his prayer book when he moved towards the better pay and shorter hours in the towns. A royal commission was discovering, or perhaps confirming, what many already knew:

> The churches have come to be regarded as the resorts of the well-to-do, and of those who are willing to accept the charity and patronage of people better off than themselves. It is felt that the tone of the services, particularly in the Church of England, is opposed to the idea of advancement; inculcating rather contentment with, and the necessity for doing of duty in, that station of life to which it has pleased God to call a man. The spirit of self-sacrifice, inculcated in theory, is not observed among, or believed to be practised by, members of these

> churches in any particular degree, and the inconsistency is very critically and severely judged. . . . The average working man of today thinks more of his rights or his wrongs than of his duties and his failures to perform them. Humility and the consciousness of sin, and the attitude of worship are perhaps more natural to him. He is not helped by calling himself a miserable sinner and would probably feel the abasement somewhat exaggerated and, in the same way, perhaps, triumphant praise strikes in him no sympathetic note.

This was not necessarily a trend. There is no evidence to suggest that the towns and cities had ever been particularly church going. There is evidence stretching from the eighteenth century that shows rural parishes more in fear of superstitions and the squirarchy than the lamentations of the parson.

The Church of Rome, largely a town-based mission, probably did better in built-up areas, especially among large pockets of Irish immigrants.

Just as social changes were fast enough to cause fads and fashions, so strategic thinking was throwing up possibilities of international confrontations that had not recently been considered. One consequence was the decision taken in 1901 to increase military spending, which might have seemed unnecessary at a time when the commercial instincts of the nation appeared quite capable of compensating for world trade shifts and new economic influences.

Britain's economy was indeed strong. However, there were clear signs that during the last three decades other economies had been rising, and this fact, combined with radical trends such as the re-positioning of the cotton industry and its market, meant that the nation was not disaster proof, as some had blindly or even arrogantly, assumed. In addition, the inability to bring the Boer War to a swift conclusion had rightly prompted forward-thinking observers to question the nation's ability to protect its overseas interests, interests that determined the British economy.

There was nothing new about these concerns. Unsuccessful campaigning in the Crimean War in the 1850s had led commercial interests to wonder if the nation's leaders were, in fact, leaders. Similar questions were posed in 1901. One main difference between the mid-1850s and 1901 lay in the fact that the inability of the then prime minister, Lord Aberdeen, to manage the Crimean War led to his resignation and the first ministry of Lord Palmerston, a strong and sometimes inspiring leader, who successfully ended the war. Nearly half a century on, however, critics of the government's handling of the Boer War were unable to produce a Palmerston. Balfour, who succeeded Salisbury, was not an inspiring figure, and the timing was wrong for a too young Lloyd George. No matter who had been prime minister, it is doubtful if he would have had different military advice – no one seemed to know how to fight the Boers in their own territory and against their hit-and-run tactics.

A second important difference was the economic climate. In the 1850s Britain was commercially invincible, largely because there was little opposition. By 1901 this advantage was fading. The Germans and Americans were now successful economic rivals, with increasingly international interests, which they knew how to sustain and exploit. Moreover, commercial nervousness in Britain was being increased by the changing social and political structure. The right to vote was extended. Educational reform, in spite of earlier Church and later Nonconformist objections, was gathering support and pace. Trades unions were now represented in the House of Commons, and the Independent Labour Party had been founded in 1900. The whole concept of leadership by right was fading – Salisbury, for example, would be the last prime minister to sit in the Lords.

By the first decade of this century Britain needed, but did not yet have, a more complex leadership aware that industrial and foreign policy had to recognize that this was an increasingly manufacturing-based nation, which had to abandon its isolationist position in Europe. Yet the manufacturing base that demanded a new style of leadership was a nursery for a social order that was determined to avoid the grim industrial environment. People who acquired great wealth through new ways of making money wanted only to get into the old system as quickly as they could. The British obsession with class meant that the newly rich industrialists sent their sons not onto the shop floor but into the public schools. Thus it was that the young men who would one day inherit Britain's industrial base received, almost exclusively, classical educations, unlike, say, their contemporaries in Germany, who were taught science and technology. The effects of this social phenomenon continued to be felt until the end of the century, but in 1901 there was little inclination to analyse the consequences.

By the first decade of the century, Britain was importing more than it was exporting, and it was only the money made within the banking and insurance institutions abroad that balanced Britain's balance of payments.

It is against this background that those who governed and those who influenced them began to feel uneasy about the nation's apparent inability to bring the Boer War to a conclusion. And these same men, born and educated to rule a manageable empire, quickly saw that empire threatened not only by the expansion of Germany, Japan, Italy and France but also by the increasing aspirations of the new King's subjects.

In the opening years of the twentieth century Australia was demanding some form of independence. Sixty years earlier Australians had wanted self-government. The 1850s' gold rush had increased the population, the economy and the demand for its own government. Apart from Western Australia, the five colonies of Australia (now known as states) were given the rights they wanted by 1860. It was not until 1901 that the whole of Australia became a single and independent dominion[7]

7 See section on twentieth century by Dr Kenneth O. Morgan in *Oxford History of Britain*, Oxford University Press (1993 edition). Canada had achieved a similar status under the British North America Act of 1867. The original Canadian provinces in the Dominion made a federation of what was then Upper and Lower Canada, New Brunswick and Nova Scotia. The

within the 'Commonwealth'.[8] The British Empire covered a third of the globe. The nations within that Empire were coming of age and beginning to identify their own interests, which were not always Britain's. It was a signal only faintly received in Whitehall.

The protection of the Empire and imperial interests had been complicated by the rapid developments in marine engineering. Steam ships had been around for a long time, but it was not until the 1870s that the technology to reuse steam through high-pressure boilers began to appear.[9] This advance in marine engineering meant that merchant ships could carry more cargo because boilers and bunkers were smaller and could go faster. Ship design produced economic expansion. It also made warships more mobile, faster, more heavily armoured (the power–weight ratio was easier to balance) and therefore more threatening – to everyone.

In 1900 a British shipyard had built the biggest ever warship for the Japanese navy. Japan had helped to suppress the Boxer Rebellion in China and was an ally. Alliances and national interest were now global, but in London cautious young Edwardians were reassessing the strength of alliances closer to home, especially future relations with Germany. Since 1714 the British monarchy had been German. The King's name was Saxe-Coburg, and the Kaiser was the King's nephew.[10] Through the line of the King's late sister, Alice, and her husband, Louis IV, Grand Duke of Hesse, the royal family included the Battenbergs – who altered their name to Mountbatten[11] – and Henry of Prussia.

Wives, mothers and sons have often plotted the downfall of their husbands, children and fathers, so even in the relatively sophisticated early Edwardian period, governments would turn on sensitivities of uncle–King and nephew–Kaiser. Earnest British attempts had been made for more than three years to bring about some Anglo-German pact.

The strongest voice in favour of an alliance came from Joseph Chamberlain, who had been appointed Secretary for the Colonies in 1895. Chamberlain had chosen this role rather than entering the coalition government as a social reformer, which his political reputation suggested might be more appropriate. In 1898, when many in Salisbury's Cabinet feared that Britain had drifted into isolationism, Chamberlain's efforts seemed appropriate, although he received scant support at Westminster and almost none from the prime minister himself. In the spring of 1898 Chamberlain had proposed a formal alliance, an idea that found some support in Germany, although not from the expected quarters. The Germans were

---

7 (from p.7) other provinces joined between 1869 and 1949. Newfoundland was the last to join.

8 'Commonwealth', as an official term of the group of states that had been part of the British Empire, was first used during the 1914–18 War.

9 Almost entirely based on the engineering of Alfred Holt in Liverpool, whose designs revolutionized commercial shipping and signalled the end of big sailing ships, although many were still trading well into the twentieth century. Holt's Blue Funnel Line became one of the most famous shipping companies of the twentieth century.

10 Kaiser Wilhelm II's mother was the Princess Royal ('Vicky'), who died in 1901.

11 See page 93.

debating huge expenditure on a new and bigger navy, and the Kaiser was obsessed with the idea of building a fleet for the high seas. It is likely that an alliance at that point would have undermined the Kaiser's argument for his fleet, a large part of which presupposed, correctly, that Britain could control the sea lanes in and out of Europe. The Royal Navy had just launched its first submarine and planned to build three 18,000-ton battleships. British naval plans presented a formidable threat to any nation with its own ambitions for naval supremacy, and as long as that threat remained, so would the political credibility of the Kaiser's naval ambitions.

Unsurprisingly, Chamberlain's 1898 offer got nowhere. In 1899 Tsar Nicholas II's foreign minister, Count Muravyov, convened a world peace conference, which was held in The Hague and discussed imposing limits on armaments. The conference achieved little, beyond establishing the International Court of Arbitration, and did nothing to allay British, and probably German, suspicions that a Franco-Russian axis threatened Europe.

In the November of that year Chamberlain made another fruitless attempt at a full alliance. Shortly after this, the Royal Navy boarded German ships suspected of running supplies to the Boers. The action played into the Kaiser's hands: increased German naval spending was approved by the government in June 1900.

That is one version of what was going on between Berlin and London. The second view suggests that the Kaiser was erratic and playing a double game, especially by 1901. Shortly after Victoria's funeral, the Kaiser told Edward VII that their two nations should be formally allied and that those in the British government who would not go along with this notion were 'noodles'. This put the King in a difficult position. He had no intention of meddling in government policy over such a sensitive and strategically important issue.[12]

With hindsight, it is easy to criticize the makers of Britain's foreign policy for not being more flexible or more subtle in the way it made overtures to Germany and responded to the often devious ploys of the Kaiser. Lord Lansdowne, the steward of that policy, was not the most imaginative Foreign Secretary, and he and Salisbury, not the enthusiastic Chamberlain, were easy targets for the Kaiser.

Henry Petty-Fitzmaurice, 5th Marquess of Lansdowne, was an Irish peer who had, until he opposed Gladstone's policy for Irish Home Rule, been a Liberal. He then became a Liberal-Unionist, then a Conservative. He had been Governor-General of Canada (1883–8), then Viceroy of India (1888–94) and, before becoming Foreign Secretary in 1900, Secretary of War.[13] He was criticized for failing to sort out the Second Boer War, but he was unlikely to change his mind about the Germans because they were openly supporting Paul Kruger and the Boers. Lansdowne's credentials were either hopeless or, considering the difficulties he had witnessed, ideal. Whatever one's assessment of Lansdowne, he was hardly a lone

12 Ironically, Edward VII had just made the Kaiser a field marshal in the British army.

13 Until the October 1900 election Salisbury had been prime minister and Foreign Secretary. After the Khaki Election Lansdowne became Foreign Secretary and St John Broderick became War Secretary.

voice. After all, the prime minister himself did not want an agreement, although he had not directly stopped Chamberlain from trying to negotiate one.

Salisbury's scepticism was reflected by the 'noodles' of Whitehall and St James's, who believed that they had good reason to be cautious of any overture from Wilhelm II. Most thought that he was an erratic man who did not command the authority of his own government. Moreover, the idea of getting into an agreement with Germany, or any other European power for that matter, was fraught with diplomatic and strategic danger. Would a formal alliance mean, for example, that each side was automatically linked to obligations that the other had made with third parties? If, say, the Triple Alliance of Germany, Italy and Austria-Hungary was threatened, would an Anglo-German treaty mean that Britain would have to go to the defence of one or all of its members?

These questions arose because Britain had pursued a largely isolationist policy, almost since the date of Nelson's victory at Trafalgar in October 1805. That victory had encouraged a general acceptance that Britain indeed ruled the waves, a dominance that grew as the Empire expanded. While Britain was strong at sea, the confidence in Empire was justified, which might appear to be at odds with an isolationist foreign policy. However, in the mid-Victorian period the truly powerful nations were European, and the most powerful was Britain. But Britain's interests were not European. Her investments, commercial and political, lay far beyond Europe and a distancing from continental European politics.

By the mid-1890s there was a clear division in Europe. On one side was the Triple Alliance, concluded in 1882, which was a complicated system of agreements protecting Germany and Italy from an attack by France, and all three partners from an attack by another party. On the other side was the alignment of France and Russia, which was such a powerful alliance that Germany could see the possibility of war in both directions.

The immediate result was that Germany and Austria-Hungary identified a future common enemy and closed ranks, and the Germans began to prepare for a war they believed inevitable. By the time Salisbury came to power in 1895 he had to face the fact that the Russo-French alliance meant that Britain's two likeliest enemies represented a formidable feature of his foreign policy and that Britain would have to revise the deployment and basing of her most successful military capability, the navy. The corollary of this thinking was that if Britain wanted to maintain her navy in the Mediterranean, Egypt was the only remaining option. Salisbury's admirals had but one idea: if Britain wanted to command the high seas, it had to have a fleet that was larger than that of the most likely enemy. If the enemy joined in alliance with another potential threat, the navy had to be bigger than the combined fleets of France and Russia.

No wonder there were those in Berlin who saw this logic not as an instance of Britain looking to her defences but of Britain building a threat that could be turned on Germany.

Hitherto, although Britain's actions were partly governed by what was happening in continental Europe, it was not taking an active part in those events. Moreover, if it had taken part, Britain would have needed to maintain a standing army in Europe – unless of course it was in alliance with a nation that already had a big military organization.

We can now begin to see why many believed that an arrangement with Germany was vital. Germany could look after Europe on the land; Britain could guarantee the high seas and, in so doing, make it near impossible for the Kaiser to justify his plans to expand the German fleet. At the same time, they would be formidable opposition to a Franco-Russian axis, and Britain would be protected from a future threat.

The Kaiser had believed that Britain and Germany could properly guarantee the peace of Europe and that a definition of Europe would extend from the Atlantic to beyond the Urals. European interests meant protection from the Russians and their ambitions in the Far East – an area of great interest to both the Germans and British.

Salisbury's government wished to keep the Russians out of the strategically and commercially important Far East. The Russians had ambitions in Korea, and the Japanese, who opposed the Russian policy, approached Britain as a potential ally. An alternative would have been a Russo-Japanese pact, but that was unlikely at the moment. The British policy of keeping Russian Far Eastern ambitions in check was in line with Japanese thinking, and towards the end of 1901 an Anglo-Japanese agreement was drafted for signature in January 1902. But here is an example of the Kaiser's flexible diplomacy. The Germans had suggested closer ties between Japan and Britain partly because it suited them to have the Russians believe there was something else to worry about, so Edward VII suggested that the Kaiser be told of the Anglo-Japanese pact. The Kaiser let the Tsar know about the treaty to prove how wrong the Russians had been in standing aside from criticizing British policy in Africa.

As the Kaiser played his double game, he failed to understand that the agreement between Britain and Japan would redirect Russia's interests towards Europe and the Middle East and so threaten Germany's own security and commercial interests.[14]

For all this double-dealing, there remained in London an awkward attempt to balance the imagined advantages of isolationism with the dawning realization that Britain was no longer the single great power. But an alliance with Germany remained a proposition with more against than for.

By the spring of 1901 the Foreign Office had not rejected any overtures, although it clearly believed them to be false, but nor had it given up on its own efforts to bring about some sort of understanding. Draft treaties were prepared

14 The Germans were building a railway to Baghdad. Although it was never finished, it signified the depth of German interest in the region.

to which Lord Salisbury added caustic memoranda suggesting caution. By the summer it was clear that there would be no pact. The German press were campaigning against the British concentration camps in South Africa, and Chamberlain, the champion of closer understanding between the governments of Berlin and London, made his attack in response. In December all hope of a workable and trusting alliance was officially postponed but unofficially abandoned.

The German ship-building programme was put in hand, and as early as 1901 many people believed that war was inevitable.[15] Britain's isolationism was coming to an end.

As *The Times* recorded, the last month of the first year of the new century 'witnessed the greatest triumph of applied science'. The Italian physicist Guglielmo Marconi built a 164-foot high aerial at Poldhu, on the Lizard peninsula in Cornwall, and sent the Morse code signal dit-dit-dit across the Atlantic. At the end of 1901 the century of communications had truly arrived.

Deaths
Benjamin Harrison (US president)
William McKinley (US president)
William Stubbs (historian and prelate)
Henri de Toulouse-Lautrec (French artist)
Giuseppe Verdi (Italian composer)
Queen Victoria
Charlotte M. Yonge (novelist)

1902

JANUARY 1902 opened in London with the sounds of New Year bells for the moment smothering the wheezing of fumigation bellows. The British capital was suffering from an outbreak of smallpox, which had started the previous spring. At first few understood the consequences, but by January more than 2000 people had died, quarantine ships were moored in the Thames, and houses were being fumigated. The population of Greater London had reached more than 6.5 million, and medical teams were finding it difficult to control the spread of the disease because, for reasons ranging from embarrassment to ignorance, there was too little public co-operation. Seeing what was happening in England, the French ordered everyone to have smallpox vaccinations.

15 Whatever the later assessment of Erskine Childers's character and motives, his novel *The Riddle of the Sands* (1903), which warned of a German invasion, should not be overlooked when reading about this period. Also, there is evidence that shortly before he died in 1898, Gladstone believed that war with Germany was inevitable.

The misery of disease was not to overshadow the political and industrial dramas of 1902: a coronation, a new prime minister, the end of the Boer War and the new Education Act.

First, there was the question of the coronation. Victoria had died in January 1901, and a year later was deemed an appropriate time for the new monarch's coronation. The ceremony was arranged for the last week in June, but the Earl Marshal and his fellow planners of pageantry had not allowed for the King developing appendicitis. Two days before the ceremony, his doctors operated and the champagne remained unopened until August. In July, as a sop to a disappointed nation, royal summer parties were held and half a million of the poorest people in London were given a coronation dinner paid for by the King and the breweries.

In May 1902 the Boer War came to an end when the Boers arrived in Pretoria to surrender to Lord Milner (whose miscalculation must be blamed for the length of the conflict) and to the commander of the British forces, Lord Kitchener of Khartoum. The war had lasted for more than two and a half years, during which 22,000 British soldiers had died, 16,000 of that number dying not in battle but of disease. There is no record of the numbers of Boer dead, but it is thought that at least 20,000 died in British concentration camps.

The settlement terms, known as the Peace of Vereeniging after the Transvaal border town where agreement was reached, were simple and predictable. Britain's annexation of Orange Free State and Transvaal was now unquestioned. English became the national language, although Dutch could be used in schools and law courts, and there was an undated promise of self-government. Britain was to pay for the rebuilding of the Boer farms that had been destroyed.

Perhaps the importance of Vereeniging was the modest terms of the settlement. It was an agreement that made no harsh demands and promised a reasonable reconciliation. Indeed, within four years, Transvaal had self-government, which was followed by that of Orange Free State. The Boer leaders, Louis Botha and Jan Smuts, were instrumental in maintaining that peaceful relationship with the government in London, and there was to be a relatively straightforward transition to the Dominion of South Africa in 1910.[16]

Although the Boer War was a staff college illustration of diplomatic futility and military incompetence, the government in London did not suffer. In October 1900, encouraged by Joseph Chamberlain and buoyed by good news from the Boer War, Salisbury was persuaded to call an election. From the colour of the army's new uniform, khaki, it was known as the Khaki Election. Salisbury was returned with a 134-point majority. If any political difficulty emerged, it was not the sitting Conservatives who suffered, but the Liberals. The Gladstonian rump and the younger radicals, especially the thirty-nine-year-old David Lloyd George, had opposed the war. The more conservative Liberals, among whom were Herbert

16 The four provinces of Transvaal, Orange Free State, Cape of Good Hope and Natal.

Henry Asquith (1852–1928) and Robert Burdon Haldane (1856–1928), had tended towards the government view – that Britain had not started the conflict – so it was the Liberal leader, Sir Henry Campbell-Bannerman, who suffered a split among his supporters and not Salisbury.

Vereeniging meant that Salisbury could at last rest. He had wanted to step down for two years, and he was now in his seventies. Born in 1830, the year Wellington was prime minister and Cobbett published *Rural Rides*, Salisbury had been in and out of government since 1866 and had succeeded Disraeli as Conservative leader in 1881. He was tired and far from well. The war was over and Salisbury could go; he did so within weeks of the settlement.

The new prime minister was his nephew, Arthur Balfour. Arthur James Balfour was a slim, urbane and detached character, with soft eyes and full, slightly drooping moustache, who seemingly summed up all the charm and sense of security of Edwardian England.[17] Balfour entered Parliament in 1874 when he was twenty-six years old. Twelve years later he was in his uncle's Cabinet as Secretary for Scotland. A year later he became Secretary for Ireland. He opposed Irish Home Rule and, by making concessions, made the petition for even limited independence unlikely. He called it 'killing Home Rule with kindness', although he showed little kindness in the ways he sanctioned tough actions against protestors, earning the sobriquet 'Bloody Balfour' after the Mitchelstown massacre of 1887.[18] Balfour's next job was Tory leader in the Commons, a similar arrangement to Disraeli's when he was heir apparent to Lord Derby.

By 1902, however, Balfour may not have been the party's first choice to succeed his uncle. It is sometimes said that Joseph Chamberlain could easily have been a candidate, had he not been badly injured in a cab accident, but Chamberlain was only in the Cabinet because it was a coalition; he was not a Tory. In addition, he was a Nonconformist, and it is unlikely that the Conservatives would have allowed a radical and a non-Anglican to have led them.[19] The other candidate was Sir Michael Hicks Beach, who had been Salisbury's Chancellor of the Exchequer, but nothing came of that, probably because Hicks Beach did not want the job. He had become disillusioned with many in his party and was happy enough to go to the House of Lords as Lord St Aldwyn.

When Balfour became prime minister he had been in Parliament for more than a quarter of a century and for much of that time he had been involved with the inner workings of the party. By 1902 Balfour had few illusions about the health of the Conservative movement. The Khaki Election may have gone its way, but the Tory Party, senior partner in the coalition, was increasingly uncertain and dissatisfied.

---

17 Anthony Wood, *Nineteenth-Century Britain, 1815–1914*, Longman (1960).

18 Balfour is said to have told the authorities in Ireland: 'Do not hesitate to shoot.' It is more likely, however, that this instruction came from Plunkett, the Cork magistrate.

19 Chamberlain resigned the following year to campaign against free trade, an issue that helped to bring down the Tories.

Questions were asked about the whole concept of government, but reassessments were not being brought about by any violent opposition to the way in which Britain was governed. It was far more that people were thinking of what was being governed than how that government operated. Society was more transparent than it had been during the politically formative years of the old guard. Education and relative prosperity played their part, and there was still an instinct for the eighteenth-century Protestant belief in national superiority.

Now there was, in addition, a wider spread of the population with an intelligent interest in their own and their nation's future. While as much as 70 per cent of the population was reasonably paid and not unreasonably nourished, this still meant that 30 per cent of the nation lived below the poverty line. The Labour movement, now called the Independent Labour Party, was beginning to be a home for this group. There were still legal restrictions on what a union could do, although workers' representation had made enormous progress since the swingeing Combination Acts of a hundred years earlier had banned combined attempts at wage bargaining. The failure of Robert Owen's Grand National Consolidated Trades Union and even the Tolpuddle Martyrs were beyond most living memories.

The commercial good times of the 1840s and 1850s had encouraged workers to unite. The Miners' Association came into being in 1841, the Engineers' Union ten years later, and the 'Chippies' (the Amalgamated Society of Carpenters and Joiners) in 1862. Six years later the Trades Union Congress, the TUC, was set up. By 1871 the unions had proper legal standing, and within a decade the non-craft, the unskilled workers, were being organized.[20]

Balfour understood the union movement, as well as the hopes of the growing and better educated middle class. And it was education that was in the forefront of his thoughts. Some believe that the measure that became known as the Balfour Education Act was one of the most important pieces of education legislation in the whole century. The work that was done to prepare the way for the Bill was under the direction of the man who was really the architect of the Act, Robert Morant, a civil servant at the Board of Education. Morant was not simply a civil servant given the task of drafting legislation; he was an enthusiast.

Secondary education was, in general terms, administered through three systems: the school boards under the Elementary Education Acts and the borough and county councils under the Technical Instruction Act. Morant had studied how secondary education worked in other countries, and he believed that the school board system did not work and could not be made to work. He engineered a judge's ruling during a complicated test case over a dispute between a school board and the London local authority. The court decision was instrumental in undermining the authority of education boards throughout the country by stating that the boards had no rights that allowed them to maintain day and evening

20 For a deeper understanding of the background see E.P. Thompson, *The Making of the English Working Class*, Victor Gollancz (1963).

classes for further education. This was the point Morant had wanted to make. His view was that internal politics in school boards were damaging and the almost universal bickering added nothing to the already inefficient administration. The court ruling effectively abolished the school board system, which, in turn, meant that secondary education, including the growing provision of technical teaching, would be brought under the control of borough and county councils.

There remained the position of the established Church in education. Church schools would now be maintained through the rates. The Church of England did not mind because many of its schools were unfunded, but the Nonconforming churches saw this as a subsidy for a decaying system. The Bill went through and became law by the end of 1902, but the debate did not end there. Lloyd George led the charge for his countrymen. Wales was almost entirely Nonconformist, so why should the Welsh pay for Anglican schools? Some local authorities refused to administer the system, and the government was forced to bring a Defaulting Authorities Act to make them do so. This clear-cut line of the debate was good for the Liberals, whose policies and ideals had become unfocused and muddled. Nonconformity gave them a unifying purpose.

It is easy to see that the debate's intensity reflected more than some petty desire for control of education. Teaching at all levels was moving at a pace never before seen. The two Acts of 1902 and an amendment, passed in 1903, meant that elementary schooling was now funded by ratepayers. Even schools outside this system, therefore – those once described as voluntary schools – were monitored by local authorities, which could, and did, lay down the rules of, for example, religious education.

With local control came a simple structure that spread from how and what children were taught, to the standards and the pay scales of teachers and to the numbers they taught. This did not mean the immediate righting of all the elementary education wrongs. There was not, for example, enough money to create facilities and new schools. Classrooms remained crowded and facilities few. But there was no regression. Every year, almost everything that happened in basic education was an improvement on what had been there the previous year.

Britain was leading the technological and scientific evolution. Electronics were becoming commercial realities instead of laboratory experiments. Radio signals would be heard across the world. Medicine was a developing science, not simply a caring profession. Education could no longer be regarded as desirable; it was a vital element in the social, commercial and industrial life of the nation. There were those, like Morant, who perfectly understood this.

Better education did not simply mean elementary teaching. If more children were taught to read and write, more could have some secondary schooling. This was not yet universal, but the numbers, through the grant-aided schemes, rose rapidly. In the decade following the 1902 Education Act, the numbers of pupils in grant-aided secondary schools, including the old grammar schools, more than doubled. By 1914 about 200,000 youngsters were receiving higher education.

The next step was too far for most to take because there were few universities at the turn of the century. Apart from Oxford and Cambridge, English universities had their origins in the nineteenth century, and London and Durham, founded in the 1830s, were considered old establishments. University reform began in the 1870s and was influenced not simply by a desire for education. Gladstone's reform of the Civil Service had meant that instead of patronage, open examination was the way to the steady and lucrative occupations in the nation's bureaucracy.

The spread of the new colleges through the country owed something to the standing of London University. As a teaching institute, London University was small, yet it offered examinations to external students and colleges. A remote college could give its local students the advantage of a London University degree. Consequently, colleges sprang up in the main towns and cities and, apart from the courses they taught, provided homes for those who might have gone to Oxbridge had they not been Roman Catholics or Nonconformists.

The next stage of the development came when first Cambridge and later Oxford started the teaching extension system of adult education from which, in 1903, came the proposal for a Workers' Educational Association. If anyone wondered why the WEA was needed and what it could achieve, there was no better model than the man who founded the organization, Albert Mansbridge. Mansbridge was born in 1876 and had left school by 1890. He got a job as a clerk, but he joined the extension classes running from King's College, London. This was an important stepping stone, and Mansbridge became an evening class teacher. His idea for higher education for working men was taken up and the WEA was born. By the time war began in 1914 a total of 145 WEA classes were up and running throughout the United Kingdom.

The advance towards further and higher education came from the existing colleges, such as the ones in Manchester and Birmingham, and out of this system came the first modern university. The colleges in Leeds, Liverpool and Manchester were grouped together and patriotically called Victoria University. The main difference was in the examination board. Until 1884 the colleges' students sat the London University external examination. Now the colleges could set their own papers.

Throughout this revolution women had to fight for a place in the higher education system. In 1848 Queen's College, London, had opened for women, but there was little else. By the 1870s there was the Girls' Public Day Schools Company (later Trust), based on the North London Collegiate School, opened by Frances Buss in 1850, but again the problem was a lack of higher education. Unless places were provided for young women, where would the women teachers come from?

The small provincial colleges and Victoria University pioneered higher education for women on the broader scale that was necessary for general education. In 1849 Bedford College in London became the first degree-awarding college for women, but the older universities offered little to women. In 1870 women in Cambridge were allowed to attend some, but not all, lectures, but in 1873 Girton College was opened. Four years later a Girton student, Agnata Ramsay, was the only student (male or female) to get a First in the Classics tripos. She did not receive her degree, however. Only men were allowed that. In 1890 a Newnham woman headed the mathematics class list. Again, she did not receive a degree. In 1921 women were offered 'degree titles', but it was not until 1947 that Cambridge gave women the same university status as men. If this was the slow progress at one of the great institutions, imagine the battle faced at the start of the century.

Birmingham University was opened in 1900, making Birmingham the first city to have a modern university of its own rather than a mix of colleges from other cities and towns. In 1903 the three colleges of Victoria University were separated once more and the Manchester and Liverpool schools re-opened as universities in their own right. In 1904 Leeds followed. In 1905 Sheffield opened. Four years later it was Bristol's turn to have its own city university.

In 1902, however, the main education debate was at a more fundamental level. The Act that Balfour introduced had one particular strand that Chamberlain could not support: religious instruction would be that of the Established Church.[21] As we shall see, the questions of religion in schools and the debate over free trade and tariff reform were without answers that would suit all sides and hold together the already stretched coalition government.

Deaths

John E.E.D. Acton, 1st Baron Acton (historian)
Samuel Butler (writer)
Elizabeth Cady Stanton (US suffrage leader)
Bret Harte (US writer)
Cecil John Rhodes (colonial administrator)
Charles Lewis Tiffany (US jeweller)
Émile Zola (French novelist)

1903

THE YEAR 1903 opened not with the discords of political in-fighting but the clear-tuned trumpets of Empire.

On 1 January India proclaimed its loyalty to its Emperor, Edward VII, at a durbar. Seated on a state-dressed elephant, the Viceroy, Lord Curzon, led a gold-draped and bejewelled procession into Delhi. When the line reached the saluting base, the elephant knelt and the King's man stepped to earth and thence to a gold and white dais, where he sat in viceregal splendour to receive the expressions of loyalty from dozens of princes, led by the blue-coated Nizam of Hyderabad.

21 The British debate was measured compared to what was going on in France, where the government was trying to ban religious teaching in schools that did not carry official approval. Many religious orders were refused permission to teach, and soldiers were sent into monasteries to enforce the policy.

If now this seems bizarre, we must remember that in 1903 there remained a pride in being part of this far-flung Empire, although that membership had its obligations. In February soldiers from the Punjab went to Somaliland to join British forces fighting Mohammed bin Abdullah – the Mad Mullah as he was called – who claimed to be the Mahdi and who continued to harass the British until 1920.

In London the government was deep in its own battles. The arguments over education and free trade were getting more intense, and Chamberlain's voice was stronger than most. The Education Bill had become law and Chamberlain was tied by its terms, but his natural political constituency was among the Nonconformists, who did not agree that public money should be spent on spreading Anglicanism in schools. For the moment, however, that debate would have to rest – free trade and tariff reform were at the head of the political agenda.

Free trade is the import and export of goods without tariffs and quotas. Placing active restrictions on trade by law and tax probably dated from the late thirteenth century when, because wool was such a valuable export, all English wool had to be shipped to a designated continental port, originally Bruges and later Calais, called the 'staple' port, and the shipping could only be carried out by members of the Company of the Staple. In effect, these wool merchants monopolized the export of wool. By 1617 the export of wool was banned, but by then the staple had fallen into disuse.

During the early seventeenth century more countries came to rely on commerce, and the general concept of what came to be called mercantilism was born. This was the origin of the 'balance of trade'. Mercantilists supported the view that Britain should be a net importer, and a system of variable duties – export and import duties – was imposed. The system was stifled by its own regulation, however, and in the eighteenth century Robert Walpole abolished dozens of these taxes and tariffs and moved the nation away from mercantilism. In 1776 the Scottish economist and philosopher Adam Smith published a slim volume, *Inquiry into the Nature and Causes of the Wealth of Nations*, in which he considered the consequences of economic freedom, and the movement towards freedom of trade began in earnest. Pitt the Younger moved towards further tariff reductions, and in 1846 Robert Peel succeeded in repealing the Corn Laws (the perfect example of trade barriers) in an endorsement of the belief that an economy should stand on its own feet.

This philosophy was fine as long as the world demanded British goods. By 1902 Britain held a third of world trade in its ledgers, but competition and changing markets were making inroads into the accounts, and a number of politicians began to see what was happening. Among them was Joseph Chamberlain.

Chamberlain had made his name as a social reformer, although as a member of Salisbury's Cabinet he had devoted his energies to colonial affairs, which were less controversial than domestic issues. He was thus better able to survive in the coalition government of Conservatives and Liberal Unionists. Almost a decade earlier, however, Chamberlain queried the value of free trade, and in 1902 he was among those who raised the idea once more.

Leaders of the self-governing colonies[22] lobbied Chamberlain at the Imperial Conference that was held in July 1902. They wanted the government to exempt them from paying the 5 shillings (25p) import duty on corn, thereby giving corn-growers within the Empire an advantage over non-Empire producers, a system known as Imperial preference. Chamberlain felt that adopting this scheme would not cost the British consumer anything and the government would not lose much revenue. It would be an inexpensive gesture to the colonies, which had sent troops to help Britain with her battles in Africa. It was not to be, however.

During the winter of 1902–3, while Chamberlain was visiting the four African colonies, Charles Ritchie, the Chancellor of the Exchequer, and Balfour scuppered any plans Chamberlain had for Imperial preference. The Budget announced in April 1903 abolished corn import duties altogether, not just for colonial producers. If no country paid tariffs no country was disadvantaged, including the colonies – which was not what they had wanted. They wanted preferential treatment, and Chamberlain still wanted it for them.

In May Chamberlain went to Birmingham, where he launched a campaign for a complete reform of the tariff system:

> I believe in a British Empire, in an Empire which, although it should be one of its first duties to cultivate friendship with all the nations of the world, should yet, even if alone, be self-sustaining and self-sufficient, able to maintain itself against the competition of all its rivals. And I do not believe in a Little England which shall be separated from all those to whom it should in the natural course look for support and affection – a Little England which shall thus be dependent absolutely on the mercy of those who envy its present prosperity and who have shown they are ready to do all in their power to prevent its future union with the British race throughout the world.[23]

Although his speech did not break new ground, it was in direct opposition to government policy, and it was effectively the signal for a change in understanding the relationship between those who governed and the governed and how government was exercised. The economic policies of government dated into the first part of the previous century. This did not mean that free trade was valueless, nor was it considered wrong in the sense that a Radical might find it unfair. But was not free trade classless? You got what your product was worth on the open market – there were no privileges in the corn exchange, the metal market or the

22 Australia, Canada, Cape Colony, Natal, Newfoundland and New Zealand.
23 In Chamberlain papers and quoted, at greater length, in Julian Amery's *Life of Joseph Chamberlain*, Macmillan (1969).

cotton dealing room. This was Gladstonian fairness: the ability to make something popular because it appeared to be fair.[24] Gladstone had promoted free trade, and Chamberlain was no Gladstone, certainly not on tariff reform. It was not easy to explain that taxing food was in the nation's interest, and the argument that increased revenues meant benefits for the electorate was not an easy one to make.

In the first decade of the twentieth century Britain did not have a welfare state, and the poor had to depend on charities. Chamberlain tried to develop the idea of old age pensions, and he talked about imposing tariffs and using the revenues for social reform: the British would get social benefits while the colonies received recognition for their support in the worst of possible times, war. This was not entirely true, but it certainly made sense as a platform for Chamberlain's reforms. If Chamberlain had been able to keep social benefits at the forefront of his campaign, he might have avoided the political schism that followed.

Chamberlain was still part of a coalition Cabinet in which the Conservatives were the majority party and the prime minister was a Tory. They were kept together by their opposition to Home Rule for Ireland – hence the title, Unionist – but it is unlikely that Chamberlain was trusted by anyone but his closest followers. Now he was talking about getting rid of free trade, which had been indelibly written into every code of Tory thinking since Adam Smith had published *The Wealth of Nations*. How could Chamberlain be propounding anything but a radical doctrine that should be avoided by his Tory colleagues in Cabinet? Here was the basis for the split in the government, although not all Tories thought that Chamberlain was wrong. Some of his colleagues, although supporters of free trade, thought that it was wrong for the times, and even Balfour could not see the point in continuing the nineteenth-century doctrine of free trade.

As the debate grew more intense, Salisbury, the last prime minister to sit in the House of Lords, died on the fiftieth anniversary of his first election to Parliament. He had been Conservative prime minister three times (1885–6, 1886–92 and 1895–1902). Salisbury would certainly not have even considered Chamberlain's tariff reform argument. So why did his nephew, Balfour? The answer may be that he was more of a political philosopher than a politician, or it may just be that he could always see both sides of an argument and therefore had no strong views of his own.

Balfour was not on Chamberlain's side, but he did see tariffs as a potential weapon against other countries that also imposed tariffs. He believed that tariff controls could be used as a weapon so that eventually all tariffs would equal out and the whole world would turn to a new form of free trade. Tariffs would thus stand sentry over the new system, and any nation that bent the new rules would face the threat of tariffs.

---

24 Peter Clarke, *Hope and Glory*, Allen Lane (1996), pages 24–5.

Chamberlain's arguments – that tariffs repaid colonial loyalties and would pay for social reforms in Britain – were easier to understand, but he does not seem to have considered the fact that the revenue collected from tariffs would not pay for pensions or social security hand-outs, particularly if the economic circumstances changed and more people become eligible for payments. The only clear thing in that summer's debate was that Chamberlain could no longer remain in government and argue his case. So in August he resigned.

Chamberlain's going presented Balfour with opportunity and a conundrum. The prime minister was neither a free trader nor a tariff reformer in the sense Chamberlain understood, so when Chamberlain resigned, Balfour took the opportunity to get rid of the hard-liners in the Cabinet, including Ritchie. In his place as Chancellor he appointed Chamberlain's son, Austen Chamberlain. This encouraged the tariff reformers but did not stop the splits, and it was on this subject that the MP for Oldham, Winston Churchill, a supporter of free trade, left the party the following year and joined the Liberals.

Typically, Balfour's supporters thought first and foremost about party unity. No matter what happened, the Conservatives had to hold together, and this was, of course, long before the days of party discipline. Some Tories leaned towards tariff reform, others towards free trade. (Party historians might usefully compare 1903 with 1996 and 1997.) Balfour continued to act as a mandarin rather than as an emperor and was little use to the future of the Conservative Party.

Chamberlain and his supporters felt confident, and the Tariff Reform League was formed with the aim of turning the colonies, the British Empire, into a structured trading bloc. The by-products of this would be new markets for Empire goods and social benefits for the electorate. Chamberlain, now free of Cabinet responsibilities, travelled around the country giving speech after speech, but always with the same message. It is worth remembering that there was no radio in 1903 and, as all music-hall entertainers understood, it was possible for Chamberlain to play twenty different halls in a month and make exactly the same speech.

The most competent of Chamberlain's opponents was Herbert Henry Asquith (1852–1928). Asquith was a self-made man, a Liberal, once Gladstone's Home Secretary (1892–5) and a man who had annoyed many of his fellow party members for supporting the Imperialists against the Boers (whom many radicals regarded as 'freedom-fighters') during the Second Boer War. Asquith now became a champion of free trade, cheering those of his colleagues in the Liberal Party who had doubted his credentials. He was marked as a potential leader, perhaps someone who would replace Henry Campbell-Bannerman, who had been Liberal leader in the Commons since 1899.

The debate centred on visual images rather than economic or political substance. Big and small loaves were displayed at the meetings. Supporters of free trade produced a large loaf and said that was what free trade meant for the electorate while a small loaf was used to show what they would get if they voted for tariff reform. The arguments in favour of Imperial preference (which were not easily illustrated with loaves and buns) all but disappeared, but by the end of the year there was sufficient reason to believe that this single issue would decide the fate of the government. Curiously, Chamberlain himself appeared to believe that it was the Education Act that would eventually bring down Balfour's administration.

Although neither the education nor tariff reform debates went away, it is doubtful if the British public thought them the most important issues of 1903. There was plenty to attract and hold attention elsewhere.

In October an organization was founded in Manchester by Mrs Emmeline Pankhurst and her daughter, Christabel. Called the Women's Social and Political Union, its slogan was 'Deeds not Words'. The group was not yet called suffragettes (that was a tag given them in 1906 by the *Daily Mail*), but no matter what its name, the modern movement was on the march.

A few days later another radical group met, this time in London. Led by Vladimir Ilyich Ulyanov, better known as V.I. Lenin (1870–1924), it was called the Russian Social Democratic Labour Party and was known as the Social Democrats. Lenin's supporters, the Bolsheviks (the Russian word for majority), decided that there had to be a revolution in Russia but that instead of a general uprising it should be organized on a military staff basis.

At home people went about their everyday business in more mechanical ways than their fathers had dreamed about. In London a new street, Kingsway, had just been named after Edward VII. The signposts were hardly dry before the thoroughfare was clogged, and a royal commission inquired into the seemingly continuous traffic jams in the nation's capital. Public transport was seen by some as an answer, and the first electric tram took to the streets with the King on board to show its importance.

But there was no stopping the motor car. Oldsmobile was making 4000 automobiles a year, and a consortium formed the Ford Motor Company, with Henry Ford as its chief engineer.[25] In Parliament the need to regulate the numbers of motor cars was taken seriously enough for a Bill to be introduced that would make it necessary to register a car and give it a number, although suggestions that the government should introduce driving tests were rejected.

In America Wilbur and Orville Wright took off from Kitty Hawk, North Carolina, in the first successful powered flight. They made four trips, none lasting for more than a few seconds, but heavier than air travel had arrived. At the other extreme, in Paris pedal power reigned. Henri Desgrange's brainchild for a grand bicycle competition set off in tremendous style. Sixty competitors raced south from Paris to Lyons, Marseilles, Toulouse, Bordeaux and Nantes and back to Paris. Only twenty survived the nineteen days' cycling, but the Tour de France was born.

25 Ford owned only 25 per cent of the shares at that time.

At the other side of the world, in March 1903 Robert Falcon Scott, Ernest Shackleton and Edward Wilson were trekking further south than any men had done. They reached 80 degrees south, even though their dogs had died and they were forced with very crude equipment to pull their own sledges there and back to McMurdo Sound.

This was the also the year in which the first western was made – a 21-minute film called *Kit Carson* – and the biggest hit on Broadway was a musical called *The Wizard of Oz*.

If these triumphs promised much, elsewhere man was proving that his instinct for violence and crude regard for civilization was as strong as ever. On Easter Day between forty and fifty Jews were murdered and 'some hundreds' of Jewish women were raped at Kishinev in Russian Bessarabia. The attacks came after the murder of a Christian child the previous winter. Rumour had it that he was murdered by Jews, although later evidence suggested that the authorities had spread that rumour. Tsar Nicholas II had done little to protect the 5 million Jews living in Russia, and there is much evidence of officially inspired persecution.

In August the future of Zionism and a homeland for Jews was discussed at the Zionist Congress in Basle. The British suggested Uganda, offering the thought that it was one of the few places that protection from persecution could be guaranteed. But the main opposition to the idea came from the representatives from Kishinev – the scene of the killings mentioned above. They said that as Palestine was their biblical homeland, nowhere else would do. The Uganda plan was rejected, although many Jews at the Basle conference had thought it sensible.

Also in April the spectre of yet another Balkan war appeared. The Turks mobilized more than 200,000 troops for Macedonia as civil unrest against Turkish authority grew. Bulgarians and Albanians were bent on getting rid of Turkish rule, and it was a Bulgarian group that killed 165 men, women and children in one attack on a Muslim village close to Monastir (now Bitola). In the same region, two months later, the King and Queen of Serbia were assassinated in their palace in Belgrade. But this news was of hardly any significance by September, when the Turks in Macedonia showed their determination to put down any attempt by the Macedonia Revolutionary Committee to rise against the Sultan's rule. Returning to the villages around Monastir, the Turkish troops systematically murdered some 50,000 men, women and children. The Balkans were living up to their reputation as a centuries-old killing ground.

It was against this background that the British government announced that it was to build a new naval base in the Firth of Forth. The distance from the base to Germany was not a day's steaming. In spite of the talk of treaties and agreements of understanding, there was every sign that, as Gladstone had privately observed, the construction of the new German fleet made war between the two Teutonic cousins inevitable.

Deaths
Robert Cecil, 3rd Marquess of Salisbury (politician)
Richard Jordan Gatling (US inventor)
Paul Gauguin (French artist)
Camille Pissarro (French artist)
Herbert Spencer (philosopher)
James McNeill Whistler (US artist)

1904

THE YEAR opened to tensions between Japan and Russia. The Japanese wanted to protect their interests in Manchuria, where the Russians opposed them. The Russians had ambitions in Korea, where the Japanese opposed them. Both sides had sent troops into the disputed areas and looked set on confrontation. A diplomatic offensive was mounted to avoid what would be war in an important strategic and commercial area and one likely to involve other states. In February 1904 a conference was held in St Petersburg, but no solution to the differences could be found, particularly as the Russians believed themselves to be militarily superior.

As we have seen, Britain's isolationist tendency was based partly on a suspicion that alliances with one country could drag the nation into a war with a third country with whom it had no particular quarrel. Towards the end of January 1904 it seemed that the differences between Japan and Russia might not be settled, and Britain and France were drawn together. France had a treaty with Russia; Britain had one with Japan; and Germany had suspected for some time that a Franco-Russian axis posed a threat to its own security.

In April the French and British governments signed the Entente Cordiale, a term that almost immediately established itself in the diplomatic language of the twentieth century and that was the basis for the Anglo-French alliance in the First World War. The agreement to maintain cordial relations supposedly ended the differences between France and Britain over colonial territories in Africa. For Britain it meant much more, however. The Entente was not meant as a signal that Britain would join the dangerous alliances of continental Europe, but it was a sign that the foreign secretary, Lansdowne,[26] realized that isolationism was drawing to a close. It was Lansdowne who had negotiated the Anglo-Japanese Treaty of 1902 and the Entente Cordiale itself. Moreover, his long-term aim was to protect Britain from a war against the Germans, who in spite of their offers of alliance, were developing a large blue water fleet and therefore an expansionist policy that could threaten Britain's interests.

26 Henry Petty-Fitzmaurice, 5th Marquess of Lansdowne, was an Irish peer and, following the death of Salisbury, the Conservative leader in the Lords between 1903 and 1916. See page 9.

Events in Korea and Manchuria, on the other side of the globe and outside the empire, could have repercussions in twentieth-century Britain, and it is against this background that on 1 February 1904 Britain and France agreed that neither would get involved should the St Petersburg talks break down.

It quickly became clear that the Japanese had anticipated failure in St Petersburg. At midnight on 8–9 February Japanese boats fired the relatively new weapon system, the torpedo, at Russian ships moored in Port Arthur in northeast China. Two Russian battleships and a cruiser were crippled, blocking the main channel into port so that the Russians could not put to sea. The Japanese struck at two more Russian ships on the west coast of Korea and captured seven others. The Japanese had command of the sea and within months had turned about the Russian army based in Manchuria, which had crossed into Korea. Without its naval power and with an army strung out and almost back in its base, the Russians could do little to stop the Japanese landing in Korea. In April the Russian Far Eastern flagship, the *Petropavlovsk*, was mined off Port Arthur and went down with nearly 800 men, including Admiral Makarov, the commander-in-chief. The biggest loss to the Japanese occurred when a Japanese battleship hit a Russian mine and sank with 400 men on board. The only other major loss for the Japanese navy was when more than 200 sailors perished after two Japanese ships rammed each other in dense fog.

These events on the other side of the world were important to Britain because it was inevitable that an escalation of the war would spread elsewhere. The Russians had no option but to reinforce their Far Eastern fleet – or what was left of it. That meant sending ships from the Baltic. When the Russian flotilla got into the North Sea it ran into mist off the Dogger Bank. The nearest Japanese vessel was across the other side of the world, but given the existence of the Anglo-Japanese treaty, we might imagine the discipline and the nervousness of a fleet sailing through waters that were nominally commanded by a potential ally of Japan's.

The conditions were poor, and when Russian look-outs spotted vessels off the Dogger Bank on 21 October, they assumed they were hostile warships and opened fire. In fact, they had seen British fishermen – one trawler was sunk and two fishermen were killed. The Russians claimed that two Japanese torpedo boats, of the type that had started the whole war, were hiding among the fishermen, and they refused to apologize. Public furore in Britain over what was called the Dogger Bank Incident was considerable. In the end the Russians were forced to agree to a tribunal of investigation and to pay compensation claims. Meanwhile, the Russians, in what was becoming the biggest war for more than thirty years, were being humiliated.

There was another perspective for the European onlookers of this first exhibition of twentieth-century warfare. The Japanese success showed that warfare was now a science and not an art form to be executed by cavalry officers, who continued to believe that the greatest fighting vehicle was a horse, whose days were numbered if not over. The tactical lessons on display in the Far East could not be immediately adapted for the British military system – no army, navy or, later, air force could change quickly – but changes in the army and navy were taking place. Efforts were being made to bring it from the mid-nineteenth century into some order that corresponded to the realities of planning for war as the best way of defence.

The Russo-Japanese War did not trigger British military reform, but it endorsed the need for it. Shortly after he became prime minister, Balfour appointed himself chairman of the Committee of Imperial Defence, a group of ill-informed Cabinet ministers. Balfour brought on board admirals, generals, colonial service officers and, wisely, the Chancellor of the Exchequer. In those days there were no such things as Cabinet minutes, but now the Committee of Imperial Defence had, thanks to Balfour, a permanent secretary and notes were kept of the committee's discussions. Here was the basis for reform. A sub-committee set about the task of convincing a hidebound establishment that if Britain were to avoid the sort of débâcle seen in Africa and to prepare for war in Europe, change had to begin at the top.

The sub-committee of three consisted of Colonel Sir George Clarke (later Lord Sydenham); Admiral Sir 'Jackie' Fisher, the often controversial First Sea Lord, who gathered around himself a group of like-minded followers known as the Fishpond; and Lord Esher, who was a close friend of the King. In February 1904 they alarmed many people in Whitehall by proposing that the army should follow the navy's example and have a board, which would be called the Army Council. This would mean getting rid of the post of commander-in-chief in the army, and one person who was not happy with the plan was the commander-in-chief, Lord Roberts, who had led the campaign in the Boer War. But the committee's proposal was voted through, and Roberts was pensioned off by a grateful nation.

But the committee had not gone far enough. What the army really needed was a proper general staff, and what the government needed was a committee of the Chiefs of Staff. That was not to come until the 1920s, and its effective structure was not developed until the 1990s. Such lack of foresight in the early 1900s should not be overly criticized, for this was a navy and army scarcely out of the nineteenth century. It was a navy that dreamed still of Trafalgar and an army that based its mobility on the only reliable vehicle available to it – the horse. It was, in fact, a perfect example of how we should judge the times as they were and not with all the apparent sophistication and hindsight now at hand.

The most radical reform took place in that most conservative of services, the Royal Navy. Advances in naval engineering and science had been faster than most sailors could imagine, but this was a navy that still thought in terms of sailing ships and one in which most senior officers and ratings had trained in sailing vessels. In the early 1900s the advances in ship construction, boiler and steam reciprocating engineering and mechanical inventiveness were outstanding. The first computers (mechanical ones) were, for example, already in place for gunnery range finding. Such innovations meant that the effects of advanced technology were likely to be felt in the navy sooner than in the army – but not sooner than in the German navy. Admiral Fisher understood this perfectly.

In 1904 Fisher became the First Sea Lord. Within six years he had scrapped more than 150 vessels, overhauled the training system and redeployed Britain's naval strength to counter the growing German naval threat. He oversaw the design of a new era of giant battleships, the Dreadnought class, the first one of which was launched in 1906, rendering 'all earlier battleships obsolete'.[27]

Fisher's position was strengthened by the appointment of a new minister, the Earl of Cawdor, who was brought in as First Lord of the Admiralty[28] from outside the Cabinet. Cawdor had first sat as an MP (as Viscount Emlyn) in 1874, although he had not been much noticed. His reputation was made as the imaginative and visionary chairman of the Great Western Railway. The Fisher–Cawdor team was a good one, although it was short lived.

HMS *Dreadnought* had been built quickly and secretly. She was launched in February 1906 and completed by October – a remarkable ship-building achievement in any age. If anyone doubted the significance of the German naval plan, they had only to note that as soon as the Germans learned about *Dreadnought*, they began widening the Kiel Canal so that they could bring through their own, larger, vessels into the North Sea. This was an enormous undertaking and diverted energy and resources that the Germans could hardly afford. But the Germans had the incentive: if the British were building, so must they.

Cawdor and Fisher planned to lay down four Dreadnought class battleships every year, a scheme that put Britain far ahead of the German fleet-building programme and, on paper at least, was the perfect deterrent to war. They had no doubts that the growing German fleet had a single objective: to defeat the Royal Navy and therefore Britain. Without the fleet, Britain was isolated from its overseas interests. But big ships alone could not protect global responsibilities, so those ships had to be based where they could do real damage to the enemy, not just snipe around the edges. Three new commands were set up: the Mediterranean, the Atlantic and the Channel. The plan that Fisher and Cawdor set in train looked very positive in 1904, but two years later, there was a new government and the building programme was set aside. Once the programme lost way, so did its deterrent value. The curtailing of the Dreadnought programme allowed an advanced German naval plan that encouraged them to believe that any coming war was winnable.

Balfour may have been able to reform the army, but he failed to act on party discipline, and the increasingly divisive debate over tariff reform and free trade

---

27 Captain S.W. Roskill RN, *The Strategy of Sea Power*, Collins (1962), page 101.

28 The First Lord is the naval minister, a civilian. The First Sea Lord is the uniformed officer in charge of the navy. The nomenclature is complicated by the rank of Admiral of the Fleet. An Admiral of the Fleet never officially retires, but it is the First Sea Lord who is the active service, senior officer.

continued. Furthermore, he was about to lose one of his brightest MPs, Winston Churchill. When the issue of abandoning free trade arose, Churchill the radical was there to oppose. He 'emerged at once as one of the most vociferous supporters of free trade,'[29] and his support was genuine, not merely a ploy for political campaign medals. The Conservative Association at Oldham was so alarmed by his speeches against the prime minister Balfour and by his plan to form a local free trade group that it told him it no longer had confidence in him and he could not be their candidate at the next election.

Churchill was now taking advice from the rising star of the Liberals, David Lloyd George, and openly talking about crossing the floor. The battle over free trade had brought him to the conclusion that the Liberals were about to be crushed between big business and organized labour and would not survive the pressure. Equally depressing, or so he thought, was the likelihood that the Conservatives would simply become the party of capitalism and therefore be one-dimensional, with all that would mean to the electorate. In the Commons on 2 March 1904 he observed:

> It was always found in the past to be a misfortune to a country when it was governed from one particular point of view, or in the interests of any particular class. . . . Every country ought to be governed from some central point of view, where all classes and all interests are proportionally represented . . . I venture to think that even in modern days that principal to some extent extends to our government.

Churchill's position could not now be doubted. He supported a censure motion against his own government (against the British use of Chinese labour in South Africa) and Balfour would take no more. On 29 March, as Churchill rose to speak, the prime minister got up from the front bench and left the Commons.

On 18 April Churchill agreed to stand as free trade candidate for Northwest Manchester and to be supported by the Liberals. This was the young radical, a man who would never be confounded by the party and its ways, but his final speech during a trade union debate on 22 April was a sad affair. He became incoherent and sat down without finishing. It is not unnatural to recall the moment when his father, Lord Randolph Churchill, ended his political career in the House in similar confusion – except of course, the younger Churchill's career had hardly started. Never again did he go into any chamber without pages of notes marked to the last ad lib.

On 31 May Churchill finally crossed the floor and took his seat on the Liberal benches next to Lloyd George and, poignantly, in the place in which his father had sat.

★

29 Martin Gilbert, *Churchill: A Life*, Heinemann (1991), page 154.

Away from Whitehall there was far more interest in the everyday novelties of life than in the possibilities of war with Germany or the intricacies of the debate over free trade.

On 12 March the first mainline electric train went into service between Southport and Liverpool. For those less impressed with trains than motor cars Henry Royce displayed his first motor car, and on 4 May he went into partnership with Charles Rolls. By 1904 there were so many cars that number plates were introduced. But with more cars came congestion – there were 3000 cab drivers in London alone – and a Board of Trade commission began to look for ways to solve London traffic jams. Motor cars were no longer simply for the rich. There was already a motor show at Olympia, and Chas. Jarrott & Letts, which had car showrooms in Great Malvern Street off Regent Street in the West End of London, were selling a Standard 7 motor car for £150. It looked what it was: a self-powered, open-topped horseless carriage, with a leather bench seat and dashboard.

Reliability became a watchword. The argument against the car was that it would not only break down but that there would be no one about who knew how to fix it. In 1904 the triumph of motor manufacturers was the reliability test. The Siddeley Car Company claimed that its new 10 horse power model would provide 5000 miles of trouble-free driving. Convenience rather than exclusivity became a selling feature, and an advertisement appeared that insisted that the car was the best means of getting out of the cities because the driver and passengers did not have to wait for a train but could go direct to their destinations. Here was a message that was to last a hundred years.

Car theft was not unknown, but thieves were far more interested in spare parts. For those undertaking long car journeys in this first decade of the century there were few garages and even fewer parts to be found. Until the 1930s it was common for a motorist to take a host of spares including cans of petrol.

The Metropolitan Police had a new scheme to help it catch thieves. Scotland Yard had started its fingerprint section, and by the end of 1904 had a collection of 70,000 prints. These, the police said, would revolutionize not so much the detection but the conviction of burglars.

Cheating of a different kind, which sadly shows how little is new, took place at the 1904 Olympic Games, which were held in St Louis, Missouri. One of the marathon runners was disqualified when it was discovered that he had thumbed a lift. But there was much celebration at the gallantry of the winner, the English-born Tom Hicks, who was so distressed during the 3½-hour run in temperatures of around 90°F (32°C) that he kept himself going on strychnine and brandy.

Those who wanted to spread the good – or bad – news had taken to writing letters. More than 2.5 million letters were delivered in Britain in 1904, and the British had caught the latest continental European craze: the postcard. In 1904 alone the British sent more than 600,000 cards to each other.

⋆

It was inevitable that there would, in general terms, be more of everything, and there were now more people and more houses. The population was increasing at a rate of about 1 per cent a year, and the migration from the countryside to the more regular work and higher wages in urban areas continued. Britain now had more of what had been newly termed conurbations than any other country in Europe. Congestion was beginning to overwhelm town planners, hence the idea of the Garden Cities, of which the first, Letchworth in Hertfordshire, had been begun the previous year.

The increased populations in the commercial and industrial towns faced an everyday hazard that simply could not be avoided: pollution. The growth in the number of houses in London, in particular, combined with increased numbers of minor industries and power stations, all relying on coal, meant that the capital was so polluted that a ginger group, the Coal Smoke Abatement Society, wanted London to be declared a smokeless zone.

Even though the signs of increased prosperity were evident on all sides, it should not be forgotten that 250,000 people were living in workhouses and that more than 800,000 were on poor relief. If we look at the statistics for, say, the previous fifty years, we can see that more people were officially paupers than at any time since the 1880s. This meant that about one in every forty people in England and Wales was 'on the Parish'. Similar statistics in the eighteenth century show that times were hardest in the same places. At the beginning of the twentieth century there were still, in percentage terms, more poor in East Anglia and the Northeast than anywhere else. The charity foundations now talked about destitution during the coming winter on a scale not seen for a quarter of a century. In 1901 a survey by Seebohm Rowntree,[30] *Poverty: A Study of Town Life*, emphasized the differences in the nation's prosperity and large groups of its peoples, and showed that in York more than a quarter of the population were miserably poor.

While the poor begged, audiences at the Duke of York's Theatre in London were entranced by the make-believe world of James Barrie's *Peter Pan*. Nor did it do the hungry much good that the most modern building to be built in London that year – and the first to have a steel frame – was the Ritz Hotel.

But good as well as bad news spreads. In 1904 what was happening in the workhouses, in the Ritz and as far away as Manchuria was going to be easier to broadcast thanks to John Fleming at London University. Fleming had made a radio valve, which would eventually do away with crystal sets.

Not that this would have impressed Arthur Balfour, who was contemplating Christmas in Downing Street. It was to be his last.

30 The son of Joseph Rowntree, the chocolate manufacturer, Benjamin Seebohm Rowntree (1871–1954) succeeded his father as chairman of the company but devoted most of life and a considerable amount of money to the study of social questions that others often ignored. The Rowntree Trust remains a major funding source for many academic studies.

Deaths

Anton Chekhov (Russian playwright)
Antonín Dvořák (Czech composer)
Henri Fantin-Latour (French artist)
Theodor Herzl (Hungarian Zionist)
Paul Kruger (South African politician)
Samuel Smiles (writer and social reformer)
Sir Henry Morton Stanley (journalist and explorer)
Sir Leslie Stephen (critic and writer)

1905

BRITISH NEWSPAPERS at the end of 1904 and early in 1905 were filled with reports of violence and repression in Russia. Hardly a month passed without some protest against the Tsar's rule, and on Boxing Day 1904 the Tsar had issued a public decree promising that there would be improvements in the way people lived. He said he would look at people's grievances and the way the government was organized, but he was too late.

In January 1905 a young Russian Orthodox priest, Father George Gapon, led a march of workers to the Winter Palace in St Petersburg. They were carrying a petition asking for better conditions in their daily lives. They got within about 30 yards of the palace when the Tsar's guard opened fire. The correspondent of *The Times* was there, and on 22 January the newspaper carried the following report:

> The strikers in the front ranks fell on their knees and implored the Cossacks to let them pass, protesting that they had no hostile intentions. They refused, however, to be intimidated by blank cartridges, and orders were given to load with ball.
>
> The passions of the mob broke loose like a bursting dam. The people, seeing the dead and dying carried away in all directions, the snow on the streets and pavements, soaked with blood, cried aloud for vengeance. Meanwhile, the situation at the Palace was becoming momentarily worse. The troops were reported to be unable to control vast masses which were constantly surging forward. Reinforcements were sent, and at 2 o'clock here also the order was given to fire.
>
> Men, women, and children fell at each volley, and were carried away in ambulances, sledges, and carts. It was no longer a workman's question. The indignation and fury of every class were roused.

Five hundred of the workers, their wives and their children were killed that day, and it seemed impossible that there could be a return to the notion of kingship in Russia. This was the concept, developed in Saxon Britain, that in return for their allegiance, a monarch would protect the people from their enemies – including the government. So the peasants chose the Tsar as the only conduit for their grievances. Anything else would have been seen as an act of treason. His portrait was carried on that demonstration, but by the end of the march Nicholas II's image lay in the snow of St Petersburg alongside the bodies of his people and the boot prints of his Cossacks.

This was a bloody winter for Russia, at home and abroad. In January 20,000 Russian troops had surrendered to the Japanese at Port Arthur. In March in Manchuria the Russian army of nearly a quarter of a million men was routed in a twelve-day battle by the Japanese. Some 200,000 died in the battle near the ancient capital of Mukden. But worse was to come.

At the end of May the Japanese sank the Russian fleet at Tsushima. It was an astonishing naval victory, and in maritime history probably ranks with the Battle of Trafalgar. For more than a year the Russians had gathered together their most important fleet in the Baltic and had sailed for Japan to try and dominate the Japanese navy – this was the fleet that caused the Dogger Bank Incident the previous year. The fleet left Vigo, was reinforced, sailed south and separated off the Straits of Gibraltar. One group port-hopped down the west coast of Africa (they were coal-burners and had to bunker whenever possible) and round into the Indian Ocean to rendezvous off Madagascar with the other group, which had gone through the Mediterranean and the Suez Canal. This was a huge naval deployment and one requiring complex management. The next, and most important, leg was the long haul across the Indian Ocean and the South China Sea, heading for the Russian base at Vladivostok. They never got there.

Eighteen months after they had left the Baltic the Russian ships were ambushed as they came out of a fog bank by Admiral Togo's Japanese battle group. Thirty-eight Russian ships sailed into the Strait of Tsushima. Thirty-five of them were either sunk or knocked out, and nearly 5000 officers and ratings were killed. The humiliation of the Russian navy was complete. The authority of the Tsar and the Russian *nomenklatura* was threatened.

None of this was in the interests of Britain, France or Germany, who had the common aim of maintaining international stability. Instability threatened commercial interests and also, even more dangerously, threatened to involve onlookers, including the United States. As early as 1 January 1905 Wilhelm II urged Nicholas II to stop the war, and on the following day President Roosevelt offered himself as mediator in the conflict. The Japanese knew their strength, however, and it was clear that the Tsar was already losing control of his people and of Russia's political system.

On 27 June the most significant protest of all took place in the Black Sea. The flagship of the Russian navy, the *Potemkim*, was standing off the Black Sea naval base at Odessa when the crew mutinied. This was not an action taken in isolation. Odessa had been suffering a violent general strike for some days, and the navy was utterly demoralized by a string of defeats in the Far East. The news of the disaster at Tsushima had reached the *Potemkim*; the word from St Petersburg was of political upheavals; there were almost daily reports of protests, most ending in violence; and the ship itself was standing offshore because there was anarchy on the streets of Odessa. The trigger for the mutiny was squeezed, perhaps inadvertently, by a young rating, who was pushed forward by his mates to complain about the appalling food being served to the ship's company. The sailor was shot by the ship's first lieutenant, the officer responsible for the running of the ship and discipline. The ship's company mutinied and the captain and some of the officers were hurled overboard. The battleship *Potemkim*, its defiant crew and their leader, a sailor called Matshushenko, entered the folklore of the Russian Revolution.

In Odessa itself the protests were unabated, and the authorities, fearful that the mutiny would spread ashore, sent 50,000 troops to the town. They had to kill 2000 people before order was restored. They could stop the rioting, but they could not stop news from spreading, and a general strike was called in St Petersburg.

The mutineers held out for more than a week, surrendering on 8 July not to the Russian authorities but to the Romanians, who refused to hand them over because, they claimed, the sailors were not terrorists but had committed a political act. This was perhaps one of the first examples in modern history of an extradition demand being refused on these grounds. Eventually, the Russians did get the sailors, eight of whom were convicted of mutiny.

By now the Russians were downcast on all fronts. The governor of Sakhalin Island, off the Siberian coast, surrendered just three weeks after a reinforced brigade of Japanese troops landed. This was the first invasion of Russian territory by Japan, and it seemed impossible that the Russians could expect any kind of victory. On 2 August Russian and Japanese diplomats began talks in America. By September the war was over and the Russians were forced to pull out of Manchuria and to recognize Japanese claims in Korea.

As if this diplomatic humiliation was not enough, Russia was in the grip of its worst famine in a decade; there were demands for a proper parliament to be elected; the oilfields in Baku were burning; and more than a thousand were dead after a battle between Russian Armenians and Tartars. By October the whole of Russia was on strike. Russian troops had mutinied in Vladivostok, where the majority of soldiers now appeared to be disloyal to the Tsar.

In Odessa up to 1000 Jews were massacred by organized gangs of workers. Throughout the Ukraine and Byelorusse gangs known as the Black Hundred shot Jewish men and cut to pieces Jewish women and children.

At the year's end a demonstration of students and workers developed into a week-long battle with the Tsar's troops. The firing began when the workers and students proclaimed a provisional government with plans to set up a new government in St Petersburg. Yet another Red Flag was hoisted and once more the Tsar's troops were sent in. At the time it was reported that some 10,000 had died although it is very likely that many of the casualties were people caught up in what was going on rather than taking part in the attempted revolution.

Here were the violent origins of the Russian Revolution that was to take place twelve years later and affect the whole of Europe.

We can understand Britain's story only when we know the outside influences that made politics and commerce take the directions they did. Therefore, even the briefest anecdotal view becomes important.[31] For three-quarters of this century the aftermath of the Russian Revolution either dominated or was the codicil to almost every long-term foreign policy of successive British governments. Even by 1905 it was increasingly difficult to ignore events in the Far East. The Japanese victory changed the balance of power there and, perhaps more significantly, the defeat of the nation's navy and the army had an enormous reaction among the *nomanklatura* in Russia. A ruling class faced with the devastation of the military power on which they relied for their existence could do little more than turn a hard face to social and political reform. It is true that the Tsar promised, and even set in motion, better government, but the combination of defeat and internal unrest encouraged revolution.

Even though Britain did not get directly involved, it knew full well that there was a danger that the instability in Russian society would have an effect throughout Europe that would touch Britain and, inevitably, its relations with Germany and France.

For the time being, however, Balfour was relaxed. More important to him than events in Russia was that traditional role of a Conservative leader, attempting to hold the party together. This was a Unionist government formed of Tories and Liberal Unionists, who had joined in coalition in 1895 when the Liberal Unionist leader in the Commons, Joseph Chamberlain, and the leader in the Lords, Lord Hartington, joined Salisbury's government. But as we have seen, the end had come. Chamberlain was campaigning for tariff reform up and down the country, while Balfour quietly worked against the free trade hard-liners in Cabinet. Both were to lose.

The most significant moment came in the Commons in the winter of 1905. There had still been a chance that Chamberlain and Balfour could join forces, which would have left the rump of Liberal and Conservative free traders in a minority. But that rump was well structured, and it now included the young Winston Churchill who had, as we have seen, used the issue as his reason for defecting from the Conservative to the Liberal benches. The defection of an MP, especially over such an emotive issue, would not normally be worth more than passing interest, but Churchill was to become one of the dominant figures of the twentieth century and one of a handful representing all that the Conservatives stood for.

---

31 For an authoritative view of this period see *A History of the Soviet Union* by Professor Geoffrey Hoskings, Collins (1985) and, for a broader view of these events in the context of twentieth-century history, see Martin Gilbert's three-volume *A History of the Twentieth Century*, HarperCollins (1997).

Churchill's debate within himself reflected the political uncertainties felt in the early 1900s. Which way would the political climate take Britain? His defection intensified the prime minister's dilemma. The party was split, and Balfour could not repair it. His own position was clear: he was for tariff reform but opposed the dogmatic supporters of unfettered free trade. Balfour, it might be noted, always believed there was a middle way.

This may not explain the half measures he took to get out of the free trade versus tariff reform debate, but when we try to understand why Balfour behaved as he did, we should remember that he did not appreciate that power was no longer about ruling the state but was now about governing for the nation's people.

In a speech in Manchester Balfour suggested that tariffs could be used against some countries, especially if they were trying to dump cheap goods into Britain. He also proposed the closer commercial ties with the colonies that Chamberlain had always wanted. By March Chamberlain's supporters agreed with him, but the Liberals, who supported free trade, regarded Balfour's proposal for what it was – a not very well thought-through compromise – and they believed it could be easily defeated. The motion in the Commons was on the financing of any arrangement. Even the Tories, Balfour's own people, could not be relied on when it came to deciding 'how much'. The Liberals forced a vote.

At this point Balfour made a tactical error. He ordered his own people not to vote and led them out of the Chamber. In political terms, he had badly miscalculated. Here we see once more how one topic cannot be considered in isolation, for Balfour wrongly judged that the Liberals were likely to split, not on tariff reform, but on Irish Home Rule. He believed that the two would-be Liberal prime ministers, old Lord Rosebery and Sir Henry Campbell-Bannerman, would be in opposite camps over this crucial issue – as, indeed, they were – but what Balfour did not know was that Campbell-Bannerman had out-manoeuvred him.

In November Campbell-Bannerman had delivered a carefully choreographed series of speeches, which he directed not at the government but at a specific target within his *own* party, Lord Rosebery. Rosebery had served in Gladstone's Cabinet and had been Liberal prime minister, albeit briefly, in 1894. Now, in 1905, Rosebery thought he could return to Downing Street.

In a speech delivered on 23 November Campbell-Bannerman suggested that Home Rule for Ireland was on the cards but that those cards would not be dealt quickly. Rosebery, in an ill-judged response made at Bodmin two days later, declared his opposition to this programme and said that he could not serve a prime minister who followed it.[32] Rosebery thought he had the support of senior Liberals for his position, a view that encouraged Balfour in his belief that the Liberals would split over Home Rule. However, there was no split in the party

32 Campbell-Bannerman was the only person who could be prime minister if Balfour's administration fell.

because Campbell-Bannerman had already got the support of the men who mattered, including Asquith, and his position was sound.

Balfour realized that he would have to go because the free trade debate could not be won without the clear-out that a change of government would bring, but he also knew that a general election was to be avoided. He could not trust the electorate to support him. So, he took what was, in those days, still a tactical alternative. He simply resigned.

The next constitutional step was for the King to ask the leader of the party with the next highest majority to form a government. Balfour judged that the Liberals would be unable to hold themselves together, and some Liberals felt the same way and advised Campbell-Bannerman to refuse the premiership and force the election Balfour did not want. Campbell-Bannerman believed, however, that should he duck the premiership now, the electorate was unlikely to have faith in him at a later date. It was much better that he should take the job and go to the country later, when he was sure of his power base.

On 5 December, therefore, at the age of sixty-nine, Henry Campbell-Bannerman became Liberal prime minister. Balfour was gone and with him the ghosts of Victorian Toryism. Campbell-Bannerman had been born in 1836, the year before Victoria came to the throne. He was a son of the sometime Lord Provost of Glasgow, Sir James Campbell,[33] and in 1868 he became Liberal MP for Sterling. By the 1880s he had became a convert to Home Rule for Ireland, following the Liberal leader, Gladstone.

In 1905 his main rival for the Liberal leadership – and the government – was Rosebery, who had succeeded Gladstone as prime minister in 1894. Although Rosebery was only in Downing Street for a few months, he remained the Liberal leader in the Lords, but his leadership of government and party was undistinguished. The Rosebery family is perhaps better remembered in racing rather than political circles.[34]

Campbell-Bannerman had built a very solid political base. He had held ministerial jobs in Gladstone's first two governments – in 1884–5 he had been Chief Secretary for Ireland, and the following year he had joined the Cabinet as Secretary for War – and he was the political force behind such army reform as there was in the first half of the 1890s. He was a competent, if not an outstanding, performer, and when he took possession of 10 Downing Street at the end of 1905, few doubted his right to be there.

Campbell-Bannerman was careful not to lose touch with anyone in the parliamentary party, especially the trio of Liberal Leaguers (a group formed by Rosebery) who, he imagined, would form the core of his future Cabinet – Asquith, Haldane and Grey. His immediate task, however, was to prove wrong the Balfour hypothesis that the Liberal Party would split.

33 He added Bannerman to his name in 1872 to comply with an inheritance he received that year.

34 Rosebery's horse, Cicero, won the Derby in 1905.

It was a team of some distinction that attended that first Cabinet meeting in December 1905. H.H. Asquith was Chancellor of the Exchequer, Herbert Gladstone, the son of the Victorian prime minister, was Home Secretary, Sir Edward Grey was Foreign Secretary, and the Earl of Elgin[35] became Colonial Secretary. Haldane became Secretary of War and was later to be one of the more thoughtful military reformers of the twentieth century. Even the lower orders of the Cabinet were exceptionally talented. They included Augustine Birrell at Education, John Burns, who was put in charge of Local Government, and, as President of the Board of Trade, David Lloyd George. Churchill became a junior minister in the Colonial Office.

For those who remember Lloyd George for his leadership in the 1914–18 war, for scandals about bought peerages and for his burning Welsh oratory, it is worth noting his time at the relatively obscure Board of Trade. It was Lloyd George who brought in the Merchant Shipping Act in 1906 and the Patents Act in 1907 and who, the following year, set up the Port of London Authority.

By the end of 1905 the Conservative rule had gone and the Liberal revival, which would blossom then perish under Lloyd George, had begun.

While the politicians changed seats, the electorate was taken up with headier matters. At Crystal Palace in February two Frenchmen landed a hot-air balloon in which they had flown across the Channel.

In London the increase in the number of vehicles on the streets led to such a steep rise in the accident rate that the London County Council proposed setting up a motorized ambulance service to get crash victims to hospital. The public was now well into its love-hate relationship with the car, and groups sprang up to reduce its use. The speed limit was set at 20 miles an hour, and there were even police speed traps to enforce it. An association was formed to protect the motorist from the authorities – it was called the Automobile Association.

Those Londoners who were not injured by the increasingly quick motor cars were endangered by an outbreak of typhus – a reminder of the crowded and sometimes wretched conditions in which many Londoners lived, particularly in the East End.

After the pestilence came 100 mph gales, which stormed across the country, leaving the dead amid damaged buildings from coast to coast.

It was in April 1905 that a Frenchman, the psychologist Alfred Binet, invented a process that would be the basis of examinations for school children (as well as an excuse for intellectual snobbery) that would last for the next hundred years. Binet introduced the intelligence test, which claimed to be able to distinguish between knowledge and intelligence. While a person's learning curve increased or decreased, Binet had found that intelligence was a constant.

---

35 Elgin, the 9th Earl, was the grandson of Tom Elgin, the man who brought the marbles from the Parthenon to London at the turn of the eighteenth century.

Someone who had probably never heard of Binet but who was demonstrating the test of intelligence over which scientists would battle for decades to come was the German physicist, Albert Einstein. In July he published his theory of relativity, which set out to prove that there is no such thing as an absolute in time and motion and that everything is relative to the starting point.

If thinking about Einstein's theory was going to cause a headache, help was at hand. In October 1905 the first aspirins went on sale, although they were of little help to the anxious supporters of Christabel Pankhurst and Annie Kenney, the first suffragettes to be jailed.

Finally in 1905, someone returned from the dead. Arthur Conan Doyle had killed off Sherlock Holmes by the hands of the dastardly Moriarty at the Reichenbach Falls, but thousands of readers of *Strand Magazine* (where the Sherlock Holmes stories appeared) demanded to know what had really happened to Holmes. It was inconceivable that he was dead. Conan Doyle bowed to the inevitable and brought back the character of whom he had surely tired. *The Return of Sherlock Holmes* was published to the delight of his fans and the incredulity of his devoted physician, Watson.

Deaths

Dr Thomas Barnardo (philanthropist)
John Milton Hay (US diplomat)
Sir Henry Irving (actor)
Adolf Menzel (German artist)
Jules Verne (French writer)

1906

ON THE second Saturday in January 1906 Britain went to the polls. In those days there was not a single polling day; instead, voting was spread over two weeks, with the big towns and cities voting first and the country districts following. As the results appeared during the rest of the month, they were posted on billboards. The full result was not declared until 7 February.

This was the Liberal triumph that the party had been promising itself since the days of Gladstone. The reaction against tariff reform was overwhelming, and even Arthur Balfour lost his seat. The previous election had been in 1900, when there had been 560 constituencies. In that election there had been 184 Liberal MPs; now there were 400. In 1900 there had been 402 Unionists; now there were 157. Significantly, there were now 30 Labour members of Parliament. The political balance had shifted.

It is from this point that we can talk about the Labour party. The socialists had campaigned as the Labour Representation Committee (LRC), which had been formed in 1900. After the election, the LRC was restructured, at the same time changing its name to the Labour Party.

Although the election had clearly endorsed free trade, tariff reform had not disappeared. The issue split the Unionists, strengthening those who were left, which should, at least, have cheered Joseph Chamberlain. Within a few months of the January election he suffered a stroke, however, and although he lived for another eight years, he was lost to British politics.

The puzzle of this period is the way in which someone with the intellectual depth of Balfour could be so wrong-footed. A political philosopher, he had, in political terms, the disadvantage of being able to see both sides of an argument, and he lacked the essential quality of the most successful politicians – single-mindedness. By some definitions Balfour was a Whig whose instinct was to lead the country at the bidding of the Book of Common Prayer: the nation should be quietly governed. He seems to have failed to understand that the nineteenth-century style of governance had disappeared and been replaced by a more abrasive system and one that was exercised in public.

As for the Liberals – a group born of Whigs, radicals and Peelite Tories – they should have been able to achieve anything they wanted in the new Parliament, where they could count on the support of the Labour Party and more than eighty Irish Nationalists. This arithmetic did not, however, apply to the Conservative-dominated House of Lords, which was quite adept at turning over government legislation. This was certainly the case when the Commons wanted to amend Balfour's 1902 Education Act. The Lords did not reject the Bill; they simply made sure it was bogged down until the government withdrew it.

The House of Lords should not be blamed entirely for boring government. Neither the Liberals as a party nor Campbell-Bannerman as its leader had a 'big idea'. There was no major policy programme to catch the public imagination, apart, of course, from free trade. Free trade could be summed up as cheap food and most people would vote for that, as they had. But the country already had a free trade policy, so there was no legislation to bring forward. It began to look as if the 1906 election had produced a government that tinkered rather than reformed.

Campbell-Bannerman himself appeared to have less energy once he was in power. He was deeply affected by the death of his wife, and this, combined with the stress of all that had gone before, appeared to overwhelm him. He had a number of heart attacks and died within two years of assuming office.

The effects of the new government on British foreign policy were not much greater than they were on domestic policy. Britain's foreign interests were still taken up by the Empire, and in 1906 it is worth remembering that Britain 'owned' 20 per cent of the globe, and Edward VII was King to more than 400 million people in thirty-three countries.[36]

36 Gibraltar, Cyprus, Malta, Gambia, Sierra Leone, the Gold Coast, Nigeria, Cape Colony, Bechuanaland, Rhodesia and Nyasaland, Kenya, Uganda, British Somaliland, Egyptian-Sudan, Egypt, Aden, India, Ceylon (Sri Lanka), Burma, Malaya, Hong Kong, Canada, Bahamas, Bermuda, British West Indies, Honduras, British Guyana, Falkland Islands, Australia, New Zealand, British New Guinea, Seychelles and Mauritius.

The new government found itself involved in the so-called Moroccan question, which had first reared its head in 1900 and which involved the three main European players, France, Britain and Germany. The French claimed authority over the kingdom of Morocco, where the Moors began a campaign of protest and raids against them. In 1902 Britain had major interests in Egypt; the French were still in Morocco; and German interests extended into the Mediterranean and across Africa. It is clear that here were the seeds of dispute and instability: the French did not want the British to interfere in Morocco; the British did not want the French to interfere in Egypt; neither country wanted Germany to interfere in what they regarded as their affairs.

Potential conflict between France and Britain in Africa had been one of the reasons, as we saw in 1904, for the Entente Cordiale, which stipulated that each country should stay out of the other's business. Diplomacy is rarely as simple as that, however. Spain was hoping to extend its influence and claimed part of Morocco high in the Rif Mountains. So began the conflict between the Spanish and the Moors.

In 1905, however, the Germans identified an opportunity to create tension between Britain and France and so, it hoped, weaken the Entente. They also wanted to curb French influence in the area. In March the Kaiser travelled to Tangier and declared support for the Sultan and announced that Germany had interests in Morocco (which it did not). For the remainder of the year the diplomatic crisis continued, and it was unresolved when the new Liberal government came to power. The question Campbell-Bannerman faced was, if France and Germany fought over Morocco, would Britain not feel obliged to go to France's help?

The Germans demanded that an international conference be held, ostensibly to clarify the position of both France and Spain in Morocco, but actually to see how far Britain would be prepared to go in its support for France. The conference was held in January 1906 in the Spanish town of Algeciras, across the bay from Gibraltar. A peaceful solution was agreed and the Germans suffered a diplomatic defeat. They had made it known that they fancied what they called 'a prompt war' with France, and although Britain would not commit itself to defending France, one positive and long-term action came of this diplomatic and military test.

The allies had come to the realization that although war had been avoided this time, circumstances might arise in which they would have to fight. How would they meet that test? Moreover, if they were right in believing that Germany was spoiling for conflict, were they the only states to be tested? With Campbell-Bannerman's blessing – although he did not tell the whole Cabinet – France and Britain started to hold informal military talks, which continued on a regular basis until 1914.

When it came to the question of third-party involvement, the British and Belgians started to explore, quietly and unofficially, what should be done if the Germans invaded any Belgian territory. These talks were initiated by Belgian concerns at reports that the Germans were building long railway platforms at obscure countryside spots close to their frontier. Long platforms are not for commuters but for lines of troops waiting to embark to the front line.

The Moroccan Question and the Algeciras Conference should not be forgotten. Five years later the Germans again chose Morocco as an arena for sabre rattling. Four years after that, the Anglo-French entente was tested to its limits, this time in Flanders.

Events at home also required Campbell-Bannerman's attention. When Parliament opened in October 1906 there was a protest from the suffragettes, eleven of whom were arrested and jailed. They had believed that a new Liberal government would rapidly advance the cause for 'one woman, one vote'. They were wrong.

For some, a more pressing matter than equal voting rights was what to do about the people who were trapped in poverty. Lloyd George observed that even though Britain was the richest nation on earth, 10 million people lived in conditions close to destitution, and whether his figures were correct, he was reminding people that the social conditions for the poorest could not begin to approach those of the richest, among whom the latest fashion was to drink champagne with every meal. In a speech to the Society of Social Service of North Wales Wesleyans (a society of modest habits), Lloyd George said that drink caused 60 per cent of the nation's poverty and that it was the most 'urgent problem for our rulers'.

That summer these social problems were, for the moment at least, largely ignored by the majority of Edwardians, who had just returned from their holidays. Dressed in full skirts, straw boaters and blazers, the more fortunate had gone to the seaside. In temperatures of 90°F (32°C), they were probably glad, particularly if they were from the southeast, to get away from London, for yet again the capital was grappling with the problems of traffic, and the spectacular open-topped buses were being hauled off the streets by the police because they were too noisy. There were now more than 700 buses on regular routes and 40 per cent more were about to arrive.

Beneath the streets tunnels were being dug at an unprecedented rate. Two new railway lines were being built: one ran between Finsbury Park and Hammersmith and passed beneath Piccadilly Circus; the other ran from Baker Street to Waterloo. The original underground tunnels had been dug as big trenches, which were then covered. The new lines were much deeper and were round and came to be called tubes – the origin of the expression coming from the tunnel and not the train.

What was happening above and below ground in London over-shadowed a political shift. The London and borough elections were taking place, and the general election success enjoyed by the Liberals just nine months earlier was not to be reflected at local level. The Tories were getting back into power at the cost of the Liberals, who were also losing out to the newly organized Labour Party. Voters had a new home.

*

International diplomacy and local democracy were of little avail when it came to natural disasters. In the Pacific as many as 10,000 people were swept away by winds and tidal waves; hundreds died in Italy when Mount Vesuvius erupted; and more than a thousand people died in San Francisco when the city was hit by yet another earthquake. But none of this was anything compared to the tragedy that had been sweeping through India for the past five years. In 1906 it was estimated that some 3 million people had died from a plague carried by rats.

Problems of a different kind were arising in the north as hopes of a democratic resolution to the unrest in Russia vanished when the first parliament, the Duma, was dissolved. It had lasted for just two months but had so few powers that no one in Russia believed that the reforms promised by the Tsar would come to pass. Disaffection among workers, students and academics had spread to some of the most important and powerful elements of the army, and it could only be a matter of time before there was challenge to the Tsar himself.

But there were bright spots in the calendar. Kellogg's Corn Flakes made their first appearance on the nation's breakfast tables, and on Christmas Eve 1906 the first radio broadcast was made. It came from a Canadian, Reginald Fessenden, who had worked for both Thomas Edison and Westinghouse. The century of communications swept on.

Deaths
Paul Cézanne (French artist)
Pierre Curie (French chemist)
Henrik Ibsen (Norwegian writer)
F.W. Maitland (historian)

1907

IN WESTMINSTER, where there had been hopes that the radical traditions of the Liberal government would bring in social and constitutional reforms, the opening months of 1907 offered no promise of change.

The women's suffrage moment, which had expected that the Liberals would have sympathized with their aims, were disappointed. In his March column in the *Illustrated London News*, the novelist and sometime Liberal polemicist G.K. Chesterton took up the matter:

> I incline to think that a great mass of women voting just at present would make just as little difference as a great mass more of men voting would make. I think the extending of the franchise from males to females would, under existing conditions, make just about as much difference as the extending of the franchise from males of twenty-one to males of twenty. . . . If voting is only putting a cross against certain names submitted by a party caucus, then certainly women

> could do it as well as men. But voting ought not to mean this: voting ought to mean arguing for hours and hours in a public house and interrupting people and hitting the table. . . . In short, voting, if it means anything, means doing all the thing that males have always done – notably, fighting, drinking, and talking about everything and nothing.

Few people took much notice of Chesterton on women's suffrage, apart, perhaps, from his friend Hilaire Belloc, who had become a Liberal MP in the 1905 election. They might have well spent time doing so, because there was little to excite them in the House. Apart from Lloyd George's Merchant Shipping Act and the Patents and Designs Act, there was no legislation for them to push through. It was as if social reform was no longer a subject for the great party of social reform.

The Trades Disputes Bill, which had got through the Commons at the close of the previous year, was the work not of the Liberals but of the Labour MPs. It was, in any case, an almost incomprehensible piece of legislation, which had to be revisited. Also the work of Labour MPs was the legislation that gave schoolchildren free lunches. Even the proposal for school health checks came from the backbenches.

The first three major pieces of legislation – on education, trade disputes and voting – were a test of what the new government was capable of doing rather than of what it wanted to do. Of more importance was the Education Bill. The Liberals had included this in their election manifesto, and on the question of the Church and schools it certainly had a clear policy. The Bill went through the Commons with its large Liberal majority. The Lords turned it down. The reformers who believed that the Upper House had to be controlled were stirred.

In 1907 a new Bill was drafted, but it never reached the Commons Order Paper, as the House turned to what were, at the time, quite contentious measures concerned with reforming land tenancy agreements: the Smallholdings Bill, the Irish Evicted Tenants Bill, the Small Landholders (Scotland) Bill and the Land Values (Scotland) Bill. Once again it was the House of Lords that stood in the way of legislation. The two Scottish Bills were thrown out and the other two were unrecognizable and worthless by the time they left the Lords.

Campbell-Bannerman moved a government resolution that the decision of the Commons should be the ultimate means of putting through legislation. He wanted a system that would allow the Lords and the Commons to come to quiet agreement over any Bill, and he suggested that if a Bill could not get through the Lords and if the government was persuaded that it should, a group of peers and MPs should meet to see if there was any way that compromise could be reached. If that did not work, the process would be repeated through the Commons, through the Lords and, if necessary, through an ad hoc committee of both. He said that if the process did not work for a second time, six months later the Bill would actually become law, not in its original form but in the wording that it had when it was sent to the House of Lords on the second occasion. This resolution was carried in June 1907 by a majority of 285. The Lords ignored it.

Here was a crucial step on the path that was leading to what became a head-on collision with the House of Lords just four years later. What was happening now was a signpost to the most major piece of legislation to reform the powers of the Lords that was seen until 1999.

One important social reform, hardly noticed today, was carried. At the beginning of the century Britain was an intolerant society. Identifying oneself as belonging to the Church of England hardly signified one way or the other, but being a Roman Catholic prevented people from all kinds of promotion and even from access to higher education – at Oxford and Cambridge Universities, for example, a Catholic would never be appointed to the senior teaching posts. Britain needed teachers, and in 1907 the architect of so much of the nation's educational reforms of the period, Robert Morant, rewrote the regulations that stopped non-Anglicans being admitted to training colleges:

> In no circumstances may the application of a candidate be rejected on the ground of religious faith or by reason of his refusal to undertake to attend or abstain from attending any place of religious worship, or any religious observance, or instruction in religious subjects in the college or elsewhere.

While the prime minister's attention was turned to domestic and constitutional matters, the Foreign Office was issuing warnings of what it believed were German plans to rule the whole of Europe. Some analysts believed that that was, indeed, part one of the greater German ambition. The conclusion was triggered when Gustav von Schmoller, the Chairman of the German Colonial Policy Committee, insisted that Germany must increase its colonial expansion. The German Socialist Party, which opposed expansion and used it as a platform for the elections to the Reichstag, found themselves totally out of step with the German voters and lost the election to the Kaiser's supporters.

The War Office rumblings about a threat to the state's security was not simply a reactionary cough from the armchair generals. Early in February Britain's new battleship HMS *Dreadnought* set a speed record between Gibraltar and Trinidad of a constant 17 knots. The government had promised to order three more Dreadnought class vessels but was about to cut the naval defence estimates. Extra money was being spent on the army, with the formation of a new 160,000-man British Expeditionary Force (BEF), which was part of the restructuring programme that had begun under the previous government and would form the basis of British army operations until the end of the Second World War.

The most far-reaching reform came under the stewardship of Haldane, whom Campbell-Bannerman appointed as Secretary for War in 1905 and who oversaw the restructuring of the army. In 1906 Haldane established the General Staff of seventy-two officers, and it was he who, in 1907, pushed through Parliament an

Act that gave Britain the first Territorial Army. But Haldane was not given a free hand nor an open cheque. Campbell-Bannerman insisted that Haldane should not interfere with the system of battalions (groups of about 650 men) that Edward Cardwell had put in place during the nineteenth century. The institutions and society of the Edwardian army were in many ways as hidebound as those Cardwell had faced forty years earlier. It is unlikely that any lesser mind than Haldane's would have succeeded in 1907, and he had one great advantage that Cardwell did not: most of the brightest senior officers in the army were on his side. But as Cardwell had found, it is not always the brightest officers who have the most influence in high places.

The combination of Boer War, German political and military activity, and new technologies meant that reform would have only one chance. Unlike the reforms of the 1980s and 1990s, there would be no opportunity at this time for another masterplan to end all masterplans. There is a parallel to what happened to British army reforms in the 1990s with Haldane's reforms in 1907. If Haldane could show major financial savings – in other words, if he could reduce the army budget – he would get the support he needed in Parliament from the radical benches of the Liberal Party. This he did. He saved £3 million, bringing down the army's budget to less than £28 million. The combined army and navy budget for 1907 was just £59 million, the lowest it had been for many years and the lowest it would ever be.

The Expeditionary Force of seven divisions (the tank was still to be invented) was so thoroughly thought through that it was the formation that was sent to France seven years later. Moreover, Haldane made sure that there would be a considerable reserve of men to take the places of the huge casualties the planners expected.

Perhaps the greatest irony of the Haldane reforms was that he had taken Germany as one of his models. He had, after all, become familiar with the German system in his student days at Göttingen.

Preparing for defence is about preparing for war, but treaties and protocols can be as important as the numbers of divisions. At the end of August 1907 the government signed what was to become the Anglo-Russian Convention or the Anglo-Russian Entente. To get an immediate idea of why this agreement was important, we should remember two other treaties: the Franco-Russian Alliance of 1894 and the more recent Entente Cordiale, agreed by France and Britain in 1904.

Ostensibly, the 1907 agreement between Russia and Britain was designed to prevent diplomatic and even military conflict not in Europe but over Tibet, Afghanistan and Persia (now Iran). Britain had direct interests in Tibet and Persia and did not wish the Russians to use the area as a route south to the Indian Ocean. Such was the Russian need for warm-water ports (a subject still being discussed at Soviet and then Russian naval conferences in the 1980s and 1990s) that the other part of the agreement, that covering Persia, was more contentious.

In 1907 Persia was in an advanced state of social, economic and political decay. The Tsar, Nicholas II, had sent his engineers south to help the Shah of Persia build roads and railways and Cossacks to act as officers in the Shah's guard. If the regime in Persia collapsed the Russians could move their armies along the roads and railways they had helped build, knowing that the forces they had put at the Shah's disposal would have already taken command. It was a simple example of military planning: infiltrate an advance guard and provide the infrastructure and you have pre-positioned a command and control system to be used when the opportunity arises.

Probably the only country that could have stopped Russia was Britain, and if, at this stage, Britain had lost interest in its international role outside Empire, Russia would have been free to take over Persia when the time was right. The tension was eased by the August agreement between the two nations, which, while not an actual treaty, did allow each side to settle their differences in the area amicably by defining their own particular spheres of interest.

There was now, and not by design, a triangle of treaties, precisely the sort of thing that Britain had been avoiding at the turn of the century. Forty years later the arrangement was held up as a fine example of diplomacy and defence when on 4 April 1949 the North Atlantic Treaty Organization was founded with the unwritten slogan 'an attack on one is an attack on all'.

In 1907, then, appeared the template that would be used in just two years' time for the agreement between France, Britain and Russia that became known as the Triple Entente and that was a direct counter to the Triple Alliance of Germany, Austria and Italy, which Britain had so carefully avoided just a few years previously. It is now clear that the arrangements with France and with Russia were, in effect, weighing out the alliance that would one day set itself against Germany. However, in the late summer of 1907 no one knew when that day would come.

Events around the world were hardly suggestive of peace. In South Africa a new law was passed demanding that all Indians living in the Transvaal had to be fingerprinted and had to carry a registered identity card. Anyone who ignored this regulation would lose their right of residence in the Transvaal and could even be deported. In theory, the law had to receive royal assent in London, and the new Colonial Under-Secretary, Winston Churchill, had said that it would not be accepted. But the Transvaal had become self-governing, and so the law could exist as an ordinance that amended an existing and more benign law that had received royal assent.

The leader of the group opposing the fingerprinting was a young lawyer who had served as a sergeant major in the Ambulance Corps. His name was Mohandas Gandhi. Gandhi was jailed, but General Smuts was quick to understand that keeping Gandhi in prison would make him the focus of more protests against the fingerprinting law. Smuts and Gandhi met privately, and in return for some amendments to the ordinance, the South African Indian agreed to call off his protest and to register. It was the first of many compromises to tempt Gandhi and to upset some of his more aggressive supporters.

As for Russia, there were no signs of peace anywhere. In March 1907 there was an increase in the number of attacks being made on Jews, particularly on the 15,000 who had survived in Odessa. In St Petersburg troops were used to disperse 40,000 people who were demonstrating against Nicholas II as he opened the new Duma. Three months later, it was closed when the prime minister, Pyotr Stolypin, claimed that some of the deputies were plotting to overthrow the Tsar. The garrison in St Petersburg was put on full alert and any thoughts of protest were abandoned.

Japan's military success in Korea had led to riots. The Japanese had assumed total power over the country's administration, including local government, and had forced the Emperor of Korea to abdicate. As soon as the rioting started, Japanese soldiers moved in, took out the leaders and executed them.

In India two days of rioting in Calcutta began after a students' rally. Matters were made worse when the British Labour Party leader, Keir Hardie, told a local newspaper that the situation in India was as bad as that in the Balkans. By November new powers had been given to regional administrators to ban all public meetings.

And Britain itself did not escape violence. Four civilians died in August when a riot began in the Falls Road area of Belfast. A crowd gathered after two men had been arrested, and fighting broke out. Mounted troops charged the crowds, and although they dispersed they soon gathered in other parts of the city.

More peaceable was the first Boy Scout camp, initiated by Baden-Powell, the hero of Mafeking. Twenty of his scouts were taken across to Brownsea Island in Poole Harbour where, apart from camping, BP taught them tracking, how to light fires and first aid. This was the beginning of the Boy Scouts Association.

Rudyard Kipling was the first English writer to be awarded the Nobel Prize for Literature, while an American visiting Britain, Mark Twain, received an honorary Doctorate of Letters from Oxford University.

In Dublin the New Abbey Theatre put on J.M. Synge's play, *The Playboy of the Western World*. There was rioting and people going to the theatre were arrested, all because the hero boasts that he is a big man in the West of Ireland because he has killed his father. The play was considered to be amoral and a slur on the Irish people.

The directors of the Cunard Line were celebrating. On 11 October their ocean liner *Lusitania* crossed the Atlantic in 4 days, 19 hours and 52 minutes, beating by 11 hours and 45 minutes the previous record, which had been held by the German ship, the *Deutschland*. Cunard remained justifiably proud of its four-funnelled transatlantic liner, and in its posters and brochures the ship was hailed as 'the fastest and largest steamer now in Atlantic service'.

In 1907 the world saw the first performance of the Ziegfeld Follies, and one of the most popular songs of the year was entitled 'If Those Lips Could Only Speak'.

Another event in the art world left some speechless. A new style of painting by a young artist called Pablo Picasso appeared. *Les Demoiselles d'Avignon* represented five jagged pink female nudes, supposedly whores, seen from different perspectives. The art world seemed to be caught napping, and in 1907 some people even thought that this was Picasso's practical joke.

Deaths
Marcelin Berthelot (French chemist)
Edvard Grieg (Norwegian composer)
J.K. Huysmans (French novelist)
Sully Prudhomme (French poet)
Sir William Howard Russell (war correspondent)
Francis Thompson (poet)
William Thomson, 1st Baron Kelvin (scientist)

1908

THIS WAS a year of political change in Britain. Campbell-Bannerman had suffered a number of heart attacks, and the day after what was to be his final speech in the Commons on 12 February it became clear that he could not carry on. Asquith, his deputy, took charge, and on 6 April Campbell-Bannerman resigned. Sixteen days later he died.

Sir Henry Campbell-Bannerman was highly regarded, but some historians have found it hard to understand why he was so popular. Perhaps his strengths lay in his age and in the fact that he spanned the two great cultures, both politically and socially, of the Victorian and Edwardian periods. He had been a minister in Gladstone's government of the 1880s, and his notion of what Britain stood for was peculiarly tempered by imperialism, almost ancient military ritual (of which he was a brave reformer) and the accelerated technology that presented opportunities for expansion as well as industrial exploitation. Yet his Cabinet pushed through little remarkable legislation, largely thanks to the House of Lords.

If there was a notable success of his government, it was the way he arranged the future of South Africa, but even this was done secretly, and few of his Cabinet were even asked their opinions on the matter. Campbell-Bannerman manipulated the political procedures to make Transvaal self-governing, although there was much opposition to this move at Westminster. He persuaded his Cabinet that self-government was right and then guided the legal procedure by letters patent, rather than a full Act of Parliament. He contrived the same arrangement for the Orange River Colony, as it then was. It was not until after his death that all the provinces came together, and by then all but the most sceptical and reactionary at Westminster saw the sense of what he had done.

When the King was told of Campbell-Bannerman's resignation, he was on holiday in Biarritz, and rather than disrupt his holiday and return to England, he had Asquith come to him. Thus it was that Herbert Henry Asquith, the Chancellor of the Exchequer, became the only British prime minister to kiss hands in a foreign hotel.[37]

Asquith was a Yorkshireman, and as far as the electorate was concerned he was far removed from the Whiggish and impressionistic figures that had gone before, especially Balfour. As one writer observed: 'His type was at this time more familiar in big business than in high politics; fond of high life, but nothing of an aristocrat, and as distinct from Grey or Balfour as earthenware from porcelain.'[38]

He had entered Parliament in 1886 as the member for East Fife and tended to the left wing of the Liberal Party. In 1892 he had been Gladstone's Home Secretary at a time when Gladstone's Home Rule for Ireland Bill had been defeated in the Lords. Asquith well understood the need to reform not the power, but the use of power in that place.

This was the man who, at the age of fifty-six, gave up his desk at the Treasury to Lloyd George and moved into 10 Downing Street. He carried with him the Budget for 1908.

The important element of Asquith's Budget was not the price of sugar nor the provision of new warships for the navy, although there was considerable debate about both. The main feature was £1.2 million for something quite new: non-contributory old age pensions. Providing for the increasing numbers of elderly people had not been a high political question until the 1900s. For centuries the British had made some provision for the needy. The Poor Laws of 1536 had helped some of those who had nothing, but even then means had to be found to put 'sturdy beggars'[39] to work. In the eighteenth and nineteenth centuries the Board of Commissioners had continued that philosophy, making poor houses as unpleasant as possible to deter the 'indigent poor' from seeking their shelter.

Being old does not mean being poor or lazy, of course, but the predicament is similar. The elderly need money. By 1907 many old people were living too long for the coffers of the charitably minded friendly societies, many of which were small and localized and limited in what they could do. In the 1880s a campaign began, largely led by Joseph Chamberlain, urging the government to follow the German model of providing a pension to people who had made contributions up to the age of sixty-five. Asquith's scheme, instead of starting at sixty-five, was to begin when people reached the age of seventy, a decision that ran counter to all the evidence suggesting that by the time people got to their mid-sixties, few were capable of supporting themselves. The scheme did have the financial advantage of being some sort of social reform. But because pensions could not be collected until the age of seventy, the Treasury had estimated that fewer people would actually be alive to collect their pensions. Those who did manage to hang

---

37 R.C.K. Ensor, *England 1870–1914*, Oxford University Press (1936), page 406.
38 Ibid.
39 See Christopher Lee, *This Sceptred Isle*, BBC Books (1997), page 183.

on would get 5 shillings (25p) a week. If both the husband and wife survived until they were seventy years old they would get 7s 6d (37½p) between them. In addition to age, the Bill stipulated that:

> The person must satisfy the pension authorities that for at least twenty years up to the date of the receipt of any sum on account of a pension he has been a British subject, and has had his residence, as defined by the regulations . . . in the United Kingdom. The person must satisfy the pension authorities that his yearly means as calculated under this Act do not exceed thirty one pounds ten shillings.

The Treasury was determined that the Bill should include sufficient anomalies to safeguard against bad claims. For example, a woman would lose her pension rights if she married a foreigner because she automatically lost her nationality. The foreigner, however, got a pension because he was married to an Englishwoman. Nevertheless, despite its limitations, the 1908 Pension Act was one of the most important pieces of social legislation to pass through Parliament in the twentieth century. At first, the Lords were inclined to oppose it, but they sensed that the mood of the country was for the Bill and that the Commons might well choose this as the issue on which to challenge the future of the Upper House. They backed down.

They did not retreat on another Bill brought that intended to amend Balfour's 1904 Licensing Act. Heavy drinking, even among the very young, was commonplace, but the licensing trade was quick to organize opposition to the Bill. The Tories supported the trade, claiming that the Bill was a direct attack on a major private industry. The Peers rejected the Bill on its second reading and so added to the case for its own reform.

Asquith dominated his Cabinet and shone beyond his reputation on the backbenches. Like all good captains, Asquith put his ablest, not just his favoured, officers in the most important jobs. Winston Churchill became President of the Board of Trade at a time when there were enormous commercial pressures on the government. Haldane remained Secretary for War, and Herbert Gladstone stayed at the Home Office. Sir Edward Grey was still Foreign Secretary, and Walter Runciman was brought in to run Education.

By choosing Lloyd George as Chancellor, Asquith was putting someone quite unlike himself into the job. Although both were, in a middle-class manner, self-made men, Asquith was regarded as a Balliol-educated barrister, whereas Lloyd George proudly saw himself as a country lawyer. As Chancellor, Lloyd George's task was to balance the increased financing of older people against a budget that was too small to cope with the real costs. When government supporters persuaded Asquith to include the really poor – that is, those people already on poor relief – up went the cost. Here was the beginning of a dilemma that was to haunt party managers, election campaign directors, social service ministers and Chancellors of the Exchequer for the rest of the century. The dilemma of how to protect the aged from the financial impossibilities of living so long took root in 1908.

For Asquith and Lloyd George the fiscal conundrum was compounded by legislation that meant the rearranging of the Poor Laws. And then along came the admirals. Campbell-Bannerman had embarked on a programme of cutting back the Dreadnought-class battleship programme. Four vessels had been promised; this was cut to three, and then two. In a new journal, *The Nation*, Campbell-Bannerman had explained his thoughts on world arms reductions. The Germans condemned the article as trickery, and not even the offer of disarmament would encourage the Germans to cut their own warship programme. Indeed, Admiral von Tirpitz increased his building rate to four ships a year. The reduction in the Royal Navy's development, promised under the plan put forward by Cawdor,[40] was about to have an inevitable but frightening impact on government. And this came about because of a change of mood in Germany.

The Kaiser, Edward VII's nephew, was falling from grace in his own country. On 28 October 1908 the London *Daily Telegraph* had carried a long interview with Wilhelm II in which he played on his Englishness and even claimed that Germany was a truly anglophile nation. Here was a test of strength, not between Britain and Germany, but between the Kaiser and his own government. Wilhelm II's pronouncements on international relations were seen by the German government as direct interference in the making of foreign policy, and the decline in the Kaiser's influence over German politics and in particular his influence over the military can be dated from this moment in 1908.

The British government in 1908 could no longer ignore Germany's military programme. The political battle for Dreadnoughts was to run over into 1909.

Of more immediate concern to Asquith's government were events in Russia and Persia.

Edward VII accepted an invitation to visit his kinsman, Tsar Nicholas II, at the Baltic port of Reval.[41] The news of the visit disrupted business in the Commons when the Labour MP Keir Hardie said that the Tsar was a murderer and that the King's visit condoned his crimes. Many at Westminster found the cruelty shown towards the Russian peasantry and, especially, towards ethnic groups intolerable. Circulating among MPs was a statement from the Jewish Relief League claiming that the Tsar fully supported the anti-Semitic pogroms that were conducted against thousands of Russian Jews. Officials travelling with the King raised the question of the treatment of Jews but made no progress.

Of more than passing interest to the royal party was the impressive display of German naval power they saw as they passed through the Kiel Canal, a waterway

---

40 See page 28.

41 This visit turned out to be the last of a British monarch to Russian soil until Elizabeth II's visit in 1994.

still being widened to give the fast-growing German battle fleet easy access to the North Sea.[42] The Germans regarded Edward's visit as politically and militarily provocative, even though the King made a point of not including ministers at his meetings with the Tsar. German suspicions were heightened when the Tsar returned to Reval in July for an official meeting with the president of France, Clément-Armand Fallières. In light of the insecurity felt throughout Europe, the Kaiser's commanders felt encouraged to raise their own questions of vulnerability and the need to continue the building and training programmes in the army and navy.

The second of three foreign affairs events in 1908 had the Foreign Office searching for its strategic assessments of Russian interests in Persia. Earlier in the year, Russian troops had been sent south when Turkish troops were reported to be entering Persia. The movement against the Shah's rule was gathering pace in Tehran, and on 22 June the Cossack imperial guard entered the capital and savagely put down the attempted take-over by liberal reformers. Britain was inclined to support the liberal leadership and did not believe that this was the end of the reform movement. Nor was it the end of Russian ambitions in the region.

Significantly, at the end of July 1908, the Shah of Persia was forced to restructure his parliament, and the model for this new tool of democracy was not Westminster, but the Russian Duma.

The third sequence of events to exercise Sir Edward Grey, the Foreign Secretary, was instability in Turkey and yet another crisis in the Balkans. For six months, since the beginning of 1908, the Foreign Office had anticipated a complete break-down in stability in that part of Europe.

From the main protagonists in the affair we get the modern phrase that signifies a group that has no time for the old ways, Young Turks. The Young Turks were disrupting and challenging every institution in Turkey. The Sultan, Abdul Hamed II, had decreed that the country's constitution was in abeyance, but the revolutionaries, the Young Turks, demanded that the Ottoman (Turkish) parliament be recalled and that all national and ethnic groups should be able to send delegates to the forum in Constantinople (later Istanbul).

The Balkans had long been a tinderbox that could easily light fires throughout the region. Different groups lived in states that were legally Turkish but were basically self-governing. Some of them lived in Bosnia-Herzegovina, which was actually governed by Austria-Hungary, which theoretically controlled lands and peoples that could too easily be agitated into revolution by what was happening in Turkey.

The British, together with the French, German and Russians (who supported the Slavs living in the Balkans), realized that Austria-Hungary would attempt to take over some of the region. Russia had an agreement with Austria-Hungary that

42 See page 28.

neither state would interfere with the stability of the Balkans, but the situation was further complicated by the growing German influence in Turkey.

In 1908, therefore, Asquith's government was faced by increased tensions in areas where Britain had a traditional interest but was unwilling to get involved in any new dispute. The Germans were looking to their own interests, which were threatened by instability. And the Russians were threatening war if Austria-Hungary disturbed the status quo ante. On top of all this, there was a natural instinct in Macedonia – where there always seemed to be an anti-Ottoman demonstration and encouragement for every Balkan grouping whether national or ethnic – to take part in this regional agitation.

Russia could be bought off, but this was a temporary solution, because the Russians believed that the Habsburgs (the Austro-Hungarian Empire) had promised them compensation, which would mean that the Russians would not mind changing the agreement that they had signed as long ago as 1878. Either the Russians did not understand what the Austro-Hungarian offer meant, or the other side did not, or the whole thing was deceitful diplomacy.

In October 1908 Austria-Hungary annexed the land it had intended to take. The Russians complained long and bitterly that they had been cheated, but the Germans sided with the Habsburgs. This meant that the Russians had to risk fighting Germany and Austria-Hungary at the same time – which would be a hopeless prospect. Moreover, the French would not help Serbia, and Russia's pliant province would be overrun. The Russians were in an impossible position and backed down.

The Dual Monarchy of Austria-Hungary and Russia were ancient enemies in the Balkans, and once again war had only just been averted. Russia's pride was deeply wounded, and, more seriously, Russia had been unable to defend what it believed to be its rights in the Balkans. It was only three years since the Russian army and fleet had been annihilated by the Japanese, and the unrest that had started as a direct consequence of that defeat would lead inexorably to the Revolution. In consequence, Russia began a rapid programme of military rebuilding and restructuring.

Thus, as Europe approached the end of 1908 Russia, Germany, Britain and, to some extent, France were building up their armed forces and strengthening their supply lines.

In October the British government announced that 24,000 men were to be recruited as extra troops in the Special Reserve and that thousands more would be needed in the dockyards to work on warship repairs. This decision may have had as much to do with unemployment as it did with strategic caution. There were now more than a million paupers in Britain; a million more were jobless. There was no mechanism to create jobs and some important industries had long been declining. World prices and increased production elsewhere meant that the cotton industry that had been the backbone of the economy of Lancashire, which had produced millions of yards of cloth for export each year, was in terminal decline.

Agriculture had been in decline since the early 1880s and the migration from the poorly paid countryside to the better paid urban districts had continued.

The management of the labour force and the relationship between jobs and government policies would now have to reach a level of sophistication never before thought necessary. This was to be a three-cornered contest in which industry, government and workforce would struggle for most of the century.

The headline writers had much more cheerful moments to record, and one in particular that said much about Britain's relations with France. In May the Franco-British Exhibition was opened in Shepherd's Bush, London, where a 200-acre site had been cleared to build twenty-five exhibition halls and pavilions. The centrepiece was a collection of white oriental palaces over a lake setting. It was named White City.

Not all demonstrations in London reflected political harmony. June saw the biggest ever demonstration by the suffragette movement. Some 200,000 gathered in Hyde Park, the ladies wearing hats and green, purple and white sashes, led by Emmeline Pankhurst's daughter, Christabel.

The still sparkling White City was the venue for the 1908 Olympic Games. For the first time there was a Winter Olympics, although this was confined to ice skating, which in July took some organizing. The highlight of the Games was a competitor who did not win. The Italian marathon runner, Dorando Pietri, became the hero of the crowds when he entered the stadium completely exhausted, wearing a singlet with a crudely written no. 19 on his chest and long, baggy shorts. He staggered and fell. He got up, staggered and fell again. Officials ran to his help and encouraged him on. He finished long before anyone else but had to be disqualified because he had been helped. The nation was devastated. Pietri was devastated. Queen Alexandra was devastated. And so in the spirit of the Games, unrecognizable to the Italian's grandchildren, a special gold cup complete with ornate lid was found, engraved and presented to the plucky Pietri by a gracious Queen Alexandra.

A less energetic sporting hero was making his last appearance in April. W.G. Grace, the bearded and most celebrated of cricketers, had decided to give up the first class game shortly before his sixtieth birthday. He had begun playing first class cricket in 1865 and in his career had scored more than 54,000 runs and taken more than 2800 wickets.

Kenneth Grahame wrote *The Wind in the Willows*, and W.H. Davies wrote *Autobiography of a Super-tramp*. Jack Johnson became the first black man to win the world heavyweight championship. Ernest Rutherford was awarded the Nobel Prize for chemistry. Edward Elgar's First Symphony was premièred in the Free Trade Hall, Manchester. But the most glittering end to an often dangerous 1908 took place in Amsterdam, where the Cullinan diamond was cut. When the workshop had finished holding its breath they had produced eight perfect diamonds, seven of which were made into a necklace for Queen Alexandra.

If the idea that diamonds were a royal girl's best friend was not glitzy enough, the ultimate world of make-believe was. In America a new film was made, *The Count of Monte Cristo*. For the first time the film industry had decided on the perfect location, simply because of the reliable weather. It was called Hollywood. As the job queues lengthened in Britain, it was reported from America that more than 100,000 people were already employed in the American film business.

Deaths
Antoine-Henri Becquerel (French physicist)
Sir Henry Campbell-Bannerman (politician)
Stephen Grover Cleveland (US president)
Joel Chandler Harris (US writer)
Ouida (novelist)
Nikolai Rimsky-Korsakov (Russian composer)

1909

WHILE EUROPE took a step closer to war, Westminster moved to the brink of political anarchy.

Few achievements come without conflict, and so it was in 1909 in the British constitutional system. During the opening years of the twentieth century the composition of government and its attitude to the House of Lords had shifted. We have already noted that one continuing problem facing Campbell-Bannerman's government had been opposition, not in the Commons, but in the House of Lords. There was nothing new in this – it was, after all, part of a revising chamber's job to challenge legislation – and it was not long since Tory peers had ruined Gladstone's second Home Rule Bill; the 1884 electoral reform Bill got through only after long negotiations between Gladstone and Salisbury; all the legislation of Rosebery's year-long government was blocked; and the peers had rejected and ejected the 1906 Education Bill and made the Land Bills of the following year quite unworkable. They even interfered with that most popular piece of legislation, the 1908 Old Age Pensions Bill.

Confrontation was inevitable, but it was important for the government that it was a crucial piece of legislation because confronting the Lords was to offer a challenge to an essential part of Britain's constitutional heritage and law-making process and could not be undertaken lightly. The test of constitutional strength needed public backing, and that would come only if the legislation in question was something *all* the people wanted. Only one piece of government business affected the whole nation, the Budget, and the detail and principle of Lloyd George's 1909 Budget became the battlefield on which the future role and power of the House of Lords would be fought. It was a particularly important finance Bill.

Events in Europe had made it clear why the army had to be modernized and why the navy needed extra Dreadnoughts. In addition, the new old age pensions, which were proving enormously popular, were running at 400 per cent above the original estimate, and the country needed a new road-building programme. More than £15 million had to be raised by new taxation, a sum, say, at 2000 prices that would need a 'crisis budget'. About £600,000 a year came from motorists through taxes on petrol and licences to drive. Death duties were now to produce £4.4 million. There was to be an increase in tobacco and spirits duties of £3.5 million, and another £2.6 million was to come from liquor licences. Income tax would rise from 1s to 1s 2d in the pound, and for the first time something called super-tax was introduced and aimed at those with incomes of more than £3000 a year. The higher income duties and especially the new land value duties, effectively a 20 per cent capital gains tax on land values, affected few commoners, but many in the House of Lords.

In return for this taxation the country was going to get warships, old age pensions and labour exchanges (the Edwardian equivalent of job centres). There was even a green section in the Budget – there was to be a Development Commission for the countryside. This was a Budget that apparently offended few and cheered many, even though the increase in liquor licences would probably upset the brewers, who had recently, so they thought, managed to persuade the peers to kill off the Licensing Bill. The violent reaction to the Budget had a much deeper cause: the debate over free trades and tariff reform had not gone away. Lloyd George was raising through increased taxes money that he might otherwise have got from import duties. Joseph Chamberlain had promised that raising revenue through tariffs was the way to finance social reform. Lloyd George was getting the money from the people themselves. The tariff reformers did not like the Budget.

This probably would not have mattered in public terms and would not really have been enough to cause the collision between Lords and Commons, had it not been for the most vitriolic attacks on the Budget that appeared in the newspapers owned by the Harmsworth Press. Harmsworth, who became 1st Viscount Northcliffe in 1919, owned the *London Evening News* and had started the *Daily Mail* in 1896. He and his brother, later Lord Rothermere, bought the *Sunday Despatch* and, in 1903, had produced the first newspaper for women, the *Daily Mirror*. In 1908, the year before the Budget, and after a long legal battle, Northcliffe had bought *The Times*. This then was a formidable media battalion set against Lloyd George. But the Chancellor appeared unperturbed.

The objections to the Budget from members of the House of Lords, especially those that appeared in the press, were counterproductive in terms of public opinion, which saw the rich getting angry about having to put relatively small amounts into the public purse for the benefit of the less well off. Moreover, the Lords did not organize their opposition very well and Tory supporters of free trade had no real case to argue. Balfour, the former prime minister, had no real influence, and where once he had been able to command a middle way, he now could find little support among any but those with extreme views, and this neither suited him intellectually nor gave him the gravitas of an elder statesman.

What followed, in retrospect, seems to have been unnecessary. The Conservatives, the loyal opposition, were politically against the Budget. They made the mistake of forcing the pace and opened the challenge, which was what the government wanted if they were to show the people that peers challenged the constitutional right of the Commons (and therefore the people) to decide how it would raise taxes and spend the money it raised. The Tories were really saying that the fiscal management of the country was less important than a political confrontation with the government.

During the summer of 1909 the main opposition had come from the Tories in the Commons because the Finance Bill had not yet reached the Lords. This was the summer that Lloyd George came to the fore of the political class. His speech, on 30 July, is remembered as one of the finest of Edwardian politics, but it was easy for him to present the Tory peers as caricatures from the pages of *Punch* magazine. More serious opposition to his tactics came from within the Cabinet, but he could rely on the prime minister. Asquith bore the brunt of Cabinet criticism and put his own reputation on the line, standing shoulder to shoulder with Lloyd George – which is why many never forgave Lloyd George for turning on Asquith seven years later.

Although the Lords felt they had a right to amend Money Bills, there was no modern constitutional precedent for the Lords rejecting a Budget. To do so, raised two issues: constitutional precedence and, more important, the reaction of the people. If the Lords rejected Lloyd George's Budget, Asquith would have to hold a general election in which the real issue would be: 'Do you agree or disagree with the action of the House of Lords?'

If the government lost that election, the House of Lords and not the House of Commons would effectively become the legislative chamber and the nation's government would revert to the hereditary peers. This was the constitutional issue that Lloyd George had brought to a head. The matter was so important that Edward VII himself became involved, and he made the private suggestion that a political bribe could be offered to the Lords and the Tories, which amounted to the same group. The King suggested that if the Lords agreed the Finance Bill, Asquith's government would be willing to call an election in the New Year. This was rather an inept solution, and it seemed the King had not grasped the constitutional principle.

In November 1909 the Finance Bill went through the Commons. The Lords rejected it, and the prime minister, Asquith, immediately tabled the resolution:

> That the action of the House of Lords in refusing to pass into Law the financial provisions made by this House for the service of the year is a breach of the Constitution and a usurpation of the rights of the Commons.

This meant that there had to be a general election. Yet votes alone would not decide the outstanding issue: the Budget had not been passed.

*

The more cheerful news of the year included the opening of the Victoria and Albert Museum in South Kensington and the revolution in classical ballet with Diaghilev's productions of *Prince Igor* and *Les Sylphides*, performed by Nijinsky and Pavlova.

The first colour films to be seen in Britain appeared in Brighton, and in London H.G. Selfridge, who had worked in Marshall Field & Co. in Chicago, returned to Britain and opened London's first department store in Oxford Street; it became one of the largest department stores in Europe.

More dangerously, Louis Blériot became the first man to fly across the English Channel, landing at Dover Castle on 25 July 43 minutes after leaving Calais. The summer was very English and for a moment Blériot was lost in cloud. A French reporter saw him through a break in the clouds and waved the tricolour to guide him to his historic landing and the £1000 put up by the *Daily Mail*. Blériot had better luck than Count von Zeppelin who had, a couple of weeks earlier when trying to fly one of his airships to Berlin, hit a pear tree and was late for lunch with the Kaiser.

A hazardous journey ended in triumph, when Commander Robert E. Peary became the first man to reach the North Pole. Guglielmo Marconi, however, did not have to travel far to receive his honour, the Nobel Prize for his work on the development of the wireless.

In Belgium the chemist Leo Baekeland had accidentally invented a synthetic material that would soon be used as the casing for Marconi radios. From Baekeland came Bakelite.

Deaths

Geronimo (Apache leader)
George Meredith (novelist and poet)
Algernon Charles Swinburne (poet)
John Millington Synge (Irish playwright)

CHAPTER TWO

THE ROAD TO WARS 1910–1919

1910

THE YEAR opened with the nation preparing for a general election in January, but it was not prepared for the death of the King. Edward VII died at the beginning of the summer and was succeeded by George V. For the moment, however, nothing mattered more than polling day.

The Conservatives lost as they had expected to, but there was no Liberal landslide. The Liberals had 272 seats, as did the Unionists (Conservatives 237, Liberal Unionists 35). The Labour Party (with 40 MPs) and the Irish Nationalists (with 82) would vote with the Liberals, and as long as they continued to do so, the Tory Unionists would effectively be in a minority of 124. In 1909 the Irish Nationalists had voted against the second reading of Lloyd George's Budget (although they abstained on the third reading) because they objected to the increase in the tax on alcohol. The Labour Party felt that it should vote against the government on principle and, no doubt, to prove its independence to its grass-root supporters.

These differences were overcome by the unifying objective of reforming the House of Lords, and the majority of 124, which was effectively the largest government majority since 1832, would make that possible. Asquith did not want to bring down the Lords, merely to revise their powers, but one obstacle stood in the way of reform: Ireland and Home Rule.

The debate over Home Rule had its origins in the 1801 Act of Union between Britain and Ireland. In 1870 the Home Government Association (later the Home Rule League) had been formed, bolstered by about sixty Irish MPs at Westminster. A decade later these MPs held the balance of power between the Liberals and Tories. Gladstone, who became a convert to Home Rule for Ireland, introduced a Bill that would have given the island self-government in 1886, but it was defeated because the Liberal Party was split. When Gladstone returned to power in 1893 he produced a second Home Rule Bill, which passed through the Commons but was thrown out by the House of Lords.

By 1910 the importance of Home Rule was becoming clear. As soon as the election result was declared the government wanted to get the Finance Bill through, and the Irish MPs, led now by John Redmond, were willing to support the Liberal government in the Budget debate and in its desire to reform the Lords, but there were conditions for this support, notably that Asquith had to give some guarantees about Home Rule.[1]

The common aim was to bring the Lords into line, but the Tory peers, who were almost entirely opposed to Home Rule, could just as easily veto a Home Rule Bill as they could the Budget. It was up to Asquith to find some way of circumventing the Lords in their present mood.

It was said that before the election he had asked the King if the Upper House could be threatened with the creation of as many new peers as it took to get legislation through. Events in 1832 were a precedent for this. After the general election, Asquith told the House of Commons that he had had no such plan, but this was not true. In fact, the King had rejected the 1832 precedent and had told Asquith, on 15 December 1909, that he would not approve the creation of new members of the House of Lords unless and until there was a second general election the following year – that is, in 1910.

The dispute damaged Asquith's credibility. In a speech in the Albert Hall, London, on 10 December 1909 he had said that the Liberals would not form a government unless they could 'secure the safeguards which experience shows us to be necessary for the legislative utility and honour of the party of progress'. Yet even his Cabinet was not united. A simple Bill that would stop the Lords veto might have satisfied John Redmond and his fellow Irish MPs, but there were those in the Cabinet, including the Foreign Secretary, Sir Edward Grey, who wanted to go much further. More radical Liberals saw this as an opportunity to reform the hereditary system, although for Asquith himself that would be a reform too far.

The Commons business managers set about producing the Parliament Bill. Their first task was to get the principle of the Bill voted through. Three separate resolutions were introduced on the floor of the Commons covering general legislation, financial legislation and the interval between general elections. At this stage a government could exist for seven years. Under the new resolution, the life of a government would be limited to five years. These resolutions were accepted. Then came the Parliament Bill itself and then the Finance Bill, which would make the Budget measure law. That went through the House of Commons on 27 April and was sent to the Lords.

The prologue to the Parliament Bill noted that the greater ambition was to make the Lords a Chamber based on a 'popular' (elected) rather than a hereditary footing, but the time was not right to insist upon that. We have, nevertheless, the

1 In the 1990s peace campaigners in Northern Ireland pointed to the emergence of Mandela's South Africa as an example of what was possible. There was nothing new in this comparison. In 1910 politicians pointed to Campbell-Bannerman's success in resolving differences in South Africa as a template for Irish Home Rule.

beginnings of change in the House of Lords. Asquith was not alone in accepting that legislation could start in the Lords, but he believed that government-drafted laws should not perish there. Grey and his supporters wanted a vigorous but largely elected second chamber, and all reformers saw the Lords as a revising committee rather than as a blocking chamber. Asquith was certainly not willing to spend too long contemplating what was now before him: a group of aristocratic muggers going about their task for either reactionary or political (or both) reasons.

Reasonably confident that the constitutional crisis had been thus far managed, the House adjourned, but while the MPs were away, Edward VII died on 6 May. He was succeeded by his second son, who became George V, because his eldest son, the Duke of Clarence, had died in 1892.

George V, an intelligent man, understood the constitutional debate over Lords reform and suggested a constitutional conference. Asquith's Cabinet did not like the idea, but Balfour saw its sense although he did not have the support of the Unionist majority. The existing stalemate would mean an election, however, so the conference met, in secret, at 10 Downing Street on 16 June 1910. Eight men sat around the long Cabinet table. On the government side were Asquith; Lloyd George, the Chancellor; Augustine Birrell, the Chief Secretary for Ireland; and the Earl of Crewe, the Colonial Secretary. The other four men in the room were the key members of the opposition: Arthur Balfour; Austen Chamberlain (Joseph Chamberlain's son), who had been Chancellor in Balfour's Cabinet; the Earl of Cawdor, Balfour's sometime First Lord of the Admiralty; and the Marquess of Lansdowne, Balfour's former Foreign Secretary. These names suggest that that the views of the House of Lords would be well represented but unlikely to be changed. No accurate minutes of the meeting were taken, however.[2]

The constitutional conference lasted until November but ended in failure. The eight did not disagree on the constitutional issue but on the Conservative Unionists' determination to stop Home Rule for Ireland. There was agreement that the Lords would not reject the Budget. There was also an understanding that if the Lords rejected a Bill in two consecutive years there should be a combined sitting of Lords and Commons to decide what should happen to it. However, the Conservatives would not agree that *all* legislation could be referred to the joint sittings, and they were particularly concerned that no constitutional or structural bills would be considered. The Conservatives said that constitutional bills could be decided only by a referendum.

The Liberals would have gone along with the Conservative and Lords on most constitutional bills, but not on Irish Home Rule, and if one person at that conference was responsible for its failure on the Irish question, that person was Lansdowne, who, although sitting with Balfour's group, was an Irish peer and had been a Liberal. Having opposed Gladstone's Home Rule for the Irish Bill, Lansdowne joined the coalition of Liberals and Unionists. He later joined the

2 In 1910 not even Cabinet meetings had minutes.

Conservatives and had become the Conservative leader in the House of Lords, remaining in this position until 1917, when he was criticized for suggesting a compromise for peace with Germany. There is no doubt that Lansdowne's position on Ireland was consistent: he had opposed Gladstone, and nothing he had heard at the constitutional conference had changed his mind.

Asquith went to see the King, and it was agreed that he would not call an election until the Lords had voted on the Parliament Bill. The Bill was sent to the Lords who, in the expression of that place, 'postponed the consideration of it'. The peers produced their own plan, one that reflected Campbell-Bannerman's 1907 proposal.[3] A money Bill would be allowed through without the assent of the peers as long as it had been before a joint Lords–Commons committee, with the Speaker[4] having a casting vote and being happy that whatever was being proposed was indeed a money Bill. With certain provisions, anything the Lords rejected could still become law if it had been passed by the House of Commons in three successive sessions of Parliament. The third point was the reduction of the life of a Parliament from seven to five years.

Two years earlier, in 1908, the Cawdor committee on reform had recommended an upper chamber in which about 20 per cent of the members should be elected or chosen rather than sitting there by right of birth. In November 1910 peers voted for a reform that would have meant that:

> in future the House of Lords shall consist of Lords of Parliament: (a) chosen by the whole body of hereditary peers from among themselves and by nomination of the Crown; (b) sitting by virtue of offices and of offices held by them; [e.g. a law officer] (c) chosen from outside.[5]

This may sound like a serious proposal for reform, but at the time (and probably rightly) most saw the Lords proposal as nothing more than political tactics.

Asquith announced that Parliament would be dissolved on 28 November. The Conservatives knew their campaign would have to avoid any debate on Lords reform and the right of veto (which the voters seemed to want). Their best chance was to oppose Home Rule for Ireland, and Balfour added a promise that there would be a referendum on free trade and tariff reform.

The election took place in December and the two main parties tied: Liberals 272, Unionists 272, Irish Nationalists 84 and Labour 42. The Liberals had the support, albeit reluctant, of Labour and the Irish. George V understood that if the Lords continued to reject the Parliament Bill, Britain would have an enormous constitutional crisis. He was under pressure to agree to Asquith's demand for an

---

3 See page 44.

4 In practice, it would probably be the Chairman of Ways and Means; the Speaker would not preside over money Bills.

5 Hansard.

honours list packed with as many as 250 Liberal peers, appointed for no other reason than to out-vote the Conservatives in the Lords.

As MPs went away for Christmas each knew that he would return in 1911 to witness the biggest parliamentary constitutional issue and confrontation in his political lifetime.

The grandest occasion of the year was Edward VII's funeral, and the list of mourners tells us so much of the times. In addition to the new King, George V, eight European monarchs were present, those of Germany, Greece, Denmark, Bulgaria, Belgium, Norway and the Iberian houses of Spain and Portugal. Also present were forty members of other monarchies, including the Crown Prince of Serbia. This was such a royal occasion that no commoners, not even the prime minister, were included in the funeral procession.

There was another spectacular funeral in London that year. The first woman to hold the Order of Merit and the founder of the St Thomas's Hospital Nursing School, Florence Nightingale, died. The funeral service was almost a state occasion, and even Queen Alexandra, now the Queen Mother, sent a wreath. Miss Nightingale, as she continued to be known, had caught the public imagination for the work she carried out at Scutari Hospital during the Crimean War more than half a century earlier. Here once more was a reminder that at the beginning of the century, it was quite possible to know someone who had heard a first-hand account of the Crimea War. One of the wreaths sent to the St Paul's Cathedral service came from survivors of the Charge of the Light Brigade.

An even larger gathering was seen at Westminster when 10,000 suffragettes took to the streets to support a Labour motion in the House of Commons to give women the vote. Such a show of force might have persuaded a Liberal prime minister to support the Labour motion or at least to have it withdrawn on the promise of introducing legislation in the government's own timetable. Surprisingly, the Liberal government did not want to bring in an Enfranchisement Bill. Asquith said he would not introduce what he called 'contentious' legislation; he just did not believe legislation would get through both Houses. His government had a large majority over the Conservative Unionists on major issues because he had the support of Labour and Irish Nationalist MPs. He could not guarantee the same level of support for an issue like women's suffrage. Parliamentary time had to be used selectively, and in 1910 it could not cope with enormous quantities of legislation. MPs did not attend the House for the same amount of time that they did by the end of the twentieth century, because they were not paid and all had interests outside Westminster.[6]

The suffragettes marched on Downing Street, an event described in *The Times*:

---

6 It was not until August 1911 that the Commons agreed to pay each MP £400 per year.

> their increased fierceness may be accounted for by the fact that some of them have vowed to go to prison for their cause, and are prepared to commit increasingly serious breaches of the law to achieve this object. The rioters yesterday appear to have lost all control of themselves. . . . all fought with a dogged but aimless pertinacity. Some of the rioters appeared to be quite young girls, who must have been the victims of hysterical rather than deep conviction. . . . The women behaved like demented creatures and it is evident that their conduct completely alienated the sympathy of the crowd. The police behaved with self-control and good humour under the greatest provocation.

Here was a reflection of the popular opinion that suffragettes believed that only the noisiest and most violent demonstrations would force any government into bringing forward its own legislation for universal suffrage.

A more cheerful note was sounded when it was found that the trade figures were up, and in spite of unemployment and threats to the cotton industry, there was relative prosperity. A major part of the export market was to the 350 million people in the British Empire, but ominously, Britain's share of that growing market was falling. This news led to a renewal of the campaign for imperial trade preferences.

Unemployment was rising, however, and conditions for those in work were often harder than before. Eighty labour exchanges were opened throughout the country, and there were more people in the queue for work than there were jobs for them, yet the economy appeared sound.

In 1910 Britain produced more than 264 million tons of coal, about a quarter of which was for export. It was the highest production figure and export total that Britain's coal industry would ever again see. It came also in a year when miners in the Northeast coal fields went on strike, protesting not only at the pit-owners but also at their own Durham Miners' Executive. The miners' leaders had agreed a new twenty-four-hour working system of three eight-hour shifts a day, and the men rioted. Sympathy for the miners was widespread, for most people understood the hardships and the hazards of the trade. This was emphasized just before Christmas 1910, when an explosion deep in the Hulton Colliery in Lancashire killed nearly 350 men. Miners in Wales went on strike for ten months during 1910, and troops were sent in on more than one occasion, sometimes with violent results.

The miners were not the only workers facing difficulties. There was a feud between the dock- and ship-building unions and the Ship Building Employers' Federation. The Boiler Makers' Society had called several strikes, and at the time there were about 68,000 boiler-makers, two-thirds of whom worked in the shipyards. There were now nineteen shipyard unions, with a total of only 70,000 members. The boiler-makers, seen as the troublemakers, claimed that national pay agreements – a concept that would remain controversial for the rest of the century – meant that employers were able to cut rates of pay in some jobs. The Ship Building Employers' Federation confronted the unions and locked out the entire workforce, hoping to isolate the boiler-makers. The other men could not do their jobs unless the boiler-makers did theirs. The Federation won.

In October the determination of employers to challenge union pressures was seen in the Lancashire cotton industry's 700 mills. In the previous summer, strikes had started over the sacking of one worker. Early in October the owners shut down all 700 mills. The seriousness of this can be judged by the fact that the government immediately intervened. A deal was worked out and the mills reopened, but few believed the industry was settled.

Britain's cotton industry had begun to boom in the 1840s and by 1910 about a quarter of Britain's exports were cotton goods – some 5.5 million yards of cotton cloth went abroad that year. The Lancashire cotton industry was Britain's single biggest exporter.[7] At first the markets were in the United States and Europe, but in 1900 these outlets had developed their own production and Britain had to rely on countries that did not have the industrial base to convert raw cotton. This meant that the Lancashire mills were weaving largely for the eastern end of the Mediterranean, for China and, particularly, for India. Once the developing world began to make its own cloth, the economy of Lancashire would collapse. This started to happen in 1910, and within a generation the industry was in full decline.

Forty years on, Britain's cotton industry was exporting 10 per cent of what it had in 1910, and by 1960 British cotton exports were not large enough to register on any statistical scale.

Other industries were expanding, however. In 1910 Britain's steel producers enjoyed a record year: 6.5 million tonnes left the mills and, with some exceptions (notably the economic and strike-stifled period in the late 1920s and 1930s), Britain's steel production was to continue to rise, until 60 years later the industry was producing 28 million tons a year.

From almost single-workshop production in 1900 and the time George V came to the throne, Britain was producing about 30,000 motor vehicles a year. In that year it was estimated that there were 53,000 private cars on British roads and perhaps 30,000 vans and trucks (by the end of the century there would be more than 25 million).

Most people still travelled long distances by train, however, and in 1910 there were almost 20,000 miles of railways across the country, used by some 1.28 million passengers. This figure grew until 1920 when it was estimated that the railways attracted some 1.6 million passengers. It was not until then that the motor car and bus changed the habits of the British traveller, and the railways lost about half their passengers within twenty years.

★

---

7 Iron and steel made up 14 per cent of the nation's exports, coal about 10 per cent and machinery 7 per cent. In 1910 Britain became a major car exporter; 3 per cent of the value of British exports came from the motor industry.

The year 1910 is remembered for milestones far from the events of Westminster. For the first time an X-ray machine was used to illuminate a child's lung so that a surgeon could watch on a screen as he removed a nail with forceps through a small incision.

It was also the year when Dr Hawley Harvey Crippen was captured because it was possible to link up the ship on which he was travelling by radio. Crippen had murdered and then chopped up his wife, Cora Turner, in their house in Camden Town and hidden her beneath the cellar floor. In July 1910 he escaped with his mistress, Ethel le Neve (dressed as a boy), and boarded the SS *Montrose*, which was sailing from Antwerp to Quebec. They were booked as Mr and Master Robinson. The master of the *Montrose*, Captain Henry Kendall, thought it odd (which it would have been in 1910) to see the two 'men' holding hands and used his wireless to notify the police in Britain. The chase was on. Scotland Yard's Chief Inspector Walter Dew boarded the *Laurentic*, a faster ship, and got to Canada before the *Montrose*. He slipped aboard disguised as a St Lawrence River pilot. Crippen was caught, taken back to London for trial, found guilty of poisoning his wife and was hanged[8] in London on 23 November 1910. Crippen was, therefore, the first criminal captured by the still relatively new gadget, wireless.

In moments information could reach almost anywhere in the world. How incongruous that armies were still so reliant on horses. Even though motor vehicles were being built and an expected German offensive was just four years away, the military demand for horses was considerable. It was estimated, in February 1910, that on the outbreak of war the British army would need 170,000 horses and would need the same number every six months. Britain's horse breeders could easily meet that demand in 1910.

It is tempting to look on Edward's monarchy with nostalgia, yet the long Edwardian summer was an illusion. Those nine years were sometimes the most bitter in British social and political life. It was, too, the period in which the nation was heading inevitably for the most horrendous war it had ever fought. If the Edwardian Age has an epitaph, it was the period in which the British peoples began to lose the innocence of surprise and be left with not much more than amazement. Invention and innovation ran so quickly together that very soon people would no longer be overwhelmed by advances in science and technology.

Deaths

Mary Baker Eddy (US founder of Christian Science Church)
Edward VII
O. Henry (US writer)
Julia Ward Howe (US suffragist)

---

8 Hanging for murder was not abolished in the United Kingdom until 1965 and for arson in 1971. Treason and piracy with violence is still (1999) a hanging offence.

William Holman Hunt (artist)
Robert Koch (German scientist)
Florence Nightingale (nurse)
Charles Stewart Rolls (manufacturer and aviator)
Henri 'Douanier' Rousseau (French artist)
Leo Tolstoy (Russian writer)
Mark Twain (US writer)

1911

THROUGH THE LONG Christmas holiday and into the New Year, prayers were said for the guidance needed by the nation's political leaders as they prepared themselves for the constitutional debate that would decide the power of the House of Lords for the rest of the century.

It is not known how devoutly the nation prayed that its politicians would receive divine guidance. Britain claimed to be a religious nation and the Church of England was established by Parliament, but it was not a church-going nation. The figures for the Anglican Church are usually balanced on Easter Day, this being one of the festivals on which members of the church were required by law to attend. On Easter Day 1911 2.29 million communicants attended the Church of England to be ministered to by 23,193 clergymen. There were nearly 800,000 Methodists, 419,000 Baptists, 494,000 Congregationalists and, in Scotland, 1.22 million Presbyterians. The Roman Catholic population of the United Kingdom in 1911 was 1.71 million, of whom more than 900,000 were regular worshippers. The power of prayer and political management were about to be tested.

On 21 February 1911 Asquith introduced the Parliament Bill and three months later it received its third reading. The battle was not to be conducted on the floor of the House of Commons. The Lords, perhaps anticipating a constitutional revolution, were themselves debating the reform of their own chamber. They made little progress, although Lansdowne proposed that there should be a second chamber of 350 peers, who would be chosen by four methods. The only group there by absolute right were a bench of bishops, the law lords and the royal princes. The second group would be composed of 100 hereditary peers selected by other peers. The third group would be 120 peers selected regionally by MPs. The fourth group would be nominated by the Crown, in reality the government, and would reflect the balance of parties in the House of Commons. This was a serious model for an improved yet still unelected second chamber, and the proposal got as far as a second reading in the Lords. This framework, claimed as original, resurfaced in 1999.

On 23 May 1911 the Parliament Bill arrived in the House of Lords. During the next six weeks it was radically amended and returned to the Commons. If there was a sense of tactical politics here by the Conservative leader in the Lords, Lord Lansdowne, it was soon usurped by a group of die-hard Tory peers. On the Bill's third reading in the Upper House on 20 July, speeches from the celebrated judge, the Earl of Halsbury, and Lord Willoughby de Broke defied the Parliament Bill. Their interventions, while not arguing any new constitutional issue, met with such approval that the House seemed heading towards a constitutional precipice.

There were now two groups. The Hedgers, led by Lansdowne, were trying to contrive delays and even compromise. The Ditchers were trying to preserve the power of the Lords. Lansdowne knew that Asquith was determined and he knew, too, that the King, however reluctantly, might have to approve a long list of political peers. It was Lansdowne's duty, never mind political sense, to tell his colleagues what to do. He should have led. Instead, he asked them what they wanted to do.

The situation was saved by Lord Curzon, who assessed the real strength of the die-hards and lobbied to have them outvoted. It was not easy, and they even had friends in the Commons. On 24 July, in what has been called 'a scene then without precedent', Asquith was barracked continuously by the supporters of the die-hards. Nevertheless, the Commons rejected the Lords' amendments and sent the Bill back to the Upper House. The result was, as an earlier duke would have remarked, a close run thing. On 10 August 1911 the Parliament Bill was passed by 131 votes to 114.

If the Lords had continued to reject that Bill the Liberals would certainly have asked the King to create 250 new peers and could have got through the Parliament Bill, a total reform of the House of Lords and Home Rule for Ireland. That single measure in 1911 would have gone some considerable way to forestalling the troubles of the island of Ireland for the rest of the century.

If the battle for Westminster was over, there remained in Whitehall a belief that the battle for Europe was still to come. The Anglo-German diplomatic relationship had steadied itself since the high tensions of the Balkan emergency three years earlier,[9] but the simple arithmetic of the size and structure of the expanding German high seas fleet could not be ignored. Nevertheless, the Germans had every reason to be equally cautious about the British.

The Germans thought that war with Russia was very possible, and they were anxious to guarantee Britain's neutrality. There was no question of Asquith's government – or any other government – siding with Germany, but the Germans went as far as to hold a series of discussions about limiting its new fleet. The talks continued for about a year, but they were fruitless. Germany offered little except what the Foreign Secretary, Grey, regarded as arrogance.

No matter what the Germans offered, Britain would not have withdrawn from the Entente Cordiale nor its protocol with Russia.

In January 1911 a sub-committee of the Standing Committee of Imperial Defence was appointed. This working party's task was to write and then edit

---

9 See page 53.

something called *The War-Book*, which became the best known document in early twentieth-century British military planning. In it was entered what each department had to do in the event of war.

Although the government was making suitable plans, it did not wish to do anything that could provoke a confrontation, and when, for example, more than two years earlier Field Marshal Lord Roberts had proposed army conscription, his plan had been rejected as being so provocative that it might actually cause a confrontation.

The first act of provocation came from Germany in the summer of 1911; it was the Agadir Crisis. Under the terms of the agreement reached at Algeciras in 1906, France and Germany had agreed not to interfere with each other's interests in Morocco. In April 1911, when the Sultan of Morocco was threatened by rebellion, French troops were sent to the capital, Fez, to protect the Europeans there. Sir Edward Grey, the Foreign Secretary, thought that the French had stretched the terms of the Algeciras agreement by so doing. The Germans suspected that the French actually intended to take over Morocco.

At this time, if a country's rights were affronted, the state's government would expect, and usually get, some form of compensation. Germany now believed that the Algeciras agreement was worthless and that it, Germany, should receive some compensation from the French. The Germans sent a gun boat, the appropriately named *Panther*, to the Moroccan port of Agadir, and three alarm bells sounded in the Foreign Office. First, it was clear that the Germans would be willing to go to war over this issue. Second, Britain had some sort of responsibility towards France. Third, and perhaps in the long term most importantly, if the Germans established a port at Agadir, they would have an Atlantic naval base that would potentially threaten the balance of sea power in Europe.

Grey called in the German ambassador and told him that Britain would never agree to any rearrangement of military power in Morocco without being a partner to it. This amounted to a warning to Germany to back off, although Asquith and Grey were anxious to keep the crisis from reaching boiling point. The Chancellor of the Exchequer, Lloyd George, had a different approach. In a speech on 21 July Lloyd George publicly warned the Germans that this could lead to war. He said:

> I would make great sacrifices to preserve peace. . . . But if a situation were to be forced upon us, in which peace could only be preserved by the surrender of the . . . position Britain has won by centuries of heroism and achievement, by allowing Britain to be treated, where her interests were vitally affected, as if she were of no account in the Cabinet of Nations then I say emphatically that peace at that price would be an humiliation intolerable for a great country like ours to endure.

Here is Lloyd George, a known friend of Germany, telling that nation's leaders that unless it backs down Britain will go to war. There was noisy support for the government in Germany, but there was a quiet realization of where the Agadir Crisis could lead. In November 1911 the *Panther* was withdrawn and the confrontation – apart from the compensation – was over.

Again, Germany's action had brought the British and French closer, and Asquith's government believed that if France were to become a victim of German aggression, public opinion in Britain would support military intervention on the side of France.

This was a year of great occasions: the confrontation between the government and the House of Lords; the seven-hour coronation service of George V on 22 June; and the achievement of the Norwegian, Roald Amundsen, on becoming the first man to reach the South Pole on 14 December. 'Everything went like a dance,' he said. Captain Robert Scott reached the Pole a month later on his second attempt.

It was also the year that saw Balfour stand down as leader of the Conservative Party when he announced that he was to resign because of failing health. He did not give up his political career, however, returning to government during the First World War, initially as First Lord of the Admiralty and later as Foreign Secretary.

Balfour's party was not in good health. Defeated and outwitted, it looked for new leadership, and the two men who might have expected to have a reasonable chance of taking over from Balfour were Walter Long and Austen Chamberlain. Long had been president of the Local Government Board in Balfour's 1902 Cabinet and later Chief Secretary for Ireland; he had considerable support on the backbenches. Chamberlain had been Balfour's Chancellor following the resignation of Charles Ritchie. He, too, had a coterie of backbench followers.

Neither Long nor Chamberlain had enough support to become outright leader, so the party sought a compromise candidate, and the man they chose was the Canadian-born Andrew Bonar Law. Law's parents were Scottish, and he had been educated in Glasgow before becoming an iron merchant. Law had become an MP only eleven years earlier during the Khaki Election of October 1900 and did not have the standing of previous leaders. He did, however, represent a new mood among a sufficient number of the party to get him elected. Law's job was to hold together the party in the Commons.

Winston Churchill had joined Asquith's government in April 1908 as President of the Board of Trade. He had stayed there until 1910, when Herbert Gladstone, the Home Secretary, was sent off to be Governor-General of South Africa and Churchill became Home Secretary. It was in this role that in January 1911 Winston Churchill supervised the breaking of the siege of Sidney Street.

The story began with the deaths of three policemen, who were supposedly assassinated by three anarchists. The three men were tracked to 100 Sidney Street in the East End of London. As police approached the house, they were shot at and one of the policemen was wounded. The army was called in, and by the end of the morning 1000 troops and armed police had sealed off the house.

Winston Churchill, a veteran of punitive raids and charges, arrived to take charge. The army set up a Maxim gun and two 13-pounders, while the Scots Guards took up position with their rifles and the police with their double-barrelled shotguns. Shortly before one o'clock in the afternoon, after hundreds of rounds of ammunition had been fired into the building, smoke was seen coming from the roof. The fire brigade was alerted. Churchill, believing either that the armed men inside made it too dangerous for the firemen or that at this point they would be smoked out, ordered the fire brigade to withdraw. The house burned to the ground as the troops, the policemen and Churchill watched. Two bodies were found in the remains, but the third anarchist, known as Peter the Painter, escaped.

Anarchy was a convenient word that seemed to suit the times. In the same month as the events in Sidney Street occurred, a Russian Jew was murdered on Clapham Common, and it was assumed that an anarchist was the murderer. In Mexico the revolutionary leader Emiliano Zapata (remembered for his moustache) was roaming the north and south of the country under the slogan 'Land and liberty'.

In late autumn, anarchy spread across China. In Shanghai Dr Sun Yat-sen, the Chinese revolutionary leader, was elected as president of the new Chinese Republican government.

In Kiev, the Russian prime minister, Pyotr Stolypin, was shot while he was sitting just yards from Nicholas II at the opera. He died a week later.

In Britain unrest was not confined to the green and red benches of Parliament. Armed troops and police had to be called out to put down increasingly ugly riots. The country was on strike.

The strikes had started with the seamen, who were demanding more money. The ship-owners backed down, which was surprising because before the strike the seamen were among the most disorganized of the unions. Other unions decided that if the seamen could get what they wanted, so could they. The strike spread to the docks, the lightermen on the Thames and the railways. In Llanelli, South Wales, as eighty railway wagons were set on fire, nine people died. Six of them died when the fire set off an explosion in the trucks; the other three were killed by soldiers, and bayonets were fixed against a mass of railwaymen and their supporters.

The railwaymen were on strike in support of the dockers, who carried banners reading: 'War declared! Strike for liberty!' In Liverpool two rioters were shot dead.

By August much of the country was at a standstill. The capital had no buses because there was no petrol, and in some cities food was so scarce that famine warnings were issued. The navy sent three warships to the Mersey to protect merchant vessels waiting to unload. It was estimated that 200,000 people were on strike, and at least 50,000 armed troops plus naval officers and ratings were on duty.

In Liverpool policemen were escorted by soldiers carrying rifles, and the city was without electricity because no coal was getting to the power stations.

★

Despite the unrest, the Chancellor, Lloyd George, was not distracted from the most difficult task facing him in 1911. In May he introduced legislation to set up the National Insurance scheme. Because this was a Money Bill it needed the full attention of the Commons once the Parliament Bill had been returned from the House of Lords. As a result, the full debate did not get under way until the autumn.

The concept was not original. There had been a form of national insurance in Germany since the late 1880s, and Lloyd George's proposals used the German system as a model. Contributions from government (2d), employees (4d) and employers (3d) would be recorded as stamps in National Insurance cards.[10] The main difference of Lloyd George's scheme was the use of unions and friendly societies to help arrange the benefits for their members.

This Bill met such an obvious need that it is difficult from the perspective of the end of the century to imagine that it would be opposed by anything other than amendments for its improvement. But the Conservative Unionists took against it, and they were supported (perhaps urged) by the extreme elements of the press, notably the Harmsworth Press, directed by Alfred Harmsworth, by then Lord Northcliffe.

Coming, as it did, so soon after the confrontation with the Lords, the legislation got through and became law by December 1911. It provided a high note on which the Liberal government would face the New Year, although, strangely enough, it was not one that would gain them many votes.

As the year ended, the population seemed happy enough as it whistled and hummed the top two tunes of 1911 – 'I'm 21 Today' and 'Alexander's Ragtime Band'. The more highbrow might have travelled to Dresden for the opening night of Richard Strauss's new opera, *Der Rosenkavalier.*

It was, however, MPs who broke most cheerfully for Christmas. Until 1911 Members of Parliament were not paid; in that year they voted themselves £400 a year.

Deaths
Sir William Schwenck Gilbert (writer)
Gustav Mahler (Austrian composer)
Carry Nation (US temperance agitator)
Joseph Pulitzer (US publisher and journalist)

1912

1912 WAS the year of the *Titanic.* On 15 April the four-funnelled, unsinkable ship sank, with the loss of more than 1500 lives. The story has been often told, but less often remembered is that in the icy Atlantic that night was born the expression 'And the band played on'.

---

10 Lloyd George did the arithmetic and coined the phrase, 'ninepence for fourpence'.

Closer to home, both Asquith's government and Bonar Law's opposition were concerned about the increasing number of strikes in Britain, the continuing debate about Home Rule for Ireland, the continuing build-up of the German army and the navy, another war in the Balkans and the growing influence of Lenin and Josef Vissarionovich Djugashvili, later known as Joseph Stalin.

The coal strike began in February 1912. Britain was in the middle of a severe winter, with temperatures falling to as low as –35°F (–37°C) and thousands dying of hypothermia. More than a million other people were out of work because of the strike. In March the government introduced a bill that would give the miners a minimum wage that was below their demands. Even though Labour MPs voted against it, the measure was passed and for the first time the principle of a minimum wage was written in law. On 11 April 1912 the National Conference of Miners voted to return to work.

By then the government's mind was on weightier business. Irish MPs held the balance of power at Westminster, and Asquith's government had to commit itself to a new Home Rule Bill. Home Rule did not mean independence; rather, the Bill would give the Irish the right to govern their domestic affairs. Both the earlier Bills (1886 and 1893), which would have gone further than this, had been defeated, the first because the Liberal Unionists defected and the second because the Lords opposed it. In May 1912 the third Bill reached its second reading in the House of Commons and came up against the sharp opposition of the Ulster Unionists.

British politicians had often failed to understand the power of the Ulster Unionists. Even Charles Stewart Parnell, the Protestant Anglo-Irish MP who had led the campaign for Home Rule in the 1870s, had observed that Protestants, apart from the landowners, did not really oppose what he called 'a full measure of autonomy to Ireland'. Now the leader of the Nationalist Party was Parnell's successor, John Redmond (1856–1918), who had supported the concept of Home Rule since the 1880s and had become the leader of the often fragmented Nationalist MPs in 1900. Under his leadership, the Nationalists supported the Liberals after the 1910 election for one purpose, to achieve Home Rule.

Since February 1910 the leader of the Irish Unionists in the House of Commons had been Sir Edward Carson, the Dublin QC, who had been the MP for Trinity College, Dublin, since 1892. He had been Solicitor-General for Ireland in 1892 and for England in 1900–6; he was a charismatic figure, who became something of a hero among Irish Protestants. In the autumn of 1911 Carson stood before an audience of 100,000 members of Ulster Unionists Clubs and the Orange Order and declared they were on a course that could lead to collision of the most severe form. He told them to oppose Home Rule and to plan for a break-away state – the Protestant Province of Ulster. Here then, in simple and contemporary form, lay the origins of Northern Ireland.

The Protestant communities refused to go along with what would effectively have been a federal island of Ireland. Here was a group of people, totally loyal to

Westminster, who believed that Westminster was actually on the point of giving its long-standing enemies domestic control over their affairs. In 1912 Carson and the Protestant Unionists believed that the Home Rule Bill would be passed and that they would be controlled by Dublin. They refused absolutely to countenance the possibility. Indeed, on 5 January 1913, recognizing that a unilateral declaration of independence from the rest of Ireland would have to be enforceable, Ulster Protestants applied to local magistrates for permission to set up a militia. This was the beginning of the Ulster Volunteer Force (UVF). Once the UVF had come into existence, it was clear that any protest would not simply be in self-defence.

It seems that Asquith completely failed to understand what the future would bring or that he had no sense that he could change the conditions that would bring about the separate entity that would be Ulster. He must have had advice from Grey, his Foreign Secretary, and probably from Churchill, who, from all documentary evidence, seems to have understood the predicament of the Ulster Protestants and the fact that they were unbending. In addition, there was an opportunity to amend the Bill. After it had got through the second reading, the Bill had gone into Committee, when, on 11 June 1912, it was proposed that four of the Irish counties, Londonderry, Antrim, Armagh and Down (all Protestant), should be excluded from the legislation. The government did not want this at all, and the proposal was defeated.

Asquith's government appears to have rejected this suggestion for three reasons. First, the Irish Nationalists, on whom they depended, thought only of One Ireland. Second, Tyrone and Fermanagh might easily have been included with the original four counties, but they contained Roman Catholics and Protestant-Catholic families, and separating them from the rest of Ireland could prove difficult. Third, Belfast was such an industrial success that it was assumed, wrongly, that the island was not economically viable without Belfast.

It is as easy to criticize Asquith's apparent lack of foresight as it is to reject Carson's position. The position of Andrew Bonar Law, the leader of the Conservatives, was quite different. Bonar Law might have been seen as a moderate and thoughtful debater in what was, after all, a serious piece of constitutional legislation. Instead, he over-committed himself – and his party – and took to the soapbox. In the summer of 1912 he said that he would personally support any degree of resistance decided upon by the Ulster Unionists and that he believed that the majority of Britain thought the same way. When the Ulster Volunteer Force had been organized, he stood alongside Carson on the saluting platform. He even encouraged incitement in the army.

The Tories now found that they had been committed to supporting the extreme actions of people who opposed legislation that had been proposed by the democratically elected government. By the end of the year the position of the Ulster Protestants was the basis of the Conservative Party's opposition to Home Rule. The Bill went through the House and, predictably, was rejected by the predominantly Conservative House of Lords.

The third Home Rule Bill could become law under the new Parliament Act, however. In two years' time it could be on the statute book because the House of Lords could now only delay, rather than veto.

There was now a further conundrum facing the government: the matter of universal suffrage. In 1911 Asquith had promised that in 1912 there would be another attempt to bring in legislation. The suffragettes were determined to keep their protest in the public eye and to underline their arguments with violent demonstration. Property was smashed, including the windows of the increasing number of department stores that were springing up in London. The demonstrators were working on the principle propounded by Emmeline Pankhurst: 'Is not a woman's life, is not her health, are not her limbs more valuable than panes of glass?'

In July 1912, however, the Women's Social and Political Union became factionalized. Christabel, who was all for violence, broke away from the Union and left England (and the law) for Paris, from where she organized a militant campaign in Britain. Empty houses were set alight, petrol bombs were put into pillar boxes, a school was burned down and small bombs exploded. The orchid houses at Kew Gardens were destroyed and paintings in public galleries were slashed.

In the end, it was neither the actions of Asquith's government nor the agility of the police force that stopped the suffragettes, but the outbreak of war in 1914. Even so, it was not until 1918 that women were given the vote, and then only to those over the age of 30 with certain property and education qualifications. It was not until 1928 that equal voting rights were given to women.

Britain was only two years away from war with Germany, although attempts continued to be made to put off what now seemed inevitable. Grey, the Foreign Secretary, had even proposed an Anglo-German equivalent of the Entente Cordiale. This came to nought because there could be no understanding with Germany unless Britain reneged on its agreements with France and Russia. Germany's war was likely to be with France and/or Russia; but if Britain and France had an exclusive treaty of understanding the likelihood of either France or Russia going to war was slim. Yet Britain was irrevocably linked to the defence of France, especially after the Agadir Crisis of 1911.

The government's position did not command universal respect within Parliament. Some MPs remained committed to the nineteenth-century policies of isolation from Europe (though not from Empire) from which Britain had emerged at the beginning of the twentieth century. The isolationists argued, with reason, that bilateral arrangements with European nations would involve Britain in a war that was not of its making.

Early in 1912 Haldane (by now 1st Viscount Haldane), the Secretary of War, went to Germany to discuss the possibility of what would later be called the lowering of the arms race. What he got was an insistence that if there was a war,

Britain should stay out of it. This, of course, would not be possible, for apart from the commitments made under the Entente, a successful German invasion of France would have given the Kaiser's army and Tirpitz's fleet access to the Channel ports, including Calais – just 21 miles from Dover.

In some senses, however, almost medieval arrangements continued to exist between the two nations. There were exchanges of officers, and senior members of the Cabinet, including Churchill, by now First Lord of the Admiralty, were welcome observers at German army exercises.

The real problem in Europe was the instability that was grumbling away in the Balkans. This is not the place to unravel the complex story of that region, although a simplified version might begin with the observation that the dual state of Austria-Hungary was threatened on all sides. The Romanians wanted to assert what they saw as their national rights in the 'provinces' Bokovina and Transylvania. The Italians wanted to expand into Trentino and Trieste. The Slavs wanted to control the region of the Balkans that included Dalmatia, Croatia and Bosnia-Herzegovina. There were confrontations between Czechs and Germans and between Poles and Ruthenians. In the Hungarian capital, Budapest, socialists rioted and demanded the right to vote. Austria-Hungary was an ally of Germany, but Germans living in Prague were treated as second-class citizens.

An additional complication had been created by the Italians, who, in the autumn of 1911, had attacked Turkish territory in North Africa. Tripoli had been bombarded and the Turks were driven out. The Italian navy then attacked the Red Sea ports of the Yemen. Yemen was part of the Turkish (Ottoman) Empire, and the Arabs there, who did not like the Turks, set against their colonial masters. This, in turn, had the effect of working against the Young Turks, who had ruled in Constantinople (Istanbul) since 1908.

Austria-Hungary had warned Italy not to attack Turkey itself, and now the Kaiser tried to act as mediator between Italy and Austria-Hungary, although, of course, there was the additional dimension that German interests in Turkey had to be protected as well as the position of its ally, Austria-Hungary. In protest at being told what to do by the two allies, Italy launched an attack on the Dardanelles, but it had little stomach for the fight and quickly concluded a peace with Turkey. Italians, Germans, Turkey and Austria-Hungary were once more talking to each other.

Now it was the turn of the Albanians, who rebelled against Turkish rule. The Turks were forced to send their best soldiers to fight the Albanians, who immediately took to the hills of Macedonia. At the same time the Serbs in Macedonia were fighting the Bulgarians, whom they accused of taking Serb territory.

The confusion was increased because Serbia, Montenegro, Bulgaria and Greece – the four Christian states in the region – formed an alliance. At first they did nothing to capitalize on the fact that Turkey did not seem to know which way to turn to fend off yet another revolt, but their real interest was to claim territorial rights over Macedonia and Thrace.

The Albanians seemed to gain territorial advantage over the Turks when they captured Pristina, a town that has become well known in the late 1990s as the centre of yet another Serb assault on the province of Kosovo. An attempt was made to deal with the Albanians, but they wanted autonomy, although it seems unlikely that in 1912 they believed they could shake off Turkish rule entirely. Nevertheless, full of their own success and potential, the Albanians threatened to march on Salonica.

At this point the Turks gave up all attempts at negotiation and sent in a bigger and better force. The Albanians were scattered into the mountains in northern Macedonia, where they established what was virtually a state within a state. By the summer the Bulgarian and Serb Macedonians were demanding that their national governments should go to war with Turkey and drive them out of Macedonia. The four allied Christian states mobilized on 30 September.

All the European powers, using Austria-Hungary and Russia as intermediaries, tried to stop the war, but on 10 October Russia and Austria-Hungary announced that if war broke out they would support Turkey. Serbia, Montenegro, Bulgaria and Greece took no notice. Turkey's army in Thrace was obliterated by the Bulgarians; the Serbians beat the Turkish army in Macedonia; and the Greeks forced yet another army at Elassona to surrender. Salonica fell on 8 November, and Monastir was taken on 18 November. The Turks were forced into a position where they could do nothing more than defend their capital, Constantinople.

Yet again the continuing connections between Balkan conflicts and west European interests are revealed. Russia and Austria-Hungary said that they would defend Turkish territorial rights. Austria-Hungary demanded that Serbia give up her claims on Albania and to the Turkish Adriatic ports. The Russians supported the Serbs, for if the Serbs controlled those ports, Russia would have access to them. Austria-Hungary would be landlocked and Russian naval vessels would have forward bases for the Mediterranean. Germany and Britain understood this only too well.

In November 1912 Franz Joseph, Emperor of Austria-Hungary, asked the Germans for help. The Kaiser called together his Chiefs of Staff, and they concluded that if the Russians were allowed to support the Serbs, Germany would have to go to war and, given the existence of the Franco-Russian alliance, this would mean that France would join in and, when this happened, Britain would support France.

Russia regarded itself as the protector of Slavonic Christian Orthodoxy. It did not, however, have any desire to get into a war. The Serbs could not expect to go to war with any success against Austria-Hungary without Russia's support, so Serbia, for the time being, withdrew its claims to Albania.

This uneasy truce did not remove the spectre of what was potentially a horrifying conflict, with the Russians heading south and the Germans heading east to collide in the Balkans. If – or when – war broke out, Germany could control the whole of Continental Europe and Britain would be vulnerable to Germany's future ambitions and, as in the eighteenth century, would be stretched to protect the global, colonial and commercial interests that kept the nation financially afloat.

Sir Edward Grey now became the key player in the peace process. Ambassadors from all the warring factions and European powers met in London. What is known as the London Conference was, in fact, two conferences. At one session the protagonists in the Balkan War discussed peace terms. The Balkan allies – Greece, Bulgaria, Montenegro and Serbia – did not want to give up any of the territory they had taken. Russia, Austria-Hungary and Germany had their own interests, of which an overriding desire was to keep the Russians from the Adriatic. The French and the Germans supported the Slavs. Grey adhered to the Foreign Office axiom that its role is to lie for its country, and even though he was supposed to be the impartial chairman of the conference, he did, in fact, support Austria-Hungary and Germany.

Although a peace agreement was signed in 1913, no one in the Balkans was particularly satisfied, and the region continued to smoulder.

The Germans, meanwhile, increased army conscription from 280,000 men a year to more than 340,000 men. Higher taxes were levied on an already over-taxed nation, and the nation's gold reserves were increased. Work on widening the Kiel Canal was speeded up to guarantee access to the North Sea for German battleships in the Baltic. By the following year, 1913, the Germans appeared to have decided that war would start at the earliest in August 1914 – and so it did.

There is a military footnote from the Balkan War that had broken out. Britain, France, Russia and Germany were able to observe how well basic weaponry was working in battle conditions where barrels are over-used, maintenance is inadequate and logistical trains are stretched. The Serbs, for example, had done better with French-built big guns than had their enemies with German weapons. It was an insight not lost on the Chiefs of Staff in Berlin, Paris and London.

As if the crisis in the Balkans wasn't enough, Asquith now had to deal with what has come to be known as the Marconi Scandal. In March 1912 the government announced that the British Marconi Company had been appointed to build a chain of wireless stations that would link Britain with the countries of the Empire, thus helping maintain strategic military interests.

The decision was announced by Herbert Samuel, the Postmaster General, and because it was a government contract, the terms were laid before Parliament, although discussion was delayed until October. This was an enormous project. Wireless communication was in its infancy – it was, after all, only eleven years since Marconi had managed to send the first signal across the Atlantic – and this would be one of the biggest contracts, if not the biggest contract, ever awarded in the new world of radio.

Shares in the Marconi Company soared, and the rumours began. It was said that some ministers, including Herbert Samuel and Sir Rufus Isaacs, the Attorney General, as well as Alexander Murray, Lord Elibank, a former Liberal Chief Whip, and, most damning of all, Lloyd George, the Chancellor of the Exchequer, had wangled the contract for Marconi in order to make money out of the shares.

At first, they all seemed to be in the clear because none of the ministers nor the Master of Elibank held shares in the British Marconi Company. But then it was discovered that they did own shares in the American Marconi Company, although they had not bought the shares until five weeks after the announcement that the company had got the contract.

One of Sir Rufus Isaacs's brothers was on the board of the British Marconi Company, and he had offered his brother the American shares. Sir Rufus Isaacs had, quite rightly, said no, but later, those same shares came to him via yet another brother, and it was this block of shares that had been split between the ministers. If Sir Rufus Isaacs's brother had not had the connection with Marconi, it was asked, would the shares have been available to them? The ministers claimed that all was above board because the American company had no interest in the contract. Then why did they buy them? And why did they not say they had bought them when the matter was debated in the Commons?

The Attorney General and Lloyd George apologized to the House for their errors of judgement in buying the shares. The Liberal backbenchers were inclined to accept that there had been folly rather than corruption and accepted the apologies. The leader of the Conservative Unionists, Bonar Law, saw this as an opportunity to make political capital and proposed a motion declaring that the House regretted their action. If the House of Commons had gone along with Bonar Law, both the Attorney General and the Chancellor of the Exchequer would have been forced to resign. Eventually, a House of Commons select committee exonerated the minister.

Far away from scandal, Captain Scott had at last reached the South Pole, only to die on the return journey, and the French took control in Morocco. In the year that Woodrow Wilson became president, New Mexico became the forty-seventh and Arizona the forty-eighth states of the union. This was also the year in which Carl Gustav Jung published *The Psychology of the Unconscious*.

In February 1912 Albert Berry became the first man to jump successfully from an aeroplane with a parachute. Barnsley beat West Bromwich Albion in the FA Cup, and the Fifth Modern Olympic Games were held in Stockholm. The waxed jacket appeared in the autumn of 1912 – it was called the Barbour.

The first performance of Ravel's *Daphnis et Chloë* was given in Paris, and, in the year the first film censor was appointed, the first Keystone Cops film was shown. The Royal Navy launched the world's biggest battleship, *The Iron Duke*, and the Kaiser launched the world's biggest liner, the *Imperator*.

Deaths

Rev. William Booth (founder of Salvation Army)
Samuel Coleridge-Taylor (composer)

Joseph Lister (surgeon)
Jules Massenet (French composer)
Robert Falcon Scott (explorer)
August Strindberg (Swedish playwright)
Wilbur Wright (US aviator)

1913

IN 1913 the combined population of the British Isles was about 46 million, with the growth rate below 1 per cent a year. In spite of the medical profession's objections, the 1911 National Insurance Act was beginning to bring benefits to the sick and unemployed between the ages of sixteen and seventy. In January maternity benefits were paid for the first time. The eighty newly established labour exchanges were finding some work, although not enough to make a great impression on the unemployment figure of some one million men. To protect the workforce, there were now almost 1300 registered trade unions with a total membership of more than 4 million. Nearly 10 million working days were lost through stoppages in this year, although this was an improvement on 1912, when 41 million working days had been lost.

In spite of the shift from the countryside to the urban conurbations, a trend that had increased steadily over the last forty years, about 1.5 million people still worked on the land and in the trawler industry. This total compared with 1.3 million miners and 1.3 million bus, train, truck and taxi drivers. By far the largest of all the so-called occupational groups were the 6 million workers in manufacturing industries.

In spite of all the social and industrial unrest, Britain continued to be a law-abiding society – in the official jargon, there were fewer than 100,000 'crimes known to the police' in England and Wales.[11]

The nation was also beginning to feel the benefit of the 1902 Education Act, which had abolished school boards and replaced them with local education authorities. These had built new secondary schools and given grants to grammar schools. The Workers' Educational Association, which had been founded in 1903, had improved adult and further education. In 1907 between 25 and 40 per cent of free secondary school places had been reserved for children from elementary schools. In just a decade the percentage of twelve- to fourteen-year-olds at school had risen to nearly 60 per cent.

An often unremarked aspect of the 1902 Education Act was that it provided for medical inspections in schools. In December 1913 a report from the schools'

---

11 It is difficult to make comparisons with the latter part of the century, when the figure had climbed to 6 million. Changes to the Criminal Justice Acts redefined what was and what was not an indictable offence. For example, the doubling of crime figures from 1970 onwards had more to do with the 1969 Theft Act than it did with lawlessness.

medical inspectors made grim reading. Of 6 million school children examined, more than 3 million needed urgent dental treatment. One in twelve of the children in elementary school was diseased and suffering the effects of a poor diet. Up to 10 per cent needed treatment for eye problems. The report included a long list of hitherto unreported disabilities including poor hearing, heart disease and tuberculosis.

When 1913 opened, politicians were still seeking a way out of another problem, Ireland. Asquith has been accused of doing little to ease the passage of the third Home Rule Bill through the House of Commons, but the political process was now running its course, and energetic campaigning could easily have disrupted its progress. There were certainly problems enough, and it was even felt that the King might abdicate over the Bill. Augustine Birrell, Chief Secretary for Ireland, is known to have contemplated resignation on more than one occasion.

In January the government proposed that the people of Ireland should be able to vote using a system of proportional representation. This was done in the hope that it would placate the Protestant minority and was the origin of the use of proportional representation in Ulster but nowhere else in the United Kingdom for the rest of the century.

In February agitation for democracy in another area took a violent turn. Suffragettes planted a bomb in Lloyd George's golf villa at Waltham Heath. The explosion destroyed the building, and men who were working on the villa had been due to return just 20 minutes after the bomb exploded. Emmeline Pankhurst said the attack was justified, but she was sentenced to three years' imprisonment for arson. There were indications that the movement's tactics were alienating public support, and a number of suffragettes were attacked during a rally in Hyde Park the following month.

The high point, if that is how it can be described, for the suffragettes came in June 1913. Emily Davison, who had been a member of the Women's Social and Political Union since 1906, threw herself in front of the King's horse, Amner, during the Epsom Derby. She died four days later and became the heroine the suffragettes were looking for. Her funeral procession attracted thousands. Her coffin was drawn from London on an open carriage accompanied by an honour guard of suffragettes and twelve clergymen at its head to her home village of Morpeth, County Durham, where she was buried. It took four carts to carry the wreaths that had been sent from all over the world.

Three days later the violence was resumed. Seven suffragettes were charged at the Old Bailey with conspiracy and found guilty. One of the leaders was Sylvia Pankhurst, Emmeline's second daughter, who was serving a three-year prison sentence but had been paroled on condition that she took no part in demonstrations. The police who tried to arrest her were stabbed and poked by the hat pins and umbrellas of her supporters.

★

The most important event of 1913 was the ending with the Treaty of London of the Balkan War that had broken out in 1912 (see page 77). The treaty reduced Turkish territory in Europe to the area around Constantinople and the Straits of Bosphorus and the Dardanelles; Crete was ceded to Greece; Bulgaria gained Adrianople (Edirne); both Serbia and Bulgaria gained territory in Macedonia. No decisions were taken about Albania or the islands of the Aegean.

For those who have wondered why war broke out in 1914, an understanding of the conflicts in the Balkans, especially the war of 1912–13, is essential. The reason Germany had warned its ally, Austria-Hungary, not to fight Serbia in 1912 was that the government in Berlin could see that such a conflict could quickly spread throughout Europe, and Germany was not yet ready for that kind of war. In February 1913 Helmuth von Moltke, the German Chief of the General Staff, had said that he believed war would come, but he thought that the German people had to be prepared and they were not yet ready.

The German Chancellor, Theobald Bethmann Hollweg, gave many speeches warning of the dangers of further conflicts with Slav states. He went out of his way to tell the Russians that in spite of the history of Teutonic–Slavonic animosities, he did not believe that circumstances would contrive to bring Russia and Germany to the battlefield on opposing sides. Nevertheless, the German high command was not looking only across the North Sea or to France as potential aggressors. Germany was accelerating its army and naval building programmes because it knew it would have to fight on more than one front.

Turkey was regarded as the linchpin in any future conflict in that region, and all the countries had some direct interest in its military structure. The British were helping to rebuild Turkish defences in the Dardanelles. The French had men in the influential interior and economic ministries. The Germans controlled the modernization programme that was under way in the Turkish army.

In October 1913 Austria-Hungary issued an ultimatum to the Serbs to get out of Albania within eight days or accept the consequences of war. The Serbs did not withdraw. The importance of the Austro-Hungarian ultimatum should not be overlooked, for it was an indication that Austria-Hungary was willing to act without the consent of the other European powers, none of which had expected it to do so. Or it may be that one country, at least, expected Austria-Hungary's reaction, for it is unlikely that the Emperor Franz Joseph had not considered what support he would get from Germany if he delivered the ultimatum to the Serbs. The Germans either knew what was going on and could not do anything about it, or they knew and encouraged Austria-Hungary. The Kaiser certainly expressed his support for the idea of ridding Albania of the Serbs.

The first Morris Oxford car was built in a converted garage at Cowley. On a much grander scale, the first moving assembly line in the motor industry was started up in Michigan. This was a revolution in car production, and it was the brainchild of Henry Ford. For the first time a moving assembly line would enable mechanics to bolt, screw and fix parts to the Model T Fords as they passed in front of them. Ford could now build one of his Model Ts in less than three hours, and he expected to produce a quarter of a million of them in a year.

In Britain, in comparison, the car industry was turning out 34,000 motor vehicles a year. There were now nearly 350,000 motor vehicles, including wagons, on British roads, and the increased congestion on the roads was causing concern. A House of Commons Select Committee Report[12] said there had been a 500 per cent increase in road deaths caused by motor buses since 1907.

In February the nation mourned a hero, Robert Falcon Scott. His expedition to Antarctica the previous year had ended in disaster when he and his team had become trapped by a blizzard and ran out of food. The frozen tent in which they had taken refuge on their return from the South Pole had been found by a search party, and on 14 February a memorial service was held in St Paul's Cathedral for Captain Scott, Edward Wilson, H.R. Bowers, Edgar Evans (who did not perish in the tent but died after a fall on the Beardmore Glacier on the way back from the Pole) and, of course, Captain Laurence Oates, whose final words became famous: 'I am just going outside, I may be some time.'

Less often recorded was the opening on 2 February of the world's largest railway station, Grand Central in New York, and in October the largest transport construction project ever undertaken was completed when what has been called 'the greatest liberty man had ever taken with nature' reached a climax. A huge dynamite explosion was used to blast open the Panama Canal.

In that same year London heard the first British performances of Igor Stravinsky's *The Firebird* and *Petruschka*. While London had been polite and in some instances delighted by Stravinsky's music, there were riots in Paris on the opening night of Diaghilev's production, with choreography by Nijinsky, of Stravinsky's *The Rite of Spring*. Those who did not attend the opening night might have decided to tuck themselves up with a good book, perhaps the first volume of Marcel Proust's *À la recherche du temps perdu*.

A footnote to cultural entertainment was written in November 1913. In South America the tango was regarded less as a ballroom dance than an erotic rite, and the Germans seemed to have understood this. Not only did they ban soldiers and sailors from dancing it, but they instructed them to avoid any families that did so.

Deaths
Alfred Austin (poet)
Rudolf Diesel (German engineer)
J. Pierpoint Morgan (US financier)
Garnet Joseph Wolseley, 1st Viscount Wolseley (soldier)

12 House of Commons Select Committee Orders 14, 1913.

1914

THE GREAT WAR, or the First World War as it is often, if not altogether accurately, known, started in 1914 and ended in 1918 (see Appendix 1, First World War Diary on pages 469–79). The year, however, was nearly half done when the heir to the throne of Austria-Hungary, the Archduke Franz Ferdinand, was assassinated in Sarajevo, the capital of Bosnia, on 28 June, and the war did not start until August.

In January 1914 Lloyd George delivered a speech against the build-up of weaponry in Europe, which he saw as organized insanity, but the government's immediate problems lay in Ireland. Bonar Law, the Conservative leader, continued to attack the plans for Home Rule, claiming that there would be an inevitable 'drift to civil war'. His prophecy, which had been proclaimed with relish rather than regret, was illustrated towards the end of February when the Ulster Volunteer Force staged a huge military exercise in County Tyrone. By now the UVF had at least 100,000 members, and it had grown easily and legally, because Asquith's government had not had the foresight to proscribe paramilitary forces in the United Kingdom. In just twelve months the UVF's first commander, General Sir George Richardson, had turned the organization from a group of enthusiasts to a reasonably well-drilled force.

On 5 March the Irish Home Rule Bill was introduced into the House of Commons. On the following day, the Ulster Defence League issued thousands of pledge forms to those who opposed the break-up of the Union. One of the government's proposals was that any of the counties could, by using the electoral system, 'opt out' of Home Rule for six years. The Ulster Unionists did not like this. What would happen, for example, if in a general election the British electorate as a whole endorsed Home Rule? In those circumstances any county that had opted out would, presumably, have to opt back in. Moreover, only the counties of Antrim, Armagh, Derry and Down commanded the natural Protestant majorities necessary for an opt-out. The government proposals were rejected by the Unionists.

At this point the argument was broadened. The leaders of the die-hards, the group that had opposed the Parliament Bill, suggested that the peers should refuse to pass the Army Bill. Constitutionally, the army and navy existed by an Act of Parliament that had to be renewed each year. If the Lords rejected the Bill, there would, in theory, be no army by the end of April 1914. Believing only in their own cause and perhaps not even contemplating the wider European dilemma, the Unionists in the House of Lords, led by Lord Willoughby de Broke, supported the proposal. Worse still, so did Bonar Law. The government had to act quickly. Churchill, by now First Lord of the Admiralty, stationed one of the navy's battle squadrons off Ulster as reports came into Whitehall of civilian unrest, the growth of the Ulster Volunteer Force, large arms shipments being landed for the militia and disaffection among some of the regular soldiers stationed in Ireland. Sir Edward Carson denounced Churchill as 'the butcher of Belfast'.

The commander-in-chief in Ireland, Major General Sir Arthur Paget, was told to reinforce his troop deployments in Ulster. We now come to the most bizarre sequence of events which, from the point of view of the end of the twentieth century, seem almost impossible to believe. Instead of doing what he was told, Paget went to London to see the War Minister, J.E.B. Seely. Paget believed that it would not be possible to carry out the deployment of reinforcements and that he might find himself having to order his officers to fight against their fellow countrymen. Moreover, many of his officers were Ulstermen, so Paget told Seely that he wanted any Ulster-born officers to be allowed to quietly go away while this emergency lasted. When asked what would happen if their loyalties were so torn and that they might go off and join the Ulster Volunteer Force, Paget said that he was certain that his officers would give assurances that they would not do so.

Here was a major general questioning his orders and wringing concessions from the Secretary of War. Whatever his reasons, Seely agreed.

Paget called together his senior officers at the headquarters at the Curragh, near Kildare, and told them that those with homes in Ulster would be allowed to 'disappear'. An officer who did not have a home in Ulster should, if he objected to any operations in the North of Ireland, resign. The brigade commander, General Hubert Gough, and all but thirteen officers of the Third Cavalry Brigade, resigned their commissions rather than possibly having to obey orders that might involve their having to force Unionists into accepting Home Rule. Officers in the Infantry Regiments responded in the same way.

Instead of taking firm action, the War Office called them to London for consultations. At a Cabinet meeting it was agreed that: 'An officer or soldier is forbidden, in future, to ask for assurances as to orders which he may be required to obey.' But Gough and his colleagues demanded a written guarantee that the army would not be called out to force the Home Rule Bill on Ulster. Once again Seely backed down, and a form of words was cobbled together that ostensibly gave Gough what he wanted. He even got the Chief of the General Staff, Sir John French, to initial the document. Gough, who was later to be knighted and command the Fifth Army in the First World War, returned to the Curragh as a hero.

Parliamentary and public anger at the Curragh incident was intense, and it was obvious that the army 'mafia' had to be dispersed. But nothing was done because the government knew full well that war was imminent and to have torn to shreds the army at that point would have been the equivalent of military suicide. Seely and Field Marshal Sir John French were subsequently forced to resign (although they would be back), and the prime minister repudiated the assurance that had been given to Gough. Sir Henry Wilson, the Director of Military Operations, who had gone along with the whole appeasement of the mutineers, escaped unscathed. He had his own sympathies with their cause: he came from a prominent Irish Catholic family.

*

As if this was not enough, in February the suffragettes returned to their campaign of violence when they burned down two Scottish mansions and Whitkirk Parish Church in East Lothian. In March the suffragettes staged two demonstrations, one in Trafalgar Square and the other in Glasgow. Sylvia Pankhurst was arrested on her way to the London demonstration. Emmeline Pankhurst was arrested in Scotland. Another suffragette, Mary Richardson, took a butcher's meat cleaver into the National Gallery and slashed Velázquez's *The Rokeby Venus*. Miss Richardson claimed that she had tried to destroy the Venus, the most beautiful woman in mythological history, 'in protest at the government's destruction of Miss Pankhurst, the most beautiful character in modern history'. The London magistrates sentenced Miss Richardson to six months' imprisonment. Sylvia Pankhurst was rearrested under the Cat and Mouse Act, officially the Prisoners (Temporary Discharge for Ill-health) Act of 1913, which had been passed to stop hunger-striking suffragettes becoming martyrs. Prisoners would be released but rearrested as soon as they were again fit. Mary Richardson was less fortunate and was subjected to forced feeding. The violent protests continued nevertheless. On 1 June the suffragettes set fire to the parish church at Wargrave on the Thames, and a week later Sylvia Pankhurst was arrested again.

Elsewhere in Britain, events continued very much as normal. On 1 June the General Post Office took over the Portsmouth Telephone System, which had been in private hands. This left the City of Hull as the only place in Britain with its own telephone network. Hull kept its own telephone system until the end of the century. On 14 June London was struck with a horrendous downpour: 4 inches of rain fell in four hours, and many Londoners died as a result of the floods.

In Oxford a group of archaeologists announced that they had discovered from early Babylonian tablets the story of Noah and the Flood, and a medical team at the Middlesex Hospital in London announced that it had successfully relieved cancer tumours with radium treatment.

On 17 March Churchill, as First Lord of the Admiralty, presented the biggest ever navy budget to the Commons. He told the House that it was his intention to put eight squadrons of warships into service in the same time it took Germany to build just five. He was accused of warmongering.

While Churchill was asking for £2.5 million more for the navy, 100,000 Yorkshire miners were striking for a minimum wage, and by 4 April 40,000 more miners had come out on strike. Building workers in London were also on strike, but being held off by the employers. One estimate showed that they had lost more than £400,000 in wages since they came out on 24 January; the same report claimed that many of the families of the builders were close to starving. There was no sign that the building workers were going to get what they wanted until the railway and mine workers came out in their support together with some of the smaller unions, including the Association of Cricket Ball Makers. By the summer some 2 million workers were striking, and by that time the lost wages of the builders had gone up to £1 million. It was probably no comfort to them that in May 1914 the Chancellor, Lloyd George, increased the rate of supertax.

In that year anyone earning £3000 would pay 5d in the pound on top of their normal income tax. Anyone earning more than £7000 a year would pay an extra 1s 4d in the pound. Standard income tax in the Budget began at £1000 a year, on which the tax payer would be charged 10d (slightly less than 5p) in the pound. That summer, as one group of ministers prepared for war, another wondered if the nation would be at a standstill and unable to attend the event's opening.

In Russia the imminence of war had not been ignored. The government announced it would increase the army by 400 per cent, from 460,000 to 1.7 million men, and by the spring of 1914 Russia had the biggest army from the Atlantic to the Urals. Germany was the next biggest followed by France, Austria-Hungary, Italy and then Britain. The British army included contingents sent from other parts of the British Empire, and the generals knew they would have to rely on these overseas regiments if war was declared.

On Sunday, 28 June 1914, the heir apparent to the dual monarchy of Austria-Hungary, the Archduke Franz Ferdinand, was assassinated in the Bosnian capital, Sarajevo, by the Serb nationalist Gavrilo Princip. The archduke's wife, Sophie, Duchess of Hohenberg, who had tried to protect her husband, was shot in the stomach, and she too died.

Few were profoundly upset at the passing of the archduke, who had been enormously unpopular in both Budapest and Vienna. Princip, the assassin, may have been a Serb but he was also an Austrian subject; however, because the assassination had taken place in Sarajevo and therefore on Serbian soil, the Austrians saw it as good reason to attack Serbia. The Emperor, Franz Joseph, wrote to ask the Kaiser for his support. The answer came by return of messenger, for Wilhelm had long made it clear that if Austria should attack Serbia, Germany would 'draw the sword' alongside its friend. The uncertainties lay in how the other powers would react.

The Russians were on the side of the Serbs. But this was a quarrel between Austrians and Serbs and not between Germans and Serbs. Therefore, if Germany intervened it would do so to support Austria, not on its own behalf, and in theory, therefore, Russia should not be antagonized.

On 23 July Austria-Hungary issued an impossible ultimatum to Serbia: Austrian officers were to be given *carte blanche* to act in Serbia to investigate Serbian complicity in the assassination. In addition, Serbia was to join with Austrian forces to fight so-called subversive movements against Austria-Hungary, which amounted to a take-over. The Serbians had two days to comply with the ultimatum, and at the end of that period, Austria-Hungary would go to war. The timing of the ultimatum was perfect, for we might remember that in 1912 the German high command had estimated that it would be ready for war by August 1914.

The Kaiser understood the need to maintain some element of surprise – after all, there had been perhaps a nervous, if optimistic, lull since the assassination – so he avoided raising any suspicions by ostentatiously going off in his yacht to Norway.

The British government, which was attempting to resolve the issues raised by the Home Rule Bill and was distracted by what it believed to be the real possibility of civil war in Ireland, apparently knew nothing of the Austro-Hungarian threat until Sir Edward Grey heard about it twenty-four hours later, on Friday, 24 July. Grey offered to mediate – just as he had done (successfully) in the Balkan Wars of 1912–13. The Italians and French agreed that there should be a conference in London, but the Germans rejected the proposal. The next day, 25 July, the Serbs capitulated on all but a couple of points, which they offered for arbitration among the elders of Europe. The Austrians rejected the capitulation and declared war, as they had always intended to do.

The speed with which the whole of Europe now went to war gives the impression that the continent had waited so long for this event that everyone concerned understood that nothing that could be said or done would prevent the conflict.

On 29 July the Tsar of Russia, Nicholas II, ordered the mobilization of more than a million troops. Britain told Germany that the Kaiser could not rely on British neutrality, and Germany promised that no part of mainland France nor Holland would be overrun and that any invasion of Belgium would be put right after the war.

On the following day, 30 July, Wilhelm announced that he would order German mobilization unless the Tsar told his soldiers to stand down. The next day the Kaiser issued a formal ultimatum to his cousin the Tsar that unless Russia stopped mobilization within twelve hours, Germany would declare war on Russia. The Kaiser then turned on France, warning them on 31 July to stay out of the war or, in the formal language of the day, 'sought guarantees of their neutrality'.

The Italians, who were nervous about their future as a nation state – Italy had existed for only about fifty years – declared that they would keep out of the war.

On 1 August Germany declared war on Russia and two days later declared war on France. Britain then told Germany that, under the Treaty of London signed in 1839, it would defend Belgium's right to remain neutral and, having placed the Royal Navy on mobilization level, would also protect the French coast.

Germany invaded Belgium on 4 August and on the same day the prime minister, Asquith, went to the House of Commons to announce that the breaking of the 1839 Treaty (in which Britain, France and Germany guaranteed Belgium neutrality) meant that Britain was at war with Germany.

By the end of August soldiers in the British Expeditionary Force of about 70,000 men had crossed to Belgium and were dying at Mons. By 23 August the British Expeditionary Force was in retreat.

★

We might well ask who among the European leaders actually wanted to go to war. The British government certainly did not. Nor did the French and Belgian governments. So what of the three great personalities, the Tsar, the Kaiser and the Emperor?

The Tsar, Nicholas II, who was described by David Lloyd George as feeble and simple-minded in this matter, could not possibly have wanted war, even for some Machiavellian reasoning that it might divert attention from his personal and national troubles.

The Kaiser, Wilhelm II, is sometimes seen as the mercurial person who was driven to the idea of war almost as a form of military alcoholism. Perhaps if he really understood that there was to be a conflict, he believed that it would be nothing more than one in which Germany would support Austria against the Serbs. In his diary the Kaiser claimed that he was totally surprised by the news of the Austrian ultimatum to the Serbs, and he goes some way towards suggesting the view that he had taken his annual yachting holiday in order to divert attention from the crisis:

> During my stay at Balholm I received but meagre news from the Foreign Office [i.e., the German foreign ministry] and was obliged to rely principally on the Norwegian newspapers, from which I received the impression that the situation was growing worse. I telegraphed repeatedly to the Chancellor [Count Theobald von Bethmann Hollweg] and the Foreign Office that I considered it advisable to return home, but was asked each time not to interrupt my journey.[13]

As the above quote shows, the Kaiser said that he had heard from the newspapers and not from the Chancellor in Berlin of the Austrian ultimatum to the Serbs and that it was the newspaper reports that prompted his return to Berlin. The implication is that the German High Command and Bethmann Hollweg were determined to go to war and preferred that the Kaiser, whom they regarded as a weak man, should keep out of the way.

What about Franz Joseph, Emperor of Austria-Hungary? There is little doubt that the Emperor wanted war, but to what extent he imagined that the war would involve the whole of Europe has never fully been explained.

Could it really be said that Bethmann Hollweg, the German Chancellor, Grey, the British Foreign Secretary, or Viviani, the French prime minister, were statesmen enough to prevent the war that perhaps any one of them might have wanted but whose consequences none of them could have foreseen?

Lloyd George claimed that if there had been warnings that war was imminent, senior members of the government were unaware of them. This is not as unlikely as it may at first appear. During the eight years that Lloyd George was a Cabinet

13 Wilhelm II, *My Memoirs, 1878–1918*, privately translated and published, pages 241–2.

minister, there is no record that the senior ministers ever got into deep discussion about security in Europe. Equally, there are no Cabinet minutes to support this idea. It is quite possible that, apart from the prime minister, the Foreign Secretary and the Minister for War, no member of the Cabinet was given any of the details of the arrangements that existed between Russia, France and Britain in the event of war with Germany. Lloyd George claimed that the hesitation displayed by Britain about going to the aid of France broke all the understandings that existed between the two countries.

In the days before war was declared on 4 August 1914 the British government was far more concerned with the possibility of civil war in Ireland. After all, instead of high-level meetings after the assassination of Archduke Franz Ferdinand, what did Asquith, Grey, Churchill and Lloyd George observe in Germany? The Kaiser went yachting in the Norwegian fjords, and Bethmann Hollweg went off to his estates in Silesia. The man in charge of the German Foreign Office went on honeymoon, and the Chief of the German General Staff, Helmuth von Moltke, went to a spa to take the cure. The Russian envoy to the archduke's court in Vienna was away on annual leave, and the French president and prime minister were journeying home after a state visit to Russia. This was hardly the atmosphere in which anyone in the British Cabinet would readily lay down his briefing papers on the situation in Ireland and raise questions about the possibility of war. Lloyd George is absolutely certain that if there were signs that should have been noticed then no intelligence came the way of the Cabinet.

> I cannot recall any discussion on the subject in the Cabinet until the Friday evening [24 July] before the final declaration of war by Germany. . . . Mr Churchill recalls the fact that on that Friday . . . we met in the prime minister's room in the House of Commons to discuss once more the Irish crisis, which was daily becoming more menacing. When the discussion was over the Cabinet rose, but the Foreign Secretary [Sir Edward Grey] asked us to remain behind for a few more minutes as he had something to impart to us about the situation in Europe. When we resumed our seats he told us, for the first time, that he thought the position was very grave, but he was hopeful that the conversations which were proceeding between Austria and Russia might lead to a pacific settlement. So we separated upon that assurance. On Saturday [25 July] Sir Edward Grey left for his fishing lodge in Hampshire, and all other ministers followed his example and left Town. On Sunday came the news of the landing of arms by Nationalists at Howth, near Dublin, and of a conflict with the military which arose out of that incident. The excitement over this event overshadowed, for the time being, the Continental situation. . . . Sir Arthur Nicolson[14] . . . became so alarmed about the situation on this Sunday, that he took immediate steps to bring Sir Edward Grey back to London. War was

14 Permanent Under Secretary (i.e., Head of the Foreign Office) and later Lord Carnock.

> declared by Austria on Serbia two days later and by Germany and Russia five days later. Even then I met no responsible minister who was not convinced that, in one way or another, the calamity of a great European war would somehow be averted.[15]

It appears that the government simply was not up to decision-making on such an important level. On 24 July the Russians had asked Britain to join with France and itself in a triple alliance against Austria. On 30 July the French president, Raymond Poincaré, had repeated the Russian request. The Russians and French obviously wanted Britain as an ally, but there was something deeper to it than that: while they sensed Germany would go to war, ostensibly on Austria's behalf, against France and Russia, they believed also Germany would not declare war if it thought Britain would join in.

It is possible that earlier action and a declaration by the British government would have presented the potentially strong front that the Russians and French believed would scare off Germany, but there is no real evidence to suggest that the Chiefs of the German Staff expected to do anything but fight on three fronts. Moreover, anyone with a minimal grasp of military operations would understand that the German Chiefs of Staff would already have planned to fight France, Russia and Britain and most certainly would not go into any war assuming anything else.

In military terms, the order of battle and the deployment of armies and navies involving millions of men, thousands of miles of troop transportation and thousands of vehicles and ships required such meticulous planning that there would have been no time to update the plans in light of the surprise intervention of Britain, and it must therefore be assumed that German plans were drawn up on the assumption that the British army and navy would participate in the war.

Once war had been declared, Britain's immediate problem was how to defend Belgian neutrality. The importance of this neutral state had been recognized since Palmerston's time, but most members of Asquith's Cabinet held the same opinion of the 1839 treaty as the Kaiser – it was not worth the paper it was written on.

Here is one defence for Sir Edward Grey against charges of vacillation. How could he declare any earlier than he did that Britain would go to war over Belgium if half the Cabinet disagreed?

Furthermore, the Great War cannot simply be seen as an event started in Sarajevo. We have to revisit the years of Otto von Bismarck (1815–98) and his rebuilding of Germany into a society geared to what the British army would later call ruthless military efficiency. In the 1870s we saw the seemingly unstoppable expansion of Germany under Bismarck. Under the Kaiser, the Germany sown by the legendary Bismarck grew to a point where R.C.K. Ensor in his *History of*

15 David Lloyd George, *War Memoirs*, Odhams (revised edition 1939).

England observed that arrogant megalomania and a distinctive preference for methods of violence became the national vices of prewar Germany, making the country 'an object of alarm to every leading nation save her Austrian ally'.[16]

From the end of the twentieth century, this view may itself seem as bellicose and uncompromising as the form it criticizes, but again we have to observe the times, rather than simply a late twentieth-century perspective of them. We need to remember that the other great powers – Russia, France and Britain – were just as imperialistic as Germany. The difference is likely to lie in the fact that Germany was willing to be far more ruthless in the way it maintained its imperial ambitions. We must also remember that at the beginning of the twentieth century Britain instinctively wished to preserve its isolationist policies – that is, its isolation from alliances in Europe. Britain retained a large and effective navy in order to protect the trade routes from and to the Empire. It also saw that to engage in any alliance could mean getting involved in another nation's wars. The involvement with France and the Entente Cordiale was a much bigger step in Britain's European policy than the contents of the understanding suggest.

The search for a scapegoat for Britain's involvement in the Great War ends with Sir Edward Grey, the Foreign Secretary. This clever but indecisive man spent many years trying to placate Germany and persuade that country that it was not under threat. Many in Germany believed that this conciliatory approach of Grey's meant that Britain would never stand alongside France. What might have happened had Britain had not gone to war? Without Britain's involvement, there would have been no American support. Moreover, once Germany had taken over Continental Europe it would have thought, at the very least, about sweeping up the edges, including the British Isles, which by that time would truly have stood alone. Germany would have long forgotten the concept that Germany should look after the security of the land mass while Britain guaranteed the seaways.

Whatever the 'what ifs', the fact is that on 4 August Britain was at war with Germany, and the simplest group to deploy to that war was the Royal Navy. In July the fleet had been on exercises and was supposed to have dispersed to its home ports on 24 July. On 26 July the First Sea Lord, Prince Louis of Battenberg,[17] countermanded the dispersal order and so the Royal Navy, although not fully armed and fuelled, was perhaps in a better position for war than Cabinet indecision might have suggested.

Churchill, the First Lord of the Admiralty, was anxious to take advantage of this and was for taking the battle to the German fleet at the first opportunity, and he had Royal Navy ships shadowing a German battle cruiser and a light cruiser. Asquith refused to let Churchill go ahead because, at that stage, war had not been

16 R.C.K. Ensor, *England 1870–1914*, Oxford University Press (1936).

17 Anti-German feeling led the Battenbergs to change their name to Mountbatten. Prince Louis was the father of the future First Sea Lord, Lord 'Dickie' Mountbatten of Burma.

officially declared, even though the British ultimatum would expire at 11 o'clock that night. As soon as the hour had chimed, Churchill sent a signal to the navy: 'Commence hostilities against Germany.'

The commander of the British Expeditionary Force, Field Marshal Sir John French, claimed the war would be over by Christmas, and the only voice of authority to scoff at this notion was the old campaigner Field Marshal Lord Kitchener, who had been appointed Secretary for War. In his opinion this was going to be a long-drawn-out affair, and he immediately made a public declaration that the army needed 100,000 fresh recruits. A line of volunteers formed outside the newly opened recruiting offices.

There was another queue outside the Bank of England, but this time of people demanding to exchange their bank notes for gold. Certainly someone was going to have to pay the costs of the conflict, and in November 1914 Lloyd George produced a war budget. The war was already costing about £1 million a day, even at 1914 prices. On 8 August the House of Commons had agreed a government credit of £100 million, but Lloyd George now wanted to double that, and he warned the House that he was going to need even more, money that would either have to be borrowed and added to the National Debt or raised through direct taxation.

The complication of war on this scale is that it would cause considerable inflation. Industry would benefit, especially the export trade provided that the seaways could be kept open. Even the Channel and Mediterranean ports became doubly important because a lot of manufacturing output would head for Continental allies whose own industrial base was either threatened or destroyed. This meant that there would be a lot of money circulating, and it would be easier for the government to claw some of that back in taxation. If Kitchener was right, however, inflation would eventually become deflation and the surplus cash would disappear. So Lloyd George doubled income tax to 2s 8d in the pound and doubled supertax. The duty on beer went up from 7s 9d to 25s a barrel and the duty on tea from 5d to 8d a pound.

At least 10 million men were killed in action during the Great War: Germany lost 1.8 million, Russia lost 1.7 million, the French 1.4 million and Austria-Hungary 1.3 million. Britain and the Empire lost 947,000 troops, and 615,000 Italian men died in action. As many as 335,000 Romanians and 325,000 Turks were killed, 90,000 Bulgarians died and the Serbs lost 55,000 troops; when all Serbian deaths were accounted for, a quarter of the population was dead. The Americans, who had not joined the war until late in 1917, lost 48,909 men. None of these figures includes the hundreds of thousands of civilians who died either directly as a result of fighting or indirectly from disease and deprivation.

This was a European civil war that involved every continent except Antarctica. It came at a time when weapons engineering had developed systems that would change the way in which wars would be fought for the rest of the century. When the longbow appeared in the twelfth century it completely revolutionized warfare. In 1914 either the tank, the submarine or the aircraft would have had a similar devastating effect, but all three came at the same time and at a stroke changed the whole concept of warfare. Together they delivered such a barrage of firepower that destruction was inevitably on a more gruesome scale than ever before.

The power of the new machine-guns could rip a company of men to shreds in seconds. The new naval weapon, the submarine, could take hundreds of lives with a single torpedo. For the first time, civilians could be reached beyond the battlefields. Aircraft could drop crude explosives. Mines could sink hospital ships and passenger liners. The latest weapon of all, the tank, could change a battle's direction, threaten the safe and defend the vulnerable within minutes.

Millions of men, barely trained and living in appalling conditions across the continent of Europe and beyond, were moved around as cannon fodder in days. Tens of thousands of defenceless civilians could be slaughtered in ethnic retribution under the cover of war. All this could happen and all this did happen between 1914 and 1918.

When it was over the war left widows, orphans, the fatherless and whole nations starving. National infrastructures were destroyed. Industries were broken and some had even disappeared entirely. Financial institutions, desperately needed for recovery programmes, were ruined. Monarchies had disappeared for ever; Germany, Austria, Russia and Hungary were all now republics. Constitutional changes had occurred that would never be reversed; the scale of the war, its intensity and its span caused governments to take upon themselves powers that they did not relinquish after the conflict.

There is a footnote that might be explored elsewhere. Into the Great War folklore was woven variations on the phrase 'the lost generation'. It is true that thousands upon thousands of Britain's youngest men died. One-third of Britain's working men were in the army: in the last full year of the war, more than 4 million men were in the armed forces. It has been estimated that when the 'great push' against the Germans came in 1918, the majority of the foot soldiers were teenagers. Certainly, during the four years of conflict men died who would have normally expected to live.

A generation was raped. Yet many of them might easily have left Britain for the colonies and North America, and others would have died of natural and unnatural causes. Perhaps the lost generation was not as large as we sometimes imagine when we look at the terrible casualty figures.

It seems wrong to single out dead sons because they were public figures or became so. Every name on every cross in every war cemetery is a public figure. It is, nevertheless, inevitable to reflect on what might have come from some who perished. What might Lieutenant Rupert Brooke, who died on his way to the Dardanelles, ironically from a mosquito bite, Edward Thomas and Isaac Rosenberg have written after the war? Wilfred Owen was killed just seven days before the Germans surrendered, and he left behind the classic war poem, 'Futility'. In 1915

Julian Grenfell was killed on the day that his poem 'Into Battle' was published in *The Times*.

> If this be the last song you shall sing,
> Sing well, for you may not sing another.

What else might Saki (H.H. Munro) have written? It is only possible to imagine the music that might have come from that most English of composers, George Butterworth.

But others did survive. Laurence Binyon lived to write, 'They shall not grow old'. Robert Graves was presumed dead in one battle and had a shock when he read his own obituary. Siegfried Sassoon, whose simple expression 'Sister Steel' summed up the patriotism as well as the hopelessness of the trenches, received the Military Cross. Another was awarded to Edmund Blunden.

Those who survived were changed by what they had seen, including three future prime ministers, Anthony Eden, Clement Attlee and Harold Macmillan, who felt their lives shaped in the conflict.

No one was spared death; the meek fell as well as the mighty.

Deaths
Joseph Chamberlain (politician)
Frederick Sleigh Roberts, 1st Earl Roberts (soldier)
Count Maximilian von Spee (German sailor)
Sir John Tenniel (artist)
George Westinghouse (US manufacturer)

1915

IN 1915 Churchill was First Lord of the Admiralty and a member of Asquith's Cabinet, and it was he who gave the political direction for what became known as the Gallipoli expedition, which was undertaken because of the inability of the British and French to make any advances on the Western Front, where they were, truly, entrenched.

The plan was to land at Gallipoli, force a passage through the Dardanelles and overpower Turkey, thus removing the Ottoman Empire from the war. The navy was ordered to force the passage through the Dardanelles, but the operation, launched in February 1915, was a failure. Between April and August ten divisions of British and Australasian troops were landed and suffered devastating casualties – 250,000 men died. The campaign was called off in December 1915. The withdrawal took a month.

Churchill, who had been badly advised, was blamed for the disaster and was forced to resign. The naval deployment that went so terribly wrong in trying to breach the Dardanelles had been suggested by two admirals, de Robeck and

Carden, and confirmed by the First Sea Lord, Jackie Fisher. Fisher wrote to the prime minister denouncing Churchill, and in a letter containing six ways of winning the war, he said that one of them would be to sack Churchill from the Cabinet.

The details of what happened and the bizarre behaviour of Fisher have been described elsewhere, but they give an insight into what it was like to conduct a war from Whitehall as well as into the animosities and conflicts between Churchill and the First Sea Lord.[18]

Fisher resigned in protest at the Dardanelles expedition, and Churchill was effectively sacked. He went to the Western Front, not as a minister, but as a soldier. On 18 November 1915, in the uniform of the Queen's Own Oxfordshire Hussars, Major Winston S. Churchill crossed to France to join his regiment. In time he was promoted Lieutenant Colonel and given command of the 6th Royal Scots Fusiliers. But he remained an MP, returning occasionally to London and never losing touch with politics. By 1917 he was back in London and government, his credibility high. Churchill had touched the war, and it him.

The country was slowly realizing that the war, which was to have been over by Christmas 1914, had in five months taken the lives of more than 100,000 British soldiers.

There is a truism that in wartime a nation pulls together. That was not entirely true. At the end of February 1915 Scottish munitions workers went on strike for more pay. In July 200,000 miners walked out for the same reason, and it was a month before the dispute was settled.

The government had another anxiety. For more than a decade there had been increasing concern about levels of drunkenness in the country, especially in factories, but attempts at legislation had been opposed by the Conservatives, who spoke for the brewing and distilling industries. In 1915 considerable evidence was adduced to show that heavy drinking among munitions workers, many of whom were now women,[19] was commonplace. Lloyd George announced higher taxes on alcohol, claiming that Britain's biggest enemies were 'Germany, Austria and drink'. Lord Kitchener, the Secretary for War, said that excess drinking had led to the supplies of shells and bullets to troops on the Western Front being disrupted. A group of businessmen even asked the government to introduce prohibition, such were the problems caused in factories by excess drinking. On 8 April the King announced that the royal household was now a drink-free zone, and Lord Kitchener declared himself to be an abstainer. However, apart from banning alcohol, ministers were at a loss to know how to counter increasing consumption.

---

18 Particularly see Martin Gilbert, *Churchill: A Life*, Heinemann (1991).

19 When the war started many women had volunteered to go into factories as part of the national effort. Thousands of them from the age of fourteen were working twelve hours a day and seven days a week – for which the average wage was 32 shillings (£1.60).

One measure was announced in October 1915: buying other people drinks was to be illegal and anyone caught 'treating' would be liable to a £100 fine.

From May 1915 Britain had a war government, a coalition, and in the autumn Reginald McKenna, the new Chancellor of the Exchequer (Lloyd George had been appointed Minister of Munitions), introduced the biggest and most demanding Budget the country had ever seen. Income tax was raised to 2s 11d in the pound[20] for everyone earning £130 per annum; this meant that income tax had gone up by 40 per cent. In addition, there was to be a 50 per cent increase on customs duties for tea and tobacco. Tobacco imports were actually stopped altogether later in the war.

Between 1914 and 1918 there was not a community in Europe, including the British Isles, that was not scarred by the war, but, true to the cliché, life went on.

Although in February it was decided that the 1916 Olympics, due to be held in Berlin, should be postponed and the Lawn Tennis Association announced that the grass court championships at Wimbledon would be suspended until the war was over, the Jockey Club decided that racing would continue. Horses destined for the Front were hardly good bloodstock, and thoroughbreds had to be kept in training and so they might as well be raced. However, there were two changes of plan. The army had taken over Epsom Downs, so the Derby was run at Newmarket, and the Grand National would run at Gatwick.

It is true that one of the hit songs of 1914, 'Keep the Home Fires Burning', was full of nostalgia for those who boarded the troop ships, but a more foot-tapping song heard in all the dance halls was 'St Louis Blues'. In London Sir Joseph Beecham, the father of the conductor (later Sir Thomas Beecham), opened a new season of Russian opera with the bass Fyodor Chaliapin. The Old Vic Shakespeare Company was set up by Lilian Baylis, and three premières transfixed London concert-goers: Ralph Vaughan Williams's *A London Symphony*, Delius's *On Hearing the First Cuckoo in Spring* and Ravel's *Daphnis et Chloë*. If this sounds a cosy world of English culture as the home fires burned, it soon came under attack by the new group of artists led by Wyndham Lewis – the Vorticists. They went so far as to produce a manifesto, called *Blast*.

Not all artists stayed at home, however. The government sponsored an official war artists scheme through the Ministry of Information. Sir John Sargeant and Sir George Clausen were established, representational artists, but that did not stop the starker paintings appearing from so-called modernists, such as Stanley Spencer and the Nash brothers, Paul and John. Paul Nash's study of a shattered battlefield, *We Are Making a New World*, summed up the misery of the conflict without showing the gore. Even society painters were not excluded. Sir William Orpen, a sought-after portraitist, might be better studied for his horrific canvas *Dead Germans in a Trench*.

20 This is about 15p, but at 1915 prices this was unprecedented.

While the war took its toll, Alexander Graham Bell was working out the science to make the longest-distance telephone call ever known between New York and San Francisco. The technology was to revolutionize communication and decision making. The war weary, if not quite teetotal, took refuge in the cinema, where audiences were higher than ever. The biggest attraction of 1915 was Charlie Chaplin in one of his best known films, *The Tramp*. For those who wanted to curl up with a good book, Somerset Maugham published his autobiographical novel *Of Human Bondage*. The great actress, Sarah Bernhardt, returned to the stage after having her right leg amputated earlier in the year; she had injured it during a production of *La Tosca*.

Deaths
Rupert Brooke (poet)
Edith Cavell (nurse)
W.G. Grace (cricketer)
Keir Hardie (politician)
Aleksandr Scriabin (Russian composer)
Booker T. Washington (US educator)

1916

THE WAR was forcing British industrial society to change, particularly in terms of the workforce. In a single year there had been a 2 million increase in the number of women employed, and the government wanted more women in the factories and fewer men. At the moment, the army and navy were still all-volunteer forces, but this was about to change.

The Military Service Bill, which would allow the government to call up single men, was laid before the House, but the Home Secretary, Sir John Simon, was so against conscription that he resigned. The Trades Union Congress voted to oppose it, and on 27 January the Labour Party Conference produced an overwhelming vote against conscription. More than half a million single men had refused to volunteer, although about the same number of married men had volunteered, but were being kept in reserve because it was recognized that the married man was still the bread winner and the social consequences of parting families was not underestimated. Despite the widespread opposition to the measure, by the end of January 1916 the King had signed both the Military Service Bill and legislation to extend the life of the existing Parliament by a further year.

The Military Service Act introduced compulsory military service for all single men between the ages of eighteen and forty-one. In May the act was extended to include married men, although with the proviso that married men would not be drafted as long as recruiting ran at 50,000 men a month. To mitigate the social consequences of the Acts, grants were available to help with, for example, mortgages and even schooling, which for teenagers was almost exclusively fee paying.

The effects of the war were spreading to the countryside. The decline in agricultural output had begun in the 1880s, largely because it was cheaper to import than buy home-grown, but the war meant that Britain could no longer guarantee the safety of the sea lanes and, therefore, food supplies. The nation had to dig, as well as fight, for victory, and the government started a recruiting campaign for 400,000 women to work in the fields, and many of the women who came forward in response to the campaign came from another industry, domestic service.

In the first years of the twentieth century even modestly well-off families had domestic servants, but in 1916 a publicity campaign was directed towards those families who employed large staffs. They were urged to release both male and female servants for war work, even if this meant shutting down parts of the grander houses.

The social consequences of industrial change were significant. A man might take home a weekly wage of £5; his wife doing the same job might be paid less than one-third of that amount. The government was forced to announce equal pay for women, with the proviso that it would depend on proving that women were doing as good a job as the men. But the precedent had been established.

Many men objected to women workers, and in some communities the introduction of female staff was a social change too far. In March 1916, for example, the proposal to allow women into the Liverpool docks was abandoned when the men simply refused to work with them.

A more immediate restriction on industrial output was industrial action. Emergency powers had restricted wage bargaining and striking, and the atmosphere was further soured by trade unions that were against conscription and not necessarily on moral grounds. Most union members simply did not want to go to the Front.

From the very start of the war, one of the centres of unrest was on Clydeside. By March 1916 a small number of striking workers in the munitions industry had almost brought to a standstill the supply of guns needed on the front line. The Clyde Workers' Committee was at the base of this unrest, and the trade union leadership had lost control of that part of its membership. The Clydesiders were supported by workers in other key unions, and they knew they could hold up munition supplies. The strike leaders were arrested on 28 March, but this did not frighten the workforce, especially when it was learned that the government had a secret plan to widen the scope of conscription.

The resolve of those who were against conscription cannot have been weakened when the casualty lists started arriving in July 1916 from the latest battle, the Somme, which lasted from 1 July until 18 November. In the first half hour of the battle 20,000 British soldiers were killed, and according to one calculation there were more than 1.3 million casualties in the four and a half month period. In military terms, nothing was achieved.

By November 1916 few, dug-in in their factories, felt a burning need to volunteer for the front line trenches.

★

In 1916 a royal commission was established to investigate yet another danger facing the population, especially soldiers – venereal disease. Prostitutes haunted every army camp. So did syphilis. By the autumn of 1916 the army had more than 50,000 'reported' cases, but of equal concern was what to do about the cases that had not been reported. The Health Boards wanted reporting and examination compulsory, but this was thought to be unacceptable, largely because social disgrace would send soldiers to back-street quacks rather than to professional medics. The royal commission found that in Britain's largest cities as much as 10 per cent of the population was infected with syphilis and even more had gonorrhoea.

In 1914, at the outbreak of the war, Asquith's government had been distracted by Irish Home Rule. The problem had not gone away, and in April 1916 there were five days of revolution in Dublin, which became known as the Easter Rising.

Padraic Pearse, who commanded the Irish Republican Brotherhood (the IRB),[21] and James Connolly, with the Irish Citizen Army, led 2000 armed men into the centre of Dublin on Easter Monday. Pearse announced that he was now the president of the provisional government of the Irish Republic. Between 24 and 29 April fighting continued non-stop through the streets of Dublin, and the rebels took over the Post Office, in Sackville Street. The British soldiers of the Royal Irish Rifles and the Dublin Fusiliers covered the building, and the navy was called up to bombard the Post Office. Eventually, Pearse and Connolly were forced to surrender, and they, with twelve others, were executed.

Initially, there had been little support for the IRB, but the executions of the ringleaders inevitably led to their martyrdom. After the deaths of Pearse and Connolly and the internment, albeit short lived, of other rebels, who included Michael Collins and Eamon de Valera, public sympathy started to shift towards the Republicans, and it is strange that the British government did not understand that this would be the reaction to the heavy-handed response to the rising.

It must not be overlooked that the government was fighting an increasingly horrendous war, and the Cabinet was under enormous stress.[22] The future of Ireland had been at the forefront of government policies for decades, and there was a realization that rebellions threatened the very structure of the United Kingdom. If we put the Easter Rising in this context, there is no need to be an apologist for Asquith's government to understand that an immediate, even inept, response was all that could be expected. Whatever the reasons behind the government's response, the result of the executions and imprisonments was predictable, and the 1916 Easter Rising became a date mark for the Republican movement against British rule and the continuing support of others who ordinarily would have been indifferent to the cause. There was now no way in which the government could

21 In 1919 the IRB changed its name to the Irish Republican Army, the IRA.

22 The vexed question of conscription, which was opposed in Ireland, was important enough to make Asquith warn his colleagues that the government could fall if it were not resolved.

force through conscription in Ireland, and in the following month, May, the idea was abandoned.

There was one character whose involvement became a thorn and then a dagger in Britain's side. He was a former British consul in Africa, Sir Roger Casement. When he left the foreign service, Casement became such a committed Irish Nationalist that when the war broke out, he went to Germany to canvass for aid to the Sinn Fein cause. His involvement in the Easter Rising was an attempt to smuggle German weapons into Ireland. This attempt was foiled, and Casement was arrested, tried and found guilty of one of the five fourteenth-century acts of high treason – warring against the monarch within the monarch's realm or adhering to the monarch's enemies. He was hanged in Pentonville Prison on 3 August 1916. Casement, too, went into the martyr's book and was never forgotten. His bones were returned to Dublin in 1965 and given a state funeral.

If there was any ray of sunshine in British life that spring, it was the introduction of British Summer Time, or daylight saving time as it was then called. But there was little warmth felt in the political life of the prime minister. Anti-Asquith articles appeared, particularly in *The Times*, accusing the prime minister of indecision and failure to prosecute the war. The articles carried the inevitable inference that he was responsible for the deaths of young men at the Front.

There can be no doubt that Asquith's leadership was less than vigorous. The war was in stalemate, and the campaign in the Dardanelles had turned to fiasco. The prime minister was vulnerable. Lloyd George, now the Minister for War, wanted the Cabinet to be reconstructed so that a smaller committee assumed responsibility for the war effort. Some of his advisers, including the Ulster Unionist leader, Sir Edward Carson, and, probably, Lord Beaverbrook believed it was impossible to achieve this under Asquith, but when it was put to him on 1 December the prime minister promised to think it over. By the end of the day, he had produced several counter-proposals. As the war continued, Britain's most senior Cabinet members were bargaining like members of the trades unions they so opposed.

By Monday, 4 December Lloyd George had increased the pressure on Asquith so much that the latter told his private office that he could not see his War Minister. On the same day the King told Asquith to dissolve the government and try to form a new one. At the crux of this decision was the continuing insistence by Lloyd George that a new War Committee had to be formed. Letters sped across Whitehall between Lloyd George and Asquith, and at one point, Lloyd George threatened that if he had to resign he would publish all the memoranda and letters from Asquith. In other words, he was determined that if he went, Asquith would be brought down with him. Asquith had lost.

On 5 December Asquith offered his resignation to George V, and Bonar Law was asked to form a government. Asquith refused to serve under him. On 7 December 1916 Lloyd George became prime minister.

Deaths
William Merritt Chase (US artist)
Henry James (US writer)
Horatio Herbert Kitchener, 1st Earl Kitchener (soldier)
Jack London (US writer)
Ernst Mach (Austrian physicist)
Sir Hiram Maxim (inventor)
H.H. Munro – 'Saki' (writer)
Grigory Yefimovich Rasputin (Russian mystic)
Henryk Sienkiewicz (Polish writer)

1917

IN MILITARY lore the year 1917 is remembered for Passchendaele, the small village captured at the end of the Third Battle of Ypres – Wipers, as the British soldiers called it. This was the battle of quagmire, when men drowned in mud before they could be machine-gunned.

In international lore 1917 was the year Nicholas II, Tsar of Russia, abdicated. It was the year of the Russian Revolution, an event that for seventy years was to influence every aspect of British and American foreign policy. From 1917 the world started to live with communism.

The rest of the story of the twentieth century cannot be told without even the simplest explanation of why it happened. This was not a sudden change by Russians who did not like their monarch and wanted to lead the people to freedom. The opposition to the Tsar had been as much a feature of nineteenth-century Russia as the violence with which it had been put down.

The trigger that led to the end of the 300-year-old Romanov dynasty[23] occurred in 1905, when the Russian army and navy were defeated by the Japanese. After the defeat in the Far East revolution broke out in St Petersburg, and it was obvious even to Nicholas II that there had to be changes. As a gesture towards democracy, the Tsar instituted the Duma, a parliament, which first met in May 1905 but achieved nothing.

The relative industrial success of Russia put further demands on the state but also led to further demands from the people. These same pressures occurred in other countries, but in those the democratic process was reasonably established. In addition, no other nation had the huge physical difficulties of Russia. It was a nation stretching over ten time zones, from the Baltic to Alaska, in which lived more than a hundred nationalities. It was a nation of ethnic and geophysical extremes, rich in natural resources, many of which were locked deep beneath permafrost.

---

23 The first Romanov was Michael, who became Tsar in 1613. Although we speak of Nicholas II being the last of the Romanovs, in fact his brother, Grand Duke Michael, was nominally Tsar for one day after Nicholas's abdication.

By 1914 Russia's economic growth was beginning to outstrip that of the other two European powers, Britain and Germany. The industrial base was expanding, and there were even signs that the agricultural system was beginning to meet the needs of the huge population. This was largely due to the tenant farmers, *kulaks*, who had an incentive to find efficient ways of harvesting crops. Yet even the economic growth did not dissipate the sense of revolution. The murder of the autocratic prime minister, Pyotr Stolypin, in 1911 and the first publication in 1912 of the Bolshevik newspaper *Pravda* were parts of the unstoppable revolution, and by 1917 men such as Lenin, Stalin and Trotsky were internationally recognized as revolutionaries.

Just as the military defeat, humiliation and hardship had sparked revolt in 1905, so the dreadful conditions and abject miseries endured during the First World War fed the protests that would lead to the final revolution. On 3 March 1917 there was a strike at a munitions factory in Petrograd (as St Petersburg was now known). The workers went on strike after the factory was closed because of shortages. Rumours of bread rationing sparked riots in the capital, and within a week there were as many as 300,000 on the streets. This was a protest not simply about hunger and job losses but about the authority of the Tsar himself. In 1905 the crowds had marched and the Cossacks had slaughtered them. This time, with a few exceptions, the Cossacks refused to put down the protesters. On that day in 1905 the marchers carried their petition to their guardian, the Tsar. The Tsar failed them. This time the petition was against the Tsar.

But even its leaders did not grasp the fact that the Revolution was starting without them. Lenin was still in exile, as he had been for the last ten years, and the Germans actually smuggled him back, hoping that he would pull Russia out of the war.

Nor did the Tsar understand what was going on. He was not in the capital but at his military headquarters more than 400 miles away, relying on his ministers for information. It seems likely that he was not told the full story and that he was, in any case, distracted by the progress of the war. He sent a telegraph to the leaders of the riots, ordering them to stop the protests. At last, realizing the gravity of the situation, he sent more troops with the orders to put down the riots. This time they did open fire, and forty people were killed. The president of the Duma, M.V. Rodzianko, telegraphed Nicholas and told him anarchy was breaking out, that the government was paralysed and that some of the troops were firing at each other. Rodzianko added that any procrastination at this stage would be fatal.

On 12 March he once more telegraphed the Tsar. His message was simple – tomorrow would be too late to prevent the fall of the dynasty. The Tsar left his military headquarters by train for Petrograd, relying on his troops to stand alongside and behind him. But those very soldiers, more than 300,000 of them, had joined the rioters and marched not behind the Tsar but behind the placards that condemned him.

The Duma set up a provisional committee for the restoration of order with

Rodzianko at its head but with the socialist leader, Alexander Kerensky, as a member. Then came one of those acts that would be written into the same revolutionary log as the events on the battleship *Potemkin*. On Tuesday, 13 March sailors on board the Russian cruiser *Aurora* mutinied in Petrograd and murdered the captain. By the following day, even though the Tsar had still not reached Petrograd, he was told that he should make concessions and bow to the authority of Rodzianko's Committee. Now there was no going back. Even his own people were accepting the authority of the provisional committee. On 15 March the Tsar abdicated, and the provisional committee asked Prince Lvov to form a provisional government. A new word had been added to the lexicon of political history: 'soviet', which means council. The first soviet was elected by the protesters in Petrograd.

The battle for control was not simply between the workers and the Tsar. It was between the revolutionaries and the workers. The real power base within the opposition to the Tsar was held by the Mensheviks, a group within the Social Democratic Party. The Bolsheviks, who included Lenin, were in a minority. In fact, in Russian, Bolshevik means majority and Menshevik means minority. The contest that followed eventually led to the triumph of Leninism and then Stalinism, which is why the events of 1917 are often called the Bolshevik revolution, although that is not strictly accurate.[24]

This brief outline of the events of the Russian Revolution in March 1917 is enough to show the real distractions of the war against Germany and Austria. Add to it the industrial unrest in Britain and the events in Ireland, and there is an indication of how difficult it must have been for a Cabinet to prosecute a war and to get on with the everyday business of running a country whose children still had to go to school, whose families still had to be fed, whose social and constitutional futures still had to be planned and who could not be expected to set aside four years of their lives behind a patriotic flag simply because their leaders had been part of a system that had been incapable of preventing war in the first place.

The second major event of 1917 was the entry of the United States into the war. America had emerged as a world power in the late nineteenth century, with strategic interests in its own hemisphere and in Asia more than in Europe, but its industrial and economic growth meant that it could not cut itself off from the world of stocks and shares and trading floors in Europe.

From the outbreak of the war the Germans had needed to keep America out of the conflict, which makes it difficult to understand why the Germans continued to torpedo passenger ships, when inevitably Americans would be included among the victims.

The first public protest in the United States came in May 1915 when a German submarine torpedoed and sank the Cunard Line's *Lusitania*. Among the 1400 who

24 See Geoffrey Hosking, *A History of the Soviet Union*, Fontana (1985).

died were 128 Americans, including the multi-millionaire Alfred Vanderbilt. President Wilson had adopted a strictly neutral policy, but with such prominent people as his predecessor, Teddy Roosevelt, describing the sinking as an act of piracy, the administration's stance was difficult to sustain. Even Wilson's Secretary of State, William Bryan, believed America should join the war.

Ships continued to go down and Americans with them. In mid-1915 President Wilson told the Germans that America would not be bullied off the high seas. Two days later, on 25 July, the Germans sank two American merchant ships; the next month the White Star liner, *Arabic*, went down with twenty-six Americans on board. At the same time the new Secretary of State, Robert Lansing, started an enquiry in Washington, D.C., into German espionage in the nation's capital.

Even in 1915 Wilson's policy of neutrality had not meant totally abandoning the European war effort, and millions of dollars of gold shipments were arriving in Britain to pay for armaments. By 1916, however, it was clear that the United States would have to come into the war if it continued for much longer. The US army was enlarged and the navy ordered new ships.

In April 1916 Wilson warned Germany that the United States would break diplomatic relations if the Germans continued its campaign of submarine warfare. The Kaiser replied that Germany would cut back its activities but that in return the Americans would have to oppose the Royal Navy's blockade in Europe. The US National Guard was increased to almost half a million men.

Towards the end of 1916 Wilson attempted to see if there was any way the war could be stopped by negotiation. This was welcomed by the Germans but not the British, but then in February 1917, another American vessel was sunk, this time off the coast of Sicily.

On 3 February 1917 the president announced that diplomatic relations with Germany were at an end and on 26 February the Americans began arming their ships. The New York State National Guard, the navy and militia were called up, but Congress was still reluctant to get into the war. Many legislators could see no reason to put American lives at risk for a war that was not theirs. By March, Wilson had to call a special session of Congress, simply to discuss what to do next, and it was not until the first week in April, after a sometimes heated seventeen-hour debate, that the Senate voted by 90 votes to 6 to support the president.

On Friday, 6 April President Woodrow Wilson signed the declaration of war against Germany; the first American troops arrived in France on 27 June.

Less well documented at the time but of great significance was a document that became known as the Balfour Declaration. The former prime minister, Arthur Balfour, was now Foreign Secretary in Lloyd George's Cabinet. For some time discussions had taken place about the future of Palestine as the Jewish homeland. This, even in 1917, was a concept with obvious dangers. The view in the Foreign Office was that the Turkish (Ottoman) Empire was about to be destroyed and its territories in the Middle East would be carved up into areas of influence.

In 1917 this region was nothing like the neatly parcelled states that we see today in our atlases. The countries did not exist behind borders. For example, the huge kingdom of Abdul Aziz Ibn Saud was not created until the 1930s, when it became Saudi Arabia.

Zionists, however, were not waiting to go to the Holy Land. There were already 50,000 Jews living in Palestine; but so, too, were ten times that number of Arabs. We can see that both the British and the Zionists had something to offer each other: the Jews would need protection, which the British could give, and the British could then claim territorial influence in a region that was strategically and commercially important.

On 9 November 1917 the Balfour Declaration (probably not actually written by Balfour) was sent to the leading Zionist, Baron Guy de Rothschild. The wording was simple and unequivocal:

> His Majesty's government view with favour the establishment in Palestine of a national home for the Jewish people, and will use their best endeavours to facilitate the achievement of this object, it being clearly understood that nothing shall be done which may prejudice the civil and religious rights of existing non-Jewish communities in Palestine, or the rights and political status enjoyed in any other country.

This text was to achieve great notoriety, but it had a more immediate purpose. If Britain could be assured of a foothold in Palestine – never mind the half a million Arabs already there – it would also give Britain an ascendancy over France, which saw Syria as its sphere of interest. The reason for this is simple: Palestine lies between Syria and the Suez Canal, that most essential conduit between Europe and the Asian and Far Eastern shipping lanes, which were crucial to commercial survival in 1917.

A month later, Britain's ambitions for Palestine were encouraged when General Allenby took the Ottoman surrender of Jerusalem. The Holy Shrines were immediately protected. Soldiers were placed outside the Christian churches, and sentries from Allenby's Indian Muslim contingents were posted at the Islamic shrines.

Deaths

Elizabeth Garrett Anderson (doctor)
William F. Cody – Buffalo Bill (US showman)
Edgar Degas (French artist)
Émile Durkheim (French sociologist)
Mata Hari (Dutch adventuress)
Scott Joplin (US composer)
Auguste Rodin (French sculptor)
Sir Herbert Beerbohm Tree (actor-manager)
Count Ferdinand von Zeppelin (German inventor)

1918

THE WAR that was supposed to have been over by Christmas 1914 continued into 1918, and few people could have believed that it would be over by the following Christmas.

In January meat rationing was imposed when the government decreed that two days a week should be meat free. The poor were encouraged to eat cheaply because the only way of getting around the meat ban was to have a meal that cost 1s 2d or less. The better-off could have nipped along to the smart hotels in London where on the meatless days it was possible to rub by on a lobster.

The government was again concerned about agriculture, but the war was showing what terrible prices the nation could easily have to pay not only for its food supplies but for its timber. Throughout much of the nineteenth century Britain's forests had been almost continually destroyed, and at the outbreak of the war less than 6 per cent of Britain was covered by woods and forests. The importation of timber, especially softwood from the Baltic, was hazardous, so in January the government, again thinking ahead through its committees and encouraged by a report from the Forestry Commission, decided to plant 2 million acres of forests.

Another example of how the country had to be run as a peacetime organization as well as one on a war footing came in March 1918 with the introduction of H.A.L. Fisher's Education Bill. This really continued the work that had been begun at the beginning of the century with Balfour's Education Act of 1902. Fisher was an academic who believed passionately in the right of education among the youngest, which was not a universally held view. The Bill ensured for the first time that all children would stay on at school until the age of fourteen. This was almost as far as he could go, although he did propose part-time education for children aged between fourteen and sixteen years. It was not until 1944 that everyone in Britain became entitled to secondary education.

Although Fisher increased the powers of Local Education Authorities, he could do nothing about class sizes, which grew simply because more children were kept at school. Fisher's idea for part-time education included continuation schools, giving rise to the expression, continuing education. Fisher also had in mind that all teachers, wherever they taught, should have similar rates of pay. A review committee, under the chairmanship of Harry Burnham, the Unionist MP, now assessed all teachers in all areas. For the rest of the century teachers' pay was worked out according to the Burnham Scale.

Britain was continuing to expand its democracy, and in 1918 the new Representation of the People Bill appeared before the Commons. About 60 per cent of the male adult population had the right to vote, but women were not allowed to vote. The war had identified an anomaly in accepted voting rights: not only was it very difficult to produce an accurate electoral register, but in addition, if men who were fighting for their country were to be registered as voters, why should not women, also fighting for their country, not have a vote?

In 1916 the prime minister, Asquith, had referred the question to a Speaker's Conference, a standing meeting presided over by the Speaker of the House of Commons. The question of electoral registration, which would normally require the full residence of the voter, was circumvented by permitting six months' residence as qualification. The conference further recommended that women should be given the vote but only if they were occupiers of a house. Finally, the age at which women would be allowed to vote would be higher than for men.

MPs found themselves in an impossible situation. Those who might still vote against such proposals simply because they were set in their minds continued to vote against. Those who until then had been undecided or open to persuasion were persuaded by Asquith, when he observed that the war effort of British women demanded that they be given a vote. The Commons approved. The Bill did not immediately go through the Lords, however, where the objections to the Bill had nothing to do with suffrage for women but with *how* people voted.

The peers considered proportional representation, although eventually this was dropped. Under the Representation of the People (Equal Franchise) Act of 1918, women who were over the age of thirty and who were rate-payers, or married to a rate-payer, could vote. Later that year a Bill was passed allowing women to become MPs.

The new democracy was tested at the end of the year in what was known as the Coupon Election, the general election called immediately after the war had finished. The prime minister, David Lloyd George, and the leader of the Conservatives in the coalition government, Bonar Law, had sent a 'coupon' – a letter of approval – to approved candidates indicating that the candidates would not be opposed by other pro-coalition candidates. In effect, this was election rigging of candidates in order to preserve the coalition in government, which many members of all parties no longer wished to do. Importantly, this showed the division between Lloyd George's Liberals, who supported coalition, and Asquith's Liberals, who did not. Of 531 'coupon' candidates, 468 were elected, 133 of them Liberals, and 335 Conservatives. Asquith lost his seat and, partly thanks to Lloyd George, the Liberals were finished as a single great party.

The greater interest at the time was how women voted. How they voted is still difficult to determine from anything but anecdotal evidence, but the opinion of the time was that most women had voted as their husbands did. This trend continued well into the final quarter of the century.

A total of 1600 candidates had stood in the 1918 election, but after all the expectations, no more than 17 women were adopted. The only one elected was a Sinn Fein member from Dublin, Countess Markievicz, Constance Gore-Booth. But she refused to take her seat because she refused to swear an oath of allegiance to the monarch.

If the common interest was exercising minds in Whitehall, the common good was on the agenda of the relatively new Labour Party. The party had been formed in

1906 through a simple name change from the Labour Representation Committee (LRC). The origins of the Labour movement lay in the nineteenth century, especially in the growing influence of the trade unions.

Another influence on the movement was the Fabian Society, named after the Roman general, Quintus Fabius Maximus, who fought Hannibal. His tactic was to be patient but, when the time was right, to strike swiftly and with steel. This was the credo of the Fabian Society. It was not a revolutionary group, but had been set up in 1884 with the aim of establishing a socialist state through philosophical argument and the accepted passages of democracy rather than through the violent means championed elsewhere. The godparents of the society were the Webbs. Sydney Webb had been a civil servant; his wife, Beatrice Potter, was the daughter of an industrialist. The Webbs studied industrial reform, trade unionism and local and regional government and their writings became required reading for all British socialists. Their physical memorial is the college in London that would soon become internationally famous, the London School of Economics, which they founded in 1895, and the house journal of British socialism, the *New Statesman*, which they started in 1913. It was the Webbs' report on the Poor Laws that showed what was possible in setting up the welfare state forty years later.

Membership of the Fabian Society was not confined to political philosophers. George Bernard Shaw was one of its most celebrated members and it was he who edited *Fabian Essays* in 1889. H.G. Wells was also a member, and so was a future prime minister, Clement Attlee.

In 1918 Sydney Webb and Arthur Henderson, the Labour Party Secretary and a member of the War Cabinet, were largely responsible for the reorganization of the Labour Party. It was Webb who wrote the outline of what became the Labour Party's most famous constitution. This was the first declaration that the party would, if it became the government, nationalize many of the major industries, including banks and other commercial institutions. In the document, approved by the party on 26 February 1918, were the words that would inform every socialist and supporter of the Labour Party until the 1990s. It was, according to the declaration, the pledge of the Labour Movement:

> To secure for the workers by hand or by brain the full fruits of their industry and the most equitable distribution thereof that may be possible upon the basis of the common ownership of the means of production, distribution and exchange, and the best obtainable system of popular administration and control of each industry or service.

Until 1996 the words, known as Clause Four, appeared on the back of every Labour Party membership card.

In July 1918 the headline writers had more interesting copy – responsible sex. Dr Marie Stopes had published a book, *Married Love*. This was 1918 – imagine the scandal. Here in public was a discussion of the sexual habits and duties of married people plus the almost unspoken issue of contraception.

In that same month, July 1918, came news from Russia that sent shudders through the royal courts of Europe. On 16 July Nicholas II and his family, together with their doctor, servants and dog, were shot and stabbed to death on the orders of the Bolshevik leaders. The murders took place in a cellar in Ekaterinburg, where the Romanovs had been kept prisoner since 30 May. This was not simply the revenge of the socialist revolutionaries; deeper motives lay behind the killings.

When the Bolsheviks took control, they had set up the Red Army (beneath the banner of Communism, the Red Flag) and, the security police, the Cheka. Civil war was inevitable. In the Ukraine Tsarist generals organized what was called the White Volunteer Army. Elsewhere, Alexander Kerensky, who had been deposed by Lenin, had organized the Czech Legion of about 45,000 men in Siberia. However, it was the White Volunteer Army and the Red Army that would battle for future control of Russia.

So convinced were the Western Alliance of the need to make sure that Lenin was at least challenged, they took the side of the White Russians. On 2 August the British army, supported by French and Polish contingents and an American Marine group, landed at Archangel. The fighting went on until 1920 and the Allies eventually had to withdraw. The Red Army was successful; the Bolshevik Revolution was secure.

It was in this atmosphere that the Romanovs were murdered. Ekaterinburg was on the line of advance of the White Russians, and it must have been clear that an army raised by officers loyal to the Tsar would at least try to rescue the royal family. The people in charge of the Romanovs were not sophisticated political philosophers nor were they military tacticians. Moreover, they understood that all orders now came from the centre, so they asked Moscow what should be done about the Tsar, his family and his servants. They were told that it was up to them, and the Bolshevik workers handed the Romanovs over to the Cheka. It was they who executed them.

Deaths

Claude Debussy (French composer)
Raymond Duchamp-Villon (French sculptor)
Gustav Klimt (Austrian artist)
Nicholas II (emperor of Russia 1868–1918)
Wilfred Owen (poet)
Edmond Rostand (French playwright)
Frank Wedekind (German writer)

1919

THE WAR over, Britain had to attend both to promises made in earlier years and to the pressures of the present. In 1917, for example, India had been told that it could have 'responsible government', although there was no question of independence as the Indian National Congress and its leader, Gandhi, wanted. But in April 1919 there came an incident that was indicative of the tone of the British rule and of Gandhi's form of opposition until independence was achieved. The British army killed 379 demonstrators at Amritsar. Some commentators believe that this was the point at which British rule in India lost all credibility. The British were simply not prepared for what followed – Gandhi's protest campaign of civil disobedience. The Raj did not know how to cope with this opposition and never would.

When 1919 opened the war was over but neither continental Europe nor Britain had much future to celebrate. Close to a quarter of a million British workers were on strike, by far the largest group being miners who simply wanted a shorter working week. The Miners' Federation wanted the pits nationalized and a six-hour day for its members. The London Underground came to a standstill over shorter hours, and in Glasgow there was a general strike that became so unpleasant that the sheriff had to read the Riot Act.[25] The strikers in George Square were not much impressed, and it took a police foot and mounted charge to disperse them. Vehicles were overturned and shops were looted. Behind this demonstration lay yet again the demand for shorter working weeks without any reduction in pay.

Similar protests were common throughout Britain, and they were accompanied by increased unemployment and crime.

During the war there had been full employment, but Lloyd George's government was now faced with the task of how best to demobilize 4 million able-bodied men, many of whom had no job to go to. The nation was not yet – and perhaps never would be – a country fit for heroes.

At first it was decided to release from the forces all those soldiers who had civilian jobs to go to, which in practice was likely to include a large number of men who had not been in the army for very long. It is not difficult to imagine the thoughts of the soldiers who, having served King and country in the worst of all wars, were now being told that they would have to stay on until it was convenient to let them return to civilian society.

There were mutinies in army camps in France and on the Kent coast. Three thousand soldiers staged a protest demonstration on Horse Guards Parade. Another group, this time Canadians, mutinied at their barracks in Wales. The Canadians

25 The Riot Act was passed in 1715 following Jacobite unrest. Its basic provision was that if so-called riotous assemblies of twelve or more people failed to break up after the Riot Act, forbidding them to be there, was read publicly and formally to them, they would be guilty of riotous assembly. This was a capital offence.

were not looking for jobs – they simply wanted to go home – but their discharge and embarkation were delayed, or so it was said, because there were not enough ships. In March an attempt to bring the mutineers to order led to some of them being killed.

There was, too, a widely held view that the events in Russia might bring about increasing industrial unrest in Britain, a factor that was in the back of the minds of ministers as they confronted the problem of demobilization. Churchill, the War Minister, was of the opinion that immediate action was necessary rather than some philosophical debate about the long-term consequences. Soldiers without jobs to go to would get gratuities and the longest serving should go first. The pay-outs would have to be found from diminishing government coffers, which increased the stress on the public purse at a time when there was increased activity from trade unions, although it should be remembered that many had called their members out on strike even in wartime.

By the summer, probably thanks to Churchill's initiative, 80 per cent of soldiers who were due for discharge had been demobilized. Contrary to past experiences, many of them went straight back into industry. There were jobs to go to and there were markets for British goods, but there appears to have been a simple flaw in the industrial management and forecasting.

Consider what industries would have sprung up as a result of the developments taking place throughout the world if there had been no war. The automobile industry had gone from workshop production to conveyor belt assembly line, and Henry Ford had produced his one millionth motor car in 1917. The wireless industry was now sophisticated enough for global communication stations to be built. Pharmaceuticals were leaving laboratories at a faster rate than ever before. Engineering and manufacturing systems had been refined, especially in the United States. New forms of tool making and cosmetic fabrication were opening up industries that simply made things look better. Chemical production was not only producing in bulk but was also introducing processes that had wide-ranging industrial and social repercussions, including the development of celluloid, which had such implications for the film industry.

When a nation goes to war much of its industrial base and effort is geared to that confrontation. Although engineering innovations occur in wartime, by and large in 1914–18 British industry did not develop in the way it might have done in peacetime.

In 1919, therefore, the government was faced with the need to reconstruct and restructure British industry. Conflict with the trade unions seemed inevitable, and in February 1919 a conference of industrialists and employers heard the railway workers' leader, James Thomas, demand that British workers should have more money and greater profits from the boom they believed would come in postwar Britain. The first step was to dispense with the war effort in the factories. Women were the first to go, and within almost twelve months there were fewer women working than there had been before the war.

Everyone wanted to be free of wartime restrictions, but the flaw in the argument was a belief that government and industry could simply harness the wartime effort in peacetime and return to the concepts and systems of prewar Britain. The advantages of a wartime economy were that it remained under close examination and direction, but this was soon forgotten. Tariffs on trade, both at home and overseas, were removed as were price controls. Gold exports were freed, and the government allowed the pound to find its natural value. Hitherto, it had kept pace with the dollar. What was inevitable had not been foreseen.

By the end of 1919 wholesale prices in Britain were nearly three times their prewar levels. Up went wage demands, a stance that was encouraged, ironically, because industry was then very rich and many wage demands were met. Inflation followed, and for the next two years the government even had to maintain food rationing.

Industrial relations had not improved with the end of the war. The three most powerful unions, the miners, the railway and the transport workers, controlled the flow of goods and people throughout Britain and were aiming to put into practice their plans for nationalization. Several commissions were established to try to work out some arrangement between government and workers, but they were unsuccessful. The railwaymen became impatient, and in September 1919 they went on strike.

The politicking of this strike was effective. Auckland Geddes, the President of the Board of Trade, under which the railways still operated, refused to meet the demands of the railway workers. Ten days later Lloyd George settled with the National Union of Railwaymen. James Thomas, the NUR General Secretary, was triumphant. But Lloyd George, had isolated the NUR from the other unions, and it now had no reason to join in a general strike – unless it was out of sympathy – because its members had got what they wanted.

In September the Trades Union Congress demanded that the coal mines be nationalized. A few days later, on 22 September, Britain's 50,000 foundry workers struck for more pay. In October teachers, whose pay had been frozen during the war, demanded increases of 100 per cent.

Policemen tried to set up their own trade union, but the government refused to recognize it. Industrial action was called for July and more than 6000 police officers were dismissed for going on strike. With the police striking, crime increased and the army had to be called out to cope with rioting and looting.

The Labour Party Conference added to the prospects of industrial chaos by voting that workers could be called out for political reasons and not simply for higher wages or better conditions.

Some changes in the way the nation was governed survived the war and some of these, especially the restructuring of departments of responsibility, were carried through into the peace. The immediate change in political tempo that wartime brought had meant the nub of British government, the Cabinet, was unable to cope with the complexities of running a war and a country. The man who eased the burden of government was Maurice Hankey, a civil servant who was the Secretary to the Imperial Defence Committee set up in 1912. It was Hankey who saw the need for a Cabinet Secretariat. His system survived both the war and the rest of the century.

One of the reasons that Lloyd George had needed a new government – apart from the fact that the existing one had overrun its peacetime mandate – was that he needed the country behind him when he went to the conference table around which would be decided the future of Germany and a postwar settlement agreed.

As early as January 1918, in a speech to Congress, President Wilson had delivered a fourteen-point peace plan. His proposal provide a useful perspective on the effects of the four-year conflict.

1. Open covenants of peace [in other words, no secret deals].
2. Freedom of navigation.
3. Removal of trade barriers.
4. National armaments to be reduced to the lowest level possible for national domestic safety.
5. Free, open minded and impartial adjustment of colonial claims.
6. Evacuation of all Russian territory.
7. Evacuation of Belgium.
8. All French territory to be freed and Alsace Lorraine to be returned.
9. The frontiers of Italy to be readjusted.
10. The people of Austria-Hungary to be offered autonomy.
11. Romania, Serbia and Montenegro to be evacuated.
12. Turkish parts of the Ottoman Empire to be assured of sovereignty.
13. An independent Polish state to be established with access to the sea [the Baltic].
14. An association of nations to be formed to guarantee independence and territorial integrity.

It was the fourteenth point that was intended to make sure that the world would not see another war, and it was approved by the twenty-seven states attending the Paris Conference. It led to the setting up of the League of Nations.

The immediate way forward to what would be yet another Treaty of Versailles was to reach agreement on the future of Germany and to meet demands that the Germans should pay for the war. The task was ostensibly simple. The enemy had been a coalition of Germany, Turkey, Bulgaria, Austria and Hungary. The war had effectively ended the dual state of Austria-Hungary and the Habsburg Empire that had controlled it. The Ottoman Empire had also gone. Most items on the agenda of the peace conference, therefore, concerned the redrawing of frontiers.

The Italians had great difficulty in agreeing what should be done about Fiume (Rijeka), which was the Hungarian outlet to the sea but now separated from

Hungary. Here was yet another contention of Balkan proportions that the Italians would not allow to be overlooked. Meanwhile, the French and the British were quietly carving up the Ottoman Empire, much to the annoyance of the Americans, who could do very little about it as they had never actually been officially at war with Turkey.

Although these were indeed important issues and ones that would have consequences for the rest of the century, the focus of that conference had to be Germany.

Many Germans did not believe that they had been defeated. Germany was not yet occupied, and it still had freedom over its own plans for government. It still had its army. The abdication of the Kaiser necessitated a radical constitutional change, and the Germans were doing that themselves. Even as the Allies were meeting at the Paris Peace Conference, the Germans were sitting down in a newly elected national assembly, not in Berlin, but at a small town called Weimar, to discuss the future of the nation. It was from this town that the Weimar Republic was born.

The Weimar Republic immediately established voting rights for everyone over the age of twenty. The system of *Länder*, or states, was dominated by Prussia, whatever the ambitions of some of the leading lights of the new republic. Prussia could not be ignored, largely because it included the great Silesian coal fields and the industrially important Ruhr valley. It also dominated much of the police force in Germany. Whatever the people of the new Republic hoped for, Prussia would continue to dominate them.

The major powers assembled in Paris did believe that they were now living on a settled continent. The war was over, but not the fighting, which this time was ideologically inspired. In most capitals, including Berlin, there was a movement to replace whatever government struggled to emerge from the war with communism. In January 1919 in Berlin itself there was an uprising against the new system. The revolutionaries came from a group called the Spartacists, which had been founded in Munich by Max Levien, a supporter of Lenin, and was named after the slave who had led the revolt against the Roman Empire in the first century BC. The group's name was eventually changed to the German Communist Party. The Spartacist revolution in Berlin was led by two communists, Karl Liebknecht and a woman who has joined the list of European political martyrs, 'Red' Rosa Luxemburg. Barricades were set up, and the Spartacists demanded a socialist and Bolshevik republic. Troops were sent to deal with them and did so. Both Luxemburg and Liebknecht were arrested and murdered on their way to prison. 1200 of their supporters were killed in January 1919 and the Communist uprising was put down.

Further south, the Bavarian socialist party, which was led by Kurt Visnier, had been set up in December 1918. In Hungary in March 1919 Belakun seized power, planning to link up with the Red Army, which was still fighting the White Army. On 6 April the First Bavarian Socialist Republic was set up in Munich, with Ernst

Toller at its head. It survived a week. But another took its place, until that too was put down on the unforgiving orders from Berlin. In Vienna it seemed that the Austrian capital was about to succumb to yet another communist revolution but that was suppressed.

These revolutions, sometimes in the name of the Bolsheviks, were unsuccessful. But in Paris, many of the delegates were learning that socialism and communism were movements that would not be confined to Russia.

No one was invulnerable to anarchy. Even in Britain police were watching a group of anarchists, who were arrested in August 1919 for planning a communist plot to overthrow the government. On 23 March Benito Mussolini set up his Fascist Party in Italy. On 19 February the French prime minister, Georges Clemenceau, was shot and wounded by an anarchist. But such an attack on 'The Tiger', as Clemenceau was called, did nothing to curb his singled-minded ambition to rid France of what he saw as the continuing threat of Germany before whose threat anarchy paled.

The so-called victors of the war carried on talking in Paris and dividing up Europe, eventually producing the document known as the Treaty of Versailles. The hundreds of articles and clauses of the treaty referred only to Germany. A second treaty, agreed in September 1919, dealt with Austria.

The Treaty of Versailles had a single purpose: Germany must never again be a threat to peace. Alsace Lorraine was returned to France, and regions of Prussia and Silesia were restored to Poland. Denmark was given part of Schleswig. Germany's entire colonial possessions were declared mandated territories and nominally put under the control of the League of Nations, and the Allied powers were supposed to occupy the Rhineland for up to fifteen years. In order to prevent Germany from building up its military resources, the army was limited to 100,000 men while the navy was to have no more than six battleships, twelve cruisers and twelve destroyers.

Then came the 'fine'. Article 232 of the Versailles Treaty said that the Germans had to pay repatriations to the victims and victors. In 1921 that figure was fixed at £6.6 million. It was an impossible demand and was never paid. It was impossible that Germany would accept the treaty. Its Cabinet did not and resigned.

While German anguish was public, not every member of the victorious alliance was happy with the terms. The French wanted the most out of the Versailles Treaty, and President Poincaré went further than any other leader in seeking the complete crushing of Germany. He saw Prussia as a completely separate issue and declared that he could see no way that a peace could be signed to include the Prussians.

Of all the nations, Britain was probably the easiest to satisfy. The main threat at the beginning of the war as far as British strategic sensitivities were concerned had been the German high seas fleet. That had surrendered, and the bulk of it, seventy ships, was lying at Scapa Flow in the Orkney Islands. On the day that the Treaty was concluded, 21 June (it was not signed until a week later), the German commander of the captured fleet, Rear Admiral von Reuter, ordered the skeleton crews on board the vessels to scuttle them. The sailors went below and opened the sea-cocks to let water into the hulls and then escaped into the ships' boats. All but one battleship, a cruiser and some smaller vessels went to the bottom.

Von Reuter was carrying out orders. The ships had gone to Scapa Flow at the end of the war because there was an armistice. As far as he was concerned (and he was quite correct), an armistice was an agreement to stop fighting for a period; it was not an end to war. With the signing of a Treaty, the armistice had come to an end. His orders were that no German ship should be surrendered.

The Americans found themselves ensnared in bilateral disputes, but President Wilson had no great demands to make on Germany now that it was overthrown. His single interest was the establishment of the League of Nations, whose constitution was written into the Treaty of Versailles. The role of the League of Nations was not unanimously accepted. The Americans and the British saw it as a sensible talking shop that would resolve international disputes before they broke into war. Others, particularly the French, were more single minded, and Clemenceau believed that the League's objective was to make sure the Germans were never in any position to go to war again. The French also wanted the League to become an instrument to maintain the wartime alliance – in other words, he wanted it to be a formal arrangement of the Entente Cordiale with some guarantee that America would not opt out of any strategic plan to keep Germany down.

It is interesting to note that when France joined NATO after the Second World War, it was not so much through fear of Stalin's Russia – the reason for NATO's formation – but because France still feared Germany. Moreover, the French were still looking for a mechanism that would keep the Americans in Europe.

However, for that moment on the afternoon of 28 June 1919, all eyes were on the ceremonies at the Palace of Versailles. After five months of discussion, drafting and re-drafting, the 200 pages of the peace treaty, with its 440 clauses, was signed. Lloyd George was not alone when he reflected on what was a flawed document. As he result of it, he believed, the allies would have to 'fight another war all over again in 25 years at three times the cost'.[26]

Perhaps the most significant event of the year, and one that would hang over the whole world following the end of the war to come, came in 1919. It was announced that a scientist, Professor Ernest Rutherford (1871–1937), of Manchester University, had 'split' the atom.

Deaths

William Waldorf Astor, 1st Viscount Astor of Hever (financier and journalist)
L. Frank Baum (US writer)
Louis Botha (South African politician)
Andrew Carnegie (US industrialist and humanitarian)

26 David Lloyd George, *War Memoirs*, Odhams (revised edition 1939).

Sir Wilfrid Laurier (Canadian politician)
Ruggero Leoncavallo (Italian composer)
Adelina Patti (Italian soprano)
Pierre-Auguste Renoir (French artist)
Theodore Roosevelt (US president)

CHAPTER THREE

THE ROARING TWENTIES 1920–1929

1920

THE ROARING TWENTIES were supposed to be the years of flapper fun, innovation and the Jazz Age,[1] but not everyone was draped in the thin silks of changing fashions. Some wore shrouds, for this was the year in which Lenin gripped Russia, Hitler emerged as the leading figure of the National Socialist German Workers' Party, the United States refused to join the League of Nations and ratify the Treaty of Versailles, the Black and Tans were sent to Ireland and the IRA murdered fourteen British officers and officials in cold blood.

By the beginning of March the civil war in Russia was running out of steam. The White Russian army, led by the former Tsar's generals, was losing both battles and allies. The British, American, Japanese, Greek, Polish, Romanian and French masters were beginning to pull out their armies, which totalled some 90,000 infantry and which were equipped with the latest military inventions, tanks and planes. As summer turned into autumn, the Red Army crushed the rebellion.

In another part of Europe another conflict was beginning. Germany was not united in defeat. It had never been a single state in the sense that everyone had common understanding and worked for the good of one nation. As the French had long insisted, while it was possible to treat with Germans, it was impossible to apply the same rules to Prussians. While the Allies dished out honours to each other,[2] Germans seethed over what they called the Versailles 'diktat' and fought among themselves for control of the vanquished nation.

In January anti-government demonstrators were gunned down by government troops in front of the Reichstag, but the government could not prevent extremist groups from springing up in most parts of the country. A new Bavarian group, the German Workers' Party, soon to become the National Socialist German Workers'

1 From *Tales of the Jazz Age* by F. Scott Fitzgerald, first published in 1922. See also *This Side of Paradise* (1920).

2 President Woodrow Wilson was actually given the Nobel Peace Prize, even though his own country refused to ratify the Versailles Treaty, which was virtually Wilson's fourteen-point peace plan (see 1919).

Party, began demonstrating against capitalism and Jews. A former corporal, Adolf Schicklgruber, who now called himself Adolf Hitler, emerged as the group's spokesman.

Not all the demonstrations were inspired by socialism. Towards the end of February 1920, the Social Democratic government that had emerged from the setting up of the Weimar Republic was challenged by a group of the old guard, led by Dr Wolfgang von Kapp, which claimed that it wanted to prevent the Bolshevik revolution from spreading to Germany. Kapp proclaimed himself Chancellor, but the government outwitted the would-be revolutionaries. A general strike was called that paralysed the nation. The French watched knowingly. They regarded the attempted coup not as a move against Bolshevism but as a blatant attempt to restore the Prussian monarchy.

In June the Allies told the Germans that they must pay £12.5 million in war reparations. The British economic philosopher, John Maynard Keynes, who in 1919 had published a study of the Treaty of Versailles, *The Economic Consequences of the Peace*, had warned against the foolishness and futility of bleeding the German economy dry. He had shown that the treaty was more than a simple matter of redrawing boundaries and reducing military power and predicted that it would bring Europe to its knees. Under the treaty, however, the Germans had to give up valuable industrial areas. Their economy was already in ruins, so they had little chance of earning the money that the Allies were demanding from them.

The Treaty of Versailles stipulated that Germany had to cut its army to 100,000 men, hand over major weapon systems (including aircraft) and abolish conscription.[3] But the Germans had not done as they had been ordered: they still had 150,000 men under arms and had refused to disband the security police. Given the armed anarchy within the country, there were those who sympathized.

There was little sympathy, however, with the decision of the US Congress not to join the League of Nations. No matter how hard he tried, President Wilson could not carry the legislature. The heart of US objections was Article 10, which committed member states to defend any other member that was attacked. The Americans objected to this, just as Britain had been loath to join the alliance of Germany, Italy and Austria at the turn of the century. In addition, a large group in Congress did not like the idea of Britain having extra votes, even though these were actually held on behalf of the dominion members.

When a compromise on these first two objections was produced, President Wilson refused to vote for a watered-down agreement. Wilson was, however, in no position to fight the obstruction by the Congress – he had suffered a stroke and was very ill. In the presidential election that November, the new president, the sturdy Republican Senator from Ohio, Warren Harding, had a landslide victory. If America was to ratify the Treaty of Versailles, it would have to be rewritten.

---

3 Churchill, the War Minister, had announced in February 1920 that Britain's non-conscript army would be 220,000 strong.

The first meeting of the Council of the League of Nations was held in London in February 1920. It agreed to set up the International Court of Justice, which was progress, but the League needed the United States. It had fifty-three members but no authority to enforce any rulings with anything other than sanctions. Any country that objected to its treatment could resign – as did Germany when Hitler took over. If the League had any value it was its use as a cover for often bilateral agreements, including, for example, the San Remo Conference, held in April 1920, which carved up the Middle East and parts of Africa.

In April it was agreed that the former German and Turkish territories taken during the war should be ruled under mandates directed by the League of Nations. This is how Britain came to rule Tanganyika (now Tanzania), the Cameroons, Jordan (Transjordan as was), Iraq and Palestine, while France was granted mandates over Syria and Lebanon. Britain had been especially anxious to obtain the mandate over Palestine. Together with interests in Egypt, Britain would then be in the most influential position to guard the strategically important Suez Canal. Zionist groups also welcomed Britain's mandate, because the Balfour Declaration of 1917 would be written into the agreement. Although Jews already lived in Palestine, alongside some half million Arabs, the Declaration meant that they were on the way to having an internationally recognized homeland and that recognition would be underwritten by Britain.

The most pressing concern in Britain was not the Holy Land nor the discussions taking place around the conference table of the League of Nations. In 1920 Ireland was at the forefront of the Cabinet's mind. The whole of the island of Ireland was still within the United Kingdom, with the headquarters of government residing at Dublin Castle. In the 1918 general election all seventy-three Irish seats, apart from those in Ulster, had been won by Sinn Fein, with 47 per cent of the Irish electorate voting for a party that intended that Ireland should be independent from Great Britain.

After the election Sinn Fein set up an Irish Parliament, the Dáil Éireann, and Eamon de Valera was elected as the Dáil's president. The British government said the Dáil was illegal, but Sinn Fein ignored edicts from London and began to govern as if it had assumed independence. This was not a peaceful and democratic period in Irish history.

The Irish Republican Army (IRA) had been formed in 1919. It was commanded by Michael Collins (1890–1922), a doomed, romantic figure from Cork. He came to prominence in the Easter Rising[4] and later as one of the MPs elected during the 1918 campaign. The British offered a large reward for his capture, but Collins's intelligence gathering was good, and he had more than one sympathizer among the British, so he remained at large. Like many branded 'terrorists', Collins became part of the 'democratic' process for peace. It was not the

4 See page 101.

British who eventually got Collins, but his own people. His political agreement with the British and his signing of the Anglo-Irish Treaty in 1921 led to his downfall and his murder at the hands of the Republicans.

The Chief of the Imperial General Staff, Sir Henry Wilson, is said to have claimed that Ireland could be brought to heel only by full-scale war, and by 1920 Britain was, effectively, at war with the Republicans. It reinforced the Royal Irish Constabulary – which was totally unsuited to fighting the IRA – with the Black and Tans, so called because of the khaki and dark green uniforms. The Black and Tans were mostly ex-soldiers, whose ruthlessness soon earned themselves and the British government an unenviable reputation.

Lloyd George wanted a more conventional solution than war. The Government of Ireland Act would establish two parliaments – one in Dublin, the other in Belfast – and a Council of Ireland. The IRA would recognize neither parliament, however, although, predictably, the Ulster Unionist Council accepted the concept of a parliament in Belfast. At the end of March the Home Rule Bill went through the Commons, but there were many, including Sir Edward Carson, who saw it as a recipe for yet more conflict. In April, on the anniversary of the Easter Rising, the IRA burned down twenty-two Inland Revenue offices and 122 police stations. Some 300,000 Irish workers went on strike in protest at the British treatment of prisoners.

In May Londonderry became a battleground between Unionists and Republicans. The army appeared helpless, and reinforcements were sent. The Constabulary could no longer go about its normal police work, never mind its bewildering anti-terrorism task, and the murder of policemen and soldiers became everyday events. The death toll rose. By the end of 1920 martial law, thought to be the appropriate response to uprisings in less stable societies than Britain's, had been imposed in large areas of Ireland, which, for the moment, remained in the United Kingdom.

Deaths

John Arbuthnot Fisher, 1st Baron Fisher of Kilverstone (sailor)
Max Klinger (German artist)
Amedeo Modigliani (Italian artist)
Robert Peary (US explorer)
John Reed (US writer)
Max Weber (German sociologist)

1921

IN JANUARY the prime minister of the coalition government, David Lloyd George, held a house-warming party. He was the first prime minister to move into Chequers, the Tudor mansion in the Chilterns, 30 miles from London, which had been given to the nation by Lord Lee of Fareham and which became, and has remained, the prime minister's official country residence. Lloyd George was not, however, going to enjoy the tenancy of Chequers for long. Postwar Britain was unwell.

Although Britain was not alone in experiencing economic difficulties – even enormously rich America had 3.5 million unemployed – there were more than a million people out of work in Britain, and the government was forced to raise unemployment benefit from 15 shillings (75p) a week to 18 shillings (90p) for men and from 12 shillings (60p) to 15 shillings (75p) for women. The benefit was paid for six months of the year.

On paper, Britain should have been reasonably well off, even if not rich, but the arithmetic was something of a chimera. During the period 1920–24, for example, there was a net balance of payments of £1.61 million, but this was entirely due to 'invisible' earnings (insurance and so forth). Imports still far exceeded exports. Moreover, in addition to the effects of war, Britain was gradually losing the cushion that had historically been provided by trade with the Empire.

Socio-economic arguments were of little value on the streets, and the only weapon available to threatened industries was strike action. By mid-June more than 2 million men were involved in pay negotiations or in industrial action. In March the miners believed that the much talked-of alliance with the railway and transport unions would force the pit-owners to reach agreement – the miners' action was against the privately owned mines, not against the government – but the government declared a state of emergency, and in April coal rationing began. The railwaymen and the transport unions, which had promised to support the miners, at the last moment failed to do, and the first big effort at cross-union support failed.

This did not lead to industrial peace, however. The decline in the Lancashire cotton industry that had been predicted for so long was evident to all. The Indian market had more or less vanished, partly because India was now buying from elsewhere and partly because it was now manufacturing its own cotton goods. When the Prince of Wales paid an official visit to India in 1921, Gandhi organized demonstrations against cloth imports. For Gandhi the issue was very simple: the British, the masters, had made fortunes from Indians who needed cotton cloth. If, as Gandhi now did, every Indian learned to spin his or her own cotton, there would be a symbolic protest as well as an actual step towards establishing India's own cotton industry, which would be a positive move towards independence.

Keynes told Lloyd George that if Britain was to be prosperous again, fundamental policy changes had to come about, among which should be a concentrated effort to make Germany prosperous. It is easy to see why people who had given so much during the war found it difficult to accept a hypothesis that declared that it was necessary to make other people rich before they could become rich themselves. The French, too, had suffered at the hands of the German army and appeared determined to reduce Germans to a condition of twentieth-century serfdom. The French also found it hard to accept the larger argument that a prosperous Germany was less likely to result in extreme government. Nationalism too often arises when people blame minorities, especially alien minorities, for national misfortune. This is not to say that what was to follow did not find sympathizers in Britain. Although from the perspective of the end of the twentieth century it is difficult to accept that in the 1930s there were people in Britain who admired Hitler's Germany, if we try to understand what was happening in Britain in the aftermath of the First World War and the treacherous social and economic circumstances that arose then, the source of the sympathy may be quickly identified.

In addition to the economic problems, the government continued to be beset by violence in Ireland. More troops were sent from England as the war with the IRA intensified, and in January tanks appeared in Dublin itself. New orders for martial law were posted across the island. The intensity of the fighting is revealed in the horrific catalogue of deaths in the first short weeks: on 20 January six policemen were killed, three days later eight were killed in a gun battle with the IRA, and at the end of the month three more policemen died at the hands of the IRA. On 1 February troops torched houses in retribution for the deaths of the three policemen. The violence continued on 11 February when the IRA murdered an Irish police informer, while on 16 February eight members of Sinn Fein were killed by the army. Four days later a former soldier was taken from Cork Hospital and murdered by Sinn Fein. And that was just the first two months of the year.

In the spring the IRA stepped up its campaign by attacking relatives of police officers. Both sides were directing their pressure towards the political events of May 1921, when elections to the two new parliaments were due to be held. Of the 128 Southern Irish seats, Sinn Fein won 124. Eamon de Valera, who had already been appointed by Sinn Fein as president of the Dáil, became the official leader of the Southern Irish Parliament. Sir James Craig (1871–1940) became the first prime minister of Northern Ireland. The Southern Irish still wanted a united Ireland, and the Ulster Unionists believed that the establishment of the parliament in Dublin was the first step towards their betrayal by this, or some future, British government – a belief that survived for the rest of the century.

The important matter was to stop open warfare. De Valera agreed to talks with Lloyd George but rejected an idea that had originally come from South Africa – that Ireland should become a dominion. General Jan Smuts, the South African leader, had advised George V that the only solution to Ireland was independence within what was now being called the Commonwealth. In July a peace conference in Dublin agreed, surprisingly, to a truce, but differences were so great that talks to resolve the future status of Ireland were called off because de Valera would attend only if he were regarded as the head of an independent state.

In October 1921 a conference did open in London. In the early hours of the morning of 8 December 1921 the British government bowed to the political and military inevitable. A document was signed, the Anglo-Irish Treaty, establishing the Irish Free State as a self-governing dominion within the Commonwealth. The six counties in the northeastern part of the island did not agree to be part of the Irish

Free State. They declared that they must have self-government, but within the United Kingdom. Here lie the origins of Southern and Northern Ireland, and here lies the cause of the bitterness felt by the extreme Nationalists at having failed to achieve their object of an entirely united Ireland and also at having to accept the oath of allegiance to the British crown.

This was a political settlement that did not please, and would never satisfy, the IRA. Nor did it stop the violence. When he signed the Anglo-Irish Treaty on behalf of the Irish, Michael Collins had signed his death warrant. He died in an ambush in Cork the following year.

There were high points in the year, which saw the fiftieth anniversary of bank holiday Mondays. The Bank Holidays Act of 1871 had established public holidays when banks would be closed in England and Wales – Easter Monday, Whit Monday, the first Monday in August and Boxing Day – and over the years to these had been added Good Friday and Christmas Day. The fiftieth anniversary of Sir John Lubbock's 1871 Act was treated as a national celebration.

There was a moment of international celebration when in Canada Charles Best and Frederick Banting isolated insulin. Until this point, diabetics had died because their bodies could not create sufficient insulin to cope with the sugar in their blood. The work done by Banting and Best saved and prolonged millions of lives, especially those of young people.

Deaths

Enrico Caruso (Italian tenor)
John Boyd Dunlop (inventor)
Georges Feydeau (French playwright)
Engelbert Humperdinck (German composer)
Prince Pyotr Kropotkin (Russian anarchist)
Camille Saint-Saëns (French composer)

1922

IN 1922 Britain's coalition government finally collapsed. It had come into being during, and because of, the First World War and had continued to exist for another four years to keep Lloyd George's Liberals – not Asquith's Liberals – in power with Bonar Law's Conservatives. Now the coalition was finished, and so was Lloyd George.

Lloyd George was the man who had won the war. His image was that of a country lawyer and he was known to be a great orator, but he lost his reputation as a 'man of the people' because of democracy. The rise of the Labour Party gave the working classes an acceptable and more encouraging alternative. Moreover, the Liberal groups within the coalition had fragmented, and fewer MPs now regarded Lloyd George as their natural leader. Who could he turn to for political support?

The Conservatives, out of office since 1906, remained, of course, but they no longer needed him.

Lloyd George was now a prime minister without a party. To add to his problems, the economy was in a mess, and the promised strategy for industrial relations had not materialized. Ireland was a compromise waiting to turn sour. The question of control over Germany and the payment of reparations was another area of compromise, and, of course, Lloyd George had sold off political honours in return for election campaign expenses.

At one point he offered to resign and hold a general election, but the person who might have replaced him, Austen Chamberlain, did not want the job – at least, not then. If he was to be successful in a general election, Lloyd George needed the Conservatives, and for that he needed a triumph of some kind. As others had done and others would do, he searched for it in foreign policy. In April 1922, largely at Lloyd George's instigation, an international conference was held in Genoa to resolve international relations with Lenin's Russia (which became the Union of Soviet Socialist Republics in December 1922), and, as it turned out, almost any other subject that could be put on the agenda. The Americans refused to attend and the conference was a failure. Lloyd George believed that the Russians should get full war reparations from the Germans and that the Germans should not be allowed to trade with the Russians until they had fully paid the reparations. This pleased the French, who had attended the conference only to make sure Germany was made to pay in full. Even though the Americans had sent an observer to the talks, nothing could be properly discussed and nothing could be resolved.

Lloyd George returned from the conference with little hope of surviving as prime minister. He had one lifebelt left. The Turks had lost the Ottoman Empire during the First World War, and all that remained to them was land in Asia (Anatolia) and Edirne, the Turkish part of Europe. There was a great movement to prevent the complete disintegration of the nation. The head of state was Sultan Mehmet, whose headquarters were in Constantinople, on the western side of the Bosporus waterway. The spiritual leader of nationalist Turkey was Mustafa Kemal, who was based in Ankara, in Asian Turkey, in direct opposition to the sultan. Kemal opposed the sultan's support for the Allies. They had soldiers in Constantinople and in the Bosporus (the entrance to the Black Sea), including Chanak, supposedly the neutral zone on the 'eastern' (the Asian) side of the Dardanelles. The third element in this triangle were the Greeks, who were in Anatolia (the Asian part of Turkey).

By August 1922 Kemal's army had forced back the hated Greeks and was poised to take Izmir (Smyrna). The British saw an evacuation of Greeks troops as the only hope for a peaceful settlement. Kemal would not stop once he had driven the Greeks from Asia Minor back into Balkan Europe, however, and there was no reason to believe that he would leave the rest of the Allies alone. Churchill, by then Colonial Secretary, warned the Cabinet that if the Turks succeeded in driving the

Allies from the Bosporus, Kemal would control the Gallipoli peninsula and the Dardanelles (the entrance to the Aegean) and, therefore, the Mediterranean. Churchill regarded this as the most strategically important point in the world after the western approaches to the Atlantic. If the waterway were taken, the prospect of yet another Balkan war loomed.

Bulgaria was on the European side of the waterway, and a Bulgarian-Turkish alliance would be a confident and ambitious force in the region.

In September Lloyd George proposed that Britain's wartime Balkan allies should be asked to fight Kemal. The Allies, about 7600-strong, would be no match for Kemal's forces, which had already defeated the Greeks, and there were substantiated reports of hundreds, maybe thousands of Armenians being massacred. He appealed to the dominions for help. New Zealand agreed, but, mindful of the disaster of the previous Gallipoli campaign and because they had not been consulted until this point, Australia and Canada refused. Of the 7600 Allied troops, 1000 were British, and then, on 18 September, as they prepared to face Kemal's army, the French and Italians decided to pull out.

Lloyd George said Britain could stand alone. He did not know, however, that his Foreign Minister, Lord Curzon, had signed what became known as the Paris Note with the French and Italians. This was a secret agreement that a peace conference could resolve the situation without the terror that a full confrontation would surely bring. Lloyd George would not hear of a British withdrawal to the Gallipoli side – that is, the European side of the waterway – and the British commander was instructed to threaten Kemal that the British would retaliate if he did not withdraw his forces. The British commander, General Harrington, sought wiser counsel and did not deliver the ultimatum.

In the Sea of Marmara, the giant 'lake' that sits between the Bosporus at its northern end and the Dardanelles and Gallipoli peninsula at its southern end, there is an island called Mudania. The two sides met on the island. At first the talks were unsuccessful because the Turks said they would move into Thrace on the European side. The French and Italians agreed to this, but the British did not.

On 6 October the Mudania Conference was adjourned, and on the following day British political unity evaporated. Hope had been at Lloyd George's hand; now it deserted him. Andrew Bonar Law, who had resigned from Cabinet because of poor health, wrote to *The Times* to say that Britain could not stand alone. He used a phrase that went into the handbook of British diplomacy and strategic thinking when he said that Britain 'cannot act alone as the policeman of the world'.

Four days later agreement was reached in Mudania. The Turkish claim to European Turkey was recognized. Mustafa Kemal, or Kemal Atatürk as he is known, had succeeded. The following year he was elected president and is remembered as the father of modern Turkey.

The Mudania Convention of 11 October 1922 was a peaceful settlement to what had threatened to become a terrible war. It was also the trigger for Lloyd

George's going. War had been avoided, but its shadow had hung too heavily over the British people. A week later, the Conservatives left the coalition government that had held together since 1915. It had come about because of war, and the catalyst for its ending was the threat of another conflict.

On 16 November 1922 the general election returned the Tories to power, and Andrew Bonar Law became prime minister. Of David Lloyd George, Stanley Baldwin, a future Conservative prime minister (whom Lloyd George mocked as being too honest), said that he had destroyed his own Liberal party and would, if allowed, destroy the Conservative Party. The historian A.J.P. Taylor noted that he was: 'devious and unscrupulous. . . . He aroused every feeling except trust.' He was also the prime minister who had won the First World War.

Deaths

Alexander Graham Bell (US inventor)
George Cadbury (philanthropist)
Michael Collins (Irish nationalist)
Alfred Charles William Harmsworth, Viscount Northcliffe (publisher)
Marie Lloyd (music-hall comedienne)
Marcel Proust (French writer)
Sir Ernest Shackleton (explorer)
Georges Sorel (French philosopher)

1923

IT WOULD BE difficult to describe Andrew Bonar Law, who replaced David Lloyd George as prime minister, as the twentieth-century's most distinguished politician. He had replaced Balfour as the leader of the Unionists in the Commons in 1911 and had served in the War Cabinet as Chancellor of the Exchequer when Lloyd George had become prime minister.

Bonar Law's Cabinet was what Winston Churchill called the 'second eleven'. It was a not very demanding club, and he left his ministers to get on with their ministries. There were moments when Bonar Law's inclination to 'undo' Lloyd George could have had damaging results. At one time, for example, he wanted to rid the Cabinet of its most important innovation this century, the Secretariat set up by Hankey.[5] But it came to nothing. The Secretariat was too well established.

Bonar Law believed that unless all else had failed, the prime minister should not interfere in the workings of any department, and by this policy Bonar Law was perhaps unwittingly making the prime minister a more powerful figure because ministers had to give an account of themselves without falling back on the mantra of joint responsibility. How good a premier Bonar Law might have been, we were never to find out. He had to resign within the year as he had cancer of the throat.

---

5 See page 115.

Lord Curzon, the Foreign Secretary, was regarded as the obvious successor, but the King sent for Stanley Baldwin. Bonar Law's brief time in Downing Street had not really been months of lost opportunity, because he was not the man, intellectually nor, by then, physically, to provide dynamic leadership. And neither was his successor. Baldwin was, however, a very clever political manager, which Bonar Law was not.

Baldwin became prime minister on 21 May 1923, although he was not elected leader of his party until seven days later when he was proposed by Curzon, who must have been a disappointed man. It is said that Curzon believed Baldwin to be a man of the utmost insignificance. He was wealthy and had made his considerable fortune through the iron trade, and he had given a quarter of his fortune to the nation to help pay for the war. He was a good speech maker, although most of his papers were written by one of the assistant secretaries in the Cabinet Secretariat, Tom Jones. If Baldwin added any literary marks to the first drafts, it would be pleasing to think that they reflected some genetic influences – he was a cousin of the writer Rudyard Kipling.

Whatever Baldwin was or was not, it may be that in 1923 Britain had a prime minister who was first and foremost an excellent chairman of the board. At first, he changed little, although until the end of the summer he continued to be Chancellor of the Exchequer as well as prime minister. In August 1923 he made Neville Chamberlain Chancellor for a year, then Health Minister; Chamberlain served him well and continuously until he became prime minister himself in 1937. Chamberlain and Baldwin complemented each other. While Baldwin was the thoughtful pig-fancier, who would think through a way of bringing the two sides of an argument together, Chamberlain was more abrasive and the kind of person who might be tempted to bang heads together (although this may not be a description that some would recognize when they remember Chamberlain's dealings with Hitler).

Many Conservatives were worried about the rise of the Labour Party, but Baldwin applied his boardroom logic to the reality of what this meant for British politics. He could see that there was a need to work with the socialists rather than simply believing they could be beaten and would go into decline. Ramsay Macdonald, the Labour leader, even went as far as to say that Baldwin had a philosophy that was not that far removed from Labour's.

Baldwin inherited record unemployment figures, and most major industries were being threatened by strikes. In October the government announced that it would spend up to £50 million on unemployment benefits, and from a figure of 1.54 million for 1922, the unemployment total had been brought down to 1.275 million by the end of 1923.

A week later, however, Baldwin returned to a subject that his party had hoped had been banished – free trade and tariff reform. He wanted the support of the Cabinet and of Parliament to introduce protectionism. The timing of his announcement was not unconnected with the meeting in London of the Imperial

Conference. The representatives of the colonies said, as they had always said, that they wanted the dominions to be able to send their produce to the United Kingdom without having to pay import tariffs but – and this was the old argument – other countries would have to pay duties.

Baldwin could not expect to tax imports without British exports being taxed in return by other countries. Unless Baldwin was deliberately trying to provoke a political argument, he appears not to have understood the relatively simple economics of imports and exports. Could he really have believed that by putting protectionist tariffs on imports, British-made goods and materials would get more of the home market? That seems unlikely.

Baldwin said protection was such an important issue that there had to be a public mandate for any policy change, and a general election was called for December 1923. Once again, British politicians lined up for free trade or for protectionism. The Conservatives came out as protectionists. The Liberals, now led by the former prime minister, Asquith, were for free trade. The Labour Party's platform on protectionism versus free trade was unclear; its main policy was the nationalization of the three major industries, electricity generation, the railways and coal mining.

The vote went against Baldwin's plan for protectionism. The Conservatives won 258 seats, the Labour Party 191 seats, and the Liberals 151 seats. Baldwin's election had backfired. The Conservatives were down by about ninety seats, having lost 107 to the Liberals and Labour, although having won eighteen from them. The election arithmetic suggested that the Liberal and Labour MPs were capable of defeating the government at the first debate. Here was a potential step-change in British politics. If the government lost a vote in the House and the prime minister resigned, the King would have to send for the leader of the party with the next highest number of seats. If that happened, Britain would have a Labour prime minister for the first time. That was the prospect facing politicians as they left Westminster for Christmas 1923.

In Rome Mussolini's fascists arrested hundreds of socialists, and in Munich in January Hitler attempted, albeit ineptly, to mount a *coup d'état*. The National Socialist Party held its first congress, and that winter Munich was festooned with the ancient design of the crooked cross, the swastika – once a symbol of good fortune. At that meeting Hitler demanded that the government seek to have the Treaty of Versailles revoked.

The Germans had done their best not to pay anything, even though the original amount of reparations had been reduced, and in January the French and Belgian governments sent 100,000 soldiers with instructions to return with 'goods in kind' collected from the mines, forests and industrial heartland in the Ruhr valley. Germans went on strike, demonstrated and sabotaged factories and transport. Industrial output fell. Within the first four weeks of January, partly prompted by the arrival of the French and Belgian soldiers, the Deutschmark dropped from its New Year value of 7000 to the US dollar to 18,000 to the dollar. The slide against the pound was even more marked. At the beginning of January the Deutschmark had stood at 85,000 to the pound sterling; by the end of January the mark stood at 220,000 to the pound. The Deutschmark really was no longer worth the paper it was written on.

The French wanted to take over the Ruhr, with its great towns of Essen, Duisburg, Mülheim and, slightly to the northeast, Dortmund, because this was the industrial base of the whole German nation. The British and the Americans objected, and Bonar Law pointed out that the industrial strength of the Ruhr was the only hope that the German economy had of ever recovering. Without that recovery, the political, social and military consequences for the nation, and Europe, could be devastating.

The Americans, faced with their own political difficulties, had decided they had been too long in Europe. They could see the signs of things to come, and on 6 January 1923 the Senate voted to withdraw American troops from Germany.

Raymond Poincaré, the French prime minister, and his defence minister, André Maginot (after whom the line of defensive tunnels and gun emplacements was named), declared that the French would remain in Germany until they were satisfied that the Germans had paid for the suffering they had caused France during the Great War. French troops blocked supplies to other parts of Germany, and German industrialists who did not co-operate faced court martial. When German workers tried to stop French soldiers taking trucks from the Krupp steel works at Essen, the French opened fire, killing nine Germans and wounding dozens more. The directors of the factory were blamed and arrested. Count Krupp von Bohlen, the patriarch of the steel family, was sentenced to fifteen years' imprisonment, although he did not serve the term.

None of these draconian measures achieved the effects desired by the French and Belgians, and the German economy declined still further. By the autumn, brokers could no longer value the Deutschmark, which had dropped to 200 million to the pound. German workers were carrying their wages in bags and boxes and barrows, knowing that they would be devalued by the time they reached home. In addition, the passive resistance being shown by workers under the French occupation meant that German industry was not producing enough to support itself, let alone earning money through exports.

The French determination to get what it perceived as its due did, however, succeed in uniting the Germans.

Briefly in 1923 political attention shifted to the Soviet Union where in March Lenin had a stroke. The previous year he had suffered a mild stroke, but now he was unable to move. Who would succeed him? Grigori Zinoviev, the chairman of the Comintern (Communist International), was the outside candidate, but the two most powerful men after Lenin were Joseph Stalin (1879–1953), the Communist Party's General Secretary, and Leon Trotsky (1879–1940). While Britain settled down to the prospect of its first Labour government, the Russians were about to be ruled by Stalin. And Hitler was building his power base in an increasingly nationalistic Germany.

The year had been another of postwar turmoil, but there had been moments to delight the British. Lady Elizabeth Bowes-Lyon married the then Duke of York, little thinking that one day she would be Queen.

This was the year of one of the best known photographs in English soccer history. The Empire Stadium at Wembley had been built for the British Empire Exhibition, which was to be held in 1924–5, but it also became the venue for the cup final, the first of which was played there on 28 April 1923. This was a sell-out but also nearly a disaster of overcrowding. The stadium was designed to hold 100,000, but by kick-off time almost 190,000 fans had got in. They spilled onto the pitch, forced by weight of numbers from behind. It could have been a riot but for the presence of a single policeman. PC George Storey, mounted on his white horse, saved the day and nudged the crowd back beyond the touchlines. Bolton Wanderers eventually beat West Ham.

A month later, another sporting achievement captured the headlines. The Surrey batsman Jack Hobbs became only the third man (after W.G. Grace and Tom Hayward) to complete the magical hundred hundreds in first class cricket. The first 24-hour Le Mans race took place, and Sir Henry Segrave became the first British driver to win a Grand Prix race.

A less noisy reception, although sometimes crackly, was given to a new programme transmitted from the British Broadcasting Company's Savoy Hill studios. The programme was called *Woman's Hour*.

The Nobel Prize for Literature went to W.B. Yeats. No Peace Prize was awarded in 1923, which is hardly surprising as there was very little peace.

In September in Japan almost 200,000 people died in an earthquake that was felt across almost 10,000 square miles. A few weeks later, the regent emperor, Hirohito, survived an assassination attempt. In Spain the archbishop of Saragossa was not so fortunate, and nor was the one-time Mexican revolutionary, Pancho Villa, who was murdered by a rival family.

Deaths

Sarah Bernhardt (French actress)
Gustave Eiffel (French engineer)
Warren G. Harding (US president)
Andrew Bonar Law (politician)
Katherine Mansfield (writer)
William Doud Packard (US inventor)
Wilhelm Conrad Roentgen (German physicist)

1924

THIS WAS the year in which Lenin died and in which the United Kingdom had its first Labour prime minister and quickly lost him partly thanks to a forged letter.

On 21 January the Conservative government was defeated in Parliament. Stanley Baldwin went and George V called on Ramsay MacDonald to be prime minister. Asquith had insisted that MacDonald be given the chance, probably because he knew that the fragility of its Commons majority would mean that the Labour government would not last and that he, Asquith, would soon be called on to form another government. He was right on the first count but wrong on the second.

James Ramsay MacDonald (1866–1937) was the social opposite of any previous prime minister. This was no champagne socialist. He was a Scot, born in Lossiemouth, who had become a leading figure in the Independent Labour Party, which he had joined in 1894, becoming its secretary by 1900. The evolving Labour Party was riven by factions at a high level. As secretary, MacDonald had to be more than an excellent administrator; he had to balance differing ideological interests, and this he did. To become prime minister, especially in the economic and political climate of early 1924, he would need all these skills – particularly as he had no experience whatsoever of government.

Just eighteen months earlier the Cabinet had included Viscount Cave, the Marquess of Salisbury, the Marquess Curzon, the Duke of Devonshire, the Earl of Derby, Viscount Peel, Viscount Novar and four baronets. It was as if Bonar Law did not know any commoners. MacDonald's Cabinet might have been expected to reflect working men's clubs and trade unions rather than the unnumbered doors of Pall Mall and St James's, but he got together a moderate Cabinet, which included Haldane, the Liberal politician and the man who had remodelled the army and established the Territorial Army. He had been Lord Chancellor in Asquith's Cabinet (1912–15), and now here he was as Lord Chancellor under MacDonald, partly because he was the best man to oversee the new Committee of Imperial Defence.

Philip Snowden (1864–1937), the MP for Blackburn, became an orthodox, sometimes bitter and even occasionally deeply intellectual Chancellor of the Exchequer. Snowden was a social reformer who would not have been out of place in the Liberal politics of the late nineteenth century. He wanted the greater good for the greatest number of people, but he was a believer in the 'kitchen table' philosophy of economics: if a family wanted something, the family had to balance its budget to get it. Social reforms, no matter how pressing, had to be paid for from within that budget. On an international scale such an approach would lead to the type of free trade budget that the nation would normally have expected from a confident Liberal government.

People at the far left of the party were kept out, including George Lansbury (1859–1940). Lansbury had become a Labour MP in 1910, although he resigned in 1912 to fight for the suffragettes, which was not a popular enough platform to get him re-elected for his seat at Bow and Bromley until 1922. Lansbury was not an idler, however, and he went off and founded the *Daily Herald* in April 1912 (which, after many transitions and changes of ownership, became the *Sun*), personally editing that paper until 1922. It was then that the *Daily Herald* became the Labour Party's official newspaper. To leave a man like Lansbury out of the government was a major decision. It certainly pleased the King, who disliked him intensely. So the MacDonald Cabinet, which was composed largely of trade unionists (albeit moderate ones), was able to demonstrate that there was another way than that of the traditional ruling classes.

The new government had little power, however, because it did not have the parliamentary majority to support any plans that it might have had for government. Clause Four of the Labour Party constitution, about taking the primary industries into common ownership, could not be put into practice without the right economic climate, enormous planning and an intricate knowledge of the country's bureaucracy and institutions, a sizeable working majority in the Commons and support in the Lords. MacDonald's government had none of these things. Perhaps its most important deficiency was its parliamentary standing. We should not forget that there had not been a general election to put the party in power, and Ramsay MacDonald as prime minister was in the same position as Stanley Baldwin had been: there were 191 Labour MPs, but 258 Conservatives and 158 Liberals. The government could be brought down at any time if the Liberals and the Tories voted together.

This was, nevertheless, an opportunity for Ramsay MacDonald to show a future electorate that the Labour Party was capable of government and that it was not bent on the rape and pillage of British society for left-wing ends. Without experience of handling the machinery of government – only Haldane and Arthur Henderson had ever been in Cabinet – this was an almost impossible task. But James Wheatley, a businessman, became Minister of Housing. Here was an opportunity and it was taken.

Wheatley understood that there was an enormous need for affordable housing but also that the need could not be met quickly. There were three elements in providing accommodation for people who did not have much money: the availability of housing at modest and therefore probably subsidized rents; a building industry that could make this happen; and the time required to get houses built. What is surprising is that this subject had not featured much in Labour Party discussions, certainly not at any official level. In the short time for which even the most optimistic socialist believed that the Labour Party would be in power before an election had to be called, Wheatley wanted to get through legislation, or amendments to existing legislation, that would provide a long-term solution to the problem of low-cost housing.

The Housing Act of 1924 answered those who questioned the need for, and practicability of providing, social housing. First, he made sure that the building industry would find it worthwhile to expand. If the building industry did not grow there would be insufficient skills and it would not be sufficiently attractive to investment to make the plan work. He encouraged expansion and investment by promising that the Wheatley Housing Plan would be in operation for fifteen years so that the industry could plan ahead. The practical and short-term solution was to guarantee subsidies for twenty- and forty-year periods. The subsidies were increased and the responsibility for providing housing was given to local authorities. Finally, Wheatley insisted that a large part of the building programme had to be for houses that could be rented.

Wheatley's Housing Act did not solve the problems of the very poor, nor could it get rid of existing poor housing and the landlords who made such huge profits from it. The term 'slum clearance' was not yet in the political language of Britain, but within ten years Wheatley's Act had done more to provide low-cost housing than any other legislation and had, for the first time, introduced housing as a political as well as a social issue.

The only other advance made by the first Labour administration was in education. The new Chairman of the Board of Education (later to be called a Secretary of State) was Charles Trevelyan. Trevelyan was not one of the trade union MPs. He was the son of Sir George O. Trevelyan, who had been responsible for radical social reforms in India during Victoria's reign; the historian, George Macaulay Trevelyan, was his brother. Trevelyan had been in education for much of his parliamentary life and had been the Liberal Parliamentary Secretary to the Board for six years until he resigned in 1914 because he disapproved of the war. In 1922 he became a Labour MP and was the ideal man for MacDonald to send back to the Board of Education. It was Trevelyan who set up the consultative committee that would lead – though not in his lifetime – to the restructuring of elementary education for decades to come.

Both housing and education were long-term projects. In the short term there was no money to pay for any policy that involved major expenditure, but the main issue for this first Labour government was unemployment. When MacDonald went to Downing Street in January 1924 about 1.2 million people were without jobs, but there was nothing that the new government could do for them. It is strange that the Labour Party did not appear to have a strong policy on unemployment. No one, for example, seems to have put forward the idea that the capitalist system should be replaced by a socialist system that would achieve the same objectives as capitalism did except that profits would be more equitably distributed. There were few who said that the economy could be altered by public works. No one suggested, for example, that if the government built a road it would become the employer of those needed to build it and that this would help bring down the numbers of people out of work.

There was another problem that the government could not resolve. MacDonald had no formula to end the increasing number of strikes. A Labour government, largely financed by the trade unions, was now prepared to use the method it had previously opposed, the Emergency Powers Act. Certainly, MacDonald's government must have caused many voters to sigh with relief: a Labour government did not mean Leninism. Others, including Churchill, believed, however, that if Labour were elected for a full term, the political and social mischief would begin. He claimed that the country was being softened up for left-wing government.

By this time Churchill was no longer sitting with the Liberals. As a supporter of free trade he had crossed the floor of the House from the Conservative to the Liberal benches in 1904 but had not rejoined the Tories. When a by-election was called in March 1924 in one of the Westminster constituencies, rather than seek the seat as a Tory he stood as an Independent Anti-Socialist. Although he was supported by the Beaverbrook and Rothermere press, he did not win. Many Tories wanted him back in the party, but his views on free trade were unshakeable. It was only in June 1924, when Stanley Baldwin, still leader of the Conservatives, publicly renounced tariffs, that Churchill felt that he could, at last, rejoin the party.

As well as being prime minister, MacDonald had kept for himself the post of Foreign Secretary, and he was faced, as any British prime minister in 1924 would have been, with the intractable problem of the future of Germany and the debate that had gone on since 1919 over war reparations – how much Germany should pay and what form those payments should take.

On the very day before Ramsay MacDonald became prime minister, the British government knew that it had to consider its future relations with a potentially powerful nation, the Soviet Union. On 21 January 1924 Lenin died at the age of fifty-four. He had suffered a stroke in 1922, and two further attacks in the following year had led him to step down from power. Such was his reputation, however, that even though he had no practical grasp on power, his very breathing was power enough. The Russian Revolution had become known as his Revolution.

The Council set up to succeed Lenin included Leon Kamenev, Grigori Zinoviev and Joseph Stalin. Alexis Rykov became the new president of the Council of Commissars, but the real struggle for power was to be between Stalin, Kamenev and Zinoviev on one side and Leon Trotsky on the other. As we know, Stalin would win and Trotsky would be assassinated.

For the next nine months MacDonald did not have to concern himself over much with events in Moscow, although it would be a letter, supposedly written by Zinoviev, that would partly turn the British electorate against him. Ramsay MacDonald's major foreign policy decision was what to do about Germany and Britain's ally, France. Britain tried to tread between French sensitivities that demanded that the Germans pay for their sins between 1914 and 1918 and the overwhelming economic logic that bringing Germany to its financial knees not only reduced to rubble a desperately needed market for British goods but encouraged nationalism and therefore instability.

An American banker, Charles G. Dawes (1865–1951), who was soon to be vice president of the United States, submitted a scheme to the Allied Reparations Committee. The Dawes Plan was a working proposal for the payment of realistic reparations rather than the immediate postwar instinct to bleed Germany to its military death. The Germans accepted a vastly reduced financial fine but one that was achievable, although acceptance in the Reichstag was not by a huge majority. How was Germany to pay anything at all, let alone the 2500 million Deutschmarks a year that had been agreed? The only possible system had been arranged by Dawes: Germany would be given an initial loan of $200 million in order to balance her economy. The payments to the Allies would come partly through taxes and partly from industrial profits. At last it had been recognized – more importantly accepted by France – that the kitchen table school of economics was right: that Germans could not pay up unless they had the money to pay their way. One aspect of the agreement, which immediately reduced tension between France and Germany, was that the French agreed to pull out their troops from the Ruhr within a year. Some of the credit for persuading the French, and indeed the Belgians, to accept the Dawes Plan should go to Ramsay MacDonald.

Many people recognized, however, that although it was important that the German economy be restructured, this could not be done overnight, even with the setting up of an independent German bank, and that the resulting nationalism and political upheaval would not go away.

And now we come to the general election of November 1924 and the events that corrupted public opinion or so it was long believed. The story begins in the public mind long before the Labour Party came to power. The party had been sympathetic to the Russian Revolution but did not even begin to suggest that the same sort of thing should happen in Britain. MacDonald was, in fact, openly criticized by Russian communists, who thought him no better than a middle-class and insincere socialist.

Three events influenced, although they did not decide, the outcome of the general election.

MacDonald had become prime minister in January 1924, at a time when more than a million of his natural supporters were out of work. Many in his party saw the untapped Russian market as a way of revitalizing the British economy, and MacDonald did what neither Baldwin nor Lloyd George had done: he recognized the Soviet government. MacDonald's administration had to deal directly with the Soviet Union and attempt to get back money that had been owed since the days of the Tsar. The Russians were willing to repay some of the money, but they also wanted a big loan. (Perhaps they had seen how lenient the Allied powers had been towards Germany, which had received a loan and even an understanding that it would not pay war reparations until it could afford to.) After many false starts, an arrangement was made that was broken on the British part by prominent left-wing members of the party. Russia was to get its loan and a settlement of its debts. The Conservatives objected immediately.

Apart from the fact that the country was in no state to hand out loans, this was seen as an arrangement between socialists, exactly the sort of thing that Churchill was to warn against. The Liberals, on the other hand, were in a difficult position. In principle they agreed that a loan should be made to the Russians, but Lloyd George had not given up hope of getting back into Downing Street and he persuaded the bulk of the Liberal Party to attack what he called a fake loan to the Bolsheviks. Asquith, who was really the leader, had to go along on the oldest principle of leadership – see which way the mob is marching and then get in front of them.

At the beginning of August 1924 a British communist, J.R. Campbell, wrote an article in *Worker's Weekly* telling British soldiers in Ulster that in no circumstances should they shoot when ordered to do so. Campbell's article had no more effect on the military and public mind than did the banners and similar articles of the 'Troops Out' movement sixty years later. Campbell was, nevertheless, charged with inciting mutiny, a prosecution that many people thought was quite unnecessary. Pacifist members on the Labour benches had said similar things themselves and not always when they were protected by parliamentary privilege. Through lobbying of one form or another, the government, and this meant MacDonald, gave instructions that Campbell was not, after all, to be prosecuted. Sir Patrick Hastings, the Attorney General, dropped the case. The Conservatives leapt at the opportunity to claim that this was blatant political interference with justice.

The government faced a censure motion in October. Asquith, the Liberal leader, did not want the motion to be tabled and attempted to get the matter heard in a select committee. MacDonald rejected the proposal. The government faced the motion and went down by 364 votes to 191.

Asquith was bitterly disappointed because he knew that the only way that the King could constitutionally call on him to form the next government (as the next biggest party) was if the government were defeated by a Conservative-only vote. MacDonald could constitutionally go to the country.

Just before polling day, a copy of a letter supposedly written and signed by Grigori Zinoviev, the chairman of the Comintern, was given to the editor of the *Daily Mail*. The letter, which was addressed to the recently formed Communist Party of Great Britain, instructed British communists to prepare for revolution and to set up cells within the armed forces. The Foreign Office, which also had a copy of the letter, heard that it had gone to the newspaper and decided to pre-empt the sensation publication would cause by releasing it on 24 October.

The Zinoviev letter was a forgery. Although, then, few were absolutely certain. So the damage was done. The Conservatives denounced the government as being friends of communists, even though the letter itself warned British communists to beware of MacDonald's government.

The Conservatives, while not suggesting that MacDonald had anything to do with it, were able to suggest to the electorate that in light of this socialist threat, what the country needed was the firm hand of Conservative government. The election followed four days later.

It is difficult to prove that the fudged financial arrangements with Russia, the Campbell case and the Zinoviev Letter turned the electorate against MacDonald's government, but it may be assumed that parts of the electorate were influenced enough to turn out on polling day. More people voted that October than ever before. It is likely that Liberal voters went over to the Conservatives. Of the 615 MPs at Westminster, 419 were Conservatives, and probably almost 100 of those seats had been taken from the Liberals. The Labour Party now had 151 seats – more than before, but they had put up more candidates – and the Liberals were down to a political rump of 40 MPs. Asquith was gone and the Liberals now lined up, although in not very good order, behind Lloyd George.

Once again Stanley Baldwin was prime minister. He had, of course, made it possible for more people to vote for him than in the previous election because he had wisely abandoned his campaign for protectionism. This meant that all those who had passionately defended free trade could return to the Conservative fold, most famously Winston Churchill. He did not stand in this 1924 election as a Conservative but as the Constitutional candidate for Epping in support of the Conservative programme. Surprisingly, considering his experience and obvious talents, Churchill became Chancellor of the Exchequer, a job he seemed hardly suited for.

Elsewhere the Irish declared an amnesty for terrorist prisoners; the BBC started broadcasts for schools; and Sir Edward Elgar became Master of the King's Musick. E.M. Forster published *A Passage to India*, and George Gershwin wrote *Rhapsody in Blue*. Eric Liddell and Harold Abrahams ran like chariots of fire at the Paris Olympics.

In Egypt Howard Carter uncovered the golden effigy of Tutankhamun, and Sir Leigh Stack, the British Governor-General of the Sudan, was assassinated in Cairo. Mussolini imposed press censorship; and Hitler, who had been in prison for the past eight months on charges of high treason, was freed to become leader of the Nazis.

In the United States Metro Pictures, Goldwyn Pictures and the Louis B. Mayer Corporation merged to become MGM; and Charlie Chaplin married the sixteen-year-old Lita Gray.

Deaths

Frances Hodgson Burnett (US writer)
Ferruccio Busoni (Italian composer)
Joseph Conrad (writer)
Gabriel Fauré (French composer)
Anatole France (French writer)
Victor Herbert (US composer)
Franz Kafka (Austrian writer)
Vladimir Ilyich Lenin (Russian communist)
Edith Nesbit (novelist)

Giacomo Puccini (Italian composer)
Sir Charles Villiers Stanford (composer)
Thomas Woodrow Wilson (US president)

1925

A CHILD born in 1925 would be old enough to fight in the Second World War, a war that would begin in just fourteen years' time. Between now and then, Britain would come off the gold standard, women aged twenty-one and over would be allowed to vote, and the nation would go through the Great Depression and have a National Government. Hitler would become Chancellor of Germany, and Franklin Delano Roosevelt would become President of the United States. Edward VIII would abdicate, and idealists from around the world would fight in the Spanish Civil War.

Some of these events – notably the changes in Britain's monetary policy, the rise of Hitler and the decline of the economy and consequent industrial unrest – could have been anticipated by Stanley Baldwin's Conservative government, which had come to office following the election in November 1924.

The new Cabinet was rather unbalanced. Churchill, who had no record as an economist, became Chancellor of the Exchequer and proved to be a rather indifferent one at that. Baldwin's reasoning was that it would be better to have him in the Cabinet rather than free to develop a faction of his own supporters or even join forces with Lloyd George (whom Baldwin detested). Curzon, who might have expected to become Foreign Secretary, found himself in the less politically threatening role of Lord President. Curzon had been a Lloyd George man, but in this instance, Baldwin was not acting from spite – he really did need someone at the Foreign Office who would bring a fresh and more friendly policy towards France. Curzon had always been hostile to the French, but, as it turned out, he died in March 1925.

Austen Chamberlain, who was a Francophile, went to the Foreign Office as a signal of Britain's good intentions, while Lord Birkenhead, a great lawyer, who had reformed property law, went to the Indian Office. Chamberlain's appointment to the Foreign Office proved to be a success. He was instrumental in the almost year-long negotiations for a formal agreement between France, Germany and Belgium that they would not in future settle disputes by military means and that they would recognize their post-1919 frontiers. This non-aggression pact, known as the Treaty of Locarno after the Italian town in which it was signed, was guaranteed by Italy and Britain. Although with hindsight the pact may be regarded as ineffectual, its provisions remained the basis of peace in Europe until March 1936, when Hitler occupied the Rhineland.

Locarno suggested to the British government that it no longer had any obligations in continental Europe, but by the 1920s a policy of isolationism towards Europe was impossible, even with Britain's huge colonial responsibilities. No British government could ignore, for example, the events unfolding in the Soviet Union. Stalin had got rid of Leon Trotsky, who had been the Commissar for War, from the Politburo. He had never been a political animal but had not been forgiven for opposing the Bolsheviks and supporting the Mensheviks in 1917. There was more to this than Stalin's desire to extend his control over the power base of the Soviet Union. Stalin was, after all, powerful, and all he needed to do was to be certain of the loyalty of the most powerful group in the whole Soviet Union – the army. Trotsky had, for the past seven years, been the commander-in-chief of the army. Now that he was gone from power, together with hundreds of supporters arrested by the Cheka, the security police, nothing stood in Stalin's way of taking complete control.

Further south, Mussolini was assuming similar powers in Italy, where he was now an unopposed dictator.

In Germany Hitler made his first public appearance since getting out of prison, and the state of emergency that had existed in Bavaria was lifted at the same time as the ban on the Nazi Party. In Berlin Field Marshal Paul von Hindenburg became the first directly elected president of Germany. Hindenburg had no public plans to replace the new Republican constitution with a monarchy, but it was no secret that he wanted to see a Kaiser on the throne of Germany. In Munich on 18 July, shortly after Hindenburg's democratic installation as president, Hitler published the first volume of *Mein Kampf*, which has been variously described as his philosophy and his collection of diatribes, especially against the Jews.

In London, meanwhile, all interest was on Churchill's first Budget. In April 1925 the Chancellor turned to one of the defining economic acts of the first half of the twentieth century, the 1919 legislation that suspended Britain's economy to the value of gold, the gold standard. Currency, whether it was a dollar or a pound sterling, was kept at the value of a fixed weight of gold. Sterling was bought for gold. If someone sold sterling, the British government would pay in gold. At the beginning of the First World War those gold payments were suspended. Economists, particularly Keynes, regarded the gold standard as monetary heraldry, a reflection of the past. Churchill, however, returned Britain to the gold standard. This was a mistake: gold was not in circulation; new sovereigns were not minted for circulation; and there was no longer the economic, industrial and social climate that allowed the economy to be manipulated to maintain that standard as there had been in earlier decades. Keynes was right, but he was not Chancellor. Income tax was down to 4 shillings in the pound, which was riding on a ten-year high in the foreign exchanges.

Even in 1925, the future of India was a contentious political issue. The previous year, riots in Madras and Bombay were blamed on Mahatma Gandhi, whose quiet, non-violent leadership was far more difficult to contend with than the sort of violence Britain had handled elsewhere in its colonial history. The British were going to need a strong mind at the Indian Office, and Birkenhead, with his experience as Attorney General and his controversial part in the Irish settlement of 1921, could have been a deciding factor in bringing India into the Commonwealth. As it turned out, Birkenhead's was a bad appointment, and by 1928 he had gone to spend more time with his City directorships.

After twelve lean years for cricket enthusiasts, the MCC had beaten the Australians in a Test Match. The latest fashion craze for men, Oxford bags, was causing more debate than the economy. Industrial dishwashers were being modified for the home. The Royal Navy was flexing Britain's global muscles and setting up a naval base at Singapore. The government was helping to pay for Britons who wanted to go and live in Australia.

Noël Coward had three plays in the West End, *The Vortex*, *Fallen Angels* and *Hay Fever*. The Charleston was the rage of flappers in the ballrooms, and parents suspected their children were dancing with the devil. Charlie Chaplin's film *Goldrush* had opened, but there was no rushing in London's Piccadilly. The first traffic lights were put in. The following year congestion was so great that a one-way traffic scheme had to be introduced around Trafalgar Square and Hyde Park Corner. A new law made it possible for the first time to jail drunken drivers.

In London there were two medical 'firsts': Henry Souttar carried out the first successful operation to repair damaged heart valves, and the first use of insulin for diabetics began at St Bartholomew's Hospital.

In America F. Scott Fitzgerald published *The Great Gatsby*. Bernard Shaw was given the Nobel Prize for literature in recognition of his play *St Joan*. 'No doubt,' he remarked, 'it is a token of gratitude for the sense of world relief that I have published nothing this year.'

Deaths

Queen Alexandra (consort of Edward VII)
George Nathaniel Curzon, 1st Baron Curzon (politician)
John French, 1st Earl of Ypres (soldier)
Sir Henry Rider Haggard (writer)
Alfred Milner, 1st Viscount Milner (colonial administrator)
John Singer Sargent (US artist)
Erik Satie (French composer)
Rudolf Steiner (Austrian philosopher)
Sun Yat-sen (Chinese politician)

1926

THIS WAS the year of the general strike, the year in which the carefree image of the twenties looked very frayed. But alongside the poverty and industrial failure there was success. Using the heads of two ventriloquist dummies as images, John Logie Baird transmitted electrical signals by wireless. At the other end, the wireless signals were remixed as electrical signals using a cathode ray tube. The pictures were only just visible but they were there – and so was television. Ten years later, in 1936, the BBC was to start its first television broadcasts.

In the House of Commons MPs were digesting a report that said that broadcasting should be run by a public corporation and that rejected any idea of following the American system of uncontrolled transmission. The previous year the managing director of the British Broadcasting Company, John Reith, had appeared before a House of Lords enquiry into broadcasting. He told the peers that he wanted the ban on news broadcasting before 7 o'clock in the evening (which was in place to protect the morning newspaper from being beaten to late news) to be lifted. Reith reassured their lordships that his announcers all spoke with what he called 'the right pronunciation of the English tongue'. By 1926 the British Broadcasting Company[6] was already transmitting 10,000 programmes a year, mostly talks and music, and special broadcasting was going into 1000 schools every year.

The government had to turn its attention to a more serious problem than broadcasting – poverty. The economic and industrial decline experienced in Britain was a facet of postwar Europe, which could be easily seen in the unemployment figures. Although the numbers were high, there had been something of a decline in recent years. For example, in 1921 there were 2 million unemployed, but in 1922 the figure had fallen to about 1.5 million. The figure continued to fall in 1923, 1924 and 1925, but it went up again in 1926 to nearly 1.4 million. By 1932 it would be 2.7 million. This was at a time when the population of England and Wales was less than 40 million and that of Scotland less than 5 million.

None of the political parties had any understanding of how to resolve the problem. Industrial output was part of the answer, and by the middle of the decade it had reached prewar levels, but the further contradiction in the unemployment figures can be explained by an often overlooked fact: the workforce was not a static unit. One reason more people were out of work was that the population was greater and more people were looking for work. Another reason was that, while new industries emerged, older ones disappeared.

In 1926 most of the unemployed were in the traditional industries that had fed the home market and, more importantly, the export trade. The difficulty for the exporters was that many of these industries – cotton most obviously – were operating within a declining British market. Other countries had become major exporters and Britain needed to bring down the price of its own goods, but

6 The British Broadcasting Company had been established in 1922, not as a public body but by the radio manufacturers; it became the British Broadcasting Corporation under a royal charter granted in 1927.

Churchill had returned the nation to the gold standard at too high a rate and the pound was too strong – a complaint from exporters that was to echo for the next three-quarters of a century.

By July 1925 it had become official government policy that workers had to take pay cuts. On past evidence, industrial action against what many union members regarded as an unfair practice would appear to have been inevitable. There had been more industrial action in previous years than there was in the difficult times of 1925 when there was still hope that the conflicts could be resolved by negotiation. In spite of general impressions, there is evidence that people from the shop floor to the boardroom understood that the long-term solution relied more on restructuring out-of-date industries than on cross-table bargaining.[7] This might, indeed, have worked if it had not been for the wage cuts.

It did not matter which government was in power. Even Ramsay MacDonald's Labour government had not inspired confidence within the trades union leadership. Moreover, industrial action more often than not centred on the troika of transport, the railways and coal mining. By the mid-1920s it seemed quite natural to expect that industrial action, if it came, would be in the coal mines. Industry used coal and homes were heated by coal. Trains could not run and ships could not sail without coal. To bring out the miners was to bring out Britain.

The coal industry had not actually been in too bad a shape; now the situation was deteriorating. Britain's two main European competitors, Germany and Poland, had been slow to recover in the immediate postwar period, but when they did so in the mid-1920s they were able to undercut the price of coal from British mines, which were losing money by 1926.

One way out of the problem was to modernize the coal industry, but where was the money to come from? The pits were privately owned and the government would not give more public subsidies to private enterprise. In addition, there was a difference in the approach of the miners, led by their president, Herbert Smith, and that of the Trades Union Congress (TUC). The TUC was far more moderate and thought that it would be possible to negotiate a settlement. It took over the negotiations on behalf of the miners, believing it would be able to achieve a settlement rather than leading the country into a confrontational strike. The miners would not accept the TUC's position, however, and Herbert Smith was convinced that one major strike, with other unions, particularly the transport unions, coming out in support of the miners, would bring the government and pit-owners to their knees.

For their part, the pit-owners would not listen to the miners and nor would they accept conciliatory noises from the government. In public the government said that this was a problem for the pit-owners.

---

7 See Kenneth Young, *Baldwin*, Weidenfeld & Nicolson (1976); A.J.P. Taylor, *English History 1914–1945*, Oxford University Press (1965); and Martin Gilbert, *A History of the Twentieth Century, Vol. One 1900–1933*, HarperCollins (1997). Also discussed in Christopher Lee, 'Perceptions and Illusions of Twentieth-century Events', unpublished Cambridge lecture series (1989).

Pit-owners had told the miners in 1925 that they were going to cut their wages. The government shifted its position and offered a subsidy, which would have meant some £23 million being put into the pits, ostensibly to maintain wages at 1925 levels until the summer of 1926. As a delaying tactic, a royal commission was set up under the chairmanship of Herbert Samuel to examine ways of modernizing the industry, but the members of the commission did not know very much about coal mining, a fact that the report they eventually produced made abundantly clear.

The government was still not committed to the coal industry, and the TUC was left with a simmering dispute. The railway and transport unions were beginning to argue that if the miners' demand for a national boycott of coal was accepted, they – the railway and transport unions – would be in the front line of the dispute because they were the people who actually moved the coal to the factories, to the docks and to the hearths. But they wanted support. Effectively, this would mean a national strike.

The government started to dust off its emergency plans. The nation was split into eleven regions, roughly coinciding with the grand military districts envisaged by Cromwell and maintained under major generals until the late 1990s. These regions would have commissioners with absolute and dictatorial powers; they would be isolated governments. This would be the first test of the motor car. Previous administrations had recognized the crippling power of stopping the railway system, but now the petrol engine could be used as an alternative form of transportation.

In March 1926 the royal commission outlined its proposals for modernizing the coal industry, but its recommendations could not deter the miners since those proposals would take years to implement. Moreover, no modernization plan, especially one that looked to the facilities of the miners, would ever be agreed by the pit-owners. In any case, the commission's main recommendation was that the industry needed to cut wages, and any chance of the two sides compromising – the miners accepting a wage reduction and the owners agreeing improvements – evaporated.

On 1 May the strike became unstoppable when the pit-owners locked out the miners and when, in response, the general council of the TUC gave the go-ahead for a national strike, beginning on 3 May:

> The prolonged efforts of the Trades Union Congress General Council and the Miners' Federation have failed to effect a satisfactory settlement of the mining dispute. A situation of the utmost gravity has been produced by the action of the mine-owners in locking out more than a million mine workers, and by the failure of the government to make any acceptable proposals to enable the industry to continue without any further degradation of the standards of life and labour in the coal-fields pending reorganization.
>
> The General Council, with the full approval and co-operation of the accredited representatives of the trade unions, has been compelled to organize

> united resistance to the attempt to enforce a settlement of the mining problem at the expense of the miners' wages. . . . Unless a settlement . . . is reached before midnight on Monday the workers in these essential industries will be withdrawn. The trade unions disclaim all responsibility for the calamity that now threatens. Their action is not directed against the public. Responsibility for the consequences that must inevitably follow a general cessation of work lies with the mine-owners and the government entirely.

In addition to the miners, railwaymen, dockers and bus and tram drivers came out, but oil and petrol lorries were allowed through, as were lorries carrying food.

On the afternoon of 4 May 1926 Baldwin told the Commons that there could be no negotiations because the TUC, by ordering a strike, was effectively making an attempt to take over government. He saw the TUC action in giving the green light for a general strike throughout Britain as a quite separate matter from the miners' dispute.

The government was willing to talk to the miners but not now to the TUC, which Baldwin accused of political anarchy. The dispute had never started as a general strike and not everyone was called out at first, but the government saw it for what it was – a general strike in all but name. The Emergency Committee on Supply and Transport, the basis for the regional seats of government, was activated, and troops were moved as a warning of the seriousness of the situation.

Emergency supplies, including fuel and food, were already in place, and the non-striking public responded. Some of the 6000 members of the Organization for the Maintenance of Supplies signed up as volunteer dockers and drivers, and what might later be called the 'Dunkirk spirit' developed. The MCC even announced that cricket would not be interrupted. This was the first general strike in British history, and Asquith, by now in the House of Lords, rose to his feet on 4 May:

> Can there be a more lamentable fact than that, at a time when we are all in the international sphere hymning the praises and propagating the doctrine of disarmament, here at home, in the free-est of all the free countries of the world, we should be witnessing a resort on an unexampled scale to one of the cruellest because of the most discriminating of all forms of warfare?
>
> For the essence of a General Strike is this – that it inflicts the maximum of loss and suffering upon the innocent mass of the common people, who are not parties to the industrial dispute, who have taken neither the one side nor the other in it, who have no interest in it whatever except the common interest, which we all have as members of a community of inter-dependent relationships in the misfortunes and embarrassments, whoever is responsible for them, of one of our greatest industries.

Winston Churchill established himself as the editor of a newspaper called the *British Gazette*, printed for the duration of the dispute on the presses of the *Morning Star*.

By 11 May he and his assistant, J.C.C. Davidson (1889–1970), at the time a junior naval officer but later Viscount Davidson, were publishing more than 2 million copies, in which he described the strikers as 'the enemy'. Churchill's wife, Clementine, set up a canteen for the people who were producing the *British Gazette*.

By the end of the first week the strike was beginning to collapse, and on 12 May the TUC backed down and officially called it off, although the miners, who had never believed that the TUC had its interests at heart, remained on strike. The TUC had failed in its main objective: the strike was intended to bring the government and miners to the negotiating table. This ploy had failed and so, therefore, had the TUC.

Apart from the Church of England and Lloyd George, there seemed very little establishment and political support for the miners, who after all, had a recognizable moral and industrial case. But the government remained adamant that it would not be bullied, and on 12 May Baldwin used the BBC (still a private company) to broadcast once more to the nation. He said that it was not the government's intention to laud the tactics used against the TUC nor to lord it over the miners, who he said, 'have failed in a mistaken attempt'.

The miners, although ill organized and poorly funded, were not easily persuaded by political argument. They were stubborn and remained so, even after Baldwin's broadcast. The pit-owners had triumphed, for the moment. The TUC had backed down. The government, in spite of promises to implement the report of the royal commission, had stood aside from the dispute between miner and owner, and the pit-owners now felt free to do what they liked. So they did.

The miners and their families went hungry, and although they held out until 12 November, starvation and misery drove them back. They were now worse off than once they had been. They had to accept lower wages and to work longer hours to get those wages. The pit-owners also insisted on introducing district wage agreements, which defied the most important industrial demand of the workers, a national wage. The private industrial sector completely controlled the unions, and the pit-owners were the biggest single employer in the country.

The example of the miners' strike did not spread, and employers in other industries, by and large, did not attempt to cut wages, as many had wanted to.

The 1926 strike represented a watershed in industrial action. There were far fewer striking days a year in the coming decade than there had been in the previous ten years, but the world was now heading for the Great Depression. For the moment, however, there would be a three-year buffer in the misfortunes of most working men and women because, in general terms, people were better off between 1926 and the start of the financial and economic collapse of 1929.

Asquith's intervention in the Lords drew little response. Their lordships had listened politely, but Asquith was tired and his long career was coming to an end. He was leader of the Liberal Party but had neither the energy nor the vision to rally his troops to come up with new ideas on industrial relations, which was an important failure at a time when industrial relations were undergoing such radical change. There were tensions within the trades unions as well as within the political parties over the right route to take towards decent wages, conditions and, above all, the novel thought that the workers needed to understand their industries if those industries were to survive. A new generation of trades unionists, including men such as Ernest Bevin and James Thomas, had emerged, who were willing to think about the future rather than march on the present, but the Liberals did not seem to understand this opportunity. As A.J.P. Taylor noted: 'The elderly Liberal leaders forgot their liberalism when threatened by (imaginary) social revolution.'[8]

Lloyd George, still an immense influence on rank-and-file Liberals and, because of his accumulated wealth, popular with the Liberal treasury, supported the government but demanded negotiations with the miners. Asquith was unimpressed by his arguments, and he had not forgiven Lloyd George for the way the Welshman had plotted against him in 1916. This long-felt animosity did the party no good at all. On 1 June Asquith felt it necessary to write to the Liberal Chief Whip, Sir Godfrey Collins, and ended the letter with the following:

> I see that it is insinuated that I have been the perhaps passive vessel of personal animosities. My record in those matters is well known to my fellow countrymen and I can afford to disregard base imputations upon my honour. I am this month completing forty years of service to the Liberal Party. For a considerable part of that time I have been its leader, and I have honestly striven during the last two years to recreate and to revive the broken fabric of Liberal unity. It has been a burdensome, and in some of its aspects, a thankless task. I will not continue to hold the leadership for a day unless I am satisfied that I retain in full measure the confidence of the party.

Most of the shadow Cabinet went to Asquith's defence, but they pointed out that the differences in the past had to be completely forgotten otherwise there could be no reconciliation between Lloyd George and Asquith. This was difficult because not only did Lloyd George refuse to co-operate with Asquith and follow his leadership but he also set up a separate Liberal headquarters for himself with a separate accounting system. Lloyd George was further criticized for refusing to support Asquith's suggestions on how the strike could be resolved and for even refusing to meet his Liberal colleagues when the strike was at its peak. The shadow Cabinet claimed that it had done its best in the interests of Liberalism to work with Lloyd George but concluded that it was impossible.

In spite of this expression of support, Asquith could not stay long. In mid-June at the National Liberal Federation (the party assembly) at Weston-super-Mare, the Council of the Liberal Party published what it called its 'unabated confidence in Lord Oxford [Asquith was now the Earl of Oxford and Asquith] as leader of the Liberal Party'. It continued:

8 *English History 1914–1945*, Oxford University Press (1965).

> The Council expresses the hope that for many years to come these outstanding qualities will continue to inspire the party which, in spite of recent differences, earnestly desires to retain the co-operation of all Liberals in pressing forward a rigorous and constructive policy of social and industrial reform.

But Asquith was not there to hear it. He was ill, and his doctors had told him not to attend. For the next two months he rested at Castle Howard. At the beginning of October he sent to his closest Cabinet friends and supporters what he described as a confidential and secret memorandum. It began with the observation that:

> The disintegration of the Liberal Party began with the Coupon Election of December 1918, it then received a blow from which it has never since recovered . . . the Liberal members in the new House were reduced to a handful of little more than thirty. The bulk of the original parliamentary party deserted to the coalition. . . . Those were the darkest days for Liberalism that I have ever known.

The long pages of this memorandum were, in fact, his valedictory and his irrevocable letter of resignation.

Asquith, now seventy-five years old, was a disappointed man. Baldwin spoke of Asquith's ability not to take advantage of others simply for the sake of scoring political points, a characteristic that Lloyd George regarded as a weakness in both men, but it was a quality mentioned in a letter to Asquith from the Foreign Secretary, Austen Chamberlain, who wrote: 'You have kept a high standard of dignity, of loyalty to colleagues and friends and of courtesy to opponents.'

In the context of the whole of the century it is not important to dwell on Asquith's life and departure from politics. However, it is an opportunity to remember that the transition from Victorian Britain to a political and industrial nation on the threshold of the most terrible depression and a war of unimaginable proportions was managed by people like Asquith, whose formative years were wholly devoid of the precedents needed to handle that transition. Between Gladstone's going and Asquith's the world had changed more than ever before, but the political and international institutions necessary for those times and the times to come were not in place. The League of Nations, for example, the first international organization to be established, was totally ill equipped to offer alternative solutions to the conflicts that were then festering. The monetary and fiscal policies of a large trading nation such as Britain were based on concepts that now had to be managed in a sophisticated manner rather than the patrician style that had suited Britain until the 1920s.

In spite of their many failings, leaders like Asquith deserve greater study if we are perhaps to understand why the twentieth century went in the direction of disaster.

In October Asquith resigned as leader of the Liberal Party and Lloyd George took over. He had two advantages in addition to intellect and charisma: the editor of the *Manchester Guardian* was a great supporter of his, and the Lloyd George Fund made large donations to the party at a time when it could scarcely make ends meet. For the time being, therefore, the Liberals imagined that a return to power was possible, and they set about the practical politics of social and economic planning – something that Baldwin's Conservative government failed to do.

Events elsewhere in 1926 were also to have a direct effect on Britain.

Benito Mussolini had almost completely established his grip on Italy, where he had been known as Il Duce since 1922.

In the Soviet Union, meanwhile, Stalin had begun to consolidate his power base, ridding himself of some who had been his close supporters, including Grigori Zinoviev, who in 1922 had helped start the process that led to Trotsky's downfall. Another to go was Lev Kamenev, who had been one of the leaders of the Bolshevik movement in 1917 but who was now dismissed from office because of his support for Trotsky. The charge was one long favoured by monarchs everywhere, including those in England – Kamenev was denounced as an enemy of the state. By the end of 1926 the new men, beholden to Stalin, were being slotted into place, including Anastas Mikoyan, Vyacheslav Menzhinsky and Nikolai Bukharin. None would be safe.

A trend was emerging in Britain for people to be told, officially, what was good and what was bad for them. In 1926 a paper published by the Institute of Hygiene claimed that young women were using drugs, cigarettes and alcohol to cope with the stresses of the flapper style then in vogue. The fashion for shorter and thinner dresses was encouraging increasing numbers of women to diet, and women were now smoking more than ever before, as advertising began to aim directly at them. In January 1926 the increased number of cases of cancer of the mouth was linked directly to cigarette smoking. Meanwhile the recently established Food Council was promoting the idea of standard measurements to overcome short measures.

No short measure was given by Alan Cobham. In March he was welcomed back to Croydon aerodrome by the sort of crowds that normally turned out for film stars after his 16,000-mile return flight from London to Cape Town.

In the United States experiments into another form of flight were under way. Robert H. Goddard had produced the first rocket to be powered by liquid fuel. Goddard believed that this was the future for space travel and that with careful development his 4-foot-long rockets could become giants and go into space.

The mystery of 1926 was not in space but concerned a vanishing lady. In December Agatha Christie, already a celebrated novelist, seemed to disappear. Her car had been found in Surrey but no one knew where she was. A maid at a hotel in Harrogate, Yorkshire, recognized her from a newspaper photograph, and her then husband, Archie Christie, travelled to Yorkshire to bring her home. Despite a host of theories, no one ever really got to the bottom of the mysterious affair at York.

The year ended on a rowdy note when the audience at the Abbey Theatre, Dublin, started fighting at a performance of a new play by Sean O'Casey, *The Plough and the Stars*. London audiences were more restrained and welcomed *The Plough* even more warmly than they had the same author's *Juno and the Paycock* the previous year.

Stars of another kind twinkled in London. Fred Astaire and his sister, Adele, were appearing in George Gershwin's *Lady, Be Good!* at the Empire Theatre and bringing down the house with the fastest of the numbers, 'Fascinating Rhythm'.

Deaths

Alexei Brusilov (Russian soldier)
Antonio Gaudí (Spanish architect)
Harry Houdini (US magician)
Claude Monet (French artist)
Annie Oakley (US sharpshooter)
Rainer Maria Rilke (German poet)
Rudolf Valentino (US actor)

1927

THIS WAS the year that the British Broadcasting Company started broadcasting as the British Broadcasting Corporation under the austere direction of John Reith. There was plenty for the new service to talk about, including a special warning that had been issued by the British Medical Association on the increasing number of deaths from cancer. The Health Minister, Neville Chamberlain, said there had been a 500 per cent increase in cancer deaths since the last century.

Churchill introduced his third Budget in which, to recoup some of the £150 million that the miners' strike had cost, he put up taxes on wine and tobacco. Two days later Baldwin announced to the Commons that the government would introduce a Bill granting the vote for all women over the age of twenty-one. A week later debate on higher education began, but although teachers' unions said that the school leaving age should be raised from fourteen to sixteen, this did not actually happen until after the Second World War.

In the Commons Labour MPs walked out after they had failed to filibuster the government's Trade Disputes Bill, the Conservative government's reaction to the general strike of the previous year. The Bill restricted the activities of trades unions, making 'general and sympathetic' – that is, secondary – action illegal. It also attempted to limit the flow of funds available to the Labour Party by imposing the system of 'contracting in' for the political levy. In addition, civil servants were no longer able to join TUC-registered unions. The Bill became law in July; it was repealed in 1946.

An altogether less abrasive subject, but one nonetheless capable of exciting terrible schisms, was about to be debated. The Church of England had published its proposals for revising the Book of Common Prayer and immediately reawakened the long-simmering differences between the evangelical and Anglo-Catholic wings of the Church. In July Convocation approved the revisions, but Parliament, reminding the nation that it held power over the Church, rejected the changes. The Solicitor-General, Sir Thomas Inskip, suggested that it was too inclined towards the Church of Rome, and many MPs spoke against the change in the marriage service in which the bride no longer promised to obey her husband. The Prayer Book was sent for a rewrite, in a direct confrontation between the government and the Church that could not be properly settled without a constitutional debate. But this was not about to happen. The Archbishop of Canterbury was Randall Davidson, who, as Dean of Windsor, had been a great favourite of Queen Victoria. Davidson announced that he would resign in November 1928 because he felt so strongly about the rejection of the new Prayer Book in the Commons. The revised Book of Common Prayer was approved by the House of Lords but was twice thrown out by MPs, among whom was the Home Secretary, Sir William Joynson-Hicks. Joynson-Hicks's public warning to the incoming Archbishop of Canterbury, Cosmo Lang, was that he should not get involved in the politics of Britain, by which he seems to have meant that he should not decide what should and should not be read in the Prayer Book.

Cosmo Lang was to become one of the most celebrated archbishops of Canterbury in the twentieth century. He was a firm believer in the revised Book of Common Prayer, but it could not be denied that the Home Secretary had a spiritual as well as a political point: the numbers of believers in what Lang and his curates preached was falling. In spite of the automatic assumption that being British meant being 'C of E', there is no statistical evidence that Britain was a Christian country.

What was not revised was the military instinct that war would come within twenty years. The military hypothesis was that defeat in the First World War had played on German minds and that the increasing population of that country would encourage expansion that would be impossible to contain within the existing boundaries. In January, in line with the Dawes Plan, the Allies gave up their control of Germany, handing over the responsibility to the League of Nations. In May Adolf Hitler held a Nazi rally in Berlin, the first such event to be organized in the German capital.

Elsewhere, the Treaty of Jeddah was signed, marking British recognition of the state set up by Abdul Aziz Ibn Saud, Saudi Arabia. By the end of January, the Civil War in China had reached such proportions that the British government ordered a division of soldiers to protect the British community in Shanghai, and a squadron of twelve cruisers and a flotilla of nine destroyers stood off the coast of China. Also in January bubonic plague broke out in Lisbon.

In February the BBC reported that Malcolm Campbell had set a new world land speed record, having driven *Bluebird* at more than 174 miles an hour across Pendine Sands in Carmarthenshire, but in March Henry Segrave beat Campbell's record when he drove the *Golden Arrow* at more than 203 miles an hour at Daytona Beach in Florida.

Henry Ford produced the 15 millionth Model T, and in his plane *The Spirit of St Louis* Charles Lindbergh covered the 3600 miles between New York and Le Bourget, collecting a prize of $25,000 for making the first non-stop transatlantic flight.

In Paris the talk was of a performance of Edouard Lalo's intricate *Symphonie espagnole*. The violinist was the ten-year-old Yehudi Menuhin.

In April the American swimmer, Johnny Weissmuller – later a screen idol as Tarzan – set three new records to be the first man to hold every freestyle record from 100 yards to half a mile.

This was also the year in which one of Joanna Southcott's boxes was opened. Pandora did not escape. Instead the box contained a few pamphlets, a linen night cap, a purse and a book entitled *The Surprises of Love*.

Visitors to London could stay at the Park Lane Hotel, which opened with the boast that it was the first hotel to have a private bathroom for each bedroom.

Deaths
Georg Brandes (Danish writer)
J.B. Bury (historian)
Isadora Duncan (US dancer)
Juan Gris (Spanish artist)
Jerome K. Jerome (writer)
Gaston Leroux (French writer)
Hudson Maxim (US inventor)
Henry Petty-Fitzmaurice, 5th Marquess of Lansdowne (politician)
Samuel L. Warner (US film executive)

1928

IN THIS year occurred what is quite possibly the most important discovery of the twentieth century. At St Mary's Hospital, London, Alexander Fleming discovered a mould that attacked bacteria. The mould was penicillin. Fleming surprised many by pointing out that the growth, *Penicillium notatum*, could be seen every day on stale bread. Even more obvious, and therefore unremarked, was the way he discovered it. Fleming looked at a mould and noticed that around it were rings that were quite bare. Why should this be? His answer was simple: the mould must be producing something that killed the surrounding bacteria or prevented a bacterium growing. This was one of the few high points in a year that presaged disaster, both economic and military, throughout the world.

★

Baldwin's government was not in good health and nor, in fact, was the prime minister, who was walking with a limp and a stick after a fall at Chequers. As each day passed he grew grumpier with his lot and even his own party: 'Every morning I am full of faith, hope and cheer. By lunchtime, I have lost a great deal of it and by evening I have given up all hope of this world and the next'.[9] He even seemed short tempered with the very people who were putting into practice what he thought were reasonable policies, particularly those concerned with the ever-increasing difficulties of unemployment.

By mid-1928 unemployment had risen to over 1.3 million. The policy of developing new industries could not produce an immediate response to unemployment. It was impossible to shut down one industry that was no longer viable in national and international markets and simply begin something new the following day. So the government's insistence that weak industries should simply strip themselves of money-losing sections was never to be a reasonable proposal. There was the additional problem that Baldwin did not have particularly good advisers: one would tell him that a department was badly run, while another would tell him that the same department was well looked after. Churchill, usually an innovative strategic thinker, failed to bring imagination to the Treasury.

One of the greatest burdens on any minister was being carried by Neville Chamberlain, the Health Minister. Chamberlain, the son of the great radical, Joseph Chamberlain, and the brother of the Foreign Secretary, Austen, had gained his experience in local government, and it is not altogether surprising that his reforms were designed to improve conditions and at the same time make local government more efficient. The connection between health and local authorities was close, and health boards and social security boards often doubled with the work that was being done by a county council.

In November Chamberlain introduced legislation to abolish the boards of guardians that had administered the first plank of poverty relief, the Poor Laws. Here was an example of an antiquated and often arbitrary system confusing the work that was supposed to be done within the fledgling national health authorities. Taking the 1902 Education Act as an exemplar, Chamberlain got rid of the boards of guardians and gave their authority to the public assistance committees in the counties and local boroughs. At the time there were sixty-two counties and more than eighty county boroughs in England and Wales. Although Chamberlain's reform does not seem to be a particularly radical advance in local government, within less than thirty years the county and borough councils had assumed control over most education, public health, water (except in London), gas and electricity, housing, and health and public assistance matters. The reform provided the electorate with a means of identifying the authority responsible for providing services to them. People talked about 'going to the town hall' to see what 'they'

9 Recorded by Tom Jones; quoted in Kenneth Young, *Baldwin*, Weidenfeld & Nicolson (1976).

were going to do about 'it'. Chamberlain had brought responsibility as well as provision closer to the people. This did not mean that government was off the hook, however.

Baldwin and the Cabinet understood that they could not run the country by handing responsibility – and therefore budgets – to local authorities. So, although local authorities appeared to have enormous powers they had to work within the constraints that 20 per cent of local funding came from central government in the form of grants.

Baldwin felt himself considering his most important objective – the voter. Although he was under no great pressure to do so and was opposed by two members of his government, Winston Churchill and Lord Birkenhead, Baldwin planned to lower the age at which women could vote from thirty to twenty-one (the same as the male voting age) and to give them the same residential qualification as men. The only anomaly remaining allowed what were known as business and university votes. For example, a man at Oxford would have a vote where he lived and another at his university, a system that continued until 1948. Giving women a vote at twenty-one brought 5 million more people onto the electoral register. In May the House of Commons passed the Equal Franchise Bill, and the most famous campaigner for women's votes survived long enough to see it through; Emmeline Pankhurst died the following month at the age of seventy.

In the same month the Bank of England was given permission to issue new currency, the £1 and 10 shilling notes, and there was a large increase in the use of a relatively new form of currency, the cheque book.

At the end of November and the beginning of December there was great concern at Buckingham Palace for the health of George V, who was suffering from what was described as congestion of the lungs. Queen Mary took over her husband's duties, and the Prince of Wales returned from a tour of Africa to be at his father's bedside. By 2 December George V could not breathe without oxygen bottles. Two days later, on the Tuesday, the government appointed a Council of State to act in his stead. The following week surgeons operated on his lung and the King, and his nation, breathed more easily.

In August France and the United States agreed the Treaty for the Renunciation of War in Europe, which is better known as the Kellogg-Briand Pact, after Frank Kellogg, the US Secretary of State, and Aristide Briand, the French Foreign Minister. The Pact, subsequently signed by sixty-five nations, renounced war as an instrument of foreign policy. Unfortunately, it failed to specify how aggressors might be punished. It was notable, however, because the first person to sign it was Gustav Stresemann, the German Foreign Minister, and because the Americans had become involved in European politics. The Pact went some way towards compensating for America's continuing refusal to get involved with the workings of the League of Nations, which had, after all, been the brainchild of President Woodrow Wilson.

In Russia, Stalin tightened his grip about the necks of his political opponents. In a purge that was a sign of things to come he sent thirty opposition leaders into exile, including Leon Trotsky, who was deported to the wilderness of Alma-Ata on the Russo-Chinese border. Stalin was not entirely unopposed. Trotskyite supporters held demonstrations, even in Moscow, but Stalin's secret police, OGPU, which had replaced the Cheka, arrested the leaders.

China was experiencing a terrible famine, partly because of the continuing war between the Nationalists under Jiang Jie-shi (Chiang Kai-shek) and the communists, which showed few signs of coming to an end. In May Jiang Jie-shi launched an attack on Beijing. Britain was more concerned about the potential threat to its commercial interests, especially in Shanghai, and about the possibility that the conflict would spread and involve the Soviet Union.

On the whole, however, Britain was paying more attention to stock markets around the world than to the increasing instability of Europe and to events in China and Russia. In the spring of 1928 Wall Street shares started to tumble at a faster rate than ever before. At first this was seen as a sign of crisis to come, but in fact it had more to do with a run on aircraft shares and irrational dealing. By the late autumn the recovery was so great that trading was not only back to normal but had approached abnormal levels, and in November the New York Stock Exchange had to shut down for a day to clear a backlog in trading of nearly 7 million shares. The more thoughtful in the British Treasury saw this not as a vigorous expression of free enterprise but as a harbinger of a storm to come. By the following autumn the world would have witnessed the Wall Street Crash.

Figures published for the previous year showed that Britain's birth rate continued the decline that had started at the beginning of the century and would not be arrested, but good news in the field of public health came in July, when the government announced that it would be possible to eradicate smallpox through the use of concentrated vaccine. Less welcome news was heard in August when the Imperial Economical Committee announced that more Britons smoked cigarettes than any other nation. There seemed to be two reasons for this: the decline in pipe smoking among men, who were taking up cigarettes, and the increase in smoking among women.

If smoking did not kill the population, road accidents certainly did. The accident rate had started to increase in 1921, and by September 1928 an average of fourteen people were being killed every day and nearly 150,000 people a year were injured. The numbers of cars on Britain's roads relentlessly increased. In August Morris Motors launched the Morris Minor, and in October the Motor Traders Association announced that anyone earning £400 a year could afford to buy and run a motor car. Hyde Park Corner was said to be the world's busiest traffic junction, and driving tests became compulsory.

In February the archaeologists working on Tutankhamun's tomb announced that its final excavation had uncovered jars that held the boy king's vital organs.

After seventy years the twelve volumes of the *Oxford English Dictionary* were finished.

Malcolm Campbell regained his world land speed record when he drove *Bluebird* at more than 206 miles an hour along Daytona Flats in Florida.

In June Amelia Earhart touched down in South Wales, becoming the first woman to fly the Atlantic. The twenty-nine-year-old Miss Earhart landed her sea plane just in time. Fuel was rapidly running out, and she had to throw out pieces of the aircraft to stay in the air. A landing that did not end successfully occurred near Spitsbergen in the Arctic Circle when Roald Aumundsen – the first man to reach the South Pole – was killed when he crashed his sea plane while trying to find an Italian airship that had crash-landed in the Arctic. The airship and its crew were eventually rescued by a Soviet vessel.

At the Olympic Games in Amsterdam Lord Burghley won the 400 metre hurdles which was celebrated partly because he was the first non-American to win it.

At the beginning of 1928 three notable Englishmen had died: Thomas Hardy, Douglas Haig and H.H. Asquith. Each had represented times past and not simply because of their ages. Asquith, the longest serving prime minister of the century, had overseen the transition from Gladstonian England to the realities of postwar economies and international alliances. Haig, the British commander during the First World War, had sat on the bridge spanning the military world of cavalry charges and the increasingly mechanized system of war. He had not anticipated, understood or adapted to the changes. Thomas Hardy had deliberately remained in times gone by. The poet, who was to be best remembered for his novels, portrayed an image of a Wessex country that people wanted to see to compensate for the world in which they now lived and that Haig little understood and of which Asquith, in his darker moments, despaired.

Perhaps the most lasting moment of 1928 and one that would affect the whole world for the rest of the century was a new film, *Steamboat Willy*. Its star was Mickey Mouse.

Deaths

Roald Amundsen (Norwegian explorer)
Herbert Henry Asquith, 1st Earl of Oxford and Asquith (politician)
Field Marshal Douglas Haig, 1st Earl Haig (soldier)
Richard Burdon Haldane, 1st Viscount Haldane of Cloan (politician)
Thomas Hardy (writer)
Sir Ebenezer Howard (reformer)
Leoš Janáček (Czech composer)
James Ward Packard (US inventor)
Emmeline Pankhurst (suffrage leader)
Dame Ellen Terry (actress)
Sir George Otto Trevelyan, 2nd Baron Trevelyan (historian)
Stanley John Weyman (writer)

1929

ALTHOUGH 1929 will be remembered as the year of the Wall Street Crash, second thoughts might bring to mind that in the same year Britain elected its second Labour government. Ramsay MacDonald's government of that year was the first to have an all-Labour Cabinet.

Baldwin had decided in 1928 that he would go to the country, and he did so in May 1929. Despite the long notice, the Conservative Party was not really prepared, but eventually the campaign settled on the theme that Baldwin was the man to trust. The nation probably thought so, but the voting system produced a different outcome. Here was a perfect example of the first-past-the-post method not reflecting the electorate's intentions. About 22.5 million people voted in the 1929 election. The Conservatives got more than 8.5 million votes but only 260 seats; the Labour Party got fewer than 8.5 million votes but 288 seats; and the Liberals received 5.5 million votes but returned only 59 MPs.

It was said that young women, voting for the first time after the 1928 Act, voted against the government. There may have been some truth in this, but the evidence remains largely anecdotal and not statistically proven. The Conservatives were certainly still regarded as a largely patrician group, who appeared to believe that they needed no special political programme to govern.

By 1929, with Asquith gone and Lloyd George back at the helm, the Liberal Party was revitalized. 'We can conquer unemployment' claimed its election banner, and its new policies planned to do so by creating jobs – building roads, railways and houses. But, as was to be the case for decades to come, the Liberals were too early with their ideas. Moreover, not all Liberal candidates understood the ideas sufficiently well to explain them to the biggest electorate the nation had ever had. Most damaging of all, no great institution and no big newspaper (about 90 per cent of which supported the Conservatives) stood up in all the muddle to declare that the Liberals had got it right. Moreover, Lloyd George once more failed to carry his party with him. People could vote Conservative or Labour without necessarily being Tories or socialists. But people had to 'feel' Liberals to vote for them.

The alternative was Labour. Many new voters would not have remembered a Liberal government, but the public now regarded Labour as a proper party and a credible alternative in government. It had been in government before and had shown it had something to offer. MacDonald and his colleagues did their best to preserve the public image of being members of a coherent political party that did not operate in a den of socialist revolutionary fervour, just as they had succeeded in doing in their short time in government in 1924.

MacDonald's immediate concern was unemployment, then at 1.2 million and rising. He gave the job of sorting it out to Margaret Bondfield (1873–1953), Britain's first woman Cabinet minister, who was appointed Minister of Labour. The previous solution had been to modernize, to cut out production waste, to lay off people where necessary and, as we saw in the 1926 miners' strike, to cut wages. This remained the most logical answer to the predicted industrial stagnation.

One of the most draconian methods of reducing unemployment figures was odd, coming as it did from a Labour government. Some long-term unemployed were made to work in a series of special camps. There were twenty-five places in England, Wales and Scotland, from Glenbranter in the north to Haldon in the southwest. The work was often futile – rock breaking, hole digging and tree felling – and today we might call them labour camps. The official files on these camps seem to have been destroyed.

For the moment, however, the British economy appeared to be sound, and the unemployment figures, though high, were not unduly alarming in percentage terms. So, MacDonald turned his attention to foreign affairs.

Arthur Henderson (1863–1935) had been appointed Foreign Secretary. Henderson was an iron moulder by trade, and he was one of the dedicated socialists who had built the Labour Party at the turn of the century. At various times between 1908 and 1932 he had been chairman of the party, but his childhood in Glasgow and then in the foundries of Newcastle, together with his deep religious conviction, did not suggest a typical background for the Foreign Office. Henderson was, however, to confound cynics in that first year in power.

In August a conference was held in The Hague to discuss, yet again, how much Germany should pay in compensation for the First World War. The world decline in trade had affected Germany, where unemployment was high and climbing. So great was Germany's war debt that it was estimated in June 1929 that it would take until 1988 for the country to finish paying reparations. The government was losing control.

A new repayment schedule had been arranged in June by a committee chaired by an American banker, Owen Young. The Young Plan meant that Germany would pay an initial $7.8 billion between 1929 and 1966, when new arrangements for the rest of the money would have been made. The money would go to an international bank of compensation. Unlike previous demands, the money would not be used to cover the costs of repairing France from damage caused by the Germans. Instead, the $7.8 billion would, in broad terms, go to the Allies so that they could pay off the debts they had run up during the war; most had borrowed money from the Americans. There were still those in Germany who resented having to pay a single Deutschmark to anyone, and the Young Plan added fuel to the nationalist fire.

This then was the background when Arthur Henderson, accompanied by Philip Snowden, the single-minded Chancellor of the Exchequer, went to The Hague in August. The conference agreed the Young Plan and it was further agreed that Allied control of the German economy would be dropped, thus restoring the country to full independence. Henderson proved to be a clever chairman, facilitating the early withdrawal of the Allies from the Rhineland, which pleased both the Germans and the Allies, who really did not want to be there.

Henderson then turned his attention to the League of Nations, which had become little more than a talking shop with many expansionist ideas. The French prime minister, Aristide Briand, had even proposed a United States of Europe. The origins of Briand's idea lay in 1923 and the Pan Europa movement, which had been founded by Count Coudenhove Calurgi. Pan Europa had a lot of supporters, including the back-bencher Leo Amery, but in 1929 the British had no real overseas interests apart from the Empire and perhaps a growing relationship with the United States. However, Willy Graham, the President of the Board of Trade, spoke in favour at the conference, emphasizing the concept of a free trade area. Even Gustav Stresemann, the German Foreign Minister, welcomed Briand's idea, although in 1929, given the state of Franco-German relations, European federalism could not have been regarded as a serious proposition.

Despite Graham's speech and the fact that other politicians, including Philip Noel Baker, Arthur Henderson's Parliamentary Private Secretary, accepted Briand's idea, MacDonald's Cabinet insisted that nothing should be done that would jeopardize the League of Nations, which they believed could play an important role in world security and economic growth. Henderson continued to promote the work of the League and at the same time won the confidence of the Germans and the French, particularly on disarmament. He even managed to get agreement that a world disarmament conference should be held in February 1932. In 1929 this was considered a huge success, but by the time the conference met, Henderson had left the Foreign Office and Europe's hopes of disarmament were fading fast.

Predictably, perhaps, the greatest disagreement was over naval power. At the Washington Conference of 1921–2 nine countries, including the United States and Britain – but not Germany – negotiated three agreements. One of these was a collective guarantee of China's independence. The second was a four-power treaty, signed by France, Japan, Britain and America, which promised to maintain the political and military stability of the Pacific region. The third was a naval convention by which five of the nations present at the conference – Italy, France, Japan, America and Britain – agreed to regulate the sizes of their navies, which effectively limited the building of new ships for the Royal Navy.

The Conservatives had resented this curtailment on naval expansion, so MacDonald took action. Two years earlier a conference in Geneva had tried, but failed, to reach fresh agreement on levels of naval force, so in October 1929 MacDonald went to the United States to persuade the Americans that the whole naval disarmament issue had to be rewritten. His efforts bore fruit in January 1930.

In October 1929, Henderson re-established diplomatic relations with the Soviet Union, which had been broken off two years before. There is no record of George V's emotions on shaking hands with the ambassador representing those who had murdered his cousin just a decade earlier.

★

Headlines were about to be made elsewhere, however. On 19 October the New York stock market recorded its biggest day of selling. The financial panic had started. On Thursday, 24 October 13 million shares were dealt on Wall Street, but by 11.30 in the morning no one knew the value of the stock that was being traded. At noon the major banking houses met at the offices of J.P. Morgan. The company's senior partner, Thomas W. Lamont, noted that 'there has been a little distress selling on the Stock Exchange'. During the afternoon the major banks were trying to reassure the markets and there was some buying. Four days later the London Stock Exchange fell.

The Wall Street Crash was not the total disaster since painted. There had been a constant rise in prices since 1924, with a slight levelling off in 1926, followed by a huge jump between 1927 and 1928. During this four-year period it was possible to float the most bizarre company and people would buy stock in it. Yet, beyond Wall Street and Threadneedle Street, there were the signs of an enormous slump.

Americans were protected by their nation's natural resources and sheer wealth from many of the things that were going on beyond their borders. International commodity prices had started to fall in the late summer. Russians, for example, were selling cheap timber, which meant that major exporters such as Canada and Scandinavia were losing money. In addition, the much encouraged increase in world production failed to reach markets because there was not much money about.

Although some Wall Street stock actually closed up on the day's trading on 24 October, by the end of the year about 22,000 American businesses had gone to the wall. Some of these would have gone anyway, but the real damage was caused by the more than 400 banks that crashed in 1929.

Lloyd George could point to the policy that he had put forward before the election as the solution to the government's economic difficulties as well as the contribution to righting the world economy. It was, he could say, happening in America, where Congress was putting money into federal road-building programmes to provide jobs and where the railroad operators agreed to maintain wage levels and increase construction programmes to safeguard as well as to provide jobs.

Matters on both sides of the Atlantic were, perhaps inevitably, made worse by the instincts of the middlemen, the suppliers and retailers. Frightened that they would not be able to sell goods, they cancelled orders. In consequence, manufacturers had fewer orders and everyone, including the workforce, suffered.

MacDonald set up a ministerial committee to look at ways of cushioning the effects of the slumped economies. Lloyd George and John Maynard Keynes were pushing their plans for borrowing and building to create jobs and outlets for manufacturing industries, and many in the Cabinet wanted the prime minister to agree to the Liberal scheme, but he would not.

George V was extremely concerned but could find no one to explain the depths of the economic difficulties. It was said that the only person in MacDonald's Cabinet that he trusted was the flamboyant James Thomas, the Lord Privy Seal.

'Tell me, Mr Thomas,' said the King. 'What state is my country in?'

Thomas thought for a moment and then replied: 'If I were you, I'd put it in your wife's name.'

In the Balkans the state of the Serbs, the Croats and the Slovenes was brought under one official name, Yugoslavia. In Australia the Labour Party came to power. In Afghanistan Mohammad Nadir Shah, the rebellious warlord, became King. In London the government said Britain was to have national parks, and it also announced that in future all London buses would be red (they had previously been yellow and red). Red, green and amber traffic lights were introduced.

Three remarkable books appeared in 1929 – Erich Maria Remarque's *All Quiet on the Western Front*, Robert Graves's *Goodbye to All That* and Ernest Hemingway's *A Farewell to Arms* – and Thomas Mann was awarded the Nobel Prize for Literature.

We should not pass by 1929 without a look at its lighter moments. George Gershwin's musical *Strike up the Band* opened. The first Academy Awards were presented. Joan Crawford married the nineteen-year-old Douglas Fairbanks Junior. *Popeye* appeared for the first time.

On a more gruesome note on 14 February seven members of Bugsy Malone's gang were murdered in a Chicago side street by members of Al Capone's gang. The killings went down in history as the St Valentine's Day Massacre.

Deaths

Carl Benz (German engineer)
Emil Berliner (US inventor)
General William Bramwell Booth (head of Salvation Army)
Georges Clemenceau (French politician)
Sergei Diaghilev (Russian impresario)
Wyatt Earp (US lawman)
Ferdinand Foch (French soldier)
Hugo von Hofmannsthal (Austrian writer)
Lillie Langtry (actress)
André Messager (French composer)
Archibald Philip Primrose, 5th Earl Rosebery (politician)
Gustav Stresemann (German politician)

CHAPTER FOUR

THE COALITION DECADE 1930–1939

1930

THE YEAR opened with unfinished business from 1929. At the end of January the five-power naval conference gathered to rewrite the Washington Treaty. The London Naval Arms Conference, which was opened by George V, was attended by Britain, the United States, France, Japan and Italy. Britain, the United States and Japan agreed to limit the numbers of their cruisers, submarines and destroyers. No major warships – the big battle class vessels – would be built for five years. Italy objected because it wanted the same number of vessels as France, and within two years the Japanese had ignored the treaty altogether. Perhaps the agreement's greatest value was that it made clear that Britain and America had common interests, one of which was their future attitudes to the Soviet Union.

Other unfinished business from the previous year concerned the Briand plan. Although it had been discussed in Paris and again in Geneva in 1929, the full details of the Frenchman's plan for a federal Europe were not published until May 1930, which coincided with a Pan Europa Congress in Berlin. The Conservative opposition supported Briand but said Britain's future lay with its Empire.

In July Henderson, the Foreign Secretary, minuted that the Cabinet opposed the Briand plan because it would weaken the League of Nations and possibly the Empire. The memorandum further suggested that an 'independent European Union . . . might create inter-Continental rivalries and hostilities'. The French naturally supported Briand, the Italians (equally naturally) did not, and the Germans appeared to say that their reaction would depend on Britain's reaction. The Dutch and the Belgians were in broad agreement, but there is no evidence that either believed that it would get very far.

What destroyed the Briand plan was a proposal to use the League of Nations to set lower tariffs and customs duties. As a last resort, the League agreed to Briand's proposal to set up a committee to enquire into European union, and although nothing came of it, it was a marker for the future. There is nothing but fanciful evidence that its failure was responsible for the Second World War; it is unlikely that any plan would have been able to prevent what was going on in Germany.

In March 1930 the German Parliament, the Reichstag, confirmed the Hague Agreement, but the Social Democrat government could not disguise the opposition. Hitler's National Socialist Movement and another opposition group, the German National People's Party, together with the Catholic Centre Party, objected to the Young Plan.[1] It was seen not as an agreement but a 'diktat'. German nationalism was further inflamed.

By now 2.5 million Germans were out of work, and nationalism was growing as quickly as unemployment. In the elections held in September, the number of members of Hitler's National Socialists rose from twelve to 107. They attended the opening of the Reichstag wearing their Nazi uniforms, while outside Nazi supporters marched through the streets, shouting 'Down with the Jews'.

For the time being the spectre of Nazi dominance had not greatly impressed itself on the British Cabinet, which was more concerned with violence of another kind. The move for Indian independence was growing, and Gandhi's doctrine of civil disobedience and the total rejection of violence was increasingly ignored by Indians wanting independence. In 1926 Britain had thought to change the way in which India was governed. Lord Irwin (later the Earl of Halifax) went to India as Viceroy and concluded that the subcontinent should become a dominion as, say, Canada was – that is, a self-governing nation within the Commonwealth. In 1927 Baldwin had set up a commission to examine the future of India, chaired by Sir John Simon, former Attorney General (1913) and Home Secretary (1915–16) and future Lord Chancellor (1937–40). It took three years for his commission (which included Clement Attlee) to report. This frustrated Irwin, who in October 1929 gave up on Simon and announced that India would become a dominion. It was not enough. Two months later, Irwin's train was bombed.

In January the All-India National Congress passed a resolution, proposed by Gandhi, demanding independence, and to underline this, the next month Indian nationalists planted a bomb in the British Museum. In March a more potent demonstration took place. Britain had imposed a law making it illegal for any other body than the government to produce salt. The symbolism of this act was not lost on Gandhi, who marched 300 miles from Ahmedabad in Gujarat to the sea at the Gulf of Khambat. When he reached the sea, Gandhi picked up a piece of natural salt. He had broken the law and was arrested.

Mahatma Gandhi had achieved the status of a god-like figure. He had always insisted that the way to independence and the fulfilment of a dignified nation was through peaceful conflict. Many of his followers were frustrated by this quiet campaign, and there were riots and deaths. Martial law was declared in different parts of India, and by the end of May the Viceroy was forced to announce a series of emergency laws.

When Simon's report finally appeared in June, its main recommendation was to

1 See page 160.

turn India into a federation of states with self-governing provinces. The report also recommended that there should be negotiations to explore powers for establishing a central government. The weakness of the report was that the commissioners had never spoken to Gandhi. The Indian princes did agree to talk to the British, however, and they liked the idea of a federation, which seems to have encouraged Gandhi to relax his position on non-co-operation. Now began an intricate dialogue between Gandhi and the Viceroy that would last for a decade and a half.

Further west MacDonald's government had to think carefully its Middle East policy. Britain's administration in Egypt had produced nothing but diplomatic and military headaches. In the summer of 1930 the Royal Navy was sent to stand off Alexandria as nationalists threatened the whole state and the safety of foreigners.

Henderson, the Foreign Secretary, thought that Britain should give up the administration of the country and pull back British forces to the Canal Zone. The Egyptians wanted far more than this, including control over the Sudan, which had been under direct British administration since 1924. The Foreign Office, however, saw Sudan as a strategically important state that should be kept under British rule.

Britain was now in further difficulties in Palestine. It will be remembered that in 1917 the Balfour Declaration had indicated that Britain favoured a national home for the Jewish people in Palestine. At that time there were already about 50,000 Jews living in Palestine. There were also half a million Arabs. The potential for conflict between Zionism and displaced Arabs was already obvious. The Balfour Declaration was, and was to remain, the most forceful commitment by Britain to a Jewish homeland, and there was not a Zionist who would shrink from making Britain keep its promise. The migrating Jews began to buy land from the Arabs or in some cases simply to fence it off. Since Allenby's victory in 1917–18, Palestine had been a British mandated territory – that is, Britain was responsible for the future of Palestine and its peoples.

In the autumn of 1930 MacDonald's government said that Jewish emigration to Palestine should be all but stopped. The Zionist reaction can be imagined. The fundamental differences between the Jews and the Arabs in Palestine could not be reconciled by some ideology founded on a Westminster model of democracy and common interest. Furthermore, the restriction on emigration had to be achieved in Palestine, but the volume of emigration was increasing because of the rise of nationalism in Russia and, particularly, Germany, where as early as 1929 Nazis were openly campaigning against the Jews.

There is a sense that 1930 was a year in which major issues to come were ticking over. In foreign policy, the London Naval Treaty, for example, which promised to limit the number of warships that could be built, looked good on paper but in practice restricted the building of a deterrent force and therefore made confrontation more likely. The Simon Commission on India could not bridge the gap between imperialism and independence.

At home, unemployment had risen above 2 million, yet the only radical proposal appears to have been the notion favoured by Keynes and Lloyd George of using public money to spend the nation's way out of the dilemma. The inadequacies of government applied across the political spectrum, for by 1930 a nation like the United Kingdom could no longer hope to control all its interests but still did not understand the administrative, economic and strategic means that were necessary to compensate for these failings.

The government did introduce the Coal Mines Act in 1930. The 1926 coal strike, which brought about the general strike, had been a conflict between the miners and the pit-owners, who wanted the miners to work longer hours but accept wage cuts. The Coal Mines Act gave the miners a seven and a half hour working day. By now Ramsay MacDonald's minority government relied on the Liberals, but the arrangement was crumbling. The Liberals wanted electoral reform, pointing out that in the 1929 election they had got 5.5 million votes but only 59 seats whereas the government had just 3 million votes more but 500 per cent more seats. In May 1930, without firm promises of electoral reform, Lloyd George withdrew his support in the Commons.

MacDonald had another problem to contend with. He had appointed Sir Oswald Mosley as Chancellor of the Duchy of Lancaster specifically to deal with the problem of unemployment. Mosley was an erratic figure who had been a Conservative and an Independent MP and was now a Labour junior minister. He saw only one way to deal with unemployment and that was through massive public spending and intervention in industry in order to generate jobs and markets. His boss, James Thomas, and the rest of the Cabinet rejected Mosley's plan, which was, in effect, an extension of the scheme proposed by Lloyd George and Keynes. Mosley walked out of the government and his job was given to the quiet Clement Attlee.

Mosley went his own way, becoming leader of the British Union of Fascists in 1932. His marches with the black-shirted Fascists against London Jews led to the 1936 Public Order Act, which banned political uniforms in Britain and gave the government powers to ban marches if it were believed that they would lead to incitement.

Lord Beaverbrook, the Canadian-born newspaper proprietor, launched his political party the United Empire Party in 1930. He was dissatisfied with the way in which Baldwin led the Conservatives and could not accept the logic of their defeat in the 1929 election nor their inability to dissect and criticize the government. Baldwin, on the other hand, was quite willing to accept that MacDonald's government was right in most cases. He was suited to consensus politics.

Helped by Rothermere and the *Daily Mail*, Beaverbrook attempted to change the tempo of British politics. The United Empire Party, as its name suggests, was intended to take Britain back to what he saw as the 'good old days'. Beaverbrook wanted Baldwin to promote the simple political policy that the British would buy all the Empire's commodities in return for British manufacturers selling their goods to the Empire. Beaverbrook's party did not last, but its sentiments and his determination for Empire became the theme of his greatest publication, the *Daily Express*, well into the 1970s.[2]

Deaths

Arthur J. Balfour, 1st Earl of Balfour (politician)
Robert Seymour Bridges (poet)
Lon Chaney (US actor)
Randall Thomas Davidson, 1st Baron Davidson of Lambeth (archbishop)
Sir Arthur Conan Doyle (writer)
D.H. Lawrence (writer)
Fridtjof Nansen (Norwegian explorer)
Miguel Primero de Rivera (Spanish dictator)
F.E. Smith, 1st Earl of Birkenhead (politician)
Dr William Spooner (cleric)
William Howard Taft (US president)
Alfred von Tirpitz (German sailor)

1931

THE GREATEST political upheaval in living memory in peacetime Britain occurred in 1931: the Labour government fell and was replaced by a National Government, an all-party government. In British politics coalition governments are normally reserved for wartime emergencies, but in 1931 the enemy was a collapsing economy.

MacDonald's government was not a failure, however, and had seen through significant legislation. The Statute of Westminster of 1931 gave the dominions independence from the United Kingdom. It was designed to replace the 1865 Colonial Laws Validity Act, which allowed Britain to veto locally made legislation. In 1926, at the Imperial Conference, the dominions were reclassified. They were now called autonomous communities within the British Empire and were described as being within 'the British Commonwealth of Nations'. The Statute of Westminster therefore was the parliamentary ratification of this 1926 process which meant that the parliaments in Australia, Canada, the Irish Free State, Newfoundland, New Zealand and the Union of South Africa had legislative independence. It was to this body that the Viceroy Lord Irwin had wanted to attach India.

The government also faced up to the vexed question of London Transport. This existed in two forms – buses and Underground. The Labour government set up

2 In 1977 at a celebration to mark the thirtieth wedding anniversary of the Queen and Prince Philip, the *Daily Express* editor's speech contained many references to the glories of Empire and Commonwealth.

the Transport Board, one effect of which was that the buses would subsidize the unprofitable Underground. London had its first trolley buses, twenty years after they had appeared in Yorkshire. Coincidentally, the *Highway Code* was first published in 1931, and in January a new Road Traffic Act came into effect. From this time Britain was to have traffic policemen, and every motorist had to carry third-party insurance.

Arthur Greenwood, the Health Minister, began a huge programme of slum clearance, and the dreadful accommodation was gradually replaced with subsidized housing. Not all basic ambitions were satisfied. Sir Charles Trevelyan at the Board of Education drafted a School Attendance Bill to raise the school leaving age from fourteen to fifteen. The opposition came from Roman Catholic MPs on the Labour benches, although this had more to do with the religious debate than it did with the raising of the school leaving age, and the Bill fell in the Lords. Trevelyan resigned. He did not go on a point of principle but in frustration. Like many senior Labour MPs, Trevelyan disliked the soft approach of MacDonald to government. Trevelyan believed that MacDonald should have pushed this important piece of legislation, which was, after all, a continuation of the work started in 1924. This was not MacDonald's style, however.

A quiet approach did not mean a lack of thought. When the Liberals pressed for a change in the voting system, Labour considered the idea of proportional representation and offered something called the 'alternative vote'. An alternative vote is simply a way of redistributing the seats among the other parties. When the subject was revisited in 1998 the model had already been discussed sixty-seven years earlier. The government's plans to bring in alternative voting also had to contend with the university constituencies, which Labour saw as totally undemocratic and wanted to abolish on the principle that one person should have only one vote. As with so much electoral reform, the House of Lords blocked the Bill. In July 1931 the government planned to use the Parliament Act to push through this legislation. If it had done so it would have maintained the support of the Liberals in the voting lobbies, but it did not get the chance. The government fell in August.

In the summer of 1931, therefore, the Conservative and Labour parliamentary parties were agreed on most major foreign policy and political decisions, while the Liberals and Lloyd George were pushing radical proposals that had no chance of getting through. More importantly, however, was the fact that the Parliament of 1931 had no ideas for overcoming the slump in world trade and the economic consequences that were being felt in Britain.

The after-effects of the 1929 Wall Street Crash were still being felt, and economies around the world had not recovered with the American Stock Market. Less money was being spent globally; therefore, fewer goods were sold. The effects on an economy like Britain's were twofold. Because cheap goods and raw materials were available on the world market, Britain was able to import as easily as and in some cases more easily than ever before. In return, Britain's manufacturing market had to struggle against rising prices. When we look at the world depression we find the anomaly that although there were more people out of work, those with jobs were better off than they had been for some time. One, perhaps over simplified, way of describing this phenomenon was that although wages were not going up, many prices were coming down.

In the middle of this illusion – that Britain was prosperous in spite of what was going on elsewhere – the Labour government had to produce a Budget. In 1931 Philip Snowden was no nearer balancing Britain's budget than twelve months earlier when he was still trying to make sense of the accounts left by Winston Churchill. Social security payments had increased because more people were out of work; at the same time, fewer people were paying taxes. The result was that the inland revenue income was less than in the previous year.

In February 1931 Sir George May, a former senior executive of the Prudential Insurance Company, was asked to chair a committee to recommend measures that would balance Britain's budget. Snowden hoped that the May committee, which included two senior trade union members, would give him the authority to introduce a high taxation, low expenditure Budget by the autumn of 1931. This would be the great test of conciliation politics. Before Snowden could even draft his autumn Budget, two reports appeared – a Treasury report and the May report.

A Treasury committee, chaired by Lord Macmillan, published a report criticizing the conventional way of financing government and managing the economy. Here, in the summer of 1931, was broken the illusion of Britain as a great trading nation. As we have noted, at the beginning of the century, Britain did not have a balance of trade on which it could survive. The figures were, and always would be, balanced by the so-called invisible earnings of insurance, banking and shipping. Now in 1931, with the decline in world trade, the more vulnerable elements of this triangle were bared.

The May report appeared at the end of July. It has been described as reeking with panic and ignorance. John Maynard Keynes, the Cambridge economist, described it as foolish. May said, for example, that unemployment relief should be cut by 20 per cent and that the dole should be financed from existing income. He also said that taxes should not be raised to pay for public spending.

The May report had said many of the things that Snowden had wanted it to say, and he could therefore produce an autumn Budget, citing the report's evidence for his fixation with a balanced budget. But first there had to be an enactment of government ritual – a committee was set up to examine the findings of another committee. This was a Cabinet committee consisting of Ramsay MacDonald himself and his trusted advisers, Philip Snowden, Arthur Henderson, James Thomas and Willie Graham. Instead of meeting immediately, however, the five fixed their first session for the last week in August and went on holiday.

On 11 August the prime minister hurried back to London. Overseas speculators were selling the pound. There was no single economic reason for a run on sterling. It had more to do with international financial juggling of where money could be bought at one rate and loaned at another. It relied on the lifeblood of international financial trading, rumour. There had been a banking collapse in Vienna, and German banks had produced a rescue package but had lost money in doing so. In the same way as a bookmaker might lay off bets, so financial rates are laid off in the money markets. The City of London was awash with short-term foreign deposits and long-term loans at reasonably low interest rates. When the Germans started to sink they could not or would not honour their debts, and the London banks caught the cold. A lot of British banking assets were held in Germany. The Germans were now in deep financial crisis and those assets were frozen. The Bank of England handed out Britain's gold reserves to the troubled London banks, and soon the Bank of England had to borrow money, which it did from other bankers, this time in the United States and France. The French and Americans wanted guarantees, the chief of which was exactly what Philip Snowden had tried for – a balanced Budget. Only the government could bring in the political measures that would satisfy the world markets.

Cutting unemployment payments would reduce government expenditure and would even scare the rest of the workforce into accepting wage freezes if not wage cuts. All the work that had been done since the general strike of 1926 was theoretically to be undone.

This was the position when MacDonald and his Cabinet colleagues were called back from their holidays in mid-August. The only person with any strong views on what to do was Snowden. MacDonald did not have the intellectual or political authority to carry through the draconian budgetary measures. On 20 August the unions rejected the cuts proposed by Snowden.

By then, more than 2.7 million people were registered as out of work. No wonder that the government was awaiting the reaction of the TUC, then meeting in Bristol. Given the political influence of the TUC, this was no longer simply an economic crisis.

Three days later, nine of MacDonald's twenty Cabinet ministers threatened to resign rather than accept the cuts. These were not lightweight members of the Cabinet, and they included Arthur Henderson, perhaps the most respected minister at MacDonald's table.

By the third week in August it was clear that the government could not go on in its present form, even though no one could see an alternative way. MacDonald could, constitutionally, resign so that a Conservative–Liberal coalition could form a government under Baldwin, leader of the second biggest party at Westminster. It would then be up to that coalition to put through the cuts and take the consequences.

One person who would not be in that coalition or a candidate for its leadership was Lloyd George, who had prostate cancer. His place was taken by Herbert Samuel. Samuel suggested there should be a National Government, headed by Ramsay MacDonald. Baldwin supported the idea and so did George V. MacDonald went along with this, some think too quickly.

On 24 August 1931, therefore, MacDonald became the prime minister of a

National Government. The Cabinet contained four Labour members (MacDonald, Snowden as Chancellor of the Exchequer, J.H. Thomas and Lord Sankey, the Lord Chancellor), two Liberals (Herbert Samuel and Rufus Isaacs, now Lord Reading) and four Conservatives (Baldwin as Lord President of the Council, Neville Chamberlain, Sir Samuel Hoare and Cunliffe-Lister).

It was agreed that once the economy – the national emergency – was resolved the National Government would be dissolved. The government was an agreement among the senior politicians at Westminster. It had not been endorsed by the body politic of the three parties, although Liberals and Conservatives, with a couple of exceptions, gave the Cabinet their blessings.

However, just as the Liberals distrusted Lloyd George and the Conservatives distrusted Baldwin, so MacDonald did not have the political and moral support of the Labour Party. He seems not to have understood that the Labour movement would not rubber-stamp proposals formulated by the parliamentary hierarchy. The parliamentary party suspected that policy was being dictated by bankers, and on 31 August, just one month after the appearance of the May report that was intended to salvage the economic crisis, feelings within the Labour Party were so strong that the Hampstead branch, MacDonald's local branch, expelled him.

There were, moreover, no quick results. At the beginning of the month the French and American banks had given the Bank of England a credit note of £50 million. By 26 August, the day after the National Government was formed, the Bank had lost 80 per cent of that £50 million. Money was still running out of London, and overseas investors in the pound had not regained any confidence. The swift and decisive action that MacDonald had promised could not have been heard in the overseas markets. More money was needed. Once again, Britain went to the French and Americans for help. The government got £80 million, but this time it went into the Treasury rather than the Bank of England.

In just two working weeks there had been an increase of more than 47,000 in the number of those unemployed, and the figure was rising. The Finance Bill went to Parliament. Snowden's Budget combined with the new credit loan might have saved the government from any further runs on the pound, but foreign confidence took another knock on 15 September when the fleet mutinied at Invergordon.

In the Budget income tax went up, unemployment benefit was cut by 10 per cent and all government salaries were reduced, including those of civil servants, the judiciary, teachers, the police and the armed forces. Even George V entered into the spirit of things and took a cut of £50,000 a year in the civil list payments.

The May report had suggested that rates of pay in the armed services should be 'consolidated' on those paid in 1925.[3] These cuts were now incorporated in the

3 The Anderson committee report considered that costs of living had fallen and therefore naval pay should be cut by around 25 per cent. The argument against this included the fact that many ratings had joined up at the higher wages and expected them to continue. A compromise was reached, but May was now proposing a return to the Anderson recommendations – hence the further fury of the navy at the cuts.

Budget proposals for reductions in government employee wages, and, not surprisingly, the 12,000 ratings in the Atlantic Fleet, which had deployed to Invergordon on the Cromarty Firth, were angry. They had not been told about the cuts until they had sailed from Portsmouth; moreover the cuts were considerable. Foreign investors do not like military mutinies directed at government policies, especially as only two weeks earlier the Chilean fleet had violently mutinied for the very same reasons – wage cuts.

The demands of the sailors were quite specific and written out by Able Seaman Len Wincott in HMS *Norfolk*. He and a few ratings had formed themselves into 'a sailors' soviet'. They borrowed a portable typewriter from the ship's executive officer and typed out their manifesto, which was read to the ship's company and, later, to the House of Commons:

> We, the loyal subjects of His Majesty the King, do hereby present to the Lord Commissioners of the Admiralty our earnest representations to them to revise the drastic cuts in pay that have been inflicted upon the lowest men on the lower deck. It is evident to all concerned that these cuts are the forerunner of tragedy, poverty and immorality among the families of the men of the lower deck. The men are quite willing to accept a cut, which they, the men, think within reason, and unless this is done, we must remain as one unit refusing to serve under the new rates of pay.

Len Wincott cleverly reflected the views of many of the 12,000 ratings in the fifteen ships at Invergordon that September. The navy did the most sensible thing and put the ships to sea so that they could return to their home ports. The mutiny was soon over because the Admiralty undertook to review the pay rates. The cuts were limited to 10 per cent, which settled the matter for all time.

The events at Invergordon came on 15 September. Foreign reaction led to further runs on the pound, and four days later Britain's reserves were exhausted. On Sunday, 20 September, the government was forced to devalue the pound and come off the gold standard. Emergency legislation was pushed through the House to stop more gold withdrawals from British assets and to deter foreign speculators. The pound dropped overnight from $4.86 to $3.40, a decline of 30 per cent. The Invergordon mutiny did not cause the crisis but it did make it irreversible and pushed the government over the edge.

By October it was clear the government could not continue in its present form. The National Government had a limited life. Its function had been to balance the pound and the budget, but how far it had achieved these objectives is unclear. The devaluation gave an impression that enough dramatic action had been taken to save the economy, so what was the government to do next? A general election was called for 27 October.

The difficulty facing all parties was to find a platform for that election. The only sensible course was to preserve the apparent unity of the past few weeks and not put to the test individual Labour, Conservative or Liberal policies, even if they would have made sense. MacDonald was muddled. It seems likely that the only person he trusted with his true thoughts was the Conservative leader, Baldwin, to whom he wrote in the first week of October:

> We are in a dreadful mix up and unless we can get out of it disgrace is to be ours. The best way to escape from an entanglement is to see how we got into it. I have done what I have done to try and save this Country from a financial crisis. . . . The United Cabinet for a majority of the new House will be Conservative in all likelihood . . . for us to have to resign before the New Year and leave a Conservative majority in power for five years would cover us in much ridicule . . . this is the root of the whole matter.

MacDonald was under considerable stress. All the suspicions that his party had had were now to be seen as true. MacDonald – one of the architects of the Labour Party, the long-time secretary of the Independent Labour Party – was about to go to the country and return with exactly what his ramblings had predicted, a predominantly Conservative government. This would be his doing. The first Labour prime minister would soon preside over a Conservative Cabinet, no matter how it was described.

When the results were declared the supporters of the National Government had 554 seats of the 615 in the House of Commons, of which 473 were Conservative. Labour candidates won just forty-six seats, and every former Labour minister, with the exception of George Lansbury and MacDonald himself, lost his seat. MacDonald, who had stood in the face of fierce and spiteful opposition as the National Government candidate for his Labour constituency of Seaham Harbour, held it.

There were twenty seats in the Cabinet. The Conservatives took eleven of them, the Liberals had five and MacDonald's National Labour Party had four. MacDonald was prime minister and Baldwin was Lord President of the Council. Baldwin, ever the manager, was the centre of power. Neville Chamberlain became Chancellor of the Exchequer, and Philip Snowden went to the House of Lords. There was no place for Lloyd George nor for Winston Churchill, who had left the shadow Cabinet in January after criticizing Baldwin's policy towards India.

Other, less momentous, decisions were taken at Westminster in 1931. In April for the first time MPs voted to allow cinemas to open on Sundays although a lot of people were already going to the 'flicks', as they were called, on the Sabbath. In May people were looking up at Auguste Piccard, who ascended in a balloon and reached more than 52,000 feet from earth to become the first man to float in the stratosphere. A little lower down, the world's tallest building, the Empire State, was opened in New York. Down to earth, traffic jams were caused in Bedfordshire when thousands of people visited the county's latest attraction; Whipsnade Zoo opened on 23 May. In June, an electric tote was used at the Ascot races for the first time.

Farmers were marooned and livestock were penned in after an epidemic of foot and mouth disease.

In the concert, music halls and theatres Malcolm Sargent conducted the first performance of William Walton's *Belshazzar's Feast* and Noël Coward produced his latest show, *Cavalcade*. Ninette de Valois transferred her ballet company from the Old Vic in south London to a new site in north London called Sadler's Wells. One of her new ballerinas left the Ballets Russes to join her at Sadler's Wells – Alicia Markova. At the age of fifteen years, Yehudi Menuhin gave his first London performance in Beethoven's Violin Concerto, which was conducted by Sir Thomas Beecham. Their music could be heard in a new company formed in November 1931, when HMV and Columbia merged and called themselves EMI.

Deaths
Bix Beiderbecke (US musician)
Arnold Bennett (writer)
Sir Jesse Boot, 1st Baron Boot (drug manufacturer)
Thomas Alva Edison (US inventor)
Joseph Joffre (French soldier)
Sir Thomas Lipton, 1st Baronet (businessman)
George Herbert Mead (US philosopher)
Dame Nellie Melba (Australian soprano)
Sir William Orpen (artist)
Anna Pavlova (Russian ballerina)
Arthur Schnitzler (Austrian playwright)

1932

THE WORLD of 1932 was an uncertain place. Japan invaded China. Hermann Goering became president of the Reichstag and the Nazis were the largest party in the German legislature. The French president, Paul Doumer, was assassinated by a Russian anarchist. Stalin carried out a further purge of opposition politicians. In the United States 12 million people were unemployed; in Britain, the figure was 2.75 million.

Britain was still ruled by a National Government. There were no Labour, no Conservative and no Liberal policies, just a simple arrangement to manage the United Kingdom. That was the theory. Ramsay MacDonald knew, however, that the National Government would be dominated by Tory policies. The Conservatives wanted taxes on imports – in other words, Britain was once again faced with the old debate over free trade and tariff reform.

Imports rose because traders believed the Conservatives would have their way, highlighting part of the difficulty of the transition from an economy finding its natural level, which it continued to do, and a government trying to manipulate it on the basis of the floating pound. The additional stress came from the fact that the managers were not very good. The Economic Advisory Council, which had been established two years earlier, had little energy and even less understanding of the subject even though the committee included businessmen, trade unionists and economists. On one side was the argument for paying less and getting more; ranged against it was the view of those who supported the idea of paying more and introducing protection through tariff reform. The Conservatives' view was simple: imposing tariffs would make it more expensive for people to sell goods to Britain and therefore there would not be so much competition from foreign imports. None of this would affect Britain's exports, however, because the public would buy more British goods since they would be cheaper than foreign imports. This, in turn, would mean that profit margins could be adjusted, and British exports would be even more competitive.

By January 1932 the Cabinet had before it a formal proposal from a committee it had established to examine the balance of trade, which strongly recommended protectionism – that is, the imposition of customs duties to protect British goods.

The Liberals, traditionally opposed to tariffs and therefore supporters of free trade, threatened to walk out of the Cabinet. The Cabinet was 'saved' by a suggestion from Quintin Hogg, who was now Secretary for War. He suggested there was absolutely no reason for the Cabinet to agree; it was a perfectly democratic process to have disagreement. This preserved the nonsense that the National Government was unified government. But this was not a proposal for some minor piece of legislation. The committee's recommendation represented a fundamental change in long-standing government ideology – the transition from free trade to protectionism.

The Conservative-inspired legislation, the Import Duties Bill, went to the Commons in February and had passed through both Houses by the end of the month – the Lords, of course, being dominated by the Conservatives. Imports from the dominions were exempted, although this did not mean they were getting preferential treatment as the Chancellor's father, Joseph Chamberlain, had advocated at the beginning of the century. The then prime minister, Arthur Balfour, had tried to support Joseph Chamberlain by suggesting that, once they had been imposed, tariffs could be used as a bargaining chip with other industrial nations until protectionist duties cancelled each other out and the whole world reverted to free trade. This convoluted argument had done Balfour's government no good at all. It now resurfaced from the mouth of Neville Chamberlain who insisted that import taxes could be used to bargain with other countries.

For the moment, there were no taxes on food imports – stomach taxes, as they were known. British agriculture had not fed Britain for half a century and anything that raised the price of food would have been unpopular, and it is perhaps for this reason that the Import Duties Bill raised no widespread public debate.

This great adventure into the economics of trading and national management was as far as the MacDonald government went.

The following month, April, Neville Chamberlain presented his National Government Budget to the House. It was hardly ground breaking: he cut the arms budget; he fiddled with prices and pay; and he reduced the level of revenue raised from direct taxation. He did not balance the national books.

In July and August an Imperial Conference was held in Ottawa. This should have been a gathering dedicated to Joseph Chamberlain's memory. He had wanted to protect the dominions – Canada, Australasia and South Africa – and to acknowledge the enormous debt Britain owed them for their support in, for example, sending troops to fight in the Boer War. Just as it had not worked in Joseph Chamberlain's time, so it failed in 1932. The dominions themselves had just as many problems as Britain. The Canadians still wanted preferential treatment for their wheat; the Australians wanted the same for their meat. There was a widespread fear of taxing imports of food into Britain, but Chamberlain could see good reason for them; Baldwin was against them. The straightforward approach of imposing taxes and giving preferences was too cut and dried for political manoeuvring, so there were bilateral agreements that turned into fudges. Philip Snowden, MacDonald's one-time Chancellor of the Exchequer and now in the Lords, resigned in protest. The Liberals went with him. MacDonald was left with his back to a wall of Conservatives.

The government of Britain still did not know how to cope with the depression. The lesson, impossible to practise in Britain, was to be demonstrated in the United States, which was about to get its most inspirational leader of the century, Franklin Delano Roosevelt.

In America in the summer of 1932, 20,000 ex-soldiers and their families marched on Washington. They were demanding $24,000 million in hand-outs. The Bonus Expeditionary Force, as they called themselves, thought they had persuaded the Congress to support them, but they had not. Herbert Hoover, the out-going president – although he didn't then know that – sent troops to burn down the tent city in which the Bonus Expeditionary Force camped.

Elsewhere in America the industrial and farming landscape was desolate. In November 1932 the Governor of New York State, Roosevelt, defeated Hoover in the Presidential Election. It was one of the biggest changes in American political history, for at the time the differences between Republican and Democrat were more marked than they would be later in the century. FDR, as Roosevelt would become known, was the Democrat by whom future candidates would be measured. He would also become the longest serving president, because at that stage in American constitutional history the president was not restricted to two terms in office. In that year's election Roosevelt won forty-two of the forty-eight states.

When he became president in 1933 Roosevelt introduced what he called the New Deal. As Keynes would agree, America planned to spend its way out of the depression. There would be new highways, railroads, energy-creating industries and farming and more bank regulations. The New Deal had two aims: to restore the economy on a long-term footing and by doing so get back to work the more than 11 million jobless or about 20 per cent of the workforce.

In Britain there was no such vision, no such system and no such wealth to create a New Deal for the United Kingdom.

By 1932 about 40 million people lived in England and Wales, about 4.5 million in Scotland and about 4.2 million in Ireland.[4] Some 5.5 million children went to elementary schools and more than half a million had further education. There were just 30,000 undergraduates.

The birth rate was falling and did not much recover for two decades. It is difficult to identify a single reason for the decline. One reason may have been male contraception, which had become more widely available during the First World War to counter the spread of venereal diseases. A second reason could well have been that the postwar economy brought hardship. Less money made people think more of the cost of children, although among those working in the worst affected industries, the birth rate does not appear to have dropped at an exceptional rate. Indeed, in some cases, it increased.

The economic influence on birth rates may have had more to do with the opportunities to spend money. This was an age of invention. Vacuum cleaners, electric ovens, irons and boilers were making homes more comfortable and the kitchens and sculleries less of a drudge. Here was the beginning of the dormitory town and semi-detached Britain. Houses had, for the first time, garages. Anyone earning, say, £400 a year, could afford to buy and run a car – as long as they were not running something else, like a second or third child.

There was, too, more suburbia and more to do in it. The nation in 1932 went to the cinema to see Johnny Weissmuller in *Tarzan the Ape Man* or Boris Karloff in *Frankenstein*. The higher brows could wrinkle to Aldous Huxley's *Brave New World* or listen to Britain's newest orchestra, the London Philharmonic. Further afield, the BBC began its overseas broadcasting service and at home, George V made the first royal Christmas broadcast.

Deaths

Aristide Briand (French politician)
George Eastman (US inventor)
Charles Gore (cleric)
Kenneth Grahame (writer)
André Maginot (French politician)
John Philip Sousa (US composer)
Giles Lytton Strachey (writer)
Rin Tin Tin (canine actor)
Edgar Wallace (writer)

---

4 Accurate figures are available only every ten years. These figures are based on low population growths estimated in 1931 and for Ireland in 1936.

1933

ON 30 JANUARY 1933 occurred one of the deciding moments in the history of this century. It was the day on which Adolf Hitler became Chancellor of Germany.

Hitler was able to do this because the incumbent Chancellor, Kurt von Schleicher, could not gather enough support in the Reichstag, the parliament, and because the President, Hindenburg, refused to dissolve it. Instead, Hindenburg followed the constitution – which was exactly the same as Britain's – and asked the leader of the biggest single party to form a government. Adolf Hitler was that leader.

In Britain, few people seemed aware of the signs and dangers of Nazi Germany. Churchill, referring to Hitler, even wrote that he 'admired men who stand up for their country after defeat'. Lord Irwin, soon to inherit his father's title and become Lord Halifax, believed that he could apply the same philosophy to Germany and Hitlerism as he had in India. It was all psychological. It was all to do with dealing with inferiority complexes.

MacDonald, still the prime minister, was preoccupied and muddled. Baldwin, the Conservative leader and the true power within the National Government, was more interested in the personality of Hitler than his power within Germany. It would take at least a year before the alarm bells began to ring and then only softly. The *News Chronicle*, which reflected the Liberal Party, was one of the first to announce that Hitler's appointment was a 'good and necessary thing'. Considering there were 7 million people out of work – almost three times as many as Britain – and little prospect of overseas trade providing relief or financial reserves, this seemed to be a general view.

It remains a curious fact that there was no urgency in the examination of Hitler's rise to the German Chancellery. Perhaps no one expected him to last. There was, moreover, a generally accepted view that Japan, not Germany, posed the greatest threat to Britain's security.

The Times of 7 February, reflecting the thinking of Sir Maurice Hankey who was both Cabinet Secretary and Secretary to the Committee of Imperial Defence, seemed unclear what line to take on Hitler:

> The successive messages of our Berlin Correspondent during the last few days leave no doubt about Herr Hitler's method of conducting an election campaign. It is to make no pronouncement of policy in the ordinary sense of the term, but to proclaim a political creed, to impose it with all the resources of official power upon the whole nation and to denounce, malign and thwart its opponents, open or supposed . . . the most active and ruthless exponent of this plan of political extermination is Captain Goering, one of the three Nazi members of the Cabinet, who is Deputy Commissioner for the Interior in Prussia, as well as being the first German Minister for the Air. . . . Herr Hitler is . . . continuing as Chancellor the methods which have made him the leader

> of the largest party in Germany and won him a place among the dramatic figures of Europe. All the world is asking the question – and asking it for the most part sympathetically – whether the street-orator will become an efficient ruler, and whether the leader of a movement can also become the leader of a Government; whether in fact the agitator will prove himself an efficient ruler, and the demagogue a statesman . . . it has been a comparatively simple matter to capture the imagination of German youth, to exploit discontents, to enrol and organize the idle of a country that likes to be organized, to criticize and condemn existing institutions and to heap the blame for the prevailing impoverishment and suffering upon the heads of successive governments. Now scathing indictment and irresponsible clamour will have to be succeeded by steady work and sobriety.

The view from Printing House Square was generous. The following month the Reichstag was set on fire. The belief was that this might have been deliberately started by the Nazis in order to blame the opposition to Hitler's authority. Hermann Goering was reported to have arrived at the blazing building to announce that this was a communist crime against the new government: 'We will show no mercy. Every communist must be shot on the spot.'

The SA (Sturmabteilung), the paramilitary wing of the Nazi party, took over the policing of the country. A decree, aimed at communists and Jews, enabled the SA to arrest and imprison without trial.

In March 1933 elections were held in Germany. There were four main groups: the Social Democrats got 7 million votes, the communists got 5 million and the once-powerful Centre Party got fewer than 4.5 million votes. The Nazis increased their vote to more than 17 million and now had 288 of the 647 seats in the Reichstag. This was not enough for Hitler, however, and the newly elected communist representatives were refused entry to the Reichstag. Outside the building and far beyond it Hitler's Brownshirts were at work, moving from town to town systematically beating Jews.

On 9 March 1933 the SS (Schutzstaffel) opened the first concentration camp just outside a town called Dachau, not far from Munich. As the SS moved through Germany, so Hitler swept through the political system. The Bavarian government was ordered to replace its Minister of Interior with one of Hitler's men. Opposition newspapers were shut down. Any gathering apart from Nazi rallies was banned. By March 1933 the prisons were estimated to be holding 40,000 Jews and opposition leaders. The swastika now flew alongside the imperial flag of Germany (it became the official German flag in August 1935), and Hitler and his supporters wore Nazi uniforms.

Hitler promised full employment. To achieve that there would be a new law to alleviate the distress of the people and the nation. The bill that went through the Reichstag meant the end of the Weimar Republic and its constitution. By the end of March, the Enabling Bill was being used to get rid of Jewish teachers and civil servants. All Jewish businesses were to be boycotted. Stars of David were splashed across doors and windows of Jewish shops and the slogans 'Jews Out' and 'Perish Judah' appeared overnight.

There was more to come. In July 1933 Hitler declared that only members of the Nazi Party would have absolute German citizenship. On 25 July the Nazis announced that they planned the compulsory sterilization of the imperfect: the deformed, lame, blind, deaf and those suffering from serious hereditary deformities were to be forcibly sterilized.

Jews marched through London to draw attention to what was happening in Germany, but there was no great political reaction. Britain went through the motions of criticizing Nazism at a session of the League of Nations, and Churchill and the almost forgotten Austen Chamberlain made noises. Some people, however, were already talking of the coming war. When the Royal Disarmament Conference had opened late in 1932, the Labour and Liberal Parties had believed that disarmament was the way to prevent war. In 1933, however, the Chiefs of Staff seized on what was happening in Germany as good reason to build more weapons. Weapons in the hands of other nations threatened war. Others believed that the League of Nations would be the forum in which war could be avoided through debate.

The Germans and the French were still arguing over the consequences of the First World War, and neither country had accepted its financial and political consequences. The Germans were insisting that they should have the same level of weaponry as the French, and in September 1933 the French produced a compromise: the Germans could have equality but only if Britain promised to announce that, if France were attacked, Britain would fight alongside the French. The British did not agree. The French then agreed to German equality but only for a limited period. Hitler refused to accept this and walked out of the talks in October 1933. There was no point in continuing a disarmament conference without Germany.

Worse still, on 14 October Hitler ordered his delegates away from the League of Nations and withdrew German membership. In November 1933 a referendum was held in Germany to support Hitler's withdrawal. According to the official figures, 95 per cent of the nation – including inmates of Dachau – supported the decision to pull out.

In the Commons there was open discussion about the possibilities of war and it was Baldwin who observed that advances in air power made it inevitable that the bomber, as he put it, would always get through. Yet no voice was strident enough to alert the government.

So where were the prophets? Not in politics, that's for sure. In September 1933 H.G. Wells had published *The Shape of Things to Come*. In it he had argued that by 1940 Germany and Poland would be at war.

In general, in Britain, the disquiet that might have been felt about the treatment of Jews in Germany did not overwhelm the British conscience. Germany was still a popular place to go on holiday. Many admired what was happening there. It was also becoming more the fashion to believe that after two decades of inquests Germany was not entirely to blame for starting the First World War. No great animosity was felt towards the German people. Equally interesting, there was a general anti-war mood in Britain. This, for example, was the year of the Oxford Union resolution: 'This House will not fight for King and Country.' Although this did reflect a general anti-war feeling, it did not, as many have said, give Hitler the impression that Britain would keep out of any future European war.

There was, however, a greater argument that wars could be prevented if people realized why they started. Accidental conflict was a popular debating point, as, too, was the argument that wars would start if nations built huge armouries. More relevant for the situation in 1933 was the notion that if a nation was unhappy – that is, if it was internationally maltreated – it might go to war if efforts were not made to cheer it up. Germany was the perfect example. It had been stripped of its assets to pay retributions, so what was happening now was understandable. The movement to say enough was enough was growing, and it was nothing more than Keynes had argued immediately after the 1914–1918 war. Bleed Germany and no corn would be grown; instead, there would be discontentment and, ultimately, nationalism – which was what was now happening.

But if all this is important now, there seemed as much, if not more, interest in what was happening to English cricketers in Australia that winter. The MCC captain, Douglas Jardine, had started to use what were technically called leg theory tactics. This meant putting lots of fielders on the onside of the wicket (the side to which the batsman has his back when taking strike). A fast bowler then runs in and pitches the ball on the line of the batsman's body and legs. The sharply rising ball is difficult to hit and can be struck properly in only one direction – towards the fielding cordon. The English fast bowlers were hitting the batsmen as often as the bat, and this became known as the body line tour. So strong was the protest, so intense the rivalry that it was raised at government level. At one point it even threatened relations between Australia and the United Kingdom. Perhaps it would not have been so controversial if England had not won the Ashes series.

A less contentious sporting event was taking place in America. Sir Malcolm Campbell, once again in *Bluebird* and once more at Daytona Beach in Florida, set up a new land speed record of 272 miles per hour.

On the other side of the world a British biplane, the *Westland Wallace*, became the first aircraft to fly over Mount Everest – exactly twenty years before it was climbed by Edmund Hilary and Sherpa Tenzing, or nine years after George Leigh Mallory and Andrew Irvine, who may have reached the summit in 1924.

Perhaps the politicians should have taken more notice of the three biggest hit tunes of the year: 'Smoke Gets in Your Eyes', 'Who's Afraid of the Big Bad Wolf?' and 'Stormy Weather'.

Deaths
Calvin Coolidge (US president)
John Galsworthy (writer)
Stefan George (German poet)
Sir Edward Grey, Viscount Grey of Fallodon (politician)
Ring Lardner (US writer)
George Augustus Moore (Irish writer)
Sir Frederick Henry Royce (engineer)
Louis Comfort Tiffany (US designer)

1934

IN JANUARY 1934 the Nazis began the sterilization of the so-called inferior Germans. More than 50,000 were sterilized in the first year. The Psalms were rewritten to remove any reference to Jews. In February a series of Nazi rallies began during which the demonstrators raised their right arms and swore allegiance to Hitler.

Baldwin, the Conservative leader in the Nationalist Government, was more aware of the dangers of Nazism than was the prime minister, MacDonald, and concerned about Hitler's politics. The German Chancellor's personality seemed to intrigue Baldwin. He was encouraged by Joachim von Ribbentrop, a sometime wine merchant who had joined the Nazi Party in 1932. Ribbentrop was to become Hitler's most influential foreign adviser and by the following year he had been appointed ambassador to London. He recognized the authority of Baldwin and the fact that although Britain had a coalition government, it was dominated by the Conservatives and that Baldwin was the most important member of the Cabinet. Ribbentrop asked Baldwin to go to Berlin. But he never did.

It is important to remember that a great deal of attention was being paid, not to Germany, but to Japan, and the Chiefs of Staff rightly pointed to Japan as the best armed of Britain's potential enemies. There is, however, some indication that not all politicians suffered strategic myopia when considering Germany. In the Commons in March 1934, Baldwin had to speak for the increased budget for military aircraft. He had been talking about getting an agreement at the World Disarmament Conference, and although the conference did not break up until May 1934, Baldwin seemed to be anticipating that breakdown and its consequences for Britain:

> If all our great efforts for an agreement fail, and if it is not possible to obtain equality in such matters as I have indicated, then any government of this country – a National Government more than any and *this* government – will see to it that in air strength and airpower this country shall no longer be in a position inferior to any country within striking distance of our shore.

That meant Germany, but Britain continued with its plan, not always understood by some others, including the French, of tacitly supporting German rearmament.

The French, still concerned that Germany would invade (a fear that would persist until the early 1950s), accused Hitler's government of increasing its weapons industries. The Germans denied this, and other powers within the League of Nations had no sure means or inclination to do anything about it.

But events in southern Germany that summer suggested that all was not well in the Nazi camp. On 30 June 1934 took place the Night of the Long Knives. Hundreds, perhaps thousands, of members of the SA were executed in Munich and Berlin that night, including Ernst Röhm, the SA's Chief of Staff. He was asleep in a hotel bed when a Nazi unit woke him, pulled him outside and shot him. Josef Goebbels, head of Nazi propaganda, claimed that the SA was plotting to overthrow Hitler. The Night of the Long Knives removed any suggestion of a socialist revolution against Nazism. Within two months and the death of President Hindenburg in August, Hitler had assumed absolute power in Germany. He announced that there would be no president in future and that he, Hitler, would now be known as Führer and Chancellor of the Reich. He took over as commander of the armed forces, and all sailors, soldiers and airmen had to swear an oath of allegiance, not to Germany, but to Hitler personally.

In September 1934 a rally was held at Nuremberg, where ranks of thousands of Nazis gave a demonstration of total allegiance to their leader. By the end of October the German army was three times the size of the 100,000 permitted under the Treaty of Versailles.

In the House of Commons Winston Churchill said that the German air force would, within three years, be twice the size of Britain's, and he added that German armament factories were approaching wartime production levels. Within four months Germany would be on the march to reclaim lost territory and the League of Nations would do nothing about it.

Poland could read the signs as well as any neighbour might do and began conscripting young men for the army. In July a Nazi unit assassinated Austria's Chancellor, the dictator Engelbert Dollfuss. Mussolini ordered troops and aircraft to Italy's border with Austria. Alexander I, King of Yugoslavia, was assassinated by a Croatian terrorist while he was on a state visit to France.

The National Government was still trying to rescue the economy, and the building industry was certainly playing its part. More money than ever before was being loaned to would-be house buyers. This had two advantages: it was an indicator of growing fortune for the middle classes, and it was providing jobs. The Housing Ministry announced that more than 280,000 council houses were to be built in Britain and that some 100,000 men would be employed in building them.

If there was a boom time in building there was a slump in farming. The Potato Marketing Board was forced to start an 'eat a potato' campaign. At the beginning of the century, potato and bread had been part of the staple diet. But in 1934 the annual conference of the Fruit and Potato Trades Association declared that women were too worried about their figures and had cut out potatoes. This was the beginning of the slimming craze that swept through Britain in the mid-1930s. The Central Council of Recreative Physical Training was set up to promote healthy activities to keep people trim.

If the average Briton wanted to tell friends about the latest dieting fad, perhaps they were doing so on the telephone. In 1934 more than 800 million calls were made and there were twice as many telephones as in 1933.

In November, far away, a journey of another kind was beginning. The communist leader, a peasant by the name of Mao Zedong, was besieged with his peasant army in Kiangsi by the Nationalist armies of Jiang Jie-shi. The only way out for Mao and his followers was a 6000-mile march to the safety of Yenan. The long march had begun. It would take a year for him to reach Shensi Province in northwest China and the beginnings of the Chinese communist dynasty.

Deaths
Marie Curie (French physicist)
Frederick Delius (composer)
Engelbert Dollfuss (Austrian politician)
Sir Gerald du Maurier (actor-manager)
Sir Edward Elgar (composer)
Roger Fry (artist)
Paul von Hindenburg (German politician)
Gustav Holst (composer)
Sergei Kirov (Russian politician)
Arthur Wing Pinero (playwright)
Raymond Poincaré (French politician)

1935

IN 1935, the Germans marched into the Saar, the Italians into Abyssinia, the Japanese into Peking, and Stanley Baldwin into 10 Downing Street, for the third time.

In 1935, too, George V celebrated his silver jubilee. But it was not a happy year in Britain, as the economic depression continued to bite into the social fabric of the nation. The cotton and coal industries were particularly badly hit. The cotton workers had gone on strike in 1932 when mill-owners cut their wages, and from more than 800,000 members at the beginning of the decade, membership of the National Union of Mineworkers had fallen to fewer than 600,000 – a 25 per cent drop in the workforce. Miners had once been in the largest union in the country; in 1935 they were overtaken by the Transport and General Workers Union (TGWU). Other unions reflected the changing patterns in British industry, and there was growth within the Amalgamated Engineers' Union and the Electrical Trades Union. The harsh conditions in industry meant harsh conditions in homes. Men joined regiments like the Brigade of Guards, not because they felt called to the colours but because they were hungry.

In February 1935 MacDonald received a deputation of senior churchmen to discuss the case for raising the school leaving age. Among them was the Archbishop of York, pleading his case for keeping young teenagers at school:

> We ought, I think, to keep in mind not only the educational advantage of their being in school but the great social advantage of their not being at that time thrown into the open labour market or faced with the possibility of compulsory idleness. I know, of course, that provision is being made to obviate the latter evil, but nonetheless the in and out experience which is often all that can be secured for those who are given the kind of additional education provided for juvenile unemployed is necessarily very limited as compared with a continuous course in the schools . . . There is the special evil of unemployment . . . Whatever may be the effect of raising the school age upon the problem of unemployment – and I cannot myself doubt that it would relieve that problem at least to some degree – it would bring to an end the problem of juvenile unemployment.

At this time there were more than 2 million people out of work, the crime rate was rising (it had increased by more than 50 per cent in five years), and industrial unrest was so bad that by the end of the year there had been about 800 strikes and stoppages. That meant not much less than 2 million working days lost – all this in a nation desperate for economic and social recovery.

The Saar was important to the German economy because it was the major coal-mining area of the nation. It was taken from Germany after 1918 and administered by the League of Nations as part of the compensation package agreed under the Versailles Treaty, by which France was given the coal-mining rights in the Saar for fifteen years. In January 1935 a referendum was held among the 500,000 Saarlanders, who voted overwhelmingly to be reunited with Germany.

By February British troops had started to pull out of the territory and on 1 March the Saar was handed over to Germany. Within twelve months Hitler would have swept aside the last flimsy pages of the Treaty of Versailles and ordered his troops into the Rhineland, even though there were doubters among his own military advisers.

There was now no disguising Hitler's intentions. On 6 March Hermann Goering announced that Germany needed in excess of the 400,000 troops that it had (under the Treaty of Versailles it was only allowed 100,000). Sir John Simon, the British Foreign Secretary, was sent to Berlin to talk to Hitler, but instead of showing any weakness, the Führer demanded that Germany be allowed to have a 500,000-strong conscript army and announced that Germany should have an air force the same size as Britain's and a 400,000-tonne navy. The Luftwaffe was established on 11 March.

In April ministers from France, Britain and Italy met at Stresa and announced that they would oppose German rearmament, but they omitted to say how they would do so. They did, however, guarantee Austria's independence and agreed on future co-operation. The Lord Privy Seal, Anthony Eden, went to Moscow to meet the Foreign Commissar, Maxim Litvinov, but there was little the Soviet and British governments could do other than refer their anxieties to the toothless League of Nations.

Hitler's next move was to join up with East Prussia by annexing parts of Czechoslovakia. In April 1935 the German navy announced that it was going to build a submarine flotilla of twelve U-boats. By now the Treaty of Versailles was worthless, and in the summer the Germans announced they were embarking on an even bigger naval programme.

In Germany Jews were now being described as subhuman and the Nazis banned Jews from marrying anyone other than another Jew. The evil being perpetrated in Germany was not Hitler's alone. He had surrounded himself with men like Hermann Goering, Heinrich Himmler and Joseph Goebbels, who instituted and carried out some of the most terrible peacetime and wartime policies in Hitler's name.

In early March the British government produced a military White Paper. There were to be more ships and, significantly, newly designed air defence systems. Three months later the government decided that the Royal Air Force was to get a 300 per cent increase in aircraft and that within two years the RAF would have 1500 planes. By the end of the year the Germans had proposed that there should be limits on the numbers of squadrons both sides had. British plans were made to give the RAF a new squadron every week.

Stanley Baldwin, still the most powerful man in Ramsay MacDonald's Cabinet, admitted that it was no longer possible to reduce British defences and expect others, especially Germany, to follow suit. The Germans said that this increase in military spending was a good enough reason for the Germans to increase theirs. Baldwin pointed out that German rearmament was contrary to Hitler's public pronouncements that it was looking for peaceful relations with the rest of Europe.

In April only Denmark, a neighbour of Germany's, failed to condemn German rearmament when it was debated at the League of Nations. It is not thought that Hitler was much concerned by the tone of the debate. In June Britain initialled an accord with Germany that claimed to limit the size of the German fleet to a little over one-third of that of the Royal Navy; the German navy was already smaller than that and was supposed to be within the naval agreements of the Treaty of Versailles. The Cabinet had decided that this was a reasonable limit and that Germany would follow it. The immediate result was that Germany began a major naval building programme.

In Britain it was not a simple task to build masses of planes, tanks and ships. There was still a National Government because there was still no structured way out of the economic depression. To compensate for the hardships being experienced throughout the country, the government had found it necessary to see what social reforms could be brought in quickly. So great was the problem of dealing with growing dole queues that the newly established unemployment assistance board was never quite able to cope with the demands.

We should remember this background when we consider the criticisms that British politicians did not do enough to prepare for war. It was not easy to sell the idea of rearmament to a nation that could not hear the sound of gunfire.

Labour ministers had never quite understood the possibilities of war after the Treaty of Versailles. They believed neither that German rearmament would lead to warfare nor that the enormous reparations should continue. There were those who thought that Germany should be given back her former colonies and that German claims on Poland and Czechoslovakia should be met. For their part, the Conservatives saw greater danger in the increased powers of Stalinism. To them the communist threat was an alien ideological virus that, if not contained, would spread across Europe and certainly into Britain.

Although Britain and France worked together in the League of Nations and should have concerned themselves with the future of Europe, in practice only France did so. Once more, it appeared that Britain was wary of becoming involved in Europe or European politics and strategic thinking. The chiefs of the armed forces and the civil service were less sanguine. They had contingency plans for rationing and a wish list of weaponry they believed had to be delivered as a deterrent to German ambitions.

Baldwin was unsure of levels of public support for a potential war, and in June 1935 some 11.5 million people responded to a questionnaire, asking, in general terms, if they agreed that it was right to go to war to stop aggression. Some 6.75 million people agreed that it was. Baldwin was interested that this meant almost 5 million people disagreed. Yet the great hope of peace, the League of Nations, had far from unanimous support among the British.

Cynics were proved right in October when Italian soldiers marched into Abyssinia (Ethiopia). The invasion had been long expected, for Italian interests in the Horn of Africa had strategic as well as territorial overtones reaching back to the nineteenth century. The carve-up of colonies and former colonies was about to begin. For the whole year the Italians, who governed the colonies of Eritrea and Italian Somaliland, had continuously fought a border war with the neighbouring Abyssinians. The Emperor of Abyssinia, Haile Selassie, referred the border dispute to the League of Nations, but the League was quite incapable of outmanoeuvring the double-dealing between France and Italy over Abyssinia.

The French, who believed that Germany would eventually move into Austria, asked the Italians to help when that happened. The Italians agreed. In return, the Italians wanted a chunk of Abyssinia. The French would support their cause in return for help in Austria. In October the Foreign Secretary, Sir Samuel Hoare, told the Commons that this was a great test for the League of Nations and that if it failed, 'the world will be faced with a period of danger and gloom'.

By November the League believed it had an answer: it would impose economic sanctions on Italy. Sanctions were being broken by the end of November, but their imposition meant Mussolini's Fascists had reason for even greater control in Italy. Il Duce nationalized the Italian banks and drew up a list of major industries that he would take into his ownership.

By the following spring the capital of Abyssinia, Addis Ababa, had been taken and Italy now had its Empire. The Christian Emperor fled to Palestine and thence to exile in London. The British abandoned all pretence of sanctions, and the League of Nations turned its back. By 1935 no one could pretend that any of the pacts that had been agreed around the world could prevent conflict if, like the Italians, a nation saw its best interests served in war. It was difficult to argue against the Chiefs of Staff and senior civil servants when they said that disarmament had done little to deter rearmament.

'The Statement Relating to Defence', which appeared in March 1935, was a document of considerable political and military importance. It reflected the mistrust of Germans, the fear of Russians and the need for America that would lead in less than fifteen years' time to the establishment of the North Atlantic Treaty Organization (NATO). Here was the basis for the post-World War Two notion that an alliance was needed 'to keep the Germans down, the Russians out and the Americans in'.[5] In 1935, however, this philosophy gave Hitler an excuse for rearmament at an ever faster rate.

By June MacDonald could no longer cope. Baldwin noted: 'It was tragic to see him in his closing days as prime minister, losing the thread of his speech and turning to ask a colleague why people were laughing.' MacDonald stepped down on 7 June, but he did not leave the government and the government did not fall.

Baldwin was once more prime minister, MacDonald became Lord President of the Council, and his son, Malcolm MacDonald, joined the Cabinet as Colonial Secretary. Sixteen of the twenty-two Cabinet places were held by Conservatives, among them Anthony Eden, who became Minister for League of Nations' Affairs, the first time one had been appointed. This was supposedly a reflection of the National Government's belief that the future security of Europe was based on international agreement. Churchill did not get into the Cabinet. Interestingly, Baldwin observed that Churchill got so involved with anything that he did, that he should be saved and so be fresh as a wartime prime minister. This was in 1935. In July, however, Churchill was appointed to the Air Research Committee.

Scientists and engineers had to decide how to apply new technologies and to what. This was the year that a new system, initially for detecting aeroplanes, was tested. It became known as RADAR, Radio Detection And Ranging. The

5 Attributed to Lord Ismay, NATO Secretary General 1952–7.

committee, encouraged by Baldwin, understood that air power did not simply mean numbers of aircraft. Unless new technologies were introduced in the right places and in the right systems, the Royal Air Force would be good for ceremonial fly pasts but not much more.

Within twelve months, the Hurricane and the Spitfire were being developed. Automatic gun turrets and variable pitch propellers were now moving from drawing boards to hangars and would change the way in which air combat was planned until the introduction of the jet engine.

Baldwin had a more immediate matter to attend. In October he went to the ageing George V and told him he wanted to call a general election. He had promised, when MacDonald stood down, that the election would not be on party lines. It took place in November 1935, and only 71 per cent of the electorate bothered to vote.

Once more the Conservative vote was so great that this was in effect a Tory government. There were 432 Conservative MPs, 154 Labour MPs, which was a considerable improvement, and only 20 Liberals, who simply could not contest any more than 25 per cent of the seats.

The government was again caught up with the future of India. MacDonald and Baldwin were determined that India would join Africa, Australasia and Canada as a dominion power. There was now a Government of India Act, passed in 1935, which would provide provincial government and central power invested in the Viceroy. In practice this was nothing to do with the democratic settlement of India, but had a great deal to do with Britain not being ready to hand over full power and having too many vested interests, including the whole apparatus of the Raj, even though Indians were beginning to take over some posts.

Furthermore there is no evidence that beyond London people were much interested in the future of India. It was a place that could provide a greater social standing for those without much money. It was common enough, for example, for young officers who could not afford to hunt two days a week with a fashionable regiment in Britain to go to India.

Baldwin was immersed in another drama. The scene shifted back to Abyssinia and the Franco-Italian arrangement. Britain had kept its distance, but now it became involved, in a very grubby way. The Foreign Secretary, Sir Samuel Hoare, made an agreement with the French prime minister, Pierre Laval, that Italy would be allowed to keep the best parts of Abyssinia without any objections from France or Britain. The Hoare-Laval Pact was seen as a despicable arrangement that contradicted the League of Nations' position and excited popular anger towards the Italians.

Anthony Eden, the Minister for League of Nations' Affairs, could not politically nor personally stomach the agreement. He told Baldwin that he would resign unless Hoare was reprimanded and the Pact abrogated. Hoare refused to back down. Baldwin, seeing the damage this was doing to his new government, sacked him, and Anthony Eden was appointed Foreign Secretary. Baldwin and Eden were clearly right, and Hoare was wrong. The fact that he was so wrong, makes it difficult to believe that he came to such an agreement with Pierre Laval on his own initiative. If, on such an important issue, he had even tacit approval within the Cabinet, as he most certainly did, then the whole affair left few in credit and the League of Nations in its death throes.

Drama of a more traditional kind, but reflecting even more sinister politics, took place in the theatre. T.S. Eliot's *Murder in the Cathedral*, which dramatized the assassination of Thomas Becket, was produced in the Chapter House of Canterbury Cathedral. It was one of the few dramas, perhaps the only one, to have transferred from a cathedral to the London stage. John Gielgud, Laurence Olivier and Peggy Ashcroft were playing just down the road in *Romeo and Juliet*.

On a lighter but noisier note, George Gershwin's *Porgy and Bess* opened in New York. Benny Goodman formed his jazz orchestra. In publishing, Allen Lane brought out a new kind of book. Instead of having a hard back, this was a paperback, and he called the imprint Penguin Books.

Deaths
Alban Berg (Austrian composer)
Edward Carson (jurist and politician)
André Citroën (French manufacturer)
Alfred Dreyfus (French soldier)
Paul Dukas (French composer)
Arthur Henderson (politician)
Oliver Wendell Holmes (US jurist)
John Jellicoe, 1st Earl Jellicoe (sailor)
T.E. Lawrence – Lawrence of Arabia (soldier and writer)
Max Liebermann (German artist)
Huey Long (US politician)
Józef Pilsudski (Polish politician)
Henri Pirenne (Belgian historian)
G.W. Russell – Æ (Irish writer)

1936

GEORGE V died at Sandringham on 20 January. His coffin was taken that night on a farm cart across to Sandringham Church. Behind the cart trailed estate workers and his riderless cob, Jock. On 28 January the royal countryman was laid to rest at Windsor. George V was succeeded by his eldest son, Edward, who had been born in 1894.

The story of Edward VIII and Mrs Wallis Simpson, a divorcee, has often been told, but although the abdication did not publicly surface until December 1936, it had been a constitutional dilemma for much longer. From our standpoint at the end of the century, it is not always easy to comprehend the importance, in 1936, of the monarch in Commonwealth life. The dominion prime ministers and Baldwin advised the King not to marry and added that the people would not find Mrs Simpson acceptable as their Queen. There were very strict laws of succession. Edward proposed that he would remain King but Mrs Simpson would not be Queen; any children of the marriage would have no right to the throne. Baldwin opposed the plan.

In what seems an unthinkable discipline in the late 1990s, the national newspapers in 1936 agreed a code of silence over the affair. The foreign press was under no similar obligation, however, and the news became known. On 11 December Edward VIII gave a radio broadcast from Windsor Castle. He told his people that he had found it impossible to discharge his duties as King as he would wish to do so 'without the help and support of the woman I love'.

The next day, Saturday, 12 December 1936, Prince Albert became King and would be known as George VI. The new King was forty-one years old. As a youngster he had been a cadet at the Royal Naval College, Osborne, and had fought at the Battle of Jutland in 1916. In 1923 he had married Elizabeth Bowes-Lyon. The elder of his two daughters, Elizabeth, who was ten years old, was next in line to the throne.

In continental Europe the Spanish Civil War was of more immediate concern. This was not simply a confrontation, it was a cause. In 1936 a general election in Spain brought a left-wing coalition into government. The army could not accept the result, and on 16 July it marched on Madrid. At the head of the army, General Franco expected a relatively easy path to control of Spain. But the Popular Front, the Republican government, called on the partisans and factory workers and waiters and labourers to repel the old guard and they did. Others interfered. Mussolini's Fascists supported Franco as did, to a lesser degree, the Nazis. The Soviet Union supported the Republicans.

The French were alarmed about the war going on across its borders. Léon Blum had just become the first socialist prime minister of France at the head of a Popular Front government, was nervous that the idea of revolution might spread. The British also became politically involved.

The Spanish Civil War entered intellectual folklore. Romantics and idealists, most of whom had never been to Spain, decided to go to the war and help the Republicans. The war attracted the deeply intellectual as well as the ill-educated, the famous and soon-to-be-famous, among them Ernest Hemingway, George Orwell and Laurie Lee. About 2000 British people joined the International Brigade on the side of the Republicans, of whom 500 were killed.

A diplomatic fiasco and international humbug followed in short order. The League of Nations could play no part in bringing the Civil War to a conclusion, with other governments agreeing to a French and British proposal that no one should get involved on either side. Needless to say, they did. The Italians sent tens of thousands of soldiers to help Franco. The Soviet government said they would send help to the Republicans if others were sending help to Franco.

At first, the Labour Party in Britain, which might have been expected to support the Republicans, agreed to support the policy of non-intervention. They changed their minds when it was seen that non-intervention was failing to bring the war to an end. One difficulty was to translate British political thought into what was happening in Spain. Did, for example, a political group that supported the Republicans incline towards a Popular Front in Britain? Would not that imply support for communism? The Conservatives had no brief for the Republicans, and if pushed, their instinct was to support Franco. But Nazis and Fascists were fighting on the side of Franco, so how should they feel about Hitler?

It was this political discussion and the idealism of the 2000 who joined the International Brigade that made their mark on British social, political and intellectual history in the 1930s rather than the future of Spain, for which few cared.

By 1936 Britain was not an unprosperous country. The economy had risen since the difficult days of 1929. With that prosperity had come a rise in the cost of living. Neville Chamberlain, who had cut income taxes in earlier years, raised taxes in 1936. This was simply 'tiller economics'. He claimed that the country was returning to prosperity.

With that relative prosperity – relative in the sense that some had and many more had not – had come a rise in the cost of living. But Britain was spending what it had, and, if it was on motor cars, according to the correspondent of the *Illustrated London News*, H. Thornton Rutter, it was spending it well:

> Motorists are receiving splendid value for their cash in the 1936 cars. . . . Take the new 14hp Wolseley as an example of high value for the price demanded. This is listed at £200 for the saloon and £235 for the de-luxe model. Both give the same road performance, and the difference in price is due to a sliding head. Triplex glass to all windows, instead of safety glass for the front screen only, a dual arm screen wiper in place of a single arm, chromium plated lamps replacing the black enamel finish, chromium plated front and rear bumpers . . . and chromium plated frame to bonnet louvres additionally provided. So who would not pay the extra £15 for the de luxe 'Fourteen' Wolseley, instead of saving that small amount and buying a car wanting in these necessary equipments?

There were now more than 2.5 million vehicles, including 400,000 vans and about 1.5 million private cars. By the 1990s there were more than 22 million private cars.

In 1936 there were about 20,000 miles of railways, a figure that had halved by the end of the century. Because of population growth and a more mobile society, however, there was not a similar decline in passenger levels. In 1936 around 800 million passengers travelled those 20,000 miles of tracks. By the 1990s the same numbers of people were travelling on half the lines.

The mining towns, the mill cities and the Welsh valleys did not always share in the prosperity that Chamberlain saw. There remained enormous poverty, and four specific areas – Tyneside, West Cumberland, Scotland and South Wales – were officially recognized as economically depressed in 1934. Even with a £2 million budget, there was no chance of helping these regions without attracting new industries to replace those worked out. The alternative was the national assistance payments, which were now in the hands of the national assistance boards.

The average family – mother, father and a couple of children – needed at least £6 a week to keep above the poverty line, but the average wage was not much more than £2 a week. The north–south divide was now demonstrated with a poignancy that may have moved people but did little to change their circumstances.

On 5 October 200 unemployed men began to march from Jarrow, where there was 68 per cent unemployment, to London, but when they reached London, Baldwin refused to meet the marchers. To his mind, the march could lead to civil war. The marchers held a rally in Hyde Park (organized by the Communist Party of Great Britain, which lost them the instant support of Labour politicians) and then went home. Plans would not help the people of Jarrow. The case for planning was fine in a large and wider society with plenty of natural resources, ideas, markets and, above all, money. The British economy had resources that, apart from manpower, were in decline, and the country seemed unable to replace old industries with new ones. Loading public money into the economy tended to stimulate those parts that were already prosperous or becoming so. The declining industries continued to decline. It was now that John Maynard Keynes published his *General Theory of Employment, Interest and Money*. This was the purse theory of supply and demand. If there is not enough demand for that which is produced, depression follows.

The answer to the problem was simply an extension of what he had long preached: interest rates should be cut to put more money into circulation, government money wealth should be spent on public works, and the obsession with a balanced budget should be abandoned. The notion of spending out of a depression did not work in every society. Roosevelt had more success in America than Baldwin or his successors would have in Britain, but even FDR was no magician. His strongest message came in January 1937 when he declaimed at his inauguration address: 'I see one third of a nation ill-housed, ill-clad, ill-nourished.'

But there was one good American idea floated successfully in England. In September 1936, Hollywood came to the United Kingdom when J. Arthur Rank opened the first British Hollywood-style studio at Pinewood in Buckinghamshire.

If anyone had money to spare, a thirty-seven-year-old businessman, who had previously worked in a fun fair, recognized a gap in the holiday market. Billy Butlin opened his first camp on the site of a sugar beet field near Skegness. If all a family had was pretend money, the latest board game from America was the safest way to spend it. The game Monopoly appeared in the shops.

Deaths
David Beatty, 1st Earl Beatty (Admiral)
Louis Blériot (French aviator)
G.K. Chesterton (writer)
George V
Alexander Glazunov (Russian composer)
Maxim Gorky (Russian writer)
A.E. Housman (poet)
Frank Hornby (inventor)
Rudyard Kipling (writer)
Federico García Lorca (Spanish writer)
Hiram Percy Maxim (US inventor)
Ivan Pavlov (Russian physiologist)
Luigi Pirandello (Italian writer)
Oswald Spengler (German writer)

1937

IN 1937 George VI was crowned king, Ramsay MacDonald died, Baldwin retired, Chamberlain became prime minister, Stalin's purges continued and eight of his generals were executed, the Japanese bombed Shanghai, the Germans bombed Guernica, the British government announced that it had plans to evacuate the capital in time of war and that air-raid shelters were to be built and Wallis Simpson became the Duchess of Windsor.

Baldwin's handling of the abdication meant that his image as a safe pair of hands was assured. It has been argued that Baldwin and Cosmo Lang, the Archbishop of Canterbury, had meant to get rid of Edward VIII all along. Baldwin's doubts about the prince's behaviour and his style were not his alone. George V had also wondered aloud about the suitability of his son to be king. Even the intelligence services watched the monarch and Mrs Simpson, who had had friends in the German embassy. Baldwin had said that the Cabinet would resign if the King went against their advice.

This was the background to Baldwin's mental and physical state in 1937. It was time for him to retire. Not enough is made of the utter weariness of a prime minister who was attempting to hold together a foreign policy threatened from Japan, India, Palestine, Germany, Russia, Spain and even America. Add to that the domestic difficulties over the economy and social change and the political in-fighting at Westminster. The safest of political hands might be wearied of their work.

By 1937 Baldwin was exhausted. He looked about him and decided that he had done almost everything that could have been done to prepare the nation for the war that he saw as inevitable. In February he delivered the Defence White Paper. Unilateral disarmament was firmly written in the logbook of failed policies. Baldwin now laid the guidelines for a new policy of deterrence and, as he told the House, ineffective 'deterrence is worse than useless'. For the first time, money would have to be borrowed to pay for national defence.

On 28 May 1937 Baldwin resigned and was succeeded by Neville Chamberlain, the son of the great radical of the late 1890s and early 1900s, Joseph Chamberlain, and the brother of Austen Chamberlain, who had shared the Nobel Peace Prize with Charles Dawes for putting together the Locarno Pact. Austen Chamberlain might, in fact, have been considered for higher office, but Baldwin more or less told him he was too decrepit. He died later this year.

Neville Chamberlain was now in his late sixties. At the beginning of the First World War he had been Lord Mayor of Birmingham and his only important government offices had been as Minister for Health in the 1920s and, for the six years before he became prime minister, Chancellor of the Exchequer. He was well acquainted with the state of the economy and the industrial and social influences on it.

Chamberlain was ordinary at a time when the country would have liked an extraordinary leader. He had no great grasp of foreign affairs, but he did understand Germany more than many give him credit. His reputation is that of appeaser, but it could be that he was simply aware that Britain was not yet ready for war. Nevertheless, RAF aircraft delivery rates were increasing, and those ship yards that could were working exclusively on military tonnage. This was to be the biggest naval programme since the Great War.

Chamberlain's Cabinet was still a National Government. Taking his place at the Treasury was the Home Secretary, Sir John Simon, one of the last long-serving Liberals, although he was certainly not in the radical mould of Lloyd George. Malcolm MacDonald, the son of Ramsay, was Dominion Secretary. Halifax became Lord President of the Council; he later become Foreign Secretary and believed that he should have been prime minister instead of Churchill at the beginning of the war. Anthony Eden was Foreign Secretary; Samuel Hoare was Home Secretary; Leslie Hore-Belisha (after whom the Belisha beacon was named) was Secretary for War; Viscount Swinton was the Air Secretary; and Sir Alfred Duff Cooper was the First Lord of the Admiralty. Only Halifax and Eden had the experience and capabilities that Britain needed in 1937.

Eden was the only member of the government to be trusted by the Foreign Office. Chamberlain, assisted by Sir Horace Wilson, one of his most trusted advisers, probably understood what was going on abroad even if he knew less of what Britain should do about it. The internecine warfare in Whitehall was unhelpful.

Sir Robert Vansittart, the senior civil servant at the Foreign Office, practised the most arrogant form of Whitehall warfare. His position was clear: German ambitions must be resisted and loudly. So he dropped hints to well-known rousers, including Churchill, and to the editors in Fleet Street and stirred up the debate on what Britain should do about Hitler's Nazis. Whatever spinning and leaking was going on, only Chamberlain and his innermost Cabinet carried the responsibility for going to war, and for the moment at least they had other matters before them.

In 1937 the Irish Free State, which had been created in 1921, became Eire. It was still a member of the Commonwealth and kept that name until 1949, when it became the Republic of Ireland. In 1937 the British government was in the hands of the Irish leader, Eamon de Valera. Britain gave British citizenship to all Irish, and Britain's three naval bases in Eire were given to the Irish government. This was seen was not only as a concession too far but as strategic folly, for what would happen to those bases if Britain went to war with Germany? For the British Cabinet there was a breathing space in Anglo-Irish relations, and although the Irish had not given up the outstanding issue – the reunification of the whole of the island of Ireland – Republican terrorism was stilled, for the moment.

Elsewhere Chamberlain was faced with an even longer story of internal security that was seemingly insoluble. The pogroms against Jews in the Soviet Union and Germany were leading to accelerating migration to Palestine. The government appointed a royal commission, chaired by Lord Peel, to decide the future of Palestine, over which Britain still held a mandate. In July a White Paper recommended that two-thirds of Palestine should become an Arab country and one-third should be a Jewish homeland. The sensitive question of the Holy Cities of Nazareth, Bethlehem and Jerusalem would be resolved by their being administered by Britain.

In August the World Zionist Congress rejected the British plan, but an ordinance restricted Jewish immigration into Palestine. The great exodus had begun in Europe not, as we know, bound to an ordinance from the British authorities in Palestine. By 1939 the Balfour declaration had been abandoned, but the Zionist cause had not.

At home, ministers put their minds to education, industrial reform and social services – each overshadowed by the prospect of war.

In April the National Defence Contribution Tax was introduced. It was supposed to be revenue taken exclusively from arms manufacturers, but it was virtually unworkable and had to be abandoned. In its place a 5 per cent profits tax would be raised. The money to pay for Britain's defences was supposed to be either in place or in the pipelines of the Treasury.

Gradually, the consensus in the House of Commons necessary to maintain the rearmament programme was being reached. The Labour Party found it difficult to vote for increased defence spending but agreed to abstain rather than vote against, but enough Labour MPs opposed abstention for newspapers to give the impression that the party itself opposed rearmament. Chamberlain's personal dilemma was that although he saw the logic of rearmament he saw there were too many expensive domestic issues that were still unresolved.

This is no more than a clue to Chamberlain's approach to Hitler during these two crucial years in European history. Chamberlain believed that Germany could be talked out of war. He was not hampered by the political philosophy of his predecessors and peers and could accept that Germany was no longer the downtrodden, vanquished country of 1918. He saw as simple logic the fact that Germany would, if left alone, become the controlling power in eastern Europe, given the practical politics of Europe and the undeniable power of Nazism. In truth, Chamberlain's greatest crime was that he appeared incapable of thinking beyond day-to-day politics and therefore came up with day-to-day solutions to problems. He had no vision.

A politician with greater insight died in 1937. On 10 November the Commons gathered to pay homage to the illegitimate son of a Scottish farm worker. Ramsay MacDonald was dead. The current Labour leader, Clement Attlee, spoke of MacDonald's campaign for socialism. The prime minister praised his skill in foreign affairs. The truth was that MacDonald, one of the persistent architects of the twentieth-century Labour Party and Britain's first Labour prime minister, was a discarded figure at Westminster. His own party detested him.

This was a period of cultural and social achievements. There were, for example, now more than 800 millionaires in Britain. A general increase in wealth meant that 3.35 million people were now paying tax, which was 50,000 more than the previous year and it included the fact that 250,000 people had been put into a bracket where they did not have to pay tax at all. Some of the lost revenue was made up in the £88 million gathered by the Treasury in death duties.

If not everyone was wealthy enough to be a big tipper at the booming number of city restaurants, they could leave the latest coin under the plate. In March 1937 was introduced the twelve-sided threepenny 'bit'.

In the theatres, publishing houses and galleries artists and writers were deeply moved by the war in Spain. In Paris Picasso showed his damning protest of the German bombing of the Basque capital, *Guernica*. George Orwell, deeply angry over the conditions of the unemployed and poor, published *The Road to Wigan Pier*. He did not sit by to read the reviews but was fighting in the Spanish Civil War. Ernest Hemingway was sending despatches from Madrid to an American news agency, and Arthur Koestler, working as the *News Chronicle* correspondent, was captured by Franco's troops, sentenced to death but survived.

The most rapturous applause in London in 1937 was for an eighteen-year-old English girl, Peggy Hookham. She made her debut in *Giselle* at Sadler's Wells and promised and had the brightest future in English ballet. Miss Hookham, in need of a more artistic name, became known as Margot Fonteyn.

In Britain, there was a typhoid epidemic, and a new emergency telephone number, one that would last the century: 999.

Deaths

Sir James Barrie (writer)
Sir Austen Chamberlain (politician)
Baron Pierre de Coubertin (French sportsman)
Amelia Earhart (US aviator)
George Gershwin (US composer)
Jean Harlow (US actress)
H.P. Lovecraft (US writer)
Erich Ludendorff (German politician)
James Ramsay MacDonald (politician)
Guglielmo Marconi (Italian inventor)
Tomáš Masaryk (Czech politician)
Maurice Ravel (French composer)
John D. Rockefeller (US industrialist and philanthropist)
Ernest Rutherford, 1st Baron Rutherford (physicist)
Bessie Smith (US singer)
Philip Snowden, 1st Viscount Snowden (politician)
Edith Wharton (US writer)

1938

ON 30 SEPTEMBER Neville Chamberlain returned to Heston Aerodrome from Munich, waving a piece of paper and telling the people of Britain: 'I believe it is peace for our time.' The next day the Germans marched unopposed into Czechoslovakia. On 9 November came Kristallnacht, Crystal Night, when German storm troopers attacked German Jews, beating and killing them. They burned down their synagogues and smashed and looted their homes and shops. Berliners stood by, applauding the beatings and murders. It was reported that Hermann Goering, on being told that there was not enough glass in Germany to repair the damage, said they should have broken less glass and killed more Jews.

It is easy to understand why, early in 1938, Neville Chamberlain was seen as an appeaser. But from such actions at some periods, myths emerge. Was Chamberlain an appeaser and did his Foreign Secretary, Anthony Eden, resign because he was? We might remember that Hitler was not the single concern of the British government in 1938. Italy and Spain were important factors in government considerations. It is also worth bearing in mind that in 1938 the German army was weak. Finally, it must be remembered that Russia had not yet signed the pact with Germany that was to create uncertainty in British minds.

If we understand these points we can begin to see that the question of whether Chamberlain was an appeaser is complex, although the historically accepted answer that he was, appears to stand.

Was Munich appeasement? On the face of it, yes, of course it was. But was it a desperate stalling for time? Had Chamberlain at last come to see that war was inevitable but believed that more pieces of paper would buy time in which to reverse the slow-down orders to the British weapons industry, which would be able to gear up for the war to come?

Eden did not resign, as sometimes claimed, because he believed Chamberlain had not stood up to Hitler. In fact, Eden was effectively fired by Chamberlain, who put him in a position where he had to jump before he was pushed. Eden disagreed with Chamberlain over the importance of Italy's intervention on Franco's side in the Spanish Civil War. Eden had never shown much regard for the Italians, thinking they were opportunists. Nevertheless, the Italians were the only people capable of dissuading the Germans from going into Austria, and being nice to the Italians in 1937 might just have prevented that. Eden was wrong from the start. He did go some way towards reaching agreement with Mussolini, but an agreement not to get involved in the Spanish Civil War was always going to be ignored by the Italians. None of this eased Eden's diplomatic pique.

In the early months of 1938 Chamberlain was still trying to bring Italy into the equation as an ally against Hitler's expansionism. Eden insisted that Italy should be pushed to withdraw troops from Spain. Had the discussions with Italy over Austria started the previous summer, something might have come of them, but now it was too late. Eden would not let go, however, believing that Mussolini really intended to support Hitler over Austria in return for Hitler supporting Italian ambitions in the Mediterranean countries. Chamberlain demanded that Anglo-Italian talks be opened as soon as possible, but he must have known that this would force Eden to resign, thus effectively sacking him, especially when the prime minister had overwhelming Cabinet support. Eden went and was replaced by Lord Halifax, the gaunt figure we often see in newsreels with Chamberlain in the 1938–9 version of the shuttle diplomacy to avert war. They failed – but then, Eden would have failed, too.

By 1938, no matter what Chamberlain's ambitions may have been, Britain was having to prepare for the worst – and not simply by building more ships, planes and tanks. Aircraft design had advanced so far that for the first time in their history everyone on these islands would be vulnerable to war. In continental Europe people were used to being criss-crossed by armies. In Britain, with a few exceptions during the First World War, the British had not been touched in their homes by warfare. All this was about to change, for the bomber did not distinguish between the military and its civilians.

So great was the air threat that an Act of parliament had already set up air-raid precautions. In January 1938 *The Times* ran a specially commissioned and detailed inquiry into, as its main headline declared, 'Defence Against the Bomber'. Very sensibly, the investigation had started in Germany. The first day of the report was rather blunt.

> The problem is immense but its elements are simple. Lord Baldwin declared some time ago that the frontier of Britain now lay on the Rhine. He said this to prepare the country for a huge armaments programme. No one has yet thought of preparing the country for the even bigger plan of civil defence by declaring that our first line of defence is the Thames. Yet that is the fact. No minister has really taken the public into his confidence over the question of air-raid precautions. The House of Commons debates have been scrappy and ill-informed. . . . The public who have noticed only the sensational superficialities of newspapers, have the most fantastic ideas about the nature of aerial warfare, the dangers of gas, and the futility of resistance. Misleading analogies have been drawn from the wars in China and Spain. As a result there has been general apathy and a lack of critical, informed interest.

Could Britain be completely taken over by the prospects of war? In January 1938 the vision of children being issued with gas masks was sinister enough, but there were distractions. A new image appeared for the first time in January of that year – seven images, in fact, Happy, Sleepy, Bashful, Sneezy, Grumpy, Dopey and Doc – when Walt Disney's first full-length cartoon, *Snow White and the Seven Dwarfs*, arrived in February.

Edwin Lutyens produced designs for a National Theatre and in the same year was elected president of the Royal Academy. In May the Marquess of Bute, who owned great tracts of land in the capital of Wales, completed the biggest single property deal ever in Britain when he sold half the City of Cardiff for £20 million. The following year, the Duke of Norfolk followed Bute's example and sold Littlehampton, which had been in the family of the Earl Marshal of England for centuries, as part of the Norfolk estates controlled from the family seat at Arundel in West Sussex.

A spectacular piece of theatre took place in the United States on Halloween. CBS radio broadcast a dramatization of H.G. Wells's novel *The War of the Worlds*. It is doubtful that any piece of theatre has had such an impact on real life, when the young actor, Orson Welles, announced into the microphone: 'Ladies and gentlemen, I have a grave announcement to make . . . Strange beings who landed in New Jersey tonight are the vanguard of an invading army from Mars.' New York panicked. Thousands of listeners rushed into the streets, many of them leaping into their cars to drive out of the city to escape the Martians. This overreaction might have been the power of radio and the adaptation as well as of Welles's performance. It might, too, have reflected an international unease over what was going on in Europe that had spread – perhaps subconsciously – as far as the United States.

The BBC was broadcasting more weighty entertainment when it transmitted the first television performance of an opera. The fact that it was Richard Wagner's *Tristan und Isolde* was coincidental to the international tension caused by Germany's actions in Europe.

Deaths
Mustafa Kemal Atatürk (Turkish politician)
Nikolai Bukharin (Russian politician)
Fyodor Chaliapin (Russian bass)
Gabriele d'Annunzio (Italian writer)
Max Factor (US make-up expert)
Ödön von Horváth (German writer)
Edmund Husserl (German philosopher)
James Johnson (US writer)
Sir Henry John Newbolt (writer)
Joe 'King' Oliver (US jazz musician)
Konstantin Stanislavsky (Russian actor)
Thomas Wolfe (US writer)

1939

The Second World War started in September. By late autumn Britain had landed more than 150,000 troops in France. Within two months 200,000 tonnes of British shipping had gone down, including an aircraft carrier, HMS *Courageous*, and the battleship, *The Royal Oak*. Thousands of sailors were lost with their ships. By the end of the year, the pride of the German high seas fleet, the pocket battleship *Graf Spee*, had been scuttled in the River Plate. Germany and Russia had invaded Poland.

That is how the Second World War of the twentieth century began. It is not the purpose of this book to record the history of the Second World War; that has been done elsewhere and in the space that it demands. Instead there is a diary of the war years (pages 480–6), which shows the major events of the war and is, for those who find it difficult to follow the strategic and military implications of that period, probably more valuable.

The world of social reform, poverty, business, education and industrial relations did not stop for the war, and it would be a mistake to believe the popular image that everyone in Britain was pulling together against Hitler. There were still discontent, industrial disputes, crime and some evidence that by no means everyone thought the war justified.

In Europe there was fighting from the Atlantic to the Urals. Even neutral Switzerland became involved as a clandestine conduit for agents, escapees and temporary lodgings for millions of dollars' worth of treasures, bonds and cash.

In Asia the war extended from the Bosporus to the subcontinent deep into southeast Asia, and up into China and across to Japan. Australasia sent troops and ships and aircraft to all the theatres of war. The Pacific Islands became terrible battlegrounds, and Pearl Harbor's greatest fame was that it was the Japanese target that brought America into the war.

Canadian troops were the first from the dominions to be sent to Europe. The United States itself entered the war at a late stage but made the difference between defeat and survival, by making massive war loans to the European allies long before it joined the confrontation.

Later in the conflict, Nazis would escape to South America. After the sinking of the *Graf Spee* in the River Plate there was no question that the 'Sixth' Continent was more than a spectator.

In Britain the preparations for war were poorly managed. Moreover, not all Cabinet members understood the depth of the crisis nor the fears of those whom Britain had promised to defend. Britain had had an understanding with France since the signing of the Entente Cordiale in 1904. That agreement had led, more by accident than design, to Britain and France standing shoulder to shoulder in 1914 against Wilhelm II's Germany. France expected similar support in 1939. Chamberlain was telling his Cabinet that British policy was to prevent France from being drawn into a war with Germany because Britain did not want to be involved in that same war. What would happen if France, having given up on any hope of British support, came to an arrangement with Germany? The result would be that Germany's frontier with Britain would have moved to the Channel coast and the British Isles would be so much more vulnerable. Halifax and Chamberlain told the French that Britain would provide two divisions to reinforce France but that it was up to the French to hold the whole of the Western Front without any more aid from Britain.

It was only in 1939 that British policy started to change and that Chamberlain could no longer hide from his Cabinet the concerns of France, the real threats of war and the depths to which Britain would be involved. Yet Sir John Simon, the Chancellor, supported by Chamberlain, still opposed huge increases in the budget for the army. In late February Lord Halifax began to move away from the Chamberlain–Simon position. The prime minister and the Chancellor were right to emphasize the need for air defence – subsequent events endorsed their position – but they were not right to believe that it should be carried out to the detriment of spending on the army.

The Cabinet began to see the truer picture and it nodded through a proposal to increase the size of the British Expeditionary Force and the Territorial Army. But Sir John Simon and Neville Chamberlain could still restrict the amount of money to be spent on the essential updating of the army – even as late as February 1939.

On 14 February the Germans had launched the battleship, *Bismarck*. The Home Office now believed that war was so likely that air-raid shelters, which had been developed under the guidance of Sir John Anderson (later 1st Viscount Waverley) and which became known as Anderson shelters, were to be delivered to thousands of homes throughout London.

Intelligence reports suggested that Hitler was about to enter Prague and intended to invade Poland. The march into Prague meant that Britain had to introduce conscription – as it stood, the army was undermanned. Chamberlain opposed conscription, even though he knew that war would involve millions of men. He was frightened of the trade unions and believed that the TUC might call out its workers from the munitions factories, as had happened in the First World War. The response was to double the size of the Territorial Army. But again, here is an example of politics on paper being of more value than the practical solution to an overwhelming problem. It would take at least twelve months to train a part-time soldier. Even then he would not be much good unless called up on a full-time basis. Moreover, the training process itself would divert scarce resources, including trained men, from the regular army. It was clear Cabinet's decision was nonsensical, a fact understood by both the German and the French.

By early September 1939 the British army was preparing to go to war with an Expeditionary Force that would not have been equipped to fight the previous war. At a time when the government was announcing plans to evacuate 2.5 million children, it was considering sending to two fronts an army that had none of the guns that had been ordered, a carpark full of tanks instead of the more than 1600 that were scheduled, and a transport system that, as Montgomery wrote, consisted of civilian vans and lorries.

Chamberlain's days were numbered, but there were still practical decisions to be taken. Imperial Airways (the forerunner of BOAC and, in turn, British Airways) shut down all passenger bookings. Chamberlain went to France for talks, but before he had decided the true value of those discussions, HMS *Courageous* was sunk with the loss of 500 sailors. Chamberlain needed a new Cabinet, and it had to be bipartisan.

The Labour and Liberal groups refused to join, although they promised that they would not stand in the way of government decisions. Eden was brought back as Secretary of State for the Dominions, but he was not in the Cabinet. The spectacular appointment was that of Churchill, who had, since resigning from Baldwin's Cabinet, been in the political wilderness. Chamberlain made him First Lord of the Admiralty, the post he had held in 1914.

New government departments were set up to regulate and administer the dissemination of information and news, to control food supplies and to oversee national service. There would also be a Department of Economic Warfare.

Conscription had started for 250,000 men over the age of twenty. If this seems a small number, we have to remember that although the procedures for the call-up were in place, the difficulties of handling and processing even 250,000 new and untrained recruits were enormous.

Butter and bacon were rationed in November 1939 and petrol prices were increased. In December, sugar and meat were rationed. The trades unions were called into government departments and unwritten guidelines discussed. By December 1939 the government had its first industrial dispute: women munitions workers were demanding equal pay with men.

The government had other concerns, too. In February Britain recognized the government of General Franco, who entered Madrid in March. The United States also recognized Franco's government. The Spanish Civil War was at a standstill, and the Republicans, whom so many idealists had supported, were finished. The war would be ended on All Fools' Day 1939.

A war of another kind was going on in Britain in 1939. The IRA began a bombing campaign in London, Manchester and Birmingham, and the Central Electricity control room in south London was bombed. The IRA issued an order that all Irishmen should join in the battle against Britain and that British armies should leave Ireland. IRA suspects were arrested, and in July new anti-terrorism legislation was introduced into the Commons. Such was the realistic prospect of an increased bombing campaign that the public was banned from visiting the House of Commons gallery and passengers were not allowed to carry suitcases on London buses. The government in Eire began a series of measures that were supposed to restrict the movements and the activities of the IRA, and opposition to British measures against the IRA waned when an IRA bomb killed five people and injured fifty others in Coventry's main street, Broadgate, in the summer.

Arrangements were also being made for a new Palestinian state to be established by 1949.

In America a greater sensation than the war was seen in the cinema, where the film *Stagecoach* opened in March; its cowboy star was John Wayne. In June 1939, with war not yet declared, the World Fair opened in New York, followed in August by *The Wizard of Oz*, making seventeen-year-old Judy Garland an instant star. While they were in a downtown recording studio, Glen Miller's Band recorded *In the Mood*.

In April the Australians elected a forty-four-year-old lawyer, Robert Menzies, as prime minister. He would dominate Australian politics for more than a quarter of a century and become known Pig Iron Bob.

In January Al Capone was released from prison on health grounds. King Farouk was proclaimed Caliph in Cairo, and more than 30,000 Chileans were killed when a single earthquake destroyed the major cities of Chillan and Concepción.

Deaths

E.M. Dell (writer)
Havelock Ellis (writer)
Douglas Fairbanks (US actor)
Anthony Fokker (US aircraft designer)
Ford Madox Ford (writer)

Sigmund Freud (Austrian psychiatrist)
Zane Grey (US writer)
W.B. Yeats (Irish writer)

CHAPTER FIVE

THE IRON CURTAIN FALLS 1940–1949

1940

BRITAIN BEGAN 1940 in a freezing northerly wind. For the first time in more than half a century the Thames froze, and for the first time since 1918 ration books, with their coupons, were kept by every household. People registered with a shop for general groceries and with their local butcher for meat. The traders passed on to the Food Office a list of the supplies they expected to sell based on the registrations, and the Food Office lists were forwarded to the Ministry of Food.

The ration book became the most important single item in any home, and the system appeared to work. Even the royal family was known to keep strictly to the rules, as many visitors to Buckingham Palace later testified. Those with money, especially in the countryside, could always find extras, of course, and in some cases, quite a lot extra.

Curiously, rationing went some way to improving the nation's health. In the late 1930s probably as much as a third of the population were living on very basic and often unhealthy food. The rationing programme set nourishing diets with whatever might be available. Consequently, it was possible for the whole nation and not just two-thirds of it to be better fed in wartime than in the previous decade of peace.

The IRA campaign that had started in January 1939 continued. In February 1940 two Irish terrorists were hanged in Birmingham. The security problems worsened because internment camps had to be arranged for Germans too. The fear of insurgents was real enough, and a nationwide poster campaign began with the theme, 'Careless talk costs lives'. A lot of the posters were amusing – in one, for example, Hitler was shown sitting on a bus behind two nattering ladies with the caption 'You never know who's listening!' Another, perhaps more telling, showed a ship torpedoed by a U-boat. The caption read: 'A few careless words may end in this.' The flagship of the British merchant fleet was the new liner, the *Queen Elizabeth*, which steamed at full speed across the Atlantic into an anchorage by New York.

★

By the beginning of May Neville Chamberlain was thoroughly disliked and commanded little respect. On 8 May, after a British setback in Norway, he was forced to go to the Commons for a vote of confidence, which he lost; even some of his own colleagues voted against him or abstained.

There was a desperate need for a coalition, but Labour leaders refused to serve under Chamberlain nor under the man who expected to be prime minister, the Foreign Secretary, Lord Halifax. As Baldwin had predicted, Churchill was the obvious wartime leader.

The sight of Churchill was enough to inspire the public, but not all his political colleagues thought so highly of him. In June 1940 his wife, Clementine, decided that he should know and wrote to him on Sunday, 23 June. At first she could not bring herself to let him see what she had written but four days later sent him a new version of her letter:

> My Darling,
> I hope you will forgive me if I tell you something that I feel you ought to know. One of the men in your entourage (a devoted friend) has been to me & told me that there is a danger of your being generally disliked by your colleagues & subordinates because of your rough, sarcastic & overbearing manner – It seems your Private Secretaries have agreed to behave like school boys & 'take what's coming to them' & then escape out of your presence shrugging their shoulders – Higher up if an idea is suggested (say at a conference) you are supposed to be so contemptuous that presently no ideas, good or bad, will be forthcoming. I was astonished & upset because in all these years I have been accustomed to all those who have worked with & under you, loving you – I said this & I was told 'No doubt it's the strain' –
>
> My Darling, Winston – I must confess that I have noticed a deterioration in your manner; & you are not so kind as you used to be.
>
> It is for you to give the Orders & if they are bungled – except for the king, the Archbishop of Canterbury & the Speaker you can sack anyone & everyone – Therefore with this terrific power you must combine urbanity, kindness and if possible Olympic calm. You used to quote: 'on ne regne sur les ames que par le calme' – I cannot bear that those who serve the Country and yourself should not love as well as admire and respect you – besides you won't get the best results by irascibility and rudeness. They *will* breed either dislike or a slave mentality – (Rebellion in War time being out of the question!).
>
> Please forgive your loving devoted & watchful
>
> Clemmie

In the edited version of *The Personal Letters of Winston & Clementine Churchill*[1] Mary Soames says that no answer exists to this letter. 'But Winston surely took it to heart.'

---

1 Mary Soames (ed.), *Speaking for Themselves*, Doubleday (1998).

In the Palace of Westminster Churchill was sometimes seen as a self-centred, medal- and money-seeking individual. Even in his finest hours he still had to suffer the pettiness of political enemies who could never forgive.

As even the laziest student of 1940 knows, these were dark days. The British Expeditionary Force was pushed back to Dunkirk by the end of May, and Operation Dynamo was mounted to evacuate Dunkirk. Here was a major defeat turned into a national triumph. This was a nation that was proud of the little ships that had carried out the operation and was relieved to get back its soldiers – and doubly relieved that the Germans were not following them. For the moment the land battle in Europe was over for the British: the Germans would be in Paris by 14 June and Chamberlain would be proved right that all that stood between Britain and capitulation was the Royal Air Force and the Royal Navy, fighting the remorseless Battle of the Atlantic.

The Battle of Britain was about to start. The blitz was launched on London in September 1940, and Churchill would be ready to paraphrase another speech that reminded the nation that 'never in the field of human conflict was so much owed by so many to so few'.

The effects of the bombing were devastating. There was not a community in the United Kingdom that did not feel vulnerable. On 13 September 1940 even Buckingham Palace took a direct hit. The Queen remarked: 'I'm glad . . . It makes me feel I can look the East End [of London] in the face.'

Oblivious to the darker reasons of war and the wretched futures of so many in Europe were the children in Britain, especially those in the capital, who were being moved out. They were the evacuees. In the autumn of 1939 a group had left London for the countryside. Hilda Marchant recorded the moment in *Women and Children Last*:[2]

> I watched the schoolteachers calling out their names and tying luggage labels in their coats, checking their parcels to see there were warm and clean clothes. On the gates of the school there were two fat policemen. They were letting the children through but gently asking the parents not to come farther. They might disturb the children . . . every now and then the policeman would call out a child's name and a mother who had forgotten a bar of chocolate or a toothbrush had a last chance to tell a child to be good, to write and to straighten her hat . . . On one side of Gray's Inn Road this ragged crocodile moved towards the tube station. On the other, were mothers who were waving and running along to see the last of their children. The police had asked them not to follow, but they could not resist. The children scrambled down the tube.

2 Victor Gollancz (1941).

Britain was now caught in what would be the most horrifying demonstration of military power and hatred that the world had ever seen.

A hatred of a different kind wafted through the Kremlin. Throughout the 1930s Stalin had carried out purges of his real and potential political enemies, and men like Zinoviev, Bukharin and Kamenev were executed. Thousands were sent to the gulags and never seen again. Perhaps the most spectacular execution was carried out on the former army commander, Leon Trotsky, whose name had come to be applied to all opponents of Stalin – Trotskyites. Stalin had accused him and exiled him further and further from the seats of power. On 21 August 1940 Trotsky, still a Bolshevik, was assassinated in Mexico City when Ramon Mercader stabbed him with an ice pick.

There were cheerful moments, however, especially in the early days of the war. Walt Disney's feature-length cartoons *Pinocchio* and *Fantasia* were released in 1940, and Joan Fontaine appeared in Alfred Hitchcock's *Rebecca*. Charlie Chaplin's film *The Great Dictator* may have been a parody, but its message that nations should live together in peace seemed out of date by 1940. More romantic was Katharine Hepburn's appearance in *The Philadelphia Story*.

Two novels were the highlights of the literary year: Ernest Hemingway's story of the Spanish Civil War, *For Whom the Bell Tolls*, and Graham Greene's novel *The Power and the Glory*.

The young Princess Elizabeth made her first broadcast to the nation. Also broadcast, on 9 November, was the news of the death of Neville Chamberlain, who died from cancer at the age of seventy-one. Old animosities were temporarily set aside.

Deaths
Sir John Buchan, 1st Baron Tweedsmuir (writer)
Mrs Patrick Campbell (actress)
Neville Chamberlain (politician)
Walter P. Chrysler (US manufacturer)
Herbert Albert Laurens Fisher (historian and educationist)
F. Scott Fitzgerald (US writer)
Marcus Garvey (Jamaican nationalist)
Eric Gill (artist)
Harold Harmsworth, 1st Viscount Rothermere (publisher)
Paul Klee (Swiss artist)
George Lansbury (politician)
Sir J.J. Thomson (physicist)
Leon Trotsky (Russian communist leader)

1941

THE SECOND WORLD WAR proved that Britain was no longer an island. German bombers brought the war to civilians, and all the peoples of these islands were caught in the crossfire of war. Never before had they been deliberate targets.

On the night of Saturday, 10 May, 550 German aircraft flew over London. When they were gone 1400 Londoners were dead and 5000 homes had been destroyed. The Chamber of the House of Commons had been destroyed and a quarter of a million books had been destroyed in the British Museum. More than 2000 fires were still burning when dawn broke. This had been the biggest single air raid in nine months of the blitz. By its end in May 1941 20,000 Londoners had been killed and more than that number injured.

Feelings against the Germans was never as strongly 'anti' as might have been thought, however. Those who prosecuted the war in Whitehall had views that ranged between astonishing extremes. According to the late Jock Colville,[3] he was dining with Churchill, de Gaulle and Duncan Sandys one evening in March:

> We talked of Germany and the Germans. De Gaulle said that the important thing for people living in an occupied territory was to remain aloof and superior. The Germans knew that they were inferior beings and were susceptible on the point. . . . Duncan Sandys was bloodthirsty. He wanted to destroy Germany by laying the country to waste and burning towns and factories, so that for years the German people might be occupied in reconstruction. He wanted to destroy their books and libraries so that an illiterate generation might grow up. . . . The P.M. said he was in no way moved by Duncan's words. He did not believe in pariah nations, and he saw no alternative to the acceptance of Germany as part of the family of Europe. In the event of an invasion he would not even approve of the civil population murdering the Germans quartered on them. Still less would he condone atrocities against the German civil population if we were in a position to commit them.

Churchill's public mood was to cajole and encourage, but while he was telling the nation that the British would 'not fail mankind at this turning point in our fortunes', Rommel's Africa Korps was landing in Tripoli.

The age-old task of the propagandist in wartime was now desperately needed in Britain. In April 1941 the Air Minister was sent a memorandum by one of his officials that went some way to explaining why, in this second year of the war, civilians were sceptical about the work of the Ministry of Information.

> I believe the basis of the trouble to be the old 'Service' attitude of mind, founded on memory of when armies conducted campaigns out of England,

3 John Colville, *Fringes of Power*, Hodder and Stoughton (1985).

> independent of home control, with slow communications between the field of warfare and the British public, and in a spirit which said that the civilian's job was to ask no questions, to pay his taxes in order to keep up the Armed Forces, to take off his hat when the Colours marched past, and generally to regard himself as a necessary but unfortunate adjunct to the glories of military life.

Another official publication, *British Life and Thought*, tried to explain just who the British were in 1941:

> Events have moved fast in the last two years and history is being written in letters of blood and fire. What has been the effect on the Englishman of these events? Exactly what anyone who knew him and understood him would have predicted . . . His reluctance to think the worst of men, his faith in human nature and in the emergence of the better side of that nature gave him a hope against hope which remained with him until the last moment. Yet the same tenacity for which he thought was right, the same fierce resentment against what he thought was bullying, the same savage resistance to cruelty – all these things lay deep in his nature as they have always done throughout his long history.

It was now recognized in Whitehall that propaganda had to contend with the justice of the cause and not simply the concept that the British were right because, well, they were British. A secret Cabinet paper indicated how Government was thinking:

> Propaganda should emphasize clearly: (a) what we are seeking to defeat. (b) what we are seeking to preserve and create . . . The question is not whether the old order shall prevail over the new, but whether the new order should be based on the Christian Ethic, the scientific spirit, and the rule of law, upon which Western civilization has been chiefly built. Propaganda should therefore be directed towards representing every social and economic upheaval which war involves not as an inconvenience but as an opportunity.

Churchill was aware of the need to use public images to win wide support for the war. The greater need was to give the nation hope, and Churchill believed that hope had to come from the other side of the Atlantic. But, in the spring of 1941, there was increased tension between the United States and Britain. Britain needed ships; the United States had ships to spare. So the Americans gave Britain fifty destroyers, but in return for the destroyers, Britain had to give the Americans ninety-nine-year leases on bases in the West Indies. Worse, the destroyers were obsolete. Colville remembered:.

> The P.M. met Lord Moyne and Cranbourne, Herschel Johnson and Winant, the new US ambassador, in the Cabinet Room at Number Ten, to discuss the vexed

problem of the American bases in the West Indies . . . the West Indian Colonies themselves, the oldest of the Crown, are resentful and their feelings are shared by many people here in view of the conditions which the Americans have demanded and which amount to capitulations. Both sides are haggling and ill-feeling has arisen. . . . The Colonial Office are frightened that in the heat of conflict we shall cede much that will afterwards be most regrettable . . . But the P.M. is ill-satisfied with the point of view expressed by his colleagues. He believes that the safety of the state is at stake, that America in providing us with credits will enable us to win the war which we could not otherwise do, and that we cannot afford to risk the major issue in order to maintain our pride and to preserve the dignity of a few small islands. I think this view is statesmanlike, but America, if she persists, is going to arouse a lot of bitterness in England and set back the cause of Anglo-American unity.

On 7 December 1941 Japanese aircraft attacked Pearl Harbor. As Churchill later reflected: 'So we had won after all!' America was about to join the war. There is every evidence that until that point Churchill believed that it was entirely possible that Hitler would succeed. He was much cheered by Pearl Harbor but not by the news three days later that the Japanese had attacked the British naval flotilla in southeast Asia and HMS *Prince of Wales* and the *Repulse* had been lost.

In January Amy Johnson, the most celebrated female aviator of her day, crashed into the Thames estuary while ferrying aircraft for the RAF and was killed, but on the whole, the British were happier to be diverted from the news of disasters at the Front and at sea.

In 1941 they mourned the passing of James Joyce, whose great work, *Ulysses*, had been banned as obscene in Britain. Joyce had gone into exile from his native Dublin in 1904. His final, long – and lesser – work, *Finnegans Wake*, was yet to be popular. There was the beginnings of a notion that this might be the most obscure book ever written by a genius.

Virginia Woolf drowned herself in the River Ouse in Sussex. A writer less likely to feel out of control was the humorist, P.G. Wodehouse. There was a flurry in the British press and in Parliament when Wodehouse made a radio broadcast from Germany to America. He was in Germany because he had been put in jail in Upper Silesia, having been captured by the Germans at Le Touquet where he had a house. For the first twelve months or so of the war, he was kept in prison camps and even a mental home. His broadcasts from Radio Berlin were pure Wodehouse: 'How to be an Internee without Previous Training.'

Another humorist was hard at work but to a quite different audience. In July 1941 Noël Coward's comedy *Blithe Spirit* opened in London. In New York Walt Disney's *Dumbo* got its first showing. If *Dumbo* did not aim to boost morale in Britain, Tommy Handley's radio show *ITMA* – 'It's That Man Again' – did. It was a groundbreaking BBC comedy of one-liners and national catchphrases. The other favourite show was *Sincerely Yours*, a musical programme to boost morale in the forces. The generals did not much like it to begin with – they thought the way to boost morale was to put out a programme of stirring military marches – but the troops had other ideas, as did the nation, and the star of the show, Vera Lynn, quickly earned her nickname of the Forces' Sweetheart, and went on to sing her signature tune, 'We'll Meet Again', for another fifty years. She also sang the hit of the year, 'The White Cliffs of Dover'.

Deaths
Sherwood Anderson (US writer)
Robert Baden-Powell, 1st Baron Baden-Powell (soldier)
Henri Bergson (French philosopher)
Louis Brandeis (US jurist)
Louis Chevrolet (US manufacturer)
Sir Arthur Evans (archaeologist)
Sir James G. Frazer (anthropologist)
Sir Hamilton Harty (composer)
Amy Johnson (aviator)
James Joyce (Irish writer)
El Lissitzky (Russian artist)
Jelly Roll Morton (US musician)
Ignacy Jan Paderewski (Polish politician and pianist)
Sir Rabindranath Tagore (Indian writer)
Sir Hugh Walpole (writer)
Wilhelm II (former German Kaiser)
Virginia Woolf (writer)

1942

IN 1942 the English language got a new word, quisling. Vidkun Quisling had been leader of the Norwegian Fascist Party since 1933. When the threat of German invasion could no longer be ignored, Quisling did all he could to delay mobilization and then collaborated with the Germans. In February 1942 he was rewarded by the Germans, who made him prime minister. In 1945 he was rewarded by his countrymen, who tried him as a traitor. He was shot.

British thoughts were in Southeast Asia. Singapore had fallen to the Japanese, and the expectation was that the Japanese would move further south and west until they swept to the littoral states of the Indian Ocean. The news of Singapore came just two months after the sinking of the *Repulse* and the *Prince of Wales*. The effect on morale was predictable. For many, the loss of a ship creates a greater sense of loss than a setback in a land battle. The land battle moves on. A warship cannot be recovered. Furthermore, the vessel is not anonymous, and when a ship's company perishes, it is as if with the name of the vessel, each man is known to the nation.

By 1942 there was clearly a need to limit the amount of fuel that was being used. The threat to shipping from German U-boats meant that the price of each gallon of oil was being paid for in the lives of merchant seamen. The amount of fuel that could be brought into the United Kingdom was limited. Logically, the coal-mining industry should have been booming but was not. It was producing less coal and there were fewer miners because they were leaving the industry to earn more money in the munitions factories.

There was a sound case for fuel rationing, but public and political objections were strong enough for the government to postpone plans, especially when they were deliberately leaked.

The nation mourned every time a ship went down and a sailor on home leave was a hero in every bar – unless that sailor was a merchant seaman. These unarmed heroes manned the lifelines of Britain during the war, but such was the ignorance of the public that merchant seaman were often openly abused and refused the social – in some cases the official – privileges offered and taken by the officers and ratings of the Royal Navy. There was a general feeling that these seafarers, because they were not in the King's uniform, were somehow avoiding the war. Yet between 1939 and 1945 50,000 merchant seamen perished at sea.

In March 1942 one of the most famous and most controversial cartoons of the war appeared in the *Daily Mirror*. The efforts of the merchant seamen were not lost on Philip Zec, the political cartoonist, and when petrol prices were increased, he produced a cartoon of an exhausted and dying sailor clinging to a large hatchboard in a turbulent Atlantic. He used a government announcement for the caption: 'The price of petrol has been increased by 1d – official.'

This open criticism angered Churchill and most of his Cabinet. Ironically, it was the Home Secretary, Herbert Morrison, who was given the job of warning the *Mirror* that it would be shut down unless it toed the line. In the political debate, the cause of merchant seamen all but disappeared.

In the middle of the war other and often controversial issues would not be silenced. Education, social and welfare reform could not be left on a warm stove to simmer without fear of boiling, and one such problem was India. When Churchill became prime minister it was clear that there would be split opinions at Westminster and in Whitehall on the future of India. The Viceroy, the Marquess of Zetland, was in favour of reaching an understanding with the Indian Congress Party and its leader, Mahatma Gandhi, that once the war was finished India would get its independence.

Churchill, however, was opposed to Indian independence and appointed Leo Amery, who had been born at Gorakpur, as Secretary of State for India and Burma. Both men must have understood that, in the long term, independence was inevitable. Under the 1935 Government of India Act the subcontinent could have become a dominion in all but name by the time the Second World War began. Relations were not helped by the high-handed way in which Britain, without consulting Indian politicians, declared that India was at war with Germany.

Dominion status was promised, but the Indian National Congress dismissed this offer and asked Roosevelt to help them get independence. In August 1941 the Americans and British had signed the Atlantic Charter, which asserted the two countries' commitment to the rights of self-determination, self-government and free speech for all nations. The Indians believed that this concept of equality allowed them independence, but Churchill's view was that the Charter did not apply to members of the British Empire. Roosevelt continued to press the case of the Indians, but there is no evidence that Churchill responded.

Churchill's view was not supported by all his Cabinet. Ernest Bevin, who was Minister of Labour and National Service and who was to become one of the more far-seeing Foreign Secretaries of the century, believed that Churchill was being too unbending. Bevin's political leader, Clement Attlee, drafted a Cabinet memorandum that concluded that a representative of the British government with power to negotiate within wide limits should be sent to India.

Churchill was forced to agree when faced with threats of Cabinet resignation, which would have led to a politically impossible situation in wartime, especially so in the winter and early spring of 1942 when the continuing setbacks – against the Japanese in the Far East and the Germans in the Western Desert – not only shook confidence in the War Cabinet but in Churchill's own position as prime minister.

In March 1942, therefore, Sir Stafford Cripps, who had been ambassador to Moscow and was now Lord Privy Seal, was sent to India. The rejected offer of dominion status made in August 1940 was still, as far as Britain was concerned, on the table. The two future leaders of the subcontinent, Jawaharlal Nehru, the president of the Indian National Congress, and the Muslim leader, Muhammad Ali Jinnah, could see the sense in using that 1940 proposal as a basis for negotiation, but no negotiations or constitutional decisions could ever be made in India without the express agreement of Gandhi. Gandhi rejected the offer.

There was not much that Cripps could do, but President Roosevelt felt more could be done. Roosevelt was reflecting a large body of American public opinion that believed that Britain should get out of India. On 12 April he wrote to Churchill:

> The feeling is almost universally held that the deadlock has been caused by the unwillingness of the British government to concede to the Indians the right of self-government not withstanding the willingness of the Indians to entrust technical, military and naval defense control to the competent British authorities.

Churchill was angry. He had backed down as far as he was willing to go. He did not want Indian independence, yet he had agreed to promote dominion status by the end of the conflict. He had given the negotiations to Sir Stafford Cripps, a man whose views he probably loathed. Churchill's first instinct was to pen a long explanation of his position and his doubts to Roosevelt. This document was never sent, but the note that he did send and the inevitability of his views being represented in Washington, made it very clear that he not only disagreed with Roosevelt but resented the way in which the Americans were interfering in what Churchill believed to be British domestic policies.

Roosevelt backed off. Both men understood that nothing should come between the Anglo-American alliance against the Nazi Axis.

Yet the India question would not go away. In August the All-India Congress passed a resolution that Britain should leave India. It was followed by yet another campaign of civil disobedience, and Gandhi was arrested again. He would be kept under house arrest and would later go on hunger strike and later still be released, but for the moment Churchill and his Cabinet could get on with trying to contain the war.

In the summer of 1942, despite the political changes and the fact that Air Marshal Sir Arthur Harris had taken over bomber command and Montgomery now commanded the Eighth Army in the desert, there was no indication whatever that Churchill had got it right. At the beginning of July there was a sense that the political consensus was falling apart. The government knew the strength of feeling against its policies, the outcomes of which were largely beyond its control.

By the late autumn, however, the mood had changed. The Soviet armies had started to hit back against the Germans west of Stalingrad, and in November came the turning point in the Western Desert. On the night of 30 October Montgomery launched the Battle of El Alamein, and by 8 November Rommel had retreated into Libya. By 13 November the Allies had recaptured Tobruk.

The nation needed to rejoice and Churchill made sure they did. For the first time since 1940 church bells rang out.

Women were, as they had in the First World War, assuming more powers and responsibilities. But in addition to helping the war effort, they were faced with the despair of being apart from their children, who had been evacuated from the cities. Dr Shirley Summerskill, speaking in the Commons, saw very clearly the changing importance of her gender in everyday life and understood some of the agonies of women who were still being treated as if they mattered little. The subject of the debate was evacuation:

> I thought I would listen to the Minister on the radio because I was experiencing the same sensation as other mothers. I appreciated the attributes of the Minister,

> his lucidity, his fluency and so on, but what the Minister, and the whole Government, and the BBC, have not yet realized is that on the radio they are now in contact not with a few women in their homes, the rest of the listeners being men, but that as every day passes the vast audience which the radio reaches is more and more composed of women. As the men are going into the Services [and] are doing overtime at night we shall find that soon almost the whole audience will be women. Yet what do women hear every night? Do they hear a woman who understands the problems of the war? No. . . . the only thing that matters to me are my children running round me. They have my face, my hair, my eyes . . . and the minister comes and says in a statesman like way, 'The train will leave on Thursday. You are to be evacuated. The teachers are ready, get things packed, put the tags on.' . . . And then he goes on to explain that it is a question of dispersal, that if a bomb drops on a place in the country it will not kill so many people as if it drops in a crowded town.

It might seem remarkable, given the horrors of 1942, how much normal life was going on. People still insisted on taking their holidays although restrictions in travel made this increasingly difficult. Daily shopping became harder, partly because there were not as many shops, and home deliveries were far less common than before the war. But the nation still went to football matches and cricket matches, and they certainly went to the cinema. Some of what they watched was propaganda. The most popular film of the year was Noël Coward's *In Which We Serve*, which was based on the sinking of Lord Louis Mountbatten's ship HMS *Kelly*. Audiences broke into applause and cheering. The film of 1942 was *Casablanca*, with Humphrey Bogart and Ingrid Bergman. It was a war film that would remain a classic of any genre for the remainder of the century.

Any young lady dressing up for the cinema that year picked up a trick learned from shortages. It was impossible for all but the best connected to get stockings. So before a night out in 1942 bare legs were tinted with gravy browning and an ink line was drawn up the back to simulate a stocking seam – it was great . . . except when it rained!

Deaths

John Barrymore (US actor)
Franz Boas (US anthropologist)
Sir William Bragg (physicist)
George M. Cohan (US actor)
George, Duke of Kent
J.B.M. Hertzog (South African politician)
Walter Sickert (artist)

1943

LLOYD GEORGE, the 'man who won the Great War', was eighty years old in 1943. He would not live to see the end to this confrontation but for the moment, thousands of telegrams arrived to mark the great man's birthday.

This was the year the war tide turned. In January the Germans surrendered at Stalingrad, and the Allied leaders flew to Casablanca to discuss the next stage of advancing the war rather than defending against it. The only dull glow at the conference was General de Gaulle, who was put out because Roosevelt and Churchill had not kept him informed that the Allies were going to invade French North Africa. Moreover, de Gaulle believed himself to be the only French leader in the world, and he felt that this dignity had been compromised by having to meet General Henri Giraud, the commander-in-chief in French North Africa. Churchill later remarked that the greatest cross he had to bear during the war years was the Cross of Lorraine, the symbol of de Gaulle's Free French army.

Rommel was now in retreat in Tunisia; the Japanese had retreated from the Solomon Islands in the Pacific; Guy Gibson and the dambusters had flown Barnes Wallis's bouncing bombs against the Möhne and Eder dams; the battle for the Atlantic was now turning with the introduction of the defended convoy system; more merchant ships (except in March 1943) were getting through; the Allies landed in Italy. The Italians signed an armistice and executed a complete about-turn by declaring war on their erstwhile ally, Germany. The German battleship *Scharnhorst* was sunk, and the talk now was of the invasion of Europe.

By the end of 1943 D-Day was still eighteen months away, but so confident were the Allies that General Dwight D. Eisenhower was appointed to plan the Normandy invasion. The Deputy Supreme Allied commander would be Air Chief Marshal Sir Arthur Tedder, while Field Marshal Montgomery would command the army in the field.

Away from the war, a new name was becoming more widely known by the early 1940s, Sir William Henry Beveridge (1879–1963). Beveridge was a Scot, born in India, who had been educated at Charterhouse and Oxford. He had shown his authority as a planner and an economist in the earlier part of the century. He joined the Board of Trade in 1908 and became the director of the newly founded Labour Exchanges in 1909–16. It was then that he published a memorable report, simply entitled *Unemployment*.

After the First World War Beveridge retreated to the relative safety of academic life. He was director of the London School of Economics (LSE) until 1937, when he moved to Oxford as Master of University College, a lodge in which he lived until the end of the Second World War. Like many senior academics, he sat on commissions and committees throughout his time at the LSE, and not surprisingly he was drawn into the war effort. In 1942 he had, for example, been asked by the President of the Board of Trade, Hugh Dalton, to draw up plans for fuel rationing.

In 1941–2 Beveridge had, perhaps against his will, been chairing the committee looking at the future of the social security of the nation. His first interest was unemployment, and he really wanted to examine the future of the organization of labour. In the early 1940s it was very clear that if Britain was to survive unaided in the postwar economic slump that was inevitable, long and deep consideration had to be given to the future and structure of the work force, the position of the trade union system, the methods of pay negotiations, wages tribunals, training and apprentice systems and the ever-vexed problem of the immobility of successive labour forces.

So why did Beveridge get involved with social security and not the future of the British labour system? In 1940 the Minister of Labour, Ernest Bevin, did not get on with Beveridge – the social and political chemistry did not work between them – and Arthur Greenwood, Minister without Portfolio, was given the job of looking at social security. It was Greenwood who appointed Beveridge as his committee chairman. In February 1942 Greenwood went, but Beveridge soldiered on; so did the resentment he felt towards Bevin and, probably, Churchill.

In April 1943 Beveridge began a private enquiry into the circumstances in which postwar Britain should provide jobs, and his book, *Full Employment in a Free Society*, was published in 1944. The book captured enormous attention, but the government side-stepped Beveridge with its own White Paper, which showed little of the depth that Beveridge had brought to the subject after more than thirty years of study.

Industrialists and industrial scholars still refer to *Full Employment in a Free Society*, even though it is his report on the future of social security – the Welfare State[4] – for which he is popularly remembered.

The concept of a Welfare State was not new. In its simplest form – looking after the people – even Henry VIII had discussed some form of public health for his people. The model for the twentieth-century version lay not in Beveridge's mind, but in Germany. The national insurance scheme introduced before the First World War had been based on the system developed in late nineteenth-century Germany.[5] Smaller countries were better able to cope with looking after tinier populations than Britain's, and New Zealand and Sweden, for example, were already experimenting with welfare systems.

During the period between 1918 and the start of Beveridge's inquiry, there had been marked progress in Britain's own welfare system. There was, for example, a Ministry of Health, and its remit was broader than its title at first suggests – it looked after the running of local government and house building. But was not a large part of local administration and the provision of housing an essential task of maintaining the health of the nation?

---

4 The expression 'welfare state' was coined by the Oxford Professor of International Relations, Alfred Zimmermann, in 1934.

5 See page 73.

Until the Beveridge plan was enacted, Britain's Welfare State was established to cope with the have-nots – the weakest in society. After Beveridge, everyone, in theory, was part of the Welfare State. But the revolution he fostered was kept at bay until after the war. His *Report on Social Insurance and Allied Services*, the Beveridge Report, came before the government in February 1943, but at first the government – perhaps too busy, perhaps disappointed in some areas – did not give his plan for a cradle-to-the-grave Welfare State the universal acceptance he might have expected. The government did not like the idea, for example, that in any nationally funded health service, there would still have to be funding for a private medical service. The British Medical Association objected to the proposals – it had raised similar objections to the National Insurance Act in 1911 – but the objections that mattered came from within the Cabinet. The Beveridge Report was the basis for what the government believed was necessary, but the Cabinet would not commit itself to a date to start the system.

A backbench revolt was led by Emmanuel Shinwell and the Labour MP who would eventually be put in charge of setting up the National Health Service, Aneurin Bevan. They wanted the immediate implementation of Beveridge's proposal, but on 23 February 1943, the protest having been made, they stepped back, knowing full well that for the moment there was no way in which a political schism on the Beveridge Report – which they believed would eventually be accepted – should damage the political unity necessary to maintain the political will of the war effort.

Eventually the Beveridge Report was accepted and became the basis of every government's social security programme until the end of the century.

Another social innovation arrived at this time with a new scheme for collecting tax. In the late autumn of 1943 the government announced that the best way of making sure everyone paid fair tax was to change the system by which it was gathered. Previously people had told the Inland Revenue how much they earned, and the Inland Revenue had told them how much they would have to pay in taxes. Now the government intended to give everyone a personal tax code, which would be applied to every person's wages. The government would take tax at source, and the wage-earner would have what was left. In 1943 the scheme was christened pay-as-you-earn (PAYE).

The fact that people were thinking of what would happen after the war rather than just the next stage of the conflict was yet another example of the optimism that was beginning to be felt throughout the British Isles. It was at this time, for example, that John Maynard Keynes developed a plan for a world bank and a global monetary fund that would bail out countries whose economies could not recover by themselves. The money would be loaned from the International Monetary Fund, in return for the debtor nation accepting the Fund's guidelines for independent recovery.

But there were others who recognized that there would always be the needy, no matter how many grandiose schemes were designed. The previous year, 1942, a small group had met in the University Church of Saint Mary the Virgin, Oxford, to discuss ways in which they could get food and clothing to refugees caught in the European war. The meeting decided to establish a charity that would call itself the Oxford Committee for Famine Relief, Oxfam.

In 1943 a more immediate comfort was being delivered to the battlefields of Europe. Infected wounds were now being successfully treated with penicillin.

Deaths

R.G. Collingwood (historian)
Lorenz Hart (US lyricist)
Leslie Howard (actor)
John Harvey Kellogg (US inventor)
Jean Moulin (French patriot)
Beatrix Potter (writer and illustrator)
Sergei Rachmaninov (Russian composer)
Max Reinhardt (Austrian director)
Oskar Schlemmer (German artist)
Wladislaw Sikorski (Polish politician)
Fats Waller (US musician)
Beatrice Webb (sociologist)

1944

THIS WAS the year that the Allies launched the D-Day landings into Normandy, General Douglas MacArthur kept his promise to return to the Philippines, some children in Britain saw street lights for the first time, Rommel committed suicide, and the Allies announced plans to set up a world organization called the United Nations.

On 6 June the Allied troops of the 21st Army Group, commanded by Montgomery, landed in Normandy. The details of those landings and what followed are set out in meticulous detail elsewhere.[6] It is sufficient to say that during the first fifteen days of that offensive, there were more than 40,000 Allied casualties – killed, missing and wounded.

Once the soldiers had left British shores and landed in continental Europe, the war was not over for the civilians left behind. Before Normandy was cleared, the Germans began their V1 (doodle-bug) and, from September, V2 flying bomb raids.

But if 1944 is mostly remembered because of the D-Day landings, it was also the year in which the government made two historic announcements for the future

---

6 For an accessible account, see John Keegan, *The Second World War*, Century Hutchinson (1989), which might be read as a prelude to Hugh Thomas, *Armed Truce, The Beginnings of the Cold War, 1945–6* (1986).

welfare of everyone in the United Kingdom. A White Paper promised the setting up of a National Health Service, and R.A. Butler produced an Education Bill.

R.A. 'Rab' Butler (1902–82) was to become one of the most important Conservative politicians in the postwar years, and some believe that he should have been prime minister in 1957 and again in 1963. His most significant contributions to British politics were the reorganization of the Conservative Party after the 1945 election defeat and, more importantly, the 1944 Education Act.

Butler had to take forward the Fisher Education Act of 1918 and project what children would need in the coming decades. There was a parallel between the setting up of a health service and the development of secondary education in Britain in the 1940s – those who could afford the private system within both services got a better deal. This was certainly true in education and was, in many ways, a more important inequality, simply because education was needed by everyone all the time whereas the health service was largely needed in emergencies only.

In 1944, 90 per cent of the children in England and Wales went to state schools, and the vast majority stayed on at school only until the age of fourteen. Since 1902 the Board of Education had paid far more attention to the grammar schools, which were attended by those who had got through examinations. This meant that a very small proportion of children were getting a proper secondary education. The facilities in the grammar schools, both in terms of teachers and classrooms, were far superior to those in other schools. For example, the average secondary school class was about twenty-five, but in the elementary schools it was common to have classes of more than forty, and classes with fifty children were not unknown.

Since the Fisher Act of 1918 attempts had been made to change the system, but none of the new ideas had been particularly successful. One of the major problems for advancing the system of education was the British attitude to education in general. The Board of Education was considered an unglamorous part of the government system, and the Education Minister was never considered a high flyer – most, certainly in the 1930s, lasted less than two years in the job. This, then, was the job that Butler, an enormously intelligent former academic,[7] took on in 1941.

Education had become a major issue, partly because of the evacuation of children, which had revealed the different standards of education that were achieved in different parts of the country. Moreover, moving nine-year-olds from London to, say, Hampshire, meant someone had to make the decisions about schooling, a difficulty that was fuelled when hard-boiled children from inner London were suddenly thrown into the gentler classrooms of the Home Counties and beyond.

Just as the Board of Education did not attract the best brains, it has to be said that some of the committees of inquiry, even though they had recognized that

7 Butler had been a fellow of Corpus Christi College, Cambridge, in 1925–9.

there was a problem, had come up with less than compelling reforms. In 1943 the Committee on Curriculum and Examination in Secondary Schools, under Sir Cyril Norwood, reported that natural scholars should be sent to grammar schools, those good with their hands to technical schools and the rest to elementary schools – which they would rename secondary schools. However carefully future plans were disguised, this is more or less what happened.

Butler understood the need to be seen to examine ways in which the public schools might be more closely connected with the state system, and his inquiry, the Fleming Committee (named after its chairman), suggested that public schools should take 25 per cent of their intake from the state system. The local authorities, it was suggested, would pay. Not much came of Fleming.

Butler introduced the Bill in January 1944. By May it was through both Houses. The Board of Education disappeared and its president became Minister of Education. This was big advance – it was a recognition of the importance of schooling not only in the British social and political system but also in the budgetary process.

In its basic form the Butler Act raised the school-leaving age from fourteen to fifteen by 1947 and, looking ahead, laid down a school-leaving age of sixteen by 1970. The three forms of secondary education – secondary modern, technical and grammar – were to be free.

Religious education was to be compulsory in every school curriculum, and every school day had to begin with an act of collective worship. Behind this clause, which was included after furious debate within the churches and between church and government, was a stark fact of life in 1944. Britain was no longer a Christian nation. The government had, therefore, decided that as it could no longer rely on teaching staff to provide morning worship on a voluntary basis, schools would have to be told to do so.

If we are to understand why Butler did not bring about the fundamental changes in education that were required to overcome the class differences were considered objectional, we must look once more at the times rather than with hindsight. The system of grammar, technical and secondary modern schools in many ways perpetuated a class system that by the 1990s was widely unacceptable, but Butler's legislation went as far as it could without being blocked. And it made the sort of leap in the education system that was to carry state schooling through into the 1960s, when the time was right for further change. Indeed, when the radical changes of the 1960s and 1970s had worked themselves through to the 1990s there were some who looked back with envy to the teaching methods and standards the Butler Act had brought about. It is fair to regard the Butler Education Act of 1944 as the most important social reform of the first half of the twentieth century.

During the First World War President Woodrow Wilson had put forward the idea of the League of Nations, although the United States itself never joined. Now, in

August 1944, the four great powers – America, Britain, China and Russia – met at Dumbarton Oaks, a mansion in Washington, D.C. The meeting was to decide on a forum that would guide the future of world security. This was more than idealism. It was crystal clear that a mechanism had to be established that would prevent conflict arising rather than simply doing something about it once it started.

A lesson of the Second World War was the way in which it was impossible to avoid the obligations of alliance. This had long been an especial fear of Britain, and was the reason for its hesitancy over becoming involved in Europe through the obligations imposed by the Triple Alliance. Alliances, the reasoning ran, meant that nations might be called upon to take part in a war that really had nothing to do with them. Equally, war might start because an aggressive member of one pact would feel courageous because it had ready-made military allies. If an instinctively isolationist nation like the United States was reluctant to get involved in a mini-alliance, why should anyone believe that Congress would ratify a global pact with its potential for multiple dangers. It was also, for example, no longer clear if the Monroe Doctrine[8] still applied.

Ultimately, however, the four powers at Dumbarton Oaks agreed on the need for the global security body, and on 9 October it was announced in Washington, London, Peking and Moscow that an organization called the United Nations would be established and that every nation in the world would be invited to join.

But there was still more change to come in the old world order. On 1 July 1944 a conference of more than 1300 delegates from forty-four countries opened in the American state of New Hampshire at a place called Bretton Woods. Their task was to make sure that the world did not repeat the mistakes that followed the First World War. John Maynard Keynes and Harry Dexter White of the US Treasury Department set out to convince the conference that once the war was over a monetary system had to be agreed that would prevent international economic crisis.

Their message was simple: monetary instability produces political instability produces war. Keynes and White were persuasive.

By 22 July it had been agreed to set up two agencies of the United Nations: the International Bank for Reconstruction and Development (which became known as the World Bank) and the International Monetary Fund (IMF). By the end of 1945 both agencies were established. The IMF was to be the administrative means of organizing loan funding that would, it was hoped, maintain currency stability. The World Bank was designed to provide investment capital for the developing world.

---

8 The statement of US policy, put forward in 1823, proclaiming the existence of a separate political sphere in the western hemisphere; US opposition to further attempts at European colonization; and a policy of non-intererence with existing European colonies or European affairs.

A third, although in the long run less powerful, agency was established in 1947. This was a debating and talking shop that could actually fix trading rates; it became known as the General Agreement on Tariffs and Trade (GATT).

The term Bretton Woods survived for nearly three decades as the system for fixing currency rates against the dollar. The advantage of the system was that it helped industrial and world trade growth and therefore helped to achieve, certainly until the end of the 1960s, a certain amount of the economic stability that the original Bretton Woods Conference had sought.

While the international order was setting up new security systems the tenor of the war could be gauged by the fact that Britain felt confident enough to shut down Dad's Army. The Home Guard had been set up in 1940 and at one time more than 1.7 million men and women were members.

Anticipating the end of the war, British tailors were getting government orders for 'demob' suits. Restrictions on cloth had been eased, and tailors could now make suits with turn-ups, which until then had been banned as an austerity measure just as had pleats in women's skirts.Rebuilding for the future had already started in the most practical sense. In 1944 the government announced that it would be necessary to build between 3 and 4 million houses after the war. In a document entitled *Design of Dwellings* the government painted a glowing picture of bigger and better equipped houses for everyone who wanted them.[9]

The more immediate problem was what to do for people who had no homes at all because of bombing, and the rush of returning servicemen, whose lives had been disrupted by the war. One answer was the prefab. Half a million prefabricated houses were to be built. They would be a standard size, shape and design, and they would be built in factories that normally manufactured car and truck bodies. They could be erected by relatively unskilled workmen in a weekend. Inside would be two bedrooms, a living room, a kitchen and a bathroom. The plan was to fit them with the latest gadgetry and fold-away tables to make easy living in a single storey of not much more than 600 square feet. They were meant as temporary housing relief, but many survived well into the 1980s and later.

A long-running battle between teachers and the government was finally won, appropriately in the year of the Butler Education Act. Women teachers were at last to get the same pay as their male colleagues.

Not all industrial differences ended as easily. In March 1944 nearly 90 per cent of Welsh miners went on strike, and only forty-four of the 200 pits in South Wales were working. Many of those pits were producing the quality of coal needed to power the railways and to fire merchant and warships, most of which were still coal burners. Coal was also used for the furnaces in munitions factories. The Welsh miners wanted extra money because it was harder to mine in Wales than it was in,

---

9 This document was published by the Ministry of Health, which still had responsibility for housing.

say, Durham and they wanted cheaper coal for themselves. The government realized they could not take the same attitude in wartime as they had done in peacetime and leave it to the pit-owners. Within three weeks, the miners had got what they wanted and Britain's ships, trains and factories got their coal.

In April home-based troops were driving London buses because the drivers were on strike. Anyone who thought that the easing of the threat of a German invasion would mean that Britain would be able to slip back into peacetime living was to be disillusioned. By the end of April the Labour Party, more confident of its political position than ever before, was demanding that its leaders and government nationalize the big industries, coal, gas and electricity generation.

Throughout the war the entertainment industry had continued to perform and had been seen as an essential part of national morale boosting. Laurence Olivier had been in the Fleet Air Arm; now, in 1944 came his film, *Henry V*, with music by William Walton. When he was not filming, Olivier was performing in *Richard III* at the Old Vic's temporary home at the New Theatre in London, the company's own theatre in Waterloo Road having been bombed. Ralph Richardson was appearing in *Peer Gynt*. James Agate, the theatre critic, described the *King Lear* of one of the last classic actor-managers, Donald Wolfit, as 'the greatest I have seen'.

The public could mourn as well as applaud. The architect, Sir Edwin Lutyens, whose designs of grand imperialism spread from New Delhi to the English countryside, who was the last man to build a castle in Britain[10] and who had designed the Cenotaph in Whitehall, died. So did the bandleader, Glenn Miller, whose plane went missing on a flight over the English Channel.

The war was not over yet. To come were the horrors that would be exposed in the concentration camps, the carnage of the British bombing of Dresden and the ultimate symbol of war that would be carried for decades to come – the mushrooms of Hiroshima and Nagasaki.

As the world moved into the final year of World War Two, a prophetic letter was sent to Winston Churchill and President Roosevelt by Niels Bohr, the Danish physicist and the founder of the Institute of Theoretical Physics. Bohr had worked on nuclear physics with Rutherford at Manchester University. At the beginning of the war he had escaped to America and was now working on the atomic bomb programme. Bohr saw the power of the invention. Here is part of his letter to Churchill and Roosevelt:

> A weapon of unparalleled power is being created. Unless some international agreement about the control or the use of the new active materials can be obtained, any temporary advantage, however great, may be outweighed by a perpetual menace to human society.

10 Castle Drogo, near Chadford, Devon.

Deaths
Marc Bloch (French historian)
Arthur Stanley Eddington (astronomer)
Jean Giraudoux (French writer)
Wassily Kandinsky (Russian artist)
Stephen Leacock (Canadian economist and humorist)
Sir Edwin Lutyens (architect)
Glenn Miller (US bandleader)
Piet Mondrian (Dutch artist)
Edvard Munch (Norwegian artist)
Sir Arthur Quiller-Couch (writer)
William Heath Robinson (artist)
Romain Rolland (French writer)
Erwin Rommel (German soldier)
Antoine de Saint-Exupéry (French aviator and writer)
Dame Ethel Smyth (composer)
William Temple (archbishop)
Orde Charles Wingate (soldier)
Sir Henry Wood (conductor and composer)

1945

IN DECEMBER 1944 the Germans had made the last great effort to reverse the seemingly inevitable victory of the Allies. Led by Field Marshal von Rundstedt, the Germans had punched at the Allies' front line across Belgium in an attempt to penetrate the Ardennes Forest just as they had in 1940. It was the Allies' weak point, because Eisenhower was using Montgomery and his 21st Army Group in the Netherlands and General Paton's Third Army was far to the south.

It seemed that the Germans wanted to sweep up to Antwerp, thereby cutting off the Allies' logistical train, and then to hold the Allied advance, thus prolonging the war. The great advantage the Germans had was that they faced very little threat from the air because of bad weather. This was the Battle of the Bulge, but it was short lived. By January, in deep snow, the Germans were being pushed back. By March Field Marshal von Rundstedt had been replaced by Field Marshal Kesselring, and German resistance began to crumble.

For both sides there was still much to do and much horror to face.

On 27 January the Russian army was advancing through Poland when it captured Auschwitz, the Nazis' 'death factory'. On 30 January a Russian submarine sank a German liner *Wilhelm Gustloff* in the Baltic. The ship was taking refugees from East Prussia to supposed freedom. Some 7000 people went down with the ship – the biggest single loss in any one ship during the whole of the war.

In mid-February 1945 one of the most controversial actions by the Royal Air Force and the head of RAF Bomber Command, Air Chief Marshal Sir Arthur Harris, took place. Eight hundred Lancaster bombers flew sorties over the supposedly safe town of Dresden, the Florence of Germany. Twelve hours later more than 400 American B17s continued the bombing. Hundreds of tons of high explosives and incendiary bombs flattened Dresden in the biggest fireball seen in Europe. No one knows how many people perished, although some reports speak of 400,000 casualties, of whom 130,000 were killed. Why would the Allies want to bomb Dresden at this stage of the war? To Harris the answer was simple: terror bombing was far more likely to destroy a nation's morale and therefore its willingness to continue to fight than the bombing of military targets, which were often mobile and could be replaced.

Jock Colville, Churchill's secretary, remembers Harris dining at Chequers, shortly after the raid.

> Before dinner, while waiting in the Great Hall for the P.M. to come down, I asked Sir Arthur Harris what the effect of the raid on Dresden had been.
>
> 'Dresden?' he said. 'There is no such place as Dresden.'

Certainly in Downing Street at the time, the targeting of Dresden was not regarded as being any different from the bombing raids over Berlin, Hamburg or Cologne, as Colville suggests:

> A principal reason for the Dresden raid was the intelligence report, received from the Russians, that one or possibly two German armoured divisions had arrived there from Italy on their way to reinforce the defence of the eastern front. Churchill was on his way back from Yalta when the raid took place and since it was in accord with the general policy of bombing German towns massively, so as to shatter civilian morale, I do not think he was consulted about the raid. He never mentioned it in my presence, and I am reasonably sure he would have done so if it had been regarded as anything special.

The concept of so-called strategic bombing was not new and should not be laid entirely at the door of 'Bomber' Harris. The US Eighth Air Force was carrying out daylight precision bombing raids and had 1000 B17s and B24s in Britain alone. Moreover, in order to drop bombs in daylight, the big aircraft needed fighter escorts. It was not until mid-1944 that fighters with enough range to get deep into Germany and back were available. It was thanks to the Anglo-American P51 Mustang that the long-range bomber escort became a success.

Between the late autumn of 1944 and the spring of 1945 this programme of strategic bombing wrecked Germany's economic system. The anti-aircraft fire that was the mainstay of the German protection – the Luftwaffe being either stretched or unable to fly against the Mustangs – also meant that men who should have been on the front lines were dragged back into defensive positions.

It is generally accepted that about 600,000 German civilians were killed by bombs. It is also thought that about 20 per cent of those killed were children.

It is also true that Bomber Command suffered terrible losses: 55,000 Bomber Command air crews were killed in the Second World War, and as the military historian John Keegan observes, that total was 'more than the number of British army officers killed in the First World War'.

The unremitting bombing campaign against civilians was one the British people tried to sweep from their minds or to justify it by saying that they were only doing what the Germans had started to do. Air Chief Marshal Harris was later ostracized, and he was the only senior British commander who did not receive a peerage after the war. Whether it was because the British were ashamed of what had been done in their name or because they had not imagined that they might have brought themselves to Hitler's level has never been conclusively argued.

What is abundantly clear is that the myth that grew up about the British wartime image of 'fair play' was just that, a myth. An island race, with centuries of uncompromising warrior history, chose to disguise some of the methods by which it had prosecuted the war.

As the bombing of Dresden was taking place Churchill, Roosevelt and Stalin were meeting at Yalta in the Crimea. It was at this conference that the wartime Allies carved up Europe.

In April 1945 President Roosevelt died. He was sixty-three years old and had collapsed with a brain haemorrhage and never regained consciousness. Vice President Harry S Truman became president of the United States at the age of sixty-one.

In Britain on 23 May 1945 Churchill resigned as wartime prime minister but formed a caretaker government that would run the country until elections could be held. It would have been possible to maintain the coalition only if the Labour Party had agreed. There can be no doubt that Churchill wanted to do this until the Japanese had surrendered, and he even promised to push through legislation that would lead to the setting up of the Welfare State, but Clement Attlee and the Labour Party understood that their time had come. There was no longer a need for a coalition government, and in any case, the Conservative Party was badly organized and in no position to fight a general election campaign. The Labour Party was.

On 15 June 1945 the Parliament that had begun nine and a half years earlier came to an end. The general election would be held on 5 July.

Churchill appeared to be totally unable to accept the thought that he would no longer be prime minister. He described the Labour Party as extremist and claimed that any Labour government would 'have to fall back on some form of Gestapo' because they found the concept of a free Parliament 'odious'.

The mood of the nation had changed, however. The joy that came with the ending of the long and costly war was real enough, but here was a simple example of the difference between the people and their politicians. The people wanted to get on with their lives, but Churchill was trapped in triumph. People knew medals would not buy health care, food and schooling. Even so, the war had taught the electorate what their fathers had not understood: that only unbreakable international agreements and economic recovery would prevent a future generation, perhaps even themselves, having to go through the whole grim process once more. A public survey taken in 1938 had shown that only about 30 per cent of the electorate understood what was meant by British foreign policy and what it was. Now in 1945, three-quarters of the electorate understood foreign policy and wanted to see a system of international agreements in place.[11]

The politicians in the 1945 election realized that people wanted something much better than they had before the war. Beveridge's proposals represented that 'something'.

It was also the case that, as the war drew to its close, people were increasingly sceptical of government. There were anecdotal reports that the idea of Beveridge had been used to keep up morale in a time of great depression. Some thought that Churchill's promise to institute welfare reform was nothing more than a ploy to keep him in Downing Street. The electorate would not allow that.

Although the country went to the polls on 5 July, the count could not be completed overnight because there were 3 million votes from servicemen and women to be gathered from across the world. During the three-week delay Churchill went off to the Potsdam Conference, a gathering of the three major allies – the Soviet Union, the United States and Britain – which eventually led to Soviet domination in eastern Europe and confirmed Poland's frontier with Germany. But Churchill did not see out the conference.

On 26 July the election results were declared: Labour had 393 seats and the Conservatives 213; the Liberals had taken twelve seats, and there were twenty-two Independents. Churchill thought the people thankless, but they had voted in a Labour government with an election slogan 'Let us face the future'. The anxieties and discontents of the late 1930s had not been assuaged by five years of war.

Clement Attlee now joined Truman and Stalin for the resumed Potsdam Conference. The war was over and Stalin would not give an inch on his new boundaries, and he dismissed any thought of open, democratic elections in those east European countries that were now controlled by the Soviet Union. In August 1945 the new Foreign Secretary, Ernest Bevin, described the contrived elections in Soviet-dominated eastern Europe as 'one kind of totalitarianism replaced by another'.

Few were listening. The news was now from Japan. On 6 August an atomic bomb destroyed Hiroshima and another on the 9th wasted Nagasaki. William T. Laurence of the *New York Times* was in one of the aircraft:

> Observers in the tail . . . saw a giant ball of fire rise, as though the bowels of the earth, belching forth enormous white smoke rings. Next they saw a giant pillar of purple fire, ten thousand feet high, shooting skyward with enormous speed.

11 Mass Observation, *The Mood of Britain*.

> By the time our ship [aircraft] had made another turn in the direction of the atomic explosion the pillar of purple fire had reached the level of our altitude. Only about 45 seconds had passed. Awe-struck, we watched it shoot upward like a meteor coming from the earth instead of from outer space, becoming ever more alive as it climbed skyward through the white clouds. It was no longer smoke, or dust, or even a cloud of fire. It was a living thing, a new species of being, born right before our incredulous eyes.

This was the end of the war. Attlee, now Prime Minister, said that the new weapon meant 'a naked choice between world co-operation and world destruction'.

Returning troops into civilian life were a logistical problem as well as a financial headache. When Ernest Bevin announced that 750,000 would be out of uniform by the end of 1945, he made sure that the mistakes made in 1918 about who should go first did not happen again. Troops were put in two classes, A and B. Those in class B were to come out immediately because they were tradesmen and craftsmen, such as plumbers and builders. Those in class A, the majority, would be released after class B and would go according to their age and the length of time they had been in the services. Class B soldiers could not be allowed to cheat the system. A building worker had to go back into civilian life as a building worker, and if it were found that he had become, say, a used-car dealer, he would be recalled.

The next priority was to find the servicemen work. Returning servicemen were given a booklet called *Resettlement Advice*. Men would get their 'demob' suit, and women would get clothing coupons and money – it was thought that although men might not mind wearing the same light grey chalk-striped suit, women would object to having to wear the same dress.

There were schemes for resettlement, and training and education grants were available. Provision was also made for the reserved occupations. Some people had never served in the forces because they were in jobs that were vital to the prosecution of the war. It was now decided that these people would be conscripted into the army to take the place of the servicemen and women who were returning to civilian life.

The other group returning from the war were children. Evacuees had begun to return in September 1944, yet by 1946 nearly 40,000 evacuees were still away from their original homes. Some had lost their parents, killed on active service or during the blitz.

There was, too, a lack of housing. The planned 500,000 prefabs could not accommodate all the people, including servicemen and women, whose homes had been bombed. In addition, many suffered from tensions in family life, especially when husbands had been away for a long time.

Food was in short supply, and at the end of the war meat was harder to get than it had been the previous year before the war had ended, and rationing of bacon and fat was increased rather than decreased.

The austerity applied even to clothing. It would take time for textile production to return to prewar levels, partly because of labour shortages, so clothing rations were to continue. In 1947, when the young Princess Elizabeth married Prince Philip of Greece, she had to get extra coupons for the material for her wedding dress.

Songwriters, playwrights, authors and actors had a good war. Paul Nash, John Piper, Laura Knight, Stanley Spencer and Graham Sutherland painted the war for posterity and the galleries. But the biting brush-strokes that had led so many generations that came after the First World War to wonder at the futility of it all were missing. Nor did the Second World War produce the sort of poetry that came from the First World War. The First World War produced poets by and large, the Second World War produced poetry from those who were already poets. There was little of the starkness and horror in the writing or painting (Zec's cartoons excepted) that would inspire the reader and watcher.

Deaths
Béla Bartók (Hungarian composer)
Theodore Dreiser (US writer)
Anne Frank (German diarist)
Joseph Goebbels (German politician)
Heinrich Himmler (German politician)
Adolf Hitler (German dictator)
J.B. Huizinga (Dutch historian)
Käthe Kollwitz (German artist)
Simon Lake (US naval architect)
Pierre Laval (French politician)
David Lloyd George, 1st Earl of Dwyfor (politician)
Benito Mussolini (Italian dictator)
George S. Patton (US soldier)
Vidkun Quisling (Norwegian soldier)
Franklin Delano Roosevelt (US president)
Paul Valéry (French writer)
Anton Webern (Austrian composer)
Newell Convers Wyeth (US artist)

1946

ON 5 MARCH, in the small town of Fulton, Missouri, Winston Churchill delivered a speech that was to illustrate the suspicions and fears between East and West for forty years to come. The speech included the phrase: 'From Stettin in the Baltic to Trieste in the Adriatic an Iron Curtain has descended across the Continent.'

The wartime ally, the Soviet Union, had eastern Europe in its grip. Stalin believed that the West was as much a threat to his society as Churchill believed Stalin's was to his, and now, rescued from Hitler, Poland, Czechoslovakia, Hungary, Romania, Bulgaria and half of Germany fell to another dictator. Only Tito's Yugoslavia broke away.

It was into this world that the Attlee government began Britain's own revolutions.

Attlee, who kept for himself the defence portfolio, had about him some of the finest minds and activists in postwar British politics. Herbert Morrison (1888–1965) was Lord President of the Council; Arthur Greenwood (1880–1954) was the Lord Privy Seal; Hugh Dalton (1887–1962) was Chancellor of the Exchequer; Ernest Bevin (1881–1951) was Foreign Secretary; James Chuter Ede (1882–1965) was Home Secretary; Sir Stafford Cripps (1889–1952) was President of the Board of Trade; Tom Williams (1888–1967) would be one of the most respected Agricultural Ministers of all time; Emmanuel Shinwell (1884–1986) was the Minister of Fuel and Power; and as Minister of Health Attlee appointed the huge figure of Aneurin Bevan (1896–1960). Ellen Wilkinson (1891–1947) became the first ever female Education Minister in Britain.

Unlike MacDonald's Labour government, Attlee's had a radical programme, and his government intended to honour Clause Four of the Labour Party Manifesto that had first appeared in 1918,[12] to implement social security reform and to start the National Health Service. It would also take the first steps towards dismantling the Empire.

Aneurin Bevan introduced the National Health Service Bill in March; the Bill was enacted on 6 November although it was not implemented until July 1948. It was designed, in simple terms, to nationalize the hospitals, which was what, after all, made the huge difference to the health system. By nationalizing hospitals and doctors' surgeries, which would be paid for by weekly tax contributions, their facilities would be available to everyone who needed help. There was some discussion about whether this move would really benefit patients. The *Guardian* of 22 March was uncertain:

> Doubtless all doctors will explain that he will get the same treatment in either case and many doctors will mean it but the patient will not believe it. Poor patients will claim their rights and be convinced that they are getting an inferior service, rich patients, and many others who cannot really afford it, will insist on paying fees in the expectation of preferential treatment, and will go elsewhere if they do not get what they are paying for. This, in short, is a false freedom that can only survive to the extent that it is abused. It must inevitably poison the doctor-patient relationship. It is the reef on which this splendid venture with all its prospects for developments might founder at the

12 See page 110.

> outset. Whatever else the Parliamentary Labour Party may decide to let pass in the way of provisions that conflict with its declared policy it must draw the line at this.

The British Medical Association had never supported anything but private medicine. Early in the century, when Lloyd George was introducing his National Insurance Bill, the BMA told its members not to co-operate. The BMA had not changed its view. Dr H. Guy Dain, chairman of the BMA council, was reported as saying that it was up to individual members to decide whether they would co-operate with the scheme. However, he continued:

> Unless it were modified considerably the association would advise its members not to participate, but Dr Dain emphasized that until their members had made their views known there was no way of assessing the collective opinion of the profession.

Eventually, the collective opinion would, of course, rely on both state and private systems working alongside each other. The higher purpose of the National Health Service Bill was to give to those who had not. It was not to take away from those who had – unless, and this was the big unless – it stopped the poorer getting the treatment they needed.

The first job for the new Minister for National Insurance, James Griffiths (1890–1975), was to implement the 1945 Family Allowances Act. Under it, and without a means test, every family would get a weekly allowance for every child after the first-born. The first payments were made in August 1946 to more than 2.5 million families. Griffiths's next task was to put through the 1946 National Insurance Act, the biggest social reform since the National Insurance Act of 1911. Under the 1946 Act every woman between the ages of sixteen and sixty and every man between sixteen and sixty-five would be insured in sickness and in health and, most importantly, in old age.

Griffiths, Bevan and the too-often overlooked successor to Butler, Ellen Wilkinson, were to be the leaders of social and educational reform, but others too were at work in 1946. Lewis Silkin, the Housing Minister, was working on the idea of more new towns as a quick but eventually long-term way out of the postwar housing dilemma. The government eventually anticipated that twenty new towns would be needed to take in more than one million people and that the number would include the quickly expanding industrial and residential site in Crawley, Surrey, which was then largely agricultural.

Here was an opportunity to modernize building plans and to rethink the way the nation lived. The immediate task remained: to find accommodation for the homeless. Hundreds of thousands of homes had been destroyed or made uninhabitable during the war – on the east coast, for example, more than 90,000 homes in Hull had been damaged and more than 7000 were completely destroyed

– and shops from which people could run businesses and others could buy had to be replaced. A nationwide system of funding to repair war damage was established so that the rebuilding work could begin. Children's education, which everyone recognized was now a priority within the 1944 Butler Act, was being severely held back because bombed schools had to be replaced.

The problem was compounded by major shortages of building materials and skilled labour, and also by bureaucracy. Each local authority had to submit relatively complicated regeneration schemes to central government. As each month went by and building had not begun, local authorities got into further difficulties. Fewer houses and businesses meant fewer people paying rates, so that local authorities were providing services from diminishing revenue. Despite the difficulties, more than 55,000 new homes were built in 1946 and twice that number in 1947.

Then came the dip – there was just not enough money. Postwar Britain was an austere place. In February 1946, for example, there was only one week's supply of coal left in London. The wheat content in bread was reduced to the 1942 level, and in the summer of 1946 bread was rationed, something that had not happened even in wartime. The butter, margarine and cooking fat ration was cut, as was the amount of animal foodstuffs available. Meat, including poultry and eggs, was a luxury item. As the austerity deepened, the government found itself having to reissue make-do menus and urging people to go out and catch squirrels, to make a government-inspired squirrel pie.

Much of the food that was being imported into Europe was being diverted to Germany, where the agricultural industry had been virtually destroyed during the war and where people were dying of hunger. The situation was so grave there that in the opening weeks of 1946 there were predictions of famine.

Some foodstuffs were in better supply in Britain than they had been during the war, however. Bananas and pineapples returned to the shops, and in March 1946 bananas were being sold in the United Kingdom for the first time since 1939. Some children did not know how to peel these strange fruits, and they were warned not to eat too many, following the death of a child who had.

In the field of social reform the divorce laws were changed so that instead of six months, couples had only to wait six weeks between decree nisi and decree absolute. The courts reported 'a tidal wave' of divorces. In 1905, for example, there had been 670 divorces; in 1946 38,000 petitions were heard and by 1947 the figure had risen to 50,000. In May 1946 the Attorney-General, Sir Hartley Shawcross, set up legal teams with the specific task of coping with outstanding divorce petitions. Many thousands of these petitions came from soldiers, sailors and airmen and women whose domestic lives had been wrecked by the war.

The Marriage Guidance Council claimed that morals had so declined that it was estimated that four out of every ten brides were pregnant on their wedding day and that 25 per cent of children now being born were illegitimate.

★

Attlee's immediate foreign policy dilemma was India. He understood the issues well because he had been a member of the prewar commission that studied the future of India and the inevitability of independence. The problem was how to satisfy both Hindus and Muslims.

In April 1946 Sir Stafford Cripps was sent to India to discuss Gandhi's proposal that an interim Indian government should be established as quickly as possible. Cripps and Attlee saw that their plans were complicated by the differences between the Hindus, led by Gandhi, and the Muslims, led by Muhammad Ali Jinnah, but in 1946 no one spoke openly of the possibility that the subcontinent would be divided.

In May Attlee announced that India would become independent, and leaders of the Muslim League and representatives of the Hindus were invited to London to discuss details for the interim government. Within a week the Congress Party had rejected Britain's proposals. By the end of July the Muslim League had voted to withdraw its approval from the constitutional plans outlined during the Cripps visit, which it had previously accepted. The League now wanted a separate state, which would be to the north of the Hindu territory and be known as Pakistan, a name made up from *P*unjab, *A*fghanistan, *K*ashmir, *S*ind and Baluchis*tan*. By August 1946 Muslims and Hindus were fighting and dying in their thousands in India, and it was now that the Hindus, who were in the stronger position, showed their ascendancy in their relationship with Britain.

On 24 August Jawaharlal Nehru was appointed the first head of the provisional Indian government, and although Attlee personally promised Jinnah that the new arrangement would not go against the Muslims, the year ended without agreement and every sign of failure.

In the Middle East – the Near East as it was then called – Britain announced the withdrawal of its army and air force from Egypt. Strategically, the continuing concern was over who controlled the Suez Canal. Any conflict around Britain's interests in East Africa, the Gulf States, the subcontinent or Southeast Asia (including Hong Kong and Singapore) made it essential to have free access through the canal. Aircraft had limited value in transporting men and equipment, especially when flying into a defended territory. Attlee's announcement did not provide for a means of defending the Canal zone.

Across the Sinai Desert Britain was struggling with the future of Palestine, where it had to maintain its mandate until such time 'that Arab-Jewish hostility disappears'. Palestine's strategic position along the coast of the Mediterranean, surrounded by Egypt and what was then Transjordan, Syria and the Lebanon, meant frictions could escalate into war because Palestine was effectively a thoroughfare. Moreover, it contained Jerusalem, whose temple walls were Jewish shrines and whose mosques were the centres of Islam within the state.

Attlee had to face the new element in the debate over a Jewish homeland – the European survivors of the Holocaust and the Soviet and Fascist persecutions. In 1946 about 100,000 Jews were expected to move to Palestine, causing understandable indignation and fear among the Arabs there. The Jews, equally dissatisfied, wanted open access to Palestine. Britain, a co-signatory to the Anglo-American plan to partition Palestine, faced the resultant terrorism from the Arabs and, in particular, the Zionists.

The British arrested nearly 400 terrorist suspects, and two members of the Jewish underground movement, Irgun Zvai Leumi (IZL), were sentenced to death and others were given long jail sentences. IZL said it would execute three British hostages if the death sentences were carried out, and on 22 July Jewish terrorists blew up the headquarters of the British army command in Palestine, the King David Hotel in Jerusalem. Dozens were killed or wounded. Britain responded by banning Jews from going into Palestine. This angered the United States, which had a large Jewish lobby that was to influence American policy towards Israel for the rest of the century. There could be no control until there was independence; but the exodus to Palestine was under way, and shiploads of refugees were running the Royal Navy's blockade.

In the autumn of 1946 tensions in Palestine heightened, as did the differences between London and Washington. In October President Truman renewed his demand that Britain should allow 100,000 Jews to enter Palestine without delay and said that Britain should arrange to set up a Jewish state in part of Palestine. Attlee believed that the pressure of the Jewish lobby on Truman was effectively destroying the chances of peaceful negotiations with both Jews and Arabs, and throughout November and December he became more determined to resist the American and Jewish demands.

Negotiations were further complicated by splits among the Jews themselves. Haganah, the so-called Jewish defence group in Palestine, was actually fighting the two other organizations, the Stern Gang and IZL, and British servicemen found themselves the targets for almost any group. In November eight British soldiers were killed in Jerusalem and in December five died in a bomb attack. In January 1947 Britain ordered women and children to leave Palestine. The Cabinet knew the Jews would get their way, and Attlee's task was to remove as many terrorist targets as he could before they did so.

On 30 January 1946 the first session of the United Nations General Assembly took place, and Norway's Foreign Minister, Trygve Lie, became its first Secretary General. The argument over his election is an indication of how the UN was seen. The Belgian, Paul Spaak, became President, after the Soviet Union, which wanted Trygve Lie to have the job, had been out-voted. The East–West tensions in the UN were never to ease for the remainder of the century.

The UN's agenda was full from the first day: in addition to the riots between Hindus and Muslims, there was famine in India; bread riots had broken out in Paris; rioters in Cairo were demanding unification with Sudan; there was unrest in Palestine over partition plans and the continuation of the British mandate; Umberto II of Italy had been forced to resign; King Zog of Albania was dethroned and the state declared a republic; the King of Thailand, Anada Mahidol, had been assassinated; Zionists were carrying out bombings in Jerusalem; there was civil war in China; and martial law had been imposed in Indochina (later to be known as Vietnam) where the new president, Ho Chi Minh, was now in a state of guerrilla warfare against French rule.

Churchill, still a strong force in domestic and international politics and mindful of the mistakes after 1918, saw the future of peaceful co-existence in two distinct areas. He believed that the transatlantic relationship was so important that there might come a day when Britons and Americans had joint citizenship. He also believed in a 'United States' of Europe and in 1946 was proposing that Europe should have common citizenship. He recognized that a revival in Europe depended on reconciliation between France and Germany. He also knew none of this could be achieved without the Soviet Union becoming a partner in the scheme.

In 1946 opponents of a United States of Europe judged that any European alliance would antagonize Russia, but Churchill was talking about a pan-European pact, not about an arrangement with those nations to the west of the Soviet block. He was, in fact, building on the ideas of people like Aristide Briand who had wanted federalism in the late 1920s. Europe was not ready for this, however, and de Gaulle told Churchill the French would not accept a rapprochement between France and Germany.

Deaths
John Logie Baird (inventor)
Manuel de Falla (Spanish composer)
W.C. Fields (US comedian)
Herman Goering (German politician)
Harley Granville-Bantock (playwright)
Gerhardt Hauptmann (German writer)
John Maynard Keynes, 1st Baron Keynes of Tilton (economist)
Joachim von Ribbentrop (German diplomat)
Damon Runyon (US writer)
Gertrude Stein (US writer)
H.G. Wells (writer)

1947

BRITONS GREETED 1947 poor, cold and often hungry. The temperature fell to −16°F (−26°C). Rationing was increased. In January factories had to shut because there was not enough coal to keep them going. Many people were out of work, but the transport workers were on strike.

For one group a promise was fulfilled, but even so there was little joy. On 1 January the 1500 collieries in Britain were nationalized. The National Coal Board assumed responsibility for the 700,000 miners employed in an industry that was finding it difficult to take advantage of engineering and technological advances to make it more efficient. Coal exports were reaching what Shinwell, the Coal Minister, described as 'vanishing point'. Instead of cheering nationalization, miners were glum, and the high levels of absenteeism were proof of their depression. Times were hard, and for the first time, Nonconformist Welsh miners were forced to work Sunday shifts.

Homes, businesses, courts, government offices and surgeries were candle lit. One of the worst winters in living memory stopped ships from putting to sea and aircraft from landing and taking off. The freeze and power shortage lasted well into March, and gas and coal fires were banned until the autumn.

When, at last, the snows of 1947 went, there came the floods. More than 2 million sheep drowned, and spring grain crops rotted in the fields.

In June 1947, Hugh Dalton, the Chancellor of the Exchequer, told the Commons that even less food would be available, and austerity measures were imposed, backed by official slogans such as 'Work or want'. People were gradually getting back to work, but productivity was low. Mid-week sport was banned because too many were staying away from work. Here was the origin of what continental Europeans called the British disease.

The government was suffering its own stresses, including a plot – that came to nothing – against the prime minister. Attlee's greatest concern was that half the massive postwar loan from the United States was gone. Imports were immediately cut, making petrol more difficult to come by, and commercial and public transport had to be limited. Even explaining what was happening would be more difficult because newspapers were restricted to four pages, their wartime level.

The war loans from the United States had ceased when Germany was defeated, but if all the mistakes of the aftermath of the First World War were to be avoided Europe badly needed aid. America was the only nation rich enough to provide it. In June 1947 the Marshall Plan, named after the US Secretary of State, George C. Marshall, was devised, offering help for the war-devastated economies in Europe. Marshall made the point that a regeneration programme was possible only if European states understood the need to act as a combined economic unit. Here was powerful endorsement of what would become a European Union.

The aid programme was also offered to the Soviet Union and eastern Europe. Stalin refused. The United States needed a strong Europe to resist communism – by now an American phobia – and the Marshall Plan was partly intended to diminish support for communism in western Europe. The United States recognized that European opposition to communism had to be paid for, but the Marshall Plan was not instantly available. The European Recovery Programme, by which seventeen countries in western Europe received $15 billion in grant and loans, did not come into effect until 1948.

Britain had spent and borrowed to fight the war, and by the middle of the last week of August, the government admitted that it had not understood the full seriousness of the economic situation. So, two years after the end of the war, more austerity measures, harsher even than wartime emergency plans, were introduced. Foreign holidays were to be banned. Businessmen would be allowed no more than £8 a day to spend on overseas trips. Family motoring trips were stopped. Guests had to use their ration books at hotels. Gold reserves were used to pay import costs. Domestic and industrial power supplies were to be turned off in some parts of the country on one day every week.

It was the austerity Budget that cost Attlee his first Cabinet casualty. In November Hugh Dalton, the Chancellor, produced his Budget. Given the economic circumstances, this was an exceptionally solemn and sensitive occasion, but a few minutes before delivering the Budget in the House of Commons, Dalton told a journalist about the tax cuts. *The Star*, one of London's three evening newspapers, was able to carry a short report. There were no implications for the Stock Market of this advance information, but Dalton had been wrong and he resigned. His Budget never did resolve the crisis.

Two years later sterling was to be devalued by 30 per cent and Britain would still be poor.

Attlee's government was stretched in every direction. It was about to implement the greatest change in Britain's imperial history of the twentieth century, the hand-over of India to its peoples, but before it could turn to the subcontinent, there was another move to independence that the government could not ignore, that of Burma. If Burma seems of little importance at the end of the twentieth century, it is worth remembering that Burma's independence, and not India's as some think, started the post-1945 decolonization of the British Empire. Moreover, the Burmese leader assassinated in 1947 was U Aung San; his daughter Aung San Suu Kyi became the leader of Burmese pro-democracy group in Rangoon in the 1990s.

In January 1947 an agreement was signed in London giving Burma self-government. Churchill, whose enthusiasm for Europeanism did not mean that he had abandoned his support for imperialism and the concept of Empire, accused Attlee of giving away the Empire and the heritage that the 14th Army had fought to defend.

Attlee now turned to the unfinished business in India, of which Burma had been a province until 1937. By 1946 the split between Hindus and Muslims was clearly irreconcilable. At the start of 1947 Gandhi was regarded as a god-like figure above politics, while Jinnah headed the Muslim League and Pandit Nehru led the Hindus. At this time in India there were about 255 million Hindus and 92 million Muslims. There were also 5.5 million Sikhs and perhaps rather more than that number of Christians, although it is hard to find reliable figures.

In February 1947, in apparent haste, Britain entered the final stage of independence. On 20 February Lord Mountbatten was appointed Viceroy, an imperial undertaker. That Britain should need a Viceroy to replace Lord Wavell, who had once commanded the British forces in the Middle East and who had been Viceroy since June 1943, reflected the strong disagreements between Wavell and Attlee's government. Wavell had put forward what he called a Breakdown Plan. After the internecine killings that had taken place in Calcutta in the autumn of 1946, Wavell had drafted a scheme that would have meant a British military withdrawal, whether or not there was a political agreement between the British government and the two religious groups in India.

Wavell was sacked. It did not appear that way in the parliamentary record, but that was the decision.

His replacement, Mountbatten of Burma, had enormous advantages over almost anyone else who might have been considered. He was a cousin of George VI's and so had all-important caste. He had Attlee's confidence. Mountbatten understood, as Attlee did, that the problem to be tackled was not, as Wavell believed, one of security but one of almost insoluble cultural, religious and political differences. Despite misgivings from Ernest Bevin, the Foreign Secretary, Mountbatten accepted Attlee's decision that a deadline had to be fixed for the transfer of power.

When Mountbatten arrived in Delhi in March 1947, he carried with him all the trappings of royalty and, more importantly, political power for which he could wish. He had Attlee's agreement that he, Mountbatten, could take on-the-spot political decisions, which he saw as the only way he could bring about a transition by the deadline of June 1948. But even that deadline was to change.

Mountbatten had hardly unpacked when he realized that civil war would break out before June 1948. A new date was chosen – August 1947. There was just time to get the necessary legislation through Parliament.

The statement to the Commons that there would be a change was not made until 3 June 1947. A week later, a letter from the India Office to the Treasury Secretary suggests the urgency:

> To enable such legislation to pass this Session it must be introduced into the House of Commons *not later than 7 July* . . . the Bill will have to be revised in the light of the Viceroy's comments and submitted to Ministers in a revised form and finalized in the light of their views. It may be taken that this revision will take place early in the week beginning Monday, 23 June, and that final submission to Ministers will be towards the end of that week.

And a note to that letter from the India Office showed how fully the British Raj was about to end – and Britain was warning that it would have no responsibility for the consequences:

> The basic facts are:
> (a) We are now transferring power.
> (b) We have therefore no power to enforce anything whatever unless it happens outside India.

(c) Anything that does happen in India will happen because the Indians agree to it or acquiesce in it.
(d) Our only assets are the force of habit (a big one), the probability that much administrative machinery will run on because nobody has time to stop it or knows that it is running on, and the personality of the Viceroy and some of the Governors.

The legislation was put in place. There were twenty-two clauses in the Bill, covering everything from definition of territories, boundaries, what to do about the Indian army, pay, compensations, pensions, changes to the judicial system and even divorce jurisdiction.

The practical detail of packing up the Raj fell to Indian High Court judges under the chairmanship of Sir Cyril Radcliffe. Their task, to be completed within a month, was to sift through all the evidence of claims and counterclaims and arrange the practicalities of British withdrawal and supervise the separation between Hindu and Muslims. Radcliffe also had to decide where boundaries would be drawn, which services were to be retained, where compensation would be paid and even who owned what and who kept what. This last task applied right down to the lowest sections of the country's bureaucracy.

One of the most difficult administrative tasks was deciding who got Calcutta, India (Hindus) or Pakistan (Muslims). Calcutta was the biggest Indian city and economically important, especially to the Muslims. Most people in Calcutta were Hindus, however, and the city went to India.

By August 1947 Radcliffe's work was done, and late on 14 August the Indian Constituent Assembly was convened. As midnight approached, Nehru spoke:

> Long years ago we made a tryst with destiny, and now the time comes when we shall redeem our pledge, not wholly or in full measure, but substantially. At the stroke of the midnight hour, when the world sleeps, India will awake to life and freedom.

Mountbatten remained as Governor-General until June 1948, when he was succeeded by Chakravarti Rajagopalachari.

Britain had speeded up independence because Mountbatten and Attlee were convinced that civil war would erupt if they kept to the original hand-over date in 1948. But as thousands upon thousands of people tried to escape being in the 'wrong' territory at Nehru's magical midnight, so thousands upon thousands of them were slaughtered.

Attlee and Mountbatten had ducked the alternative plan, which would have been a massive influx of British troops to police an attempted transition and the unhurried transfer of Muslims to Pakistan and Hindus to India. There would have been bloodshed, but it is tempting to believe that it would not have been on the scale witnessed during 1947.

Deaths
Stanley Baldwin, 1st Earl Baldwin of Bewdley (politician)
Ettore Bugatti (Italian manufacturer)
Al Capone (US gangster)
Willa Cather (US writer)
Henry Ford (US manufacturer)
Fiorello La Guardia (US politician)
Max Planck (German physicist)
Henry Gordon Selfridge (British merchant)
Sidney James Webb, 1st Baron Passfield (economist)
Alfred N. Whitehead (philosopher)
Ellen Cicely Wilkinson (politician)

1948

THE WAR had been over for nearly three years, but Britain was still poor, although bread rationing was at last ended on 25 July. In domestic politics, however, this was a year full of hope, as Attlee's government continued to carry out the social and economic reforms it had promised. In January the railways were nationalized and plural voting was abolished. It had previously been possible for a graduate to vote at home and at university or for a businessman to vote at home and at his company. In April the electricity industry was taken into public ownership, and in July the National Health Service Act of 1946 was implemented. This meant free health care, including free prescriptions, glasses and dentures.

On 5 July nearly 1000 National Insurance offices were opened and 2751 hospitals, which had hitherto been private and sometimes public institutions, came under the control of the health boards. Just as the pits had been nationalized, so the National Health Service was nationalizing the hospitals. Bevan understood that this was the key to setting up a National Health Service – something others had overlooked. His ideas, although by the nature of planning they were not always his alone, were explained in the 1945 Cabinet paper, 'The Future of Hospital Services'. If for no other reason than accountability, the so-called voluntary hospitals – which already got most of their money from the public purse – had to be taken into public ownership. Into those hospitals and NHS surgeries went an estimated 19,000 doctors. The main opposition to this came from the doctors themselves, and in February 1948 the British Medical Association estimated that more than 80 per cent of its members were against the Welfare State. Dentists, too, were being told by the British Dental Organization that they must not join.

Bevan needed the consultants on his side, and he achieved this by promising that for the first time they would be given salaries and that they could keep NHS beds in hospitals for their private practices. There was much opposition to this, but the July launch date was safe. By the end of the year, about 90 per cent of the population had put their names on GP lists and 90 per cent of doctors were members. The Welfare State had arrived.

While progress in social reform in Britain continued, 1948 was memorable for the levels of violence that were seen in all quarters of the world. Gandhi was assassinated. The Arabs and Israelis went to war. The Soviet Union confirmed the power of its first atomic bomb, which they had tested at the end of the previous year; there was a communist coup in Czechoslovakia; and Soviet forces cut off the German capital and began the blockade of Berlin; Yugoslavia's Marshal Tito broke away from the Soviet Union. The Americans, who had started above-ground atomic bomb tests on Bikini atoll in the Pacific, admitted that the effects of the explosions were far worse than ever before anticipated

Mahatma Gandhi was shot by a Hindu fanatic, Nathruam Godse, on 30 January 1948. The founder of modern India had spent his life advocating non-violent protest. That night Pandit Nehru, the prime minister, broadcast to the Indian people:

> We must hold together and all our petty troubles, difficulties and conflicts must be ended in the face of this great disaster. The light has gone out of our lives and there is darkness everywhere.

As the new nation went into mourning and the last British troops left the subcontinent, internecine violence broke out. It did so in a country that was by no means settled after 1947. Mountbatten had stayed on to supervise the hand-over, but by June 1948 he had left. By September Indian troops had invaded Hyderabad, because the mainly Hindu state had thus far refused to join India.

In Pakistan the consequences of the unrest after Gandhi's death increased tension, and war on a massive scale appeared inevitable. The distress and uncertainty were intensified in September when Pakistan's first leader, its Governor-General, Muhammad Ali Jinnah, died from a heart attack.

Attlee's government had other problems than India and Pakistan. At midnight on 14 May the British mandate in Palestine ended. Israel was declared a state; its first prime minister was David Ben-Gurion. Here too was conflict, for Jews and Arabs refused to withdraw to the agreed lines in the Negev Desert. The Egyptians had left southern Palestine, but the Israelis moved in. The United Nations Security Council threatened to use sanctions if both sides did not stick to the original agreements.

At the end of the year, Israel and Egypt went into discussions organized by the UN but only after most of the important issues had been dropped from the agenda. War was inevitable.

Britain, France and America intended that there should be a federal government in West Germany that would have authority over the zones occupied by the Allied powers. In April, however, the Soviet Union began checking and restricting the flow of traffic, including trains, into the western sector of Berlin, partly because the Soviets believed that the Marshall Plan could undermine their authority in Germany. The blockade coincided with the introduction of the new German mark, which would be more valuable than any currency in the eastern zone.

In June the Soviet Union imposed a total blockade of Berlin. So started the twenty-four-hour, day in, day out, Berlin airlift, which was codenamed Operation Carter Paterson. During each twenty-four-hour period, as many as 200 aircraft ran the blockade, with flights landing every four minutes. The airlift continued until May 1949, and while it lasted the Allies flew in 1.6 million tons of essential foodstuffs and supplies.

During the war, some European states, notably the Norwegians, had wanted a postwar alliance to prevent future European conflicts. Now the way was opened for broad agreement on a North Atlantic alliance against Soviet political ambitions. The communist *coup d'état* in Czechoslovakia in February confirmed in the minds of people like the British Foreign Minister, Ernest Bevin, that future conflict between eastern and western nations, either by design or accident, was inevitable unless such an alliance existed.

Largely secret talks were taking place between the Americans and the British to form a North Atlantic Alliance. The negotiations were so secret that even the French were not told immediately. What the British government did not know was that in the Embassy in Washington one of its diplomats, Donald Maclean, was spying for the Soviet Union.

The Americans were, however, once again reluctant to get involved in a European pact that would drag them into another conflict. Just as Marshall had said that economic help would be available only if the Europeans pulled together, so the feeling in President Truman's White House was that it was up to the Europeans to join in some formal way against a possible Soviet attack. On 17 March 1948 the West European Union was signed in Brussels. This fifty-year mutual aid agreement was known as the Five Power Pact – Britain, France and the three Benelux countries – but its inherent weakness lay in the fact that any European defence arrangement was virtually unworkable unless it included the United States.

The Americans had now defined their own policy towards the Soviet Union. In July 1947 an essay entitled 'The Source of Soviet Conduct' appeared in the New York journal, *Foreign Affairs*. It was by-lined 'X', but the author was an official in the State Department, George F. Kennan:

> It would be an exaggeration to say that American behaviour unassisted and alone could exercise power of life and death over the Communist movement and bring about the early fall of Soviet power in Russia. But the United States has it in its power to increase enormously the strains under which Soviet policy must operate, to force upon the Kremlin a far greater degree of moderation and circumspection than it has had to observe in recent years, and in this way to

> promote tendencies which must eventually find their outlet in either the break-up or the gradual mellowing of Soviet power. . . . The issue of Soviet-American relations is in essence a test of the overall worth of the United States as a nation among nations.

US policy was henceforth that communism should be contained rather than aggressively overcome.

Not every nation saw Stalin as the greatest threat to Europe. France, for example, believed that Germany remained the greatest threat and wanted American troops and equipment positioned in Europe to stop a third German war before it could happen.

In an effort to show that the world was returning to something like normality, the Olympic Games, which had not been held since 1936, took place in London. Not surprisingly, they became known as the austerity games. New heroes were found. The seventeen-year-old American Bob Mathias won the decathlon, while the Czechoslovakian Emil Zatopek won the 10,000 metres.

And the year ended on a cheerful note when in November, Princess Elizabeth gave birth to a son, Charles Philip Arthur George.

Deaths

Antonin Artaud (French playwright)
Edvard Beneš (Czech statesman)
Sergei Eisenstein (Russian film director)
Mahatma Gandhi (Indian nationalist)
D.W. Griffith (US film director)
Muhammad Ali Jinnah (Indian Muslim politician)
Franz Lehár (Hungarian composer)
Louis Lumière (French film pioneer)
Jan Masaryk (Czech politician)
John Joseph Pershing (US soldier)
George Herman 'Babe' Ruth (US sportsman)
Kurt Schwitters (German artist)
Orville Wright (US aviator)

1949

IN 1949 Ireland became a Republic. Until May 1949 Southern Ireland had remained in the Commonwealth, but the Ireland Bill that went through Parliament, opposed by only twelve Labour MPs and two from Ulster, acknowledged the independence of the Irish Republic. With it went Ireland's status as a dominion, although the Southern Irish would still be allowed to vote at British elections. The Act included the provision that Northern Ireland would retain its position within the United Kingdom and that any change would be determined by the Parliament of Northern Ireland.

Most people in Britain were probably more concerned about their living standards than the future of Ireland. In July one of the most militant of workforces, the dockers, came out on strike yet again, and nothing moved in London's ports for three weeks. This was to be a regular occurrence for at least the next two decades until the container cargo industry began to bring about a fundamental change in the traditional system of port workings. Within not much more than thirty years the great London docks would have disappeared and eventually have been replaced by houses.

The good news was that clothes rationing, which had come into force in 1941, was abolished, while for children there was the even happier news that sweets were now 'off the ration'. Behind the joy of sugar zones was the disturbing news to the industry that the government had plans to nationalize sugar refiners. Britain's leading refiner, Tate & Lyle, drew a sugar lump character called Mr Cube, which became part of the anti-nationalization campaign that Lord Lyle himself attributed to 'long haired boys from Bloomsbury'. Lord Lyle was a Conservative.

Britain was now in debt to the United States and Canada for some £600 million. In September the pound was devalued by 30.5 per cent, which led to an immediate rise in the cost of living and essential imports. Many commodities bought overseas had to be paid for in dollars – because £1 would now be worth only \$2.80 compared with the \$4.03 it had been worth the week before. Some import costs were bound to rise. Equally, because a dollar could buy so many more pounds than the previous week, it would be cheaper to buy British exports, which would, in theory, increase. It was a political and fiscal balancing act that would face governments for the next fifty years.

Britain was not alone in its economic difficulties, and other countries had to devalue their currencies, most of which had to be measured against the dollar. The British were now, however, paying much higher prices for petrol and finding little comfort in new clothes and sweets. The milk ration had been cut to two pints per person per week, and butter was now beyond the means of many families.

In the Soviet Union Stalin was having yet another purge. The Foreign Minister, Vyacheslav Molotov, was replaced by Andrei Vishinsky, who had, on behalf of Stalin, been the public prosecutor at the prewar show trials.

By 1949 the Soviet Union was a nuclear power. It also had a foreign and military policy that appeared to threaten every western European state and the United States. From its earliest days, the United States had adopted something close to an isolationist policy, and during the immediate postwar years no one in the White House and State Department had any intention of abandoning isolationism.

As we have seen, the Norwegian government in exile in London had suggested an alliance during the early 1940s, but the driving force behind the alliance that became the North Atlantic Treaty Organization in 1949 and the man who really made it happen was not some inspired Churchillian general, but Britain's Labour Foreign Secretary, Ernest Bevin.

Bevin had none of the traditional qualifications of a British Foreign Secretary. Here was no aristocratic Curzon or Halifax. He was a Somerset lad, orphaned at the age of six, who had became a Bristol van boy, then a docker, then an official in the dockers' union. In the 1920s his ability to negotiate wage deals, against some of the country's finest legal brains, earned him the sobriquet 'the dockers' KC'. It was at this time that he helped build the National Transport and General Workers Union from a score of small guilds and bodies. During the war Churchill gave him the task of overseeing mobilization. He was an outstanding success, and it was at that time that his interest in foreign affairs and defence developed. By the time he became Attlee's Foreign Secretary, Bevin understood perfectly the dilemma facing European security. A transatlantic bridge had to be built. Only then would the Americans be on board as a deterrent and not as a hoped-for ally in some future conflict – which in the 1940s looked very possible.

Historians will generally agree that it was Bevin who pushed and cajoled, who brought together the arguments and balanced the views that led to the most momentous change in American foreign policy of all time. President Truman has been called the father of NATO. It is true that without Truman's say-so NATO would not have been formed. But without Bevin's skills Truman would never have made that decision.

In Washington on 4 April twelve nations – Belgium, Canada, Denmark, France, Iceland, Italy, Luxembourg, the Netherlands, Norway, Portugal, Britain and the United States – signed the North Atlantic Treaty Organization (NATO), which would become the basis of western opposition to Soviet military policy for the remainder of the century. Two days later President Truman observed that, if pushed, he would not hesitate in ordering the use of nuclear weapons.

The determination of the newly formed North Atlantic Treaty Organization, together with the embargoes that had been imposed, brought to an end the Soviet will to continue blockading Berlin. At the end of April the Soviets agreed to four-power talks, and the blockade was lifted on 12 May.

Less than a fortnight later, the German Federal Republic was born, with its capital in Bonn. The man who would become Germany's postwar leader, Dr Konrad Adenauer, said he believed that the new Republic and its constitution would lead to reunification with East Germany. It would not, and when unification came Adenauer would be long dead.

Inevitably for the British, one of the moments that cheered the nation came out of adversity. In March the frigate HMS *Amethyst* was trapped up the Yangtse River in China. The *Amethyst* represented everything that the advancing armies of Mao Zedong (Mao Tse-tung) hated, and it was shelled by the Chinese. It seemed that she would be sunk in the river. The captain had been killed, and the ship was taken over by Lieutenant Commander Kerans. So began a 140-mile, high-speed attempt to break out of the Yangtse. With Chinese artillery bombarding the frigate, Kerans managed to escape. The first the nation knew for sure was when he signalled the Admiralty: 'Have rejoined the fleet south of Woosung. No damage or casualties. God Save the King.' Another symbol to lift the gloom was an end to the 1939 ban on coloured lights and neon signs. In 1949 Piccadilly Circus came back to life. There were few heroes in what became the book of 1949. George Orwell, who died the following year, published *1984*. His warning against totalitarianism gave the language a new expression: 'Big Brother is watching you.'

Deaths
Tommy Handley (comedian)
Maurice Maeterlinck (Belgian writer)
Margaret Mitchell (US writer)
Edward R. Stettinius (US industrialist)
Richard Strauss (German composer)
James Henry Thomas (politician)

CHAPTER SIX

THE END OF POWER 1950–1959

1950

IN FEBRUARY 1950 the Labour government of Clement Attlee faced its first full test of popularity after the postwar years. This was the government that had promised to nationalize the great industries of coal, electricity and the railways. It was also the government that had brought about the National Health Service. Would the people blame the government for an economic crisis that was not theirs alone? Would the praise for social change compensate for the depression of the past five years that had led so many to seek their futures in far-away countries such as Australia?

In the third week of February the nation went to the polls. Boundary changes meant there would be fewer MPs: the twelve university seats had gone, as had that for the City of London. In 1945 Labour had won 393 seats, the Conservatives 210 and the Liberals twelve; there were twenty-five Independent MPs. In 1950, however, Labour won only 315 seats, the Conservatives had 298, the Liberals were down to nine and there were three others. This was the closest general election result of the century.

To say that the socialist experiment had failed is clearly untrue. That it was taking place during one of the most austere periods of the century confirmed a later American president's axiom: 'It's the economy, stupid!' It would seem far more likely that people had simply had enough of being told to tighten their belts and that the previous year's 30 per cent devaluation had not had time to filter through to wallets and purses. There was, of course, a further influence on the election – its timing. It has been long believed that Labour supporters do not go out to vote in bad weather as willingly as Tories do.

Labour increased its vote by more than a million and there was more than an 80 per cent turn-out, which should have been to Labour's advantage. The government had a parliamentary majority of just five seats, however, and the Conservatives guessed that Attlee could not survive for long.

Despite their differences over the economy, there was a common assumption among all political parties: Britain's long-term interests lay with the Commonwealth, the transatlantic relationship and Europe. The Commonwealth was the home of the colonies that Britain would have to give up. The transatlantic relationship was that British illusion, the Anglo-American 'special' relationship, which did not exist unless some circumstance arose where it was useful to both countries (that is, useful to the United States) that it should.

Europe was important as a security and economic factor in Britain's immediate future, but Britain believed that it, Britain, was the most important nation in Europe. This was no longer true. The reason for this British illusion lay in the fact that few people in Whitehall understood what was now being presented to the nation for examination: the Schuman Plan. In May the French Foreign Minister, Robert Schuman, proposed a European Coal and Steel Community, effectively the embryo from which the European Union would be born. The Schuman Plan came from Jean Monnet's idea of a greater Europe. This first step would control the industries, production and prices within a federation of coal- and steel-producing states. For Europe in 1950 the choice of coal and steel represented an understanding that these were two of the major elements (the other was energy) that would drive the domestic and export markets of Europe for decades.

By 1952 the European Coal and Steel Community would be under way, and France, West Germany, the Benelux states and Italy would be its members. Britain, however, failed to grasp its significance in August 1950 or, at least, was reluctant to sign with the others at the Paris conference to launch the community. With the memories of the 1930s and, more importantly, the Second World War so fresh, that reluctance was understandable. More likely, Attlee's government, in spite of the advice from the Whitehall bureaucracy – which was not always the dull scholarship popularly portrayed – had too much on its collective mind to analyse properly what the Schuman Plan was presenting.

Whatever the reason, the United Kingdom slipped from the front of European decision-making – an action, or perhaps inaction, of which its most favoured ally, the United States, disapproved. The US State Department did not recognize the special relationship. It wanted a strong Europe to bring about stability in the face of the increasing Soviet political and military threat. The Americans believed that even with NATO, it was in everyone's interest that Britain should be inside 'Europe' instead of pretending they were half-American.

In the summer of 1950 an event occurred that diverted Britain's immediate attention from Europe. In June the Korean War began.

Korea was a divided nation. The Americans supported the south; the Soviet Union and China supported the communist north. Japan had taken over Korea in 1910, and at a meeting in Cairo in the middle of the Second World War, the British, American and Chinese governments had met to discuss the future of Korea. At that meeting they promised to get Korea back from the Japanese and to make the state fully independent. Not long after that, the Russians were persuaded to go along with the agreement, largely because it would enable them to settle an old score that dated from their defeat by the Japanese at the beginning of the century.

An agreement was made to set up a council with four trustees – Britain, China, the United States and the Soviet Union – to see Korea through a five-year period towards democracy. Korea was then divided. The Soviet Union would take over the 8 million Koreans in the north, with their big industrial base, and the Americans would administer the 20 million, mainly peasants, in the south. The Communists in the north were unpopular at first, but they restored industries and gave away land. In the south the Korean leadership was aged; they tried their hand at democracy and capitalism, but once the Americans had left in 1949, the leaders became oppressive, allowed no opposition and were corrupt.

It is worth understanding the background to the Korean War, partly because Britain was deeply involved in it and British troops died there and partly because Korea represented a point at which the Western allies decided to make a military stand against communism.

On 25 June 1950 North Korean forces crossed the border into South Korea. A United Nations resolution condemned the North Korean action, describing it as 'an act of aggression', which in UN terms was powerful language. The UN recommended that its members go to the help of South Korea.

Korea could have become a wholly communist state had it not been for three factors: the Americans immediately sent troops, ships and aircraft; the United Nations gave its blessing for this action; and the Soviet Union failed to veto the UN action. The Soviet delegation was not at the UN when the vote was taken, because it had walked out of the UN Security Council in January 1950 when it learned that China was represented by the deposed Nationalist Chinese. This boycott meant that the UN could take decisions to which the Soviets would never have agreed. Never again would the Soviet Union put itself in such a position.

The American general, Douglas MacArthur, took command of the nominal UN force. The Royal Navy, on its summer exercises with more than twenty ships in the Far East, was put under MacArthur's command. It took a month before Britain announced that soldiers would also be sent to join US forces, who were already based in South Korea. It was not until 29 August, two months after the North Koreans invaded, that the first British troops arrived in Korea. Given the logistical arrangements, that was not so slow once the decision had been taken. Britain wanted to be seen by the White House as the staunchest and, above all, the promptest of allies. In 1950 Britain was not the world power it thought it should be, and it was believed that sending troops to fight alongside the Americans would boost British standing in Washington, where many saw it as just another European has-been.

MacArthur saw the Korean War as an opportunity to put down China, which he believed to be a threat to American interests in the Far East. His enthusiasm was not supported in Washington, however. He was taking a political initiative under the UN flag, and the British government began to wonder if the war in Korea might develop into something much greater, including another Hiroshima. China entered the war in November after the MacArthur-led UN forces had gone right to the Chinese border. However, by the end of the year, the UN was on the run – to the south. The war had turned against them, and MacArthur's days as commander were numbered. So were Britain's in Egypt.

The British kept troops in the strategically important Suez Canal Zone. In November 1950 the King of Egypt, Farouk, demanded that the British withdraw its troops so that Egypt could once more rule Sudan. The Suez Canal was the most important waterway in the region, and Britain had no intention of getting out of the Canal Zone. From this date, Britain had a major internal security operation running in the Canal area. Warships, troops and aircraft were deployed in large numbers, and riots, terrorism and the continuing threat of all-out war characterized Britain's relations with Egypt for the next six years. The conflict ended in the débâcle that was simply known in contemporary British history as Suez, and it would be the undoing of the then prime minister, Anthony Eden. Few, listening to the speech of Farouk on 16 November 1950, doubted that once more Britain was on the edge of yet another conflict.

If British MPs wanted to debate the national interests at home and abroad, they now had their own forum in which to do so. In the bombings of May 1941 the Commons Chamber had been destroyed. Now, nine years later, the rebuilding and restoration was complete, and George VI, already desperately ill from lung cancer, opened the new Chamber on 26 October.

One politician who would no longer take much part in political life was the Chancellor of the Exchequer, Sir Stafford Cripps. This was the man who had preached postwar austerity economics, but by October 1950 Cripps was too ill to continue, and he was replaced in Cabinet by one of the 1945 intake of Labour MPs, Hugh Gaitskell.

Deaths

Léon Blum (French politician)
Edgar Rice Burroughs (US writer)
Karl Jansky (US engineer)
Al Jolson (US entertainer)
William L. Mackenzie King (Canadian politician)
Harold Laski (political scientist)
Sir Harry Lauder (comedian)
Heinrich Mann (German writer)
Edna St Vincent Millay (US poet)
E.A. Milne (astronomer)
Vaslav Nijinsky (Russian dancer)
George Orwell (writer)
George Bernard Shaw (Irish writer)
Jan Smuts (South African politician)

Archibald Percival Wavell, 1st Earl Wavell (soldier)
Kurt Weill (US composer)

1951

ON 3 MAY the King and Queen opened the Festival of Britain on the transformed 27 acres of bomb site on the South Bank of the Thames near Waterloo. It was now a riverside village of pavilions, sculptures, the huge Festival Hall and the vertical cigar that was called Skylon. The centrepiece was the Dome of Discovery. The idea of the dome was to be used again for the Millennium Exhibition at Greenwich – the brainchild in the 1990s of the Labour politician, Peter Mandelson. Perhaps this concept may have something to do with the fact that Mandelson's grandfather, the Labour minister Herbert Morrison, was in charge of the 1951 exhibition.

Morrison said that the Festival of Britain had been organized so that the people could give themselves a pat on the back. Certainly the design team, led by Hugh Casson, had created shapes and spaces that reflected the fun and fantasy of what Britain hoped for in the future after the long years of austere utility designs and fabrics. Inside the pavilions were exhibitions of British technology, engineering and science. The only permanent building was the Festival Hall, and when the exhibition closed at the end of September nothing was left to remind the British of their greatness. No one had a plan to transform this working model of the nation's ingenuity into the industrial manufacturing process that would be so needed in the coming decades.

Clement Attlee's administration survived the Festival but not the year. The economy had not recovered, although the jobless figure was down to a remarkably low 253,000. With the exception of 1955, this would be the lowest peacetime jobless figure of the century, but it did not properly reflect the state of British industry nor the service sector, including the financial institutions.

Attlee was going through an upsetting period within his own Cabinet, and two issues causing particular dissension were defence spending and the Health Service, the monument to the postwar Labour government.

The Health Service had proved far more expensive than anyone had imagined, and in 1951 the government decided to introduce charges for spectacles and dentures. At the same time defence spending was being increased. Bevan regarded these policies as 'repugnant' and resigned, together with the President of the Board of Trade, Harold Wilson. Attlee, who was in hospital at the time, had no grip on his government and little hope of countering Bevan and those within the party who agreed with him.

Britain's troubles abroad were no less complex, but by now there was no Ernest Bevin at the Foreign Office. He died on 14 April, his place in the Cabinet having been taken by Herbert Morrison. Bevin was described by the historian Alan Bullock as belonging to that 'small group of men who can be said to have had a decisive impact on the history of their time'.

Second thoughts surfaced about not having joined the European Coal and Steel Community. Those doubts were reflected in the United States and in France and Germany, which made Britain's relations with those nations all the more difficult.

The war continued in Korea, and defence spending increased as more than 250,000 reservists were called up.

The ground rules of fighting the war as a UN force had changed since June 1950. The political dimension had turned into a direct conflict between President Truman and General MacArthur over the war aims: MacArthur wanted to destroy China; Truman wanted to contain the North Koreans above the 38th parallel. If MacArthur were allowed to dictate American policy, the Korean conflict could slip into the Third World War, which would be even more terrible than preceding wars because now the Soviet Union was testing atomic weapons and the United States was producing an even more powerful system, the hydrogen bomb.

On 11 April 1951 Truman dismissed MacArthur, and the United States returned to pursuing a policy of containing communism rather than attacking it. As Omar Bradley, one of the wartime commanders in Europe and the longest surviving and highest ranking general in the US army, remarked, MacArthur's actions would have resulted in 'the wrong war, at the wrong place, at the wrong time, and with the wrong enemy'.

Relieved, Britain continued to support the United States, and in Washington there was new-found warmth for the British. It was at this point that two British diplomats, who had been in the British Embassy in Washington, defected to Moscow. Donald Maclean and Guy Burgess had been working for the Soviet Union as spies and were part of a ring that included Kim Philby and Anthony Blunt. Maclean had been privy to high-level discussions about the formation of NATO, but when they were warned by Anthony Blunt that they were under investigation in Britain, both men disappeared, reappearing in Moscow in 1956.

In the Near East, discussions with Egypt were getting nowhere and there was every sign that this would turn into yet another military conflict.

There was also increased tension in Iran, as Persia had been known since 1925, where Britain had been developing oil fields since 1909. The nationalist movement in Iran had started to nationalize the country's oil fields. After rioting at the Abadan oil refinery, the Shah was forced to appoint the militantly nationalist Dr Mohammed Mossadeq as prime minister, and on 20 May the Anglo-Iranian Oil Company was told that it was to be nationalized. Britain did what it always did in this type of situation: it sent a gunboat, well, a big cruiser. At this point, the special transatlantic relationship would have been quite useful. Instead, the White House told Downing Street that the Anglo-Iranian dispute was heading for disaster.

By August Britain had been forced to open talks with the Iranians, and by the end of the month Mossadeq's government ordered British employees out of Iran. On 27 September 1951 the Iranian army seized control of the refinery at Abadan.

It was clear that as long as the occasionally theatrical Dr Mossadeq remained in power, there was little chance of any agreement being reached between Britain and Iran. The Shah, supposedly a friend of Britain, was in no position to help.

Eventually, Mossadeq was replaced in August 1953 by General Zahedi. Without the expert personnel, whom Mossadeq had expelled, the nationalized oil fields did not provide the unlimited wealth for Iran that had been foretold.

As if all this was not enough, Britain was now deeply involved in an anti-communist war in Malaya, and at the same time, extra British troops were being airlifted to Egypt as Britain tried to defend its position in the Suez Canal Zone.

In 1951 there was no need to wait for Harold Macmillan's 'winds of change' speech to understand that Britain was being kicked out of almost every foothold it had kept around the globe until just a decade earlier.

There was one other factor disturbing the prime minister: the King was terminally ill from cancer. George VI was, however, well enough to understand the state of his government. In June 1951 the King asked Attlee how long he thought he could continue because he planned to go on a six-month tour of the Commonwealth and it would, he thought, be unhelpful if he were to be away for such a long period while the government was in jeopardy. As it turned out, Princess Elizabeth and Prince Philip went in the King's place.

On 22 September, in the small operating theatre in Buckingham Palace, George VI's left lung was removed. By then the king had an understanding from Attlee that he would go to the country in the autumn and that the election would take place on Thursday, 25 October.

No one in Whitehall and no one but the absolute optimists in the Labour Party believed that Attlee would survive the general election. Nor did he.

During the campaign the Labour press accused the Conservative leader, Winston Churchill, of war-mongering and of being incapable of settling the Anglo-Iranian dispute peacefully. For their part the Conservatives attacked Labour's promises and claimed that they, the Conservatives, were the party that would build 300,000 houses a year and make Britain a better place in which to live. One of the major themes of the election campaign was military spending. Churchill himself raised the question:

> Since the General Election of 1950, an additional heavy burden has come upon us. The Soviet aggression in Korea led to a fierce war on a considerable scale. This has started an immense additional process of rearmament against aggression by Communist Russia by all free democracies of the world with the United States doing and paying the bulk . . .
>
> . . . what are we rearming for? It is to prevent Communist Russia, its reluctant satellites, and its ardent votaries spread about in many countries – some of them even here – from beating us all down to their dead level as they have done, as much as they can, to the people of every country they have

> occupied during and since the war. But rearmament is only half a policy. Unless you are armed and strong you cannot expect any mercy from the Communists; but if you are armed and strong you may make a bargain with them which might rid the world of the terror in which it now lies and relieve us all from much of the impoverished and privations into which we shall otherwise certainly sink.

Here were the seeds of what some have called a strength and others an albatross – the start of the escalation of British defence spending until it was the third, sometimes the second, biggest budget in Whitehall. It is possible to date the deliberate policy to build a so-called deterrent force against the Soviet Union from the beginning of the 1950s.

On the whole, Labour had honoured its 1945 election pledges – apart from house-building – and this very success was a weakness: there were no big issues behind which the party could unite. The small things that had not been done became much more important issues than the success of what had been accomplished.

More than 80 per cent of the electorate turned out to vote. In spite of predictions of big Conservative gains, the Tories won 321 seats while Labour clung to 295 seats. The Liberals got six seats and there were three others. As was the pattern of politics that was to be repeated over the next four decades, disaffected Liberals voted Conservative, partly because they had originally been disaffected Conservatives, voting Liberal.

On 26 October 1951, at the age of seventy-seven, Winston Churchill returned to Downing Street.

Perhaps more memorable in the public's mind than events in far-off Korea and Iran were two radio programmes that began in 1951, *The Archers* and *The Goon Show*. The former was to track public values for the rest of the century. The latter somehow represented the jumble of bizarre emotions about who and what the British felt they were and had been.

Deaths

Ernest Bevin (politician)
André Gide (French writer)
William Randolph Hearst (US publisher)
William K. Kellogg (US inventor)
Constant Lambert (composer)
Sinclair Lewis (US writer)
Liaquat Ali Khan (Pakistani politician)
Maxim Litvinov (Russian politician)
Carl Mannerheim (Finnish politician)
Willem Mengelberg (Dutch conductor)

Ivor Novello (actor and playwright)
Philippe Pétain (French politician)
Ferdinand Porsche (German designer)
Artur Schnabel (Austrian pianist)
Arnold Schoenberg (Austrian composer)
Ludwig Wittgenstein (philosopher)

1952

THE YEAR opened with the new prime minister, Winston Churchill, in Washington. He had never deviated from his opinion that the United States remained the cornerstone of Britain's – and Europe's – security and prosperity. He had understood and even proposed a need for a united Europe, but he had also considered the possibility that one day there might be such close ties between the United States and Britain that the countries would have joint citizenship.

The Americans were more likely to warm to Churchill, the grand wartime and slightly eccentric figure, than to his banker-like predecessor, Clement Attlee. Moreover, the Americans retained a suspicion of Labour, a term that has overtones for them of organized unions.

Churchill and Truman felt that the American action in Korea and the British determination to stand sentry over the Suez Canal represented a combined show of force to prove that the so-called 'free world' was not naked. Churchill told Truman that Britain's contribution to NATO would be as big as they could afford. He was also now aware that Attlee's government had supported the development of atomic weaponry, which meant Britain had to be taken as a world power.

There is some evidence to suggest that Truman, although respectful, was rather unimpressed with Churchill, who might well have appeared to have returned to Downing Street with a sense that the clock had stopped in the late 1930s.

Whatever the feelings in Washington, in Britain Churchill was the right man. He was the figurehead needed to lead the nation out of the austerity that had lasted for far longer than the public had expected and was still not at an end. The new Chancellor of the Exchequer, R.A. Butler, was ordering even more restrictions and cutting food subsidies. The cheese ration was 1 ounce (about 25 grams) a week per person. The bank rate was up to 4 per cent. Farmers were offered £5 for every acre of grazing land they put down to crops. Seven years after the end of the Second World War Britain was still broke.

Rejected in 1945, the Conservative Party had all but fallen apart. The man responsible for rebuilding it was Butler as head of the Conservative research department, and he and Frederick Woolton, the party chairman, had had the task of making the Conservatives re-electable. Part of that process was to show the party how it fitted into a comprehensive welfare society. There is no evidence, for example, that Churchill believed in Welfare State policies any more than he did in independence in India.

Churchill was not good at being in this part of the century. He neither understood nor much cared about most urgent domestic policies, including industrial relations, although he believed in the need to finance foreign policy. Britain was now fighting in Korea, Malaya and Egypt and would soon need to send troops to Kenya. Britain still had global commitments, and almost one-third of government expenditure was on the military.

A further strain on Churchill was the way he coped with events in February 1952. On 6 February 1952 George VI died at Sandringham. Princess Elizabeth and Prince Philip were in Kenya, and only a week earlier she had said goodbye to her father at London airport. It was the Duke of Edinburgh who told her that she was now Queen.

Churchill was saddened by the thought that he might not be a good prime minister to the young Queen. Jock Colville, his private secretary, wrote that when he went into Churchill's bedroom after the news was announced, he found the prime minister with tears in his eyes:

> I tried to cheer him up by saying how well he would get on with the new queen, but all he could say was that he did not know her and that she was only a child.

There now arose a minor constitutional matter over the name of the royal house, which, if nothing else, reflected badly on the ambitious Lord Mountbatten. At a party at Broadlands, the Mountbatten home, Mountbatten had told his guests that now the King was dead the royal family was the House of Mountbatten. This was quite unacceptable, and no matter what influence Mountbatten claimed, neither the Cabinet, nor Churchill, would have agreed. Prince Philip proposed that his children might be known as the House of Edinburgh, but this, too, was unacceptable. The Queen would remain the head of the House of Windsor. The drama was over, but the nasty taste had not left the constitutional lawyers' mouths.

The pressure of all this told on Churchill, and on 21 February he was poorly enough for his doctors to suggest that if he did not take it easy he might have a stroke. The suggestion was made, in private, that Churchill's load would be eased if he remained prime minister but went to the House of Lords, with Anthony Eden, then Foreign Secretary, becoming the Conservative leader in the Commons. Although Churchill might have thought this a reasonable idea, it would, in 1952, have been politically insensitive to revert to a system that had died at the turn of the century.

In May 1952 Churchill said that there had to be a period of calmness and what he called 'resolute government' to overcome all the wasteful and expensive policies of the previous government. Butler could be just as austere as Cripps, but he needed Churchill's backing for potentially controversial cuts, including some 40 per cent of the cost of keeping British forces in Germany. The offset agreement that had to be negotiated and renegotiated with the Germans could not pay the true cost to an already overstretched military budget.

The long, hot summer of 1952 failed to warm Anglo-Soviet relations. By the end of June, French, American and British foreign ministers were defining new policies to deal with the increasingly dangerous relations with the Soviet Union. This relationship was exacerbated by the increased number of East Germans who were attempting to escape to the West. By the end of the summer of 1952 they were doing so in their thousands.

Britain's military concern may have been in Korea but clear signs of the nastiest of wars, terrorism, had appeared in Kenya. This was the start of the war against the Mau Mau, a secret society of Africans committed to ridding Kenya of white settlers and its own tribal land of all settlers, both black and white. The main tribe affected by Mau Mau was the Kikuyu, whose leader, Jomo Kenyatta, would one day lead his country.

In August the Kenyan government began to impose curfews around Nairobi. The Mau Mau attacks were not directed against the white settlers, but against Africans who had refused to join them, and by mid-October the terrorism could not be contained by the Kenyan security forces. Forty or so people had been murdered that autumn, including Africans, among them Chief Waruhui. Kenyatta, who was the leader of the Kenya Africa Union, was jailed, and a round-up of hundreds of Mau Mau suspects was ordered. On 20 October troops from the British force in the Suez Canal zone started to arrive at Nairobi airport, and settlers began to arm themselves against Mau Mau.

Kenyatta was portrayed as an evil African, but his motives were more sophisticated. He had lived in England during the war and had married an English woman. When he returned to Kenya he had been branded as an agitator for raising the vexed issues of African land rights and trying to set up special schools for Africans. A newspaper article even compared him to Hitler. The 'white highlanders' – the name given to the settlers – believed that Britain was not taking their plight seriously enough and that the governor, Sir Evelyn Baring, should be tougher. The war with Mau Mau was now an official emergency and would remain so until 1960.

That late autumn the news from the United States was pleasing to the British prime minister. Churchill's wartime comrade, Eisenhower, defeated the Democrat, Adlai Stevenson, in the United States presidential election. Churchill imagined that Eisenhower would understand the special relationship between Britain and the United States. Eisenhower understood no such thing, however. The new president was more concerned with the potential military threat from the Soviet Union, but within months of Eisenhower moving into the White House, Stalin would be dead and a more dangerous period in East–West relations would begin.

In the year's lighter moments Gene Kelly splashed through the hit song of the year, 'Singin' in the Rain', and Charlie Chaplin made what he thought was probably his finest film, *Limelight*. Peggy Ashcroft appeared in a new play by

Terence Rattigan, *The Deep Blue Sea*, and a Technicolor film called *Niagara* presented Hollywood with a new goddess, Marilyn Monroe.

Deaths
Sir Richard Stafford Cripps (politician)
Benedetto Croce (Italian philosopher)
William Fox (US film executive)
George VI
Knut Hamsun (Norwegian writer)
William Morris Hughes (Australian politician)
Maria Montessori (Italian educator)
Eva Perón (Argentinian politician)
George Santayana (Spanish philosopher)
Sir Charles S. Sherrington (physiologist)
Dr Chaim Weizmann (Israeli politician)

1953

ON 2 JUNE 1953 Elizabeth II was crowned and, Britain was told, the new Elizabethan age had begun.

Apart from the coronation, foreign affairs dominated the year. Joseph Stalin suffered a brain haemorrhage and died on 5 March at the age of seventy-three. His successor was Georgi Malenkov, but old Russia hands pointed to the importance given to the person in charge of Stalin's funeral arrangements. This was Nikita Khrushchev, the leader of the Communist Party Secretariat and a senior member of the Politburo, the Soviet Cabinet. *Pravda* ('Truth'), the newspaper that Stalin himself had founded in 1912, declared that this was a time to guard against the state's enemies, both internal and external.

The Soviet Union would now go through complex and often brutal manoeuvres, including the execution of the ruthless head of Soviet security, Lavrenti Beria. Khrushchev emerged to replace Malenkov and to dominate Soviet society and East–West relations for more than a decade, and it would be Khrushchev who would be faced down by Kennedy in the Cuban missile crisis in October 1962.

After three years the Korean War came to an end with an armistice, signed at Panmunjom, that maintained the division on the 38th parallel. During the war 2 million people had died, and the tension between North and South Korea was to continue for the rest of the century.

In Southeast Asia the war in Indochina was going badly for the French – it was a war they could not win. Southeast Asia was the great test of the desire to contain communism that dominated US defence policy. The Americans were never to learn that their policy of containment would be worthless in Southeast Asia and particularly in Indochina or Vietnam, as they would learn to call it. The Secretary of State, John Foster Dulles, demonstrated the American obsession with the spread of communism. Dulles believed that if the French were forced out of Indochina, Southeast Asia would fall to communism just like 'a row of dominoes'. So the domino theory was born.

In the United States Senator Joseph McCarthy became chairman of the Senate Permanent Subcommittee on Investigations. For the previous three years McCarthy had campaigned against communism in the United States, and he claimed that the State Department was protecting more than 200 communists, although he was never able to prove this. His questioning method was crude and based, more or less, on the single line: 'Are you, or have you ever been, a member of the Communist Party?' Innuendo was enough to convict, according to the McCarthy principle. Well-known people were driven from the United States by his accusations, but in 1954 he was castigated by a majority of his peers in the Senate. Before he was finally disgraced and his ideas rejected, he had given his name to modern American witch-hunting – McCarthyism.

In Europe the news in 1953 was dominated by events in East Berlin and Hungary. In mid-June German workers began the biggest anti-Soviet demonstration seen in the Soviet zone, and they quickly attracted spontaneous support from men and women in factories, shops, schools and homes. The trigger that brought perhaps 100,000 onto the streets in support of this short-lived uprising was a government instruction to construction workers that productivity had to be increased by 10 per cent. Soviet tanks and armoured personnel carriers backed the infantry as it dispersed the demonstrators, and a curfew and martial law were imposed.

In Hungary the protest against communist domination took another form: refugees began escaping in their hundreds. Shortages of almost every kind, particularly food, persuaded many Hungarians that enough was enough, and although they were fired upon by Russian border guards and many were killed, more than 2000 Hungarians managed to escape to the West. The new Hungarian prime minister, Imre Nagy, attempted to reassure the Hungarians that the totalitarian rule would be eased.

The British response to the uprising in East Berlin and the discontent in Hungary was low key. The United Kingdom was in no position to interfere, and certainly no other nation showed any inclination to do anything other than voice diplomatic disquiet. The one Briton whose voice the world might have expected to hear, Winston Churchill, was ill.

Since the death of Stalin had been announced on 9 March, Churchill had believed that it was now both possible and proper to open a dialogue with the Soviet Union. He wanted Eisenhower to go to Moscow, but Eisenhower's advisers were against the idea because a meeting with Soviet leaders would be turned against the Western powers. Churchill suggested a meeting on mutual ground – Vienna, for example – but Eisenhower was still was not keen.

The workload on Churchill now increased because Eden was in Boston for surgery, and Churchill decided to take over the Foreign Office. Here we have a

British prime minister, almost eighty years old, who was not fit and showing the first signs of serious if not fatal illness, bearing not only the responsibility for domestic policy but also for the wars in Korea and Southeast Asia and the Mau Mau emergency. In addition to all this and just a month before the coronation, he was attempting, without encouragement (and in the face of doubts in the Foreign Office), to prepare the huge task of establishing an East–West détente. Churchill needed to know the new leaders, and the only way to achieve that was by going to meet them. He told the Commons in May 1953 that it was better to meet with a chance of generating a feeling that 'they might do something better than tear the human race, including themselves, to bits'.

The coronation may have been a welcome distraction, but on the afternoon that followed Churchill was chairing the Commonwealth prime ministers' meeting and looking for their support for, at least, informal discussions with Malenkov. It is important not to underestimate the role of the one-time colonies in Britain's policy making. Not only had they had sent soldiers into the two world wars, but they had also fought alongside British soldiers during the Boer War. In the 1950s what the Commonwealth thought still mattered. Its leaders were influential and included men such as Robert Menzies, the Australian Prime Minister, and Lester Pearson of Canada, who influenced Anglo-Canadian relations as well as the workings of the United Nations during its infancy. In 1953 everyone understood that whatever Churchill's reasons for opposing Indian independence, the age of independence for the dominions and Commonwealth had arrived. Within a decade, the process of handing power to former colonies would be almost completed.

In 1953 the changing processes of governing the colonies focused on what would become the most vexed area of the unravelling of the colonial system – Rhodesia. A Cabinet Paper laid before the prime minister expressed some of the extreme doubts that were to come true – whatever the warm feelings expressed at the coronation banquets. In January 1953 a conference was held in London between the governments of the Britain and the three central African nations of Southern Rhodesia (now Zimbabwe), Northern Rhodesia (now Zambia) and Nyasaland (now Malawi). Some of the dangers ahead were already being identified:

> Closer political association between the three central African Territories is essential . . . individually the Territories are vulnerable. Their individual economies are ill-balanced and ill-equipped to withstand the strong economic pressures of a changing world. Of the three Territories, only South Rhodesia has any significant second industries. Northern Rhodesia is very largely dependent on her copper industry, which provides over four-fifths of her exports. Nyasaland, an agricultural community, has to rely too much on a few primary products such as tobacco, tea and cotton and cannot develop herself unaided . . . Development of the largely untapped resources of this potentially wealthy area demands the combined efforts of the three Territories acting

> together. The right thing must be done in the right place. There are railways to be built; there are rivers to be harnessed; power must be developed to meet the needs of industry; food production must be expanded to meet the ever growing needs of a steadily increasing population. Such development requires expenditure of capital and material resources on a large scale.

The new postwar economic world coincided with the end of colonial rule. The people who took over were often not capable of running the economic affairs of their newly independent states, and there was no easy run-in to their administrations. Here, in the early 1950s, were the beginnings of some of the international tragedy that would become known as third world debt.

Britain's 1953 solution to the problem of Northern and Southern Rhodesia and Nyasaland was to join them together as the Central African Federation. In coronation year this was considered something of an achievement. The Africans did not agree, however, although the arrangement lasted for two prime ministers, Godfrey Huggins and the rather better known, Roy Welensky, and until 1963.

Day after day Churchill was either chairing meetings or promoting ideas that would persuade the Americans and the French that there should be a conference to include Malenkov. At last, he had, he believed, persuaded them to meet in Bermuda, but on 23 June, after an official dinner in Downing Street, Churchill got up from the dining table, faltered and then suffered a stroke. The effects were not noticeable to many other than those who knew, but by 26 June his left side was paralysed. A news blackout was put on his medical condition and he went down to Chartwell.

His determination to succeed in setting up a dialogue between London, Washington and Moscow was undiminished, however. In November he went into the Commons and delivered his first speech to Parliament since the stroke. It was an outstanding success.By December the news from Moscow did not augur well for any discussions, but Churchill was not put off. On 1 December he flew to Bermuda for talks with Eisenhower and the French prime minister, Joseph Laniel. Eisenhower was in a tough mood and told Churchill that if the Koreans broke the armistice they, the Americans, would use atomic weapons. Churchill did not get agreement for an East–West meeting. In 1953 he won the Nobel Prize for Literature, but Clementine, Lady Churchill, had to go to Stockholm to fetch it. Churchill was across the ocean attempting to manage the affairs of the world.

This was the year in which two Cambridge scientists, James Watson and Francis Crick, published their work on deoxyribonucleic acid (DNA), and another Cambridge man, the biochemist Frederick Sanger, published the results of his eight-year study into the chemical analysis of insulin. Of even greater immediate practical importance was the development of a vaccine by Dr Jonas Salk. It became known as the Salk vaccine, and its use led to the virtual eradication of paralytic poliomyelitis in industrialized countries.

No science could check the hurricane winds that hit the east coast of Britain that winter. The storms arrived at the same time as extraordinarily high tides and swept aside sea defences from the Wash to the Kent coast. Hundreds of people were drowned and thousands made homeless in what became known in British disaster lore as the East Coast Floods. Across the North Sea, more than 1000 people died in the Netherlands when the dykes burst during the same night of storms.

Just four days before the coronation Edmund Hilary and Tenzing Norgay reached the summit of Everest; they were the first to do so, although some doubts were to be raised in 1999 when the remains of George Leigh Mallory were discovered on the mountain where he had died in 1924.

Four days after the coronation, Sir Gordon Richards, the nation's most famous jockey, at last won the Derby on the 5–1 favourite, Pinza; Auriole came second. The recently knighted Richards was taking a chance – Auriole was owned by the Queen. Randolph Turpin won the World Middle Weight Championship and, after twenty years of trying, the England cricket side, or the MCC as it still was, won the Ashes.

The thirty-eight-year-old Stanley Matthews, certainly the most famous soccer player of his generation, won his first cup final medal when his team, Blackpool, beat Bolton Wanderers 3–1.

In Hollywood Twentieth-Century Fox went over to a new movie system called CinemaScope, which had stereophonic sound.

Deaths
Sir Arnold Bax (composer)
Hilaire Belloc (writer)
Lavrenti Beria (Russian politician)
Margaret Bondfield (politician)
Raoul Dufy (French artist)
Kathleen Ferrier (contralto)
Abdul Aziz ibn Saud (King of Saudi Arabia)
Mary of Teck (consort of George V)
Eugene O'Neill (US playwright)
Francis Picabia (French artist)
Sergei Prokofiev (Russian composer)
Django Reinhardt (French guitarist)
Ethel and Julius Rosenberg (US spies)
Kurt Schumacher (German politician)
Joseph Stalin (Russian dictator)
Robert Taft (US politician)
Dylan Thomas (poet)
Hank Williams (US singer)

1954

FOREIGN AFFAIRS dominated 1954 as they had 1953. By this time there was not always agreement among the Western allies, especially when the subject was Germany. At a meeting in Berlin in January between the United States, the Soviet Union, France and Britain, Britain had proposed that the way to reunite Germany would be to hold free elections in both sectors for an all-German assembly, a legislature that would lead to the government of one Germany. The Soviet Union rejected the proposal, suggesting instead a scheme for an all-German government without first holding elections. The Allies rejected this because it would have meant a tacit acceptance of the existing East German government. The Russians then suggested a European defence agreement that would replace NATO, but the Western Allies would never accept this idea. The summit ended in complete failure.

In October 1954 the original members of NATO met in London, and Germany was at the top of the agenda. No one expected reunification, so it was proposed that West Germany be made a member of NATO. This raised potential areas of confrontation with the Soviet Union, the most important of which was that it meant West German rearmament. In spite of the evident postwar rapprochement between France and Konrad Adenaeur's West Germany, the government in Paris was not alone in having doubts on this score. Germany would not be allowed to have a nuclear weapon capability even though it was a free member of the alliance, nor, constitutionally, did West Germany want to go down the nuclear path. Nor, constitutionally, could West Germany deploy her forces beyond national boundaries.

The Soviet reaction to West Germany joining NATO was the Warsaw Pact Treaty, which was ratified in May 1955, just a week after West Germany became a sovereign state.

Just as France had originally joined NATO because it feared that Germany would rise against the rest of Europe, in 1954 the Soviet Union feared Germany more than it did the United States. Considering its twentieth-century experiences in two wars against Germany this was not an altogether unreasonable fear.

France's main foreign policy dilemma was far away from Europe. After a fifty-five-day siege in a place called Dien Bien Phu, the Viet Minh defeated the pride of the French army, elite French paratroopers and Foreign Legionnaires, who had been dropped in to help defend the beleaguered French position. On 8 May the French government broke the news to its people that the 16,000-strong garrison had been either captured or killed. France went into the deepest mourning.

By July France was forced to the conference table in Geneva. Indochina (Vietnam) was to be divided along the 17th parallel, with the north under the control of the Viet Minh. The French pretended they had an honourable settlement.

Eisenhower declared that getting involved in Southeast Asia would do no more than signal a future tragedy for the Americans.

Churchill, who was still concerned that not enough was being done by the East and West to think in global terms about future security, once more went to Washington. At the end of a long weekend of talks, Eisenhower and Churchill signed the Potomac Agreement on 29 June. The six-point charter was little more than a reaffirmation of ideals for international peace.

By now, however, Churchill was getting somewhere with his wartime ally. Eisenhower agreed, in principle, that there should be a meeting with Malenkov on some neutral territory. There followed a difficult moment for Churchill's Cabinet. Churchill had decided on the homeward journey aboard the *Queen Elizabeth* that he would go to the Soviet Union. He intended to send a signal to the Kremlin from the liner. Anthony Eden, the Foreign Secretary, who wanted Churchill to retire so that he could be prime minister, tried to show his strength by insisting that Churchill was wrong to send such a communication without first consulting the Cabinet in London. Eden gave in – as he often did.

When Churchill got back to London, he told the Cabinet that he had decided that Britain would build the hydrogen bomb. Moreover, Malenkov had replied that the meeting in Moscow was on. For the first time, the Cabinet started to rebel. Eden tried once more to assert himself and objected strongly to the prime minister making decisions without discussing the issues with his Cabinet colleagues. By mid-July 1954 the Cabinet was so split that Harold Macmillan, at least, believed that it was in danger of collapse.

By then Churchill had promised that he would resign in the autumn so that Eden would become prime minister in September. Eden cheered up; but then Churchill told him that he had changed his mind and that he would stay on until 1955.

Churchill's decision that Britain should produce a hydrogen bomb was an inevitable military and political development by a Conservative government in the mid-1950s. Britain already had an atomic weapon, but the next stage was so sensitive that although it was discussed in Cabinet committee it was not revealed to the full Cabinet until the decision had been taken. Thirty years on, the Conservative Defence Secretary, Michael Heseltine, said that if, in the 1980s, Britain had not had nuclear weapons, most certainly the government of the day would not have built them.[1] So why was the decision taken in the 1950s to arm Britain with the 'ultimate' weapon, as it was being called?

First, the technology was there. Second, Britain's notional position in the world meant that it still saw itself as a super-power, although the term meant nothing then, and its military commitments were global, as had been seen just ten years earlier in the Second World War, a few months earlier in the Korean War and recently in the campaigns in Southeast Asia, against communists in Malaya and in

1 In conversation with the author.

East Africa against tribal terrorism – there was, in fact, hardly an area of the world, except the Americas, where British forces were not on active duty. In spite of the obvious terror of nuclear weaponry, a leader like Winston Churchill would believe it essential to have it in his locker, even though the thought of using it would cause him the deepest dismay. Third, Churchill understood that in future international conferences, only the powers with nuclear weapons would occupy the top table. Churchill knew that France would eventually become a nuclear power and that China was working to acquire nuclear capability.

While he had been in government Attlee had talked to Churchill about the need for an international treaty to control nuclear weaponry development and thereby prevent its use. Churchill's advice to Attlee in 1945 had been that the deterrent effect of nuclear weaponry should not be ignored. In 1954 the United States had become a hydrogen bomb power. There was no way Churchill could lag behind.

The threat of nuclear war was taken seriously enough for the government to review its civil defence programme. The effects of nuclear weapons were still largely unknown and much of the test data gathered by the British was crude. Certainly the full effects of the difference between the radiation from a ground-burst and an air-burst bomb was not understood.[2] It was from the civil defence efforts that eventually came the much derided pamphlet, *Protect and Survive*. It was unlikely that civil defence bunkers and training exercises by the United Kingdom Warning and Monitoring Organization, the Royal Observer Corps, scientific officers and emergency planning officers would be able to provide protection from the effects of the weapons, and during the next forty years it became generally understood that the main function of this whole apparatus was to provide the fabric and order for whatever society survived should there ever be a nuclear strike on the United Kingdom.

At the very time that Churchill was discussing with the United States Britain's plans to develop a hydrogen bomb, the first public demonstration of its distant effects were revealed. In March 1954 the United States tested a bomb in the atmosphere over the Bikini atoll in the Pacific Ocean. The weapon was relatively small, 12 kilotonnes, but still 600 times the power of the atomic bomb dropped over Hiroshima nine years earlier. The victims of that March test were Japanese fishermen trawling 70 miles away. The white dust that drifted onto their trawler was irradiated, and within hours the fishermen were showing all the symptoms of the few who had survived Hiroshima.

In the Near East Churchill's hopes for super-power status looked thin: Britain was being tossed out of Egypt. Britain had been in Egypt and the Sudan since the nineteenth century. Egypt had become a British protectorate in 1915 and had

2 In theory, the main effects of an air-burst weapon are direct radiation and blast effect. A ground-burst bomb explodes closer to the ground and, therefore, has a much longer term effect because, apart from blast, radiated debris is sucked into the sky (the mushroom) and later falls as nuclear radiation across thousands of miles.

become independent in 1936, although British forces and interests remained in the country, underpinning Britain's interest in controlling the Suez Canal. In 1954 the most significant nationalist figure known in modern Egyptian history appeared. In 1952 King Farouk had been deposed, and there had followed political in-fighting between General Mohammed Neguib and the leader of a revolutionary council of young army officers, Colonel Gamal Abdel Nasser (1918–70). By April 1954 Nasser had achieved complete control and had become prime minister. Neguib was president but had ceremonial powers only.

By now the British had retreated to the Suez Canal Zone, which it was determined to protect since it was the most important artificial waterway in the world. Nasser, however, forced Britain to sign an agreement that it would pull out its forces of more than 80,000 from the Zone by the end of 1956. The only concession that Nasser made was that the British should be allowed to leave their weapons and equipment in the Zone base in case they had to return quickly to defend the Arab states in the region with which they had defence treaties.

On 19 October both nations signed the Suez Canal agreement. Within two years British forces would be back, but on the offensive against the Egyptians, an offensive that would be condemned even by Britain's closest ally, the United States.

Just to the north, anti-British feeling was brewing in Cyprus. Greek flags were raised in Limassol as Greek Cypriots demanded *enosis*, union with Greece. This was a prelude to yet another war of terrorism for Britain.

Britain ended 1954 on a noisy note, the beginnings of postwar social change. Young people, who until now had more often than not behaved and dressed in similar fashion to their elders, were breaking out. This was the year that the Teddy Boys appeared, with their Edwardian frock coats, drainpipe trousers, suede shoes and sideburns. They were dancing to a new music called rock 'n' roll. While the French worried about Vietnam, Churchill about the bomb and Nasser about Egypt, young people in Britain tried to get into the cinema to see the adults-only film *Blackboard Jungle* and to shout and dance to its theme tune 'Rock Around the Clock', recorded on 12 April 1954 by Bill Haley and the Comets.

For the first time since 1939 ration books were no longer necessary. There were ceremonial burnings in Trafalgar Square and for the first time in many people's memories they could buy what they liked – as long as they had the money.

A second item to disappear was a portrait of Winston Churchill. On 30 November Churchill was eighty years old and MPs had commissioned Graham Sutherland to paint his portrait. Churchill described it as 'a remarkable example of modern art'. The portrait was taken home and never again seen in public. His wife had it destroyed shortly after Churchill's death.

In 1954 Roger Bannister became the first man to run a mile in less than 4 minutes. The world record had stood since July 1945, when the Swede, Gundur Haag, ran it in 4 minutes 1.3 seconds. Bannister, pushed on by his pace-makers,

Chris Chattaway and Chris Brasher, gave the world one of the few moments to celebrate in 1954.

To cheer up the summer Lester Piggott, who was eighteen years old, became the youngest jockey to win the Derby when he rode a 33–1 outsider, Never Say Die.

Deaths

Lionel Barrymore (US actor)
Sidonie Gabrielle Colette (French writer)
André Derain (French artist)
Wilhelm Furtwängler (German conductor)
Alcide de Gasperi (Italian politician)
Arthur Greenwood (politician)
Charles Ives (US composer)
Auguste Lumière (French film pioneer)
Henri Matisse (French artist)
Sir George Robey (comedian)
Benjamin Seebohm Rowntree (philanthropist)
Sir John Simon, 1st Viscount Simon (politician)
Getúlio Vargas (Brazilian politician)

1955

IN MARCH 1955 Churchill told Eden that he would retire on 5 April, but then Churchill had a message from Eisenhower that the two should meet Adenauer in Paris on 8 May. Eisenhower's advisers believed that the tenth anniversary of Germany's defeat would be a good time for a symbolic signing of a new western defence agreement. At the end of Eisenhower's message was the suggestion that a meeting with the Soviet leadership might be possible. June seemed the earliest opportunity. This could have been Churchill's last grand occasion in international politics and one for which he had worked so hard. He told Eden that he had changed his mind and would not now resign on 5 April. Eden lost his temper at a Cabinet meeting and asked Churchill if this meant that their agreement was at an end. The exchange must have baffled the other members of the Cabinet, who knew nothing of the arrangement between the two men. Churchill's tone at that meeting was that if Eden was not happy, he should resign.

Later that day another message came from Eisenhower saying that he would not, after all, be attending the meeting. If Eisenhower were not there, there was no way that Churchill could attend. It would be a matter for officials or, at the very most, foreign ministers. Churchill would, after all, stand down in April. On 30 March 1955 Churchill called Butler and Eden into his room. He pointedly asked Eden to sit at his right hand. He said to the two men that he had decided to go and that Eden would succeed him. Churchill was not interested in the arrangements that had to be made nor, it would seem, did he want to prolong the conversation.

At lunchtime on 5 April he held his last Cabinet meeting and went to Buckingham Palace for the formality of his resignation. The Queen offered Churchill a dukedom; he said he wanted to fight his Woodford seat at the next election. He did and romped home.

Anthony Eden immediately called an election, before the economic climate got worse, knowing that he could take with him public opinion that was devoted to Churchill. He knew, too, that housing, the greatest success of Churchill's administration, had been immensely popular – thanks to Harold Macmillan. The Tories had promised to build 300,000 homes a year. Macmillan had been given the job of making sure it happened and he had succeeded. In fact 340,000 houses were built in 1954. There was some risk in Eden's decision: historically, no government in the twentieth century had succeeded in going to the country and getting a new mandate. In May 1955, however, the Conservatives got 345 seats and the Labour Party 277 seats; the Liberals had just six seats and there were two others.

Clement Attlee, now aged seventy-two, resigned as leader of the Labour Party and went to the House of Lords as Earl Attlee. The leadership fight was between Hugh Gaitskell, shadow Chancellor of the Exchequer, who was on the right wing of the party, and the two left-wing candidates, the deputy leader of the party, Herbert Morrison, and Aneurin Bevan. Gaitskell won. Morrison, deeply disappointed, resigned as deputy leader. Although publicly said he would support Gaitskell, Bevan privately detested him, but he was now no longer a force in British politics. He would stand on the platform with Gaitskell and, along with Barbara Castle, raise the leader's arms aloft in unity, but just five years later, at the age of sixty-three, he would be dead.

That summer Eden went to the event that had eluded Churchill. The first peacetime East–West summit took place in Geneva towards the end of July. At last Eisenhower would meet with the Russians (it was Nikolai Bulganin and not Khrushchev). Churchill had not missed anything. Bulganin's agenda was no different from anything that had been heard before. The Soviets said they would dissolve the Warsaw Pact if the West disbanded NATO. More significantly, the Soviet Union declared total opposition to the unification of Germany. The tenor of East–West relations was set until the 1990s.

Eden and his Foreign Secretary, by now Harold Macmillan, had more pressing matters to consider – terrorism in Cyprus. In November Britain imposed a state of emergency.

In 1955 more than 53 million people lived in England, Wales, Scotland and Ireland. The birth rate was increasing, while the death rate was steady at about 11.5 per 1000 population. The crime rate was low compared with what was to follow in the 1960s and 1970s. In 1955 there were 438,085 crimes in England and Wales and nearly 75,000 in Scotland. These crimes were recorded in terms of 'crimes known to the police', not minor offences such as speeding, and the level would rise into the millions within a decade and treble by the end of the century. The increase was partly because certain crimes were being 'reclassified' – the Theft Act of 1969, for example, added to the categories of indictable offences. The 1950s and 1960s were the last years in which criminal activity might meaningfully be compared with previous years.

The nation could not be described as church going. The Easter Day communicants, the day on which heads in the Church of England were counted, was around 2 million, who were served by more than 18,000 clergy. There were some 2.5 million Roman Catholics, more than 300,000 Baptists, fewer than 300,000 Congregationalists, between 70,000 and 80,000 Presbyterians and about 1.2 million members of the Presbyterian Church of Scotland.

Economically, Britain had a negative balance of trade. Industries, especially coal mining, were contracting. From 1955 coal production began to fall rapidly. In 1955 some 220 million tons of coal were dug out by 695,000 miners from 850 collieries; thirty years later the output had halved, the labour force was down to 154,000 and there were 133 collieries. Ten years later still the figures were decimals of 1955 levels. The steel industry was, for the moment at least, in a better state. Production was about 20 million tons and rising; the slump did not come until after 1970. A good customer of the steel industry, ship building, was in decline. In 1955, 1.35 million tons were built in British yards. It was the last good year.

The growth industry continued to be motor manufacturing. In 1955 Britain produced about one million cars. There were more than 3.5 million private cars on Britain's roads – a million more than in 1950 – and by 1960 there would be nearly 6 million. Interestingly, the parliamentary report of that year's transport debate suggested that the British were now better mannered on the roads. Hugh Molson, the Transport Minister, told MPs:

> Because of what had been done to improve road manners in the last 20 years they could look forward to obtaining equally successful results in the future. The number of casualties for each 10,000 vehicles on the road fell from 32 in 1930 to 10.4 in 1953 and the number of children of all ages killed for each 10,000 vehicles had been reduced to one third. It was not intended to increase the number of pedestrian crossings, nor did they wish to increase the number of zones in which speed was restricted to 30 miles an hour. The Minister has asked the London and Home Counties Advisory Committee to consider whether in their area there were instances where the restrictions on speed should be abolished.

A regular feature of London and suburban roads was about to disappear. The trolley bus was being replaced by a new type of double-decker diesel. And soon new faces would be seen on the platforms and in the cabs, because here was the beginning of the influx of West Indian immigrants. The country, especially the hospitals and transport systems, needed them. Their welcome was not, however, wholehearted as some bus crews went on strike and others operated an open colour bar.

The austere state of the postwar nation had done little for industrial relations in general, and the first six months of 1955 were marked by strikes. Electricians shut down national newspapers, and dockers and railwaymen walked out over pay differentials. The situation became so serious that one of Eden's first acts as prime minister was to declare a state of emergency.

The most significant event of the year occurred on 14 May, when the Soviet Union, East Germany, Poland, Czechoslovakia, Hungary, Romania, Bulgaria and Albania ratified the Warsaw Treaty, which came into effect on 5 June. Nine days earlier the Allied High Commissioners in Berlin had shut down their offices, thus constitutionally acknowledging West Germany as a sovereign state. The Federal Chancellor, Dr Adenauer, promptly announced that the aim of West Germany was to be a united nation, and in July 1955 the Bundestag took the first political steps to establishing a West German army.

This was a difficult moment for all sides. Europe had been at war just ten years earlier, and tens of millions had died. Within five years of the end of that war, British soldiers were still fighting and many were dying, a large number of whom were conscripts, not professional soldiers. Korea would be followed by Cyprus, Malaya, Kenya and, soon, Aden. People had been told they had won the war, but not a few were wondering what sort of victory it was that left them on rations as late as 1954. Now, in 1955, those same people were seeing, in spite of the brave new world of the Schuman Plan and the European dream, the spectre of two power blocs threatening each other in Europe and each was armed with nuclear weapons.

Without discounting the often treacherous ambitions of the Soviet leadership, the view from Moscow was of a Britain that was developing nuclear weapons and sending its troops all over the world, often to put down opposition to its rule; a France that was fighting in Southeast Asia and North Africa; and a United States that was building up its forces in the Far East and establishing relations with Japan and Germany, Russia's most ruthless enemies this century. On top of all this was a new alliance in western Europe, and one that was fully armed and almost entirely encircling the Soviet Union and eastern Europe. In command of this new alliance were the Americans, also armed with nuclear weapons and, as had been demonstrated at Hiroshima and Nagasaki, willing to use them and promising to do so again against Korea if that armistice did not hold.

From the other side, NATO could see a Soviet Union that was no less ambitious than it had been under Stalin. There was a communist state building nuclear warheads, with a rocket programme and with millions of troops stationed from Vladivostok to the Norwegian border; a state, moreover, that had just completed the formalities of Stalin's cordon by forming the Warsaw Pact. Even the

Labour Party, by a narrow majority, voted in favour of German rearmament. In the Commons MPs spoke passionately of the 1930s and the lessons that might be learned. There was no turning back. All that followed confirmed the suspicions and the insecurities of the Soviet leadership, by now firmly in the hands of Nikita Khrushchev, who had deposed Georgi Malenkov in February, 1955.[3]

The British public was more interested in the great romance of 1955 than in the future of NATO and the Warsaw Pact. Princess Margaret was in love with Group Captain Peter Townsend, a divorcee. They wanted to get married, but Townsend, a former equerry to the late King and a highly decorated fighter pilot, was not suitable because of his previous marriage. Under the Royal Marriage Act of 1772, Princess Margaret could marry without the Queen's consent only if she waited a year after announcing her intention to marry. She talked to the Archbishop of Canterbury, Geoffrey Fisher, and, deeply saddened, issued a statement of duty:

> I would like it to be known that I have decided not to marry Group Captain Peter Townsend. I have been aware that subject to renouncing my rights of succession it might have been possible for me to contract a civil marriage, but mindful of the Church's teaching that Christian marriage is indissoluble and conscious of my duty to the Commonwealth, I have resolved to put these considerations above all others.

The longer-term way of life in Britain was changed on 22 September 1955 with the first broadcasting of commercial television and the first advertisement, which was for Gibbs SR toothpaste. The BBC used its most powerful weapon to counter that first night of ITV – *The Archers*, Britain's most popular soap opera, carried the sensational story of the death of Grace Archer, whom the writers decided would be burned to a cinder. Even the BBC realized that a barn fire every night was not possible. Independent television was here to stay.

On 13 July Ruth Ellis was hanged in Holloway Prison for the murder of her lover. She was the last woman to be hanged in Britain.

Deaths

James Agee (US writer)
Theda Bara (US actress)
Paul Claudel (French writer)
James Dean (US actor)
Albert Einstein (US physicist)
Sir Alexander Fleming (bacteriologist)
Arthur Honegger (French composer)

3 Malenkov was replaced by Nikolai Bulganin; but Khrushchev held the power.

Fernand Léger (French artist)
Thomas Mann (German writer)
Charlie 'Bird' Parker (US musician)
Nicolas de Stael (French artist)
Yves Tanguy (US artist)
Pierre Teilhard de Chardin (French philosopher)
Maurice Utrillo (French artist)

1956

WE NOW come to one of the most badly organized and ill-thought-through political decisions of postwar Britain – the 1956 Suez Crisis. It showed up the Anglo-American special relationship for what it was, a myth, and it finished the Conservative prime minister, Anthony Eden.

In October 1954 an Anglo-Egyptian agreement had been signed by which British troops would leave the Suez Canal Zone in June 1956. They had been there, ostensibly, to protect the neutral status of the waterway. The military charade contained in the 1954 agreement was that Britain would be allowed to reposition its military supplies and equipment in the Zone in case they needed to return to protect the area or to go to the defence of Arab states in the region. President Nasser never had any intention of honouring the treaty, however, and less than a fortnight after British troops started leaving on 13 June, Nasser nationalized the Suez Canal Company, which was run by France and Britain. It was the perfect opportunity – the British had gone and this was the fourth anniversary of the overthrow of King Farouk – and it gave Nasser absolute command of oil supplies from the Gulf *en route* to Europe.

It is possible that the whole event might have been avoided if the United States (and therefore Britain) had not turned down Nasser's request to put money into the project to build the High Dam at Aswan. Without total western financing – and the World Bank had refused to get involved – the dam, which was vital to Egypt's economic future, was prohibitively expensive. One reason the United States cooled to the idea of financing the dam was that it believed that Egypt was mortgaging itself to the Soviet Union. Nasser, who needed to modernize the Egyptian armed forces, had negotiated arms contracts with the Soviet Union and Czechoslovakia worth hundreds of millions of dollars. London and Washington saw no reason to bankroll a civilian project while Nasser was about to be a Middle East client state of the Soviet Union. Nasser, therefore, claimed that he would use the revenues from the Suez Canal to pay for the dam.

Eden declared that Suez concerned the very life of the nation and of Europe. Extra British forces were moved to Malta and Cyprus, and the United States, Britain and France proposed an international conference for mid-August. The twenty-two nations at the London conference had a direct interest in the outcome of that meeting: they all had ships that used the waterway. Nasser refused to attend.

After the conference, an international group chaired by the Australian prime minister, Robert Menzies, went to Egypt to try to persuade Nasser to accept the concept of an internationally controlled canal, although this could not have been anything more than a delaying tactic. It is at this point, in August 1956, that we can see the difference in approach between Britain and France on one hand and the United States on the other. Eden was talking about fighting to get the canal back, and the French supported him. The US Secretary of State, John Foster Dulles, who had never, as Churchill had found out, been much impressed by British imperial solutions, made it clear that the United States was not inclined towards military intervention.

Eisenhower's own strong objections to the Anglo-French military plans were made public on 5 September, and it became clear that Menzies was wasting his time in Egypt. There was no point telling Nasser that Britain and France were serious about military action when Eisenhower was telling everyone, and therefore Nasser, that the United States opposed force.

Eisenhower at this point wanted to set up a Suez Canal Users' Association, which he thought would be the way out of the crisis. He was, however, battling against British interests. Britain owned 44 per cent of the Suez Canal Company, and 5000 British-owned ships, about one-third of the total transits, went through the canal every year. The freight costs (and therefore the import costs) saved by avoiding the Cape route were enormous. In addition, many of those British ships were tankers coming from the Gulf, the biggest source of Britain's oil supplies. Moreover, ever since Disraeli had bought a controlling interest in the canal for Queen Victoria in 1875, there had been a sense that it was part of the Empire.

Dulles believed that Eden appeared not to have adjusted to Britain's role in international affairs. The Americans might have explained this to Eden in diplomatic speak of fewer syllables than they did. History might have moved in another direction, although with France's strong support – the French believed that Nasser was behind the Algerian uprising against them – this is unlikely.

Eden did not have total support at home. Mountbatten, the First Sea Lord, did not believe that Britain had the resources for Operation Musketeer, as it was called. The Chiefs of Staff had active service experience, and they understood the difficulties of planning, logistics and the positioning of ground, air and naval forces, and they recognized the problems of getting troops into an opposed landing area. There were too many recent examples of political hope over military reality for them not to have a sober appreciation of the situation.

Yet the opposition to Mountbatten's opinion was not simply the splutterings of High Tories. Gaitskell supported action, and popular newspapers set Nasser up as another Hitler. Macmillan even described him as an Asiatic Mussolini.

By this time, Eden was running foreign policy and all but ignoring his loyal but unimaginative Foreign Secretary, Selwyn Lloyd, who, at first, was not even included in the Cabinet committee set up to oversee the crisis.

Nasser was now saying that as long as Egypt's sovereignty was not debased, he was open to suggestions, but he turned down the American plan for a Suez Canal Users' Association, which would, in theory, happen anyway. While all eyes were focused on Paris, Washington and London, the Israelis started condemning Egyptian action. Israel was now involved against Egypt. It was impossible for the Americans to have joined any action against the Arabs that included the Israelis; such action would have completely destroyed American credibility in the Middle East.

On 2 October the Suez Canal Users' Association came into being. Nasser ignored it and the Soviet Union vetoed the idea at the United Nations. On 30 October Britain and France issued public warnings that the Egyptians had twelve hours to get out of the Suez Canal Zone. The following evening, Wednesday, 31 October, the RAF bombed the outskirts of Cairo and the Suez Canal. Troops from 16 Parachute Brigade were dropped outside Port Said. Marines went ashore from the Mediterranean flotilla. It all looked good in the headlines – successful landings, few casualties – but it was not a notable exercise in military planning, and it was an even worse example of diplomatic skill. The British, French and Israelis had no international support. Although their part in the operation was less publicized at the time, the Israelis, led by the future defence minister Colonel Ariel Sharon, had pushed across the border to the canal itself and south to where the Gulf of Suez meets the Red Sea.

The United Nations condemned the Anglo-French action. Eisenhower, who was about to fight an election, who had lost his Secretary of State to emergency surgery for a terminal illness and who was now being confronted by the Soviet Union over Hungary, was angry and under pressure. It was the United States that proposed the UN cease-fire, and on 8 November Britain and France accepted. The two European allies had not achieved their primary aim of taking complete control of the Zone although they had got to Ismailia.

By the third week in November, Selwyn Lloyd, the Foreign Secretary, was telling the UN that the Anglo-French action had set the conditions for UN supervision of the area and some guarantee that the canal would remain open. No one seems to have given his argument much support.

Cabinet colleagues were turning against Eden. Harold Macmillan, the Chancellor of the Exchequer, had supported the invasion; now he did not. He was under pressure from the Americans who were supporting sterling. Either Britain pulled out of Suez, or the Americans would pull the financial plug. Macmillan agreed with the Americans. This was not, as some have suggested, an about face. Macmillan's task was to manage the British economy. The closing of the canal and the disruption of oil supplies would have created a financial crisis of its own. The action at Suez, together with the uncertain world situation, had a destabilizing effect on the British government and the nation's economy.

It was too much for Eden, who had been far from well at the start of the crisis, and Macmillan knew that Eden was not long for Downing Street. Later in November Eden escaped to Jamaica for a rest, and R.A. Butler, the Leader of the

House, stood in as prime minister. As Butler tried to clean up the mess, Macmillan quietly waited for Eden to resign. He did so in January the following year, 1957.

In British political history Suez is important for at least three reasons: it brought about the departure of the prime minister, Anthony Eden; it showed that the United States would not automatically support Britain; and it proved that the days of the British punitive raiding party were over.

In the moments before the Anglo-French invasion, the British government received a note from Bulganin in Moscow. He suggested that if Britain did not back away from the threatened action, the Soviet Union would consider military action also. The Soviet Union had no intention of doing any such thing. Its intentions were far more sinister, for Soviet tanks were about to roll into Hungary. The threat to Britain had two aims: to divert attention and to notify the West that if anyone tried to stop them, Soviet rockets would be used against outside intervention.

The revolt against Russian rule in Eastern Europe had started in East Germany on May Day, when tens of thousands of East Germans had taken to the streets demanding reunification. That demonstration was put down with few difficulties. The revolt then spread to Poland. In October 1956 Poles began to demand that Soviet troops leave the country. Khrushchev himself had to fly to Warsaw to read the political riot act to the Polish leadership. The Polish leader, Wladyslaw Gomulka (1905–82), had been removed in 1951 (and kept in 'protective custody' by the Soviets) but was reinstated in 1956 as first secretary of the Communist Party, a rehabilitated acolyte of Moscow.

In Hungary the revolution was not so easily put down because it was more deeply felt and because it was a national uprising from the top and included the army. National character, local conditions and the origins of the protest made the Hungarian revolt more determined. This was no street demonstration. The Hungarians armed themselves against the Soviet Union, and in return they were put down by the force of superior arms.

On 5 November 1956, when Soviet tanks rolled into the capital Budapest, the Hungarian leader was Imre Nagy (1896–1958), the antithesis of the Stalinists, who saw ruthlessness as the only way to control the satellite states. It was Nagy who opposed all these concepts and introduced a liberal consumer society and relaxed the collectivization of agriculture. He had been dismissed as prime minister for a short period in February 1955, but as unrest in Hungary grew he was reappointed in the hope that his presence would satisfy the demonstrators. His ultimate crime, however, was to say that Hungary was going to pull out of the Warsaw Pact. In came the tanks. Nagy was eventually arrested and executed on Soviet orders, and a new government was set up under János Kádár (1912–89), who supported the Soviet intervention.

Many Hungarians were killed during the uprising, but more than 100,000 managed to escape. Those who were left understood that the revolution was over.

★

The lessons for the West of 1956 were that Britain and France had attempted to assert their rights over what they regarded as their territory and failed. The Soviet Union did the same thing and succeeded. The Americans did nothing and were probably right.

Nikita Khrushchev was supremely confident. In March 1956, three years after Stalin's death, at a meeting of the Communist Party leadership he was secure enough to denounce Stalin as a murdering despot. The following month Khrushchev and Bulganin had visited London, where Khrushchev's ebullience captured the imagination and not a little affection of the British media and people. However, he did not go down well with the Labour Party, especially with the equally excitable George Brown.

Of longer-term significance was a man in Khrushchev's team who would have more to do with shaping East–West relations than any other, Andrei Gromyko. He would soon be Foreign Minister and the respected bane of almost every foreign policy maker in the West.

This was an exciting and entertaining year in Britain. The government announced that the early evening ban on television transmissions between 6 and 7 o'clock would be lifted.

The film of the year was *High Society*, with Frank Sinatra, Bing Crosby, Louis Armstrong and Grace Kelly, who had in April 1956 married Prince Rainier II of Monaco.

The big hit of the year was 'Heartbreak Hotel' from one of the new stars of popular music, Elvis Presley.

Elvis fans may have represented the lighter side of young Britain, but there was a deeper, perhaps more brooding aspect. It was represented by the new breed known as Angry Young Men. They included Colin Wilson and, more lastingly famous, John Osborne. The expression Angry Young Man came from Osborne's play *Look Back in Anger*, which was first staged at the Royal Court Theatre in London in 1956. The fashionable view was, and continued to be, that this was a new mood of writing, reflecting what *The Times* called 'the crossness' of those in their late twenties:

> Most young men, in every age, are probably much alike. They turn the world, as far as they can, to their own account, in order to become old men as painlessly as possible. Mr Osborne, however, is dealing with that inconvenient phenomenon, the clever young man. It is he who sets his stamp upon a generation, he who gets the level at which the men of his own age will be remembered by posterity. Are we, then, to think that those who are now in the late twenties are likely to be known above all for their touchiness and their rages?

Deaths
Sir Max Beerbohm (critic)
Clarence Birdseye (US inventor)
William E. Boeing (US manufacturer)
Sir Frank Brangwyn (artist)
Bertolt Brecht (German writer)
Tommy Dorsey (US bandleader)
C.B. Fry (sportsman)
Alfred Kinsey (US sexologist)
Sir Alexander Korda (film producer)
Bela Lugosi (US actor)
H.L. Mencken (US writer)
A.A. Milne (writer)
Jackson Pollock (US artist)
Art Tatum (US musician)

1957

IN MARCH 1957 France, Belgium, Holland, Luxembourg, Italy and West Germany signed the Treaty of Rome, and what was then called the European Common Market was born. The British stayed out.

Attlee's government and the Conservative administration that followed had not wanted to get involved in the 1950 Schuman Plan for the European Coal and Steel Community, the origin of the European Union. Dean Acheson, the US Secretary of State under Truman, thought Britain's decision the greatest mistake of the postwar period, and by 1957 it is likely that many in British politics, including Macmillan, accepted that view.

Nevertheless, in 1957 the British did not consider themselves European – indeed, many probably never would do so. Britain's aloofness from Europe seems at odds with the determination shown by Ernest Bevin in the 1940s to establish NATO as the bedrock of European security. Should not the economic development have followed naturally? The interwar years had proved that economic instability in Europe would bring nationalism in its wake and, probably, the greater likelihood of war. The nations most threatened by this instability and scarred by previous generations of leaders who either did not understand or would not accept this view were France and Germany. It was natural that those countries should lead the way for a Common Europe. It was also natural that the Italians would not only follow but would need to feel important enough to be at the top table. The Dutch would go where the Germans went, and Luxembourg was really a bank and saw all the advantages of being in and every disadvantage of being forgotten.

By the time Macmillan became prime minister at the age of sixty-two in January 1957 it was too late for him to impose any direction that would lead to early membership for Britain in the EEC. Moreover, France was now stronger and had a new relationship with West Germany – largely urged by Chancellor, Adenauer – and a continuing suspicion of Britain's relationship with the United States. There was no need now for the Entente Cordiale. Any future application to join by Britain would be closely and cynically examined by any French government.

When Macmillan took over from Eden he was faced by four main problems: Cyprus, Ireland, the economy and, more immediately, relations with the United States after Suez.

In March Macmillan met Eisenhower in Bermuda. They were both pragmatic enough to set aside what had gone on in the previous October and November. The Americans had always wanted Britain to be more involved in European affairs, and Macmillan did not quibble, as long as the United States did not drift away. The Bermuda Declaration included what would be a recurring theme: that the United States was a pillar in European defence policy and that NATO was its foundation. To signify the close relationship, Britain would get American guided missiles, a move that meant that the British development in nuclear weapons capability would have two strands: the V-bomber force and, eventually, a limited missile capability. In return, Britain gave the Americans bases in Britain, even though they would go through the charade of calling them RAF establishments.

The Bermuda Conference of 21–23 March 1957 was the beginning of Britain's nuclear defence policy, and the Defence White Paper of that year declared that Britain's policy would be nuclear retaliation in the event of Soviet incursion into western Europe. The cost of conventional (non-nuclear) weaponry was becoming prohibitive to a nation still suffering from a badly performing economy, and although Britain's conscript army was, in theory, cheap, it was inefficient. So in the White Paper came the signal that the call-up would soon end.

Some conscripts were serving in Cyprus, where the terrorist operation was as difficult to control as ever. In April 1957 Archbishop Makarios, who had been exiled to the Seychelles in March 1956 (thereby being made into an absentee martyr) was told that he could return to Greece as long as he renounced the use of violence. The state of emergency in Cyprus was eased, then stood down. The optimism was short lived and wrongly judged.

Violent street demonstrations began again in October. Until this stage most of the violence had come from the Greeks, the majority population in Cyprus, for whom Makarios, who was now living in Athens, remained a focus. NATO attempted to act as a mediator, but the Greeks would have none of this because it would mean sitting at the same table as the Turks.

The Greek terrorist group on the island, EOKA (*Ethniki Organósis Kipriakóu Agónos*, 'National Organization of Cypriot Struggle'), suggested a cease-fire, but the British refused. Their main concern was that a cease-fire was not a peace agreement and that such a temporary truce would allow Archbishop Makarios back to Cyprus before the differences between the two communities had been resolved. The fact that those differences would not be resolved in the twentieth century had not sunk home.

Just as difficult to resolve were events in Northern Ireland. The Dublin government, led for the eighth time by Eamon de Valera, was forced to declare a state of emergency in Ireland in July 1957, following a series of shootings and arson attacks along the North–South border. The Irish prime minister's dilemma was to preserve government control at a time when the IRA ignored it, and his action came at the start of the marching season in Northern Ireland. The Irish security forces arrested more than sixty IRA men, and in the Dáil, de Valera was accused of helping the British when he should have thrown all his energies into enforcing the return of the six counties.

In August a similar arrest operation was carried out by the British forces in Ulster after a policemen was killed.

On the mainland, Macmillan's attention was almost exclusively centred on the state of the economy. The government was losing by-elections, and unemployment figures had increased slightly. Macmillan had been a politician during some of the worst years of unemployment, and he understood the social as well as the political effects. By the end of Macmillan's first year as prime minister, 312,000 people would be unemployed; within Macmillan's lifetime the figure would top 3 million. The so-called economic crisis of 1957 was like a mild tropical storm: spectacular, but soon gone.

Macmillan put in a new team at the Treasury: Peter Thorneycroft and two junior ministers, Enoch Powell and Nigel Birch. In mid-1957 there was a run on sterling, the reason for which is not clear, although there had been a lot of speculation over government spending and inflation. Thorneycroft relied on the blunt instrument of interest rates, raising them from 5 to 7 per cent – the highest for half a century. The danger here was that while inflation might be brought under control, unemployment would be the price that would be paid. The Chancellor wanted to cut family allowances by limiting payments to the first child only. This did not get through Cabinet, however, and Macmillan would not support it.

In spite of the economic difficulties, Macmillan was to show that he still had a mind for memorable phrases. In July 1957, as the markets tested sterling, the polls went against the government and the Cabinet began to divide, Macmillan tossed aside the economic forecasts and told the nation 'most of our people have never had it so good'. He was, of course, right to use the word 'most'.

It was not yet time for Macmillan's 'wind of change' speech, but hardly a year would pass without another country slipping away from the Empire. On 6 March the Gold Coast became independent with a new name, Ghana, and at the end of August 170 years of British rule ended in Malaya. British troops had fought the communist insurgents since 1948 in the Malayan Emergency, and the new leader of Malaya, Tunku Abdul Rahman, had been pro-British. To his mind the legacy of colonial rule was the administrative system, and it was one he urged his people not to abandon.

At home, there was to be a major change in British life as British Rail began to close some of its smaller branch lines. Parish councils throughout England petitioned the government to stop the closures, but the government would not intervene. Six years later the most swingeing cuts in the railway network, which these parishes had predicted, and the triumph of the motor industry would be proposed in the report written by Richard Beeching, the chairman of the new British Rail Board.

The railway lobbying against the closures took place on 3 October, but given what happened on 4 October, it is little wonder that hardly anyone noticed. On that first Friday in October 1957, the Soviet Union launched the first artificial satellite, *Sputnik 1*. The world was amazed. The Americans had always made much of their space programme and what they were going to do. The Russians simply did it before the Americans were ready to put their own claims into effect. Two months later the Americans attempted to do the same thing, but the rocket exploded just a few feet above the ground. This would be the pattern of American attempts to get into space until well into 1958, and Eisenhower was so concerned that he set up an agency to draw together the disparate efforts of American scientists. The following summer the National Aeronautical and Space Administration (NASA) was born.

Newspapers throughout the world sang Russia's praises, and people around the globe went out at night and searched the sky for a glimpse of the little silver football.

In the White House and in Downing Street there was a sense of foreboding, which had nothing to do with the space race. American and British attention was drawn not to *Sputnik* but to the launcher rocket. If the Russians had a rocket that was powerful enough to break out of the atmosphere and into space and to carry a satellite, it meant also that that same rocket could carry a nuclear bomb.

On 4 October 1957 headlines claimed that the space age had begun – so too had the age of inter-continental warfare. Rocket scientists had done something that successive British politicians, starting with Asquith, had failed to do: long-range rocket power now made the American people as vulnerable to the consequences of war as the citizens of Europe had been in the Second World War. The American front line was now the East German border. Thus 4 October 1957 became the most important date in postwar history.

If a generation of strategic thinking was changing, so was the age of alternative cultures. It was in 1957 that people in Britain began to hear about an American phenomenon called 'beatniks'. Many of their leaders, like Jack Kerouac, wrote about young people who simply wanted to drop out of the so-called rat race and reject the materialism that the United States had come to personify. That protest also brought with it a jargon lifted from the jazz age. People like the poet Allen

Ginsberg and William Burroughs, who became famous for his autobiography *Junkie* (1953), talked about being 'groovy' and 'hip' and 'digging'. These were all adopted ideas and philosophies from decades of jazz men.

In Britain the impact of the beatniks never had the same cultural effect as in the United States. British audiences were more interested in the television programme *Six-Five Special*. Then came the new fashion of skiffle – a band with a guitarist, someone on washboard and, in its original form, a double bass made of a tea chest, a broom handle and string. The music was often English versions of famous American songs such as 'Wabash Cannonball' and in the 1950s, the most famous of all, 'Rock Island Line'. The rising star in 1957 was supposed to be Britain's answer to Elvis Presley, Tommy Steele, who proved to be enduring and talented.

In the cinema the most notable film was *The Bridge on the River Kwai*. While the popular music industry applauded a new generation, classical music lovers mourned the death of Jean Sibelius, who in 1957 had not written a published note for thirty years.

Deaths

Humphrey Bogart (US actor)
Constantin Brancusi (Romanian sculptor)
Richard Byrd (US explorer)
Christian Dior (French fashion designer)
Jimmy Dorsey (US bandleader)
Beniamino Gigli (Italian tenor)
Oliver Hardy (US comedian)
Miklós von Horthy (Hungarian politician)
Percy Wyndham Lewis (writer)
Joseph McCarthy (US politician)
Louis B. Mayer (US film producer)
Charles Kay Ogden (psychologist)
Max Ophuls (German film director)
Sir Ernest Oppenheimer (South African industrialist)
Diego Rivera (Mexican artist)
Dorothy L. Sayers (writer)
Jean Sibelius (Finnish composer)
Arturo Toscanini (Italian conductor)
Henry van de Velde (Belgian architect)

1958

THE POLITICAL YEAR started with what Harold Macmillan called 'a little local difficulty'. His Treasury team, including the Chancellor, Peter Thorneycroft, and two ministers, Enoch Powell and Nigel Birch, resigned. They did so in protest at increased public expenditure. Macmillan was just about to go on a Commonwealth tour. Instead of cancelling the trip, he went, saying at Heathrow Airport: 'I thought the best thing to do was to settle up these little local difficulties, and then turn to the wider vision of the Commonwealth.' He did find time to appoint a new Chancellor, Derick Heathcoat Amory.

In April 1958 Amory took a little off purchase tax (the forerunner of VAT). He made credit easier too. By November, building societies could offer 99 per cent mortgages and local authorities were able to offer 100 per cent mortgages on pre-First World War properties, thus increasing the home-owning democracy and decreasing the chances of industrial workers wanting to strike.

If Macmillan thought he could deal with an errant Chancellor as a little local difficulty, he would not do so with an equally independent-minded group, the nuclear weapons protesters. In February 1958 Britain was to have American nuclear missile bases in Britain, and a group of objectors to this plan met in London on 17 February. Its leaders included Bertrand Russell, the philosopher and grandson of the Victorian prime minister, Lord John Russell; Michael Foot, the Labour politician; A.J.P. Taylor, the historian; John Osborne, the dramatist; and J.B. Priestley, the writer. They decided to call the group the Campaign for Nuclear Disarmament (CND), and the group's first chairman was Canon John Collins.

On Easter Monday 7 April, CND organized the first of its annual marches to the government's Weapons Research Establishment at Aldermaston. The first bank holiday march was peaceful, but others that year were disrupted, including the first big demonstrations against the American Thor missile bases in Britain.

CND members continued to campaign for what they saw as their logical point of view, even though they believed that the government would ignore them no matter how hard they campaigned. CND's campaign was, however, a constant reminder to the public, and particularly to government, that there was a protest movement based entirely on ethical grounds.

The security services and the police Special Branch kept files on CND members, but in the autumn of 1958 the Special Branch found itself with a more sinister task, racism. During the night of Monday, 8 September, whites provoked blacks living in Notting Hill Gate. A violent confrontation had spilled onto the streets of London. Nine white youths went to prison, but the Metropolitan Police was already issuing warnings to the Home Office that this was a far from isolated incident. The Special Branch involvement sprang from its belief that white extremist groups were behind the attacks. Ever since the 1930s the authorities were sensitive about what extremism could lead to.

Britain's overseas preoccupations continued to be Cyprus and the Middle East and there was a new problem in the cold waters around Iceland.

The reality of the difficulties in Cyprus had impressed itself on the government. The conflict there was what would become known on Cabinet briefing papers as the Cyprus Situation, and it was a dilemma that would not be successfully resolved for the rest of the century. In June 1958 Britain proposed a seven-year period of

British rule that would allow both Greeks and Turks time to work out a way in which the island could be governed. Makarios, still exiled in Athens, rejected the plan on behalf of the Greek Cypriots. The fighting resumed.

Macmillan flew to Athens, Ankara and Cyprus to talk to the main leaders, but without success, and shootings and bombings became features of Cypriot life. The British said they were implementing their plan, but Makarios continued to reject it, as did the Turks, who said it would lead to a union between the Greek Cypriots and the Greek mainland. This was probably true. It was certainly what the Greek Cypriots were fighting for.

Macmillan was also looking to the Middle East mainland, where Britain's interests were twofold, in Jordan, with the pro-British King Hussein, and in Iraq, where King Feisal and Crown Prince Abdullah were about to be toppled.

Colonel Nasser of Egypt engineered a *coup d'état* by Iraqi army officers. This was part of the spread of Nasserism – the Egyptian leader wanted to establish a United Arab Republic. Feisal II and the Crown Prince were murdered. The threat was made to King Hussein in Jordan and to President Chamoun in the Lebanon, where Nasser supported nationalists. The Americans and the British sent troops to Jordan and Beirut.

At the UN the Soviet Union demanded that British and US forces be withdrawn. In the Commons, the Labour opposition said that British policy was wrong and that confrontation between Britain and the Soviet Union should be avoided at all costs. Britain was now, however, committed to the widespread deployment of troops in the Middle East. The stand against what Nasser was trying to achieve worked, and by October British and American soldiers could start to leave the Lebanon and Jordan. For the moment, Nasserism was rebuffed.

Further north, Iceland had declared a 12-mile fishing limit, and Britain and Iceland were set for the first of the 'cod wars', a confrontation that was taken to NATO. There was no chance to mediate at that stage. The argument was simple: Icelanders said that all the fish within that 12-mile limit was theirs; British trawlermen said that beyond the conventional 4-mile offshore limit, anyone could fish. Trawlermen and navies settled in for a long confrontation.

In November, the three nuclear powers – the United States, the Soviet Union and Britain – met in Geneva to develop a nuclear test ban treaty. The conference was abandoned with nothing more than a draft treaty, although it was called a breakthrough. The three powers had proved that nuclear arms controls could be reached only on unwanted, outdated or technologically unlikely systems.

In December Charles de Gaulle became president of the Fifth Republic. France had been in domestic confusion for some time but more pertinent to de Gaulle's election were difficulties over the increasing violence between nationalists and the tens of thousands of French settlers in Algeria, who opposed independence. These French settlers had seized control of key ministries and all the signs pointed to civil war.

★

In the winter of 1958 Britain was shocked by a seemingly impossible disaster. On 6 February a propeller-driven passenger aircraft crashed in the snow at Munich airport. On board were the Manchester United soccer team, journalists and the club staff, who were on their way back from a European Cup semi-final in Belgrade. There were some survivors, but the cream of English first division football died.

That autumn Mike Hawthorn, driving for Ferrari, became world Grand Prix champion, the first Briton to do so. And the next four places went to British drivers – Stirling Moss, Tony Brooks, Roy Salvadori and Peter Collins. Hawthorn lived just three months to enjoy his glory. He was killed the following January when he crashed his own car on a road near Guildford.

In 1958 the first motorway in Britain was opened. It was not the M1, but the Preston bypass (now part of the M6), which was just 8 miles long. The new style of road signs – big white letters on a pale blue background – was designed to be read by drivers travelling at increasingly fast speeds. It was not all free and easy-going, however. In January 1958 the first radar speed traps were set up, and parking meters were introduced – Mayfair was the first place in Britain to get them. By March 1958 parking tickets were being stuck on windscreens, and in June London was getting the first double yellow lines in the country.

If it was harder to park in Mayfair, it was even harder at Buckingham Palace. The Queen decided that debs were no longer part of the new Elizabethan age. In March 1958 the last debutante curtsied to the Queen, and no more daughters would be presented at court.

Deaths

Sir William Burrell (industrialist and collector)
Ronald Colman (actor)
Robert Donat (actor)
Maurice Gamelin (French soldier)
Douglas Jardine (cricketer)
G.E. Moore (philosopher)
Imre Nagy (Hungarian politician)
Christabel Harriette Pankhurst (suffragette)
Wolfgang Pauli (US physicist)
Pius XII (pope)
Georges Rouault (French artist)
Marie Stopes (suffragette and pioneer of birth control)
Ralph Vaughan Williams (composer)

1959

MACMILLAN CALLED a general election in October. Hugh Gaitskell, leader of the Labour Party, talked about a victory for the party being important to the whole world not just to Britain, but the Conservatives won 365 seats and Labour 258; the Liberals once more had six MPs and there was one other elected. This was the third Conservative election victory in a row.

Considering the events of the latter years of the 1990s, when Tony Blair convinced the Labour Party that its old ideals made it unelectable, we might note that there was absolutely nothing new in what Blair was proposing. After the 1959 election Gaitskell suggested that the Labour Party should change Clause Four, which had been adopted as part of the party's constitution in 1918. This was the moral authority Labour claimed to take major industries into common ownership. Most voters in Britain had never heard of Clause Four, but they knew what it meant and therefore supposed they knew what it meant to vote Labour. In 1959 Gaitskell believed, just as Tony Blair did in 1996, that Clause Four had to go.

Macmillan, still at Downing Street, was now one of the most politically powerful prime ministers Britain had known. Yet, what he famously called 'events' would make almost worthless the optimism that must have come with such electoral triumph. That was in the near future, however, and his immediate task was to shuffle his Cabinet. Some members actually wanted to go, including the most important man in Macmillan's team, Derick Heathcoat Amory, the Chancellor. Macmillan could not be seen to have his Chancellor resigning, since that would look too much like government disunity and Heathcoat Amory had got the job because his predecessor, Peter Thorneycroft, had resigned over the government's spending policy. The Chancellor agreed to stay until the following summer, but Macmillan already knew what he wanted to do. Selwyn Lloyd would go to the Treasury, and the Earl of Home would go to the Foreign Office.

Macmillan needed to do something about David Eccles, the President of the Board of Trade, and the Colonial Secretary, Alan Lennox-Boyd, who were, according to Macmillan, now on only 'bawling terms' with each other. Lennox-Boyd went, and Iain Macleod, one of the brightest minds in the postwar Conservative governments, took over. His job, Minister of Labour, went to the Chief Whip, Edward Heath. One new Cabinet minister, often forgotten forty years on, was the Transport Minister, Ernest Marples, whose decisions were to have a lasting effect on the whole nation. It was Marples who launched into the nationwide motorway building programme.

In 1959 seven of the countries that had not joined the Common Market set up their own European market called the European Free Trade Association (EFTA). In November the EFTA nations – Austria, Denmark, Norway, Portugal, Sweden, Switzerland and the United Kingdom – met in Stockholm to establish what was effectively a rival organization to the Common Market. EFTA was Britain's way into Europe without damaging Commonwealth agreements, which remained an essential part of the nation's strategy in Europe and was the basis of the so-called special arrangements for imports of such commodities as New Zealand lamb and Australian butter.

★

This was the year that Fidel Castro's two-year guerrilla war against the Cuban dictator, Fulgencio Batista, ended. In January 1959 Batista went and Castro became president. The Americans, who had supported Batista, now had troubles on their offshore doorstep. Unlike Batista, Castro would not take US dollars in return for his allegiance, although the Americans were allowed to keep their base at Guantanamo for the rest of the century. From that moment, Washington spent millions of dollars on fiasco after fiasco in their attempts to get rid of Castro. These efforts were doubled when it was seen that Castro was dealing with the Soviet Union.

The American obsession with Soviet ambitions extended as far as man could see – into space. In September 1959 the Soviet space craft *Lunik 2* landed on the moon. The Russians were the first there, and although it was not a manned flight, the timing was immaculate, because it coincided with Khrushchev's visit to the United States. But the Americans weren't as far behind the Russians as some imagined. Men like John Glenn, Alan Shepard, Walter Schirra, Scott Carpenter, Virgil Grissom and Gordon Cooper were already in astronaut training, but the Soviet Union had Yuri Gagarin who, in two years' time, would be the first man in space.

The Soviet space programme was more than a technical success. It was a political and diplomatic triumph for Khrushchev. He now had complete control in Moscow. It had taken him eighteen months to recover from an attempted coup, but now Georgi Malenkov, Vyacheslav Molotov (who gave his name to the Molotov cocktail, the petrol bomb) and Lazar Kaganovitch had gone. So too had Marshal Bulganin, the straight man in the double act with Khrushchev that had so impressed the crowds in London. Now, thanks to the army of Marshal Zhukov, there was no one to challenge Khrushchev's authority.

In February 1959 Khrushchev invited Britain and the United States to take part in the summit meeting that would discuss the future of Berlin. Later that month Harold Macmillan, the British prime minister, went to Moscow.

This was part of a process that Churchill had so wanted to establish and that, in Churchill's time, Eisenhower had refused to contemplate. Now Khrushchev played to the gallery and in front of his own people refuted any suggestions that he was weak. Macmillan had gone to the Soviet Union with a long agenda. He and Khrushchev met and then the Soviet leader dismissed him. Khrushchev's office said their leader had toothache, and so for days Macmillan was left to act as a tourist and came away with nothing much more than a statement from Moscow that there had been a valuable exchange of views.

Macmillan went to Washington to talk to Eisenhower about the future of Berlin. Chancellor Adenauer refused to open any discussions with eastern Europe, however, and certainly not with East Germany. To talk to the East Germans would be tantamount to recognizing the Soviet-run state, and Adenauer was not willing to do that. Khrushchev went to Washington, supposedly to discuss Berlin, but apart from publicity stunts, including a tour of the Hollywood set of *Can Can*,

Khrushchev appeared little interested in diplomatic talk. Another summit came to nothing.

Between 1954 and 1959 more than 500 people died in the civil war in Cyprus. On one side were Turkish Cypriots, who represented about a quarter of the island population. On the other side were the Greek Cypriots.

The main players were the Turkish Cypriot leader, Rauf Denktas, the Greek Cypriot Archbishop Makarios, and the leader of EOKA, the terrorist organization, Colonel Grivas. The war cry of EOKA was *enosis*, union with Greece. In February 1959 the fighting stopped. An agreement meant that the Republic of Cyprus would be established within a year and that there would be a Greek president and a Turkish vice president. Britain would keep two bases, which the government needed. The Suez operation had shown how important it was for Britain and, if necessary, its allies to have airfields and army support facilities in the eastern Mediterranean. The coup in Iraq and the threat to Jordan emphasized that need.

Makarios eventually become president of Cyprus and, like so many against whom the British had fought, he joined other Commonwealth leaders for the grand photograph with the Queen in the Silver Jubilee year of 1977.

In August the British Motor Corporation put on display its new car, the Mini. Each one would cost a little over £500 (compared with the new Rolls Royce Phantom V, which cost £8905), and would be quite capable of doing 70 miles per hour. As a sign of the times the Mini's first difficulty was not on the road but on the assembly line. No sooner had Alec Issigonis's design been shown off than the unions went on strike for more money.

In 1959 there were about 5.5 million private motor cars on British roads and the first long and, therefore, properly so-called motorway, the M1, was opened.

Deaths

Solomon Bandaranaike (Sinhalese politician)
Ethel Barrymore (US actress)
Ernest Bloch (US composer)
Raymond Chandler (US writer)
G.D.H. Cole (economist)
Cecil B. DeMille (US film producer)
John Foster Dulles (US politician)
Sir Jacob Epstein (sculptor)
Errol Flynn (US actor)
George Grosz (US artist)
Mike Hawthorn (racing driver)
Gerard Hoffnung (musician and cartoonist)
Billie Holiday (US singer)
Buddy Holly (US singer)

Mario Lanza (US tenor)
D.F. Malan (South African politician)
George Catlett Marshall (US soldier)
Edwin Muir (poet)
Sir Stanley Spencer (artist)
Heitor Villa-Lobos (Brazilian composer)
Edward F.L. Wood, 1st Earl of Halifax (politician)
Frank Lloyd Wright (US architect)
Lester Young (US musician)

CHAPTER SEVEN

THE 1960S AND FREEDOM 1960–1969

1960

THE 1960S was the decade to which the middle-aged of the 1990s would look back and say that they supposed it was just as everyone said and wrote about – but it had not happened to them. It was the start of the generation that was to set the trends for the remainder of the century and that was to be blamed for all that was to come. For the first time, there was a generation with no memory of the events of the 1930s and the Second World War that had forced through the social changes that were now taken for granted. From now on people did not have to think about electoral reform, the need for a Welfare State or the availability of higher and further education.

Most significant of all perhaps was the fact that in the 1960s the transition from teenage years to adulthood was not interrupted because there was now no conscription. This single factor changed the appearance, ambitions and attitudes of a whole generation. In 1960 the last call-up papers were sent out to just over 2000 young men. Until the 1960s every young man who left school knew that he would have to go into one of the three services, probably the army, and by the time National Service was finished, 5.3 million teenagers would have learned to stand straight with their shoulders back. Their hair would have been cut in the 'short back and sides' style. They would have learned to look after themselves, probably for the first time having to do their own laundry, washing and scrubbing three times a day and, unless they were among the few who did National Service in the Royal Navy, shaving at least once a day. They learned to go everywhere at double speed and how to skive and get round regulations. They learned the futility as well as the sanity of authority and were reminded of their place in a society that could spot another man's station in life at parade ground distance.

When they returned from National Service the opportunity to make their own way from teenage to adulthood had been taken away.

In the 1960s the first teenagers since 1938 crossed into adult life at their own pace and in their own style. Collectively, they were able to question every frailty of authority and laugh openly at it. This freedom from National Service coincided with the revolution in broadcasting. Television was in every home that wanted it.

There were pop music stations and a music culture that was their own rather than handed down by their parents. The social and musical revolution for young people had started in the 1950s with the first chords of rock 'n' roll. Anyone who picked up a guitar could join in, and anyone who wanted to listen was welcome.

In February 1960 Harold Macmillan went to South Africa. On 3 February he addressed the South African Parliament in Cape Town and made a speech that included the famous sentence:

> The wind of change is blowing through this continent and, whether we like it or not, this growth of national consciousness is a political fact.

Behind this speech – and it was not the first time that Macmillan had used the phrase – was an understanding that decolonization could not be held back. Moreover, Macmillan was making this speech in an atmosphere of an intensifying Cold War. The prime minister saw that the battle between communism and western capitalism would not necessarily be exercised across the North German Plain.

It was a fundamental strategic belief in the early 1960s that neutrality was impossible in developing nations. Both the United States and Soviet Union tried to 'buy' emerging states with expertise, goods and grant in aid. The United States, for example, sank millions of dollars into supporting African and Asian leaders who said that the opposition in their countries was funded by communists.

Macmillan's speech was based on pragmatism, but most white South Africans saw it as unwarranted interference in the system of apartheid by which they ruled. Just seven weeks after Macmillan's address to the South African government came the Sharpeville massacre. The Pan African Congress had organized a demonstration against the pass laws, by which all non-white Africans had to carry identity cards at all times. The original idea had been that black Africans should simply not carry their cards and that, when arrested by the police, they should go quietly. The campaign organizers believed that the authorities would never be able to cope with the enormous numbers taken into custody. Instead, however, groups of Africans turned to violence. At first the violence was not directed against the authorities, and the protesters roamed through the townships demanding that their fellow Africans join the demonstration. At one of those townships, Sharpeville in the Transvaal, about 15,000 blacks confronted seventy-five armed police. The police opened fire with automatic weapons, killing sixty-nine black Africans and wounding more than 180 others. Black leaders were arrested and tens of thousands once more took to the streets when a state of emergency was declared.

When the issue was raised at the United Nations, the British and French governments instructed their heads of delegation not to support the UN condemnation of the South African government's action and the deaths at Sharpeville. Their national interests were too deeply entrenched in Africa. The Americans had the experiences of southern race riots, and to condemn South Africa would be to invite future resolutions condemning their own policies. The most popular demonstration in Britain was taken by the Sussex and England test cricketer, the Reverend David Sheppard, who announced that he would not go on the England tour of South Africa.

Apartheid would not be easily defeated by such a popular action, however. The following year, 1961, South Africa became a republic and the prime minister, Dr Hendrik Verwoerd, led his country from the Commonwealth.

In Macmillan's absence in Africa, industrial unrest at home was increasing. By 1960 the British domestic economy was growing too quickly. More people had more money in their pockets and consumer spending was rising, but the structure of the British domestic manufacturing industry encouraged imports while doing nothing for exports. The all-important trade balance was awry. In addition, because of the superficial success of the economy during the previous couple of years, demand had grown and there were more jobs. Demand coupled with low unemployment rates was beginning to lead to higher wage demands. The only crude way of fixing a spending society and at the same time strengthening sterling was to raise interest rates. The longer term effect of higher rates is to cool economic growth, to make employment prospects less certain and, thus, to steady wage demands. In 1960, however, this had not happened.

While Macmillan was away in Africa, Derick Heathcoat Amory, the Chancellor of the Exchequer, had written to him pointing out that interest rates should be raised. Macmillan agreed, and they rose from 4 to 5 per cent. The unions could not be easily satisfied without the government being criticized for buying industrial peace – which is what happened when Macmillan personally intervened (from Africa) to increase a pay offer to the railway workers. If they had struck they could have brought the country to a standstill.

Macmillan thought that a standstill of a different nature was needed, and when he returned from Africa he told Amory to produce a standstill Budget. In later years it would be described as 'a touch on the tiller' rather than as an example of the stop–go policies adopted by the Chancellors who followed. The problem with the Budget that Amory delivered in April 1960 was that it gave little indication of the government's economic course and destination, even though it reintroduced credit squeezes and hire purchase limits. It did not have the right results, and interest rates were raised by another 1 per cent within a few months. It was time for Amory to go, which he had wanted to do since the 1959 general election, and Macmillan moved Selwyn Lloyd from the Foreign Office to the Treasury.

Having replaced such a senior minister, Macmillan had to find another politician of equal standing to send to the Foreign Office. With some inspiration and not a little political bravery, Macmillan chose the 14th Earl of Home. Edward Heath became Home's deputy, with special responsibility for EEC affairs, thereby enhancing the process of Britain's application to join the Common Market.

None of this shuffling and juggling with political as well as economic figures did much for the nation's finances. The railway strike had been avoided, but as autumn approached the docks were at a standstill and the motor industry had embarked on a series of damaging stoppages.

The Americans had problems of their own. On 1 May 1960 a photographic reconnaissance plane, a U-2, was shot down over Sverdlovsk, and the pilot, Gary Powers, was captured. The Americans claimed that the U-2 was a weather-reporting aircraft, but no one believed them. The significance of the U-2 incident was that by shooting down the aircraft, the Russians had revealed that they had a missile that could shoot down high-flying aircraft. From then on the Americans understood that they had to develop satellites if they were to continue spying in safety.

The timing of the U-2 flight and its consequences wrecked what was supposed to have been a confident agenda for a summit meeting in Paris between Macmillan, Khrushchev, Eisenhower and de Gaulle. Khrushchev demanded that Eisenhower publicly apologize for sending the spy plane over the Soviet Union. Eisenhower refused, and the conference failed. In February 1962 Gary Powers was exchanged for a high-ranking Soviet spy held by the Americans.

By June 1960 Eisenhower was preoccupied by events in Vietnam. The United States was not openly involved in the conflict that was developing between north and south, but it was helping to finance the government in Laos, which was threatened by the communist group known as the Pathet Lao. Officially, the United States was only sending advisers to Southeast Asia (albeit accompanied by squadrons of aircraft), but its obsession with the domino theory – that if one country came under communist rule, its neighbours would become communist too – meant that the Americans were getting deeper into Southeast Asia.

Macmillan and Eisenhower were also increasingly concerned about the Soviet involvement in Cuba. At a meeting of the UN General Assembly in the autumn of 1960 it became clear that Khrushchev was supporting Castro and, in spite of his previous protests that he had nothing to do with communism, Castro welcomed the Soviet leader's advances.

By now the Americans, and to a lesser extent the British, had an accurate idea of Soviet military capability. During the annual Red Square Parade that November the Soviet Union publicly paraded its missiles for the first time. The coincidence of an event that had taken place the previous week was not lost. On Tuesday, 1 November 1960, Harold Macmillan announced that US nuclear submarines would be allowed to use the Holy Loch in Scotland as a permanent base.

Eisenhower had now come to the end of his two terms of office. His vice president, Richard Nixon, should have been the front runner for office, but in November the Democrat Senator John F. Kennedy scraped home the winner. If Kennedy is seen in retrospect as the most charismatic and popular of postwar American presidents, it should be remembered that he received only 120,000 more of the popular vote than Nixon.

*

On the other side of the Atlantic, France's policy of decolonization in North Africa had brought it to the verge of civil war. The 40,000 French settlers in Algeria had started their own campaign against Algerian nationalism. This was a rising by Frenchmen against the French rule of law, and the French nation was witnessing the very real possibility that its army would be turned on by its own people. Dramatically, de Gaulle dressed himself in his general's uniform and went on television. His orders were quite succinct: the French army had to overpower the settlers, who were fighting because de Gaulle had offered the Algerians self-government. In the parlance of the military, the settlers blinked, and the crisis was temporarily averted.

In December de Gaulle went to Algeria to see for himself. Self-government was, clearly, the only way to settle the crisis, and while the Muslims applauded, once more the extreme elements among the French settlers rioted. By the following spring de Gaulle had ordered the army to be on high alert in Paris. Tanks were deployed because the French army in Algeria had staged a coup and there was a real fear that the rebellious army would attempt to march on their own capital.

At the same time, just a few miles away in the Sahara Desert, the French were enacting a far more devastating policy. They had set up a test area in the desert and were now exploding nuclear weapons as part of their hurried experiments to become a nuclear power. Once that could be achieved, France, like the United Kingdom, could claim a permanent seat in any international strategic negotiations.

On 6 May Princess Margaret married a photographer, Anthony Armstrong-Jones, and in the same year Alfred Hitchcock produced a film that was to achieve cult status, *Psycho*. On stage at the Edinburgh Festival there was critical acclaim for a review, *Beyond the Fringe*, which launched the careers of Peter Cook, Dudley Moore, Alan Bennett and Jonathan Miller. On the London stage Peter Hall and Peggy Ashcroft were the prime movers in the setting up of the Royal Shakespeare Company, and Lionel Bart's musical *Oliver!* opened in London.

In a trial at the Old Bailey a jury decided that D.H. Lawrence's *Lady Chatterley's Lover*, which had been banned for thirty years, was not obscene. The trial, which had started out as a battle over censorship, was made even more famous by one of the prosecution barristers, Mervyn Griffiths-Jones, who having described the thirteen passages of sexual intercourse between Lady Chatterley and Mellors, now famously appealed to the jury: 'Is it a book you would . . . wish your wife or your servants to read?' Penguin Books sold out the 200,000 first print run in weeks.

At the Rome Olympics a new boxing hero appeared, Cassius Clay, who later became Muhammad Ali. The single achievement of the year was at sea, when Francis Chichester won the first single-handed transatlantic yacht race, setting a record of forty days. It was a prelude to an even greater achievement by the sometimes taciturn sailor, who was suffering from terminal cancer but who would become the first man to sail single-handed around the world seven years later.

Deaths
Aneurin Bevan (politician)
Jussi Björling (Swedish tenor)
Albert Camus (French writer)
Edwin Fischer (Swiss pianist)
Sir Arthur Fleming (engineer)
Walter Funk (German politician)
Clark Gable (US actor)
Oscar Hammerstein (US lyricist)
Albert Kesselring (German air commander)
Lewis Namier (historian)
Estelle Sylvia Pankhurst (suffragette)
Boris Pasternak (Russian writer)
Mack Sennett (US film producer)
Nevil Shute (writer)

1961

ON 20 JANUARY 1961 John F. Kennedy, just forty-three years old, took the oath of office and became the thirty-fifth president of the United States. The oath taken, Kennedy, coatless and hatless in wintry Washington, D.C., spoke to the American people: 'Ask not what your country can do for you – ask what you can do for your country.' As if signalling to the gerontocracy that had governed America – the outgoing president, Dwight Eisenhower, was seventy years old – Kennedy said that 'the torch has been passed to a new generation'.

But Kennedy continued the ways of the old order. He approved an increased budget to send more 'advisers', equipment and money to Southeast Asia, particularly to Laos, where the war against the Pathet Lao was stepped up. He next turned his attention to Cuba. President Eisenhower had approved a CIA plan to use Cuban exiles to launch a counter-revolution on the island. The general idea had been discussed with Macmillan, who had observed that it might be better if opposition to Castro were allowed to emerge by itself and within the island rather than have to cope with all the dangers inherent in an American-sponsored coup attempt.

In April 1961, however, Cuban exiles invaded their homeland. The force on the ground might have been large enough, but Kennedy did not have the courage to go through with the plan. The operation needed air support, but Kennedy refused to let US jets cover the landings and the advance. The CIA plan had never been a good idea and, without additional support, the April invasion turned into a fiasco. In May Castro was able to declare Cuba a socialist state. The rebels and the CIA had played into Castro's and Khrushchev's hands. Khrushchev was riding high.

A week before the Bay of Pigs disaster, Soviet scientists put another space craft into orbit. This time there was a man on board, Major Yuri Gagarin. Soviet scientists had done first what Americans said they were about to do. This flight orbited earth. When Alan Shepard Jr became the first American in space in May, the flight was suborbital and lasted just fifteen minutes. The Americans did not catch up with the Russians until John Glenn's orbit in February 1962.

Gagarin was sent on a celebrity tour, arriving in London on 14 July. He was taken to Buckingham Palace, where he lunched with the Queen and Prince Philip. Four weeks later, he might not have been made so welcome: East–West relations were fast deteriorating.

In June the world's attention had turned to Vienna, where Kennedy was to meet Khrushchev. The meeting began with smiles, but Khrushchev openly showed his contempt for Kennedy. Not unreasonably, the Bay of Pigs operation, in Khrushchev's view, revealed the Americans as the demons Kremlin propagandists painted them. Kennedy talked about the dangers of nuclear war – 'miscalculation' was the diplomatic-speak of the day – then he turned to Berlin. Here again, Khrushchev swept aside Kennedy's point of view. The president sitting opposite him had authorized the invasion of another country, was putting troops and weapons into Laos and Vietnam, had carried out bigger nuclear tests than ever before, had signed an agreement with Britain to base American Polaris missile submarines in Scotland and was encouraging the rearming and modernizing of the West German army.

So when Kennedy said that Russian plans for a peace treaty with East Germany could lead to war, Khrushchev snapped back words to the effect: 'That's your problem.'

For some time East Germans had been escaping to the West. On 13 August 1961 the East Germans closed the Berlin checkpoint. On 17 August the best the Americans, the British and the French could do was send protest notes to Moscow, calling for an end to restrictions in Berlin. The Russian response was straightforward: the Berlin Wall was built. The Allies claimed they had had no warning that the Wall was going to be built, but this is untrue. A Russian, Oleg Penkovsky, had told the British MI6 agent Greville Wynne that the Soviet authorities were considering building the wall. Penkovsky also told Wynne, who passed on the information, that if the Allied powers in West Berlin took a strong line, the wall would not be built. The authorities in London ignored both pieces of intelligence. The Russians did not. In 1962 Penkovsky was arrested, tried for treason and executed. Wynne was picked up by KGB agents and put on trial in Moscow.

The financial difficulties of 1960 had followed Macmillan into 1961, and by spring the import and export figures were so far apart that memories of the worst days of 1950 and 1951 returned.

Enoch Powell, the Minister of Health, increased National Health prescription charges, but Selwyn Lloyd's Budget in April offered no solutions. By the summer the dilemma was becoming a crisis. Wages had now risen 8 per cent on the year but output was not increasing at even half that rate. Selwyn Lloyd, a reluctant

Chancellor in the first place (he much preferred the Foreign Office), was left with few options, but one of the courses he took has crept into the language: he told Parliament that it was time for a 'pay pause'. This was the template of emergency economic planning that would eventually become an incomes policy.

The real demon was inflation. No government had ever understood how to cope with inflation. Selwyn Lloyd attempted to bring unions, industry and politicians together to plan the ways in which all three worked together, and the forum in which they were to do this was known as Neddy, after its title, the National Economic Development Council. Neddy could not sort out the economy, however.

The government could have been vulnerable to the most blistering political attacks, but it got off relatively lightly because Macmillan's greatest political ally was not his Cabinet but schisms within the Labour Party. As we have seen, Gaitskell had tried to get Clause Four amended in 1959 but had failed. He did, however, overcome CND's demands that the Labour Party adopt a policy of unilateral disarmament. Gaitskell would not be the only Labour leader to be challenged by the unilateralists; nor would he be the only Labour leader to refuse to go naked into the international arms control negotiating chamber.

Meanwhile, Macmillan was persuading the Cabinet to move, albeit warily, towards membership of the EEC. Britain's was a cautious approach. Edward Heath was in charge of negotiations with Europe, but all he could do was talk to the EEC to see if there might be circumstances and agreeable terms – agreeable to Britain, that is – for the UK to open negotiations. This tentative approach explains the Cabinet's unanimous approval. When he put the proposal to his party, Macmillan knew that he was entering difficult terrain. No one should believe that the controversies between and within Labour and Conservative governments during the 1990s over EU membership were new. The arguments and counter-arguments had been expressed, very clearly, first in the 1950s and never more succinctly than in 1961.

Macmillan's speech to Parliament in August 1961 laid out the case for joining the EEC; it was perhaps the most impressive of his premiership. Certainly, forty years later, no prime minister has improved on Macmillan's argument. Just a few sentences from that speech present Macmillan's philosophy of a confederation of European states:

> In this, as in most countries, there is a certain suspicion of foreigners. There is also the additional division between us and continental Europe of a wholly different development of our legal, administrative and, to some extent, political systems. If we are basically united by our religious faith, even here great divisions have grown up. Nevertheless, it is perhaps worth recording that in every period when the world has been in danger of tyrants or aggression, Britain has abandoned isolationism. . . . Although there has been economic union in Europe, while the rift was wide there has also been the hope of

> healing it . . . but if it should become clear that this rift will continue and perhaps deepen, then I fear that the consequences will be grave. As I said in the United States earlier this year: 'It will be a canker gnawing at the very heart of the Western Alliance.' I am sure that this consideration is in the minds of our continental friends . . . to some of whom the whole concept of our working closely in this field with other European nations is instinctively disagreeable. I am bound to say that I find it hard to understand this, when we have accepted close collaboration on more critical spheres. Others feel that our whole and sole duty lies with the Commonwealth. If I thought that our entry into Europe would injure our relations with, and influence in, the Commonwealth, or be against the true interest of the Commonwealth, I would not ask the House to support this step. . . . Most of us recognize that in a changing world if we are not to be left behind and to drop out of the main stream of the world's life, we must be prepared to change and adapt our methods.[1]

Macmillan may have impressed the Commons, but he did not impress de Gaulle. The French president never believed that the British were Europeans. He regarded them as Anglo-Americans, and in any case, keeping Britain out allowed France to maintain its superior position.

On Monday, 30 January 1961, the contraceptive pill went on sale for the first time in Britain. A week later the BBC dropped *Children's Hour* because audience figures were declining.

The 'success' for the West that year was Rudolf Nureyev's defection from the Kirov Ballet. It was hardly the diplomatic coup for which Kennedy searched. On the New York screen, classics met pop when the film version of Leonard Bernstein's *West Side Story* opened. The hit of the year was Walt Disney's; his studio had taken Dodie Smith's children's classic and turned it into the feature-length animated cartoon *One Hundred and One Dalmatians*. While theatre-goers were talking about Nureyev and Bernstein, the critics were falling over themselves to praise a book that had taken sixteen years to write, Joseph Heller's *Catch 22*.

In December 1961 there were mixed celebrations in Israel. After a lengthy operation to track him down, Israeli agents had snatched Adolf Eichmann, the former Nazi who had taken part in the Jewish extermination programme in wartime Germany. He had been hiding in Argentina until Mossad agents lifted him. On 15 December 1961 an Israeli court found Eichmann guilty and he was sentenced to be hanged. The sentence was carried out on 31 May 1962.

Deaths
Sir Thomas Beecham (conductor)
Gary Cooper (US actor)

---

1 Hansard, 2 August 1961.

George Formby (comedian)
Percy Grainger (Australian composer)
Dag Hammarskjöld (Swedish statesman)
Dashiell Hammett (US writer)
Moss Hart (US playwright)
Ernest Hemingway (US writer)
Augustus John (artist)
Carl G. Jung (Swiss psychiatrist)
Patrice Lumumba (Congolese politician)
Chico Marx (US comedian)
James Thurber (US writer)
Max Weber (US painter)
Zog I (ex-king of Albania)

1962

IN OCTOBER 1962 the world came as close as it has ever been to a world nuclear war. After the 1961 Bay of Pigs débâcle, the United States decided to impose a trade embargo on Cuba, which meant that Cubans were forced to rely on the Soviet Union and its East European satellites, and to some extent African nations, for all its trade. Castro had increasingly turned to Moscow after the Bay of Pigs affair. Khrushchev could offer advantageous trade relations, and the Soviet Union would take Cuba's staple crop, sugar, in return for supplies, such as construction materials. Khrushchev also told Castro that he would protect him from any new American-inspired adventure by basing medium-range missiles in Cuba. Castro readily agreed. Soviet strategists could argue that if American missiles were based in Scotland and Turkey, there was nothing wrong with Soviet missiles being based in Cuba. US spy planes watched what was happening and in October 1962 produced the aerial reconnaissance pictures to show what the Soviet Union was doing.

At the same time, the British agent Greville Wynne had been getting information from his Soviet contact Colonel Oleg Penkovsky that confirmed that the Soviet Union was building the sites, although the Russian double agent also claimed that the missiles were not as good as the Americans thought they were.

On Sunday, 21 October Kennedy told Macmillan that photographic intelligence had already identified six missile sites and that it was quite likely that two of them were operational. Moscow denied this. Since the summer of 1962, increasing numbers of Russian merchant ships, many carrying large deck cargoes, had been sailing to Havana. Aerial photographs of the island and the ships revealed that the ships had been carrying missile transporters.

President Kennedy had two options. He could either send in the US air force to knock out the bases or he could set up a blockade of Cuba and negotiate with the Soviet Union to withdraw the missiles. In spite of the so-called special relationship, the British government would have found it difficult to support the first action. Kennedy chose to blockade and negotiate. If his intelligence had been more accurate and he had known that more than two of the bases were operational, he might well have sent in the air force.

Khrushchev and Kennedy talked, and we know now that Khrushchev backed down. As Dean Rusk, the US Secretary of State put it: 'We're eyeball to eyeball and the other fellow just blinked.' How close did the world really come to a nuclear confrontation? Close enough for arrangements to be made for the Kennedys and their closest advisers and friends, including the British ambassador Sir David Ormsby-Gore and his family, to go into the nuclear bunkers.

By early November the Cuban bases were dismantled, and on 20 November the American blockade was lifted. Later that month the Americans agreed to dismantle their own missile bases in Turkey.

Khrushchev now understood that he had miscalculated in Vienna. Kennedy could not afford another humiliation, and Khrushchev, who had been so confident of handling Kennedy, was seen by his Kremlin colleagues to have made a major misjudgement that had resulted in the humiliation of the Soviet leadership. Moreover, a crisis in the Soviet economy – so severe that the Soviet Union could not feed itself – further weakened Khrushchev's position in Moscow. It is possible to date Khrushchev's decline from October 1962.

The crisis strengthened the myth of Britain's special relationship with the United States, but this had the effect of annoying President de Gaulle and reducing Britain's chances of joining the EEC while de Gaulle was in office. The position was worsened in December, when the United States agreed to let the British have Polaris nuclear missiles. Mindful that France was going to be thoroughly annoyed at yet another example of Anglo-American cosiness, Kennedy offered a similar arrangement to de Gaulle. It is thought that de Gaulle did not even reply.

British political life produced a minor landmark, Orpington Man. In March in a by-election Eric Lubbock, the Liberal candidate, turned a Conservative majority of nearly 15,000 into a Liberal one of nearly 8000. Orpington was not an isolated defeat for the Tories in 1962, but its loss was a loud alarm bell for Macmillan. Apart from the fact that Orpington was next to his own constituency, Bromley, the town and area represented sound, three-bedroomed, mock-Tudor Conservative voters. What he did not understand was that this was an example of the phenomenon of disaffected Tories voting Liberal because they believed it safer than voting Labour. In addition, Labour voters had voted for Lubbock because it was the best chance of unseating the Conservatives. Ignorance of Liberal policies and tactical voting were powerful allies and even more powerful enemies.

The economy was in yet another minor mess. The pay policy was not working, and Macmillan had about him an undistinguished breed of economic advisers. The image of the prime minister as SuperMac was fading fast. He was increasingly tired. The previous twelve months had seen crisis after crisis, seemingly in every area of the globe in which Britain's interests lay, and there had been almost continual domestic and industrial unrest. Not surprisingly, Macmillan was beginning to wear out. The same might have been said of the British economy.

Macmillan understood that he would have to produce a political *coup de théâtre* to divert public attention from the failings of a tired government. Selwyn Lloyd had not been a success at the Treasury, but who could take his place? The answer? Macmillan himself. Towards the end of June Macmillan's own proposals for the economy were in draft form, including outline plans for a Consumer Council and the replacement of Neddy by a National Incomes Commission. Macmillan was returning to his political roots in the 1930s for some simple economic formulae to expand the economy at the right rate.

Selwyn Lloyd did not think much of his master's plan, so Macmillan decided to get rid of him. While Macmillan was considering how this should be done, one of the few people who knew of his plans was Selwyn Lloyd's would-be successor, R.A. Butler. Butler, a compulsive gossip, talked, and the *Daily Mail* ran the story that the Chancellor was to be ditched.

On Thursday, 12 July, the Conservatives having lost another by-election, Macmillan sacked Selwyn Lloyd. Instead of lying low and licking his wounds, Selwyn Lloyd, a rather sad figure, went to the House of Commons. He had few other places to go; he had no private life and no family. But the news was out. By the following day the grumblings in Cabinet could be heard up the Strand and into Fleet Street. But still many Cabinet ministers thought that the Chancellor was the only victim. That was not to be. The country was witness to what became known as the Night of Long Knives – seven Cabinet ministers went, one-third of the most senior members of the government. The Liberal Party wit (and its future leader), Jeremy Thorpe, memorably observed: 'Greater love hath no man than this, that he lay down his friends for his life.' The Night of Long Knives was over – but much good it did the government. Macmillan, who really had handled the matter badly, found the opinion polls even more against him. Once SuperMac, Macmillan was now Mac the Knife.

There is an appropriate footnote to 1962, the year of high dramas with missiles and spies: it was the year of the first James Bond film, *Doctor No*, with Sean Connery and Ursula Andress, which was also set in a Caribbean island.

In January 1962 Decca refused to give the Beatles a recording contract, apparently in the belief that the group would never make it to the top.

On Sunday, 4 February the *Sunday Times* produced the first colour supplement to accompany a British newspaper. Live transatlantic television began using the Telstar satellite system, and it was now possible for more than 200 million television viewers in Europe to watch live American programmes. Those watching British programmes could see the first edition of the most famous British television satire of all, *That Was the Week That Was*, which was produced by Ned Sherrin. It became known affectionately as *TW3*, except in the BBC boardroom, which eventually bowed to BBC political instincts and took it off at the end of 1963. The thought of *TW3* going out during election year was too much for the majority of BBC governors, although not its 12 million audience.

This did not mean that in 1962 the conventional was undone in entertainment. Benjamin Britten's *War Requiem* brought together his haunting music and the poems of Wilfred Owen in, appropriately, the new Coventry Cathedral. David Lean's film *Lawrence of Arabia* was the screen success of the year. Andy Warhol painted dollar bills and soup cans as Pop Art was born.

The government announced that it was going to build a National Theatre and that Sir Laurence Olivier would be its director. The final Gentlemen versus Players cricket match was played at Lord's. This traditional match between amateurs and professionals had first taken place in 1806.

Even the royal family entered into the spirit of the new age. The heir to the throne, Prince Charles, was sent to his father's old school, Gordonstoun, which he quickly learned to dislike.

The world of show business was not always supremely confident. In August 1962 it, and seemingly the rest of the universe, was bewildered when Marilyn Monroe committed suicide. She had become the icon of 1950s Hollywood glamour as well as President Kennedy's mistress. The obituary writer in *The Times* called her a legend:

> Her career was not so much a Hollywood legend as *the* Hollywood legend: the poor orphan who became one of the most sought after and highly paid women in the world; the hopeful Hollywood unknown who became the most potent star-attraction in the American cinema; the uneducated beauty who married one of America's leading intellectuals.

Her last completed film was written for her by that intellectual, Arthur Miller. It was called *The Misfits*. By this time Monroe had been accepted as an actress, who did not rely on her looks alone.

Deaths

Niels Bohr (Danish physicist)
John Christie (patron of opera)
e. e. cummings (US poet)
Hugh Dalton, Baron Dalton (politician)
Clement Davies (politician)
Adolf Eichmann (German politician)
William Faulkner (US writer)
Kirsten Flagstadt (Norwegian soprano)
Sir Eugène Goossens (conductor)
Yves Klein (French artist)
Franz Kline (US artist)

Charles Laughton (US actor)
Salvatore 'Lucky' Luciano (US gangster)
Marilyn Monroe (US actress)
Auguste Piccard (Swiss physicist)
Eleanor Roosevelt (US humanitarian)
Victoria Sackville-West (writer)
R.H. Tawney (historian)
George Macaulay Trevelyan (historian)
Bruno Walter (German conductor)

1963

THIS WAS the year in which President Kennedy was assassinated. But much was to happen before events in Dallas captured the world's attention.

On 18 January Hugh Gaitskell died. He had been a modernizer, even trying to do away with Clause Four, and his ideas on how a Labour Party should govern Britain were as modern as any seen in the late 1990s. It is impossible to tell what would have happened if he had survived the virus infection that led to his death at the age of fifty-six.

The deputy leader of the Labour Party was George Brown, a volatile figure who had once so angered Khrushchev that the Soviet leader said that if he were British he would vote Conservative. There is also the story – surely apocryphal – of how Brown, who was attending an embassy reception in South America and was rather the worse for drink, asked a glamorous figure in a long red robe to dance as the band struck up. The figure turned to him and pointed out that apart from not dancing, the music was the National Anthem and he was the papal nuncio. Although that story is beloved of Labour activists, it does explain why much of the party leadership never quite trusted Brown. So George Brown came second to Harold Wilson.

In Downing Street meanwhile, Macmillan faced his biggest local difficulty of the year. John Profumo, the Secretary of State for War, had been involved with a high-class prostitute called Christine Keeler and her friend, Mandy Rice-Davies. Profumo told the Commons that he had not behaved indiscreetly during his friendship with Miss Keeler; he had, and in June he resigned because he had lied to the House. The key figure in the scandal, an osteopath called Dr Stephen Ward, had, however, told MI5, who had told the prime minister, that there was more to it than Profumo had indicated.

Ward claimed that Eugene Ivanov, a GRU (Soviet Military Intelligence) officer, was involved. Ward later committed suicide. Keeler and the eighteen-year-old Mandy Rice-Davies, Ward's mistress and before that, the mistress of a notorious London slum landlord, Peter Rackhman, went on to live and benefit from a certain notoriety. Profumo threw all his energies into charity work in the East End.

In March, Kim Philby, the third man in the Burgess and Maclean spy scandal, escaped to Moscow. He was under investigation by MI6, which knew he was a spy. They let him go.

The following month a judicial inquiry published its report on yet another spy scandal. John Vassall, a clerk in the Admiralty, had been jailed in October 1962 for eighteen years for spying for the Soviet Union. He had been handing over British secrets for six years after having been entrapped by the KGB at a homosexual party. The judicial enquiry centred not on Vassall but on ministerial responsibility. Coming as it did just at the time when the Secretary of State for War, Profumo, was involved in a sex ring, this was not a good moment for the ministers in the defence establishment. Lord Carrington, the First Lord of the Admiralty, was Vassall's boss, and he offered to resign, but the prime minister would not hear of it, and the inquiry cleared him and his deputy, Tom Galbraith, of responsibility. Nevertheless, Vassall had worked in Galbraith's office, and Galbraith's resignation was accepted.

As all this was going on, in Moscow Greville Wynne was given an eight-year jail sentence for spying and running the GRU agent, Oleg Penkovsky. Eleven months later Wynne was swapped for a KGB spy arrested in 1961. Gordon Lonsdale had been the handler in the Portland Naval Base espionage operation. Perhaps it was appropriate that the second James Bond film appeared in May 1963 and was called *From Russia with Love*.

In September an enquiry by Lord Denning criticized the prime minister and the Cabinet for failing to be more open about the Profumo affair. By now Macmillan was visibly wilting. From about July the prime minister had been feeling increasingly feeble. He had been badly wounded in the First World War and had suffered from those wounds ever since. He now had an inflamed prostate, which he did not tell his doctors about.

That he was tired and unwell was no secret, and he was already being advised to select very carefully the time that he should step down so as not to disrupt government business and cause damaging anxieties within the party. Macmillan told the Queen that he would probably go on until January or February 1964, and he intended to make his announcement at the October party conference. There were some who wanted him to stay on, and a relative upturn in the country's economy encouraged him for a moment to think that he might do so. At the end of the first week in October, however, Macmillan had a painful attack that gave all the symptoms of prostate problems. He could no longer keep it from his doctors. His own doctor, Sir John Richardson, was away at the time, and the stand-in persuaded him to go into hospital.

On one side were the party managers, who wanted Macmillan to go and get it over with. On the other side were those who believed him indestructible and wanted him patched up so that he could go on to the next election. On the morning of 10 October 1963 Macmillan was operated on. From his hospital bed, he sent a message to the party conference saying that he was going. The Conservatives were in disarray. Quintin Hogg, then still Lord Hailsham, and R.A. Butler were the front runners to replace Macmillan, and it would seem that Earl Home – Alec Douglas Home – was really brought in to stop Hailsham and Butler. But the battling was not over. Enoch Powell and Iain Macleod refused to serve under Home. It was to be a short-lived premiership.

In the same month that the Profumo scandal surfaced, March, there appeared a report that was far from titillating but that would affect the whole of the British Isles for decades. Dr Richard Beeching had been the technical director of ICI. When the British Transport Commission was reorganized as the London Transport Board, the Inland Waterways Board, the Docks Board and the Railways Board, Beeching took over as chairman of the Railways Board.

The railways, which had been nationalized by Attlee's government, now had an annual operating deficit of £159 million. Beeching surveyed his empire and found that 50 per cent of passenger stations produced only 2 per cent of the railway's revenue. He closed 50 per cent of the nation's railway stations; he closed one-third of the railway lines; he sent 8000 coaches to the scrapyard; and he sacked almost 68,000 staff. The results of Beeching's 'axe' included the closure of almost every branch line in northern Wales and the West Country and the shutting down of all passenger services north of Inverness. The unions fought him and so did the commuters. They lost. One campaign predicted that Beeching's cuts would result in the clogging up of the British road system. Ernest Marples, the Transport Minister, responded by saying it would be much simpler to build more roads. He began to do so.

On 14 January 1963 de Gaulle told the world that Britain was not a continental nation and was not qualified for full membership of the European Economic Community. As far as de Gaulle was concerned, Britain was worth no more than associate membership of Europe. Ignoring the solidarity shown during the Second World War, he claimed that the European Free Trade Association of seven non-EEC states had been set up by Macmillan in order to prevent the European Community from making progress. Above all, de Gaulle could not forgive Britain her close association with the United States. He still resented the fact that France had been kept out of the 1940s negotiations to set up NATO.

His latest evidence of the Anglo-American conspiracy was the way in which Macmillan and Kennedy had negotiated the Polaris missile deal. The fact that France had been offered the same arrangement only convinced him of America's intention to dominate Europe. The French president could never accept that America's real concern was that Europe should be able to stand alone as an economic and security organization.

In May President Kennedy had been touring the southern states where the race riots were almost monthly features of American life. Kennedy's administration was determined to push through desegregational laws. The president's brother, Robert Kennedy, was Attorney-General, and it was he who pointed out the enormous task involved not just in getting the legislation for desegregation passed but getting it implemented in the deep south.

The bigotry shown in the southern states, especially Alabama, made the place seem like another country to Boston Irish-Americans like the Kennedys. State governors, particularly George Wallis of Alabama, were openly defying federal law. When the president toured the south he praised civil rights demonstrators. Thousands of black demonstrators were arrested in Birmingham, Alabama, where Governor Wallis would not even consider court orders to allow desegregation. In June 1963 Kennedy called out the National Guard to protect blacks who were trying to enrol at the University of Alabama.

On 28 August more than 200,000 people marched on Washington in the biggest civil rights demonstration ever witnessed in the nation's capital. The main speaker was Martin Luther King. He told the crowd, which included President Kennedy:

> I still have a dream. It is a dream chiefly rooted in the American dream. I have a dream that one day this nation will rise up and live out the true meaning of its creed: 'We hold these truths to be self-evident, that all men are created equal.'

This was the atmosphere in the United States when, in November 1963, the Kennedys flew to Dallas, Texas.

Kennedy was shot through the head on 22 November by Lee Harvey Oswald, but the reason for Kennedy's assassination has never been properly determined. Oswald, who was supposed to have KGB connections, was the chairman of an obscure pro-Castro committee called Fair Play for Cuba. The emotions that began with the Bay of Pigs and continued with the missile crisis, the humiliation of Khrushchev and the enormous public differences over human rights would appear to have conspired to provide the hatred needed to make Oswald pull the trigger.

The impact of Kennedy's death was that continuing generations reflected on it, and the weaknesses of his character were glossed over. The man who was to follow him, Lyndon Baines Johnson, was to achieve more in the field of civil rights and to manage perhaps the most sordid overseas war in American history.

Deaths

William Henry Beveridge, 1st Baron Beveridge (economist and social reformer)
Georges Braque (French artist)
Guy Burgess (double agent)
Jean Cocteau (French writer)
Robert Frost (US poet)
Hugh Gaitskell (politician)
Paul Hindemith (German composer)

Aldous Huxley (writer)
John XXIII (pope)
John Fitzgerald Kennedy (US president)
C.S. Lewis (writer)
Sir David Low (caricaturist)
Max Miller (comedian)
William Richard Morris, 1st Viscount Nuffield (manufacturer)
Edith Piaf (French singer)
Sylvia Plath (US poet)
Francis Poulenc (French composer)
Herbert Louis Samuel, 1st Viscount Samuel (politician)
Robert Schuman (French politician)
Dinah Washington (US singer)
William Carlos Williams (US poet)

1964

IN THE election campaign of October 1963, the Labour Party campaigned for a new Britain after 'thirteen years of Tory misrule', but although the outcome seemed inevitable, the result of the voting on 15 October was so close that Sir Alec Douglas-Home did not give in until just before 3 o'clock the next morning. Labour had 317 seats, Conservatives 303, the Liberals nine and there was one other, the retiring Speaker. Labour had a majority of five. This would mean that the government Chief Whip would have to exercise enormous discipline over Wilson's backbenchers.

The world does not stop for the Downing Street removal van, and on the day of the British election, Nikita Khrushchev was kicked out of power in the Soviet Union. He was lucky to be on holiday by the Black Sea and suffered no more than the indignity of being overthrown. The two new leaders were Leonid Brezhnev (1906–82), the Party Secretary, and Alexei Kosygin (1904–80), who became prime minister. On the following day the Chinese exploded their first nuclear bomb and joined the most dangerous club of all, and two days after that, the Soviet Union who, after Germany feared China the most, demanded a worldwide ban on nuclear tests. There was, too, the simmering problem in Southern Rhodesia, and Wilson had not been in office a week when the white Rhodesian leader Ian Smith threatened that he would declare unilateral independence if the new government did not co-operate.

As ever, there was the troubled economy. Wilson looked at the books and concluded that the balance of payments deficit would be more than £800 million. On 26 October the prime minister was forced to issue a warning to the country, and particularly the markets, that the United Kingdom faced yet another economic crisis. He decided that there should be an immediate introduction of a 15 per cent import surcharge and a price review body. There would also be help for areas of underemployment, a review of government expenditure and a rethink on the Anglo-French supersonic aircraft, Concorde.

Things did not get better after the first hectic ten days in office.

International currency speculators were causing havoc with the pound, and James Callaghan, the new Chancellor of the Exchequer, was forced to produce an emergency budget. On 11 November Callaghan put up income tax by 6 per cent, which was supposed to cover increases in old age pensions, war pensions and industrial injuries payments. In addition, excise duty on petrol went up and a new capital gains tax was introduced, together with something new in industry, corporation tax, which would replace companies and profits taxes. The speculators went back to work.

Wilson and Callaghan concluded that the international money markets believed that the new Labour government, by increasing social benefits at a time of economic difficulties, would not be tough enough to take the measures necessary to balance the economy. Until the end of the year, Wilson, Callaghan and Lord Cromer, the Governor of the Bank of England, were in almost daily discussions as they watched the foreign exchanges. The fundamental crisis was that the only way the government could stabilize the pound, or attempt to, was for the Bank to release money into the money markets. This meant that Britain's reserves were being run down. It is estimated that at that time, Britain's convertible currency reserves, for example, dollars and sterling, together with gold reserves, amounted to no more than £1 billion. Even in 1964 that was not much.

Finance ministers and governments around the world were meeting to discuss Britain's financial crisis. This was not, to use a Macmillanism, 'a little local difficulty'. For example, before the EFTA countries could agree to step in and support sterling, they wanted a guarantee that Callaghan's new import surcharge was only a temporary measure. The first emergency action against the speculators was taken on 23 November, when interest rates were raised by 2 per cent. At first sterling steadied, but the world markets sensed this was not calculated economics but panic.

Wilson's government was having to face international financiers who could and would decide government policies. This may not have been their intention, but it was the result. Slight relief came on 25 November, when the central bankers of eleven nations offered Britain $3000 million to balance sterling against the speculators. For the moment Harold Wilson and his government could get a good night's sleep.

By 1964 Harold Macmillan's 'wind of change' had blown across Africa with such force that thirty-six states had shrugged off colonial rule. The African independence movement had started in the 1950s in the Sahara. The first to go was Libya in 1951, followed by Morocco, Guinea, Sudan and Ghana. Most of the changes occurred in the early 1960s: Chad, Niger, Mauritania, Mali, Nigeria, the Ivory Coast, Upper Volta, Gabon, the Central African Republic, Congo, Zaïre, Dahomey,

Togo, Sierra Leone, Senegal, Burundi, Madagascar, Zanzibar, Rwanda, Uganda, Somalia, Tanganyika (Tanzania) and, at the end of 1963, Kenya. In the summer of 1964 Malawi became independent from Britain, and a former Elder of the Church of Scotland, Dr Hastings Banda, became the country's first and long-lasting president. The following month, Northern Rhodesia changed its name to Zambia and Dr Kenneth Kaunda was sworn in as that nation's president.

In 1964 the only British colonies left were Lesotho, Swaziland, Botswana, Nyasaland (Malawi) and Southern Rhodesia, and it was Southern Rhodesia that sent a political schism through British politics.

On 13 April Ian Smith was elected prime minister. Smith had been a Spitfire pilot during the Second World War. In 1964 the war was well in the memories of the headline writers and the readers of papers like the *Daily Express*, whose proprietor, Lord Beaverbrook, backed him. Beaverbrook's son, Max Aitken, who became head of the mass-circulation paper on Beaverbrook's death in June, had also flown fighters in the North African campaign, so Smith had a close friend and soul-mate in what was then the most widely read broadsheet in Britain.

Smith had watched the fall of white power in Africa and was not going to let that happen in his country, where the white farmers and original settlers held the nation together. This was, after all, the region in which the legend of Cecil Rhodes had been born. Independence was unquestioned. The fight with Britain was over the government's insistence that the majority black population should be included in the full democratic process of hand-over, including elections. Even given the animosities between the two main groups, the Matabele and the Shona, Smith and his people understood that free elections would mean the wiping out of white rule. This was their homeland as much as it was that of the Matebele and Shona.

Smith was elected on the policy that he would negotiate independence with the British. If Westminster wanted to hand over the country to the black population the whites would declare independence and set up their own government in Salisbury, the capital, under their own rules. Both Macmillan and Home had warned Smith that he was following the wrong path and that some transitional system should be worked out. In October 1964, however, Smith received a political shock. The Conservatives lost the general election.

Harold Wilson, the new prime minister, immediately and publicly told Smith that any unilateral declaration of independence (UDI) would amount to treason and that the British government would take steps to recover the situation. This was the first public threat issued by the British government and it came in three parts. It began on a friendly tone by saying that everyone hoped that Southern Rhodesia would become independent and join the Commonwealth. Then came the warning against UDI. The statement declared that UDI would be an act of treason and that no Commonwealth government would recognize UDI. It stated that Commonwealth membership 'would be out of the question, with all the related economic consequences'. Finally, it made the point that Southern Rhodesians would no longer be British subjects and that the economic effects would be disastrous for them. There would be no access to the London market and culturally, socially, politically and, above all, economically, Southern Rhodesia would become 'isolated and virtually friendless in a largely hostile Continent'.

The shot across the bows did not deter Smith from what he saw to be the right course. The reference in the British statement to Southern Rhodesia being 'virtually friendless' anticipated the reality that blockades and trade embargoes would be ignored by Southern Rhodesia's friends, the South Africans.

By the following year, 1965, there was no way in which an agreement could be reached between London and Salisbury and Smith's Rhodesian Front Party declared UDI.

It is easy to decide when the Vietnam War ended. The Paris Conference began in January 1973; Saigon fell in April 1975, and the last US troops, eleven men of the US Marine Corps, were lifted from the embassy roof by helicopter. The war was over. But when did it start?

Most people will say in 1965, but the Americans had been putting money and 'advisers' into the area for many years before that. It was in 1964 that the American build-up reached a point where it was unlikely that they would pull out without making one huge effort to crush the North Vietnam forces. That one big effort would go on for nearly a decade.

At the beginning of August the North Vietnamese were retaliating on a regular basis, and the South Vietnamese government was suffering significant defeats. Already the West was learning new names and places: Saigon, Phnom Penh, the Gulf of Tonkin, Da Nang and the Mekong Delta. On 2 August 1964 an American destroyer, the *Maddox*, was attacked by the Vietnamese in the Gulf of Tonkin. The *Maddox* suffered no damage, but this was an escalation of the war for which the hawks had searched but that the doves had dreaded

President Johnson would be running for the White House that coming November, when his opponent would be the right-wing Republican, Senator Barry Goldwater. Johnson understood the need to avoid the right-wing ticket, but he knew he could not be soft on Vietnam. On 7 August, less than a week after the attack on the *Maddox*, he went to the Congress and got permission to take whatever action he thought necessary against North Vietnam. Johnson summed up his philosophy thus:

> the world must never forget that aggression unchallenged is aggression unleashed. We of the United States have not forgotten. That is why we have answered aggression with action.

Perhaps 7 August 1964 is a convenient date for the beginning of America's war in the quagmire of Vietnam.

★

The only light relief for Britain was the appearance of a new athletics heroine. She was Ann Packer who had gone out to the Tokyo Olympics hoping to win a gold medal in the 400 metres but had only got a silver, having been beaten by the remarkable Australian, Betty Cuthbert. Miss Packer, a sprinter, had signed up for the 800 metres the following day. She set a world record and picked up the gold medal. Even better she was in love. She and Robbie Brightwell, a silver medallist in the 4 × 400 metre relay team, were to marry. But one Olympic wedding does not make a summer.

Deaths

William Max Aitken, 1st Baron Beaverbrook (newspaper proprietor)
Nancy Witcher Astor, Viscountess Astor (politician)
Brendan Behan (Irish writer)
Eddie Cantor (US comedian)
Rachel Carson (US environmentalist)
Ian Fleming (writer)
Professor John Haldane (geneticist)
Herbert Hoover (US president)
Alan Ladd (US actor)
Peter Lorre (US actor)
Douglas MacArthur (US soldier)
Louis MacNeice (poet)
Simon Marks, Baron Marks of Broughton (businessman)
Harpo Marx (US comedian)
Jawaharlal Nehru (Indian politician)
Sean O'Casey (Irish playwright)
Cole Porter (US composer)
Dame Edith Sitwell (poet)
Frederick James Woolton, Baron Woolton (politician)

1965

Winston Churchill, the most memorable British statesman of the twentieth century, died on 24 January 1965. He was born in 1874, at Blenheim Palace in Oxfordshire. His father was Lord Randolph Churchill, the radical Tory and Chancellor of the Exchequer in Lord Salisbury's ministry. His mother was Jenny Jerome, a beautiful American heiress. Churchill had joined the Fourth Hussars in 1895 and had taken part in the charge at Omdurman. In 1900 he became a Conservative MP. The rest of the story we have told.

The last time Churchill had been in the House of Commons was 27 July 1964, when he had announced his retirement. The next day the House delivered a Resolution. It was the most unusual honour for any politician. To call it officially a vote of thanks is to understate the sentiment. It was proposed in the Chamber and carried *Nemine contradicente*, unanimously. That resolution may be his epitaph.

> That this House desires to take this opportunity of marking the forthcoming retirement of the Right Honourable Gentleman, the Member for Woodford by putting on record its unbounded admiration and gratitude for his services to Parliament, to the nation and to the world; remembers, above all, his inspiration of the British people when they stood alone, and his leadership until victory was won; and offers its grateful thanks to the Right Honourable Gentleman for these outstanding services to this House and to the nation.

After lying in state in Westminster Hall, where he was guarded by the Household Cavalry and Blues and Royals, Churchill was given a state funeral in St Paul's Cathedral, attended by all the royal families of Europe and, seemingly, leaders of almost every nation in the world. He was buried in a small churchyard by Blenheim Palace.

Churchill was the last MP to have sat in Queen Victoria's reign, and when he died there died the last public link with Empire.

We might add to the memorial list of 1965 the hundreds and thousands who were dying in Vietnam. Although it was yet to be officially a war, the United States was there in force, fighting what the soldiers would call Charlie Cong or, to the rest of us, the Viet Cong guerrillas.

The British, particularly young strategic thinkers like Denis Healey, who was Secretary of State for Defence in Wilson's Cabinet, had warned against American involvement in Indochina. The doctrine of containment – containing communism within its existing borders rather than directly fighting it – was still current in the Washington think-tanks, but the build-up of US personnel that had begun in 1963 had continued inexorably. At the beginning of 1964 the United States had 15,500 troops in Vietnam; by 1966 there were nearly 200,000; two years later there would be 500,000. To Denis Healey, who was on a visit to the region in 1964, it seemed that the Americans were irrevocably committed.

> When I landed in Saigon in April 1964 the Americans were everywhere but in the front line. Besides the military 'advisers' there were thousands of Americans from the CIA, the US Information Services, the Aid Programme and, of course, the Embassy. The US Army, Navy and Air Force were engaged in fighting one another, and all three were at loggerheads with the CIA and the State Department; the latter tended to share the British view that the Vietnamese government [the government of South Vietnam] was heading for a disaster from which no amount of military intervention by the United States could rescue it.[2]

By early 1965, with Lyndon B. Johnson sworn in as the thirty-sixth president of the United States, the Americans escalated their part in the hopeless war. In spite

2 Denis Healey, *The Time of My Life*, Michael Joseph (1989).

of their mass of aircraft, aircraft carriers, helicopter gunships and quick-reaction mobile formations, combined American and South Vietnamese forces had only brief successes. Instead of forcing out the Americans, President Johnson became determined to get further in. There were politicians in Europe, particularly in Britain, who found Johnson totally distasteful. Healey described him as a monster with a brutal lust for power. The president had spent many years following his hypothesis that if he grabbed someone by the most sensitive parts, the rest of him would follow. He never understood that his homespun philosophy could not apply in Vietnam. By June 1965 American ground forces were officially in the war.

Vietnam was not the only war of 1965. On 8 September Indian troops invaded Pakistan, and the Pakistanis launched air attacks on the capital, New Delhi. The border conflict had started because of rival claims on Kashmir. Wilson, fearful that China and the Soviet Union would take sides, said it was the worst threat to world peace since the Second World War. The Pakistan Foreign Minister, Bhutto, said that the Pakistanis were willing to fight for a thousand years.

By the autumn of that year Wilson had a more direct trouble to resolve. Ian Smith, playing to the gallery of nostalgia, announced UDI on 11 November at 11 o'clock in the morning. The following Tuesday, 16 November, Parliament, having sat well into the early hours of the morning, passed the emergency laws that would impose sanctions on Rhodesia.

Lord Carrington, the man who eventually found a resolution for the Rhodesian crisis – much to his personal discomfort having been told by fellow Conservatives that he had 'sold out to the blacks' – put the Rhodesian position in a nutshell in his autobiography:[3]

> When the white Rhodesians looked at some of their neighbours they saw tribal excess, cruelty and intolerance, economic ruin. They had committed their lives and fortunes to a country they undoubtedly loved, they felt it threatened by ultimate disaster. And they had come to regard this disaster as the consequence of betrayal. British governments, they had always believed, had a duty to support them, to see sense, to take realistic stock of the consequences of black rule, to stick up for them internationally. Angry at London's refusal to see things their way they, or considerable numbers of them, had backed Ian Smith's defiant assertion . . . The White Rhodesians were being defiant, resolute, somewhat backward-looking and certainly bloody minded. In a word, they were being British!

While Wilson was struggling with foreign policy, the Conservative opposition was rearranging its deckchairs. After the election defeat in 1964 the Conservative leader, Sir Alec Douglas-Home, had decided that the pressure on him to resign

3 Lord Carrington, *Reflecting on Things Past*, William Collins (1988).

could no longer be resisted. Much has been made of the pressure that came from the media – some of it openly inspired by his own party members – but perhaps the biggest damage to his leadership was done by the latest Liberal success.

In March 1965 David Steel won the Conservative safe seat of Roxburgh, Selkirk and Peebles. The Conservatives saw this as evidence that the Unionist vote was collapsing in Scotland – the homeland and political heartland of Alec Douglas-Home. The disquiet within his own party extended into the media and even degenerated into the personal attack by the journalist Bernard Levin, who referred to Alec Douglas-Home as a 'cretin'. So why did he stay so long after losing the election?

First, the local elections produced good results for the Conservatives. Second, the Labour government, with a small majority, had been going through a bad patch. Harold Wilson had sent his first choice of Foreign Secretary, Patrick Gordon Walker, who had lost his seat in the 1964 election, to the supposedly safe seat of Leytonstone in a by-election in 1965. He lost. Wilson appointed the virtually unknown Michael Stewart as Foreign Secretary. This, together with the bad local election results, gave the sense that there could be a general election at any time. The Conservative Party managers asked Home to stay. They did not want to go into a general election while trying to elect a new leader.

A third reason Home survived so long was that the possible successors to the Conservative leader were not particularly distinguished and most certainly did not have good public images. This last point should not be ignored, when it is remembered that in spite of his undoubted wisdom, Sir Alec Douglas-Home is thought to have lost the Conservatives many votes at the general election simply because he had the wrong image for the time.

The two front-runners were Edward Heath and the shadow Foreign Secretary, Reginald Maudling. Maudling was a relaxed, almost shambling, figure; Heath had better staff work. By July 1965 the groundswell among backbenchers was sufficient for Home to make up his mind that it was time to go. On 27 July Edward Heath became leader of the Conservative Party, the first non-public schoolboy to do so. Heath was also the first Conservative leader to be voted in by backbenchers, rather than being chosen by the outgoing man. Butler, who had long given up any thought that he could be prime minister, was at least thankful that the concept of patronage remained in some areas. He became Master of Trinity College, Cambridge, and was perhaps happier there than in any other place.

The old ways of the world were upset in a flutter of suitable pomposity that year when the Beatles were awarded MBEs. They had been proposed by Harold Wilson, and nine Members of the Order returned their decorations because they believed that Wilson's gesture to the Merseyside quartet had cheapened the honour.

This was the new democratic society. It was a year in which Elizabeth Lane became the first woman high court judge. It was also the year in which a new organization, the National Viewers' and Listeners' Association, was set up because the most pervasive of British institutions, the BBC, was bowing too much to modern times and becoming a transmitter of bad taste. The self-appointed censor on behalf of the British public was, as she liked to tell everyone, an ordinary housewife, Mary Whitehouse.

All these changes in attitudes and in some cases practical politics seemed appropriate in 1965, the 750th anniversary of the signing of Magna Carta.

Deaths
Sir Edward Appleton (physicist)
Bernard Baruch (US financier)
Clara Bow (US actress)
Sir Winston S. Churchill (politician)
Nat 'King' Cole (US singer)
William Thomas Cosgrave (Irish politician)
Sir Geoffrey de Haviland (designer)
Richard Dimbleby (broadcaster)
James Chuter Ede, Baron Chuter-Ede of Epsom (politician)
T.S. Eliot (poet)
Farouk (ex-king of Egypt)
Stan Laurel (UK comedian)
Le Corbusier (French architect)
W. Somerset Maugham (writer)
Herbert Stanley Morrison, Baron Morrison of Lambeth (politician)
Edward R. Murrow (US journalist)
Syngman Rhee (Korean politician)
Helena Rubinstein (US businesswoman)
Dr Albert Schweitzer (German missionary and philosopher)
David Smith (US sculptor)
Adlai Stevenson (US politician)
Edgar Varèse (US composer)

1966

1966 WAS a year in which the average Briton could have gone away and come back without missing anything politically. However, the one major event of the year was neither political nor social: England won the World Cup, beating the Germans 4–2.

The prime minister believed it was such a boost to national morale that it eased some of the pressure on his beleaguered government. Wilson even had a $5 bet with the Canadian prime minister, Lester Pearson, that England would win. Pearson paid up – in Canadian dollars.

On 20 July 1966 Callaghan, the Chancellor of the Exchequer, announced a price freeze for twelve months, increases in taxes paid on goods at the counter (purchase tax), restrictions on hire purchase and, most controversial of all, a pay and dividends freeze for six months. The Prices and Incomes Bill was too much for one of Wilson's key Cabinet members, Frank Cousins, a strong union man, who resigned. He was succeeded as Minister of Technology by Tony Benn, then known as Anthony Wedgwood Benn, who had given up his title of Lord Stansgate. The bank rate had gone up to 7 per cent and would stay there until the following January, when the so-called sterling crisis was officially at an end. It was not, but that was the way it looked at the end of 1966.

The major foreign policy conundrum remained Rhodesia. To attempt to give some sense of neutrality and impartiality, Wilson had convinced Ian Smith to meet him on board the cruiser HMS *Tiger* at Gibraltar on 2 December. Wilson carried with him a five-point plan. First and foremost was the offer to Smith, that if the two men could reach the basis of an agreement and if Rhodesia would return in the interim to the 1961 constitutional position – that is, negotiations on independence – Ian Smith could disembark from the *Tiger* as prime minister designate.

Second, the 1961 constitution would apply to all the Rhodesian people. Third, there would be a royal commission, and if everyone agreed to its findings, the British Parliament would lift sanctions. Fourth, Harold Wilson wanted Ian Smith to form what he called a broad-based government. The fifth section concerned how to keep law and order during the interim period and would require the setting up of a Governor's Defence Council.

Wilson always claimed that he asked Ian Smith if he could carry this proposal through his more right-wing colleagues and, if he could not, would the right-wingers resign? Wilson also claimed that Smith told him that it would not be a question of resignation and that he would sack them. Smith appeared to be contemplating a Cabinet of only a dozen members, including himself. The arithmetic would have meant Smith getting rid of six of his existing colleagues. The key to all this was the so-called return to constitutional rule, which meant there could be no further negotiations until Rhodesia gave up UDI.

Wilson's suspicions of Smith increased considerably when the Rhodesian leader said that he would have to telegraph proposals and questions back to his capital and his colleagues. Wilson had believed that Smith himself had the authority to negotiate a deal. This put Wilson in a quandary. He had got Cabinet backing to sign an agreement with Ian Smith, but if Smith insisted on his own consultations Wilson would have to do the same. There followed a confrontation between Smith and Wilson that was, in Wilson's opinion, vigorous.[4]

Wilson's feelings towards the end of that session were that Smith could not go very far, partly because he believed that he himself was vulnerable to a palace revolution that would be staged by the right-wingers in his Rhodesian Front Party.

4 See HMSO Command Paper 3171.

On 6 December 1966 Ian Smith rejected the British proposals. The confrontation had now being going on for more than a year. The British Cabinet had to reinforce its belief that there could be no settlement without majority rule in Rhodesia. The confrontation was now beyond politics and would go into the bush, from whence would come the eventual Rhodesian leader, Robert Mugabe.

Among the diversions of the year were the actions of George Brown, the Secretary of State for Economic Affairs. Brown was known to be having emotional conversations in Cabinet and offering his resignation at the drop of an ice cube. The present crisis was resolved with an announcement that Brown would do his duty and stay. He became Foreign Secretary.

As Foreign Secretary Brown faced a high pile of briefing notes. In Nigeria, a member of the Commonwealth, Jakubu Gowon, had staged a successful coup. In China Mao Zedong had imposed what became known as the Cultural Revolution. Its symbol became the Little Red Book, a collection of Chairman Mao's thoughts. The fear in Beijing was that the memories of why the revolution had taken place in 1949 were now dulled. Mao's Red Guards began a new long march as they spread out across the whole of China with absolute power to bring the country to the heel of Chairman Mao.

In New York the UN Secretary General, U Thant, had publicly given up on any thoughts that the United Nations could end the Vietnam War. In Africa, Bechuanaland became independent and changed its name to Botswana.

In Gibraltar, the Spanish began to enforce their claim that the colony should be returned to Spain. On 5 October 1966 General Franco, the Spanish leader, banned traffic across the Gibraltar–Spanish border at La Linea.

If the Wilson government thought there was security in Europe, this was set aside in 1966. The French, for so long suspicious of the United States and opposed to what they saw as the American control over the North Atlantic Treaty Organization, had withdrawn from the military wing of NATO. A slight difficulty here was that the NATO headquarters was at Fontainebleau, just outside Paris. On 6 October 1966 NATO decided to move from Paris to Brussels.

London may have been a city of political headaches, but it was nevertheless a smart place to be. *Time* magazine called it 'Swinging London'. Few places better reflected the 1960s image than the transformation of a slum area behind London's Regent Street. Carnaby Street was now being called Britain's boutique capital, and if you wanted to know what to look like to be part of the 1960s, you went to Carnaby Street and did your best.

Deaths

Elizabeth Arden (US businesswoman)
Vincent Auriol (French politician)
Lenny Bruce (US comedian)

Montgomery Clift (US actor)
Walt Disney (US film producer)
C.S. Forester (writer)
Christian A. Herter (US politician)
Buster Keaton (US comedian)
Paul Reynaud (French politician)
Sophie Tucker (US singer)
Randolph Turpin (boxer)
Hendrik Verwoerd (South African politician)
Evelyn Waugh (writer)

1967

IT WAS IN 1967 time to rethink Britain's global responsibilities, and Britain was preparing a defence review that would withdraw troops from the Far East. This came at a time when the country was in the almost usual economic crisis. However, the domino theory was such an important part of Washington's strategic thinking that the Americans wanted Britain to maintain what was still an impressive military capability of all three services in Southeast Asia. The Americans also knew that Wilson's government, inspired by the thinking of Denis Healey, understood that Britain really had to discard ideas about keeping an imperial-size force in a region that had clearly rejected colonial notions and to move away from a deployment that neither suited Britain's foreign policy ambitions nor her ability to finance such a force.

Healey's concept that Britain should begin a gradual withdrawal from its East of Suez responsibilities was sound, and it was, by and large, supported by his own Chiefs of Staff.

The Americans knew that the review was going on, but they wanted Britain to stay in the Far East. So Washington offered to underwrite the value of sterling as long as Britain remained. Wilson's government would not accept such a proposal. The International Monetary Fund was an alternative banker (in fact, it amounted to the same thing), but the conditions for a huge loan could never have been tolerated by Cabinet. So James Callaghan, the Chancellor of the Exchequer, had to recommend devaluation.

Barbara Castle records in her diary for 16 November that the Cabinet was told that Thursday:

> Jim began heavily, 'I have decided that the pound must be devalued . . . This is the unhappiest day in my life.' We all sat very still. He then elaborated on the recent run on the pound. We could arrange another massive loan, but the thought of going through the whole process again was sickening . . . In conclusion he said, 'This is the most agonizing reappraisal I have ever had to do and I will not pretend that it is anything but a failure of our policies.'[5]

---

5 Barbara Castle, *The Castle Diaries, 1964–1976*, Weidenfeld & Nicolson (1984).

On 19 November 1967 the pound was devalued from $2.80 to $2.40. That weekend – it was best to do it all when the markets were closed – it was worth 14.3 per cent less than it had been on the Friday. Wilson blamed everyone – the Six Day War was particularly convenient – and in a now famous television broadcast, he promised the nation: 'It does not mean, of course, that the pound here in Britain in your pocket or purse or in your bank has been devalued.' Not only bankers looked at each other with incredulity.

The central bankers were friends of Britain. After all, the world banking system cannot do well when a major power is broke. A $1 billion stand-by loan had been negotiated. Moreover, as only New Zealand, Denmark, Ireland and Israel devalued to keep pace with the exchange rate, Wilson felt confident that Britain would, as Callaghan had forecast, enjoy all the advantages of the weaker pound.

But Callaghan's failure to prevent devaluation meant he could not stay at the Treasury. He was moved to the Home Office, and Roy Jenkins became Chancellor of the Exchequer.

On 5 June 1967 the Six Day War had begun. The Israeli air force wiped out Egyptian aircraft, which were mostly on the ground, and they fought the Jordanian army in Jerusalem, which was not then in Israel. By 6 June Israeli forces had crossed the Sinai Peninsula, taking Bethlehem and the Gaza Strip from Egypt. By 7 June the Jordanians had given up most of the west bank of the River Jordan and the ancient city of Jericho. On Israel's western front the troops under General Moshe Dayan were at the Suez Canal. On 8 June the Egyptians surrendered. On 9 June the once self-assured Colonel Abdel Nasser resigned as president of Egypt, although the National Assembly demanded he stay in power. To the north, Israeli aircraft bombed Damascus, the capital of Syria, and took the Golan Heights.

On 10 June the Israelis had got as much as they could look after. They had the Sinai Desert to the Suez Canal, the Golan Heights, the west bank of the Jordan and, most important of all, Jerusalem.

The war came about when the United Nations' emergency buffer force along the Gaza and the border between Israel and Egypt (the United Arab Republic), frayed. The UN was also looking after the Port of Eilat, which was important to the Israelis because it was a way to bring in goods from the Indian Ocean. This artificial agreement for peaceful existence could not last.

From early 1966 there had been a number of border incidents on all three sides. The Palestinians living in Jordan had used it as a base from which to probe Israeli territory. The Syrians had done the same. By May 1967 the Israeli Cabinet had made it known that if the Syrian attacks continued they would retaliate. In the middle of the month the Egyptians sent troops to its border with Israel. It did so with a great deal of publicity – they were well equipped, having been supplied with armour, artillery and aircraft, together with advisers, by the Soviet Union.

On 16 May Nasser demanded that the United Nations withdraw its emergency force. It appears that the Secretary General, U Thant, took a unilateral decision to comply with Nasser's command on the grounds that no UN force could be deployed without the consent of the host nation. Less than a week later, Nasser had moved his troops into a position overlooking the Straits of Tiran. This meant that Israel's gateway to supplies was closed.

The British asked the Russians to persuade Nasser to pull back. President de Gaulle was shifting his position towards the Arabs, even though French arms salesmen had done very good business in Israel. De Gaulle proposed that Britain, France, the United States and the Soviet Union should meet to discuss the situation. Even here, with the real chance of a pre-emptive strike by either Israel or Egypt, domestic politics reigned supreme in France. Wilson wanted to go to Paris for talks with de Gaulle. De Gaulle agreed but said that the two men should not meet immediately because he was about to hold his six-monthly press conference. If he and Wilson met first and the situation in the Middle East suggested action that de Gaulle would have to either announce or answer questions about, it might look as if he, President de Gaulle, had been influenced by the British. This de Gaulle would not have.

The Foreign Secretary, George Brown, went to Moscow, where he addressed the Soviet Foreign Affairs Institute. Anyone who understood the Soviet system would have known that this would have been seen as a lecture to the Kremlin. The immediate reaction was that the Soviet Union sent a flotilla to the Mediterranean to reinforce its influence with Egypt, deployed extra submarines off Hammemet and issued a warning to Britain that it must immediately cease its support of Israel.

So now we had all the makings of a confrontation that could extend beyond the Sinai, the Golan and the West Bank.

President Johnson had no inclination to help the Israelis. It was not until much later that the Jewish lobby in the United States started picking off senators one at a time.

At the end of the first day of the war, British intelligence thought the Israelis had succeeded. In Cabinet there was what Richard Crossman called a 'desultory discussion about the Egyptian-Israeli war'. The interest was in how far the Israelis would extend their boundaries and even on this there was a general opinion that there was nothing any outside nation could do. The international regime had failed to prevent a conflict that, had it not been over inside a week, could easily have extended to an international confrontation. Whatever was said later, especially in memoirs, the British and American governments were not unhappy with the situation. In the long term that is. At the time, as Harold Wilson wrote, with Britain's economy gradually recovering from a very low ebb, the Six Day War was, well, unhelpful. The single influence on almost every aspect of industrial and domestic life was oil – or rather, the sudden lack of it. Here was the reason Britain wanted to keep control of the canal.

★

Relations between Britain and France continued to be unhelpful. The previous month President de Gaulle had again vetoed Britain's attempt to open negotiations for Common Market membership. De Gaulle talked about formidable obstacles, and it was clear that Britain could never join the Community while de Gaulle remained in power. However, an indication of Wilson's belief that EEC membership had all-party support came in mid-May when his government pushed through a resolution in support of Britain's application. The vote was 488 for and 62 against, those who voted against being evenly split between Labour and Conservative. It was the biggest majority of the century.

In London the film version of *Half a Sixpence*, starring Tommy Steele, opened in London – unlike some currencies, this one would run and run and show a big return.

Deaths
Konrad Adenauer (German politician)
Clement Attlee, 1st Earl Attlee of Walthamstow (politician)
Sir John Cockcroft (physicist)
John Coltrane (US musician)
Sir Victor Gollancz (publisher)
Che Guevara (Argentinian revolutionary)
Zoltán Kodály (Hungarian composer)
Vivien Leigh (actress)
Jayne Mansfield (US actress)
John Masefield (poet)
André Maurois (French writer)
Mohammed Mussadeq (Iranian politician)
Dr Robert Oppenheimer (US physicist)
Joe Orton (writer)
Dorothy Parker (US writer)
Claude Rains (US actor)
Arthur Ransome (writer)
Basil Rathbone (actor)
Sir Malcolm Sargent (conductor)
Siegfried Sassoon (writer)
Arthur William Tedder, Baron Tedder of Glenguin (soldier)
Spencer Tracy (US actor)
Paul Whiteman (US bandleader)

1968

IN JUNE 1967 the Labour government had proposed to put through a Race Relations Bill that would forbid racial discrimination in housing and employment. In theory, the Bill would protect unfortunate white people as well as unfortunate black people. Many failed to see it that way. In the same year the government in Nairobi expelled the Kenyan Asians, and the government speedily passed the Commonwealth Immigration Act in March 1968 to limit the inflow by imposing a voucher scheme.

Enoch Powell had already made speeches warning of the consequences of immigration. He was not alone, and he was getting a lot of letters as well as support from two popular newspapers, the *Daily Sketch* and the then broadsheet *Daily Express*. On 11 April 1968 Edward Heath's shadow Cabinet – of which Powell was a member – agreed to register its disapproval of the Race Relations Bill without voting against it. Powell always claimed that what he said in his speech nine days later expressed the sentiment of that meeting. In Birmingham, on 20 April, he made the speech. He talked about the dangers of increased numbers of immigrants. He talked of a coloured population of more than 3 million by 1988. These were official figures, not his. And then, finally he came to the most quoted section:

> For these dangerous and divisive elements the legislation proposed in the Race Relations Bill is the very pabulum they need to flourish. Here is the means of showing that the immigrant communities can organize to consolidate their members, to agitate and campaign against their fellow citizens, and to overawe and dominate the rest with the legal weapons which the ignorant and ill-informed have provided. As I look ahead, I am filled with foreboding. Like the Roman, I seem to see, 'the River Tiber foaming with much blood'. That tragic and intractable phenomenon which we watch with horror on the other side of the Atlantic but which there is interwoven with the history and existence of the States itself, is coming upon us here by our own volition and our own neglect. Indeed, it has all but come. In numerical terms, it will be of American proportions long before the end of the century. Only resolute and urgent action will avert it even now. Whether there will be the public will to demand and obtain that action, I do not know. All I know is that to see, and not to speak, would be a great betrayal.

Heath sacked Powell from the shadow Cabinet. *The Times* called it an evil speech. Powell always denied that he was trying to incite racial prejudice. He was, he argued, delivering a warning against the government's legislation that allowed some 50,000 dependants of immigrants into the United Kingdom each year. Powell said that the nation was 'heaping up its own funeral pyre'. And four opinion polls showed that he had us much as 80 per cent of the nation behind him.

The man who drafted the Race Relations Bill was Roy Jenkins, but now he was Chancellor. The Treasury was no hiding place.

In March sterling was at its lowest price since devaluation the year before. Gold reserves had fallen, even those in the United States, and on 9 March the World

Bank met in Switzerland and agreed that gold should be held and therefore subsidized at $35 an ounce.

Harold Wilson had often believed that the biggest threat to his administration came not from the opposition benches but from the international financial speculators. The situation by the middle of the second week in March 1968 was so desperate that Britain was asked by the World Bank to close the London Gold Market – in other words, to shut down the banks. This would involve the Queen, and a group of privy councillors went to Buckingham Palace at midnight on 14 March. The Queen was briefed and asked to declare the following day, 15 March 1968, a bank holiday. Such was the pressure on Britain from foreign banks and from the United States, that the London Gold Market was actually shut for two weeks. Sterling was suffering, as Wilson knew it would, from international speculation, and the Central Bank gave Britain $4 billion in stand-by credits.

In the southeast of England a campaign started with the theme: 'I'm backing Britain.' Soon the poster campaign was nationwide. Another slogan began appearing on small notices pasted on lamp-posts, notice boards and even on handbills stuck under windscreen wipers and its message was simple: 'Watch Out! There's a thief about.'

One of the biggest areas of crime was now among the very young. The reasons were difficult to understand although many were put forward, including less discipline in schools, a more relaxed system of education in the comprehensives and a general tenor of the times that suggested that parents were more reluctant to exercise control and children were more defiant. Whatever the reasons, the statistics were self-evident. In 1955 there were fewer than 440,000 detected crimes; in 1965 there were almost 1,134,000. It is also true that the figures were about to go up because of the 1969 Theft Act, which changed the definition of several indictable offences.

At Westminster there was a long-drawn-out debate on medicine and morality. Some MPs were trying to amend the Abortion Act, which had become law the previous year, legalizing abortion in certain circumstances. In 1964 anti-abortionists had persuaded the House to set up a select committee to examine the issues, and the MPs who had voted against the Act were trying to get the committee reconstituted as a first step to reversing the legislation. The debate would not go away. It continued for a decade, with the same group trying the same tactic over and over again.

In Vietnam the Viet Cong launched the Tet offensive. Tet, the Vietnamese word for New Year, took the war right into the heart of the American-dominated capital of South Vietnam, Saigon. Television and newspaper pictures beamed direct and in colour to the United States showed the hopelessness of the American position. There were scenes of absolute horror, including that of General Loan of the South Vietnamese army, squeezing the trigger of his silver pistol inches from the temple of a Viet Cong suspect. The photograph was taken at the moment the bullet entered the Vietnamese's head. The reaction of the American public to this seemingly unforgivable summary execution in a public thoroughfare was predictable. The American people had begun to lose faith in their leaders, in the cause in Vietnam and even in their own soldiers who were dying there.

It must be remembered that Vietnamese were also dying, and in March 1968 there was no bigger disgrace to the American army in the whole war than the manner of the dying of hundreds of apparently friendly Vietnamese in one place. In a small South Vietnamese village called My Lai, American soldiers, led by Lieutenant William Calley, burned down the village and crudely butchered hundreds of men, women and children. The reason given was that they might have been hiding Viet Cong guerrillas.

The My Lai Massacre, as it became known, was an irremovable stain in the record of the American army, made worse by the official attempt to cover it up.

In March 1968 the level of anti-war demonstrations had spread across the world. Thousands of protesters tried to get into the American embassy in London, and mounted police and demonstrators fought each other along the four sides of Grosvenor Square.

Meanwhile, President Johnson was sending thousands of extra troops to Vietnam, but public opposition and the sheer inability of the Americans to impose their military will in Vietnam meant that although the war would go on until 1973, wiser counsel in Washington was already preparing the way to get America unhooked.

The United States faced a more immediate war in its own country. It was a war with its own conscience and with the consequences of a civil rights programme that was too complex to be resolved by legislation but that did not meet the standards of wisdom and decency that should have been the norm in an enlightened country in the second half of the twentieth century. The symbol of the American civil rights protest, Martin Luther King, was murdered on 4 April 1968.

King's last words were to his friend the Reverend Jesse Jackson: 'Be sure to sing *Precious Lord* tonight and sing it well.' At his funeral in Atlanta, Georgia, almost 200,000 people followed the wooden cart that carried his coffin drawn by two mules. The mourners, who included President Kennedy's widow, Jackie, illustrated the cross-section of support for the civil rights movement and also in 1968 the inability of people with such power to make it work.

Just two months later, Senator Robert Kennedy, the brother of John F. Kennedy, died on 6 June after he had been shot by Sirhan Sirhan.

Across the Channel in May 1968 the students in Paris went on strike. It had all started in March of that year and strikes were common throughout Europe; there had even been violent scenes in London's Grosvenor Square. The origins of the protests lay in anti-American and anti-Vietnam war demonstrations. Students were arrested. Other students staged a sit-in at the Nanterre campus. The police firmly ejected the students; 30,000 were locked out of the Sorbonne. The French trade unions came out in sympathy. The students wanted reform, and they also wanted an amnesty for everyone who had taken part in the protests.

President de Gaulle, already vulnerable because of the world economic situation, was willing to discuss reforms but not amnesty. The riots in Paris reduced many streets to impassable alleyways of rubble and burned-out cars. Barricades went up. At last the full impact of what was happening not just in Paris but across France reached the very doors of the president. De Gaulle refused to resign and said that his prime minister, Georges Pompidou, would also remain. The president publicly declared that this was an attempt by the communists to take over France, and he gave enormous powers to the prefecture to deal with the rioters.

There was to have been a referendum on reforms – although what those reforms were to be was very hazy – but this could not go ahead because the internal security of the whole country was now disrupted. Moreover, with half the workforce on strike, including the printers, there was no way the government could get out referendum forms. De Gaulle was denounced on the streets and in the national assembly, which he dissolved. The strongest political voices denounced their one-time hero, and the toughest denunciation came from the Federation of the Left and its leader, François Mitterrand.

The political pundits and the activists were wrong – for the moment. De Gaulle called a general election and won. Pompidou went but de Gaulle stayed – for the moment.

Further east, the European revolution had started in a Warsaw Pact country. In January 1968 Alexander Dubček took over the Czechoslovak Communist Party. Dubček was not Moscow's man. He started to ease the controls over the people of Czechoslovakia, and so began the Prague spring, with its hope of freedom and a return to living as Czechoslovakians rather than as victims of the Allied carve-up of postwar Europe.

The Kremlin believed that Dubček and his reforms would lead to the nation demanding its independence and its withdrawal from the Warsaw Pact. There was no hope that the Soviet Union would tolerate what was going on, and in May the Soviet army moved columns of troops and tanks up to the Czechoslovak border. Nothing that Dubček said about remaining loyal to Moscow would deter the military march that had begun. By July the Russians had positioned more than 1000 tanks and 80,000 men. By the following month the Soviet force had more than trebled. On 21 August any thoughts of a peaceful solution were removed when those troops crossed the border. The Czechoslovaks went on strike to protest at the invasion.

The tanks moved on. Brezhnev had decided on what became known as the Brezhnev Doctrine: the Soviet insistence that it would use force to prevent any liberalization of its satellites.

★

This was also the year that the man whom his public had thought was the master of irony over hopelessness, Tony Hancock, committed suicide in a hotel room in Sydney.

Cecil Day-Lewis became the Poet Laureate. Dr Christiaan Barnard operated successfully and performed the second heart transplant in history, just a month after his first. At Cambridge, surgeons performed Britain's first liver transplant and fifteen-year-old Alex Smith became Britain's first lung transplant patient.

The top song of 1968 was Louis Armstrong's 'It's a Wonderful World'.

Deaths

Enid Blyton (writer)
Jim Clark (racing driver)
Marcel Duchamp (French artist)
Bud Flanagan (comedian)
Yuri Gagarin (Russian cosmonaut)
Tony Hancock (comedian)
Helen Keller (US writer and campaigner)
Robert F. Kennedy (US politician)
Dr Martin Luther King (US civil rights leader)
Mervyn Peake (writer)
Upton Sinclair (US writer)
John Steinbeck (US writer)
Sir Stanley Unwin (publisher)
Sir Donald Wolfit (actor)

1969

FURTHER ECONOMIC decline and industrial unrest were seen as an opportunity for Barbara Castle, the Employment Secretary, to publish her White Paper 'In Place of Strife', which outlined the way forward for industrial relations. The title, incidentally, was not Barbara Castle's. It came from her journalist husband who thought of it just a couple of days before it was published.

'In Place of Strife' proposed that it would be illegal to hold unofficial strikes. The government would, if the paper had gone through the House, have taken unions and workers to court. There was an enormous suspicion among many trade unionists, although not the leaders of the TUC, that this was a document designed to bash the unions into submission. In spite of all the negotiations that went on and the supposed government enthusiasm for Barbara Castle's plans for industrial reform, the White Paper was dropped. The circumstances of the time just did not allow such a radical set of ideas from a Labour government in a period of economic downturn and industrial unrest.

If Castle made a mistake, it was one of tactics. She had involved some of the unions and a few colleagues, including Tony Benn, who at that stage supported what she was proposing. However, there was never any time made for Cabinet discussion of 'In Place of Strife'. The Home Secretary, James Callaghan, was her main opponent. Castle, partly from her normal enthusiasm and partly from an understanding that long discussions would water down the proposals, wanted to bring forward a Bill that very summer. Callaghan accused her of galloping with all the reckless gallantry of the Light Brigade at Balaclava. The unions, seeing an opportunity to avoid any legislation, made a token agreement to put their own house in order. Harold Wilson saw an opportunity to do nothing, and so did nothing. 'In Place of Strife' was dropped.

Behind the parliamentary scenes there was a greater dilemma for Wilson: backbenchers and Cabinet ministers were plotting against him. One group wanted Callaghan to replace him, another group wanted the Chancellor, Roy Jenkins. One extract from Jenkins's own memoir shows why he would never become leader, and that his support for Barbara Castle might cost him dear:

> By mid-May . . . Wilson's leadership had come under even more criticism than in the previous year . . . this had the result of putting me under great pressure to abandon Mrs Castle's bill. The right of the party was more opposed to Wilson's leadership than it was in favour of In Place of Strife. Tom Bradley told me several times that the bill was the only thing standing between me and the premiership. The party, he said, desperately wanted a change of leader, but it did not want either the Bill or Callaghan. Others however, indicated that Callaghan was gaining ground, partly through his opposition to the bill, and I could no longer assume that I was the favourite son of the anti-Wilsonites. Nevertheless I was not tempted to renege on the bill in order to replace Wilson. Apart from anything else, this would be fatal for the future. The real count against Wilsonism was that it was opportunistic and provided leadership by manoeuvre and not direction. To replace him by outdoing his own deficiencies would make a discreditable nonsense of the whole enterprise.

It was equally true that if it came to a fight, at that point Jenkins was hardly likely to win, which was an altogether more pragmatic reason for not standing.

Not that this was of any comfort to Wilson, who had wanted to side-track Callaghan. Callaghan's opposition to Barbara Castle had the support of the influential trade unions. There had already been suggestions from the left wing of the party that Wilson should be replaced. It was not unreasonable for the prime minister to believe that his main threat could be Callaghan.

As far as Callaghan was concerned, Wilson was about to exclude him from his inner Cabinet, although he brought him back after his handling of the Northern Ireland situation.

Terence O'Neill, who had been prime minister of Northern Ireland since 1963, knew that his position and that of the province was in jeopardy. His task was how to bring about reforms that would satisfy the province's Roman Catholic community without giving the impression that he was sacrificing the Loyalist position and therefore the union with Great Britain.

The IRA campaign of the 1950s had not worked because it lacked support in the Province, but instead of understanding the significance of this, the Unionists (the Protestants) did not attempt to capitalize on the opportunity to make life better for the Roman Catholic community and so encourage them to continue to reject the IRA terrorists. The issues that were so contentious centred on subjects such as equal opportunities for public housing, which the Roman Catholics certainly did not enjoy. In addition, the Unionists fixed elections and local constituencies so that Protestants would always be elected. There grew up a cynical election saying in Northern Ireland: 'Vote early and vote often.'

Tension in Northern Ireland had been mounting steadily over the last few years. In April 1967 it was said that people would be rehoused in districts of Londonderry to preserve voting boundaries. O'Neill denied the allegations, but in August of the following year, formal complaints were made against the way in which Northern Ireland police handled demonstrators in Dungannon. Several Labour MPs signed a Parliamentary motion deploring this kind of action against civil rights demonstrators.

In October 1968 there had been allegations of police brutality after riots in Londonderry, and a rally was organized in Trafalgar Square to protest against Ulster police and the election system. In November parades and meetings were banned in Londonderry for one month, but the riots continued. The next month the police found hundreds of weapons during Protestant demonstrations and there was more violence in Dungannon. O'Neill sacked William Craig, the Ulster Home Affairs Minister.

In January 1969 the police reservists, the B Specials, were called out after violence erupted during a Belfast to Londonderry march. This was followed in March by the worst rioting ever seen in Londonderry, and for the first time the British army was used to guard key points in Ulster. Petrol bombs were thrown at Belfast post offices, and the water pipeline blown up. Extra troops were sent from England. O'Neill was forced to resign in April, and Major James Chichester-Clark, the Ulster Unionist, became the new prime minister.

In August 1969 the British army was sent to Londonderry. Troops tried to cut off the mainly Catholic area of the Bogside, as petrol bombs, sten guns and rifles appeared. The Protestant Apprentice Boys of Derry provoked the rioting in Londonderry. On 13 August, the day after the Apprentice Boys' march, police used CS gas against Roman Catholic demonstrators. This was the first time the canisters had ever been used in the United Kingdom.

The biggest decision of all had to be taken: the British army had to take over responsibility for security. It was described officially as aiding civil power. This was not martial law, but it was the strongest measure undertaken by a government in Whitehall over the running of the six counties. The basis of that authority was contained in a document called the Downing Street Declaration:

> Nothing which has happened in recent weeks in Northern Ireland derogates from the clear pledges made by successive United Kingdom Governments that Northern Ireland should not cease to be a part of the United Kingdom without the consent of the people in Northern Ireland . . . in all legislation and executive decisions of Government every citizen of Northern Ireland is entitled to the same equality of treatment and freedom from discrimination as obtains in the rest of the United Kingdom, irrespective of political views or religion.

Troops now went on armed patrols in the Province and would remain there for thirty years. But the British government also had to be seen to be dealing with the immediate security issue, the future of the Royal Ulster Constabulary (RUC) and their reserves, the B Specials. The B Specials were seen by many, and with some justification, as a Protestant mafia in uniform. Harold Wilson set up an inquiry into the future of the RUC, and he chose as chairman Lord Hunt. The most important section of his report – it was now October – was to get rid of the B Specials and to set up what would become the Ulster Defence Regiment (UDR).

In France, although de Gaulle had survived the student unrest of 1968, he now failed to win the support of the French people in what he saw as a crucial constitutional referendum. De Gaulle had wanted to completely restructure the administration of the country, including abolishing the Upper Senate. It went to the people in the form of a plebiscite, but only half the electorate said no, so de Gaulle resigned, his place being taken by the interim president, Alain Poher. At Westminster, more than one minister and pro-European was not sorry to see the long and broad back of the French president.

In Saharan Africa junior army officers, including a young subaltern, Muammar Gaddafi, seized power when King Idris of Libya was on an official visit to Turkey. A socialist republic was established.

In sub-Saharan Africa, one of the most wretched wars of the post-colonial continent was taking place. The Nigerians had been fighting the people of Biafra, who were rebelling against Nigerian rule. They were also starving. The Nigerian leader, General Gowon, had refused to allow Red Cross flights into Biafra because he claimed that they were being used as a cover for arms shipments. In July 1969, after considerable international pressure, he allowed some flights but international agency and government squabbling worsened the situation.

At one point in the autumn of 1969 the Red Cross estimated that at least 300,000 people in refugee camps were starving – many of them to death. By the following January, the refusal of the Nigerians to bend brought the Biafrans to their knees.

The Biafran appeal for international aid to stop people starving to death was probably the first of the major campaigns of its kind to catch international attention, largely because this long-drawn-out affair, with its pathetic images of starving children, was being beamed into every living room. So powerful were those images that campaigners could have attached almost any figure to the pictures of the numbers starving and they would have been believed. In fact, some impartial observers after the war suggested that the conditions were not always as bad as was painted.

To the north, in February 1969, a meeting took place in Cairo to attempt to consolidate the Palestinian position against the Israelis. It was at that meeting that Yassir Arafat was made head of the Palestine Liberation Organization (PLO). There was no unity, nor would there be. The Marxist leader of the Popular Front for the Liberation of Palestine (PFLP) was a man called George Habash, who had watched the attempts of all the groups and had it in his own mind that the only way to have a free Palestine was through the power of the gun and the bomb.

The BBC's longest-running radio programme, *The Dales*, the chronicles of a doctor's wife, was axed by Broadcasting House. What Dr Jim Dale would have thought of a laboratory in Cambridge, the nation never discovered. For the first time female eggs were fertilized in test tubes. The era of the test tube baby was about to arrive.

About to go away were the notorious Kray twins, Ronnie and Reggie. Together with their brother, Charlie, the twins had terrorized the East End of London, and, in that curious fascination of the underworld held by the press and the British public, had achieved some degree of celebrity. They were given life sentences on 5 March and the reign of the killers who were fêted as loving their mother was over.

On 22 April 1969 a sailor arrived back in England to become the first man to sail non-stop around the world single-handed. He was Robin Knox-Johnston. He had set sail the previous year in an international race in a small boat that he had built himself in India, called *Suhaili* after an Arabian Sea wind. So little was thought of his chances that the yachting establishment and even the national press regarded his entry with scant interest. When asked why he had entered, Knox-Johnston said that it was because he did not want a Frenchman to be the first to do what he thought the British ought to do.

In July Neil Armstrong walked on the surface of the moon, but for the time being this moment of scientific history overshadowed a less than proud moment for one family in the United States. Shortly before the landing, Senator Edward Kennedy crashed his car into the water of Chappaquiddick Island in New England. In the car was Mary Jo Kopechne, who was unable to get out. Kennedy left her there and did not report the accident. It was another distasteful episode in the history of the most famous American family of the 1960s. Mary Jo Kopechne had once been the secretary of Robert Kennedy who had been assassinated in 1968.

Deaths

Sir Harold Alexander, 1st Earl Alexander of Tunis (soldier)
Ivy Compton-Burnett (writer)
Maureen Connolly (US tennis player)
Richmal Crompton (writer)
Otto Dix (German artist)
Dwight D. Eisenhower (US president)
Judy Garland (US singer)
Walter Gropius (US architect)
Ho Chi Minh (Vietnamese politician)
Karl Jaspers (German philosopher)
Brian Jones (singer)
Boris Karloff (US actor)
Jack Kerouac (US writer)
Rocky Marciano (US boxer)
Kingsley Martin (journalist)
Ludwig Mies van der Rohe (German architect)
Saud (ex-king of Saudia Arabia)
Kliment Voroshilov (Russian soldier)
John Wyndham (writer)

CHAPTER EIGHT

THE WINTERS OF DISCONTENT 1970–1979

1970

WHEN THE 1970s began some 48 million people were living in England and Wales, about 5 million in Scotland and just under 4.5 million in Ireland, both North and South. Of the 53 million men, women and children in Great Britain, 579,000 were unemployed. Crime had risen considerably in past decades, and in 1970 there were some 1.75 million detected crimes in England, Wales and Scotland. There were 39,000 people in prison, 12,000 more than there had been twelve years earlier.

In January men and women became adults at the age of eighteen. This was the new age of majority and was in line with the law that had, in 1969, lowered the voting age from twenty-one to eighteen.

Not unexpectedly, the population of the Anglican Church was in decline, with only about 1.75 million actual communicants compared with the millions who called themselves 'C of E' on official documents. The Nonconformist church was in no better shape, however: the numbers of Baptists had declined from 318,000 to 293,000 in ten years, and Congregationalists had fallen from 312,000 to 265,000. In 1960 the Presbyterian Church of Scotland had had 1.3 million members; now it had 1.1 million members. The Roman Catholic population was increasing, having risen in a decade from around 3.5 million to about 4.2 million in 1970. There were now more Roman Catholic churches, and if previous figures are anything to go by, about 50 per cent of the Catholic population attended mass.

There was, too, a gradual increase in other faiths, which is not surprising when we consider immigration levels. There were now 6000 Buddhists, 50,000 Hindus, 250,000 Muslims, 75,000 Sikhs and 450,000 Jews. All those faiths, with the exception of Judaism, rapidly increased their numbers in Britain. The numbers of Jews began to decline in the late 1970s.

In January 1970 the Chancellor of the Exchequer, Roy Jenkins, said that he believed that the economy was improving. He told the Cabinet that during that year he expected Britain to have a balance of payments surplus of between £450 million and £500 million and that he thought that the economy would grow by about 3 per cent by the end of the year, which would be 1 per cent up on 1969.

The problem was that people wanted more money in their pay packets. Jenkins believed that the government solution to avoiding that demand would rest in a continuing message that the economy had to rebuild gradually and that everything that went with the economy, including wage demands, had to grow gradually too. Unemployment levels, often the indicator and sometimes a regulator of the short-term domestic economy, were unclear. There had not been much change during the past eighteen months, and it must have been tempting to produce a Budget that would please the electorate. It could not be done, however. Some pay increases were out of the hands of Cabinet because they came through pay review boards. The Prices and Incomes Board had reviewed the pay of the armed forces, for example, and had proposed that service salaries be increased by 25 per cent. Denis Healey, the Secretary of State for Defence, wanted to stage the payments, and after haggling with Cabinet and the Chiefs of Staff, he agreed to 18 per cent immediately and the rest later. If these figures seem enormous by the sorts of increases offered thirty years later it ought to be noted that they reflected long periods without any real increases above inflation. More importantly, the overall 25 per cent pay increase would have a knock-on effect among other sectors, especially teachers, post office workers and seamen, who were expecting 20 per cent. The country could not afford these increases.

In June 1970 Britain had a trade imbalance of £31 million. By that stage there was nothing that the government could do to present the economy in a better light to the British people. Harold Wilson most certainly would have liked to – he was about to go to the country and a general election. Throughout the campaign, the opinion polls said that Labour would be returned. Wilson had a better command of the hustings than the wooden figure of the Conservative leader, Edward Heath, and the big pay rises described above suggested to the pollsters that Labour was popular and that as far as the people were concerned, Wilson had piloted the nation through the economic storm. Wilson was the commander, the man to keep on the bridge now that calmer waters had been reached.

Heath trusted the instincts of the electorate when he campaigned that the striking unions were running the country and that the big pay rises proved it.

The pollsters were wrong. As Britain was being knocked out of the World Cup by West Germany (in Mexico on 14 June), Labour's fortunes began to slip.

On 19 June 1970 Edward Heath arrived in Downing Street. The Conservatives had won 330 seats and Labour had 287 seats; the Liberals – seemingly as ever – had six seats, and there were seven 'others', including the Republican campaigner, Bernadette Devlin (McAliskey from 1973), who stood as an Independent Unity candidate and had won a by-election in Mid-Ulster in April 1969, when she was only twenty-one years old. She was sentenced to nine months' imprisonment after being arrested while leading Catholic rioters in the Bogside, and rioting broke out in Belfast in late June when she began her term of imprisonment.

Heath set about forming what at first sight was a Cabinet of talents. His predecessor as Conservative leader, Sir Alec Douglas-Home, became Foreign Secretary, and Iain Macleod went to the Treasury. For the first time, the public learned the names of Tories who would dominate party politics for the next quarter of a century: Margaret Thatcher, Michael Heseltine, Keith Joseph, James Prior and Geoffrey Howe. But on 20 July, following an operation, the fifty-six-year-old Macleod died, and Heath lost one of the few genuine intellectuals in the Cabinet, a potentially outstanding Chancellor and the leader of the party's left wing. Anthony Barber, hardly in Macleod's league, was given the Treasury.

The new government was not to have an easy run-in. Heath had accused the unions of controlling the Labour Party, and now one of the most militant groups tested the Conservatives. On 16 July the dockers went on national strike for the first time since 1926. Heath immediately declared a state of emergency, and soldiers were ordered to stand by to replace the dockers. They were back to work the following month, but not until they had won an increased pay offer.

Almost 9 million working days were lost in 1970 because of strikes, and it is hardly surprising that one of the first important pieces of legislation prepared and brought forward during the early months of the Heath government was an Industrial Relations Bill, which proposed the setting up of the first Industrial Relations Court, in some ways recognizing the work done by Barbara Castle. The court was to have the power to fine unions, even by confiscating funds, if they failed to follow the disputes procedures designed to prevent industrial action. No Act of Parliament was ever going to bring the Heath government together with the trades unions, which had it in their power, far more than the Labour opposition did, to bring down the Tories.

In Belfast Heath's government fared no better than the previous administration. IRA snipers were at work. The army fired back, and more than fifty streets were under curfew. In August the army used rubber bullets for the first time.

There was nothing rubberized about the bullets fired by US National Guards at anti-Vietnam demonstrators. In May the protesters had marched at Kent State University in Ohio. The Guards lost their heads and four students were killed. The protests followed President Nixon's decision to expand the war in Vietnam by sending troops into Cambodia. Nixon understood the risks involved in deciding to escalate the war. There was also a risk to his future as president. His own people had, he admitted, told him that he would be so unpopular that he would not be re-elected.

That was in April 1970. By 4 May, the day after the Kent State University killings, Nixon began to say that US troops would be out of Cambodia within a couple of months. He kept his job.

If there was an American triumph in 1970, it was in the most spectacular event in the whole Apollo space programme. On the way to the moon, *Apollo 13*'s oxygen tank burst. The moon landing was abandoned, but the spacecraft had to loop the moon before heading back to earth, with its three astronauts escaping in the small lunar module. But the great drama came when the craft was ready for re-entry into the earth's atmosphere. No one knew what would happen to *Apollo 13*. It was at this point that the crew had to go back into the crippled craft because it was the only part of the whole machine that could survive re-entry. On 17 April *Apollo 13* splashed down in the Pacific. The whole world knew that the space programme was not the straightforward operation it had thus far appeared.

Deaths
Sir John Barbirolli (conductor)
Henry Bateman (Australian cartoonist)
Édouard Daladier (French politician)
Charles de Gaulle (French politician)
John Dos Passos (US writer)
Hugh Dowding, 1st Baron Dowding (air force chief)
E.M. Forster (writer)
Jimi Hendrix (US musician)
Janis Joplin (US musician)
Alexander Kerensky (Russian politician)
Dame Laura Knight (artist)
Sir Allen Lane (publisher)
Sir Basil Liddell Hart (military strategist)
Iain Macleod (politician)
François Mauriac (French writer)
Gamal Abdel Nasser (Egyptian politician)
Erich Maria Remarque (German writer)
Mark Rothko (US artist)
Bertrand Russell, 3rd Earl Russell (philosopher)
Antonio Salazar (Portuguese dictator)
William Slim, 1st Viscount Slim (soldier)
Achmed Sukarno (Indonesian politician)

1971

ON 15 FEBRUARY 1971 Britain 'went decimal', and the man who oversaw the change was Lord Fiske, the chairman of the Decimal Currency Board. The pound stayed, but the historic British coins – the half-crown, the florin or 'two-bob bit', the shilling or 'bob' and the sixpence or 'tanner' – were to be no more. The threepenny piece and the farthing had already gone. Instead of 20 shillings to the pound, there would now be 100 pennies. The logic of this decision may be obvious thirty years on, but for many at the time it was bewildering. The new coinage included a half pence piece that was so small that, some, particularly the elderly, found it almost impossible to handle. The most famous newspaper cartoonist of the day, Osbert Lancaster, called them Lord Fiske's flies – these were still the days of trouser buttons.

Edward Heath's government had made membership of the Common Market the foreign policy of his premiership. In June 1971, after hard negotiations that had started the previous year, Britain finally had an agreement that would allow it to eventually join the European club on equal terms with France, Germany and Italy. On 28 October 1971 the House of Commons voted by 356 to 244 to approve the government's decision to negotiate Britain's entry. At first glance those figures suggest that the Conservatives were for joining and the Labour opposition was against joining Europe. What the figures do not tell us is that thirty-nine Conservatives voted against their own government but that the vote was held because sixty-nine Labour MPs voted with the government. Opinion polls suggested, however, that most people in the United Kingdom were opposed to British entry.

Heath's strongest enemy was the trade union system, which was determined to bring him down. In January 1971 Britain's 230,000 postal workers went on strike, for the first time ever, demanding a pay increase of 19.5 per cent. The next month more than 1.5 million people went on strike in protest against the government's Industrial Relations Bill, which was going through Parliament and was designed to give a special court powers to fine the unions and to enforce cooling-off periods. Unemployment was now more than 800,000, the highest figure for more than thirty years.

The country needed a shift in its economic policy, but it seemed that no one was capable of that extent of strategic thinking. Chancellor Anthony Barber was forced to produce a mini-budget. There was a need to increase consumer spending, and Barber reduced purchase tax and removed all controls on hire purchase arrangements. Not even these measures could save jobs. By November 1971 the government was pouring millions of pounds into not very effective schemes aimed at cutting unemployment figures. At the height of these economic and social difficulties, MPs voted to increase the Queen's allowance, the civil list, from £475,000 a year to £980,000.

The confrontation between the British government and the IRA in Northern Ireland was growing. The first British soldier on active service to be killed since troops had been sent to Ulster in August 1969 was shot dead during a riot in the Ardoyne district of Belfast on 5 February. A new element of the war was emerging, too – sectarian killings had started. For a long time successive governments had refused to recognize that what was happening in Northern Ireland was anything more than a policing operation. Indeed, it was not until well into the campaign that soldiers were awarded general service medals for their time in Ulster.

On 20 March the prime minister of Northern Ireland, James Chichester-Clarke, resigned, having been forced out by the British. His place at Stormont was taken by Brian Faulkner. A new prime minister and the manoeuvrings of the British Cabinet would not overcome the most important change in Northern

Ireland security that occurred in 1971. There was now an open split in the IRA – the new and more violent wing was called the Provisionals. From 1971 the security forces were fighting what they called among themselves the PIRA.

The British government now embarked on one of its most dangerous policies: it began arresting and imprisoning suspected terrorists, and in August the government introduced internment without trial – 300 IRA suspects were picked up in the first week and the marching season was banned.

The security forces claimed, publicly, that the gunmen were on the run. In Belfast the IRA's Joe Cahill publicly scoffed. He said the internment operation had led to the arrest of no more than thirty of his men and was no more than a pinprick. During the first week of internment the homes of 7000 Catholic and Protestant families were torched and burned out. On 22 August the IRA put a bomb beneath the gates of Crumlin Road Prison, and on 22 September they put another one in the headquarters of the Unionist Party. The following day an IRA man shot an eighteen-month-old child. At the end of the month the Provisionals put a bomb in an Ulster pub and two people were killed. On 7 October 1500 extra troops were sent to Northern Ireland. On 23 October British soldiers killed five civilians. On 1 November two Belfast policemen were shot dead. The following Sunday two soldiers were murdered in County Armagh. On 12 November the Ulster police were armed, for the first time, with automatic weapons. On 12 December a Northern Ireland Senator, Jack Bernhill, was murdered by the Provisional IRA. As Christmas approached so did the Provisional bombers – in the week before Christmas they left explosives in a pub, killing fifteen people. That was the way 1971 ended in Northern Ireland.

The Foreign Secretary, Sir Alec Douglas-Home, was still seen as a thoroughly nice man who always looked for a gentle way out of a crisis. In September this Scottish aristocrat confounded his critics. The Soviet Union had for some time been running a comprehensive intelligence system in Britain. Apart from the natural inclination of the Russians to spy on everything and everyone, Britain was a particular target. It was a nuclear power; it was building and modernizing its fleet as well as its air force; it was the leading European power in NATO; and it had an inside track to the White House. There was, too, the most important question of Britain's entry to the Common Market. The Soviet Union was looking for commercial as well as military intelligence. There was also a big KGB and GRU (Soviet Military Intelligence) sweep of London that had been designed simply to confirm other intelligence sources. Commercial companies had been set up in and around London to act as fronts for both the KGB and the GRU. British intelligence knew what was going on and, coupled with information given by a defector, Oleg Lyalin, a KGB officer working in the trade delegation in north London, presented its report to the political head of MI6, the Foreign Secretary. On his desk was now an assessment that suggested that out of 550 Soviet officials in London about 300 were spies.

Home told his Soviet counterpart, Andrei Gromyko, to pull back the intelligence operation. Gromyko took no notice. Home wrote, formally, to Gromyko. He said that the British protest was about more than the scale and nature of the intelligence activities. His further concern, he said, was 'the frequency of the attempts which have been made in recent months to introduce into this country officials who, in the past, have been engaged in such activities'. On 4 August 1971 Home once more wrote to Gromyko about the 'inadmissible Soviet activities' that were continuing unabated. Once more Gromyko failed to reply. In September 1971 Home decided he'd waited long enough. The permanent under secretary of the Foreign and Commonwealth Office, Sir Denis Greenhill, called in the Soviet chargé d'affaires and handed him a list of 105 Russians who were going to be expelled. It was also made clear, although not officially, that although Britain expected a tit-for-tat retaliation, MI6 had given Home a second list of spies and the Foreign Secretary was quite willing to tell them to get out as well.

Two aspects of this incident are worthy of note. Harold Wilson, who had become almost paranoid in his belief that the British intelligence services were against him, had never acted on the information that was available. Part of the answer appeared in the *New Statesman*, which was then edited by Richard Crossman:

> Under the Wilson government counter-intelligence had deliberately preferred to adopt cat-and-mouse tactics. When you have detected a spy and can control his activities he may well be more useful to you than his master. Why then did Mr Heath reverse Mr Wilson's decision to play it quietly? The answer seems to have more to do with politics than with security. The Prime Minister, we judge, has decided to use this opportunity for yet another display of the kind of 'strong' Conservative government which will stand for no nonsense from foreigners, least of all from ill-informed communists under the bed. Neither temperamentally nor politically has our new-style national leader any taste for the kind of middle position in world affairs to which Mr Wilson aspired . . . How ridiculous the Kremlin has been made to look; the revelation of the brilliant British spy trap in which the blundering Russians fell makes splendid headlines. No doubt it will provide welcome relief to Tory stalwarts by showing that there is something at least the Prime Minister can deal with 'at a stroke'.

Second, no one has properly explained why Gromyko did not respond to Home's warnings (first made in 1970) and to his two letters. The truth is that, even though he was the Soviet Foreign Minister and the architect of Soviet foreign policy, Gromyko had no control over either the KGB or the GRU. Neither organization would have even considered telling him what they were doing nor would they have taken any notice if he had told them to pull back.

In the early 1970s this was an aspect of East–West relations that the West was slow to learn. Considering the nuclear arms race that was about to start, it was an enormous and dangerous gap in what was about to become an extraordinarily belligerent relationship between the two super-powers and America's senior acolyte, Britain.

In January 1971 the Commonwealth Heads of Government Conference took place in Singapore. The diplomatic game of the 1960s and 1970s at any Commonwealth Conferences was guessing which head of state would be overthrown in his absence. In 1971 it was the turn of Milton Obote, the pipe-smoking president of Uganda, who was overthrown by Idi Amin. Amin, who had been a sergeant in the King's African Rifles and an army boxing champion, went through the ritual of promising free elections, civilian rule and the release of all political prisoners. He was to prove to be one of the most pathological dictators East Africa had ever seen.

Amin did not have an exclusive right to violence in 1971 nor the years that followed. In March 1971 Sheikh Mujibur Rahman declared Bangladesh independent from Pakistan. This was no sudden burst of nationalism, for the Sheikh had won an election largely based on his brand of nationalism. East Pakistan would now be known as Bangladesh. The Pakistan – that is, the West Pakistan – army was sent in, in what became a cruel and vicious retaliation against the Sheikh. By April, what should have been the birth of a nation became the indiscriminate slaughter of thousands upon thousands of its people. Some 2 million refugees tried to escape across the border into India. They had the vicious Pakistan army behind them and the natural consequence of refugees in that part of the world in front. By June 1971 the Indians had taken the inevitable steps to close its border to stop the human flow and the cholera epidemic that came with it.

Mrs Gandhi, the Indian prime minister, knew also that what was for the moment a war between East and West Pakistan could easily become a war between India and Pakistan.

Meanwhile thousands more were dying in Bangladesh. There were horrific bouts of indiscriminate shelling and crude justice. Photographs flashed across the world of struggling Bangladeshi prisoners being hauled across the race-course at the capital Dakka, and while excited crowds stood about them, they were pig-sticked with bayonets until dead.

What the Bangladeshis could not understand was why the great powers, supposedly guardians of international order, abandoned them to the Pakistanis. It was, said most governments, an internal matter.

There were lighter moments for the nation in the sometimes unapproachable image of Edward Heath. As a child in the Kent coastal town of Broadstairs, he had been a keen dinghy sailor. He was now proving to be a talented yachtsman and became skipper of the British Admiral's Cup team of three racing yachts. Skippering his own boat, *Morning Cloud*, he led the British team to victory in the Cup, which included the toughest test of all, the 605-mile Fastnet race.

Deaths
Dean Acheson (US politician)
Louis Armstrong (US musician)
Coco Chanel (French dress designer)
Sir Alan P. Herbert (writer)
Godfrey Huggins, 1st Viscount Malvern of Rhodesia and Bexley (Rhodesian politician)
Arne Jacobsen (Danish architect)
Bobby Jones (US golfer)
Nikita Khrushchev (Russian politician)
Sonny Liston (US boxer)
Harold Lloyd (US actor)
Gyorgy Lukács (Hungarian philosopher)
Ogden Nash (US writer)
Sir John Reith, 1st Baron Reith of Stonehaven (broadcasting pioneer)
Stevie Smith (poet)
Igor Stravinsky (Russian composer)

1972

AT THE BEGINNING of 1972 the six original members of the Common Market were joined by Ireland, Denmark, Norway and the United Kingdom. Edward Heath signed the Accession Treaty on 22 January. It was the one triumph of the year and it was probably to be his lasting memorial. The remainder of the year's news was unremittingly bleak.

In January the number of people out of work exceeded a million and the figure was climbing. Wage demands were also getting out of hand. In January 1972 the National Union of Mineworkers (NUM) demanded pay rises and were turned down. So for the first time in its history the NUM called a national strike, which began on 9 January. The government declared a state of emergency, as twelve power stations were shut down, and official black-outs, lasting nine hours a day, were imposed. The train drivers' union had joined in by refusing to carry oil across picket lines. It must be borne in mind that governments did not, and still do not, wish to get involved in industrial disputes. Ministerial, let along prime ministerial, participation is a last resort in any industrial confrontation. Heath was no exception, and in February with no sign of resolution of the strike, Judge Lord Wilberforce was asked to chair an enquiry into miners' pay. Wilberforce recommended a rise of more than 20 per cent or £6 a week more – a large amount by any standards but one that the government had to accept.

The miners' strike came to an end on 28 February, and the lights came back on, but what happened after that was predictable: the other unions piled in and inflation shot up. In yet another Budget taxes were reduced – again in the hope that it would be possible for the country to spend its way out of the economic difficulties.

If by the end of 1972 Heath had hoped for political respite, he hoped in vain. The confrontation between government and trade unionism was growing, and the effect on the country was inflationary. The Heath government wanted the Confederation of British Industry (CBI) and the Trades Union Congress (TUC) to arrive at some understanding that would balance productivity with wages. Heath felt that pay restraint was inevitable in the political climate, but in anticipation of some form of statutory pay restraint, some unions were agreeing very large pay deals, including rises in double figures. Heath had always said that he would not return to the Labour government's policy of wage control, but in November 1972 the government believed that it had no choice.

A ninety-day freeze on wage increases and price increases was announced on 6 November. That ninety days would not prove enough and as the year closed, Heath already understood that the pay and wages freeze would have to continue.

On Sunday, 30 January 1972, British paratroopers opened fire on demonstrators in the Bogside district of Londonderry. When the firing was done, thirteen people were dead or dying. This was Bloody Sunday. What happened that weekend was bad enough, but then the authorities covered up evidence surrounding the shootings. The army said the troops had been threatened by gunmen and that the soldiers had retaliated. Those in the Bogside believed, with good reason, that none of this was true. Bloody Sunday guaranteed that relations between the security forces, especially the parachute brigade, and the Nationalist sections of Northern Ireland, would remain bitter for decades.

Thirty years and more than 3000 deaths on, we must not neglect the shock of that Sunday in January 1972. It would be wrong to support the political cliché that the people of England never felt that the events of Ulster were a tragedy, but Bloody Sunday did shift emotions. There was a debate in shops, homes and offices as well as among the media punditry. The following morning the editor of *The Times* summed up the confusion and its effects:

> The dreadful day's work in Londonderry will carry Northern Ireland another stage towards a finally ungovernable condition. The loss of life is heartrending. All humane people, however they may differ about all else to do with Ireland, must lament it. There is the usual flat contradiction between the official account of what happened, what some eyewitnesses are saying, and the accounts coming from within the Bogside. If the Army's account is accepted, then the IRA gunmen have directly brought on their own people so many deaths and so much suffering. If the accounts from the Bogside are anything like correct, it would seem that the IRA has now got what it has long been trying to provoke without success: a breakdown of battle discipline in the Army or a major operational misjudgement.

This is an occasion on which it is imperative that the truth of the matter be established to the reasonable satisfaction of the British people – and of the Irish people too if such a thing were possible. If what occurs does not appear in firm outline in the course of the next few days from a comparison of the testimony of credible witnesses, it will be necessary to institute a court of inquiry.

In Dublin a member of Seanad Éireann, Senator John Kelly, who was not a supporter of the IRA, wrote an open letter that summed up the political as well as the military difficulty Bloody Sunday had produced:

The effect of last Sunday's work, among ordinary people here, has been to overlay the memory of the IRA's foul deeds with that of a British deed even fouler. This makes the position of moderates in politics here in the Republic nearly impossible, as there is less and less for us to say that seems relevant or that accords with the facts of the developing situation.

Last Friday I spoke at a political dinner in county Limerick; my theme was that the British people had a conscience, evidenced not only by their reaction to Suez in 1956 but by the beneficent effect of liberal British opinion in reaching the 1922 settlement with this part of Ireland; and that our duty here was to prevent horrors from being committed in our name, leaving it to the British conscience to amend wrongs committed in theirs. This was well enough received. But if I made this speech today . . . I doubt if I would get a hearing at all, let alone a polite one, even from my own party. The Government here is launching a recruiting drive to add a few thousand men to our under-strength Army in order to improve general security; but after last Sunday I will be surprised if their enrolment proceeds as rapidly as the IRA's.

Kelly was right, in every detail and prediction. The Provisional IRA announced that its policy was 'to kill as many British soldiers as possible'. In February it bombed Aldershot, the home of the parachute regiment, killing seven. Another bomb went off in Belfast, leaving six dead and more than 140 injured.

In March 1972 the government announced that it was removing the security powers from the Ulster government of Brian Faulkner. There were talks, but Heath was adamant. Faulkner and his Cabinet were forced into a corner and had to resign, and on 25 March Heath closed down the Ulster parliament, Stormont. What was called direct rule from London was imposed, and William Whitelaw was appointed Secretary of State for Northern Ireland. Direct rule would remain in force until the end of the century. Disbanding Stormont was not a snap decision, but the talks were one sided and Faulkner believed that the decision was not only constitutionally wrong but politically inept. Although he did not go that far, Whitelaw certainly had second thoughts on the way the decision was arrived at, which is significant, because the decision affected everything that was to follow for three decades:

> There is no doubt that Brian Faulkner and his team were completely taken aback by these plans and really could not believe that Ted Heath was in earnest. As the talks continued, it became increasingly clear not only that the British Government was quite firm in its intentions, but that Brian Faulkner was not prepared to consider any such plans. He made it perfectly clear, as I remember it, that he could not recommend any such proposals to the Stormont Cabinet . . . he thought the plans insulting and completely unacceptable. . . . It was very difficult for Brian Faulkner and his colleagues to surrender operational control of the police. In addition, Unionist opinion in Northern Ireland would certainly have been outraged. Nevertheless, I still feel that if there had been more time to consider the proposals calmly, the Northern Ireland Government might have been persuaded. But as always at moments of crisis, time is a commodity in short supply. Once the nature of the talks became public there could be no delay in making a decision.[1]

The Cabinet's determination meant that time had run out for negotiations. The basic issue was whether the security forces, including the police, were controlled from within Northern Ireland or from London. The last attempt at agreement came on Wednesday, 22 March. It failed.

> Brian Faulkner and his team returned to Northern Ireland to put the position to his Cabinet the next day. Ted Heath said that the British Cabinet would also meet. However, he made it clear that at that meeting they would certainly reaffirm their position. That night I remember feeling depressed and somewhat apprehensive, for we were embarking on a collision course full of hazards.

There was general approval of Heath's action of direct rule except, predictably, from the Unionists, who believed that this had been imposed as a result of the Provisional IRA terror campaign.

In May 1972 the official IRA declared a cease-fire, but the Provisional IRA rejected it and said that it would carry on fighting. In addition, on the streets of Belfast sectarian killings were becoming increasingly common and paramilitary groups were running their own communities. Knee-cappings and beatings were commonplace.

In July there was a major change in Middle Eastern foreign policy. In the 1960s the Egyptians had signed defence contracts with the Soviet bloc, but after Nasser's death in 1970 his place was taken by Anwar Sadat. For foreign policy makers in western Europe and the United States Sadat gave the first signs that his foreign policy priorities were changing when he ordered some 20,000 Soviet advisers to

1 William Whitelaw, *The Whitelaw Memoirs*, Aurum Press (1989).

leave Egypt. The significance of this should not be underestimated. The Soviet Union had lost its foothold in the Middle East and was never to regain it.

The Middle East was not at the head of American foreign policy priorities, however. By August the Americans were on the run in Vietnam. They had pulled back from the major base at Danang. Nixon's ground army was pulling out of Vietnam. Since 1961 almost 46,000 Americans had been killed in action, and the war had cost the US treasury more than $100 billion. For the moment the Americans, continuing to believe that big is best if not necessarily beautiful, actually increased its bombing raids. It needed to bomb the Viet Cong to the conference table if it were to get out of Vietnam cleanly and with any semblance of dignity. In spite of this defeat Nixon, of course, was being seen as the president who ended the war and on 22 August he was nominated as the Republican candidate for the forthcoming elections, which he would win comfortably that November. Behind him, however, as he knew full well, was the unrelenting Watergate investigation.

In September seven men were indicted in Washington, D.C., on charges of arranging a 'plumbing' break-in of the Democrat National Committee headquarters in Washington. These headquarters were in a low-rise apartment block called Watergate. Five of the men had been captured in the complex itself, but the men who apparently conspired with them included one of Nixon's former aides, G. Gordon Liddy, and a one-time CIA officer who had worked at the White House, E. Howard Hunt.

The news that autumn was overshadowed when Black September guerrillas broke into the Olympic Village near Munich on the morning of 5 September. The Arab terrorists were demanding the release of Palestinians held in Israeli jails, and although an elaborate rescue operation in the Olympic Village was mounted, it failed. Eleven members of the Israeli Olympic team were killed, nine of them dying in the rescue attempt, together with a policemen and four of the Arab terrorists. The Israelis retaliated in the way they knew best. They bombed ten terrorist bases in the Lebanon and Syria.

In London letter-bombs from Black September were intercepted by the police, but one got through and killed an Israeli diplomat. The following month Black September hijacked a Lufthansa jet and demanded the release of the three guerrillas who had been captured at Munich. The Germans would not risk another massacre and gave in.

To understand the nervousness of governments around the world, not just the government in Bonn, it is worth noting the fear of terrorism that existed in Europe in 1972. The expression of outrage in the form of terrorism was seen as an international phenomenon. In Italy the Red Brigades had terrorized the political and judicial authority of the nation with bombings and assassinations. In Britain the IRA was widely seen for what it was – an uncomplicated terrorist group that believed it could get its way with explosives and armalites. In January 1971 the

Angry Brigade in London had bombed the home of the employment secretary, Robert Carr, and had also carried out a machine-gun attack on the Spanish embassy in London. In Germany the Red Army Faction had murdered its way across the country. Japanese terrorism had already spread to the Middle East.

At about this time governments were learning something they had not recognized about terrorism: it was no longer necessarily confined to the country in which the original protest had started. The IRA was, for example, in 1972 planning three killing rounds: in Ulster and England and against the direct focus of its anger, the British army. This was the third area of concern because the IRA believed that it could take its campaign to wherever the British army was serving, and the easiest target was in Germany. So the Germans were one of the first countries to realize that they had to counter both 'home-grown' terrorists such as the Baader-Meinhof gang and the gunmen who crossed borders in search of their targets.

Spanish terrorists claimed the right to fight for separatism but were as anarchic as the IRA or the Red Brigades. The events in France and Algeria had long meant that French security and intelligence services had a separate department dealing with that single aspect of anti-government protest.

There was hardly a major state in the whole of Europe that did not either suffer from, or fear the spillover of, terrorism. In 1972 the greatest difficulty facing governments that were trying to counter terrorism was not simply resources. It was the disparate organization of terrorism that appeared to be largely based on anger rather than the means of achieving political change. The IRA and the Basque separatists were exceptions, but in the late 1960s and early 1970s terrorism was already being seen as the real third world war rather than some anticipated conflict between the Warsaw Pact and NATO.

It is difficult to find a bright moment in 1972. Even the good news that sixteen people had survived an air crash in the Andes was tempered when it was discovered that the survivors had kept themselves alive by eating the dead.

There was light relief with the second musical by Tim Rice and Andrew Lloyd Webber. Even here there was controversy. The musical was *Jesus Christ Superstar*, and the opening night was picketed because the libretto and style were considered sacrilegious.

Deaths

John Berryman (US writer)
Maurice Chevalier (French entertainer)
Sir Francis Chichester (yachtsman)
Cecil Day-Lewis (poet)
Geoffrey Fisher, Baron Fisher of Lambeth (archbishop)
J. Edgar Hoover (US director of FBI)
Yasunari Kawabata (Japanese writer)

Dr Louis Leakey (anthropologist)
Sir Compton Mackenzie (Scottish writer)
Kwame Nkrumah (Ghanaian politician)
Lester Pearson (Canadian politician)
Ezra Pound (US poet)
Dame Margaret Rutherford (actress)
Igor Sikorsky (US engineer)
Harry S Truman (US president)
Duke of Windsor (former king Edward VIII)

1973

ON 1 JANUARY Britain, Ireland and Denmark became members of the EEC.

On the face of it, 1973 was no better than 1972, and in the post-Macmillan decade, Britain desperately needed the leadership that would move the nation on from being a one-time colonial power. In 1956, as has so often been quoted, the US Secretary of State, Dean Acheson, famously said that Britain had lost an Empire but had not yet found a role. Acheson may have been right, except for one crucial point: Britain had not lost its Empire in the 1950s. Twenty years later it was still trying to disband it, and the new role was needed not in the 1950s but in the 1960s.

Now in the 1970s, leaders like Edward Heath were trying to catch up. In the late 1940s and early 1950s Attlee's government had avoided Europe; Macmillan had tried to join but had been rejected by de Gaulle; and Wilson had fared no better. Whether Heath was right in his enthusiasm for European membership is of secondary importance to the fact that it was the only target that the nation appeared to have. The European Free Trade Association (EFTA) had never been powerful enough, partly because it was seen as a bad-tempered alternative to the EEC and partly because it would never have the full interest of the most important players in Europe, France and Germany.

Even now, 1973, Britain did not have the confidence nor the political and economic architecture to ignore its past of Commonwealth and transatlantic relations and simply and wholeheartedly get on with being a European nation. Perhaps there was still an instinct that no matter what the obligations of the Treaty of Rome, the British people were not, indeed, Europeans. They had never in their history, as the rest of Europe had, been criss-crossed by armies, political thought and cultural blurring. In the 1970s Britain did not speak any other language than English, actually or metaphorically.

Yet as Edward Heath was deep in thought about the 1972–3 prices and incomes freeze and the seemingly impossible peace plans for Northern Ireland, he was meeting the West German Chancellor, Willy Brandt, and President Georges Pompidou of France to plan that a common market would be common union by the end of the decade.

By the end of 1972 and the beginning of 1973 there was growing confidence in Bonn and Paris that at last Britain was fulfilling the demands of de Gaulle, who had said there could be no future for Britain in Continental Europe until Britain was a European-minded nation. Here at the beginning of 1973 was the confusion of nation and leadership. Heath knew what European union meant, but the people he led still saw it as a huge street market of protective tariffs, open gates for its ten stall holders and enormous subsidies. Few questioned the political price of those tariffs and subsidies.

Britain was in such an economic fix and industrial relations were so bad that the government was slipping towards the worst political winter faced by any administration since the war. Before the end of the following year the government would collapse.

The year had started badly when strikes by British Gas workers in February led to cuts in supplies in some areas, and this was followed by a one-day strike called by the TUC in May. In April pay increases were limited to £1.00 a week plus 4 per cent and in November the limits were raised to 7 per cent or £2.25 a week. In response, coal miners banned overtime working – by the end of the year there was a 40 per cent shortfall in coal supplies to power stations – leading to an energy crisis that caused the government to declare a state of emergency. The government's problems were compounded by a cut in oil production announced by Arab states in October. Although the unions, including the general secretary of the TUC, Len Murray, understood the effects of oil price rises on the economy, there was a school of thought among some union leaders that this could be turned to their advantage. Miners, for example, believed that if oil was in short supply they had the key commodity, coal, and should be paid a great deal more to dig it out. There was a further complication: some miners' leaders were not so much interested in getting a pay settlement as in getting a new Labour government for ideological reasons and because they believed that Labour's traditional ties with the unions would make it possible for a Labour government to meet future wage demands.

Barber, who was to have an unenviable nickname as a stop-go Chancellor, believed that the financial crisis in which the United Kingdom found itself was the worst in postwar treasury history. At the beginning of December there was a £2 billion drop in share prices, and by now the three strands of energy supply were in dispute – the power workers, the railwaymen and the miners. In mid-December the government understood that it had to look to the end of the winter on the assumption that there would be industrial disputes and limited fuel supplies. On 13 December 1973 Edward Heath announced that as from New Year's Day 1974, the country would be allowed to work for only three days a week. The idea was that it would save on electricity and therefore the valuable stocks already low in the power stations.

The immediate task of Heath and Anthony Barber was an emergency Budget, which was introduced on 17 December. Barber cut £1.2 billion from public expenditure, the most obvious result of which was a 20 per cent cut in the schools that were supposed to be funded and built during the next two years,

In Southeast Asia, the Vietnam War was coming to an end, and the battle had transferred to Paris, where an international peace conference agreed a four-point plan. A cease-fire between North Vietnam and South Vietnam would come into force at midnight on Saturday, 27 January 1973, and a neutral peace-keeping force would supervise that cease-fire.

By the end of February a further conference was opened to make sure that the truce became a peace agreement. By the spring at the very latest the Americans would withdraw and prisoners would be exchanged. The exchange of prisoners-of-war began in February 1973, and by the end of March the Americans had gone and the POW hand-over was complete, although there remained, for more than two decades, an American belief that some had been kept behind in North Vietnam.

President Nixon should have been riding high because of the end of the war, but on 30 April H.R. Haldeman, his Chief of Staff, John D. Ehrlichman, his home affairs adviser, Richard Kleindienst, the attorney general, and John Dean, his legal counsel, resigned. Behind their resignations lay the Watergate investigation. Watergate is important to Britain's story because in London the government, often against international opinion, could not be moved from the British view that the US was central to the western alliance, NATO. A corrupt US presidency undermined this argument. In 1972 two journalists on the *Washington Post*, Bob Woodward and Carl Bernstein, had reported that the Watergate break-in was linked to the president. Nixon denied any involvement. The importance of this was the presidential re-election campaign, and the five Watergate intruders were after information from the Democrats. Yet Nixon, a Republican, was so far ahead and so likely to be re-elected president, that there was no need for any dirty tricks. The five men were sent to prison and inevitably started talking. It soon emerged that almost everyone on Nixon's staff – excepting the political appointees such as the Secretary of State – was involved, including the president himself. The most damning evidence against the president was contained in tape recordings, which proved not only that Nixon knew what had gone on but had lied about it.

Nixon had told his advisers to deny everything. On 17 May 1973 the Senate select committee began its hearings. The key witness in that first session was to be John Dean, the White House counsel, who told the Senate committee that the Watergate break-in had been organized by Haldeman and Ehrlichman; that the ex-attorney general John Mitchell had known all about it; and that President Nixon had not only agreed that there should be a cover-up but said it was possible to find up to $1 million to buy the silence of potential witnesses. There was more to come. On 17 July another White House witness, Alexander Butterfield, said that the president had had secret microphones put into the Oval Office. The committee now knew that all the conversations that Nixon had had about Watergate had not only been recorded but that the tapes had survived.

For the rest of that year Congress fought the president for the tapes. The role of the special prosecutor, Archibald Cox, now became crucial. In October 1973 Cox demanded that the president hand over the tapes or transcripts of them. Nixon's response was to order the attorney general, now Elliot Richardson, to sack Cox. Richardson would not and resigned on the spot. Richardson's deputy, Bill Ruckelshaus, also refused to fire Cox. Eventually Nixon persuaded the solicitor-general, Robert Bork, to get rid of Cox.

Part of the tapes had been destroyed, apparently by mistake by the president's secretary, Rose Mary Woods. There were said to be five important gaps but there were also 500 tapes.

As if the president did not have enough on his plate, in August his vice president, Spiro Agnew, revealed that he was being investigated for bribery and extortion. When the charges were extended in October to include tax fraud, Agnew resigned and his place as vice president was taken by Gerald Ford.

A diversion for Nixon occurred in the autumn of 1973, when another international crisis developed in the Middle East. At the end of the first week in October, Egyptian and Syrian troops attacked Israel. The attack took place on 6 October during the Jewish festival of Yom Kippur, the holiest of Jewish festivals, and this was undoubtedly the reason for its timing. The Egyptians crossed the Suez Canal, while the Syrians attacked over the Golan Heights. Israel was unprepared, even though they had been warned of Syrian and Egyptian military reinforcements close to the border.

Israel had been on a war footing since its foundation in 1948, and every young Israeli male (and many women) did military service of one form or another. Within hours of the attack, its forces were mobilized and counter-attacking. By 12 October the Israelis had bombed the Syrian capital, Damascus, had retaken the Golan Heights and were on their way into Syria. On 14 October the Egyptians had deployed a huge tank army, supplied by the Warsaw Pact, particularly the Soviet Union, along a large front in the Sinai Desert. The biggest tank battle ever seen took place there. The United Nations called for a cease-fire but the Israelis were not finished. Their counterattack against the huge Egyptian armoured and infantry forces now cut off those Egyptians from any retreat across the Canal.

The official cease-fire between the Israelis and the Egyptians was on 11 November, but this did not stop the fighting. There were to be further clashes on both fronts but effectively the Yom Kippur War was over. Never again in the century would the Syrians and Egyptians have the strength or the desire to test the Israelis.

The effects of the Yom Kippur War were felt throughout the world. The Americans supported the Israelis and began a rapid airlift of weapons, but this policy was not supported within the European membership of NATO. The Europeans could see the bigger picture because, on 17 October, as the Americans were openly flying in aid to the Israelis, the Gulf oil states hit back at the American support for the Jews in the way they knew best: they increased oil prices by 70 per cent and, to show that they really meant business, cut back production.

The western world, particularly Europe, relied on that oil – 80 per cent of Europe's oil came from the Arab oil-exporting states. The effect on the United Kingdom, already in terrible difficulties with its economy, was devastating. Oil prices went up and there was a more than £400 million increase in the UK's oil import bill, immediately threatening an already delicate balance of payments. By the end of November the government was printing petrol rationing books and a 50 miles per hour speed limit was imposed. The Saudi Arabians told the United Kingdom that its oil supplies would be maintained but the increased prices would not be relaxed. Towards the end of December 1973 the Gulf states doubled oil prices.

The good news of 1973 was a royal wedding. Princess Anne married Lieutenant (later Captain) Mark Phillips of the Queen's Dragoon Guards.

Deaths

Salvador Allende (Chilean politician)
W.H. Auden (US poet)
Sir Eveyln Baring, Baron Howick of Glendale (administrator)
David Ben-Gurion (Israeli politician)
Elizabeth Bowen (Irish writer)
Pablo Casals (Spanish cellist)
Sir Noël Coward (playwright, composer and actor)
John Cranko (South African choreographer)
John Ford (US film director)
Sir Roger Hollis (former director of MI5)
Lyndon Baines Johnson (US president)
Nancy Mitford (writer)
Pablo Picasso (Spanish artist)
Edward G. Robinson (US actor)
J.R.R. Tolkien (writer)

1974

BRITAIN BEGAN 1974 with a three-day week in order to conserve energy supplies. Even television programmes would stop at half past ten at night. It was not so much that the television set consumed a lot of electricity but the lights in a family house that burned while people watched television did. Relations between the government and the unions had foundered on Heath's attempts to reform trade union law and to impose an incomes policy.

The miners were still operating an overtime ban at the beginning of the year (an all out-strike was called on 10 February), and the train drivers went on strike on 10 January. Once again, the country gave the impression of being cold and fed up, and petrol prices had gone up for the fourth time in twelve months. On

7 February Heath decided to call a general election, which would be held at the end of the month.

Every offer that had been put to the miners to settle their claims had failed, and many in the Cabinet believed some of the miners' leaders intended to bring down the government if they could. In January some members of the TUC had told the prime minister that he could get around any impression of having backed down by claiming that the miners were 'a special case', but the Cabinet felt that the 30–40 per cent more that the miners were demanding was far and away above what could be paid to them.

The Cabinet knew that the position had not changed with the other unions. If Heath gave in to the miners, everyone would consider themselves a special case. The Minister of Energy, Lord Carrington, announced in Parliament on 6 February: 'We are confronted today by one of the most serious crises in peace-time that any of us can recall.' By that time the NUM, sensing it had Heath on the run, would not even negotiate. Heath's administration, not the miners, would be blamed for the consequences.

There were differences in the Cabinet over the timing of the election. Heath was banking on the country understanding that the government had been honourable and had tried its best to get a solution to the miners' strike, not to save the Conservatives' political skins but for the sake of the country.

Heath went to the country with a single issue: it was for an elected government to run the nation and not the miners. The miners were challenging, as he put it, 'our whole democratic way of life'. The campaign issue was simple: Who governs Britain? Three weeks elapse between the date of an election being announced and the polling date, and a single issue such as the one posed by Heath cannot be sustained over such a long period. During the three weeks on the hustings every issue in which a party believes has to be presented, and the electorate wants to hear something new. The issue may be basic to the argument and it may be the issue on which the people eventually vote – but presentation is all. It was Lord Carrington's opinion that it was essential not to give the impression of being bloody minded.

Labour won 301 seats and the Conservatives 297. The Liberals, picking up some of the Conservative votes, had fourteen seats. There were nine Scots and Welsh Nationals, twelve MPs from Northern Ireland and two others. So, even though they had a majority over the Conservatives, Labour did not have an overall majority in the Commons. The anomaly of the voting system was demonstrated yet again, for although the Conservatives had fewer seats than Labour, they had received more votes. As in so many elections, the party that was returned to power received only about 40 per cent of the total votes cast. In February 1974, for example, the Conservatives got 37.9 per cent of the votes; in the election held in October, the Labour Party got 39.2 per cent of the votes. Moreover, in the February election the Liberals, in their best performance since 1935, got nearly 20 per cent of the popular vote but only fourteen seats.

Heath did not step down immediately. Instead, he tried to make a deal with the Liberals, even promising electoral reform. He told the Scots and the Welsh Nationalists that he would, in return for their support, introduce legislation for Scottish and Welsh assemblies. It did not work. 'Heathism', if there ever was such a style, was finished.

And so, with Heath unable to reach any arrangement with Jeremy Thorpe's Liberals, on 6 March Harold Wilson became prime minister again. On the same day he gave the miners a 35 per cent pay rise, which was twice the amount that Heath would have allowed.

The leading figure in the new government was Wilson's new Chancellor of the Exchequer, Denis Healey. The economy had been brought to its knees by the combination of government borrowing of more than £4 billion, the massive oil price rises that had followed the Yom Kippur War and the determination of the trade unions to get rid of Heath and the Tories. The economy was showing virtually nil growth, inflation was in double figures (by the middle of the year it would be 16 per cent, by the end of the year, 20 per cent) and wages agreements were linked to prices. These 'cost of living' increases were signed and had to be delivered.

The Budget Healey introduced within weeks of moving to the Treasury was a near disaster because of the Treasury figures he was working on. Once again, the Treasury's economic modelling was flawed, and Healey's first Budget was almost the opposite of what he had intended. He needed a Budget that would not make matters worse and one that could be the basis of getting on to an even keel as far as possible. He wanted a so-called neutral Budget. The Treasury figures, or so Healey has always maintained (with considerable support), produced a reflationary Budget. Some companies went under and that meant jobs went with them.

Healey had never promised that Labour was an unquestioning friend of the unions. In opposition he had been castigated at party conferences for telling delegates – especially the unions – that there would have to be controlled wage agreements, otherwise the country would go broke. It was now, once more, heading in that direction, but the unions were not co-operating. Many were simply militant, but others were way behind in the queue for a decent salary. That September, the nurses were awarded pay increases of, in some cases, more than 50 per cent. Local government employees got 13.5 per cent, teachers 32 per cent and top civil servants 28 per cent.

Wilson needed a new mandate as well as a stronger control over the lobbies if he were to get essential legislation through the Commons. In October 1974, therefore, the country went to the polls again. Wilson's overall majority was three. Healey introduced his second Budget. He believed that he now had the right figures and, if the unions responded, inflation could be reduced – even to single figures. The unions did not co-operate, and inflation rose instead of falling. By the following year, 1975, the confrontation between a Labour government and the TUC showed little sign of conforming to the stereotype of brothers in political arms.

The mood of the country in 1974 was never going to make government easy for anyone. Prices were going up; wages were not, but would. Both Conservatives and Labour governed badly, and world events conspired to make matters worse.

In Northern Ireland, the situation had worsened. The Unionists were at each other's throats, and the IRA bombing and shooting campaign had intensified.

The Northern Ireland assembly was by now on its last legs, and the leader of the Unionist Party, Brian Faulkner, had resigned, although he remained the assembly's chief executive. The assembly was responsible for the domestic running of the Province, but it did not represent the views of the increasing Catholic community and, unlike its 1999 successor, did not anticipate Sinn Fein representation.

Scenes of everyday violence may not have had an enormous effect on public opinion in England, Wales and Scotland but they have to be understood before it is possible to grasp the atmosphere and the political schisms in Ulster. It should also be noted that the violence was not carried out by one side alone. In January 1974 two Catholic workmen were murdered in public by hooded gunmen. When a Catholic man was murdered in April, the headline in London was that he was the 1000th victim. Instead of this being the catalyst for people everywhere to turn on the terrorists of both sides, it did little more than prompt an intellectual discussion on the so-called 'troubles'.

By now the bombing campaign had moved to England. On 4 February a bomb blew up a coach travelling on the M62 motorway, killing eleven people. In June an IRA bomb exploded in the Palace of Westminster; eleven people were seriously injured but none was killed. On the same day another bomb went off at the Tower of London, and this time one person died and dozens were injured. In October five more people were killed and more than sixty were badly injured when two bombs exploded in two Guildford public houses. Six days later, on 11 October, there were more bombs, this time at Marble Arch and in Pall Mall. On 22 October an IRA bomb was exploded with Edward Heath as its target. Six days later a bomb was planted under the car of the sports minister, Denis Howell.

On 7 November another bomb went off in another pub, this time in Woolwich, when nearly thirty people were injured and one person was killed. On 21 November seventeen people were blown up in two Birmingham pubs. More than 100 people were seriously injured. At the time it was believed that the Birmingham pub bombings were an IRA revenge attack. A week earlier a Republican terrorist, James McAide, had blown himself up while he was preparing a bomb in Coventry. The authorities refused to let his Republican friends give him a ceremonial burial. At the end of that month, November, the government got through the Commons its Prevention of Terrorism Act. Less than three weeks later the IRA responded with another bomb in London, which killed one person, and on 22 December 1974 yet another attempt was made on the life of Edward Heath. Somewhere in the middle of this, the IRA, almost confusingly, called a truce. No one in the security services believed it would last.

The reason for the cynicism was simple and two-fold. First, the intensity of the IRA bombing meant that the terrorists needed a breathing space. Second, and more important, the notion of a truce was far more the work of the IRA than the hard-liners within the Provisional IRA. Here was another sign that the campaign would continue into 1975 and that it would do so under the direction of the Provisional IRA.

In May 1974 the Protestant hard-liners got their way. They had worked out that the best way of killing off power sharing – with Catholics and Protestants sitting together on the executive council – was to stop the whole assembly and council being able to function. The simplest way of doing that was to bring all key workers out on strike. The Unionists organized a general strike, and the Province came to a standstill. The trade unions were against it, but there was nothing they could do, and many workers who tried to go back to work during that week's walkout were threatened by gunmen. The militant Ulster Unionists were proving that they could be just as hard line as the IRA.

The Unionists were determined to make the assembly and council unworkable because if those institutions could not govern, the Province would have to be directly ruled from London. What the hard-line Unionists wanted above everything else was not to be seen as a Province of Great Britain but as six counties within the United Kingdom. This ideology was right in as much as there is only anecdotal evidence to show that people in England, Wales and Scotland cared very much for the future of Ulster. By forcing the British government to impose direct rule, so it was believed, the responsibility for the future of the six counties would be more publicly felt. In 1974 a significant proportion of the population, the Protestant peoples of Ulster, believed that it was only a matter of time before the crown betrayed them and allowed them to be dominated by an increasingly large Catholic population and a Republican determination that the island of Ireland would soon become one country with one government, based in Dublin. It was no matter that in that year, the Irish prime minister, Liam Cosgrave, became the first Irish leader to publicly recognize Britain's authority over Ulster.

The Protestants had their way. Power sharing broke down and direct rule from London was its consequence.

On 18 May India tested its first nuclear weapon. The explosion in the Rajasthan Desert was the first public demonstration that the five existing nuclear powers – Britain, the United States, the Soviet Union, France and China – had a new member.

As if the delicately balanced Labour government had not got enough on its hands, in the summer of 1974 civil war broke out in Cyprus, and the Turks invaded the north of the island. HMS *Hermes* began airlifting British nationals from the north, but even though a cease-fire was arranged the eastern Mediterranean island was now divided, with the Turks in the north and the Greeks in the south. Here was yet another green line for successive British governments to untangle.

★

In the United States the Watergate affair continued to bring the White House into disrepute. By now, President Nixon had appointed his own man, Leon Jaworski, as prosecutor. Jaworski announced that Nixon would not hand over the tapes, but the case was stepped up when the Grand Jury announced that it believed Nixon to be guilty of being involved in a cover-up. Nixon did his best to carry on with business as usual.

By July 1974 Watergate had reached the Supreme Court. Ostensibly, the special prosecutor did not want the tapes so that he could take Nixon to court; he wanted to use the secret conversations in the trial of Nixon's former aides. It was for this reason that the president was refusing to hand them over because the American constitution said that the president's staffers should not be forced to give evidence. It was a line that President Clinton was to attempt to follow more than twenty years later; he too failed.

Congress now had the president on the run and the House Judiciary Committee voted by twenty-seven votes to eleven that he should be impeached. Nixon's only way out was a deal. The term 'high crimes and misdemeanours' was to be heard on many occasions in later years. On 8 August 1974 the threat of taking that single phrase to its constitutional conclusion was enough to get rid of Nixon. On that Thursday in August 1974 Nixon resigned. Vice President Ford moved into the Oval Office.

Among the few cheerful moments in 1974 Alexander Solzhenitsyn finally got to Stockholm to receive the Nobel Prize for Literature, which had been awarded four years earlier but because of the situation in the Soviet Union he had not been allowed to go to Stockholm to receive it.

On television, the first Teletext transmissions were made by the BBC in a service called CeeFax. Nineteen-year-old Chris Evert won the women's singles Wimbledon, and her fiancé, twenty-one-year-old Jimmy Connors, beat Ken Rosewall to win the men's finals. The West Germans won the World Cup, prompting one Fleet Street commentator to say that this was the second time this century that the Germans had beaten us at our national game, but there was some consolation because the British had twice beaten the Germans at theirs. This was considered a not at all outrageous comment in 1974 and certainly did not arouse the sort of diplomatic and political reactions that could have been expected twenty years later in a supposedly more enlightened time of the century.

Deaths

Dr Jacob Bronowski (Polish humanist)
Richard Crossman (politician)
Vittorio De Sica (Italian actor)
Duke Ellington (US musician)
Prince Henry, Duke of Gloucester
Samuel Goldwyn (US film producer)

Georgeios Grivas (Cypriot terrorist)
Georgette Heyer (writer)
Eric Linklater (Scottish writer)
Walter Lippmann (US journalist)
Kate O'Brien (Irish playwright)
David Oistrakh (Russian violinist)
Juan Perón (Argentinian politician)
Georges Pompidou (French politician)
U Thant (Burmese diplomat)
Earl Warren (US judge)
Georgi Zhukov (Soviet soldier)

1975

THE CONSERVATIVE PARTY was despondent following the two election defeats in 1974. There were those who believed that given the state of the economy and the Labour government's small majority, another election would soon follow, but wiser counsel understood that the Conservatives were in no position to offer the public an alternative. The party had to re-create itself, and at Westminster the 1922 Committee[2] executive decided that Heath should go. This was not necessarily a reflection of the opinion of the whole backbench, but the decision was almost certainly influenced by the party chairman, Edward du Cann. Du Cann and Heath had been at loggerheads since the 1960s, and there are those who, thirty years later, remain convinced that Du Cann was the instigator of the move to replace Heath for personal rather than party reasons.

It became clear that Margaret Thatcher was going to beat Heath in the first round of elections. The party hierarchy was surprised how convincingly she won – which says something about the gap between the Conservative leadership and its backbenchers.

Whatever the machinery of politics in the Conservative Party at the opening of 1975, the gap between the old guard of Edward Heath and the people now surrounding Margaret Thatcher was widening. Thatcher had an advantage in her campaign manager, Airey Neave, who was energetic, likeable and wise, but it is interesting that once Heath had stepped down from the leadership contest, only one of the four who challenged her kept her affection, William Whitelaw. The second and third challengers, James Prior and John Peyton, would hold office but would eventually go from her court. The fourth challenger during that leadership contest would eventually produce a valedictory Parliament speech in the Commons that would, in turn, bring down Thatcher; he was Sir Geoffrey Howe.

2 The committee was formed, as its name suggests, in 1922. In that year Conservative backbenchers met at the Carlton Club in London and voted to force the then Conservative leadership to get out of the coalition with Lloyd George's Liberals. They were successful: Lloyd George was forced to resign and Bonar Law became the Conservative prime minister. Lord Birkenhead (F.E. Smith) famously remarked 'the cabin boys have taken over the ship'.

On 11 February Margaret Thatcher became leader of the Conservative Party. There seemed some significance in the departure of Heath and the enthroning of Thatcher in 1975, the year in which Britain voted by referendum to stay in the Common Market. In the referendum, held in June, 67 per cent of those who voted said that they wanted to remain in the Common Market. It subsequently became clear that very few of the electorate understood what they were voting for. Analysis suggests that in 1975 Britons still thought they were voting for a European free trade area – a sort of enlarged EFTA. The consequences of loss of sovereignty and the British currency, and of the certainty that major decisions would be taken in Brussels so that eventually Westminster would be little more than the United Kingdom's town hall, were hardly debated and rarely understood.

It was, in addition, by no means certain that it was the wish of the Wilson government that the people should say 'yes'. In theory it was government policy, but of the twenty-three members of the Cabinet, almost a third voted against the prime minister. Wilson's policy was to advise the British people to vote in favour of continued membership. He did not expect unanimous support around his table and was forced to agree that so-called collective responsibility of Cabinet government could be ignored on this issue. If he had not done so it is likely that he would have lost up to seven secretaries of state, including Peter Shore, Michael Foot, Barbara Castle and Tony Benn.

Harold Wilson had showed his scepticism, not so much for the European Community but for the terms negotiated by Heath for British entry. In the previous year, James Callaghan, the Foreign Secretary, had led the negotiations to rewrite some of those terms in what was seen as Britain's favour. Wilson's additional concern was that although he could sway the majority of the Cabinet into thinking that British membership under renegotiated British terms was a sound proposition, he was unlikely to be so persuasive with the rank-and-file members of his party, including his own backbenchers. Moreover, unless he got a mandate in the form of a favourable referendum result, he faced a very public demonstration against membership when he went to his own party conference that autumn.

There was a meeting in Dublin with the other nine members of the European community in March 1975. At that meeting, new British terms were agreed. They included a possible, but not definite, refund of Britain's contribution and a not insignificant rearrangement for New Zealand agricultural products. But in 1975 Wilson had little to offer that was either new or particularly encouraging to those who had thought through the longer term implications of membership of the European Community. So split were Wilson's Cabinet and the Labour Party that when the Dublin agreement went before the Commons to be ratified on 7 April, 145 of Wilson's MPs voted against him, 33 abstained and only 137 voted for him. It got through the Commons on Conservative support.

The intensity of the referendum campaign is often forgotten a quarter of a century later. On one side was the Britain in Europe group, whose president was

Roy Jenkins. It had offices in Park Lane and 140 campaign staff. Another group, Labour Campaign for Britain in Europe, was led by Roy Jenkins's close colleague, Shirley Williams.

On the other side was the National Referendum Campaign, which was headed by the Conservative MP, Neal Marten, and the Labour MP, Douglas Jay. The No Campaign committee included Michael Foot, Barbara Castle and the by now Ulster Unionist MP, Enoch Powell.

The turn-out in the referendum was quite close to general election proportions, but if there was an anomaly in the campaign it was in the information pack sent to every voter in May, the month before the election. Three documents were sent out: one outlined the government's case, the second outlined the government's case again, because it came from the Britain in Europe group, and the third was from the National Referendum Campaign. This imbalance may seem unfair, but there is no definite evidence to suggest a correlation between the two to one vote in the referendum itself and the balance of information in the packs. No national newspaper campaigned against staying in. The British media were fully behind the government's mission, as was big business. For example, the Britain in Europe group had spent nearly £1.5 million on its campaign, whereas the National Referendum Campaign spent not much more than £130,000. The CBI estimated that around 98 per cent of its membership wanted to stay in. Hundreds of companies were told by the CBI to appoint one of their staff as a European officer who would continually explain the advantages of European membership.

Whatever the outcome in political terms for Wilson, he had kept Britain in the Common Market. What he could not do was use the same sort of organizations and funding to sort out the economy. The pound had now lost more than a quarter of its 1971 value, and inflation was running at about 25 per cent. In July 1975 a freeze was imposed on salaries above £8500 a year. Price controls were extended and there were cash limits on government spending. By August 1.25 million people were out of work, which was the highest figure in post-Second World War industrial history, and in September the TUC was forced to accept a £6-a-week limit on pay rises.

On 7 November 1975 the pound was falling even further, unemployment was continuing to rise and bankruptcies were higher than at any time in Britain's history. Britain took the nation's books to the International Monetary Fund and applied for a loan of £1 billion.

There might have been hope in the North Sea, and on 3 November the Queen formally opened the first underwater pipeline bringing North Sea oil into the United Kingdom from British Petroleum's Forties field. Thanks to leasing and mortgaging arrangements, however, Britain never did gain as much as it should have from oil revenues.

The brightest star in the firmament of international relations was the signing in August in Finland of what became known as the Helsinki Accords. There were four 'baskets' of protocols, one of which included the Helsinki Human Rights Accord. For the rest of the century the doctrine of human rights would be measured from that protocol, which was signed by thirty-five European states and the United States and Canada. Equally significantly, this was an agreement that showed what the map of Europe looked like: thirty years after the Second World War it was implicit recognition of Soviet control over eastern Europe.

Deaths

Josephine Baker (French entertainer)
Sir Arthur Bliss (composer)
Nikolai Bulganin (Soviet politician)
Eamon de Valera (Irish politician)
Michael Flanders (entertainer)
General Francisco Franco (Spanish dictator)
James Griffiths (politician)
Haile Selassie I (emperor of Ethiopia)
Dame Barbara Hepworth (sculptor)
Graham Hill (racing driver)
Sir Julian Huxley (biologist)
József Mindszenty (Hungarian cardinal)
Sheikh Mujibur Rahman (Bangladeshi politician)
Aristotle Onassis (Greek ship-owner)
Dmitri Shostakovich (Russian composer)
Arnold Joseph Toynbee (historian)
Thornton Wilder (US writer)
Sir P.G. Wodehouse (writer)

1976

In March 1976, with no apparent warning, Harold Wilson resigned as prime minister. The man who succeeded him, James Callaghan, got to know of Wilson's intention to go only five days before the announcement on 16 March. Callaghan had gone to a dinner party given by the publisher, George Weidenfeld, to celebrate Wilson's sixtieth birthday on 11 March 1976.

> The thirty or so present spent a convivial evening but Harold and I had to leave shortly before 10 o'clock to vote at the end of a debate on public expenditure . . . As if on impulse, Harold asked me to travel with him and as the car sped along the Embankment he told me in confidence the news . . . which a few days later was to astonish the country. He would call a special Cabinet meeting on the morning of 16 March to inform ministers of his intention to resign, and meantime I should begin to make preparations for the inevitable contest . . . I had hardly time to say much before we arrived in New Palace Yard. I walked

> through the Division Lobby in a bemused state, hardly grasping that the government was actually in the throes of a crisis: a large group of Labour left-wing Members were deliberately abstaining from voting in support of the government because of their opposition to the Cabinet's expenditure plans . . . 37 Labour members abstained from voting and the government suffered a major defeat by 28 votes.[3]

Harold Wilson went because he was mentally and physically tired, and he always said that he had never intended to stay long after the 1974 election. It might also be remembered that Wilson had been leader of the Labour Party for thirteen years, and he had been a front bencher since the 1940s and Attlee's government.

Callaghan had few doubts that he would succeed Harold Wilson, yet by the time the leadership election was held others had emerged as strong candidates. A formidable group now stood against Callaghan: Michael Foot, Roy Jenkins, Tony Benn (or Anthony Wedgwood Benn as he then still was), Denis Healey and Anthony Crosland. Although Michael Foot won the first ballot, Callaghan won the second ballot, as, interestingly, he had been told he would by the visiting Soviet Foreign Minister, Andrei Gromyko.

In the sometimes bleak moments of 1976 (even the wonderfully hot summer brought few moments to relax) Callaghan had to think ahead. He could not simply be Wilson's successor and carry on without his own ambitions for the nation he now led. On reflection, his list of priorities between becoming prime minister and the outside date of the next election, the end of 1989, appeared modest. They were not.

Callaghan set himself a target of reducing inflation to less than 5 per cent and unemployment to below 3 per cent. He also wanted to return to the original aims for education and housing that had been knocked off course by the economy. Constitutionally, he wanted devolution in place. With hardly any majority at all, Callaghan had little choice but to go along with this if he wanted the support of Scottish National and Plaid Cymru MPs.

Things began to go wrong from the very start. Callaghan was hardly in Downing Street when the local elections were held and the Conservatives began sweeping up council after council. Inside three weeks of the elections it was announced that sterling was worth more than 12 per cent less than it had been three months earlier, at the time of the Budget. By June the pound had dropped even further. On 28 September sterling plummeted. The pound, and therefore the economy, was in such a crisis that the Chancellor of the Exchequer, Denis Healey, turned back from Heathrow Airport shortly before he was due to fly to a conference in Hong Kong.

---

3 James Callaghan, *Time and Chance*, Collins (1987).

The government had to go to the International Monetary Fund (IMF) to borrow £2.3 billion[4] to support the pound. The bank rate was raised to 15 per cent. Mortgages went up to more than 12 per cent. As is the way in Britain – and it is not alone in this – workers went on strike to oppose public sector cuts imposed by the government to save money. It was now once more clear that the relationship between Labour and the trade unions would not sustain the agreement they had reached to keep wage demands to a minimum. Historically, the relationship between the Labour Party and the trades unions has not been anywhere near as cosy as many people think, and this was one of the occasions when this was made quite clear.

Callaghan has observed that the everyday home and foreign policy tasks and pressures facing a prime minister are, at times, overwhelming. The level of decision-making would normally be enough to bewilder a highly paid commercial executive. A quick look at the events of 1976 indicates just how many problems the government had to confront.

In January hurricane-force winds blew across Britain and twenty-two people died. Within forty-eight hours fifteen workmen were murdered in Ulster, and the decision was taken, not lightly, to send the SAS into the Province. Another 'cod war' had broken out with Iceland over fishing rights, and when this worsened in February Iceland severed diplomatic relations with Britain and a fourth warship was sent to Icelandic waters. In January bankruptcies were at an all time high.

In February a confrontation off the Falkland Islands made it necessary for the government to send a warning to Argentina to back off or face military action, and the Race Relations Bill had to be pushed through the Commons. In March, in addition to Wilson's resignation, George Brown generated some unpleasant publicity for his party when he resigned the Labour whip in protest against legislation to ban closed shops in industry. The pound fell below $2 for the first time. The constitutional talks with Ian Smith's Rhodesia collapsed. Prince Margaret and Lord Snowdon took the first steps to divorce.

In April the Rhodesian crisis worsened when Ian Smith's illegal government called up white reservists. John Stonehouse (whose chequered career included 'disappearing' to Australia) resigned from the Labour Party to join the English National Party, thus reducing the government to a minority administration.

In May a well-publicized row developed over Harold Wilson's resignation honours list, when it appeared that he was simply handing out peerages to friends, and Jeremy Thorpe was forced to resign as Liberal leader after claims about his homosexuality. Tensions in the Commons were inflamed after the Speaker had to suspend the sitting after wild scenes when the government won a vote by a single vote.

In June Anthony Crosland, the Foreign Secretary, went to Oslo and negotiated a peace between Iceland and Britain, but not without inflicting severe cuts in the

4 The most it was allowed to borrow.

deep-sea fishing industry, badly affecting the trawlermen in his own constituency, Hull. Britons were evacuated from Beirut, where the war had going on for more than a year. After the low temperatures of the winter, Britain was now suffering from water shortages, and stand pipes appeared in the streets, accompanied by increasingly frayed tempers as well as health hazards. British mercenaries were put on trial in Angola and executed. In Uganda an Air France aircraft was hijacked at Entebbe airport. On board were dozens of Israelis and non-Israeli Jews. The Ugandan dictator, Idi Amin, was helping the hijackers, who were demanding the release of Palestinians from Israeli jails. When the terrorists announced they were going to blow up the aircraft and the prisoners, Israeli commando units flew into Entebbe from Tel Aviv, 2500 miles away. They rushed the building in which the Jews were being held hostage, killed the seven terrorists and twenty of the Ugandan soldiers who were helping guard the hostages. The following month, Britain broke off diplomatic relations with Uganda.

Roy Jenkins left British politics – in January 1977 he was to become president of the EC Commission – and David Steel took over as leader of the Liberal Party in place of Jeremy Thorpe. As the drought worsened, emergency legislation was brought in and Denis Howell was appointed 'Minister for Drought' to push through the legislation.

In August the Women's Peace Movement began in Ulster. There were race riots during the Notting Hill carnival in London. Britain's unemployment figure topped 1.5 million.

In September, while the IMF loan was being negotiated, the pound continued to slide. Ireland took Britain to the European Court of Human Rights, accusing British interrogators of torturing prisoners in Ulster. In September, too, it was announced that, at the age of eighty-two, Mao Zedong had died after a number of strokes. In the way of all things in Beijing at the time, no one ever said so. Who would emerge to lead China would be of the utmost importance to Britain with its widespread Asian interests, especially in Hong Kong.

In October the National Theatre opened, three years late, and house prices fell.

In November the Conservatives won by-elections at Workington and Walsall North, taking the seats from Labour, while in the Commons the government's Dock Work Regulation Bill was defeated, as was a Bill to nationalize the aircraft and shipbuilding industries, although this was passed the following month.

In December OPEC put up the price of oil by 15 per cent.

Callaghan said that when he sat in the prime minister's seat in the Cabinet Room his dream had come true. His avuncular style could not disguise the traumatic state of the economy nor could it avert or alter the events worldwide in which Britain either had a hand or an interest. Eventually, it did rain, which was a good omen for the coming year, the Queen's Jubilee.

Deaths

Busby Berkeley (US choreographer)

Benjamin Britten, Baron Britten of Aldeburgh (composer)
Edward John Burra (artist)
Dame Agatha Christie (writer)
Dame Edith Evans (actress)
Howard Hughes (US millionaire and recluse)
Jean Paul Getty (US billionaire)
Sid James (actor)
L.S. Lowry (artist)
André Malraux (French writer)
Mao Zedong (Mao Tse-tung; Chinese politician)
Johnny Mercer (US composer)
Bernard Law Montgomery, 1st Viscount Montgomery of Alamein (soldier)
Man Ray (US artist)
Sir Carol Reed (film director)
Paul Robeson (US singer and actor)
Alastair Sim (Scottish actor)
Sir Basil Spence (Scottish architect)
Roy Thomson, Baron Thomson of Fleet (Canadian newspaper proprietor)
Dame Sybil Thorndike (actress)
Alison Uttley (writer)
Sir Mortimer Wheeler (archaeologist)
Zhou Enlai (Chou En-lai; Chinese politician)

1977

IN 1977 Elizabeth II had been on the throne for twenty-five years, and to mark the event, on 6 June she lit a huge bonfire in Windsor Great Park. Like the beacons of the first Elizabeth's watchmen all along the south coast in 1588, the flames in Windsor sparked 100 other fires from Land's End to the Shetlands. In 1977 there was no Armada in the Channel; the enemy was well ashore and in the capital.

On 29 January seven IRA bombs exploded in the West End of London, but a few days later the police were tipped off about a bomb-making factory in Liverpool. In February 1977 the IRA men captured in the Balkan Street siege were jailed for life, and in Belfast twenty-six members of the UVF were imprisoned.

In January the £2.3 billion loan from the IMF came through, but the reassuring figures that Healey had hoped for were nowhere in sight. By the time Healey came to give his Budget at the end of March there had been a 70 per cent increase in prices during the past three years. In the Budget Healey announced a reduction in income tax from 35 pence in the pound to 33 pence. The previous year he had told the unions that it was their actions that would affect the level of income tax, and he had wanted the TUC to promise low wage demands – no more than an average of 4.5 per cent. By 1977, however, the TUC could no longer control its members, and Healey was now trying to make sure that 10 per cent was the largest increase in any wage negotiations, which would probably have meant an average of about 7.5 per cent. Some companies risked higher increases to prevent industrial action and the government still had its own legislation in place, which would penalize employers who stepped out of line. An incomes policy could not last much longer. For all their public posturing, the union leaders did not have the power to make a wages policy work. The power was in the hands of the shop stewards.

On 19 February the government lost one of its brightest minds when the Foreign Secretary, Tony Crosland, died at the age of fifty-eight. His book, *The Future of Socialism* (1956), was required reading for most political scientists of the time, and it is possible that Crosland and Healey would have eventually swapped jobs. It is unlikely, however, that either of them – both intellectuals and humorists and able to see a grander picture of domestic and world politics – would have gained enough parliamentary support to have succeeded Callaghan.

Finding a replacement for Crosland was a problem for Callaghan. Healey could not be moved, not with the economy in the state it was in, and considering the talent about him, the prime minister's choices were quite restricted. He gave the job to Dr David Owen, who was only thirty-eight years old and who immediately became known as the 'Boy David' in the British press. Owen, who had trained as a doctor, had made his mark as Under-Secretary to the Navy in 1968, and in 1974–6 he had been Secretary for Health, becoming Crosland's deputy in September 1976, when his task had been to prepare for Britain's six-month presidency of the EEC that would begin in January 1977.

When Callaghan told him that he was to be Foreign Secretary he 'went white as a sheet', according to the prime minister, but his first question was whether this was just a temporary appointment before the Cabinet reshuffle that was expected in the late summer. Callaghan made it very clear that this, one of the four great offices of state, was not an interim appointment.

Confronting Owen was a formidable list of issues. The first battle would be in Europe, where he had to find a way of cutting farm prices. It was obvious to all that the common agricultural policy (CAP) was growing at an alarming rate and consuming a disproportionate amount of the overall community budget, eventually nearly 60 per cent. This could not be done immediately, however, and Owen's plan was to reach a point within two years where there would be no farm price increases. Not unnaturally, he was supported in Brussels by the new president, Roy Jenkins. In later years Owen said that if the Conservative government that followed had continued the policy instead of bowing to pressure from its large agricultural and land-owning lobby, the totally unacceptable level of financing for the CAP would not have developed to its unmanageable heights.

Owen also had to take on Rhodesia, which he visited for abortive talks in April. For the moment there was no way to break white Rhodesian grip nor to heal the deep tribal divisions between the Shona and the Matabele, differences that suited Ian Smith very well. Owen recognized that Smith was waiting for an opportunity to humble yet another Foreign Secretary.

In June Owen hosted the Commonwealth Heads of Government Conference at Marlborough House, London. Before the conference began there was the usual speculation about which leader would be overthrown while away from home. This time it was the turn of the flamboyant president of the Seychelles, James Mancham. While he and his senior Cabinet members slept in the Savoy Hotel in London, Albert René, the Marxist-leaning opposition leader, took over.

There was another aspect to the *coup d'état*, which was not reported at the time. The Seychelles are made up of almost a hundred small islands and islets scattered in the Indian Ocean. They had been a British colony since the days of the slave trade and the wars between France and England. In the 1970s Britain began to make plans for the independence of the Seychellois. The Seychellois, however, did not want to be independent. They were fiercely British and wanted to be a crown colony, rather like Gibraltar or the Falklands or even Hong Kong. Mancham, who was among those campaigning to remain British, believed that the islanders could build an idyllic tourist trade – General Gordon had called the Seychelles the Garden of Eden – and would not be a drain on the British economy. But the British government insisted that the islanders should go away, and in 1976 the Duke and Duchess of Gloucester were sent from London to take the salute as the British flag was lowered and the Seychelles flag raised, making the Seychelles an independent republic within the Commonwealth. A year later, all the warnings came true, but by then the Foreign Office was not interested, and the government had no use for the islands apart from the occasional holiday.

In Moscow, however, Andrei Gromyko did have an interest, and shortly after Albert René took over, the first overtures were made about a possible Soviet naval visit. Behind the Soviet interest was the fact that the American intelligence services, which had been generous with some of its funds, had built a satellite monitoring and signal station on top of the only mountain on the main island, Mahé.

Britain's constant foreign policy concern was its relationship with the United States. In May 1977 Callaghan puzzled the Americans when he appointed his son-in-law to the most important job in the diplomatic service, ambassador to Washington. This posting was sometimes a political rather than a career job, so close had the incumbent to be to British government thinking; this was something the Americans understand well, but the new ambassador was not even a political figure, never mind a diplomat. He was a journalist, Peter Jay, who was working in television. His background was as an economist, and given Britain's reliance on American goodwill there was some reason to counter the obvious charges of nepotism. At the time Jay was married to Callaghan's daughter, Margaret, herself a television journalist. Peter Jay later returned to the media and became the economics editor of the BBC; Margaret Jay, later Lady Jay, became leader of the House of Lords in Tony Blair's government.

Neither Owen nor Healey could hope that any of their long-term plans would come to anything without help from the Liberals, and by March 1977 David Steel and Jim Callaghan had developed the 'Lib-Lab pact' to keep the government in office and to give the Liberals a chance of influencing policy.

In the past there had been a whole series of official and unofficial coalitions between the parties, but from the 1970s onwards none of them would last for long. Edward Heath had promised the Liberals electoral reform in his attempt to retain power, and now it was difficult to see how the government could offer the Liberals anything that they really wanted given the government's economic policies. Nevertheless the first test came on 24 March, when the Conservatives forced a motion of no confidence in the Commons. If the government had lost, it was very likely that Callaghan would have been forced to call a general election. The Liberal support saved the government. Although, naturally, there were those on the backbenches of both Labour and Liberal Parties who disagreed with it, the pact survived through the difficulties of 1977 and 1978.

Perhaps the best news of 1977 took place in Jerusalem. The Egyptian president, Anwar Sadat, not only became the first Egyptian leader to visit the city under Israeli rule but he also addressed the Israeli parliament, the Knesset. The significance of Sadat's visit could scarcely be gauged, because the peace process would always revolve about Jerusalem. The road to co-existence between two ancient enemies was open.

After that meeting the Americans responded. President Carter had been warned by his own advisers that unless he took the initiative the process started by Sadat would fizzle out. Carter took the important step and said he was willing to act as an honest broker. By then some of the other Arab countries were moving against Sadat, and at the beginning of December the Egyptians were forced to break off relations with the Algerians and, predictably, the Libyans and the Syrians.

The peace process was encouraged when the most hard-line of all Israeli leaders, the Likud's Menachem Begin, told Carter that Israel was willing to give back the Sinai Desert to the Egyptians. This was yet another step too far for many Arab States, not because they did not want Egypt to get the Sinai back but because it signified a too close Egyptian relationship with Israel. Peace was not always in Arab interests.

In Czechoslovakia the first signs of an opposition that would be internationally recognized since the hopeless Prague Spring of 1968 appeared in the form of a document called Charter 77, which had been sparked by the Human Rights Act signed in Helsinki in 1975. More than 200 Czech and Slovak writers and artists signed Charter 77. Their message was that although their government had put its name to the 'Final Act', with its reaffirmation of respect for human rights, its provisions were being ignored. Inevitably, some of the Chartists were picked up by the secret police. One of them, Jan Potocka, died following his interrogation. Little known outside Czechoslovakia, Potocka became a martyr in Prague.

★

For all its economic and political low points, 1977 was a year of hope and innovation.

Clive Sinclair, the sometimes brilliant electronics inventor, produced a two-inch television screen. The space shuttle made its maiden flight, piggy-backing on a Boeing 747 to see if it was aero-dynamically sound. It was.

If you wanted to get away from Britain the way to do it was on a cheap flight to the United States. Freddie Laker started Skytrain, walk-on flights to New York, in September. The bus stop-type service would cost just £59 from Gatwick to New York, while a regular flight on another airline would cost more than £180.

On the racetrack, Red Rum was to become the most famous horse in postwar racing when he won the Grand National for the third time.

In the spring young cricketers' thoughts turned to rebellion. This was the year that the Australian media proprietor Kerry Packer signed up cricketers from all the test-playing countries to play in a series of televised internationals in Australia.

A young man who did not much concern himself with cricket, even though he came from Atherton in Lancashire, was Nigel Short. On 29 May 1977 he became, at the age of eleven, the youngest player ever to compete in a national chess championship.

In 1977 four of the world's greatest entertainers died. Maria Callas was fifty-three years old when she died of a heart attack in her apartment in Paris. By then she was a sad and lonely figure whose voice had gone. So, too, had her lover, Aristotle Onassis.

As a queen of one stage died so did a king of another. Elvis Presley died in August 1977 at the age of forty-two in his Memphis mansion, Graceland. By the time of his death he was dependent on drugs and grossly overweight.

The third death was altogether more relaxed. Bing Crosby had been playing golf on a fine day just outside of Madrid. The seventy-five-year-old crooner won his game by just one hole, had a heart attack and died.

The fourth death occurred on Christmas Day. Of them all, he was perhaps the only one who might be called a genius. He was Charlie Chaplin and he died at his home in Switzerland. There was a macabre postscript to Chaplin's death. A couple of months after he was buried, his body was stolen. It was later found, buried once more, 10 miles away.

Deaths

Steve Biko (South African activist)
Wernher von Braun (US rocket pioneer)
Maria Callas (US soprano)
Charlie Chaplin (actor and film director)
Joan Crawford (US actress)
Bing Crosby (US singer)
Anthony Crosland (politician)
Sir Anthony Eden, 1st Earl of Avon (politician)

Peter Finch (actor)
Makarios III (Cypriot archbishop)
Groucho Marx (US comedian)
Vladimir Nabokov (US writer)
Anaïs Nin (US writer)
Elvis Presley (US singer)
Sir Terence Rattigan (playwright)
Leopold Stokowski (US conductor)

1978

IN SEPTEMBER 1978 Menachem Begin and Anwar Sadat hugged each other in public and signed what became known as the Camp David Agreement – the result of long hours of sometimes faltering talks at the American president's country retreat. This was not the ultimate step in peace between the two nations but it overshadowed everything that followed. The Egyptians agreed to the setting up of regular diplomatic relations with Israel. The more militant Arab neighbours were horrified. They had not abandoned their determination to destroy Israel; here was Egypt once more moving in the direction of peaceful co-existence.

There were great dangers in the Camp David agreement for the Israeli prime minister. As Begin had already suggested to Carter, the Israelis would be willing to hand back the Sinai Desert, which they had taken from the Egyptians in the Six Day War in 1967, but many Israelis, including some of Begin's colleagues, regarded the Sinai as more than territory that enlarged the Israeli state. They saw the great desert, which stretched westwards to the Suez Canal, as a reliable buffer zone between them and the Egyptians.

Both men went politically and personally beyond advice often given in their own capitals, and in that year, Begin and Sadat were jointly awarded the Nobel Peace Prize.

There was no peace in the more immediate areas of interest for Britain. In February an IRA bomb went off in a Belfast restaurant. Fourteen people were killed. One of Sinn Fein's leaders, Gerry Adams, was charged with being a member of the IRA, whose bombing campaign shifted to Bristol, Coventry, Liverpool, London, Manchester and Southampton. Armed police began patrolling in London, and troops were sent to Heathrow Airport. In Northern Ireland three soldiers were shot dead just before Christmas, and all Metropolitan Police leave was cancelled during Christmas when the government mounted Operation Santa to stop the bombers getting to the shoppers. The general public, especially in London, was now getting a tiny idea of what the people of Belfast had lived with for nearly a decade.

In Africa, Europeans were caught up in Zaïre (now the Democratic Republic of Congo) when on 11 May 4000 Katangese from neighbouring Angola invaded the southern part of the country and moved into the copper town of Kolwezi. They and some of the Zaïrian troops who were supposed to rid the airport of the Katangese joined in what seems to have been a drug-inspired spree of killing. There were 3000 Europeans trapped in the town. France and Belgium sent a joint force to rescue the Europeans. When they arrived they counted more than 150 dead in the streets of the town, some of whom had obviously been killed with considerable savagery.

A singular form of savagery took place in Italy in 1978. A former Italian prime minister, Aldo Moro, was kidnapped in March by Red Brigade terrorists, who said they would kill Moro unless fellow terrorists were released from Italian prisons. The debate that followed was not so much with the terrorists as among the politicians in Rome. To release the prisoners would be a complete capitulation and would, it was believed, lead to a succession of kidnappings until the Italian jails were emptied of political prisoners. Moro's captors left his body in the boot of a car.

On 6 August Pope Paul VI died. On 26 August Cardinal Luciani of Venice was elected as the new pontiff, taking the name of John Paul I (a papal name taken from his two predecessors John XXIII and Paul VI). There was some surprise at the speed with which the Conclave of Cardinals had elected Luciani. He was, after all, a liberal at a time when it might have appeared that liberal thoughts had gone too far. However, it appeared that he represented a middle road in some people's eyes, along which both factions of the Vatican might walk together. Thirty-three days later, John Paul I was dead, apparently from a heart attack.

So began the search and the politicking for a successor. The power of the twenty-six Italian cardinals was considerable, but there was now a feeling that it was time to elect a non-Italian Pope. On 16 October the Italian cardinals were defeated when the new pontiff was announced – Cardinal Karol Wojtyla of Poland. For the first time since the sixteenth century, the Church of Rome would be presided over by a non-Italian. He took the name John Paul II.

Deaths

Charles Boyer (French actor)
Hubert H. Humphrey (US politician)
John Paul I (pope)
Jomo Kenyatta (Kenyan politician)
John Selwyn Lloyd, Baron Selwyn-Lloyd (politician)
Golda Meir (Israeli politician)
Sir Robert Menzies (Australian politician)
Wilhelm Messerschmitt (German engineer)
Aldo Moro (Italian politician)
Paul VI (pope)
Cyril John Radcliffe, Viscount Radcliffe (lawyer and judge)

1979

THREE EVENTS that occurred in 1979 made 1978 disappear into political and international obscurity. First, the Russians invaded Afghanistan. Second, the Shah of Iran was deposed and the fundamentalist regime of Ayatollah Khomeini began. The third event was, for Britain, the most politically momentous since the 1945 election of Clement Attlee's Labour government. On 4 May fifty-three-year-old Margaret Thatcher became prime minister.

The year began badly for the Labour government with what has come to be called the 'winter of discontent'. Entire industries closed down because of strikes caused by the government's announcement of a pay limit of 5 per cent. Public spaces became official rubbish tips because the dustmen were on strike, and even grave diggers refused to bury the dead. The railwaymen went on strike. School workers and hospital porters walked out – and that was January. By February lorry drivers were on strike and more than 1000 schools had to close because they had no heating oil.

At the end of March Callaghan's government lost a confidence motion in the Commons – the first government to do so for half a century. There was just one vote against, but it was enough; Callaghan announced that he would ask for the confidence of the country, and the date of the general election was fixed for 3 May.

There were still, however, important decisions to be taken, some of them in secret. Britain was, for example, a nuclear weapons power, and the programme was now in place to upgrade that capability. Moreover, the Americans wanted to base cruise missiles in Britain to counter what was seen as the threat from Soviet SS-20s. The idea of a western response to those Soviet systems had not originally come from United States but from a speech given by the West German Chancellor Helmut Schmidt. But this was a Labour government about to seek re-election and on very shaky ground with its own supporters over nuclear weapons. Labour had a deep rank of backbenchers and activists who genuinely believed that their party and their government should have nothing to do with a nuclear deterrent.

Polaris, the nuclear missile carried in four submarines, was old and needed to be updated. There was no sudden decision to upgrade Polaris. A secret assessment, code-named Antelope, had been made in the Ministry of Defence in 1969. When the Conservatives were returned, Ted Heath's Cabinet renamed the project Chevaline and agreed to fund it, but the Chevaline programme was badly budgeted and poorly managed, and the cost overrun was accelerating. By 1977–8 there were political as well as military and financial complications. The Defence Secretary had been convinced by the Chiefs of Staff that Chevaline was right. The prime minister believed it was necessary to continue to upgrade Polaris. Denis Healey, the Chancellor, did not agree financially nor militarily, but he chose to side with Callaghan, who after all, if necessary, could make him Foreign Secretary.

Moreover, cancellation would have cast doubts on Britain's role as a nuclear power. In 1977 and 1978 an alternative option could have been cruise missiles, but the undoubtedly better, if more expensive, Trident system was chosen.

In 1979 a decision had to be taken about the deployment of American cruise missiles in the UK. Shortly before the general election, the Defence Secretary, Fred Mulley, flew to Florida to meet the NATO Nuclear Planning Group, and he agreed to the deployment. There was no doubt that this would go through the Labour Cabinet. Thus, the real decision to base cruise missiles at Greenham Common was taken not, as many think, by Thatcher's government, but by Labour, just a few weeks before the election.

By then, of course, it hardly mattered. Mulley was not the only member of the Cabinet who felt that the Conservatives would win. At the start of the campaign, Labour was 13 per cent behind in the polls. Although by the end of the three-week campaign the percentage was down to single figures, realistic members of the Cabinet, including David Owen, never believed that Labour would be returned. Even the prime minister, Jim Callaghan, understood that British politics had completed another cycle.

Callaghan was right, and on 4 May Margaret Thatcher went to Buckingham Palace, the first woman prime minister in British history. The Conservatives had 339 seats and Labour 269; there were eleven Liberal MPs and twelve from Northern Ireland, while the Scots and Welsh Nationals had four seats between them.

On Tuesday, 8 May Thatcher held her first Cabinet. Making Cabinet appointments was not simply a matter of paying off old debts or scores; there are fundamental rules for building a Cabinet. The number of ministers is pretty steady at around twenty-one or twenty-two. Some Cabinet ministers must be members of the House of Lords, although two or three is sufficient, and today it would be unwise to appoint peers to the most senior and sensitive posts. It is, in addition, not a bad idea to have some regional representation within the Cabinet, although the electorate may not notice it. These rules applied in 1979.

Thatcher made Geoffrey Howe Chancellor of the Exchequer, and she always believed that he was better suited to this than almost any other job. Lord Carrington became Foreign Secretary; the weakness of having a senior Cabinet minister in the Upper House was to be demonstrated in 1982. Even if she had not accepted his resignation over the Falklands War, Mrs Thatcher would probably have had to have appointed another in his place in order to answer questions in the House of Commons. Keith Joseph, who had been shadow Chancellor, went to the Department of Industry instead of the Treasury because the prime minister believed that, although clever, Joseph was not tough enough for the confrontations that would inevitably follow. John Knott became Secretary of State for Trade, although he really imagined himself as Chancellor. William Whitelaw became Home Secretary and one of the closest advisers the prime minister was to have during her whole time in office.

Ted Heath, who was still extremely bitter, could probably have gone to Washington as ambassador, but he chose to stay on the backbenches.

Around the Cabinet table on the afternoon of 8 May the prime minister laid out the ground rules of what would become known as Thatcherism. Hers would be the way of this Conservative government, and she would insist on collective responsibility. The strength of her argument and the determination with which she enforced it won her a nickname among her Cabinet colleagues, Tina – There Is No Alternative.

In the early days of 1979 Thatcher was aware that she would get out of touch with her backbenchers. In theory, she would rely on her parliamentary ears, especially the Chief Whip, Michael Joplin, but, probably mindful of its origins,[5] one of her first decisions was to meet the senior members of the 1922 Committee.

The new government had to implement some of the decisions that had been taken by the Labour administration; a number of these had been made law during the closing weeks and days of the Parliament. Two important decisions had to be taken on pay rises – still one of the most sensitive issues – and the armed forces and the police were at the top of that list. Morale in the police forces was said to be at an all-time low, and the Callaghan government had set up an enquiry under Lord Justice Edmund Davies. The Thatcher government immediately implemented its findings, which introduced a new pay policy for the police. The biggest increase was to be made to the armed forces, whose pay review body had decided that the services had fallen so far behind and that morale was so low that only an increase of about 29 per cent would satisfy them. The government agreed to implement the increases in two stages.

Money could not simply be handed out without savings being made elsewhere. Prices were going up all over the country, and the immediate task was to try to control not only prices but also how public money was spent. The short-term tactic was to go for the most controllable area, the public sector, and all recruitment to the civil service was stopped.

Just as Denis Healey had found that national agreements were useless among trades unions if shop stewards refused to honour them, so the 1979 Thatcher government soon discovered that the people who were running the town halls were not at all concerned with what was going on in Whitehall as long as it did not interfere with their local, often inefficient, bureaucracies. Another step-change in 1979 was the Thatcher principle that you could not blame rising prices for inflation. Prices came about because of inflation, and a price freeze did nothing more than make industry reluctant to invest because the chances of making a profit would be limited by the price freezes.

The prime minister's first success in the new Parliament came just two weeks after coming to power. Her government forced through a division on her plans to start selling off nationalized industries.

---

5 See page 359.

Next came the Budget. On Tuesday, 12 June Geoffrey Howe cut the standard rate of income tax by 3p in the pound and the top rate was cut from 83p in the pound to 60p. This was followed the next month by public spending cuts of £4 billion. In those first two months of the administration the three principles of Thatcherism were laid before the country in practical terms: spend only what is in the nation's purse; decrease rather than increase taxes; and sell off publicly owned industries. Part of the philosophy would have a long-term political effect. For example, people would be further encouraged to buy their council houses – a policy that had been started by the Conservative government in the 1960s. Thatcher wanted a house-owning democracy. Apart from the ideology behind this, it also made political sense, since a home-owning society was far more likely to be stable than one that did not have obligations to a building society. If this could be applied at the shop floor level, so could stability. There is some, at least anecdotal, evidence to suggest that one reason that the miners' strike in the early 1980s failed was that the workers' financial responsibilities – to building societies rather than landlords – were that much greater.

In June the prime minister made her first formal sortie into what would become the hostile territory of the European Community. The meeting was at Strasbourg, and the French were in the chair. The government had already made it clear to the Germans (Chancellor Helmut Schmidt was the first head of state to visit Downing Street after the election) that it was looking for a major cut in Britain's budget contribution to the Community. The government was basing its argument on part of the agreement that had been made at the time of Britain's entry into the EEC. A crucial point of that agreement, according to the British, was that it allowed for flexibility in payments should what was called 'an unacceptable situation' arise.

In 1979 the government argued that because of Britain's other trading interests – with the Commonwealth, for example – the country was becoming a net contributor to the budget because its British tariff contribution was larger than anyone else's. One example was that by 1979 almost 70 per cent of the whole European budget was given to farmers through the Common Agricultural Policy. British farmers were doing well out of the CAP, but British agriculture was then efficient and did not get as much back from the contribution to the budget as did other countries. Hence the discrepancy in what was called the net contribution.

Much was made in the 1990s of Britain's weakening economic position in the European league table, but as early as 1979 out of the ten nations Britain had the seventh highest gross domestic product. Even so, the country was heading in the direction of being the biggest net contributor to the budget.

The prime minister may have regarded this as a logical and politically reasonable approach, but she was now in the den of European lions. The French president, Valéry Giscard d'Estaing, had his own agenda. Towards the end of that first day at the Strasbourg meeting Giscard d'Estaing proposed an end to the day's session without discussing the budget.

This was the first time that other Europeans heard Mrs Thatcher say 'no'. It had all the resonance and determination of a defiant de Gaulle. She did not get her way entirely, but it was in the Strasbourg communiqué that budgetary contributions would be discussed at the next council meeting. It would have been very easy for a new prime minister to agree with Giscard d'Estaing that the matter might be discussed at a later date. The word soon went around the European diplomatic community that Mrs Thatcher was quite capable of calling a handbag a handbag.

If the government had firm ideas on what to do about the economy, it was less certain about Northern Ireland and Rhodesia.

Margaret Thatcher's feelings towards Northern Ireland terrorism were firmly set by the events of 1979. One of her closest political and personal friends was the MP Airey Neave, who had shown consistent hard-line views towards terrorism. He had publicly declared that Sinn Fein should be outlawed since it was the political wing of an overt terrorist group, the IRA. On 30 March Neave was driving out of the underground car park at the House of Commons when an IRA bomb exploded in his car and killed him.

His would not be the only assassination in Margaret Thatcher's circle of political aides and ministers, which should be borne in mind when her position on Northern Ireland negotiations is judged.

Two weeks later, this time in Northern Ireland, the IRA exploded the biggest bomb that it had so far used, some 1000 pounds of explosive. Four policemen were killed. Little wonder that when the BBC ran an interview with a member of the Irish National Liberation Army, the prime minister personally complained to the director general. She was already formulating the idea of banning the broadcasting of any representative of a terrorist organization, including Sinn Fein, when events in August confirmed her belief that it was unacceptable to have terrorists or their sympathizers using radio and television to promote their cause and, as she saw it, apologize for atrocities. Eventually she insisted on a complete ban, which she believed would starve the terrorist of the 'oxygen of publicity'.

On 27 August the IRA carried out its most spectacular assassination. Earl Mountbatten of Burma and some of his family were out in their boat, fishing off Mullaghmore in County Sligo, where they had a family home, Classiebawn Castle, when an IRA bomb blew up their boat. The seventy-nine-year-old Mountbatten, his fourteen-year-old grandson, Nicholas, and their boatman were killed instantly; the Dowager Lady Braebourne, Mountbatten's daughter's mother-in-law, died of her injuries the following day. On the same day at Warrenpoint, County Down, a hay cart in which the IRA had planted a bomb was exploded by a remote device as an army convoy drove past. Eighteen soldiers and a civilian were killed.

Also in 1979 seven prison officers were murdered.

The Cabinet met to review security measures and to assess how they would counter the IRA publicity in the United States, from which came so much political and financial support. Thatcher went to Northern Ireland to see and hear for herself what the people on the ground had to cope with. The statistics that were put before her during that visit made plain the task ahead: 'I could not forget that by the time of my visit to Northern Ireland 1152 civilians and 543 members of the security forces had been killed as a result of terrorist action.'[6]

On 30 January Rhodesians voted for a new constitution. Since Ian Smith had declared UDI in 1965 there had been seemingly countless efforts to negotiate a settlement between Britain and Rhodesia. An expensive and not always effective blockade had been mounted, but gradually, with the bush war having greater effect, even some of the older white Rhodesian families left the country in what derisively became known as the 'chicken run' to South Africa. Change was come about, partly because there had emerged a less revolutionary wing of black opposition.

Smith's opponents were the militant rebel, Robert Mugabe, his opponent Joshua Nkomo and the two very moderate black leaders, the Reverend Ndabaningi Sithole and Bishop Abel Muzorewa. It was with the last two that Ian Smith saw the possibility of doing political business, and after almost fourteen years of holding out against black rule, 80 per cent of the 90,000 or so white Rhodesians voted in April for the new constitution that would allow black Africans to dominate the government.

On paper it looked good, but in the bush, where the rebels still fought, it looked less acceptable. On 24 April Abel Muzorewa's United African National Council won fifty-one of the seventy-two black seats in the Parliament. Mugabe and, independently, Nkomo dismissed Muzorewa as a puppet of Ian Smith, and in London, just a couple of weeks before the general election, the government refused to recognize what was going on as constitutionally legal. The election went ahead anyway, and on 1 June 1979 Rhodesia was renamed Zimbabwe and Muzorewa was appointed prime minister.

By August Thatcher, unlike Callaghan, had indicated that Bishop Muzorewa's election was at least a step in the right direction. But Commonwealth leaders convinced her that there could be no long-lasting settlement without involving the exiled and rebellious Mugabe and Nkomo, even though it was generally recognized that they would never work together. In September, with Lord Carrington now moving the debate, Nkomo, Mugabe, Muzorewa and Smith arrived in London for constitutional talks. In the third week in December, fourteen years after UDI, the Zimbabwe peace agreement was signed. The elections were held the following year, and on 4 March 1980 Robert Mugabe became the prime minister of the new state. Ian Smith's Rhodesian Front won the twenty white seats in the Parliament and Joshua Nkomo won twenty. The division between the Shona people of Robert Mugabe and the Matabele people of Joshua Nkomo was not healed. Nkomo did become interior affairs minister but it was never to be an easy relationship.

---

6 Margaret Thatcher, *The Downing Street Years*, HarperCollins (1993).

Nor was there a sense of complete ease among some very senior members of the Conservative Party. Lord Carrington, who was the undoubted architect of the arrangement, was loathed by some members of his party and he received hate mail accusing him of selling out to the blacks.

In February the footballer Trevor Francis of Birmingham City signed for Nottingham Forest for £1 million – the first British soccer player to command a £1 million transfer fee.

In March Americans turned their attention to the nuclear power station at Three Mile Island, Pennsylvania, which had developed a hydrogen bubble. The world waited for what many had predicted would be an explosion and all its consequences. Also in March the good news from Africa was the overthrow of the Ugandan dictator Idi Amin.

On 26 March, in Washington, D.C., Anwar Sadat and Menachem Begin signed a Middle East peace treaty. The PLO leader, Yassir Arafat, was so angered by this that he publicly threatened Sadat's life.

In June in Vienna the Soviet leader, Leonid Brezhnev, and the American president, Jimmy Carter, signed the Strategic Arms Limitation Treaty (SALT), which supposedly restricted both the Russians and the Americans to no more than 2250 inter-continental ballistic missiles each.

In November 1979 followers of the Ayatollah Khomeini broke into the American embassy in Iran and took hostage the whole staff, including US marines.

At the end of 1979 the world was surprised by an invasion of quite a different type, when, on Christmas Eve, the Soviet army invaded Afghanistan.

Deaths

Zulfikar Ali Bhutto (Pakistani politician)
John Diefenbaker (Canadian politician)
Dame Gracie Fields (singer)
Zeppo Marx (US comedian)
Reginald Maudling (politician)
Jean Monnet (French economist)
Louis Mountbatten, 1st Earl Mountbatten of Burma (Naval Commander)
Airey Neave (politician)
Mary Pickford (US actress)
Jean Renoir (French film director)
Nelson A. Rockefeller (US vice president)
Sir Barnes Wallace (inventor)
John Wayne (US actor)

CHAPTER NINE

THATCHERISM 1980–1989

1980

THERE WAS a change in British politics when Jim Callaghan decided that it was time to go. It was clear that Margaret Thatcher would be in Downing Street for, if she so wished, the full five-year term, but there was not a natural successor when Callaghan announced his resignation on 15 October 1980. The conflict between the left and right wings of the Labour Party had something to do with Callaghan's resignation, but it also had a great deal to do with the public impression that for the time being at least, Labour was unelectable. The two candidates who emerged in the November party election were the sixty-seven-year-old left-wing campaigner, Michael Foot, and the man who had been Chancellor of the Exchequer in Callaghan's government, Denis Healey. The result of the second ballot was a win for Michael Foot by 139 votes to 129.

The Conservatives were pleased because they saw Foot as the ideal opponent – someone who could be vilified for what would seem to be anachronistic socialist views.

In some parts of the Labour Party there were those who believed that just when it should have been moving to the centre ground of British political thinking, its shift to the left was not only bad party politics but was idiotic when what the nation needed was sophisticated political thought. In March, for example, a private enquiry showed that a Trotskyite movement, calling itself the Militant Tendency, had drawn up a programme to get absolute control over the Labour Party at grass-roots level throughout the country and to move up through the system. Among those who believed this were Shirley Williams and David Owen, and the origins of the break from the party by the group that became known as the Gang of Four – Williams, Owen, Roy Jenkins and William Rodgers – can be seen in 1980. By 1981 the group would become the unsuccessful Socialist Democrat Party (SDP), and much later they would merge with the Liberals, until the title became Liberal Democrat.

In the meantime, while Thatcher's government may have been pleased about what was going on in the Labour Party, it had its own difficulties in sorting out problems in the economy and with industrial relations. The steel workers, for example, had been out on strike for weeks. The strike had begun because some of the steel plants, including Port Talbot in South Wales, were to be closed with the loss of more than 11,000 jobs. The strike was spreading. This appeared to be against the law, and the Court of Appeal supported this view; but the decision was overturned by the House of Lords. The strike went on until April 1980, and there was no sign that the immediate economic tactics of Margaret Thatcher's party were having the desired results.

At the beginning of 1980 more than 1.59 million people were registered as out of work; by the autumn the total had risen to 2 million, which was ironic, given the Conservatives' 1979 election campaign of 'Labour isn't working'. The government believed that the reason was simply that the economy was in recession because, as the prime minister said, of increased wages and reduced production. Partly because of the system and partly because of strikes, Britain was now paying itself 22 per cent more for producing 4 per cent less. The economic and industrial climate was worsening. Energy prices, especially oil, were rising, the Public Sector Borrowing Requirement (PSBR) was unacceptably high, and there was virtually nil growth in the economy. By the following year another million would be added to the unemployment total. Although the figures were rearranged on numerous occasions from 1982 onwards to exclude some who might before that date have been included in the statistics, the unemployment totals during the next decade were so high (by 1984 there were more than 3 million unemployed) that they became an accepted, if unacceptable, part of British industrial life.

It was now, less than a year after her election, that Thatcher was identifying some of her own Cabinet colleagues as being unprepared to take the harsh measures needed to sort the economy. She was already making her mental list of 'wets'.

In March 1980 Geoffrey Howe produced his second Budget. It was virtually admitted that, as the economy turned down, there would be louder demands to spend money to get out of the downward spiral. The more public version of Howe's Budget was that there were to be higher taxes on petrol, alcohol and cigarettes. The levels of tax allowances were raised, but any idea that extra funds could be found for public expenditure could have no sound foundation because it was likely that the demands on those funds would be greater than before.

Not as a diversion but as a very real demand, the prime minister told the European Community that if it did not go along with her insistence that Britain should pay less into the European Community, she would start withholding Britain's VAT payments. In 1980 Britain was paying more than £1 billion a year into the EC budget, and it was eventually agreed at the end of May that this amount should be gradually reduced to £250 million. What the EC did not realize was that Mrs Thatcher would be back for more.

When the year opened the world's attention was focused on relations between the United States and the Soviet Union. The Soviet invasion of Afghanistan, which had begun on 24 December 1979, was being reinforced by more troops, aircraft and tanks, although the reasons for the Russian intervention were not widely understood. There was speculation, especially in Washington and London, that the Soviet government was simply expanding its empire and now hoped to move towards that elusive goal of having a warm-water port for its increasingly sophisticated surface and sub-surface fleet.

Other, wiser observers, perhaps with a greater sense of history, understood that the Islamic revolution in that part of western Asia could easily spill into the neighbouring Soviet Union and its own Islamic states. The Russians were anticipating that problem in the way they best understood – with T-72 tanks.

The first consequence in Washington was that President Carter asked Congress to postpone ratification of the Strategic Arms Limitation Treaty that he and the Soviet leader, Leonid Brezhnev, had signed in Vienna the previous June.

America's own attention in that part of the world remained focused on its embassy in Tehran, where fifty-three American hostages were held by Iranian Fundamentalists. In April President Carter sanctioned what appeared to be an almost Hollywood-style rescue attempt, which the US special troops known as Delta Force had code-named Operation Eagle Claw. The operation became a fiasco 200 miles away from Tehran, when it was found that, because of appalling staff work and planning, there were too few Delta Force helicopters. Some of the helicopters developed mechanical problems and there was no back-up. The operation was being abandoned when one of the helicopters collided with a refuelling aircraft. Delta Force escaped, leaving eight dead Americans behind them.

President Carter had to confess that the operation went with his approval. This followed months of national criticism by the American people because Carter had not been anywhere near successful in negotiating with the Iranians.

Carter's misery and humiliation were heightened when Britain's SAS stormed into the Iranian embassy in Kensington and killed four of the five terrorists who had held nineteen hostages for six days. The whole operation was caught on television and beamed around the world, including America.

Although the Iranian hostage crisis did not directly bring down Jimmy Carter, it was certainly true that by November 1980 his presidential election poll ratings were almost at the bottom of the scale. He and his vice president, Walter Mondale, could get support from only six out of the fifty states, and the Republican governor of California, Ronald Reagan, and his running mate, George Bush, swept into the White House in a landslide. There had been nothing like it since President Hoover had been defeated forty-eight years earlier.

That section of the Foreign and Commonwealth Office that was not looking after Europe, the aftermath of Zimbabwe, monitoring the events in Iran, Afghanistan and, incidentally, in Argentina, where the government was starting to show interest in the Falklands again, was carefully watching what was going on in Poland.

On 22 September 1980 Lech Walesa, an electrician in the Gdansk shipyard, became leader of a new Polish workers' organization called Solidarity. Solidarity was born out of strikes that had that year brought about the departure of the Polish leader, Edward Gierek. The balance between revolution and reform was, in Soviet eyes, impossible to manipulate. The Brezhnev doctrine was plain and had been exercised for the whole world to see: that the Soviet Union reserved the right to interfere with force if its security interests were threatened. That was how the 1968 Prague Spring had been snuffed out.

The demands of Solidarity would eventually so revolutionize the political system in Poland that Walesa himself would be president, but for the time being the trade union threatened the security interests of the Soviet Union.

There was now another force at work and one that Brezhnev had never thought of. Stalin had once been warned of the power of the Church of Rome and had scornfully wondered aloud: 'How many divisions does the Pope have?' Now there was a major difference. Since 1978, and for the first time, the pope was a Pole, and John Paul II supported Solidarity.

The Russians warned the West to stay out of the conflict, but on 11 December, after Soviet forces had been moved to the Polish border, NATO warned the Soviet Union to stay out of Poland. There was more to come, but for the moment 1980 would end with an uneasy truce on the Soviet-Polish border.

At another border, there was no longer a truce. In September 1980 Iraq invaded Iran, initiating a war that was waiting to happen. The two super-powers announced their neutrality, but they both had interests. The Americans, most of all, wanted Saddam Hussein to succeed. The Iranians had humiliated the Americans, and the mullahs of Tehran were ready to export their fundamentalism throughout the Middle East, which was not in the interests of either the United States or its client states, particularly Saudi Arabia. The war would last for eight years. Three years after that, the Americans would be leading an international force against Iraq, in the so-called Gulf War of 1991.

Almost inevitably the year could not end without a shock. On 8 December a young man in spectacles called Mark Chapman waited for John Lennon and asked him for his autograph. Lennon obliged. Later that day Chapman returned to the Dakota building in New York where Lennon lived, and as the Beatle was returning with his wife, Yoko Ono, Chapman stepped forward and shot Lennon five times at point blank range.

It was in this year that the British public came to know about Prince Charles's latest girlfriend, Lady Diana Spencer.

Deaths
Sir Cecil Beaton (photographer)
Karl Dönitz (German sailor)
Jimmy Durante (US comedian)

Alfred Hitchcock (film director)
John Lennon (singer)
Steve McQueen (US actor)
David Mercer (playwright)
Henry Miller (US writer)
Sir Oswald Mosley (politician)
Jesse Owens (US athlete)
Muhammad Reza Pahlavi (Shah of Iran)
Jean-Paul Sartre (French philosopher and writer)
Peter Sellers (actor)
Graham Sutherland (artist)
Marshal Tito (Yugoslav politician)
Ben Travers (writer)
Mae West (US actress)

1981

THE YEAR began with the news from Tehran that the fifty-two hostages held in the American embassy were to be released. Even with the announcement, the Iranian leader, Ayatollah Khomeini, believed that he had triumphed over the American president, Jimmy Carter. It was Carter who had organized the abortive attempt by the American special forces to rescue the hostages, and now in January 1981 Carter, who had paid at the polls for American bungling, was about to stand aside from the presidency and hand over to the new president, Ronald Reagan. The Ayatollah delayed the release until Carter was out of office.

In that same month in London inflation figures were falling, although at the end of the month they were still more than 15 per cent. The government was putting state aid into the motor industry, even though the hundreds of millions of pounds that were poured into the business contradicted the political philosophy of Thatcherism.

The Labour opposition was hardly in a position to attack Conservative policy, however. Labour was in the same difficulty as all defeated parties until just before a new election campaign, in that any challenge would be fended off with charges of their own incompetence. This was also the period for reforming and restructuring, although in Labour's case there was at least a public perception of infighting and unclear thinking combined with the party listing sharply to the Left. It was at this point that the so-called Gang of Four – David Owen, Shirley Williams, Roy Jenkins and William Rodgers – broke away from the party.

The origins of the Social Democrat Party, which is what the breakaway became, were not in the movements that were going on in the Labour Party in 1981. The shifts in socialist thinking had more of their origins in the early 1970s, when it was becoming clear that political parties in Britain had to be more sophisticated in their thinking. There was also a feeling that the consensus politics that had served the earlier Labour Party so well was slipping away and being replaced by a quite wrong public image of a Labour Party dominated by its left wing.

In November 1980 the election of Michael Foot as leader to replace James Callaghan was seen by some as another indication that what was supposed to be a modern Labour Party was going to be led by someone with deep socialist convictions at a time when others believed that politics had moved on from such rigid ideologies. People like David Owen were having to fight a battle inside the Labour Party that had more to do with its restructuring as seen, for example, among the Manifesto Group of MPs. Owen and his closest parliamentary colleagues – Roy Jenkins was out of British politics at this point – were trying not only to hold together but to build on the centre ground of the Labour Party. This was the important task to be faced by the party if the Labour Party was not to be dominated by any one group, including its National Executive Committee (NEC), which wanted to control the party manifesto, instead of having a broad-based political church. If there were areas of political thought that the Labour Party was not prepared to embrace, the result, or so Williams and Owen believed, would be that others, perhaps the Liberals, would fill the gap.

When one reflects on the personalities of the four founder members of the SDP, it is not surprising that they were often just as much divided as the party they were about to leave. For example, Owen and Jenkins were often far apart on the way forward in British politics, and it would not be wrong to say that Owen had at one point broken away from Jenkins's thinking and the two men for some time remained far apart. It is also important to notice the reasons why not everyone in the future SDP arrived at the same conclusion at the same time.

In perhaps over-simplistic terms, Rodgers and Williams were expressing political and social theory that would never translate into practical politics likely to attract a wide section of the electorate. Roy Jenkins was in many ways never a backbencher; he was a political animal, only really comfortable in high office or at high table. The fourth, David Owen, had a sharp mind, was a political realist and was supremely ambitious.

The crucial point of the debate within the quartet was whether to remain in the Labour Party. Jenkins, as we have seen, was hardly committed in the way that the other three were. Rodgers and Williams appeared, to those who followed it at the time, as indecisive. Owen was an altogether tougher character. In 1980 and even in early 1981, when the Council for Social Democracy was formed, Owen was still fighting. Until the point of departure from the Labour Party, he gave the impression that he wanted reform from within rather than without.

One of the issues dividing the Labour Party was Europe, but this was not a new split. In the autumn of 1971, for example, a large group of pro-European Labour MPs had voted against their own government in support of Britain's position in Europe. Those divisions remained in the 1981 Labour Party: the importance of this in our story is to show that the splits in both Conservative and Labour groupings were not phenomena of the 1990s. Mrs Thatcher's assault on the Brussels system, the confusion in the Labour Party and even the divisions among the embryonic SDP members who sought to distinguish between being pro-Europe and anti-Federalist were all difficult to understand within their own political alignments never mind among, it has to be said, a largely indifferent electorate. In 1981 the public was turned off Europe simply because no one, even those in Parliament who were supposed to explain such matters to the country, understood what was going on in the European Community and were not, therefore, capable of explaining its significance to the electorate.

This was not the only reason for the creation of the SDP. At the party conference the previous September there had been every sign that the party was once more moving to the far Left. There was little party unity. Clive Jenkins, the leader of ASTMS (Association of Scientific, Technical and Managerial Staffs), proposed a British withdrawal from the European Community. Tony Benn said that a new Labour government would extend nationalization, assume control of the movement of capital and take away all the powers of the European Commission that affected Britain. For good measure, Benn also proposed to get rid of the House of Lords.

The biggest vote, though, was that Britain should withdraw from the European Union. On the so-called card vote (whereby each conference delegate has a vote worth the numbers of people he or she represents) the conference agreed that Britain should withdraw from the Common Market by more than 5 million votes to 2 million votes. This was not enough to commit the Labour Party in government to pull out of Europe, but it was enough of an indicator to suggest it would do just that. The conference went on to vote for unilateral disarmament and, in a significant move by the left to dominate a future parliamentary party, the conference voted for a new selection process for MPs. This was the background against which Owen, Williams and Rodgers were discussing their plans, with which Jenkins would be linked once his term as president of the European Commission ended in January 1981. This is an incomplete picture, of course, but it does sketch the mood of the Labour opposition in 1981 and the reasons behind the formation of the SDP, which was to be led by three people who had held high office in government and might, if the party had been reformed, have produced the sort of Labour government that was not to be seen until the end of the 1990s.

The events within the Labour Party that forced Owen and his colleagues to leave were almost entirely the work of the party's left wing, especially the unions. The irony is that no Labour leader could reform the party until the left-wing grip, especially that of the unions, was broken. It was Margaret Thatcher who destroyed that grip, because she destroyed the power of the unions. Thatcher made Blair's reforms possible.

In March 1981 an IRA terrorist in prison started a hunger strike. His name was Bobby Sands and he was serving fourteen years for a firearms offence. His demand was that of other IRA prisoners: they wanted to be treated as prisoners-of-war not as criminals. In addition, they wanted to be kept separate from Unionist – that is, Loyalist – prisoners in the Maze Prison. This was not the first hunger strike – one had lasted fifty-five days in 1980 – but Bobby Sands was to become the most famous hunger-striker of them all, although others joined in his protest. In April Sands stood for parliament in a by-election at Fermanagh and South Tyrone. There were many doubts about the way the election was conducted, including the allegation that Catholics had been intimidated. Nevertheless, Sands was elected.

The prime minister refused to make any concessions and would not be coerced into negotiating with the hunger-strikers. On 5 May Bobby Sands died after a sixty-six-day hunger strike. On 12 May a second hunger-striker, Francis Hughes, who some believed had murdered thirty people, also died. When the news of Sands's death was announced, rioting broke out in Belfast. When the news of Hughes's death reached the streets the rioting grew more violent. On 19 May five soldiers were killed by an IRA bomb. On 20 May another hunger-striker, Ray McCreesh, died and on the following day so did the fourth hunger-striker, Patrick O'Hara. In July two more died and the rioting and demonstrations continued.

By August ten IRA terrorists had starved themselves to death. The protest did not finish until October 1981, and by that time the IRA bombing campaign had been resumed in England. On 17 October the Commandant General of the Royal Marines, Sir Steuart Pringle, was maimed by a car bomb. Later in the month a man died in Oxford Street trying to defuse an IRA bomb. In November the Official Unionist MP for Belfast South, the Reverend Robert Bradford, was shot dead by IRA gunmen. A bomb exploded in the home of the attorney general, Sir Michael Havers.

The IRA hunger protest had failed and the intelligence assessments given to the prime minister suggested that the IRA was now convinced that the best way of either driving the British out or bringing them to their knees was to maintain the bombing of the mainland and to provoke the Unionists into all-out civil war.

In April 1981 the streets of Brixton in South London exploded in flames of petrol bombs and riots. Hundreds of people, black and white, fought each other. The problems began with Operation Swamp, an attempt by the Metropolitan Police to get to grips with almost unmanageable levels of street crime. A young black man was arrested and his friends and onlookers tried to grab him back from the police. That was the spark that set Brixton on fire, but the black community leaders in Brixton said that the fuse for the riots had been laid over the years by police harassment.

South London was not alone in having to cope with violent disturbances, however. In July 1981 rioting broke out throughout England. The Home Office had been aware that fighting between local youths and the police could start at any moment on the slightest excuse. There had been fighting the previous year in the poorer area of Bristol, known as St Paul's. After the Brixton riots in April police forces throughout the United Kingdom were prepared but still surprised. On the night of Friday, 10 July rioting erupted in London, Birmingham, Hull, Wolverhampton and Preston. It was round two of the violence that had begun the previous weekend in Toxteth, a district of Liverpool.

There was no single reason for these confrontations. Some were driven by an absolute hatred of authority and the belief that that authority was persecuting deprived minorities; some were motivated by quite large groups that simply found it exciting.

Violence of quite a different kind had spread throughout the world. On 30 March 1981 the seventy-year-old president of the United States, Ronald Reagan, was shot by a disc jockey called John Hinckley III. Reagan recovered and went on to serve not only the rest of his term but also a second term as president.

The second world leader to be shot and to survive was Pope John Paul II. A student named Mehmet Ali Agca shot the pope in St Peter's Square. For a long time it was thought that the pope's would-be assassin had been financed by the KGB. There were even some who tried to link the attempted assassination to the idea that, if the pope were dead, the Polish Solidarity movement would lose its greatest international champion.

A man of peace who did not survive an assassination attempt was the Egyptian president, Anwar Sadat, who was killed while he was watching a military parade on 16 October. During a fly-past of the Egyptian air force one of the armoured cars in the parade drove out of the procession towards the saluting base. Four Egyptian soldiers jumped from the vehicle and threw grenades at the rostrum. Sadat was machine-gunned to death. It is generally accepted that Sadat had paid the price of being a peace-maker with Israel. He was succeeded by Hosni Mubarak, his vice president. Mubarak's presidency was to continue uninterrupted for a couple of decades, and in spite of many dangers and doubts, he continued the policy of peaceful co-existence with Israel.

In July there was also a moment of national splendour, a moment captured across the world with the biggest ever single television audience for one event. It was the wedding of Prince Charles and Lady Diana Spencer in St Paul's Cathedral. The famous balcony scene, when the couple broke with protocol and embraced for the hundreds and thousands of people below and the almost one billion watching on screens, promised a fairy-tale marriage.

Although it was a year of drama, it was one of cultural success. In the cinema *The French Lieutenant's Woman* and *Chariots of Fire* vied for box office honours. Andrew Lloyd-Webber's musical *Cats* opened in London. On television the commercial company Granada produced Evelyn Waugh's *Brideshead Revisited*.

On the cricket field Geoffrey Boycott became the highest scoring English test match batsman with more than 8000 runs.

Deaths
Derick Heathcoat Amory, 1st Viscount Amory (politician)
Samuel Barber (US composer)
General Omar Nelson Bradley (US soldier)
Hoagy Carmichael (US singer and actor)
A.J. Cronin (writer)
Moshe Dayan (Israeli soldier and politician)
Abel Gance (French film director)
Mike Hailwood (motorcyclist)
Bill Haley (US singer)
Joe Louis (US boxer)
Jessie Matthews (actress)
Anwar Sadat (Egyptian politician)
Harold Clayton Urey (US chemist)
Natalie Wood (US actress)

1982

ON 19 MARCH some scrap-metal dealers from Argentina landed on the remote island of South Georgia in the South Atlantic. Ostensibly, the attraction was to recover scrap metal from old ships, and official contracts gave the South Americans legitimate reason to be there. What was not legitimate was that on this occasion, the dealers raised the Argentine flag.

This was the prelude to the invasion of the Falkland Islands. The British government had had plenty of warnings of impending problems but had overlooked them. There was the added difficulty that the British ambassador in Buenos Aires was reluctant to disturb Anglo-Argentine relations by recommending strong action. Argentina had been encouraged to believe that Britain was losing interest in the future of the islands when it had been announced in 1981 that the only Royal Naval vessel kept in the area would be withdrawn. The real culprit – apart from the Argentine government which decided to invade – was the British Parliament. Nicholas Ridley, Minister of State at the Foreign Office, had devised a method by which it would have been possible to come to some agreement with Argentina over the future of the islands. The government and Parliament had not supported Ridley's suggestions, and the likelihood of conflict increased. In addition, Britain was so ill informed through its poor intelligence services and even poorer intelligence analysis that just a few days before the Argentines launched the invasion, the outgoing Chief of the Defence Staff, Admiral of the Fleet, Sir Terence Lewin, was allowed to go to New Zealand as part of his farewell tour.

No one in government – from the Defence Secretary, John Nott, down – and no one on the Joint Intelligence Committee (JIC) appeared to believe that the armada being prepared by Argentina was destined for the Falkland Islands. The best assessment was that it was about to take part in joint naval exercises with

Uruguay. All the Chiefs of Staff in Britain had spent years devising military exercises that began with the scenario of hostile forces using the cover of naval manoeuvres to position themselves for an attack on western Europe. When it happened in reality, albeit in another theatre, the incompetence of the British military and political establishment was laid bare.

On 2 April Argentina invaded the Falklands and took over the islands. The Foreign Secretary, Lord Carrington, resigned. As far as he was concerned it was the Foreign Secretary's task to be prepared and his office had not been ready. Carrington said that he accepted responsibility for 'a very great national humiliation', and he and his two junior ministers, Humphrey Atkins and Richard Luce, stepped down on 5 April. Francis Pym was appointed to replace Lord Carrington. John Nott, the Defence Secretary, offered his resignation but stayed on.

There was a large body of opinion in the JIC and in parts of the Ministry of Defence that it would not be possible to regain the islands. The Falklands lay 8000 miles or so from Britain. There was no nearby airfield from which the RAF could operate. There was no base within easy distance for ground troops. There was no runway close enough from which Britain could operate airborne early-warning aircraft. Britain had no satellites to monitor what the Argentinians were doing. This was, moreover, a private matter between Britain and Argentina, and there were no defence and treaty obligations that would bring in any military support from, for example, NATO allies. The best Britain could expect – and got immediately – from, for example, New Zealand, was that some of the Commonwealth nations would support Britain. This support would not be on the front line. It would come in the United Nations and in practical terms by some military units taking over British roles elsewhere in the world while Britain concentrated its efforts in the South Atlantic.

Within the first twelve hours of the invasion, the picture presented to Mrs Thatcher was that regaining the Falklands by military force was out of the question.

That was not how the First Sea Lord, Admiral Sir Henry Leech, saw matters, however. He immediately went to the House of Commons to see the prime minister and told her that whatever anyone else said, he believed that the Falklands could be regained and that the Royal Navy knew how to do it. Leech said he could put together a task force that could sail within a few days in what would be a great public demonstration, not just to Argentina but to Britain, of the nation's resolve to regain the islands. It was also pointed out that although the military assessment could wait, the simple formation of a task force would be a useful tool in the diplomatic negotiations that would have to take place immediately.

The task force was assembled and started sailing by the following Monday. What was hardly publicly known or understood was that the task force was almost empty of the wherewithal to win back the Falklands. It would take weeks for the ships that sailed to be properly stored, loaded with the weapons and supplies they would need and brought up to fighting readiness. The navy had the advantage that the man they put in charge of the surface fleet was Rear Admiral Sandy Woodward.[1] Apart from being an exceptional officer, Woodward had just finished an exercise that was not dissimilar to the real operation now facing him.

It is not for these pages to go into the detail of the Falklands conflict, but there are a few notable dates.

On 5 April South Georgia was recaptured, an operation whose political significance was far greater than its courageous military achievement. Throughout the conflict, attempts were made in the United Nations and through the United States to come to some negotiated agreement, but it had to be accepted that the Argentine leader, General Leopaldo Galtieri, was in no position to negotiate the withdrawal of his forces from the Malvinas, as Argentina calls the Falklands. On 30 April President Reagan publicly supported Britain's attempts to regain the islands. Without American support, especially the supply of air-to-air missiles and satellite intelligence, the British attempt might well have failed.

The next date of importance was 2 May, when the submarine *Conqueror* sank the Argentinian cruiser *General Belgrano*. More than 360 Argentinians perished. Whatever the argument posed by the threat of the *General Belgrano* and her two sister vessels, it is certainly true that that single action made sure that the Argentine navy repaired to its ports and did not re-emerge throughout the conflict.

Later that month the first British troops – apart, that is, from clandestine operations by the SAS and the Royal Marines Special Boats Squadron (SBS) – landed in the Falklands. On 14 June Argentina surrendered and the war was over. More than 900 men were killed in the conflict, which was largely due to misunderstanding, misinterpretation and, certainly in London, a complete failure to grasp the significance of three things: the determination of the military junta in Argentina to use the Falklands as a diversion from its own political problems; the military and political signals from London resulting from the decision to withdraw the *Endurance,* the Falklands guard-ship, and the rejection of Nicholas Ridley's proposals; and the inadequacy of the intelligence analysis system.

While the prime minister rejoiced in the victory (it probably won her the next election), General Galtieri was driven from office and military rule in Argentina was done for.

After the conflict in the Falklands, violence came to the doorstep of the British people.

On 20 July a troop of the Blues and Royals was trotting through Hyde Park for the Changing of the Guards ceremony on Horse Guards Parade. An IRA car bomb was exploded as they passed. Two troopers were killed, seventeen onlookers were wounded and seven horses had to be destroyed. It is perhaps not surprising that much of the outrage felt was caused by the death of the horses.

---

1 Later Admiral Sir Sandy Woodward, commander-in-chief, Naval Home Command.

Shortly before Christmas, another IRA bomb went off. This time it was in a pub in Ballykelly, County Londonderry. Sixteen people died. The terrorist atrocity was the background to a political confrontation between Thatcher's government and the Greater London Council (GLC), led by the Labour left-winger, Ken Livingstone. The GLC had invited the political leaders of the IRA, including Gerry Adams and Danny Morrison, to London. Mrs Thatcher's response was to refuse, under the Prevention of Terrorism Act, to let the Sinn Fein leaders into Britain. From that point it was clear that Mrs Thatcher would not be moved from her intention of abolishing the GLC.

Death of another kind came in November 1982, and it was a momentous political event that would have worldwide repercussions. On 10 November the seventy-five-year-old Leonid Brezhnev died of a heart attack. Brezhnev had been the overlord of the Soviet Union since he had got rid of Nikita Khrushchev in 1964. The Soviet Union was used to being run by a gerontocracy, and Brezhnev's replacement was the sixty-one-year-old Yuri Andropov, who had been the head of the KGB. By February 1984 Andropov himself was dead and was succeeded by Konstantin Chernenko, who was seventy-two and who would be gone by March 1985. So would begin the era of Gorbachev and the eventual downfall of the Soviet Union.

Violence in the Middle East continued unabated meanwhile. On 3 June Arab terrorists shot Shlomo Argov, the Israeli ambassador to London. This was not an isolated incidence of terrorism here or elsewhere, but the Israelis responded immediately with land, sea and air attacks into southern Lebanon. It was a ruthless response to a ruthless provocation that had been going on for some time. It began with the single purpose of destroying the forces of the Palestinian Liberation Organization (PLO) in southern Lebanon, but before the end of the month the Israelis were on the outskirts of Beirut itself. The operation had all the makings of a new Middle East war, but it did not come to that, when there were threats of Soviet intervention and American withdrawal of support. The Israelis were not willing to back off until they were satisfied that they had at least achieved their original aim.

By the end of August this was done. The PLO leader, Yassir Arafat, had to make an undignified exit from Beirut, and 7000 PLO soldiers were forced out of Lebanon, spreading throughout the region, into Syria and Jordan and as far south as the Yemen and the Sudan and as far west as Tunisia.

There followed a quite appalling exhibition of Israeli indifference. In September they allowed the Lebanese Christian militias into the Palestinian refugee camps of Chatila and Sabra. The militia set about slaughtering and piling high the bodies of men, women and children. This was revenge killing on a grand scale, carried out in retaliation for the killing of the Christian president-elect, Bashir Gemayel.

It was imperative that someone kept the peace in the Lebanon, and at the end of September President Reagan sent in a United States Marine Corps to resume what had been their role as peace-keepers in Beirut before the Palestinian invasion. Almost twelve months to the day later the Americans were to regret returning to Beirut. In October 1983 a truckload of explosives, driven by a suicide bomber, killed 242 US Marines and more than sixty French troops. The Americans were forced out, determined never to return.

In addition to those who died in the Falklands, in Lebanon and in Northern Ireland, 1982 was also the year in which more than seventy people died when an aircraft crashed into the frozen Potomac River in Washington, D.C.

But there were smiles as well as tears, when the Princess of Wales gave birth to William, a future King, on 21 June.

Deaths

Arthur Askey (comedian)
Sir Douglas Bader (aviator)
Ingrid Bergman (Swedish actress)
Leonid Ilyich Brezhnev (Soviet politician)
Richard Austen Butler, Lord Butler of Saffron Walden (politician)
Rainer Werner Fassbinder (German film director)
Henry Fonda (US actor)
Glenn Gould (Canadian pianist)
Grace Kelly, Princess Grace of Monaco
Pierre Mendès-France (French politician)
Thelonious Monk (US jazz pianist)
Artur Rubinstein (US pianist)
Romy Schneider (Austrian actress)
Jacques Tati (French actor)

1983

MARGARET THATCHER called a general election in 1983. It was not a Khaki Election in the sense that the election called by Salisbury in 1900 had been – then the successes in the Boer War did not mean that the conflict had actually ended, and in any case Salisbury's government was in quite a different position. Nevertheless, the Conservatives intended to capitalize on the success in the Falklands.

The previous general election had been held on 3 May 1979, and the next general election did not need to be held until 1984. However, as is the case with most governments well into their term of office, sharp criticisms of Mrs Thatcher's leadership were emerging both inside government and outside. She had begun her office with a not very strong team of ministers on the front bench. In January 1981 she had sacked Norman St John Stevas and Angus Maud, and in September of the same year she had got rid of Ian Gilmore, Mark Carlisle and Lord Soames.

It was at that point, September 1981, that she brought into Cabinet for the first time three of the strongest personalities of her administration – Nigel Lawson,

Norman Tebbit and Cecil Parkinson – who were to play important roles in the financial and political image of the Thatcher government. It was in this period, too, that she began to get rid of the so-called 'wets', those ministers who were not, she believed, strong enough to follow her dogmatic style. In that September 1981 shuffle of Cabinet she had appointed Cecil Parkinson as party chairman, which had meant getting rid of Peter Thorneycroft, one of the old breed of patrician Tories. Thatcher was attracted to Parkinson, whom she regarded as someone full of common sense and with a good accounting brain, which, considering the state of the party, was essential. Most of all, Parkinson was on what she called her 'wing of the party'.

Although both Cecil Parkinson and Norman Tebbit became chairmen of the party, they were men of very different backgrounds and different approaches to Conservative politics, and it is interesting to recall that in some ways and at various times, Mrs Thatcher managed, in spite of her reputation, to span in government the gamut of Conservative Party membership.

By the end of 1981 Mrs Thatcher had got rid of the 'wets', but it was clear at that year's party conference in Blackpool that the economic situation needed tough and sure-footed action, for while inflation was down it refused to budge from double figures. By 1983 the Cabinet, now all pro-Thatcher, was beginning to grumble. She needed the masterstroke of an election victory.

So with Cecil Parkinson as her tactitian, the prime minister went into the general election of June 1983 believing that the Falklands factor, just twelve months earlier, would not only see her through but sweep aside the complaints of the doubters.

Mrs Thatcher had clear advantages in that election. The first was the victory in the Falkland Islands, which in spite of a cynical tendency gave her a rightful (if not always welcome) claim to be a strong leader. The second was the catastrophic state of the opposition. The Labour Party was led by Michael Foot, who, despite his other qualities, did not 'look' like a prime minister. Ever since the 1960s, the use of television in politics had meant that anyone seeking to be prime minister had to look the part or, at least, to appear to be a better candidate than the alternative. Michael Foot was portrayed in the media as an anorak-wearing supporter of CND. Intellectually, of course, he was beyond Mrs Thatcher – the electorate, however, was not looking for an intellectual but a leader.

Mrs Thatcher's personality was so strong that she gave the impression that she could win the whole general election single-handed if necessary. When people criticized her for being dogmatic, she agreed with them and said that she believed in standing up for her beliefs, which struck a chord with the public. When she told the Blackpool party conference that she was 'not for turning', she had presented an image that could not be confounded. Even her handbag – in political theory a weakness because it denoted feminine authority (not feminism) – became a symbol of her strength and leadership qualities, which much of the electorate admired, especially when it was directed against foreigners.

In the election of 9 June 1983, she led, with not a little help from her friends, the Conservatives to an overall majority of 144 seats, the biggest majority since the Labour victory in 1945. The Conservatives received 42.4 per cent of the votes cast.

It was at this point that younger Labour thinkers began to understand that their party was now unelectable in the south of England and that the baggage of socialism had to be abandoned. In that summer of 1983 three political factors were clear. First, Thatcherism dominated British political and social life, even though many Tories could not stomach the prime minister's take-it-or-leave-it style of Cabinet government. Second, Fabian socialism, which had seen the electoral sense of debate and moderate government, could not be revived; the origins of New Labour may be seen here, although the structures were not yet in place to counter the militant trend that had gained so much ground because of Labour's election failures. Third, the next major confrontation would be between Thatcherism and grass-roots militancy. If the democratically elected Labour Party could not take on Margaret Thatcher, militants would actively do so. The groundwork for the political and industrial battle that was to culminate in the miners' strike was being laid.

The smudge on Mrs Thatcher's victory was not political but personal. Cecil Parkinson, who was by now Trade and Industry Secretary, was forced to resign. His former mistress, Sara Keays, had been his secretary and was now carrying his child. The news came out in the papers. Cecil Parkinson had to go and did so. John Selwyn Gummer was already party chairman in succession to Parkinson, and Norman Tebbit succeeded Parkinson at the Department of Trade and Industry.

That was in October, a time when a prime minister needed her deputies and like-minded thinkers about her. The Labour Party was regrouping, not under Michael Foot, but Neil Kinnock, whose deputy was Roy Hattersley. The Labour Party thought that this left-right combination would be enough to win the election, but there was still much to do.

Mrs Thatcher's greatest ally was not British but American. She and Ronald Reagan were political soul-mates, and when Reagan announced the seemingly bizarre Strategic Defence Initiative ('star wars') in March 1983, Mrs Thatcher was the only leader to support him publicly. Even his own people, including his Secretary of State, Alexander Haig, found it difficult to justify the programme. SDI was a programme to explore ways in which science and high technology could devise systems that would knock out incoming Soviet missiles. Research had been going on for some years before Reagan's announcement, and laboratories were working on experimental charged particle beams and long-range laser systems that could, if necessary, be space based – hence the nickname 'star wars'.

Reagan's announcement was mocked throughout the world, apart from London, but it had an effect that few at that time imagined – it forced the Soviet Union to start its own SDI research programme, which became financially crippling and contributed to the fall of the USSR.

The 'star wars' speech had another immediate effect. It enlarged the anti-nuclear debate in Britain at a time when American cruise missiles were being based at Greenham Common and Molesworth. The membership of CND began to rise rapidly. Reagan's 'star wars' ideas and Mrs Thatcher's enthusiasm for them, including a rather fanciful and entirely nonsensical notion that Britain could earn hundreds of millions of pounds of contracts by taking part, simply frightened a lot of people. The double act of the Great Communicator and the Iron Lady was just what the flagging anti-nuclear campaign had needed.

If Mrs Thatcher's election victory and President Reagan's 'star wars' speech may be considered political and strategic landmarks of 1983, there were other occasions that stayed far longer in the minds of the peoples they governed.

The more peaceful uses of space continued to attract attention, particularly when a thirty-two-year-old physicist, Sally Ride, joined the *Challenger* space shuttle crew and became the first American woman in space. Valentina Tereshkova, the Russian cosmonaut, had been the first woman in space exactly twenty years earlier. Tereshkova became a soviet minister; Sally Ride carried on being a physicist.

In the year that Britain got its first pound coin, breakfast television began (in January) when the BBC's *Breakfast Time* went on air. It was also the month that Bjorn Borg retired from tennis at the age of twenty-six after winning five Wimbledon championships and five French Open titles. Borg never did win the US Open.

In January legislation was introduced to make the wearing of seat-belts in the front passenger seats of cars compulsory. Wheel clamps were introduced in London in May.

The Thames Flood Barrier was used for the first time in February, and the winner of the 1981 Derby, Shergar, was kidnapped and never seen again in public.

In May Richard Attenborough and Ben Kingsley won Oscars for the film *Gandhi*, and the Nobel Peace Prize was awarded to Lech Walesa.

The year was marred in September when the Soviet air force shot down a South Korean airliner, Flight 007, killing all 269 passengers. As we have noted, in October more than 300 peace-keeping troops, both American and French, were killed by suicide bombers in Beirut, and in the same month more than 2000 died in a Turkish earthquake.

At least some were due to have a good Christmas in 1983, albeit illegally. Robbers got away with £25 million of gold bars from a Brinks-Mat warehouse at Heathrow Airport. It was Britain's biggest ever robbery.

Deaths
Anthony Blunt (art historian and double agent)
Sir Kenneth MacKenzie Clark, Baron Clark (art historian)
George Cukor (US film director)
Jack Dempsey (US boxer)

Arthur Koestler (Hungarian-British writer)
Donald Duart Maclean (double agent)
David Niven (actor)
Sir Ralph Richardson (actor)
Gloria Swanson (US actress)
Arnold Toynbee (historian and social reformer)
Sir William Walton (composer)
Dame Rebecca West (Irish writer)
Tennessee Williams (US playwright)

1984

THIS WAS not a year of Orwell's making and nor was it as he had imagined it might be. Orwell had described a nation under absolute state control. Thatcherism was about getting rid of state control.

In Moscow, the paradigm of modern state control, there was yet another change in leadership. Yuri Andropov, Brezhnev's successor, was now dead. The new man, Konstantin Chernenko, was at seventy-three the oldest person to become leader of the Soviet Union.

In London Mrs Thatcher had more pressing matters on her mind than the shuffling for position in the Kremlin, for this was a year of political, industrial and social unrest in Britain. It was also the year in which the government came face to face with IRA terrorism. No other administration in the history of British Cabinet government had ever been touched, maimed and even killed by forces that it had failed to overcome. Somehow, it seemed inevitable – albeit wholly evil – that the Thatcher government should be such a target for the worst form of anarchy. In this year, 1984, the IRA blew up the Grand Hotel in Brighton during the October Conservative Party conference.

The first confrontation, however, was to have a more lasting effect on the Thatcher government and on every administration that would follow for the remainder of the century.

In February 1984 the miners were negotiating a winter pay deal. Given the economic climate, the demands of the miners and the responses of government were inevitable. This was not simply a pay debate. The Coal Board was offering little more than 5 per cent, but worse still was the decision presented by the board's chairman, Ian McGregor, to close twenty pits that were not making money.

On 1 March the National Coal Board announced that Cortonwood colliery in Yorkshire was to be closed. This was the catalyst for the strike, although its cause was the determination of the National Union of Mineworkers (NUM) to oppose all pit closures. This was a challenge by the miners to a law that stated that a union could not go on strike without a national ballot. It was a clash between flying pickets and 'flying' policemen, who were brought in from forces so far away that many constables had never seen a miner in their lives. And these were not local disturbances at pit gates. On 29 May, for example, more than 5000 pickets fought what can only be described as a pitched battle with police at Orgeave Coke Works in South Yorkshire, during which more than sixty people were seriously injured. This was not an exceptional day during the strike.

On one side were the miners, led by the most militant NUM president, Arthur Scargill, ranged against, not the National Coal Board in the figure of Ian McGregor, but the most militant of all Tory prime ministers, Margaret Thatcher. Mrs Thatcher's single-minded view was that it was not a simple individual dispute – it was an insurrection.

Curiously both Thatcher and Scargill had similar strengths and weaknesses. Both were strong personalities who would not blink. Yet both understood that in the long term the greatest test would be the support each received from his and her constituency. Thatcher needed a country and particularly a Cabinet that would stand not behind, but beside her. It was winter and the industrial and living-room hearths had to be kept alight. Scargill knew that even his most militant followers would have to keep the faith with the greater campaign – as they had against the Heath government – and not melt away when times became financially hard and when, in an increasingly home-owning Britain, mortgages were unpaid.

There were too many contradictory issues arising from the simple question of law and order for the miners' strike of 1984 ever to be peacefully resolved. Nor was it. It started in March 1984 and did not end, officially, until the following March. In that period occurred the most violent confrontation between striking men and police ever seen in Britain. The strike did not come to an end because of some unanimous agreement between the two sides. The miners were beaten by the government, in spite of a national dock strike called in that same summer. The miners split – a new union was formed – and with winter approaching and their leader, Arthur Scargill, increasingly discredited, they broke ranks and drifted back to work. The promises that had been made about the number of pits that would remain open were denounced by Scargill, but when, some time later, he was more or less proved right, few cared.

From the early 1970s it had been partly accepted at Westminster that trades unions had a say in how the country was governed. This understanding had not arisen because the Labour Party had always been the tool of the unions. Organized workers did not have national political clout until the 1970s, and Mrs Thatcher recognized this and exploited it at the ballot box but resisted it in government. It is worth repeating that it was this one act that was the legacy of Mrs Thatcher, not to her own party, but to the Labour Party. Without Thatcher, the Labour Party would have found it harder (although by no means impossible) to bring about the reforms that made it electable. We should date that step-change in British politics, not from the revision of Clause Four in the late 1990s but to the miners' strike of more than ten years earlier.

The year had begun with a dramatic protest against the Anglo-American agreement to base cruise missiles in Britain. While the protesters lined the routes and fences about Greenham Common, one of the two missile bases (the other was Molesworth), a Foreign Office clerk decided to make her own protest. Sarah Tisdall, who worked in the office of the Foreign Secretary, Sir Geoffrey Howe, copied papers that contained the schedule for the missile deployment. She sent the copies to the *Guardian*. Miss Tisdall was arrested, charged under the Official Secrets Act and sent to prison for six months.

In February, while the Foreign Office watched Britain's interests in the USSR and in Lebanon, from whence hundreds of British citizens were being evacuated, the Department of Trade was learning more about the Japanese. This was the year in which Japanese industry began its colonization of little-known industrial towns in Britain – aided by generous government grants. Nissan, for example, announced that it would build an experimental car plant in Washington, County Durham.

This was also the year in which the government decided to replace O-level examinations with the General Certificate of Secondary Education, the GCSE; to abolish dog licences, the pound note and the halfpenny; to introduce 'quickie' divorces; to privatize British Telecom and the Trustee Savings Bank; to arrange the transfer of Hong Kong to China; and to expel, rather than arrest, Libyans in their embassy after one of them shot and murdered a woman police constable, Yvonne Fletcher.

The most dramatic event occurred in October. The IRA exploded a bomb at the Grand Hotel, Brighton, the conference headquarters of the Conservative Party that autumn. Four died, including the MP Sir Anthony Berry and the wife of John Wakeham, the Chief Whip. Another died later. The prime minister's reaction was, predictably, defiant. Life must go on.

Life did not always go on in Ethiopia. The famine-stricken nation became the object of an overwhelming public fund-raising event. Largely organized by the singer, Bob Geldof, rock bands joined to sing 'Do They Know It's Christmas?'

In the United States Ronald Reagan and his vice president, George Bush, won a second term, with almost 60 per cent of the popular vote.

In India there was less to celebrate. More than 2000 people were killed and tens of thousands terribly injured in December when a chemical storage tank at a Union Carbide factory leaked in a town called Bhopal.

Deaths

Yuri Andropov (Soviet politician)
Count Basie (US bandleader)
Sir John Betjeman (poet)
Richard Burton (actor)
Truman Capote (US writer)
Diana Dors (actress)
Indira Gandhi (Indian politician)
Marvin Gaye (US singer)

Tito Gobbi (Italian baritone)
Sir Arthur Travers 'Bomber' Harris (air force officer)
Joseph Losey (US film director)
James Mason (actor)
Eric Morecambe (comedian)
Mohammed Neguib (Egyptian politician)
Sam Peckinpah (US film director)
J.B. Priestley (writer)
François Truffaut (French film director)
Johnny Weissmuller (US actor)

1985

AT HOME the miners' strike came to an end after NUM delegates agreed by ninety-eight votes to ninety-one to return to work. In truth, the strike had been effectively over for many weeks. In May 1985 the Home Secretary, Leon Brittan, gave the courts and the police added powers to contain picketing and violent demonstrations of the type that had marked the twelve months.

Mrs Thatcher's relations with the Irish over Northern Ireland were complicated. She had never been happy with the way in which the Irish had been against Britain during the Falklands conflict in 1982, even though in November 1981, she and the Taoiseach, Dr Garrett Fitzgerald, had agreed to form an Anglo-Irish Inter-governmental Council. At the time this came to nothing, and its failure is testament to the increasingly frosty relationship between the two governments, when in 1982 Fitzgerald was replaced by Charles Haughey, who thought little of new British proposals for the devolution of power to Ulster.

A year later, however, in 1983, Fitzgerald was back as Taoiseach and this, in theory at least, permitted relations between the two governments to improve. There remained obvious differences, both practical and ideological. For example, the essential cross-border security co-operation between the RUC and the Garda was not working and nor was it likely to, given the deep suspicions of each other held by officers on the ground. Moreover, some of the policing proposals of the Irish were not only impracticable, they were politically and constitutionally unacceptable. The Irish had suggested that, for example, the Garda be allowed to police Republican areas of Belfast. Clearly, Mrs Thatcher's government would never have agreed to this. What is more, nor would the Garda if they thought about it. They would have been too obvious targets for bombers and snipers.

Second, there was a mutual concern about the way in which Sinn Fein was starting to gain in local elections at the expense of the largely Catholic and moderate SDLP. This was particularly important as the Northern Ireland assembly could not work without the SDLP.

The third concern was ideological. The Irish government simply could not grasp that the Thatcher government would never agree to any process that would lead to a loss of sovereignty – that is, that it would never accept a united Ireland. From the British viewpoint there were basic principles that had to be tackled. Would, for example, the Irish be willing to amend their constitution and abandon the article that claimed the six counties of Ulster? The least that could be expected was a change in the wording to drop the direct and legal claim and, perhaps, insert the hope for a United Ireland.

Certainly in Downing Street the next stage in the search for peace was the drafting of an Anglo-Irish Agreement. The basis for this would have been a Joint Security Commission, but relations worsened again in 1984 when Thatcher publicly rejected the findings of yet another consultative body, the New Ireland Forum. The main conclusions had centred on a united Ireland endorsed by a joint North–South authority. The Irish told Thatcher that if she simply rejected proposals out of hand, the IRA would gain support.

By the summer of 1985 the talks were back on course, if not an even keel. The Irish still wanted direct involvement in Ulster, including joint courts. The British insisted that whatever agreement was reached, there had to be a public announcement that no changes would be made in Northern Ireland without the majority consent of the people and that there was currently no sign of this majority. This point was the basis for the first article of the Anglo-Irish Agreement, which Thatcher and Fitzgerald signed on 15 November 1985.

Article 1 did not reassure the Unionists, who saw the agreement as the thin end of the constitutional wedge. Once more, Protestants felt they were being betrayed. By 1986 the Irish government was exaggerating its interpretation of the Agreement, and this helped to convince the Unionists that the Agreement must be opposed by all means including political, industrial and civil protest. Nothing Thatcher could tell Unionist leaders in 1985 would change this view.

If the opposition from the Unionists was predictable, so, too, was the disappointment of some of Thatcher's own people, and one of her ministers, Ian Gow, resigned in protest. In July 1990 he was murdered by the IRA.

On 11 March 1985 Mikhail Gorbachev became General Secretary of the Soviet Communist Party following the death of Konstantin Chernenko. This was the start of a new volume in the history of the Russian peoples. Gorbachev's ambition was public reform, and he wanted to change the way in which the Soviet Union was run. Within weeks, Gorbachev had announced the first slackening of the arms race in forty years, and he removed the architect of much of post-Stalin Soviet policy, Andrei Gromyko, and gave him the harmless post of president.

Gorbachev was seen as New Russia. Yet Western leaders, including both Ronald Reagan and Margaret Thatcher, could not grasp the reasoning behind Gorbachev's insistence that reform did not mean the dismantling of the Communist Party. They regarded communism as the source of all political and, potentially, military evil. Gorbachev saw, probably rightly, that if economic, political and social reform was to work in the Soviet Union, those reforms had to have a structure and even the basis of a bureaucracy. There had to be a system that could make reforms function. Gorbachev understood that the existing system could implement change because its own modernization process would be the basis for that change. Gorbachev would not survive the process, and the so-called political elite who followed, particularly Boris Yeltsin, turned the basics of Gorbachev's reforms into a drunken, corrupt, political and economic farce. Prime Minister Thatcher may have described Gorbachev as a man with whom she could do business, but she was far from the day when she would give him credit.

Thatcher had been to Washington twice in the three months before Gorbachev came to power. On the first occasion, in December 1984, she agreed to support the SDI programme, although she made a strong case for rejecting the idea that it would reduce the need for nuclear weapons. Reagan had offered to share the technology with the Soviet Union, although there were many (including the Russians) who did not believe that his policy-makers and scientists would ever let this happen, even though Reagan was undoubtedly sincere. The offer had, however, horrified Mrs Thatcher. Perhaps a consolation was that the Americans had no idea how to make the president's 'star wars' plan work in practice. By the time they did, or if they did, time and presidents would have moved on. Publicly, however, Mrs Thatcher supported the SDI research programme.

When she returned to the United States in February 1985 to address both houses of Congress, Thatcher again publicly supported SDI. But in private, she told the president that he should cut back on the rhetoric. It was not that she worried about frightening the Russians. Thatcher believed that the SDI fantasy – that one day nuclear weapons would not be needed – would influence public opinion at home, which she needed to support the government's own nuclear weapons programme and the basing of US cruise missiles in Britain.

This was the image of the prime minister when she went to Moscow that March for the funeral of Chernenko and, more importantly, a meeting with Gorbachev.

Anglo-Soviet relations were not at their best in 1985. The problems had begun with a man called Oleg Gordievski. Gordievski was a KGB officer who had been turned as a double agent by the British Secret Intelligence Service, the SIS. Just as he was about to be arrested, he was smuggled out of the Soviet Union in a pre-arranged plan by the SIS. Gordievski revealed the names of twenty-five Soviet spies in London. When they were expelled, the Soviet government, as expected, expelled twenty-five Britons from Moscow.

It was in 1985 that the world at large began to take note of what the World Health Organization (WHO) was calling an epidemic. A new acronym began to appear in the headlines, HIV (Human Immunodeficiency Virus), yet in 1985 little attention was paid to medical reports and HIV was generally dismissed as something that affected only homosexuals.

In Britain blood donors began to be screened, and the government earmarked about £1 million for research. From this moment, the red ribbons of the anti-AIDS campaign started to appear, and by 1986 a UN department was doing nothing but researching and reporting the epidemic.

In 1998 WHO reported that in 1997 5.8 million new cases of HIV/AIDS were listed. WHO claimed that one in a hundred sexually active people were HIV positive, although many of them did not know it. In the same year 2.3 million people died of HIV/AIDS, which meant that nearly 12 million had died since the syndrome was first identified as an epidemic little more than a decade earlier.

The war in Lebanon continued to claim hundreds of lives, while in Ethiopia, thousands continued to starve to death. Few of the distressed would have known about the spectacle of the Live Aid concerts in Wembley and at the JFK Stadium in Philadelphia. An estimated 1.5 billion watched throughout the world and some £40 million was raised for famine relief.

There was little that could be done to help the mourners in a series of aircraft disasters. A terrorist bomb exploded in an Air India jet as it approached the Irish coastline in June and 325 people died. A Delta airliner crashed at Dallas-Fort Worth airport. A Japanese Boeing 747 crashed outside Tokyo, and a British Airtours 737 crashed on taking off at Manchester. More than 1000 airline passengers and crew had been killed in four incidents – the worst year in civil aviation history.

This was also a year of disaster at two soccer stadia. In May more than forty fans died in a fire at the Bradford City ground and a similar number died at the Heysel Stadium in Brussels. The first event was caused by a fire. The second was started when Liverpool and Juventus supporters fought on the terraces. This led to pressure on a wall and fence. Many were crushed to death.

Also in May tens of thousands died in Bangladesh from a cyclone and a huge tidal wave. In November, perhaps as many as 20,000 died when a volcano in northern Colombia erupted, causing mud and rocks to swamp four large villages.

In London rioting on the Broadwater Farm housing estate, Tottenham, reached a violent conclusion when PC Keith Blakelock was hacked to death. This had followed rioting in Brixton after the shooting to death of a black woman during a police search of her house in September.

In Hollywood the film, *Amadeus* won eight Oscars. At Wimbledon Boris Becker beat Kevin Curren to become, at seventeen, the youngest ever winner of the men's singles. At Oxford, thirteen-year-old Ruth Lawrence, after two years' study, was awarded a first class degree in mathematics.

Deaths

Joy Adamson (German naturalist)
Laura Ashley (fashion designer)
Richard Beeching, Baron Beeching (engineer)
George Brown, Baron George-Brown (politician)

Arthur Bryant (historian)
Yul Brynner (US actor)
Marc Chagall (French artist)
Konstantin Chernenko (Soviet politician)
Robert Graves (poet)
Enver Hoxha (Albanian politician)
Rock Hudson (US actor)
Susanne Langer (US philosopher)
Philip Larkin (poet)
Sir Robert Mayer (philanthropist)
Sir Michael Redgrave (actor)
Orson Welles (US actor)

1986

THE CHANNEL TUNNEL project came to life at the start of January 1986, although Mrs Thatcher made it clear that no public money would go into the project. There were those who, perhaps cynically, observed that President Mitterrand needed the Channel Tunnel to boost his chances in the fast-approaching French elections, but there is no evidence that Mrs Thatcher committed Britain to such a scheme simply to pay off the undoubted debt owed to Mitterrand for his support during the Falklands campaign. Lack of evidence did not stop the speculation, however.

There was no speculation over what was the biggest event at Westminster during the opening weeks of 1986. This was the Westland affair, which resulted in the resignation of two Cabinet ministers, Michael Heseltine and Leon Brittan. It was also a clear sign of the potentially divisive nature of the Thatcher Cabinet. It can also be stated that the depth of ill-feeling and the issues at stake in this matter were so serious, that, as the former Chancellor of the Exchequer, Nigel Lawson, has observed: 'Margaret only survived by the skin of her teeth.'[2]

In its simplest form, the Westland saga is as follows. There were three main players: Margaret Thatcher, Michael Heseltine, who was the Defence Secretary, and Leon Brittan, who was the Trade and Industry Secretary.

The Westland Company, based in Yeovil, Somerset, was, and remains, Britain's only helicopter manufacturer. During 1985 Westland had been going out of business, but a British company was willing to save it, provided there were assurances of Defence contracts. At a private meeting at Downing Street in the late spring of 1985, Heseltine told the prime minister, Nigel Lawson, the Chancellor of the Exchequer, and Norman Tebbit, the Trade and Industry Secretary, that the Defence Ministry was not willing to put money into Westland. Tebbit said the same held true for his department, and the Chancellor said there would be no public money for the company.

---

2 Nigel Lawson, *The View from No. 11*, Bantam Press (1992).

Tebbit was about to leave the DTI, where Leon Brittan was to take over. This point is important because Brittan sided with Thatcher, even though she had shuffled him out of the important job at the Home Office to send him to the DTI. His devotion would be his Cabinet downfall.

Westland, which had been badly managed, got a new chairman, Sir John Cuckney. Not entirely coincidental with Cuckney's arrival, the American helicopter builder, Sikorsky, put out feelers to buy into Westland – something less than a 30 per cent stake was imagined. Heseltine put together an alternative plan, which would have involved a European consortium. The prime minister opposed Heseltine. First, the option was flawed because a European consortium would expect government orders to keep it afloat. Second, and this must be remembered, Heseltine was her political enemy.

Thatcher was surprised, and not a little angry, at the support shown in Cabinet for Heseltine. Her attitude stemmed partly from her personal judgement and partly from the logical view that Heseltine's support did not come from a cold analysis of the business situation but from an almost sentimental desire to oppose an American take-over. Heseltine was given four days to get concrete proposals from the European consortium, and he managed to get a form of words that he believed would satisfy the Cabinet. This was, however, not so. Heseltine was departing from the Thatcher line that the decision should be left to the Westland board and that government should not interfere.

The conflict was now played out between Brittan and Heseltine in public. Over the Christmas holiday of 1985 newspapers continued to run the story of Brittan and Heseltine battling against each other on principles that went far beyond the simple argument that government should leave Westland to sort out the problem if a long-term solution were to be found.

The matter went beyond the future of Westland. Leon Brittan authorized the leaking of a letter from the attorney general to Heseltine, in which Heseltine was warned of so-called inaccuracies in his methods. That letter had been inspired not by the law officer but by Mrs Thatcher's office. The leaking was not only a treacherous act, but for Brittan – a lawyer – quite unwise. On 6 January 1986 the attorney general threatened to resign. At a Cabinet meeting three days later Thatcher told Heseltine that he had to accept Cabinet responsibility. He responded by picking up his papers and walking out of the Cabinet room. He had resigned.

Brittan's part in the leaked letter saga (it is said that he believed that Thatcher wanted him to leak it) was now public knowledge. He too had to go.

Thatcher could easily have been removed from office by Friday, 24 January 1986, the day on which Brittan went, if he had made public Downing Street's part in the sordid politicking. He chose not to. Brittan later became vice president of the European Commission.

The importance of the Westland affair is that from that point Margaret Thatcher appeared to put no trust in her Cabinet colleagues – only her inner group of close advisers. By the time her party turned against her, she must have known that, apart from one or two, no one would shield her from the grey suits.

In international politics the most disturbing moment for the prime minister came in October 1986, when the Soviet leader Mikhail Gorbachev and President Reagan met in Reykjavik. The summit meeting was about nuclear arms control, and Reagan proposed that both super-powers should get rid of all their nuclear arsenals and develop SDI systems to protect each other from attack. The Soviet leader, predictably – as at least one of the American negotiating team had hoped – said there could be no deal unless the SDI programme was dropped. But Reagan's pronouncement that nuclear weapons might be abandoned caused the prime minister to fly to Washington at the first opportunity to put her friend, the Great Communicator, straight. Zero-Zero, as mutual abolition of nuclear warheads was called, was a zero idea. Did he want the Chinese to be the world's nuclear super-power? Furthermore, talk of getting rid of warheads made it doubly hard for Britain to resist public demands to rethink the UK's nuclear weapons programme. The term 'handbagged' was used quite widely immediately after that visit.

It took more than behind-the-scenes politicking to remove another world leader that year. Ferdinand Marcos had ruled the Philippines for two decades. He was a dictator and opposition was always short lived. In 1983 Benigno Aquino, one of the few who looked like being successful against Marcos, was murdered by Marcos's men. What Marcos had not anticipated was that this action would make Aquino into a martyr and provide a successor. At Aquino's funeral millions heard his widow, Cory Aquino, vow to continue the work her husband had started.

In February 1986 Marcos claimed that he had won the rigged general election. Even the Americans, who had supported Marcos throughout his twenty years in power, realized that public opinion had turned against him and withdrew their support. As Marcos's own cohorts turned against him, American helicopters dramatically lifted him from the presidential palace to exile in Hawaii, and Cory Aquino was sworn in as president.

Another dictator was toppled in February, Jean-Claude Duvalier of Haiti. Duvalier called himself Baby Doc; his father, also a dictator, had been known as Papa Doc and had, as now did his son, kept power by using the ruthless secret police, the Tontons Macoutes. In February 1986 the people rose against him, and Baby Doc escaped to France.

In February one of the most peaceable politicians in the world was murdered. The Swedish prime minister, Olaf Palme, was assassinated as he walked home from the cinema. His assassin was never caught, and no convincing reason for the murder has ever appeared.

There was a moment in 1986 that proved that no state could declare itself neutral to the effects of nuclear power, certainly not its fall-out. During the last week of

April the number 4 nuclear reactor at Chernobyl in the Ukraine malfunctioned. The fall-out from Chernobyl was carried around the world. Within weeks the effects were so great that, for example, a ban was placed on the butchering and selling of Cumbrian sheep. The consequences of Chernobyl would last well into the twenty-first century.

This was also the year of one of the most dramatic space accidents ever. In January, a routine US space shuttle launch ended when the *Challenger* craft exploded seconds after launching. All seven crew were killed.

The cheerful news of the year was a royal wedding in London. In June Prince Andrew married Sarah Ferguson. A sadder moment for the royal family was the death of the Duchess of Windsor at the age of eighty-nine. She was buried at Frogmore alongside her husband, Edward VIII, who had died in 1972.

At the end of that year the death was announced of the man who had masterminded the nuclear weapons arrangements with the US back in the 1960s. Harold Macmillan, publisher, First World War hero, often rebellious yet the last patrician prime minister, died on 29 December 1986 at the age of ninety-two. He would be long remembered for 'You've never had it so good' and his 'wind of change' speech in Africa. To most people he was simply Supermac. Like Churchill, he looked the part. Like Churchill, he played to the gallery.

Deaths
Simone de Beauvoir (French writer)
James Cagney (US actor)
Frank Cousins (trade union leader)
Jean Genet (French writer)
General Sir John Glubb, Glubb Pasha (British soldier)
Benny Goodman (US clarinettist)
W. Averell Harriman (US politician)
Christopher Isherwood (writer)
Harold Macmillan, the Earl of Stockton (politician)
Vyacheslav Molotov (Russian politician)
Henry Moore (sculptor)
Olaf Palme (Swedish politician)
Sir Peter Pears (tenor)
Otto Preminger (Austrian-US film producer)
Dame Flora Robson (actress)
Emmanuel Shinwell, Baron Shinwell (politician)
Tenzing Norgay, Sherpa Tenzing (Nepalese mountaineer)

1987

TERRY WAITE was kidnapped in Beirut during January 1987. He was trying to negotiate the release of hostages held by Hezbollah, the militant Party of God.

Waite remained a captive for five years, and although he was not the only person held hostage in this period,[3] for the British at least, he and John McCarthy brought the uncertain political situation in Lebanon to the forefront of public attention for almost the first time.

In February in Washington, D.C., the Tower Commission on US arms sales to Iran, now known as Irangate and inexorably linked to the hostage crisis through the duplicity of Oliver North, said that President Reagan had not deliberately misled Americans over the matter because he had simply not understood 'who was involved and what was happening'.

In Britain 1987 will be remembered for two crashes. They came within forty-eight hours of each other in October. The first was caused by the weather; the second by the uncertainties of the Stock Market system.

The worst storm in England in living memory blew through the night of 15 October and into the following morning. This was a hurricane-strength storm, which changed whole landscapes in southeast England overnight. In Sussex the countryside around villages that had not much altered in a century or more was devastated as huge oaks and remaining elms were uplifted. Fortunately, fewer than twenty people died as a direct result of the storm, largely because it happened during the night hours and few people were outside.

To give some indication of the distress and havoc caused, the London Fire Brigade had more than 6000 emergency calls in one day – the most it has ever had – and for a week afterwards about 300,000 homes in the south of England had no electricity. In Kew Gardens 30 per cent of the specimen trees were uprooted.

While this was going on, a different kind of crisis was taking place across the Atlantic – Wall Street was falling and there appeared to be uncontrolled selling. For the whole weekend governments waited to see what the financial weather was going to be like when the markets opened for trading on the following Monday, 19 October 1987. Tokyo was the first to trade, then Hong Kong. The selling was so heavy that the Hong Kong market was shut down for the rest of the week.

In London 10 per cent of the total share value disappeared, and the value of publicly quoted companies fell by £50 billion. When Wall Street opened the selling was so great that share prices fell by almost a quarter. This was, in American terms, a financial melt-down that rivalled the stock market crash of 1929 and whose consequences were expected to be greater than any other economic crisis in the twentieth century.

The responses seen in the United States and Britain reflect how economies of quite different stature react to a financial crisis such as this. The United States,

---

3 Others included John McCarthy, captured in 1986, who was released in 1991. Hostages in the 1980s included Terry Anderson, Tom Sutherland, Alberto Molinari, Joseph Cicippio, Edward Tracey, Alann Steen, Jesse Turner, Jackie Mann, Heinrich Struebig and Thomas Kemptner.

where it had started, was rich and owned the dollar – the only currency of confidence in the world. Britain was not rich and was tied into a European financial arrangement in which it had little confidence, partly because it had entered it with the pound at the wrong exchange level.

The crisis was also the first public demonstration of the ways in which international trading worked. For the past five years Wall Street had been a bull market, and in that period the price of stock had risen by 350 per cent. A lot of people had been making a lot of money. When the crash came, the 22.5 per cent drop over the previous week's trading did not, in the long term, represent such a huge loss, and given the way that stock price and management works, it was relatively easy to recover, which it did.

There was also another element of the crash that had not been present in 1929 but that now had the capacity to cause utter devastation. The world stock markets were moving towards computer-controlled dealing. The American system was already computerized, and, in the crudest of examples, it was possible to introduce programs by which shares would be bought or sold when they reached a certain level. As soon as a certain level of selling was registered, the computers would interpret that rate as a rush and the result would be almost uncontrollable dumping of shares. No one sacked the computers – and the London Stock Exchange was moving into the same method of dealing.

If there was to be a demonstration of how the markets operated, the most obvious example would be the fact that within a couple of months of so-called Black Monday, the pound was trading at its highest value for four years.

The following month an explosion of a far more wicked nature was heard, not on the world stock exchanges but, once again, in Northern Ireland. An IRA bomb exploded during the annual Remembrance Day parade in the town of Enniskillen. Eleven people were killed; sixty-three people were seriously injured. Even then, however, it was not understood in Whitehall that terrorists would succeed and eventually a British government would be forced to do business with them.

Whatever the attitude to opposition and authority revealed in London and Washington through government reactions to bombings in Northern Ireland or the Iran-Contra scandal, in China a quite different philosophy of government was shown to the world in 1987. Throughout 1986 there had been signs of dissatisfaction among students, culminating in public demonstrations on 21 December when students began protest marches in many major Chinese cities.

The students' campaign was simply defined. They wanted what they called democracy and, above all, free newspapers. Nothing like this level of student demonstrations had been seen since the late 1970s and the so-called Wall of Democracy posters. This was the time when students wrote their protest newspapers and posted them on the walls for all to read. Now the protest was to take on a new level and for a moment at least capture international attention.

The protests continued through December and January, until on New Year's Day thousands of students began to converge in Tiananmen Square in Beijing. This vision of unafraid protest registered in stark monochrome on the political minds of the Chinese leadership more than it did in the technicolour of western newspapers. Once the protest was over the western democracies, by and large, forgot this trickle of student protest, but the Chinese leadership understood perfectly what might follow. There would be changes in China, but they would be brought about not by students but by quiet revolution at the top of the Chinese Communist Party. The general secretary, Deng Xiaoping (Teng Hsiao-p'ing), retired in November 1987, although there was absolutely no question that his influence was as strong as ever.

It was not until 1989 that the student protest reawakened, and when it did it became a benchmark in the opposition not to Chinese authority but to the way in which that authority was exercised.

On 7 March 188 people died when a cross-channel ferry, *Herald of Free Enterprise*, sank as it left Zeebrugge harbour. A subsequent inquiry showed that the bow doors had not been closed before the ferry put to sea.

In another human disaster thirty people died when fire spread through King's Cross underground station in November. For the first time after this accident 'no smoking' signs went up throughout the London Underground system.

If there was a bright note to end 1987 it came in Washington. On 8 December President Reagan and the Soviet leader, Mikhail Gorbachev, signed the first ever East–West agreement to cut the size of nuclear missile arsenals.

Richard Eyre took over from Peter Hall as Director of the National Theatre in the month that Macdonald's, the publishers of Noddy, decided that the age of political correctness meant that golliwogs were banned and would be replaced in Enid Blyton's books with gnomes, who were both gender- and colour-free. The thought that even gnomes might be politically incorrect was to come later.

Deaths

Eamon Andrews (Irish broadcaster)
Fred Astaire (US actor)
Jacqueline du Pré (cellist)
Rita Hayworth (US actress)
Jascha Heifetz (US violinist)
John Huston (US film director)
Danny Kaye (US actor)
Lee Marvin (US actor)
Duncan Edwin Sandys, Baron Duncan-Sandys (politician)
Andrés Segovia (Spanish guitarist)
Andy Warhol (US artist)

1988

ON 21 DECEMBER a Pan American jumbo jet crashed at Lockerbie, killing all 259 passengers as well as eleven people in the town. It was also the month that thirty-four people died when two trains collided outside Clapham Junction in London.

These two events may have captured the headlines in Britain, but they were as nothing compared to two other disasters in December 1988. In Bangladesh more than 1000 died in yet another cyclone, and at the end of the second week in December reports began to emerge that an earthquake in Armenia on Wednesday, 7 December had claimed more than 100,000 lives.

In British politics the centrepiece of government legislation in 1988 was the Budget, prepared by Chancellor Nigel Lawson.

Lawson became known as a reforming chancellor, yet he achieved only half his aim. He had wanted to produce reforms in international financial affairs, but it was never going to be possible for a British chancellor to achieve global monetary reform, especially by the 1980s. The 1984 Budget had gone some way to reform corporate taxation, and on Tuesday, 15 March 1988 Lawson delivered his latest Budget to the Commons. In it he outlined the principles on which his reforms were based. First, he wanted to reduce tax rates; second, he would reduce or abolish unwarranted tax breaks; third, he planned to make life a little simpler for the tax payer; and finally, he intended to remove some manifest injustices from the system.

None of this was particularly new. What was different was the intention to do something about it. Lawson's decision to act was not simply ideological. There was, throughout the world, a general movement to reform domestic taxation, and as the 1980s had progressed it had become increasingly possible for money to be moved about the globe more easily and more quickly than ever before. This trend was also becoming true of manpower. In Europe especially, the trend and, increasingly, the ambition was for people to move as they wished from country to country. There was more to this than social freedom. In a continent such as Europe, where transport was relatively easy, mobility of labour was not only desirable but essential. A need in one country for craftsmen and tradesmen could be satisfied by shifting some of the surplus skills in another. This could and would extend across the hemispheres. It would not be long before, for example, British hospitals were hiring nurses from New Zealand and Australia, just as had happened in reverse in the 1940s and 1950s.

To make such change easier and to couple this movement with the international mobility of capital as well as of people, Lawson believed that it was necessary to rethink the way people were taxed. His ideas were supported on an international level. Industrialized countries were recognizing that economic prosperity would rely more than ever before on tax incentives, including lower marginal rates.

Lawson's 1988 Budget did away with the sliding scale of higher rate taxation. Until that point, the higher rate was 60 per cent and people would reach it on a sliding scale. Lawson introduced one high rate income tax, 40 per cent, and a basic tax rate of 25 per cent. It was also during the 1988 Budget speech that Lawson announced that a Conservative government ambition was to reduce the rate to 20 per cent as soon as possible.

Instead of his speech being welcomed, it caused something of an uproar. Many Labour MPs barracked the Chancellor. As far as they were concerned, reducing the higher level of taxation was simply pandering to the rich. So disruptive were the objections – a Budget speech is normally heard without interruption – that the sitting of the Commons was suspended for ten minutes.

Lawson's Budget did nothing for the British economy, of course. The international traders would have liked far more that identified the trading rate of the pound. Instead, there was nothing but compromise. Sterling was going up and the prime minister's desire that there should be no government intervention for the pound was being fulfilled. But here was a source of direct confrontation between Thatcher and Lawson. The Chancellor, for example, would have liked to have had a constant exchange rate with the Deutschmark, the most powerful currency in Europe. Thatcher, however, would not allow any intervention – either buying or selling – and Lawson could not have his way.

By now relations between Thatcher and Lawson were at a low ebb, and the battle over exchange rates was only one example of the differences between the two. One of the important aspects of getting the level of the pound right was that too strong a pound made it difficult for British industry to sell abroad and, more immediately, it was important for the pound to be trading at the right level if Britain were to join the European Money System, the Exchange Rate Mechanism (ERM).

The result of this dispute for sterling was that, instead of steadying, it continued to rise. Moreover, the media had decided that the story was not about exchange rate mechanisms but the conflict between the prime minister and her Chancellor. Within a year, in October 1989, Nigel Lawson would resign, the first Chancellor to walk out on his prime minister since Peter Thorneycroft had done so in 1958.

The discontent was not confined to the Cabinet room. In February 1988 nurses surprised many by marching on Parliament to demand higher wages. By the following month the government, perhaps a little shaken by this demonstration of angels, offered them 15 per cent.

On 28 July, along the corridor from Mrs Thatcher at Westminster, the Liberals, now called the Social and Liberal Democrats, elected a new leader. He was a former Royal Marine, who had been born in Ulster and was now the MP for Yeovil, Paddy Ashdown. The public would be seeing more of Mr Ashdown and his parliamentary colleagues, because on 9 February MPs agreed an experiment to televise the House of Commons on a limited basis.

Something that they would not agree to – especially not the government – was the publication of the memoir of the man called Peter Wright who had worked for MI5. The government had tried to stop the British media from even mentioning the memoir, *Spycatcher*, but the twelve-month injunction against newspapers could not be sustained since it was now possible to buy copies of *Spycatcher* everywhere but the United Kingdom. The government had fought an expensive and not very creditable battle in the Australian courts to stop its publication and had failed, and in 1988 the House of Lords came down against the government ban on publication. It did so not for political reasons but because the book was so widely available elsewhere.

As the publishing world observed, the action taken by Mrs Thatcher to have the book banned and the apparently duplicitous behaviour of Robert Armstrong, the Cabinet secretary, in aiding her campaign – his admission that he had been 'economical with the truth' was a gift for sketch writers on television and radio – led to massively increased sales.

Deaths
Sir Frederick Ashton (choreographer)
Enzo Ferrari (Italian designer)
Russell Harty (broadcaster)
Trevor Howard (actor)
Sir Alec Issigonis (designer)
Candido Jacuzzi (Italian engineer)
Frederick Loewe (US composer)
Seán MacBride (Irish politician)
Georgi Malenkov (Soviet politician)
Roy Orbison (US singer)
Harold 'Kim' Philby (double agent)
Kenneth Williams (actor and comedian)

1989

IN 1989 Margaret Thatcher celebrated ten years as prime minister. She had presided over 416 Cabinet meetings and changed her Cabinet eight times, including the Falklands resignations and post-election rejigging. In all, forty-seven ministers had been members of her Cabinets. By the end of 1989, few of them supported her.

Two of her most senior ministers were out of step with her political thinking – Nigel Lawson, the Chancellor, and the Foreign Secretary, Geoffrey Howe. It would be possible to add the Home Secretary, Douglas Hurd, to this list and by so doing show that the nation's three most senior Cabinet ministers were at odds with their prime minister.

In the simplest of terms, Margaret Thatcher attempted to run policy single-handed. That this was so was clear when the differences between Thatcher and

Lawson about entry into the European Exchange Rate Mechanism became public in 1988. Lawson wanted to shadow the Deutschmark and enter the ERM when the balance between the currencies was right. Thatcher was totally suspicious of any attempt to tie sterling formally to other currencies. She refused to allow stable exchange rates between the pound and other currencies to become an objective of British policy. She was not, of course, the first prime minister to have a convincing case for letting sterling find its own levels on the international money markets. In theory, the key was inflation. If inflation were down to minute levels and looked like staying that way, there might – but only might, according to Thatcher – be a case for joining.

Worse was to come. When the prime minister had an opportunity to support Lawson in the Commons, she was evasive. That fuelled media speculation that his days were numbered. Up went the pound against the mark – which was not what Britain needed. Five days later, again in the Commons, after much drafting and redrafting of statements by the offices of 11 and 10 Downing Street, Thatcher publicly supported Lawson. In some quarters that was seen as a triumph for Lawson, and that was something Thatcher found hard to accept.

When the prime minister and Howe went to a summit of the European Community (as it was then called) in Madrid in June 1989, it was without the normal close preparation of a united position. Considering that this meeting was all about the ERM and would lead to the setting up of the European Monetary Union, it was essential to have firm ideas that represented the British government position, particularly if Britain was to have a creditable basis for joining only if and when the time was right to do so.

According to Howe, he and Lawson had to insist on a pre-summit meeting at No. 10 and the prime minister agreed to meet only on the day they were to leave for Madrid. Lawson was aware that by this stage Thatcher was taking financial advice not from him, but her own financial guru, Alan Walters. At the meeting, Howe and Lawson said that if Thatcher remained unwilling to move towards joining the ERM, along the lines they had proposed, they would have to resign. It was in this unsatisfactory atmosphere that Howe and Thatcher flew to Madrid. When they reached the Spanish capital, the prime minister took her team to the Ritz Hotel and refused to join the social arrangements made by the British ambassador, which had, presumably, been approved by her office.

The big surprise of the summit was Thatcher's speech on the first day. She said that Britain would join the ERM when the time was right – inflation had to be down and there had to be progress (undefined) on exchange controls and the single market. The prime minister also said that Britain would move towards monetary union, although she did point out that Parliament would not accept a single currency. The conference was delighted. The differences appeared to be negligible. They were not.

Thatcher regarded this as victory over Lawson and Howe, while Howe, at least, thought they had got as close to their position as they could have expected.

Thatcher's trump card was that in the euphoria of her 'constructive diplomacy aimed to ensure Britain's proper part in the shaping of the future', as the *Guardian* put it, she had not committed Britain to any date for joining the ERM.

In July the media was full of stories that Howe was to be given a second minister, a Thatcherite, to run European policy. Sections of the press believed that he was soon to leave. By the end of the month, all was in place. Howe was to go and would be given the job of leader of the House. He contemplated returning to the backbenches because the leader's job would remove him from real power. An official announcement was drafted to say that Howe would act as deputy prime minister – a meaningless public relations bauble. Howe had been the longest serving Foreign Secretary of the century, and although he and Thatcher did not get on, they had between them presided over an enviable period of stable foreign policy.

John Major became Foreign Secretary, just ten years after becoming an MP.

In July 1989 Howe wrote his letter of resignation, but he filed it for future reference. When, fifteen months later, he did resign, it was his resignation speech in the Commons more than any other single statement that led to the prime minister's downfall.

The autumn did not improve tensions in Thatcher's Cabinet. She had more time for her economics adviser, Alan Walters, than she did for the Chancellor, and matters came to an inevitable head when an article by Walters appeared in an American journal. He had written that the ERM was a 'half-baked' affair and that there was no plausible reason for Britain joining it. Moreover, Walters added, the prime minister, thus far, agreed with him.

Other articles and speeches by Walters did nothing to lessen the impression that whatever Thatcher had told the European summit in Madrid, she had little intention of taking Britain into the ERM. This impression may have been mistaken at the time, since there was a strong element throughout her argument that if the time was right and the conditions were right, Britain might join. This tack was not new in government, and she was not the last prime minister to follow it.

Lawson felt strongly that Walters' influence had to be curbed. The most important aspect was not another voice against ERM (which was bad enough) but that same voice apparently convincing Thatcher that a depreciation in the value of sterling was not such a bad thing. The Chancellor was the person who had to answer to the Commons, not Walters.

On 20 October, while Thatcher was abroad, Lawson told Thatcher's parliamentary private secretary that Walters was now an impossible barrier between him (Lawson) and the prime minister. Lawson was not alone with his concerns – senior party managers felt the same way – but the strength of Lawson's feeling was not conveyed to the prime minister.

When Thatcher came back, Lawson told her that either Walters went or he did. She tried to persuade him not to go. She failed and did so for one single reason: Margaret Thatcher believed that if she were to give in – that is, to sack Alan Walters

– she would have been seen to back down. This she could not face. Lawson resigned.

For a prime minister to be so at odds with her Foreign Secretary and Chancellor that she had to appoint replacements for both within four months at a crucial time for government and country was not without omens for the future of that prime minister. It was what Macmillan would have called an eventful year.

But the relationship that the prime minister prized above all had changed. President Reagan had gone and in his place was George Bush.

In spite of what many imagined, Bush was his own man. Moreover, his Secretary of State (the US equivalent to Foreign Secretary) was James Baker. The two men, particularly Baker, had a different view of Britain's position in the world and did not go along with the Thatcher line, which was to encourage and continue the mythical special relationship. President Bush and his Secretary of State regarded Britain as a medium sized European power. Their senses of history were not dull, but nor were their concepts of *real transatlantic politik*. To Baker and the State Department, the nub of European power was Germany, and that was where the future relationship with America lay. The State Department anticipated the collapse of the eastern bloc even if they did not expect it to happen in the way that it did. Therefore, the European domino theory would centre on the power of the West German Chancellor.

Moreover, America's military interest was based not in Britain but in continental Europe. The military command was there – NATO headquarters and the Supreme Allied Commander Europe, an American general, were in continental Europe. In addition, the West Germans represented economic success. So, economics and the political importance of Germany brought any reassessment of Anglo-US relationships to a foregone conclusion. The Americans also tended to go along with the French view that the collapse of the eastern bloc was only one part of the greater strategy – a united Europe. Once again, according to the French version, Germany had a central role to play if the stability of the continent were to be maintained.

At the time, Mrs Thatcher appeared to think that the Americans were naïve to accept this version of geo-politics. But why should that have been so? The history of the whole century had reflected an American belief that Europe had to be unified. Had not the Americans always encouraged the British to be more European? The new US administration was not throwing away the past, as Thatcher seemed to think, but were continuing a policy that said simply: the special relationship would be kicked into life when it was needed but it was not needed all the time, especially if it damaged the progress towards European unity, as it had in de Gaulle's time.

When Mrs Thatcher visited Moscow in September 1989, she told Gorbachev that she did not really support the public line that was being promoted by NATO that Germany should be united. Thatcher's reasoning had a certain logic that most NATO nations (if not France) failed to follow. Thatcher did not want, as perhaps

Gorbachev misunderstood, the East Germans to continue to be communists. She wanted them to evolve their own democratic system. Unlike many caught in the euphoria of the cry for freedom that was running through Europe that year, Thatcher saw the terrible as well as the brighter consequences of sudden unification. Too many failed to understand that although western leaders could applaud the breaking down of the Berlin Wall, they would have to live with the economic and social consequences for some considerable time.

Those philosophies were about to be put to the test. The Berlin Wall came down in November 1989. Unfortunately, the West German leader of the time was Chancellor Helmut Kohl. Kohl may have been a good politician, but he was an opportunist and, on some occasions, thoughtless of the long-term and greater good of his actions and pronouncements. He may have been the longest serving postwar German leader, but he was one of the worst. When the Wall came down, Kohl was caught up in the occasion and the political opportunity. His promise that there should be, for example, a one-for-one conversion of East and West German marks was patently unwise and popularist.

It was not entirely understood that, once the first stone had been thrown down from the wall, talking about freedom rushing through eastern Europe was not much more than gesture politics. The economic, social, political and security consequences could not be settled with flag-waving and tooting car horns. The movement for democracy was not a phenomenon of 1989, but its public expression was.

Nor was this a protest that was confined to East Germany. Certainly by the spring of 1989 political change was happening throughout the constellation of Soviet satellites, including the Baltic republics.

When Gorbachev had come to power in March 1985, he wanted to reform the Soviet attitude to the way people were governed and their relations with western countries. The difficulty of this attitude to liberalism was that Gorbachev wanted an ordered transition from the post-Brezhnev period, which had not really been interrupted by Brezhnev's two successors, Chernenko and Andropov. That could not be. If the leashes were cut, people who had been kept to heel for so long would be uncontrollable. Moreover Gorbachev's *glasnost* and *perestroika* could not be contained within the Soviet Union.

Glasnost means 'freedom of publicity' or openness; *perestroika* means reconstruction and rebuilding. Here was the fundamental of Gorbachev's philosophy. He wanted the whole Soviet system to be restructured and for people to be free to talk about it. He wanted not only a great intellectual debate but also openness where there had previously been secrecy.

This was such a revolutionary concept that it would mean that people of the Soviet Union would not simply strike for freedoms but they would push until they had control of all the systems and the people who ran them. In other words, a Capitalist–Communist system. It could not be. Gorbachev's ultimate aim was an internationally integrated Soviet Union. He believed the most identifiable achievement would, therefore, be a rouble that was an international trading currency, which, of course, it was not under the communist system. It was, literally, not worth the paper it was written on. The most convertible currency in the whole of the Soviet Union was to remain, not the rouble, nor the kopeck, but *blat* – that is, influence. This traditional feature of Russian, then Soviet and once again Russian, life was to become the basis of the corrupt society that was to replace the already corrupt society Gorbachev was trying to change.

That change could not be confined to the Soviet Union and could not be controlled by the Kremlin. The more liberal and modernizing it became, the less it had to control. This hypothesis also applied to what the Russians called the Near Abroad, the Baltic and Warsaw Pact states surrounding it.

When Moscow began to loosen its grip on the leash that Brezhnev had tightened,[4] the Near Abroad was next. The people who had wanted greater freedoms saw the signs and the opportunity for them. Those who had ruled on in Brezhnevian style felt their patronage slipping away from them.

In the three Baltic republics – Estonia, Latvia and Lithuania – there was a vociferous movement for independence. Armenians, Georgians, Azerbaijanis and Abkhazians were fighting each other and taking no notice of any central authority; they were guided only by an instinct to settle old scores. There were similar disturbances in Moldova and in the Asian republic of Uzbekistan. The western floodlight was played over the Warsaw Pact states, for it was in countries such as Poland, Czechoslovakia, Hungary and, especially, East Germany where the break-up of the empire created by Stalin and maintained by Khrushchev (especially in Hungary in 1956) and Brezhnev (especially in Czechoslovakia in 1968), that the collapse of communism would come.

In January there was already a movement among some, but not all, Kremlin reformers to look beyond the party for reforming ideas. For others, the changes would take place too quickly.

The one reversed policy that had overwhelming support, especially among the young and their mothers, was the withdrawal from Afghanistan. By February 1989 the exodus was complete. For ten years Soviet forces had attempted to control Afghanistan and had failed. In that period 16,000 Soviet troops had been killed and twice that number had been wounded. History suggested that no foreign power would bring to heel the disparate tribesmen of that region; the Russians were no different from any others who had tried to prove wrong this strategic hypothesis.

Gorbachev and his Chiefs of Staff may not have entirely understood that it would not be long before their troops would be withdrawing from other states, and that the decision to do so would be forced upon them.

On 15 March 1989, exactly a month after the final withdrawal from Afghanistan, demonstrators took to the streets of Budapest and demanded that Soviet troops should leave Hungary. Two months later, the Hungarian communist

4 The Brezhnev Doctrine, see page 328.

leader, János Kádár, was stripped of his power. In June 1989 Solidarity won the Polish elections, and in August 1989 Poland elected a non-communist prime minister – the first Warsaw Pact state to do so. In September the Hungarian-Austrian border was opened, and in October the Hungarians announced that the state would become a republic. In that same month the East Germans had taken to the streets. Erich Honecker, the East German leader, was overthrown on 18 October. In November millions made their protests without fear of police retaliation. On 10 November 1989, in a seemingly spontaneous action, people climbed onto the Berlin Wall and started to hack it down. In December the Czechoslovaks also threw aside the communist leadership. Next came the Romanians and the ghastly executions of Nicolae Ceauşescu and his wife.

By the end of 1989 eastern Europe was, more or less, beyond the control of Moscow. The whole way of life of that part of the continent of Europe had been governed by repression for four decades. In four months the grip of communism had been shaken off.

But in one nation, the grip of that same political philosophy was not in the remotest sense relaxed. This was the year of Tiananmen Square in Beijing. The student protest began twenty years earlier with newspaper wall posters; then there had been the 1987 demonstrations in Beijing; now came the biggest and, sadly, the bloodiest of them all.

The signs that this was to be the summer in which the student-led groups brought their campaign to the attention of the whole world began not in June, but in May 1989. In that month, the communist leader who had started the greatest reform of all, Mikhail Gorbachev, visited Beijing. This visit was more than a routine state occasion, for China and the Soviet Union had been estranged for three decades. There was even a strongly held US State Department hypothesis that should a future nuclear war break out it would not be between NATO and the Warsaw Pact countries but between China and the Soviet Union.

On Tuesday, 16 May, in the Great Hall of the People, Gorbachev shook hands with Deng Xiaoping. This was a demonstration of what, seemingly against all prediction, was possible. Outside, there began a demonstration of what would prove impossible. An estimated 500,000 demonstrators took to Tiananmen Square, and 3000 students went on hunger strike to support, they hoped, the demands for change, including freedom for the media. For the moment, the authorities did nothing.

Gorbachev returned to Moscow for his next date with democracy, his election as president of the Soviet Union. On 20 May martial law was imposed in Beijing. The demonstrations continued. By the end of the first week in June, the protests had reached a point where many in government could see anarchy where outsiders might see democratic protest. This was no silent, flower-powered affair. Buses were set alight across the capital of China, and barricades were erected across thoroughfares.

The Chinese government saw the students as counter-revolutionaries and reinforced its authority with troops and tanks. Hundreds of demonstrators died. Thousands were wounded.

The lasting global memory of Tiananmen Square that June is of a single student standing before an advancing line of tanks.

Events in the Soviet Union and in eastern Europe served only to strengthen the Chinese leadership's resolve that any changes that might come in China would take place within the existing structure. Only then would change be orderly and not revolutionary. It was a sentiment that Gorbachev, at least, would have understood.

For the British government the events in Tiananmen Square required analysis for a more immediate consideration. Britain and China had agreed a means of handing over Hong Kong to China in 1997. Deng Xiaoping had offered the notion of 'one country, two systems', whereby Hong Kong would be allowed to continue its capitalist system even though it would be firmly governed from Beijing. Deng's proposal was based on that which the Chinese had sought to support their claim on Taiwan, nine years earlier. But in Hong Kong as well as in London people wondered if the events in Beijing that summer would mean that the meagre democracy in the crown colony would be replaced by an altogether more authoritarian regime if protests would be treated as violently as those of the pro-democracy groups in the Chinese capital. By the end of the century, any fears of the Hong Kong population had been shown to be unfounded. But in June 1989, they were not to know that.

Deaths

A.J. Ayer (philosopher)
Lucille Ball (US actress)
Samuel Beckett (Irish writer)
Irving Berlin (US composer)
Salvador Dali (Spanish artist)
Daphne du Maurier (writer)
Andrei Gromyko (Soviet politician)
Hirohito (Japanese emperor)
János Kádár (Hungarian politician)
Herbert von Karajan (Austrian conductor)
Ayatollah Khomeini (Iranian religious leader)
Ferdinand Marcos (Filipino politician)
Laurence Olivier, Baron Olivier of Brighton (actor)
Sugar Ray Robinson (US boxer)
Sir Peter Scott (artist and ornithologist)
Georges Simenon (French writer)
Sir Thomas Sopwith (aircraft designer)
Feliks Topolski (artist)

CHAPTER TEN

THE END OF PARTY POLITICS 1990–1999

1990

WHATEVER ELSE is written of 1990, for the British at least it will be recorded that on Wednesday, 28 November Margaret Thatcher resigned, forced from office not by the electorate but by the Conservative Party. The political friends she had once had were gone, either having left the office from where they might have protected her or having had enough of her vision of Britain. Her kitchen cabinet had no real power, and the Cabinet proper had had enough. Her managers of the backbenches could no longer keep her troops in line because they were no longer her troops.

Thatcher was brought down through her conviction that hers was the only way, but the issue that became the catalyst for her going was Britain's relations with the rest of Europe. Many of her most senior colleagues had a vision of Europe and of Britain's part in that Europe. That may be too simple a concept in what continued to be a complex argument, but there would have been some sense in it to a parliamentary observer in 1990.

As we have noted, Thatcher's withdrawal into an inner Cabinet might be dated from the Westland affair of 1986, but she never had total confidence in all the ministers available to her. It was she who divided ministers into people who agreed with her tough, direct approach and the others, whom she called 'wets'. She gradually got rid of the wets, especially in the late 1980s, when government departments were becoming more media conscious. When departmental reckonings also have long-term effects on a nation it is even more essential that the prime minister and the heads of those departments think as one. The battle that arose between Nigel Lawson, the Chancellor, and Geoffrey Howe, the Foreign Secretary, on one side and Margaret Thatcher on the other over the role of Britain in Europe was just the most damaging of many.

It is, perhaps, worth underlining the distinction between being prime minister and running a department of state, which is sometimes forgotten. In some ways it is easier to be prime minister. True, there are many days when two or three hours' sleep are all that is possible. There is the enormous responsibility, especially when decisions that will affect the future of the nation for decades to come must be taken. This may be a strategic military decision. The original decision to build

Britain's independent nuclear weapons is an example – the long-term implications are based on intricate arguments but the original decision is not. Even Thatcher's Cabinet, although not necessarily the prime minister herself, accepted at the highest level that whereas the original decision to have nuclear warheads was correct that same decision would not have been taken in the 1980s. In a department of state, on the other hand, a minister has a harder time from day to day than the leader of the government, inasmuch as it is necessary to become expert in a department's subject, to fight the department's case in Cabinet, to compete with other departments for Treasury funding and to defend the department in public.

Thatcher had always battled with her Cabinet. When she came to power in 1979 many of those in the government front-bench team were not especially good at their jobs; many were in awe of Britain's first woman prime minister; and there were few she could trust because of their temperament and competence. William Whitelaw was one who enjoyed her confidence, and Lord Carrington, who had served in every government since Churchill, was another. She was to get rid of her shaky ministers, but even then she was rarely satisfied, especially if, as Heseltine did, they publicly opposed her. Indeed, it was after Heseltine's resignation over the Westland affair that Thatcher seemed to withdraw into an even deeper shell, believing herself to be surrounded by fools.

That she would battle against Howe and Lawson over Europe was inevitable, but she should never have underestimated Lawson's determination to resign on a matter of principle, and she should never have underestimated Howe's memory. On 24 July 1989 she took the Foreign Office away from Howe and gave it to John Major. He was in the job for only a short time when Nigel Lawson resigned in October 1989. Thatcher needed a new Chancellor quickly, and as she looked at the talent about her it was clear she had few choices. She gave the job to John Major. Within ten years of becoming an MP, Major had risen, quite remarkably, to become Chief Secretary to the Treasury, then Foreign Secretary and then Chancellor of the Exchequer. These were the were perfect credentials for No. 10.

From the moment of Lawson's resignation on 26 October 1989 it was inevitable that Thatcher's authority would be tested, and 1990 was to be an enormously eventful year by any standards. For those who believed in such things, the omens of January's weather were forbidding. There were hurricane-force winds and severe flooding, with rivers reaching their highest levels in two decades. The pounding waves across Britain in January and February could do nothing to dampen the televised pleasure that the whole world experienced when Nelson Mandela was released from prison on 11 February.

The cheerful mood did not last long in Britain, where there seemed hardly anything that Mrs Thatcher's administration could do to please an electorate that, according to the opinion polls, was swinging strongly against it.

To replace the household rates, the government had introduced a poll tax which, according to public opinion polls, was opposed by three-quarters of the country, who thought it unfair. Those same opinion polls were beginning to show that the Labour Party was increasingly more popular than Thatcher's government, and grass-roots Conservatives could not believe that Thatcher could be insensitive to their protests. Some councillors even refused to implement the poll tax and resigned the Tory whip.

At the beginning of March 1990, when the poll tax rates were set by local authorities, demonstrations were held throughout the country, and the police were called into town halls as far apart as London and the Home Counties in the south, Newcastle in the north and Bristol and Plymouth in the west. Effigies of Margaret Thatcher were being burned outside council offices. It is likely that these demonstrations were instigated by extremists, but they nevertheless represented the opinions of an enormous swathe of Conservative as well as Labour voters. In Edinburgh the Lord Provost refused to pay the poll tax, and his bank account was frozen. So much anger was expressed in the House of Commons that the sitting was adjourned because of 'grave disorder', the first time this had happened for thirty years.

In March John Major produced his first Budget. It was generally accepted as a neutral budget – that is, it kept the economy along the same lines – but the electorate was unimpressed, and opinion polls showed Labour with a record twenty-seven point lead. When the safe Tory seat of mid-Staffordshire came up in a by-election, it went to Labour on a 21 per cent swing.

At the end of March mounted police, with riot shields and truncheons, confronted thousands of anti-poll tax demonstrators in the centre of London. Buildings were set on fire, as were cars and work sites. In April the government had to issue decrees on twenty local councils that refused to implement the poll tax. In May came the local government elections. As expected the government took a battering.

By May it seemed almost impossible for the Thatcher government to find good news on any front. Inflation was almost the highest in ten years; industrial difficulties were being announced every day; and unemployment figures were going up for the first time in four years. As the first McDonald's opened in Moscow, the Secretary of State for Agriculture, John Selwyn Gummer, felt the need to buy a beefburger for himself and his daughter, Cordelia. The bovine spongiform encephalopathy (BSE) debate was now beginning in earnest. The latest warning was that BSE could be passed on to humans. 'Not so,' said Gummer. On 30 May France joined Austria, West Germany and the Soviet Union in banning beef imports from Britain. The export of live cattle from Britain to the European Community was already banned.

Then came sad news for the prime minister. The IRA assassinated the Conservative MP Ian Gow, who had resigned from the government over the Anglo-Irish Agreement[1] and had been on the IRA hit-list for some time.

---

1 See page 401.

At the beginning of August attention moved away from Britain's domestic difficulties to the international table. On 2 August 1990 Iraqi forces entered Kuwait. Earlier in the year Thatcher had cited unrest in the Middle East as one reason for Britain keeping its nuclear weapons, and she approved the sending of British troops to the Gulf in support of what was a largely American build-up.

By October Europe was taking little notice of the Middle East because, contrary to all political and strategic sensibilities, German unification was confirmed on 3 October. It was also in October that the last chapter in Mrs Thatcher's premiership was played out. The month had started with a political surprise from Downing Street. Britain, in what appeared to be an overtly political move, applied to join the Exchange Rate Mechanism (ERM). If it was not a political tactic, the timing of the announcement was certainly opportune, coming as it did at the end of not the Conservative, but the Labour Party conference. The Chancellor added to the cheering in the City of London by cutting interest rates by 1 per cent.

Mrs Thatcher went to Bournemouth for her party conference, knowing that the government was being accused of political opportunism and that her Chancellor was being forced to juggle the economy as a pre-election gambit. The announcement of the application to join the ERM was applauded, but by the time the conference got under way there was little sign that it had much effect on the party's rank and file. The battle lines were drawn on where Britain should go next in Europe. Michael Heseltine was already leading the advance for the pro-European lobby. Howe, nominally the deputy prime minister, was encouraging the government to take part in European talks towards a single currency, which was in direct opposition to the prime minister.

Thatcher went to Rome to attend a meeting of the European heads of government, still demanding that everyone should agree that a single European currency would mean a loss of sovereignty. Her objections were ignored, and the conference agreed that a European Central Bank to control the monetary policies of all member states should be established within four years.

In spite of the memoirs written by those who were ministers at the time, including the prime minister herself, there is still confusion about why, and if, the policy changed. For example, one of the original ideas had been the so-called hard ecu. This was simply an idea to mint the ecu and allow it to circulate along with other currencies rather than forcing nations to abandon their own coins and notes. This was very much a John Major initiative. When the prime minister returned from Rome she said in the Commons that the government would be ready to move towards the 'creation of a European Monetary Fund and a Common Community Currency'. At first glance, this appeared that Thatcher was now running with the pro-Europeans, Howe, Heseltine and Lawson. The confusion came at that point because having appeared to support the hard ecu, she said that she did not believe that it would happen, and she stated quite baldly that she believed that the Commission was striving to 'extinguish democracy' and force Britain, indeed the whole of Europe, into the 'back door of federalism'.

It was clear to Geoffrey Howe that nothing had changed, and he now had no option but to resign. In his letter of resignation he said that the risks of being left behind on economic and monetary union were severe. He emphasized that much time and energy had been spent during the past decade simply catching up because of Britain's reluctance to get into Europe when the whole process had begun. He accused the prime minister of setting a mood that would make it virtually impossible for Britain to have any authority in the structure of the European Community. So he went. This was bad enough. Thatcher's team said that Howe did not disagree with policy – it was a question of style and emphasis. No one believed her spokesmen. It meant also that the pro-Europeans were about to go for the jugular. There was worse to come for the prime minister.

When ministers resign they are allowed to make a valedictory speech to the House of Commons on the reasons for the resignation. That speech is traditionally heard in silence. Normally, once it is done, the House, government and Speaker get on with political life. This was not to be the case with Geoffrey Howe – a man who was once described as being so mild-mannered that an attack from him was like being savaged by a dead sheep. In his speech, made on 13 November, he began by refuting the argument that he had resigned over style rather than substance:

> It has been suggested . . . that I decided to resign solely because of questions of style and not on matters of substance at all. Indeed, if some of my former colleagues are to be believed, I must be the first minister in history who has resigned because he was in full agreement with government policy. . . . The prime minister and I have shared something like 700 meetings of Cabinet or shadow Cabinet during the past eighteen years, and some 400 hours alongside each other, at more than thirty international summit meetings. For both of us, I suspect, it is a pretty daunting record. The House might well feel that something more than simple matters of style would be necessary to rupture such a well-tried relationship.

What was that difference or what were those differences? Howe's concluding remarks acted as a maroon to set off a flotilla of backbenchers as well as senior figures on the course that would remove Thatcher from office within weeks.

> The conflict of loyalty, of loyalty to my Right Hon. Friend the prime minister – and, after all, in two decades together the instinct of loyalty is still very real – and of loyalty to what I perceive to be the true interests of the nation, has become all too great. I no longer believe it possible to resolve that conflict from within this government. That is why I have resigned. In doing so, I have done what I believe to be right for my party and my country. The time has come for others to consider their own response to the tragic conflict of loyalties with which I have myself wrestled for perhaps too long.

There had to be an election for the leadership. The man who believed that he could win was Michael Heseltine, and when he declared his candidature, opinion polls immediately pointed to an even bigger election result. It was largely accepted in the country that Michael Heseltine had more chance of leading the Conservatives to a general election victory than any other person taking part. On 20 November, when Mrs Thatcher was at a heads of government meeting in Paris of the Conference on Security and Co-operation in Europe (CSCE), the first vote was taken. She got 204 votes, Heseltine got 156 and there were sixteen abstentions. Her majority was not big enough by four votes. There were those that believed she could still win. In Paris Mrs Thatcher said she would fight on, but she did not have enough support in her Cabinet.

There was another battle taking place, too. Many Tory ministers disliked Michael Heseltine, even though he was probably the most popular Conservative among grass-roots party members. In that scathing way of old Tories, one of them dismissed him as being so nouveau riche that he had to buy his own furniture. So the race was on to stop Heseltine. Douglas Hurd and John Major were put forward as candidates. Major became prime minister at the age of forty-seven on 27 November 1990. He would not have done so if Michael Heseltine had not challenged Mrs Thatcher in the original election. Major was Mrs Thatcher's chosen successor, and perhaps her only consolation in the whole affair was the defeat (only just) of Michael Heseltine.

West Germany beat England on penalties in the semi-final of the World Cup. It was a mixed consolation that Germany went on to beat Argentina in the final.

Deaths

Leonard Bernstein (US composer and conductor)
Aaron Copland (US composer)
Roald Dahl (writer)
Lawrence Durrell (writer)
Greta Garbo (Swedish actress)
Sir Humphrey Gibbs (colonial administrator)
Sir Rex Harrison (actor)
Sir Len Hutton (cricketer)
Gordon Jackson (Scottish actor)
Rosamond Lehmann (writer)
Alberto Moravia (Italian writer)
Malcolm Muggeridge (journalist)
Lewis Mumford (sociologist)
Terence O'Neill, Baron O'Neill of the Maine (Northern Irish politician)
Norman Parkinson (photographer)
Tunku Abdul Rahman (Malaysian politician)
A.J.P. Taylor (historian)

Paul Tortelier (musician)
Dame Eva Turner (opera singer)
Max Wall (actor and comedian)
Greville Wynne (spy)

1991

THE GOVERNMENT was already thinking of the next general election, and the prime minister introduced what he called a Citizens' Charter. This was the beginning of the concept of offering people compensation against public organizations that failed to perform. How those failures were to be gauged was not exactly worked out.

The most important change in government policy was to be the removal of the poll tax. In its place, the environment secretary, Michael Heseltine, drew up plans for a seven-tier property tax.

In the meantime, Major had to get on with the most controversial area of his policy. In June he went to the Luxembourg European summit to discuss the prospects of federalism and the moves towards a single currency. Tactically, Major achieved what he went for: the federal discussion could be sidelined and the question of deeper financial and economic union could be deferred until later in the year when heads of government would once more meet in a small town in the Netherlands called Maastricht. The decisions taken at Maastricht would live with the government and Europe for the rest of the decade.

The Maastricht Treaty committed members of the European Union to closer political and economic agreement. This was the treaty that set 1999 as the date for the introduction of the single currency. The European Commission was given extra powers and in theory the rights of the European Parliament were increased.

Major made the best of that meeting. He had, for example, apparently won the right to avoid implementing the social chapter (governing working conditions), the removal of references to federal Europe and, particularly important, an agreement that Britain would not have to sign up for a single currency on 1 January 1999.

There was more than ideology behind this. Major could not expect to win a general election (now planned for 1992) if he went into it promising the abolition of the pound, a national minimum wage and his signature on a document that talked about a federal Europe. The opposition to what Major had 'won' was based on the argument that yet again Britain had not had the conviction nor the guts nor the foresight to sign up as full Europeans and could not, therefore, be expected to enforce its opinion on how future Europe should be shaped. Now there was talk of a two-tier Europe, with the United Kingdom being members of the second division.

A more spectacular memory of 1991 was Desert Storm, the Gulf War, which had its origins in August 1990, when Iraqi troops invaded Kuwait. The United Nations passed a resolution that would allow the Iraqis to be ejected from Kuwait. A coalition of forces began to arrive in the region and for five months, like some fourteenth-century display of tabards, banners and clinking horsemen, the American-led forces arranged themselves comfortably and quite unopposed. The plan was simple. First, the Iraqi air force should either be destroyed or made useless. Second, a blanket bombing campaign would destroy the military infrastructure and the Iraqi ground force capability. Then, and only then, the coalition tanks would drive (it was presumed that they would be unopposed) the depleted Iraqi forces out of Kuwait.

This is what more or less happened. Many Iraqi pilots flew their aircraft to Iran to escape the coalition air-to-air and air-to-ground missiles. The air defence radars were suppressed and in some cases destroyed, although the bombing campaign disrupted but certainly did not destroy the Iraqi ground formations. The Iraqi navy, which was, in any case, no more than a coastal defence force, was destroyed. The coalition armoured divisions, closely supported by aircraft, drove the Iraqis out of Kuwait.

The coalition had fulfilled its mission. It should be noted that nothing in the UN resolution, nor even the most extended rules of engagement, allowed the American-led force to pursue the Iraqis across the border. There was certainly no authority to attempt to kill Saddam Hussein. Those who have later wondered why the coalition forces did not 'finish the job' should remember the parameters within which those forces then operated.

Unless the consequences of the confrontation between Saddam Hussein and the White House lead to the future use of nuclear or biological weapons, the war itself was not much more than an historical footnote.

Elsewhere there was another war and one that was to have a longer term effect.

In Moscow the movement against Mikhail Gorbachev was growing. His campaign for greater freedoms, especially of speech, meant that demonstrations were acceptable, if occasionally unwelcome. Hundreds of thousands of people now demonstrated across the western part of the Soviet Union. There had been military interventions in Lithuania and Latvia and the demonstrations were, ostensibly, against the use of force.

Here was, in January 1991, the real emergence of the main political opponent to Gorbachev. He was Boris Yeltsin, the president of the Russian Federation. It was he who accused Gorbachev of setting aside all his promises of reform by relying on, or joining with, the Communist Party old guard. The changes in the USSR were, on paper, profound. On 21 December 1991 the Soviet Union was officially dissolved, and in its place came the Commonwealth of Independent States (CIS).

Yeltsin, in some ways the Chancellor Kohl of the CIS, was determined to get rid of Gorbachev and take his job. The detail did not seem to matter to Yeltsin as long as he had power. In the Foreign Office in London doubts were raised about the ability of the new organization to survive in any constructive form, and three potential difficulties were identified. First, the economic failure of the Soviet Union had simply been transferred to the CIS. Second, the control over 27,000 nuclear warheads was unclear; even then there were rumours that some of them were being sold off privately by soldiers. Third, there was a total lack of any accountable working bureaucracy to oversee, enforce and monitor the reforms all the leaders were shouting for but none was capable of introducing.

In August 1991 the biggest revolution since 1917 occurred in Moscow when the old Soviet hard-liners, led by eight members of a mythical state emergency committee, overthrew Gorbachev, who was put under house arrest – classically, he was on holiday in the Crimea when the coup occurred. The coup leaders were overthrown by Yeltsin. After all, this was not only his great opportunity but this was happening on his territory. Gorbachev returned to Moscow and ostensibly to power, but as he was speaking to the Duma he was interrupted by Yeltsin, who strode onto the podium and humiliated the president by handing him a list of the coup backers and telling him to read out the list. Yeltsin, in the style that was to become so familiar throughout the world, was exercising his crude form of politics. The immediate result was the stripping of the Communist Party of its icons. Even the statues of Lenin and Felix Dzerzhinsky, the founder of the KGB, were roped and pulled to the ground.

On Christmas Day 1991, Gorbachev, the man who had introduced *glasnost* and *perestroika* was forced to go. He, above all Russians, understood the need for reform, but he understood that that reform could not take place in a society that was dismembering itself. The independence of the republics was, he saw, an advance in democracy. The need to stick together at a time when the very reforms everyone wanted could too easily corrupt and tear apart those same republics was even more apparent to Gorbachev. To the end of his leadership, Gorbachev understood that reforms could not work if – as everyone in the western world wanted him to – he forced the break-up of the Communist Party system. It is worth repeating that his reason was simple. The Soviet Union stretched from the Baltic to the Baring Strait. There were more than 100 nationalities and languages; it had the harshest and the finest climates in the world; there were great oil, gas and coal reserves and the second biggest diamond reserves in the world. Apart from China, it was the most powerful emerging economy on the globe. Gorbachev knew that none of this mattered unless there was a structural bureaucracy that could put into operation economic and social reforms that would harness this huge empire. The communist system was the only one that existed. At that stage, attempting to replace it would lead to an even more corrupt and unworkable system than the one that existed.

In 1991 Gorbachev asked the simple question of whether people could start a revolution simply for sausages. The answer, perhaps to his surprise, was 'yes'. The need and the desire for reform was overwhelming not simply for the freedom they had promised but also the profit.

On reflection, Gorbachev understood that he could be the interim leader only.

Because his reforms were based on consensus rather than, say, the revolutionary zeal that is too often accompanied with repressions in order that it may be enforced, he had no way of imposing his ideals. In a society such as the Soviet Union, unleashed from seventy years of communism and now for the first time publicly on the make, it was inevitable that others would be impatient at the lack of progress. By 1991 Russia was coming to resemble a political and financial Chicago of the 1920s and early 1930s. Everyone, including the most senior politicians, immediately took their financial and political cut out of the reforms. The western powers were gathering around to provide the bank balances that they believed would hurry Russia into economic prosperity. Western governments would benefit from their investment because, they believed, markets would be opened up and security would be guaranteed.

What opened up were the corrupt coffers of the new mafia of the late twentieth century, and at the head of all this was a man who had great cunning but little intelligence, who drank excessively and who had the dexterity of an ageing circus clown. Yeltsin was, nevertheless, fêted by western governments.

The new face of Russia was seen as a hero in a suit astride a tank. The lasting international vision of 1991 was not Saddam Hussein or General Schwarzkopf but Boris Yeltsin.

Deaths

John Arlott (journalist and broadcaster)
Dame Peggy Ashcroft (actress)
Frank Capra (US film director)
Miles Davis (US jazz trumpeter)
Dame Margot Fonteyn (ballerina)
Rajiv Gandhi (Indian politician)
Martha Graham (US choreographer)
Graham Greene (writer)
Gustáv Husák (Czechoslovakian politician)
Wilfred Hyde-White (actor)
Eileen Joyce (Australian pianist)
David Lean (film director)
Robert Maxwell (publisher)
Bernard Miles, Baron Miles (actor and director)
Yves Montand (French actor)
Seán O'Faoláin (Irish writer)
Lee Remick (US actress)
Sir Roy Welensky (Rhodesian politician)
Sir Angus Wilson (writer)

1992

IN 1992 the American Census Office estimated that 5.4 billion people lived on the globe. These human auditors projected that by the end of the first quarter of the twenty-first century that figure would have reached at least 8 billion. In 1992 behavioural scientists began talking about old people: we were all beginning to live longer, they said.

The population in Britain was now more than 56 million, of whom more than 51 million lived in England and Wales and more than 5 million in Scotland. There were about the same number in Ireland.

The population of England and Wales had shown an increase of no more than 0.02 per cent – in 1982 it was not much more than 49 million. In fact, the population annual growth in percentage terms in England and Wales was indicating a decline over the previous fifty years, certainly over the century. In 1892 there were almost 30 million living in England and Wales. The percentage increase at the turn of the century was about 1.2 per cent. With a few variations, the birth rate began to decline. The reasons had a great deal to do with social trends and the availability of contraception. The biggest rate of decrease had come in the previous thirty years. In 1962 the birth rate was about 0.5 per cent, but within ten years that had halved, and within a further ten years it was almost negligible.

In Scotland the population had been about 5 million since the First World War.

What had increased were the crime statistics. In 1992 in England, Wales and Scotland there were somewhere in the region of 6 million crimes known to the police. Ten years earlier there had been only half that number. It is not surprising that law and order, social reforms and Europe were the main subject in the party manifestos when the country went to the polls in 1992.

The omens were not good for Conservative Party managers. Unemployment had been steadily rising, and by the end of 1991 there were some 2.3 million out of work. It was predicted that as many as 400,000 could be added to that figure by the end of the year. These were not just poor monthly figures, which always looked worse in the winter because of seasonal short-time working in, for example, the building trades.

The December 1991 unemployment figure was more than 2.5 million; by the end of January 1992 it was 2.6 million. The Confederation of British Industry (CBI) estimated that a further 73,000 would be out of work by spring. The privatization of the nationalized industries meant job losses. For example, the Central Electricity Generating Board employed 17,000 people; it was privatized and renamed National Power. The restructuring meant that one-third of the workforce expected to lose their jobs.

Every time a batch of statistics was issued, they seemed to reflect badly on the government or at least its inability to overcome problems that no other government had overcome anyway. For example, in January car dealers reported a 300 per cent increase since 1991 in the number of stolen cars being offered for sale. The police were not at all surprised by the figure, since it simply reflected the huge increase in drug-related crime. Cars were easy targets. Some one million thefts and break-ins of vehicles took place in the year.

In the same month a report showed that in spite of the government tax concessions, Britain was at the bottom of the European league for child care. The obvious difference was that more European companies provided day nurseries than did British firms.

This was nothing compared with the deeper financial problems that faced Britain. By February 1992 the government's own figures showed that the country was now in its longest-running recession since the Second World War. Job security was not encouraged with predictions that matters would get worse before they got better. Car workers at the Rover factory at Longbridge, now owned by Honda, were having to accept the Japanese work practices that had already given some security to the Nissan employees at their plant in Washington in northeast England.

Even with a certain amount of massaging, there was no financial forecasting that could encourage the electorate to think that, in Macmillan's words, they'd never had it so good. Major had few options about the timing of the election because constitutionally he had to have an election before May. He went almost to the end of his official term. The election was held on 9 April.

John Smith, Neil Kinnock's shadow Chancellor, had the novel idea of publishing the outline of a budget that he would introduce should Labour win the election. There was nothing in it to overcome the general impression of traditional Conservative voters that there was little to be gained financially from voting Labour, and the Conservatives won a fourth election victory in a row, although with a reduced majority; the Conservatives had 336 seats, the Labour Party 271 seats and the Liberal Democrats 20 seats. John Major was now prime minister in his own right. The major change in Britain's political life was the resignation of Neil Kinnock as Labour's leader following the general election defeat. He was replaced by John Smith.

The re-election of the Conservatives had gone against many of the predictions voiced before the election. Most of the opinion polls had suggested that what was the nearest thing that Britain had thus far seen to an American brash style of election did not do Mr Kinnock's Labour Party much good. Kinnock himself believed, maybe for as long as a week before the election, that he would not win.

It was in this year that the Howe-Lawson-Thatcher battle over the European Exchange Rate Mechanism (ERM) returned to haunt the Conservatives. But the débâcle that was heading Britain's way that autumn was to turn the British economy in the government's, and therefore the country's, favour.

Britain had joined the ERM after the confrontation between Margaret Thatcher and her Chancellor Nigel Lawson and Foreign Secretary Geoffrey Howe. The man who made that possible was John Major, not when he became prime minister but when he replaced Nigel Lawson as Chancellor. In October 1990 he had surprised almost everyone in politics and in business by applying for membership of ERM. One of the reasons given for joining was that Britain's inflation rate had now come down to an acceptable level and therefore interest rates could be lowered. Indeed, on 5 October 1990 there had been a 1 per cent cut. Nigel Lawson's argument – that by controlling rates Britain could shadow the Deutschmark – was now, in retrospect, justified and so Britain joined the ERM with the pound worth a nominal 2.95 Deutschmarks. Even here, John Major had gained a concession for Britain. He got the European Community to agree that although Britain's aim would be to maintain the pound at 2.95 Deutschmarks, the UK would be allowed to fluctuate by 6 per cent either side of the rate. This was a larger fluctuation than anyone else in the ERM was allowed.

In September 1992, with John Major now prime minister and Norman Lamont as his Chancellor, all the original reservations expressed by Margaret Thatcher seemed justified. Britain had gone into the ERM at a rate that was so high against the Deutschmark that the 6 per cent fluctuation was never going to be realistic. Worse still, no currency could counter the predatory instincts of the international currency speculators and the selfish instincts of European chancelleries, even when they contradicted public expressions of unity. In simple economic terms, a group of currencies attempting to act together can succeed only if the strongest currency supports the others, and that can happen only if the government of that currency tailors its economic policies to do so. But what happens if that leading currency faces its own problems? Britain's attitude in the autumn of 1992 was that for all its promises of unity, the German economic crisis meant that the government in Bonn would look after its own and that the rest would have to make their own arrangements and ride the storm.

The pound began to fall, and speculators started to buy and sell. They were making billions of dollars while the British government, and therefore the tax payer, was losing billions of pounds. On 16 September Britain pulled out of the ERM and allowed sterling to float – that is, to let the world markets decide its value rather than attempt to maintain it artificially within the ERM. This day became known as Black Wednesday, but it was probably the best thing that could have happened to Britain's economy. This single event was the basis for an economic recovery that would set the economic agenda for the rest of Major's administration and would even benefit the Labour government when it took over four and a half years later.

That date was a long time coming in political terms because the result of the 1992 election demonstrated to the Labour leadership that the party simply had not done enough to rid itself of the image that had grown in the 1970s. In the inner sanctum of Labour's new thinking there was a realization that the days of being able to get elected on honourable socialist principles were long gone. In many respects, the election of 1992 marked the end of party political government in Britain. The electorate had been brought up on the idea that if one party thought one thing, another party would think quite differently on the same subject. This was no longer true, and Tony Blair was to prove this just five years later when he showed that it was possible for a Labour government to make itself electable by adopting Tory policies.

In the United States the Republican president, George Bush, was unsuccessful in his attempt at re-election. The Democrat, Bill Clinton, won 43 per cent of the popular vote and so became the forty-second president of the USA. There was for the first time an apparently credible third candidate, Ross Perot, who ran as an independent and who picked up 19 per cent of the vote. This was the most any third party candidate had ever won.

In Russia Yeltsin, by now president, was beginning what he thought was going to be a restructuring of Russia's social, economic and political system. His predecessor, Mikhail Gorbachev, was now exiled to a new institute for the study of foreign affairs.

If this was going to be a year of fresh starts for some people, it was also a year of new endings. All was not well in the royal family, where Elizabeth II was celebrating the fortieth year of her reign. The good news was that the Princess Royal, Princess Anne, married Commander Timothy Laurence, sometime royal equerry. The bad news was that the Duke and Duchess of York and the Prince and Princess of Wales announced their separations.

Certainly the separation of the Waleses came with some of the most bitter public relations spinning seen by members of the royal family. It was little wonder that when the Queen spoke at a Guildhall reception for her anniversary, she remarked that 1992 had been an 'annus horribilis'. It was not a year, as the Queen said, 'on which I shall look back with undiluted pleasure'.

At least the Queen did not have to live in the Balkans. It was in 1992 that NATO strategists began to warn that the political attitude of the European Union to the Balkans could too easily lead to disaster. For much grander reasoning than strategic forecasting, most European community governments took no notice.

Chancellor Kohl of Germany led the way into one of the more ill-thought-through international decisions of the decade, and no other European country had the power nor the political courage to stop him. This was all about the future of Yugoslavia, a multi-ethnic state of Bosnia, Croatia, Macedonia, Montenegro, Serbia and Slovenia. After the Second World War and until 1980 Yugoslavia had been held together by Josip Broz, or Marshal Tito as he chose to be called. During the final years of his life, although he was president, he had set up a system of rotating leadership. Yugoslavia was governed from Belgrade, but as the Serb hold over the country slipped, the provinces of Croatia and Slovenia demanded independence from Belgrade.

In eastern Croatia were large pockets of Serbs. The Serbs refused to join the new state of Croatia. Next to Croatia and Serbia is Bosnia. Bosnia consists of Croatians, Muslims and Serbians. The Muslims and Croatians, in 1992, decided that Bosnia should be independent. The Serbs, in Bosnia, refused to go along with this and began to bombard the capital of Bosnia, Sarajevo.

Every sense of political and military thinking should have suggested to the western nations that they should have no part in the battle for independence within Yugoslavia. Moreover, even the sleepiest geo-political ally understood that other states would want independence, and that Serbia would battle hard to prevent any breakaway from the government in Belgrade. The battle for independence within Yugoslavia had started in Kosovo. To understand the part of Kosovo in the modern Balkan drama one might even return to the Battle of Kosovo in 1389, which is when this small province first became central to the Balkan story.

In this century Kosovo had been overrun by Serbian and Montenegrin troops in 1912. During the Second World War it had been part of Italian-occupied Albania, but in 1945 Kosovo was annexed by Serbia. It had claimed autonomy and now wanted independence. It has been rightly claimed that Kosovo and its peoples represent centuries of belief in the Balkans that each group of peoples wish themselves to be totally independent of other groups but that each group at the same time wished to control all other groups.

In January 1992 the European Community states bowed to Germany's insistence that Croatia and Slovenia should be recognized as independent states. Once independent, those states could call on outside help, including that of the United Nations and particularly the European Community, to help maintain that independence from what would be the inevitable response of Serbia. In 1992 the European Union was forced into attempting to hold the ring in what now became known as 'the former Yugoslavia'.

The Europeans appointed the former British Foreign Secretary David Owen, who received a life peerage in 1992, as the European negotiator, and he and his American counterpart, the former US Secretary of State, Cyrus Vance, were charged with the task of bringing about a template for peaceful co-existence. The Vance–Owen combination got under way in the autumn of 1992 and continued until mid-1995. It failed.

The United Nations had already sent a protection force to the region, and by mid-September 1992 extra troops were being asked for and sent in. In October no-fly zones were established over Bosnia-Herzegovina. The shuttle diplomacy had no immediate effects, although both Owen and Vance soon learned to accept that many of the policy outlines they proposed would be as vigorously opposed in western Europe, the United Nations and, particularly, Washington as they would in Belgrade. In December 1992 the United Nations had to supply more troops. By now a UN protection force (UNPROFOR) was needed in Macedonia.

It was by that autumn that the fighting had become so intense and the diplomatic effort so disparate that contributors to the UN forces could see that they would be bogged down in the Balkans for years to come. The problem facing people like David Owen was that too many outside interests – again the European Community, NATO, the United Nations and the United States – could not agree on a common policy and, therefore, a common objective, and nor would they agree on how far they were willing to go to achieve some settlement, enforced or otherwise.

The Vance–Owen peace plan, which was put forward in October 1992, was a three-part agreement that envisaged ten provinces, based on ethnic lines. It gave a definition to Bosnia and Herzegovina as a decentralized region with, importantly, freedom of movement. There would be a high degree of autonomy for the provinces although that autonomy would not have international legal standing. There would be national local elections. In addition, Vance and Owen had drawn up a military schedule for a truce, a withdrawal of heavy weapons within a fortnight, the eventual demilitarization of the country and, so that everyone could see who owned what and where they lived, there would be a new map drawn of Bosnia-Herzegovina with the ten provinces defined. In addition, there would be an international human rights monitoring system. The plan even went so far as to outline the restoration of national services, such as banking, civil aviation, power supplies and telecommunications. Important to the presentation of that plan, Vance and Owen had deliberately not given any of the provinces ethnic labels.

Initially the Bosnian Croats had accepted the plan, and Radovan Karadžić said that the Bosnian Serbs saw the map as a basis for future negotiations but would not accept the plan. In the end, it was rejected by a referendum among the Serbs in April 1993.

By the beginning of December 1992 the UN had to abandon its relief operation in Sarajevo because the fighting was too fierce for them to carry on. The extent of the atrocities was already clear. At a Geneva conference on the war in Bosnia-Herzegovina the Americans posted the names of five Serbs and two Croats who should be listed as war criminals. They included the Serbian leader, Slobodan Milošević, the Bosnian Serb leader, Rodaban Karadžić, and his military commander, Ratko Mladic. Milošević could not care less. He was holding elections and he had, by one means or another, beaten western Europe's preferred candidate, Milan Panic.

With some desperation, the outgoing US president, George Bush, and John Major issued a joint statement declaring that any Serbian aircraft that flew into a Bosnian no-fly zone would be shot down. This indeed was fighting talk especially for those working on the ground. They would become the natural targets in retaliation to this Anglo-American initiative. As if to emphasize the setbacks for the western effort in the former Yugoslavia, Milan Panic, who had lost the presidential race, was now unseated as prime minister.

There may have been cries of fraud and cabal but the truth was as ever in Bosnia: might is the only right to rule.

Deaths
Isaac Asimov (US writer)
Menachem Begin (Israeli politician)

Willy Brandt (German politician)
Leonard Cheshire (pilot)
Elizabeth David (cookery writer)
Monica Dickens (writer)
Alexander Dubček (Czechoslovak politician)
Denholm Elliott (actor)
Stanley Holloway (entertainer)
W.G. Hoskins (historian)
Frankie Howerd (comedian)
Robert Morley (actor)
Anthony Perkins (US actor)

1993

IN MARCH Chancellor Lamont was preparing the Budget that he said would take advantage of the changed economic conditions following Britain's withdrawal from the ERM. Certainly, there was no instant success. As the Chancellor went to the Commons to announce his Budget, more than 3 million people were unemployed. His message was bullish, but might easily have been construed as 'no jam today and no jam tomorrow'. For the first time VAT was to be levied on domestic fuel, including electricity and gas.

By April Lamont was able to announce cheerfully that the recession, probably the worst since the 1930s, was being overcome. Exports were now increasing because of the pound's withdrawal from the ERM and its lower value against the dollar, the Deutschmark and the yen. Inflation was now down to 1.3 per cent, the lowest for almost thirty years, and just to show that everyone was doing their bit, the new governor of the Bank of England, Eddie George, announced that he would not rub along on his 1993 pay scale for the next five years.

If things were looking better for the government in business sections of the newspapers, they were not looking up on the political pages. This was really the beginning of John Major's public battle over Europe. There had already been, as we have seen, major confrontations with Euro-sceptics and between senior ministers and the previous prime minister. It was, however, from this point that the ratification process of the Maastricht Treaty and the prime minister's confrontation with elements within his own party over his policy towards Europe never left the headlines.

After a year's debate in the House of Commons, the Maastricht Treaty bill got its final reading. There had been 200 hours of debate. At the end of it forty-one Conservative MPs voted against their government. They were quite safe in doing so because they knew that the Labour Party, which was equally though not so publicly divided on many points, would abstain when it came to a vote. The Labour Party in 1993 would not, therefore, have to commit themselves publicly to the European process other than through the usual platitude of being at the centre of Europe.

In May the prime minister turned his attention to a matter that could not have been dealt with while his government was pushing through the Maastricht bill. He sacked Norman Lamont and appointed Kenneth Clarke as Chancellor of the Exchequer. Lamont, who had to take an enormous amount of criticism over the handling of the ERM withdrawal and who had, he believed, stood by his prime minister, did not take his sacking gracefully. His resignation speech in the Commons revealed his bitterness when he spoke of a government without power. Lamont, who had been campaign manager for John Major's successful bid to become prime minister, now appeared as a sad and isolated figure in a not very sympathetic House of Commons.

In July Major and his new Chancellor went off to the Group of Seven (G7) meeting in Tokyo. These meetings of the heads of government of the United States, Japan, Germany, France, Italy, Canada and the United Kingdom, originally the seven wealthiest nations, had been held each year since 1975. In 1993 the only person to get anything out of that meeting was someone who was not even a member of the G7, President Yeltsin of Russian. The G7 members left Tokyo with no clear ideas how to bring about world economic recovery. Russia was promised $3 billion in aid. No one seems to have had a clear idea of how that aid would be controlled or where it would go once it arrived in Russia. There were, however, those in the nether regions of Russia's bureaucracy and society who had a very clear idea of where the aid would go. Like most offers of help this one was gratefully received in personal bank accounts.

In August John Major got what he had long needed: an apparent vindication of Britain's exit from the ERM eleven months earlier. The failure at Tokyo and in bilateral negotiations among the world economic leaders had meant that nothing had been done to save the European Monetary System.

At the end of July and beginning of August the rest of Europe accepted that instead of the tight control over exchange rates, there would now have to be a 15 per cent variation on either side of a central point (Britain had wanted a 6 per cent variation, but even that had not worked). By allowing such a huge margin of variation, the other European governments had effectively done what Britain had done, but collectively: they had suspended membership of the ERM. Once again the activities of speculators in buying and selling the weak currencies, including the French franc, had caused a run on the money markets and national exchequers.

Perhaps a certain amount of irony was felt in Brussels as the European Commission met to consider yet another financial crisis of what was supposed to be the stable factor in Europeanism.

On the same day, 2 August 1993, Britain formally ratified the Maastricht Treaty, more than a year and a half after signing it.

In 1993 the British government was forced to admit that it had been having secret talks with Sinn Fein, the political wing of the terrorist organization, the IRA. The disclosure came after the prime minister had publicly denied that such talks had taken place and had even gone as far as to tell the Commons that to negotiate with terrorists would make his 'guts ache'.

Why had the talks taken place? The painful answer is that the IRA had bombed its way to the conference table. The story did not begin in 1993, of course. The momentum might have been semtex fuses, but in order to understand how those talks came about we should remind ourselves of the political attempts to reach a common solution to the events in Ulster.

The previous decade in Northern Ireland had been a period of frustrated initiatives and increased terrorist actions. In 1982, for example, the Secretary of State, James Prior, had introduced a Northern Ireland Assembly Bill, under which the assembly would resume legislative powers within the Province. Elections were held for a new assembly and 59 per cent of the votes went, not surprisingly, to the Unionists. Most of the other votes went to the largely Roman Catholic supported Social Democratic Labour Party (SDLP) and the political wing of the IRA, Sinn Fein. These two parties boycotted the assembly.

In the spring of 1983 a body called the New Ireland Forum was established in Dublin, largely at the urging of the leader of the SDLP, John Hume. The idea of the Forum was that it should come up with a consensus for unity between the North and the South – including the concept of the return of the six counties – and the following year, 1984, it publicly set itself against terrorism. The Forum was viewed with suspicion, however, because it suggested what was called a unitary state through consent and the preservation of both 'unionist and nationalist identities'. Meanwhile, the Northern Ireland assembly was trying to resolve ways of giving itself more powers and effectively devolving power from London to Belfast. Prior, who did not always see eye to eye with Margaret Thatcher, spent much time promoting discussions between all the Northern Ireland Parties and the Dublin and London governments. In September 1984 the prime minister shuffled the Cabinet and Douglas Hurd became the new Northern Ireland secretary. This was the autumn that the IRA bombed the Grand Hotel in Brighton.

Mrs Thatcher and the Taoiseach, Dr Garrett Fitzgerald, met in November for what was their second discussion at the Anglo-Irish inter-governmental council, a body that sounded more important than it was. The joint statement issued after the meeting spoke of support for the rights of both communities in the North and their joint opposition to violence. This was reasonably predictable diplomatic-speak and suggested that there was nothing new to say. Indeed, as we have seen earlier, Mrs Thatcher thought little of Dr Fitzgerald's approach and perception of the issues affecting both countries.[2]

Nevertheless, in 1985 the two met again and published the Anglo-Irish Agreement, which became known as the Hillsborough Agreement. Its language was relatively neutral. But in Northern Ireland politics there are only extreme sensitivities. So when Hillsborough declared ambitions to reconcile the Nationalist

2 See page 400.

and Loyalist communities, the Unionists, who yet again felt they were being betrayed, described the Hillsborough Agreement as a British sell-out.

The first Anglo-Irish Conference took place in December and followed one of the biggest Unionist demonstrations against the agreement seen in the Province. Unionist leaders resigned from the assembly, thus forcing by-elections. When the by-elections were held in January 1986, the Unionists campaigned on the platform that a vote for them would be a vote against the Hillsborough Agreement. They lost only one seat – to the SDLP candidate. So, the Unionists had made their point. The Unionist opposition to the Anglo-Irish Agreement was clearly made in what had, unofficially, been a referendum.

Mrs Thatcher refused to budge, and on 3 March 1986 the Unionists called for a general strike throughout the Province. This was not simply a downing of tools. It was a violent and, in some areas, bloody demonstration. Next, the Unionists boycotted the assembly. In 1987 the Unionist MPs were back at Westminster and the sympathy in London for them increased when eleven people were killed at an outdoor Remembrance Day service at Enniskillen.

The following year, 1988, saw one of the more controversial actions by British forces. Three IRA members were shot dead by the SAS in Gibraltar. Once more there were charges that the British were operating a shoot-to-kill policy. This was denied.

By 1990 the Unionists had agreed that they would take part in general discussions on the future of the Province, but nothing came of those talks, and in 1991 the British government recognized that the Hillsborough Agreement would have to be 'suspended' if there was to be any chance of peace discussions.

In 1992 the number of people who had died since the present troubles had started in 1969 passed the 3000 mark. The pressure on the move to have all-party talks and for those parties to include Sinn Fein and, therefore, the representatives and even former members of the IRA, increased in April 1992 when the IRA bombed the City of London. This was the beginning of a new campaign.

Now we come back to 1993. The bombing continued. In March two children were killed when an IRA bomb went off in Warrington; the following month an even bigger bomb went off in the City of London. In May three bombs in the Province, designed to cause the maximum financial damage, went off in Belfast, Portadown and Magherafelt. In October another bomb exploded on the Shankhill Road.

Through all this, the talking and attempts to get some agreement moved on. It was impossible for anyone to believe that an agreement could be reached between London and the terrorist groups or even between London and Dublin at that stage. Public opinion was cynical, especially when in October 1993 the president of Sinn Fein, Gerry Adams, helped to carry the coffin of IRA bomber Thomas Begley, who had killed himself and nine other people in the Shankhill Road bombing.

By the end of that month the Taoiseach Albert Reynolds and John Major showed that they were determined not to let the bombings and the intransigence of both sides overwhelm the political effort. They started working on plans for yet another initiative – that political euphemism for trying something else, almost anything else in desperation – and in mid-December came the so-called Downing Street Declaration. On Wednesday, 15 December Reynolds and Major shook hands in front of a Christmas tree and made the declaration that this new plan offered the opportunity for the Republican political wing of the IRA, Sinn Fein, to join in the talks on the future of Ulster. The price Sinn Fein would have to pay for a ticket to those talks was a public renunciation of violence.

The peace process was now officially, as it always had been unofficially, in the hands of the terrorists. Four days later the IRA gave its answer when it planted a bomb in Londonderry. The following week Gerry Adams called for talks with London and Dublin, but the cynicism of his response was proved by his insistence that the talks should be unconditional. On the Sunday before New Year's Eve the IRA delivered its 'end of year message' in the style of some terrorist monarchy. It rejected the Downing Street Declaration and made the point that the IRA offensive had consistently survived British attempts to use talks to end the conflict.

The Bosnian war, which had more or less started in April 1992, had now been going on for a year, and the failure of the international community to control events in the former Yugoslavia can be largely blamed on the determination of the Serbian leader, Milošević. An even greater reason was the inability of the international community to take a common and single line on what to do. The United Nations, the European Union and NATO all seemed to have contradictory tactics, although no one doubted the sincerity of each agency. By January 1993 the so-called Bosnian operation was expanding. The first British soldier had been killed, shot by a sniper in Gonji Vkuf.

Britain's part in this operation was increased when the government sent an aircraft carrier to the Adriatic. In February John Major went to Washington to see the newly installed president, Bill Clinton. By now both Washington and London were getting reports of Serbian ethnic cleansing, and although Major had been advised that road convoys remained the safest and most reliable way of getting food in, he promptly and publicly supported an American plan to airdrop foodstuffs and medical supplies to Bosnian Muslims. This immediately showed the great dilemma facing any attempt to arrive at a solution: no matter who was right or wrong on the ground, they had to be treated equally, or the less favoured would react violently and their friends on the outside, for example, in the UN, would reject initiatives. Led by the French, most NATO countries refused to endorse Britain's position and the American plan to airdrop supplies.

There was, however, unanimous support for the argument that the United Nations should set up the first war crimes tribunal since the end of the Second World War in some vain attempt to ward off and immediately prosecute alleged war criminals.

At the beginning of March the airdrop began. Perhaps a sad indication that this operation had not been thoroughly thought through was the fact that about 40 per cent of the American foodstuffs dropped into the Muslim positions contained pork. There was also a suspicion that the Americans were secretly flying in weapons to help the Muslims. As seemingly everyone was flying in something to help someone this breach of international agreement went unnoticed.

In March the outline of the Vance–Owen peace plan was agreed at the United Nations. It was never likely to work because it meant that territory would be given to the Serbs. Few people thought that the Bosnian Serb leader, Radovan Karadžić, would honour any plan. No-fly zones were now in place, however, and Britain's first squadron was sent to cover them.

Sure enough, towards the end of April the Bosnian Serbs dismissed the Vance–Owen plan. Their attitude was summed up by their reading of recent history. The Americans had failed to win in Vietnam and they would fail in the former Yugoslavia.

The UN immediately imposed sanctions, including the freezing of overseas bank funds, embargoes on river traffic down the Danube and on the importation of any goods, other than humanitarian aid, into Serbia. Once again it looked good on paper. Vance resigned, and in July Thorvald Stoltenberg took over as the UN representative in Bosnia (Owen remained as the European Union representative).

By June more troops were being sent to Bosnia to protect the six so-called safe havens for the Muslims. Ironically, some of the opposition in the UN to the safe haven scheme came from developing countries, which wanted tougher action because they believed that the enclaves that were being set up would eventually turn Bosnian Muslims into all but stateless refugees. In little over a year since the war began the UN peace-keepers were earning their medals. More than forty had been killed in that time and 500 had been wounded.

In July a plan to split Bosnia-Herzegovina into three autonomous republics was, on paper, agreed by the opposing sides. Even though Milošević had by then lost control over Karadžić, it was generally recognized that any agreement reached with the Bosnian Serbs would only mean that it contained a protocol they did not care about or one they did not want the other side to have. Meanwhile, more examples of war crimes were being uncovered on an almost daily basis.

The, for the moment, good news of the year was in the Middle East and Washington. After decades of war, the Palestine Liberation Organization (PLO) and Israel formally agreed to recognize each other and Israel accepted at long last that the PLO was the representative of the Palestinian people. On the White House lawn on Monday, 13 September Yassir Arafat, chairman of the PLO, and the Israeli prime minister, Yitzhak Rabin, formally shook hands on a deal that would give Palestinians some limited autonomy on the west bank of the Jordan and in the Gaza Strip. No one pretended this was the day of peace, and there were many Palestinians and Israelis who were quite determined that it would not be.

In late June the Americans, convinced that Saddam Hussein had masterminded an attempt to assassinate their previous president, George Bush, decided they should treat the Iraqi leader to a display of American fire power. They launched twenty-three Tomahawk missiles at Baghdad. The military value was obscure, and the international PR consequence not too good, as many civilians were killed.

There was one place where progress towards peaceful coexistence now seemed a reality. On Wednesday, 22 December 1993, by 237 votes to 45, the South African parliament voted itself into history. It ceased to exist in its constitutional form, and the parliament that would follow would operate under a new constitution and prepare for the first multi-racial elections that were to be held in South Africa the following April.

The year had begun in Britain with the first reports that Princess Diana wanted to divorce her husband. The story stepped up a pace with what became known in January of that year as Camillagate. This was the discovery of six minutes of taped telephone conversations between the Prince of Wales and his mistress, Camilla Parker Bowles. The intimate and sexual nature of the conversation appeared to put paid to any support the Prince might have had as the wronged man.

An aside to the daily soap opera that the Waleses' marriage had become was that the nation's bookmakers now entered the frame. They were offering odds of only 50:1 on the monarchy surviving beyond the year 2000. The Church of England, established and beholden to the establishment as it was, tended to keep out of the discussion, but the Archbishop of York, John Habgood, stated publicly that he believed that the nation would tolerate only so much bad behaviour from the royal family. What he had not entirely grasped was that increased newspaper sales, radio and television programmes suggested that the British public, indeed worldwide public, was loving every minute of it.

The events of 1993 had an uncanny historical sense of *déjà vu*. The Charles and Diana story was following almost exactly the same lines as the one that had taken place at the beginning of the nineteenth century, when the Prince and Princess of Wales, George (later George IV) and Caroline of Brunswick, married, fought, separated, divorced and used (particularly the Princess of Wales) friends in the newspapers to spread each side of the story. The public took sides and quickly supported the glamorous Princess. There was even a debate as to what would happen when the Prince became King.[3] There was even a shocking end. Caroline of Brunswick died unexpectedly, and the whole nation went into mourning in spite of the royal family's wish that they should not. So great was the mass hysteria that her coffin had to be protected in case it was stolen. She became an icon as much in death as in life.

3 See *This Sceptred Isle 55 BC – 1901*, BBC Books and Penguin paperback; also Flora Fraser, *The Unruly Queen*, Macmillan (1996).

In January the Channel Tunnel was used for the first time when Sir Christopher Mallaby, the new ambassador to Paris, decided that instead of the more conventional way of travelling to take up his appointment, he would don protective clothing and a hard hat to travel beneath the Channel in the caged workmen's train to signify the success of the ambition that until then had always seemed impossible – the physical linking of Britain and France.

Deaths

Marion Anderson (US contralto)
Arthur Ashe (US tennis player)
Sammy Cahn (US song writer)
Cyril Cusack (actor)
Les Dawson (comedian)
James H. Doolittle (US air force officer)
Billy Eckstine (US singer)
Dame Elisabeth Frink (sculptor)
Federico Fellini (Italian film director)
Dizzy Gillespie (US jazz musician)
William Golding (writer)
Jo Grimond, Baron Grimond of Forth (politician)
James Hunt (racing driver)
Joseph Leo Mankiewicz (US film director)
Thurgood Marshall (US civil rights leader)
Rudolf Nureyev (Russian dancer)
C. Northcote Parkinson (political economist)
Vincent Price (actor)
Nicholas Ridley, Lord Ridley of Liddesdale (politician)
A.B. Sabin (US scientist)
Dame Freya Stark (travel writer)
Sam Wanamaker (US actor)
Solly Zuckerman, Baron Zuckerman of Burnham Thorpe (scientist)

1994

ON THURSDAY, 12 May 1994 John Smith, the leader of the Labour Party, had a heart attack and died. Smith, who was fifty-five, was the newer face of a changing Labour Party, and most political assessments suggested that this quiet-mannered Scot was, indeed, the acceptable face of the Labour Party in the electorate's mind. Smith might well have won the next election for the Labour Party.

His successor, Tony Blair, believed that to make the Labour Party electable he would have to rid it of the last vestiges of socialism and adopt all those Conservative policies that the electorate appeared to find so attractive. There had been few signs in John Smith's writings and speeches that he was willing to abandon all the principles of the party for the sake of power. Blair had no such inhibitions.

On 21 July 1994 Blair was elected to lead the Labour Party, receiving more than half the votes in all sections of the party, the trades unions, the constituencies and the parliamentary party. Whether at that stage the Labour Party understood the extent to which it would be 'modernized' is unclear. What is clear is that there had never been a better time to challenge the Conservative government.

On Monday, 6 June the old and bold of fourteen nations returned to the beaches of Normandy. Fifty years earlier fourteen nations had begun the invasion of Europe that would bring about the end of Nazi rule. Heads of state arrived from all over the world in what was, at times, a blatantly political exercise. The real guests of honour were the survivors. More than 9000 American, nearly 4000 British and more than 2000 Canadians were among those who died in June 1994 on the beaches of Normandy. Thousand upon thousand of young, old and very old paid their respects and played laments in the graveyards at Bayeux, Beny-sur-Mer and Colleville, where lay 'the fathers we never knew, the uncles we never met and the friends who never returned. The heroes we can never repay'.

The Europhiles within the Major government reflected that the case for European unity that so split British politics in 1994 rested on the beaches of Normandy in 1944. This was no comfort to John Major, who, a week after the D-Day celebrations, suffered his worst parliamentary defeat. This was not at the Westminster Parliament but at the European assembly. The European parliamentary elections were disastrous for the Conservatives. Of the eighty-seven British seats in the European Parliament, the Labour Party won sixty-two and the Conservatives eighteen. There were now open demands for Major to resign.

At the end of the week the party chairman, Sir Norman Fowler, resigned. Fowler simply wanted to go because he felt that the party now needed a chairman who would organize it for the next general election. The grass roots of the party wanted the one man who did not want the job, Michael Heseltine, to take over. Instead Major gave it to the likeable but ineffectual Jeremy Hanley.

The week of Blair's election found John Major in such political difficulties that he had to change his Cabinet. The Major government was suffering on two fronts. First, the Conservatives were split over Maastricht, the European Community Treaty that took member states on the next stage towards closer political and financial union. Second, the government gave every impression of having run out of ideas. One of the penalties of living in a century of mass communications is that increasingly governments were expected to make things – almost anything – happen. By the 1990s it was no longer possible for a nation to be simply and quietly governed.

In August 1994 an event that most Protestant Loyalists treated with the utmost scepticism brought a hope of peace to Northern Ireland. The IRA declared what it called 'a complete cessation of military operations'. Suspicions were immediately voiced when the wording was examined, and critics pointed out that the IRA statement talked about a cessation but not a permanent ending to violence.

For some time the Dublin and London governments had encouraged Sinn Fein, the political wing of the terrorist group, to believe that if they agreed to a permanent end to hostilities, Gerry Adams and his colleagues could join the negotiations on the future of the Province. Harder-line members of the Loyalist parties, such as the Reverend Ian Paisley, insisted that the IRA could not be trusted and that, given its stockpiles of weapons and numbers of trained personnel, the violence could continue whenever the Provisional IRA chose.

In October the three Loyalist paramilitary groups announced that as from the 13th of that month they, too, would agree to a cease-fire, but they made an open condition. Their cease-fire would depend on the Republicans: if they once more started the shooting and the bombing, so would the Loyalists. Here was the consequence of no one being able to or willing to go the extra step in agreeing to a permanent cessation of violence. As it turned out, the scepticism was well founded and the cease-fire was broken.

The possibility of peace allowed the British government to bring President Clinton's administration further into the peace-making process and, as far as the British government was concerned, the next stage would depend on the momentum that the Americans might give to the process and how long the Dublin government could support what was going on in Northern Ireland.

It was essential for the British and the Americans to get on a better footing. Earlier that year they were at diplomatic loggerheads. At the end of January the British government had been furious with the Americans when they granted Gerry Adams a visa to visit the United States and to raise funds there. The American media described Adams as a statesman, and Adams, perhaps surprised by the media attention and the easy questions about peace but none about violence, took great advantage of the publicity. In London the American ambassador was formally called to the Foreign Office and a protest lodged with his government. In Washington few had been surprised at what had happened because the Irish lobby in the Senate was powerful, as was the Irish electorate, particularly in an election year.

Albert Reynolds, the Taoiseach, had relied on the Irish Labour Party for support within his ruling coalition. The leader of the Labour Party was Dick Spring, the Irish foreign minister, who had an important part to play in the peace process. By November 1994 Reynolds could no longer hold the coalition together and his two-year-old government collapsed. A month later the head of Fine Gael, John Bruton, became Taoiseach. Bruton was a right-wing politician and there was certainly public suspicion that he would not go along with the peace process so encouraged by his predecessor. The suspicions were not entirely ill founded, but the process did continue and there was no real determination in the new government to oppose the process.

In the second week of December British officials and Sinn Fein leaders met for the first time in Belfast, but whatever the political forecasting in Dublin and London, it became immediately clear that the Protestant fear about IRA weapons would continue to dominate whatever talks took place in the future. From the opening of those talks the demand was that the IRA should surrender its weapons, including explosives. At the end of the first day the Democratic Unionists, the hard-line Protestant group, observed what everyone knew to be true but few admitted publicly. As the deputy leader of the Democratic Unionists, Peter Robinson, put it: 'The IRA's path to the talks table was by violence. It represents a triumph of terror over the democratic process.' Elsewhere, both the attempted philosophical arguments of the Sinn Fein leadership and the apparent rhetoric of the Unionists was seen as irrelevant. In the Province itself, where people had lived with violence since 1969, there was a thin line between apparent rhetoric and realism. No one believed that two announcements of cease-fires were all that it would take for an agreement.

In the House of Commons there had been a bipartisan approach to Northern Ireland affairs since the early 1970s – with the exception of the renewal of the Prevention of Terrorism Act, which the Labour Party opposed. When John Smith became leader of the Labour Party after Neil Kinnock's resignation in 1992 he continued to display a determination to continue this bipartisan approach, even though there were many in his own party who believed there should be a less aggressive attitude to the Republican position. Some had even argued that British troops should be withdrawn from the Province. For example, one of those on the left of the Labour Party, Tony Benn, wrote in the 1980s:[4]

> We got dragged into a bipartisan position on Ireland. Many efforts were made to drag us out of that position and we did make a move towards a break with bipartisanship but now with support of the Anglo-Irish agreement we are back in a bipartisan posture.
>
> It is time for us to renew the campaign for British withdrawal. We have always been told you can't raise the Irish question because it is difficult and divisive, but if we had adopted a clear position a long time ago we would have made some real progress.

John Smith always balanced the 'troops out' element of his party with what he understood to be the role of the Labour Party in opposition towards Ireland, and that was support for government initiatives.

An event of greater significance was taking place a hemisphere away. South Africa had returned as a full member of the Commonwealth. The country did so thirty-three years after leaving because of apartheid. This was a momentous year for Southern Africa, when Nelson Mandela was inaugurated as South Africa's first black president on Tuesday, 10 May. Mandela's message was that South Africa would never again be known as 'the skunk of the world'. He said that it was now

---

4 Tony Benn, *Fighting Back*, Hutchinson (1998).

time to heal wounds and that 'the moment to bridge the chasms that divide us has come, the moment to build is upon us'.

As Mandela spoke in South Africa, hopes of peace in Bosnia seemed less likely than ever. A cease-fire proposal from the European Union, Russia and the United States of America was based on there being a four-month truce. During that cease-fire, negotiations were supposed to have started that would have given the Croat Muslim group 51 per cent of the land and the Bosnian Serbs 49 per cent.

The leader of the Croat Muslim group, Alija Izetbegovic, who at one point appeared to go along with this division, now went back to his original demand for not 51 per cent but 58 per cent of the territory. Moreover, Izetbegovic would not accept the length of the truce. He wanted it cut to eight weeks, largely because he believed that the Serbs, who already controlled 70 per cent of Bosnia, would use any withdrawal of forces – which a cease-fire would have to encompass – to renew their policy of ethnic cleansing. Izetbegovic was probably right. The hopes of the European negotiator, David Owen, and others involved with him in the search for peace were finished. Owen would carry on for another year but never get any closer to a conclusion. The Vance–Owen Peace Plan was perhaps the nearest anyone got to peace, but that had been in 1992. The opposition came just as much from outside the Balkans (including Washington) as it did from inside. In 1994 the attempt at a new truce to give breathing space for negotiations was scuppered, and there was little real help for any outside plan for peace. Milošević has been called the butcher of the Balkans, and Karadžić was accused of being responsible for terrible war crimes; neither label nor accusation ever concerned the two men or their followers. It was always unlikely that the conflict in the Balkans would be settled by anything but terror. After all, there were six centuries of precedent.

A permanent loss in 1994 was to the public voice of cricket. Brian Johnston, the most famous surviving voice of the BBC's *Test Match Special* team, died at the age of eighty-one. Johnston was the eternal schoolboy who saw the brighter side of everything, and his passion for the game was summed up when he remarked that he understood that some men did not care for cricket and that while he understood this, he should not like his daughter to marry one of them.

Another sporting character died in the same month. Sir Matt Busby had become a legend in the world of football, building up the great Manchester United teams of the 1950s and 1960s.

Death of a more gruesome kind was uncovered during the early weeks of the year. Police excavated a garden and house in a street in Gloucester and charged, first, the owner of the house, Frederick West and, later, his wife, Rosemary, with ten murders, including that of their daughter, Heather.

On Saturday, 12 March the first women priests in the history of the Church of England were ordained in Bristol Cathedral.

Another milestone, this time a nautical one, was reached the following month when the New Zealand catamaran ENZA NZ, skippered by Robin Knox-Johnston and Peter Blake, set a non-stop round the world record of 74 days, 22 hours, 17 minutes and 22 seconds.

Also returning home, but at a more leisurely pace and certainly without so much fuss, was Alexander Solzhenitsyn. After twenty years in exile in America, the Russian author returned to his homeland. Although he was welcomed by thousands, Solzhenitsyn remained a saddened figure. He had never believed communism could survive, but he could not accept that what had replaced it was the panacea for his own people.

In a society so used to turning to science for solutions there remained in the 1990s gaping disappointments. In the United States in April 1994 scientists at the US National Institute of Health said that they now understood better the reasons for the virtual immortality of cancer cells. As ever, the scientists had to be quick to warn the whole world of the enormous gulf between the laboratory and cures for cancer patients.

In August a more recent dilemma for medical science was discussed. In Yokohama, Japan, the tenth international conference on AIDS concluded that there was little cheerful news for the more than 17 million people now known to be HIV positive, of whom 10 million lived in Africa. One of the continuing concerns of the delegates in Yokohama was that the medical care was concentrated in the industrially advanced nations, particularly the United States. There were, the delegates were told, nations in sub-Saharan Africa where more people had AIDS than had not. The high-tech laboratories and high-cost medical treatments were unlikely to reach Black Africa.

Deaths

Sir Harold Mario Acton (writer)
Sir Matt Busby (football manager)
Cab Calloway (US band leader)
G.R. Elton (historian)
Dorothy Hodgkin (chemist)
Erich Honecker (East German politician)
Derek Jarman (artist)
Brian Johnston (broadcaster)
Keith Joseph, Baron Joseph of Portsoken (politician)
Burt Lancaster (US actor)
Walter Lantz (US film producer)
Henry Mancini (US composer)
Richard Milhous Nixon (US president)
Thomas 'Tip' O'Neill (US politician)
John Osborne (playwright)
Linus Pauling (US chemist)
John Wyndham Pope-Hennessy (art historian)

Sir Karl Popper (philosopher)
Dean Rusk (US politician)
John Smith (politician)
Jule Styne (US composer)
Donald Swann (entertainer)
Peter Thorneycroft, Baron Thorneycroft of Dunston (politician)
Billy Wright (footballer)

1995

ON 22 JUNE John Major resigned as leader of the Conservative Party, although not as prime minister, because he no longer controlled the parliamentary party. His authority had been called into question almost exclusively over his attitude to Europe, especially monetary union, and there had been weeks, even months, of speculation about his leadership, with party managers failing to bring MPs to heel. The Conservative Party confirmed its leader every autumn, and re-adoption was normally automatic. As Mrs Thatcher had found, however, when the party had set itself against its leader, an MP – preferably an obscure one – could be found to stand against the incumbent, simply to test the real support the leader might have. It was likely that a stalking horse would appear that autumn, and it was even possible that the challenge would be made by one or more of Major's Cabinet colleagues. Anticipating the possibility, Major announced that his critics should 'put up or shut up'.

One of Major's main critics and one that was ready to 'put up' against him in the election for party leader was the Euro-sceptic and Welsh Secretary, John Redwood. Redwood resigned his Cabinet post and announced his intention to run against the prime minister. An immediate effect of this was that senior Cabinet members united behind Major – they would prefer him to Redwood as prime minister. Although Major remained prime minister during this period of party electioneering, if he lost he would have to resign.

In the end, Redwood's right-wing policies and Euro-sceptic views were seen as vote losing and unacceptable, and on 4 July Major defeated Redwood by 218 votes to 89. This was not an end to party disunity, however, and the principal beneficiaries of Major's decision were the Labour team.

In the opinion of Conservative grass-roots supporters, the one person who could have successfully taken over from John Major and who would have won the next general election, which was still two years away, was Michael Heseltine. Although he had suffered a heart attack, Heseltine was now back in harness, but he could not guarantee the same level of support among his parliamentary colleagues as he could in the country as a whole. He did not run. Major recognized his importance and appointed him deputy prime minister. In the following Cabinet reshuffle the ineffectual Jeremy Hanley was replaced by the abrasive Brian Mawhinney. The only comfort for the Euro-sceptics was the appointment of Michael Portillo as Defence Secretary. This job had no value in the European debate but it gave them a strong voice in Cabinet and on the ministerial lunch circuit.

Meanwhile, the Labour Party was at work elsewhere and more constructively. Tony Blair had been touring the country, talking to Labour Party activists, including trades union members, whose support he wanted in getting rid of Clause Four, that part of the Labour Party constitution that committed the party to the public ownership of major industries. Blair had made it clear that it had to go if the party expected to convince the electorate that it was 'New' Labour and not the union-led organization that had time and time again frightened away sufficient voters for it to achieve victory in the polls. In April of 1995, at a special conference at the Central Hall in Westminster, 65 per cent of the party voted to erase Clause Four from its constitution. From that point the ethos of the Labour Party had changed, Blair's leadership was as strong as Major's was weak and the Labour Party was becoming increasingly electable as the Conservatives were becoming increasingly unelectable.

The publicity for Blair's modernization filled the newspapers and television and radio programmes, and for the following three days the media analysed his success. On the fourth day the country went to the local election polling booths. The Labour Party could have had no better run into the elections. Unemployment was at around 3 million and hardly a month went by without some new and usually contrived scare about what the Conservative government was planning to do, including the bogus notion that they would privatize the National Health Service. Even the bipartisan area of Northern Ireland's politics worked to Labour's advantage when, on the day before the elections, Major went to Ulster and faced a hostile demonstration against his handling of the peace process. This simply added to the impression that while Major was thought to be a nice man he simply was not the one to command enough respect to lead the country.

In the local elections the Conservatives lost many of their safe seats and kept control of only eight councils. The Labour Party now had 155 councils and had won 48 per cent of the popular vote – the most they had ever gained in thirty years of local elections. As ever, the electorate was not simply voting for someone else, they were voting against the existing administration.

In 1995 one of the charges against the Conservatives was sleaze. This was the year of the 'cash for questions' headlines, when two Conservative backbenchers, David Tredinnick and Graham Riddick, were suspended from the House for four weeks. It was the beginning of a widely held view, exploited ruthlessly by the opposition spin doctors, that the Conservative Party was caught up in corrupt practice. This vision was not helped when the government refused to let the Nolan Committee, enquiring into standards in public life, examine party funding.

The story of money grabbing and sharp practice was not confined to politics. In the 1980s there had grown a harsher and more ambitious group in society, which some called the 'Me generation'. The making of money, and lots of it, had become an expectation among a large section of young people. The new corporate systems, including phenomena such as the US Junk Bond market, encouraged the notion that fortunes could be made without substance. In America there was a philosophy in this period that said that chief executive officers who had gone bankrupt for millions of dollars, even more than once, should get the backing of the banks and financial institutions for their next projects because they were experienced. Even fast-growing corporations, particularly in the computer industry, supported this concept. That same phenomenon was reaching Britain in the mid-1990s, when young people, barely out of university, were given the responsibility for deals worth millions of pounds, and when one of them came unstuck, the general public saw it not as a disgrace but as a sporting spectacle or a scene from a Hollywood film.

The perfect example of this came to light in February 1995. One of the City of London's oldest merchant banks, Barings, collapsed, with estimated losses of around £800 million. At the heart of this collapse was one of its traders, the twenty-eight-year-old Nick Leeson. Leeson worked on the dealing floor of the Singapore Stock Market, and he had, single-handedly, lost £17 billion on the Japanese futures market.

There was little sympathy for Barings and a great deal of public interest in Leeson. In retrospect, the main effect of Leeson's behaviour was to add to the ledger of sleaze and malpractice that was laid often quite wrongly at the government's doorstep. There seemed almost no way in which between the spring of 1995 and the election two years later that the Conservatives were going to get away from the general impression that they had simply been in office too long.

The brightest hope in an often gloomy year was in Northern Ireland and, with hope against hope, in Bosnia.

After four years of fighting, perhaps the most vicious seen in Europe since the Second World War, the Americans had persuaded the three national leaders of the former Yugoslavia to go to formal peace negotiations in Dayton, Ohio. At the beginning of November the Americans believed they had the basis for an agreement. The Dayton Plan, as it became known, was in four parts. There would be a unified state called Bosnia-Herzegovina, which would have two self-governing federations – one Muslim Croat and the other Bosnian Serb. The two groups would take it in turns to provide a president. The whole package would be guaranteed by an international monitoring group, an implementation force. There were two other important aspects: war criminals were to be barred from office and only one group would handle foreign affairs for everyone.

After three weeks of discussions, Slobodan Milošević, the Serbian leader, Franjo Tudjman, the Croatian, and Alija Izetbegovic, the Bosnian, agreed to sign the peace agreement. The key to implementing the agreement would be a 60,000-strong NATO force. When the peace accord was signed in December 1995 all three Balkan presidents expressed reservations and few believed the Balkan tragedy to be at an end. Those at the Paris conference, where the accord was signed, understood that the next area of fighting would surely be in Kosovo. Kosovo was part of

Serbia, but the Albanians in Kosovo had never accepted the Serbian domination that had been their lot since at least 1945. The Albanian Kosovars would want independence. The lesson of Slovenia and Croatia having been learned, even by the Germans, the western nations would go no further than support the intention of an autonomous rather than an independent state. The further danger was that that conflict would spill over into neighbouring Macedonia.

Ireland had a happier Christmas. For three months the Taoiseach, John Bruton, and John Major had led discussions on the future of Ulster. Often those talks appeared to be breaking down, and at no time did anyone believe there could be a complete solution. Major's legacy was his persistence. He believed that peace was possible and he had successfully involved President Clinton in the process, although on occasion the Americans went too far for the British, especially in the freedom they allowed Gerry Adams to raise funds in the United States and to create for himself an image that lay somewhere between Irish statesman and romantic freedom fighter.

On 28 November 1995 the twelve weeks of talking between officials, ministers and prime ministers in London and Dublin came to the conclusion they had been looking for. Bruton and Major announced that they would start talks with all the political groups in Northern Ireland, including Sinn Fein. These talks, they hoped, would eventually lead to all-party talks, with everyone sitting around the same table or at least in the same building to discuss the future of the Province.

The second part of the agreement was that an international commission would examine perhaps the biggest stumbling block: the inability to find a formula whereby the terrorist groups, especially the IRA, gave up a sufficient number of its weapons to satisfy everyone that the talks were genuine and that a cease-fire was lasting. The masterstroke was the secondment of the American Democrat, Senator George Mitchell, as the chairman of the commission to work out details.

The announcement made, President Clinton flew to Ulster to turn on the Christmas lights in Belfast. He walked the Republic Falls Road and the Protestant Shankhill Road. He talked to Adams and the Protestant hard-liner, Ian Paisley. It was the turning on of the lights and the red-and-gold decorated Christmas tree in front of Belfast Town Hall that provided the symbolism that the peace process had needed.

If anyone doubted the difficulties ahead they had only to observe that even over the Christmas festival itself, the terrorists were at work. In December the IRA murdered four men, one of them on Boxing Day.

This was the year in which the Queen told her eldest son and his wife that enough spin doctoring was enough and that they should divorce.

It was also the year in which Yitzak Rabin was assassinated at a peace rally by a Jewish fanatic who believed that Rabin had given up too much for peace. Ironically, it was the fiftieth birthday of the organization dedicated to peace, the United Nations.

Deaths
Sir Kingsley Amis (writer)
Robert Bolt (writer)
Brigid Brophy (writer)
Peter Cook (humorist)
Morarji Desai (Indian politician)
Alec Douglas-Home, Baron Home of the Hirsel (politician)
Gerald Durrell (naturalist)
Gavin Ewart (poet)
J. William Fulbright (US politician)
Sir Alexander Gibson (Scottish conductor)
Carl Giles (cartoonist)
Odette Hallowes (World War Two heroine)
Sir Michael Hordern (actor)
Louis Malle (French film director)
Yitzak Rabin (Israeli politician)
Jonas E. Salk (US scientist)
Joe Slovo (South African politician)
Sir Stephen Spender (writer)
Harold Wilson, Baron Wilson of Rievaulx (politician)

1996

IN 1996, after fifteen years of marriage, the Prince and Princess of Wales were divorced. The nation's sympathies lay largely with the Princess.

Prince Charles had continued to have an affair throughout his married life. The Princess of Wales took lovers. There are centuries of precedent for such royal lifestyles. The constitutional implications should not be overshadowed by the razzmatazz of what was really nothing but a soap opera.

The deeper debate in 1996 was the suitability of Prince Charles to be king. Could a divorcee be monarch? Moreover, what would happen if he married his mistress, Camilla Parker Bowles? Would she become queen or some form of consort? The decree absolute that went through in the second half of 1996 settled nothing, especially for a nation and a media that had learned to become dissatisfied with even truthful answers.

Another constitutional debate resurfaced at the end of the year. The House of Lords voted for an important change to the British constitution as it applied to royal succession. In a complicated procedural point the peers voted to allow an approach to be made to the Queen asking her to allow their lordships to bring before Parliament a bill that would prepare the way for women members of the royal family to enjoy equal rights of succession. The immediate consequence would be for the Princess Royal to take precedence over the Duke of York in line to the throne. As a future example, Prince William (the heir apparent on his father's death) might have a female first-born child and a male second child. The first born would be in line to the throne above the second born. This Bill allowed the subject to be raised, not enacted.

If only the constitutional changes and discussions in other parts of the nation that year could have been so easily agreed.

In Northern Ireland in November the previous year there had been a terrorist cease-fire and Christmas songs and carols in Belfast. By February 1996 the celebrations seemed quite premature.

On Saturday, 10 February the seventeen-month-long IRA cease-fire was broken. The IRA exploded a bomb in London's docklands. The government announced that it would not be obstructed by what it saw as a desperate measure of the IRA to maintain control. On the following Monday thousands of demonstrators waving paper doves rallied outside Belfast City Hall. They said they were determined that peace should continue. John Major agreed and maintained that the IRA would 'never bomb their way to the negotiating table'.

The next Thursday another bomb in London was discovered, but defused, and on Sunday, 18 February an IRA bomber travelling on a bus in London blew himself up when a device he was carrying exploded prematurely. No one else was injured. Later in the year, on Saturday, 15 June the IRA blew up a sizeable chunk of the middle of Manchester. Hundreds were injured. A month later Ulster saw the worst rioting in a decade.

By now the prime minister had further political stresses in Westminster. The government majority in the Commons was reduced to two and a vote was coming up on the Scott Report into government and civil servant involvement in selling weapons to Iraq. Major won the night by one vote.

The following month worse followed, when the government had to admit that there was a possible link between BSE and Creutzfeldt-Jakob Disease (CJD). BSE, widely known as mad cow disease, had been identified in British cattle ten years earlier. The reaction was predictable. The public stopped eating beef, fast-food chains removed British beef from their menus and on 25 March 1996 the European Commission imposed a worldwide ban on British beef exports.

The government refused to instigate a mass slaughter of cattle, which was probably the only move that would have placated the other members of the European Union. The politics of the beef ban and what followed meant that British beef production had to undergo a complete change in its system of record-keeping, stock had to be slaughtered and the political bargaining had to start. It would take two years before there was any official softening of the European line against British beef.

There was in Britain another tale about livestock, whose implications were far greater than BSE. In March 1996 the scientific journal *Nature* published details of research that had been going on at Roslin Institute in Edinburgh. Scientists had taken samples from an unfertilized egg of a ewe. The maternal genes were removed from that egg and the scientists put the fertilized eggs into wombs of other ewes, which thus became surrogate mothers. The scientists had cloned sheep.

The conclusion of the research was that it was now possible to create human clones. The disturbing statement in the research was that this genetic engineering could be used soon to remove defective traits in human embryos, thus making it possible to introduce desirable ones.

In 1996 there was much discussion about the need for responsible science, but no one in the scientific world believed there was any turning back nor that there was any way in which a global ban on genetic engineering could or would be enforced.

Deaths

Spiro T. Agnew (US politician)
Michael Bentine (comedian)
Jean-Bédel Bokassa (Central African Republic dictator)
Joseph Brodsky (US-Russian poet)
George Burns (US comedian)
Marguerite Duras (French writer)
Ella Fitzgerald (US singer)
Alger Hiss (probable US spy)
Gene Kelly (US actor/dancer)
Timothy Leary (US writer)
François Mitterrand (French politician)
Andreas Papandreou (Greek politician)
Willie Rushton (writer and actor)
Sir Frank Whittle (inventor)
Derek Worlock, Archbishop of Liverpool
Sir Laurens van der Post (traveller)

1997

ON 5 SEPTEMBER 1997 Mother Teresa of Calcutta died. Often a controversial figure, she had become a symbol of selfless help to the poorest people. Her order, the Sisters of Mercy, and admirers in every capital including the Vatican were saddened by her death. She was old and had been ill.

On the Sunday before Mother Teresa died, Diana, Princess of Wales, was killed in a car crash in Paris together with her close friend, Dodi Fayed, the son of an Egyptian merchant. The public grief was worldwide.

During her marriage to Prince Charles the princess had become one of the best-known people in the world, and after her death pundits in almost every academic discipline appeared on radio and television or wrote in the press to offer explanations for the international mourning and to try to say what it meant. The truth may be simpler than the hypotheses that dominated newspapers, magazines, radio and television and academic institutions: for one week millions of people did what individuals do when a member of their family dies. They expressed grief, and because that grief was so public it was louder. The media, by its general admission, responded to that outpouring and by so doing encouraged it.

It is worth noting that once the funeral was over and the rite of passage complete, the international grief was switched off almost as suddenly as it had begun. It is too cynical to talk of mass-hysteria as the only emotion, but it is not cynical to reflect on the reasons for so many mourners simply turning away to their everyday lives almost as if nothing had happened within a couple of weeks of her death. By the 1990s society, and not just British society, had become media driven. It was now perfectly reasonable to argue that perhaps many people were beginning to act out a stereotype of their lives. By the mid-1990s consumerism, opportunity and convenience, driven by the media, meant that few decisions had to be weighed – decisions were simply taken.

It was, for example, now possible for almost any adult in Britain to invest in the international stock market without having a clue about share prices or investment policies. The tax-efficient personal equity plans, although to be short lived, in many ways reflected how it was possible to be a part of a complicated national and international process without understanding its workings or its consequences. The society heading for the end of the century no longer had to consider values; it could now simply ask the price and decide whether something was affordable.

The extension of this phenomenon showed itself in British politics. The Major government had been elected in 1992, but it had never had an easy ride in its five-year life and had never bridged the gap between policy and presentation. Policy is about what the government intends to do. Presentation is about explaining what it intends to do and convincing an electorate that it is a reasonable ambition. The big issues of, for example, Europe and the British economy were, according to most surveys, rarely examined in the media and were little understood by the British electorate. The public did understand presentation, however, and judged the government's efficiency not on the text of the drama but on the public performance. This became a self-fulfilling prophecy, for even when policies themselves were seen to be misguided, the government reiterated the mantra that it was not the policy that was at fault, but its presentation.

In 1997 the Labour Party got its presentation right. It had a corporate identity and had refined its use of creative and professional public relations and marketing systems to convince a nation that it was electable. New Labour, as it was called, went as far as to take policies of the existing government, calling them its own and, when questioned, simply saying that it could implement them better than the Conservatives.

The British electorate, fed up with the public divisions within the Conservative Party and the well-publicized, grubby self-interest of some of its parliamentarians, turned to Tony Blair. The further irony of the Labour campaign was that it was apparently endorsed by the one postwar leader who, after Churchill, had inspired the nation, Margaret Thatcher. With such tacit endorsement, the great middle-class voting bloc, with whom Blair identified far more than the working-class origins of his party, felt it safe to vote Labour.

On 1 May 1997 Labour became the governing party, with a landslide victory in the general election.

The Conservative misery was not yet over, however. John Major immediately resigned as leader of the party, but there was no obvious successor. William Hague became party leader with little chance, in the short term at least, of convincing his own grass-roots supporters, never mind the wider electorate, that he was a prime minister in waiting. For the Conservatives 1997 was the beginning of a long haul, and few believed that the right people were leading the way.

For Blair, there was every sign that his party was set for a decade to come and given the state of international politics he found it easy to assume a flattering position on that world stage. His decision, for example, to read a lesson at the funeral of Diana, Princess of Wales, suggested immediately that his publicity team would never let slip an opportunity to promote that image.

For every person who lamented the arrival of government by pager, sound bite and photo-opportunity, there were ten more who accepted that this was simply a sign of what the country had wanted for some time, namely strong and efficient government.

The constitutionalists, including the re-elected Speaker of the House, watched to see if this new approach would have a damaging effect on the authority of Parliament. The democratic tradition of announcing the government decisions to MPs was quickly ignored, and it soon became disturbingly clear that for the new government the television studio had a more important place in its presentational policy than the House of Commons.

In November 1997 the Queen and Prince Philip celebrated their fiftieth wedding anniversary. Considering the failures of the marriages of three of their children, their anniversary perhaps said more about the present monarchy and the trend to public enquiry into private lives.

It may seem that the Queen and Prince Philip had all the advantages to make their marriage work and few distractions. However, it is true that the Queen was not the only woman in Prince Philip's life during that half century, but it was not until much later in their marriage that publication of information about private lives became acceptable. Just as many editors in America sat on information about the Kennedys for a long time, so an inner circle of the royal family and several Fleet Street editors had made no sign that the marriage of the Queen and Prince Philip was anything but ideal.

The Queen's unbending sense of duty was the driving force through many difficulties of the fifty years between 1947 and 1997. Prince Philip, also, appeared to be totally devoted to the monarchy and, in spite of the wishes of his uncle, Lord Mountbatten, he was never constitutionally more than husband to the Queen. The decision had been taken early in the marriage that Philip would not become Prince Consort, and the distance of precedent was never relaxed.

In 1997 voices began to be heard calling more loudly than ever for the modernization of the monarchy. It seemed appropriate that Blair's new style of government should advise the Queen, who had for some time been holding formal meetings with members of the family and closest courtiers to discuss what might be called the 'way ahead' for the monarchy.

What was not fully recognized during these debates was the distinction between monarchy and royal family. Modernizing the monarchy was one thing; opening the royal family to inspection was unnecessary and undesirable. By doing so, the monarchy became constitutionally vulnerable. Perhaps the greater truth was that the function of monarchy, the guardian of kingship, no longer existed. It was gone at a time when the European debate showed clearly that the people more than ever needed protection from its greatest enemy, government.

The adjunct to this debate was the new government's public intent to reform the House of Lords although no alternative was explained. There was not much discussion in 1997 that an abolition of the hereditary system would one day be extended to include the politically harmless institution – the monarchy.

On 1 July Hong Kong was handed back to China. The island of Hong Kong had been ceded to Britain in the Nanking Treaty of 1842. The rest of the colony, known as the New Territories, had been held on a ninety-nine-year lease from the Chinese since 1898. The whole colony was handed back amid somewhat nervous circumstances. During the two years before hand-over, the British governor of Hong Kong pushed through legislation to give the colony greater democratic systems, something that Britain had made little attempt to do while it ruled. This was seen as a direct challenge to the Chinese. The Chinese made it clear, however, that Hong Kong would be considered a special case and not directly ruled from Beijing. Effectively, it would become a province with certain autonomy. Hand-over day came and went without, apparently, any restrictions on the Hong Kong community. Moreover, given the commercial ambitions of the emerging government of China, there was every reason to preserve the commercial instincts of the colony as a major financial centre of the Far East.

Deaths

Kathy Acker (US writer)
Hastings Banda (Malawi politician)
Diana, Princess of Wales
Robert Mitchum (US actor)
Sir George Solti (conductor)
James Stewart (US actor)
Mother Teresa (Yugoslav nun)
Gianni Versace (Italian fashion designer)

1998

THE LONGEST-RUNNING story of 1998 did not take place in the United Kingdom but in Washington, D.C. This was the year when for the first time since 1868 an American president was impeached, accused of high crimes and misdemeanours against the state.

On 21 January 1998 a formal investigation began into claims that President Clinton had an affair with a young woman, Monica Lewinsky, and had wanted her to lie under oath about that affair.

The details of the affair were contained, or so it was said, on ten tapes that carried the voice of Miss Lewinsky and a friend, Linda Tripp. The special prosecutor, Kenneth Starr, had arranged for Linda Tripp to be 'wired'. The story of Lewinsky and Clinton went back to another investigation by Starr, into claims by Paula Jones, that she had had an affair with Clinton. It was during the investigation of the Paula Jones case that Lewinsky had first denied her relationship with the president. On the tapes, Lewinsky admitted that she had falsely testified under pressure from the White House during the Paula Jones investigation.

That is the basis of the whole Clinton impeachment saga. In December the president was impeached by the House of Representatives and the following year, in January 1999, he went on trial in the Senate.

Sixty-seven of the one hundred senators had to vote against the president for him to be found guilty and therefore dismissed from the White House. Although the Republicans (Clinton was a Democrat) had a majority in the Senate, it was not big enough to guarantee a vote against the president. That was the hope of the White House defence as the Congress adjourned for Christmas 1998.

The sometimes confusing feature of the impeachment was the way in which President Clinton consistently rated highly in the opinion polls. Indeed, no second-term president had ever enjoyed such high ratings. This single factor tells us something about the American political system and how it so markedly differs from the political arrangement in the United Kingdom.

In America there are three groups: the people, the Congress and the president. The people, democratically, send congressmen to the House of Representatives and senators to the Senate. These are the legislators who work, ostensibly on behalf of the people. The greater task for a large number of them is to work at getting re-elected.

There has grown up a culture in the United States that the true democratic representative of the people in Washington, D.C., is not the Congress but the president. Each president is constantly at war with the Congress, and therefore the American people see their champion, the president, at war on their behalf. So when Congress tried to bring down the president in what was an overtly Republican political act, it was bringing down the people's champion, and the people, while not approving Clinton's morals, supported him as president.

Here again was an example of kingship. The president is the 'monarch' who will defend the people against their enemies, both foreign (military and commercial) and at home (the government). In return he has their allegiance – their vote.

The most important national event in Britain took place on Good Friday 1998. All the parties attempting to find a solution to the modern troubles of Northern Ireland reached agreement.

After thirty years of fighting it appeared that there was more than a framework for a peaceful settlement of a bombing and shooting war that had started in 1969. For the first time, albeit uneasily, Unionists and Republicans came together. The essential element of the agreement was a new, elected Northern Ireland assembly, an executive committee for the sharing of power and, crucially, institutions that would link Northern Ireland and Eire. In addition, promises were made to release Republican and nationalist prisoners, to examine ways of reforming the Royal Ulster Constabulary and to begin the process of surrendering terrorist weaponry.

This last element in the talks was crucial to the whole process and came about largely through the imagination and patience of President Clinton's representative, Senator George Mitchell, who chaired the peace talks.

By the end of 1998 more than 200 prisoners, many of them murderers, had been released from Ulster prisons, although not a single gun nor an ounce of explosive had been surrendered. Most parties looked to Sinn Fein, the political representatives of the IRA, to persuade the IRA that it should at least begin the process of decommissioning, as weapons surrender was termed. By December it was reasonably certain that Sinn Fein either could not or did not want to deliver on what the Unionists most certainly saw as its part of the bargain.

The peace process had achieved so much and had gone so far that there were those who believed it could not be unravelled. Others, not so sure, accepted that the one certainty was that Republican terrorists, in spite of the protestations of successive Westminster political leaders, had successfully bombed and shot their way to political authority in Northern Ireland.

It now remained to be seen if the Unionist leadership could and would allow the Northern Ireland assembly to go ahead by the spring of 1999 as scheduled. On New Year's Eve 1998, while many toasted the future of the Province, not a few Protestants once more voiced the thought that the British government had betrayed them by adopting a soft line towards Sinn Fein, among whose members were convicted terrorists.

The emergence of many colonial nations as independent states in the 1960s was testament to Mao Zedong's notion that power comes out of the barrel of a gun.

The most powerful of all weapons invented thus far produced a form of international terrorism from which the world had sheltered for fifty years or more. Although the Cold War had ended, the very real possibility of nuclear weapon confrontation had not gone away. In 1998 the British government produced the long-awaited Strategic Defence Review, which restructured Britain's armed forces and reflected two military factors: there was no longer a threat of war from the successor nation to the Soviet Union, even though it remained a huge nuclear power, and the United Kingdom government imagined that British forces were far more likely to be used as international firemen and UN peace-keepers. Nevertheless Britain did not stand down its nuclear forces, although the intercontinental ballistic missiles carried in submarines were expected to have a reduced role.

Here was a recognition that although the East–West confrontation was, for the foreseeable future, extinct, nuclear weapons were not. It was estimated in 1998 that in addition to the five major nuclear weapons powers – the United States, Britain, Russia, France and China – at least ten other states either had nuclear weapons or were actively in the process of trying to develop them. These countries included Israel, North Korea, Iran, India and Pakistan.

Of that number the most heated history of confrontation was between India and Pakistan. As if to confirm the sensitivities of those who doubted that nuclear confrontation could be forgotten, in May 1998 India exploded five nuclear warheads in a test programme to show that it would not be intimidated, and, as if to confirm what everybody had long expected, the Pakistan government ordered five similar explosions of its warheads.

Western governments had believed that Pakistan might carry out such tests and had pleaded with its government not to do so. Pakistan proved that no diplomatic leaning would work. Moreover, once the explosions had taken place, the only punishment the rest of the world could hand out was to impose upon Pakistan strict economic sanctions, including the withdrawal of aid programmes. While this had a sobering effect, it did not remove the nuclear weapons capability from the subcontinent.

In 1998, in spite of public declarations of intent, the chances of a successful Comprehensive Test Ban Treaty seemed far away and unenforceable. To paraphrase President Clinton's reaction, there seemed every chance that the world was about to enter the twenty-first century without having learned the mistakes of the twentieth.

Deaths

Eric Ambler (writer)
Dame Catherine Cookson (writer)
Archbishop Trevor Huddleston (missionary)
Ted Hughes (poet)
John Hunt, Baron Hunt of Llanfair Waterdine (mountaineer)
Frank Muir (writer and broadcaster)
Victor Pasmore (artist)
Pol Pot (Cambodian mass-murderer)
Enoch Powell (politician)
Roy Rogers (cowboy)

Vere Harmsworth, 3rd Viscount Rothermere (newspaper proprietor)
Alan Shepherd (US astronaut)
Frank Sinatra (US singer)
Dr Benjamin Spock (US paediatrician)
Sir Michael Tippett (composer)

THE END OF THE CENTURY

1999

THE LAST YEAR of the 1990s was not a happy one for millions of people who might have hoped that the same energies that were directed towards marking the end of a millennium might have been used to resolve their problems.

The conflicts in Africa, for example, claimed more lives and led to greater ethnic butchery than anything that happened in the Balkans, yet the world's wealthiest and most powerful nations, including Britain and the United States, failed to turn their moral crusade, let alone their cruise missiles, against the perpetrators of the wrong-doing. Human rights in China have continued to be disregarded by the Chinese government and ignored by the same nations that took on President Milošević and that have continued to fly over Iraq. And the East Timorese have had nothing more than the occasional Western newspaper article to help defend themselves against brutal oppression by the Indonesians.

During the early months of the year, across Europe and the Atlantic, foreign policy was focused on the Balkans, where President Milošević decided to rid Kosovo of its Albanian-Serb population and make it a Serbian dominion. An alliance of NATO states, enlarged by April 1999 to nineteen nations, agreed to bomb Serbia in order, it was thought, to prevent this from happening. The tactic was ill-advised, and did little to ameliorate the sufferings of the ethnic Albanians of Kosovo.

Considering what happened after the bombing started on 24 March 1999, it is important to put into perspective the events that led to this, the first war to be initiated by NATO, a supposedly defensive organization. In 1989 President Milošević took away Kosovan autonomy in order to protect the Serb minority living in the province, but in 1991, when Yugoslavia collapsed, it became clear that Kosovo would become a battleground, not just because some 90 per cent of the population of the region was of Albanian origin but because, for historical reasons, the Serbian minority regarded Kosovo as sacred territory.

In December 1992 President Bush told the Serbian leader that the United States was ready to intervene if the Serbs tried to rid Kosovo of Albanian Kosovars, and when Bill Clinton became president in 1993 he repeated the warning. But by 1996 the politicians had lost sight of Kosovo in the effort to bring some sort of peace to Bosnia. The Kosovar Albanians did not forget, however, and in 1998 they started a terrorist campaign against the Serbs and the Kosovo Liberation Army

(KLA) began to attack Serbians. The Serbs retaliated and killed KLA members and their families in Drenica.

The Americans did not take military action, as Bush and Clinton had said they would, because by now Washington was immersed in the Monica Lewinsky affair and the possibility of the president's impeachment. Moreover, Clinton's foreign policy gaze was concentrated on Russia (where the economy and President Yeltsin were in free-fall) and on Africa and China. Prime Minister Blair followed Clinton's lead.

When the United States and Europe did get round to Kosovo, it was decided that this had to be a NATO operation. The Americans believed that a diplomatic solution could be found, provided that military action was a credible threat if diplomacy failed. In May 1998 Ibrahim Rugova, the moderate Kosovo leader, warned that his country would soon be at war, and a month later the six-nation Contact Group on the Balkans (the United States, Britain, Russia, France, Germany and Italy) told Milošević that the Western countries had learned from the early days of the conflict in Bosnia and would not now hesitate to use military action. But the threats were empty.

Diplomacy was complicated when the KLA, which opposed Rugova's moderate stance, fought for and took nearly 40 per cent of Kosovo. Not unexpectedly, Milošević, who had assumed power to protect the Serb minority, struck back. NATO was unable to help. It would, it was believed, take some 200,000 ground troops to control Kosovo, but it would take months to get such a force into place and the US Congress would, in any case, be unlikely to agree to send troops into territory that was defended by Serb forces.

In the summer of 1998 a proposal was circulating in Washington that a protectorate should be established in Kosovo and safeguarded by Western troops, including Americans. That idea did not get far because it was presented in the week that the Oval Office was preoccupied with the president's appearance before the grand jury and the forthcoming mid-term elections and on the very day of the bombing of the American embassies in Tanzania and Kenya.

By October 1998 Clinton appears to have been given detailed plans for the mass-bombing of Serbia. Nothing could be implemented during the run-up to the US mid-term elections, however, and Richard Holbrooke, the US negotiator at the Dayton talks on Bosnia, was sent to the Balkans to talk to Milošević. The obvious difference this time was that Milošević regarded Kosovo as his own territory, which had not been the case in Bosnia. As a holding operation, Milošević agreed to let 1800 observers into Kosovo and to allow NATO aircraft to over-fly the province. Winter was approaching, and Milošević had nothing to lose.

At the start of 1999 the Serbs initiated Operation Potkova ('horseshoe') against the KLA, and the observers could do nothing, even when in January 1999 Serbs murdered forty-five Kosovars at a place called Racak, an event that marked the start of the Serbian ethnic cleansing of the region.

A last attempt to bring everyone to an agreement at a conference in Paris failed.

Robin Cook, the Foreign Secretary, kept repeating his assertion that Milošević had been warned, but the Serbian president does not appear to have been impressed.

The bombing began on 24 March 1999. Western intelligence reports claimed that Milošević would immediately give in, but a couple of days after the bombing had started the intelligence analysts changed their minds. Nevertheless, the bombing was under way – as was a test of NATO's credibility.

When the nineteen heads of NATO governments met in Washington for NATO's fiftieth birthday party at the end of April there was little to celebrate. For the first time in its existence NATO had gone to war. That war was being waged against a tiny power – and NATO had been found wanting. The political systems that had been designed to prevent war had broken down, and the intelligence apparatus that was supposed to give the Alliance leaders all the advantages in the modern technological and intellectual world had failed. Here was a demonstration of a new transatlantic strategic thinking. A just cause could be championed and people saved as long as no more than a handful of NATO lives were risked. In other words, no cause was worth the political consequences of many body bags. We were no longer willing to give lives in order that men might be free.

Kosovo was something of a distraction in British constitutional history, where the debate about devolution was about to be put to its most important test. During the 1997 general election campaign New Labour had promised devolved government for Scotland and Wales, and in September 1997 referenda were held. In Scotland there was a three-to-one majority in favour of devolution, but it was a close-run thing in Wales, where the turn-out was low and where those in favour of devolution won by only a narrow margin.

By devolution New Labour did not mean self-government. Scotland would have a parliament, while Wales would have an assembly. Although the Scottish parliament would be able to pass binding legislation, Westminster would retain control over major policy areas, including foreign affairs, defence, employment law, social security and border controls. The Welsh assembly would not be able to pass binding legislation. Proportional representation was used for the elections in both Wales and Scotland, with the Welsh promised sixty members, forty of them directly elected and twenty additional members. The Scots would have seventy-three directly elected members and fifty-six additional members.

The debate in Scotland turned on nationalism: would Scots really move towards independence? This was not an issue in Wales, where, contrary to popular opinion, the Welsh national party, Plaid Cymru, had never campaigned for independence.

The Scots and the Welsh went to the polls on 6 May 1999 to vote for their different forms of devolved government. In Scotland New Labour won fifty-six seats, the Scottish Nationalists thirty-seven, the Conservatives seventeen and the Liberal Democrats seventeen; there were two others. In Wales New Labour won twenty-eight seats, Plaid Cymru seventeen, the Conservatives nine and the Liberal Democrats six. New Labour failed to achieve an overall majority in either election.

Ironically, as Ulster Unionists tried to hold on to the concept of a United Kingdom, here was, perhaps, the beginning of a wider debate. Was the United Kingdom becoming disunited? Was the concept of the Union failing? Would, for example, a Westminster that was increasingly subordinate to Brussels become nothing more than the town hall, not of a United Kingdom but of England alone? The May elections in Wales and Scotland had been the beginning, not the end, of a greater constitutional debate.

A second constitutional change initiated by New Labour was the reform of the House of Lords. The government had already decided that the existing arrangement would go, but it had failed to answer one of the few valid points made by the Conservatives in 1998 and 1999: how could a government do away with the hereditary principle without first deciding what to put in its place? The more accepted models for change were similar to those proposed by Lord Lansdowne at the start of the century. It seems, in fact, that Blair had already decided but was not going to leave himself open to proper criticism by revealing his decision until he considered the time right. As the first half of 1999 drew to a close it appeared that the Lords would be replaced, in a move of supreme political irony, by a largely unelected chamber.

A third area of constitutional reform centred on the monarchy. Opinion polls suggested that by and large the nation still wanted a monarch, although there seemed to be a general acceptance that the institution might disappear within the next fifty years, perhaps sooner. There was widely held affection and respect for the Queen; less for her heir, the Prince of Wales, but more for his heir, Prince William.

If there were to be reforms they would, ostensibly, have to be initiated by the monarchy itself.[5] The strongest advice would come, as it had to, from government, but it would not be in New Labour's interests publicly to impose reform – the monarch, if not the monarchy, was too popular for that – so it was quietly agreed that political guidance would be presented in such a way that any changes would appear to come not from Downing Street but from Buckingham Palace.

The consideration of the role of monarchy in Britain offered an opportunity for a greater debate on the nature of kingship itself. In times past, kingship involved the monarch promising to protect the people from their enemies in return for their allegiance. Those enemies included government.

The British system of democracy means that there is no protection against an ever-more powerful executive. As these islands become more 'European', so the islanders become more vulnerable to a greater government. Any examination of the nature of kingship must, therefore, begin with the premise that the whole system must change.

---

5 See 1911, The Parliament Bill.

As the century draws to its end, the arguments that led to the American constitution – by which the president champions the people against the executive government, Congress – may become more attractive in the very country in which those arguments were developed, Britain. There is no new Tom Paine as we enter the twenty-first century, but in debating the role of monarchy we should not be afraid to consider whether republicanism provides the kingship that the peoples of these islands will need in the coming decades.

A fourth area of reform concerned the Church of England. There had already been some discussion within the Church of ways in which it might break away from the state and no longer be the established Church, and far-sighted clergy were privately suggesting that the whole debate could well provide the impetus towards revitalizing itself that the Church of England desperately needed.

So the century closes in many ways just as it had begun. As in the 1900s, Britain is extricating itself from a conflict it failed to prevent. As the century began, Britain was being pushed towards an alliance in Europe. Then, as now, the government was reluctant to commit itself wholeheartedly although understanding too well that such an outcome was inevitable. In the 1900s the major domestic issues were the future of Ireland, the education system, the provision of social services that the government could not afford, the monarchy and the power of the House of Lords. Most of the headlines that appeared at the start of the century would be relevant at its end.

What should we remember this century for? First, for its speed. Changes have happened more quickly in the last hundred years than ever before. Mass communications have usurped every major debate. The computer solves in seconds problems in design, engineering, science and commerce that used to take days or weeks to resolve. Yet the people who rely on them are as morally and philosophically frail as the society who hardly imagined the total reliance on the chip. We live longer and medical science has made our dying more complicated. We have learned to live with the threat of mass destruction and seem to forget – or at least, to ignore – the changes, political and scientific, that make nuclear war more, rather than less, likely.

Most of all, we have, as a race, learned not to be surprised. It really does appear that everything is possible, simply because science has championed the illusion that this is so. It may be, therefore, that the second half of this century has been the least interesting of all our centuries in that it has held the fewest surprises. The century ends with as many unsolved problems as it opened, but even this is unsurprising.

If we should learn one truth from these past one hundred years and, the more than two thousand years since our story of *This Sceptred Isle* started, it is this: what impresses today is nothing to what will impress us in the next century. Our grandchildren will be horrified by the butchery of our surgery and the barbarism of our manned battlefields, and bewildered by our failure to use our crude science, technology and wealth to make the world a safer and more reasonable place.

It may be that the American writer James Branch Cabell was right and that as the twentieth century draws to an end we should accept that, as the optimist claims, we live in the best of all possible worlds but that, as the pessimist fears, this is true.

Deaths

Sir Dirk Bogarde (actor)
Alfred Thompson Denning, Baron Denning (judge)
Basil Hume (Roman Catholic cardinal)
Ibn Talal Hussein (King of Jordan)
Sir Yehudi Menuhin (musician)
Dame Iris Murdoch (writer)
Sir Alf Ramsey (football manager)
William Whitelaw (politician)
Ernie Wise (comedian)

APPENDIX 1

FIRST WORLD WAR DIARY

1914

June

28 Archduke Franz Ferdinand assassinated at Sarajevo

July

28 Austria-Hungary declares war on Serbia
Russia, Serbia's ally, mobilizes

August

1 Germany declares war on Russia
Royal Navy mobilizes
3 Germany declares war on France
4 Germany invades Belgium
Britain declares war on Germany
6 Serbia declares war on Germany
Austria-Hungary declares war on Russia
HMS *Amphion* sunk by mine in North Sea
9 Germany and Austria-Hungary threaten Italy (which has declared itself neutral)
12 Britain and France declare war on Austria-Hungary
14–25 Battle of the Frontiers (including Battles of Lorraine, Ardennes, Sambre and Mons)
17 British Expeditionary Force lands in France
20 Germans take Brussels
23 Japan declares war on Germany
29 German governor of Samoa surrenders to New Zealanders

September

4–9 First Battle of the Marne (including Battles of the Ourcq, the Aisne and Albert)
10 South Africa sides with Britain

22 Royal Navy loses cruisers *Aboukir*, *Cressy* and *Hogue* in North Sea; 1500 men lost
23 British bomb Zeppelin base at Dusseldorf
26 Australians take German New Guinea

October
2 Battle of Arras
4 First bomb dropped on London
11 First bombs dropped on Paris
Battles of Flanders begin (including Battles of Messines and Armentières)
16 Battle of the Yser begins
19 First Battle of Ypres begins
28 Turkey attacks Russian Black Sea ports
30 Fisher takes over from Battenberg as First Sea Lord

November
1 Hindenberg becomes commander-in-chief of Eastern Front
4 Russia invades Armenia
5 Britain annexes Cyprus
10 German cruiser *Emden* sunk by RAN cruiser *Sydney*
26 HMS *Bulwark* explodes at Sheerness; 700 dead

December
3 Belgium is placed under German martial law
6 Germans take Lodz (Poland)
24 Germany now has 578,000 prisoners of war

1915

January
1 Military Cross (MC) introduced
5 Russia crushes Turkish 9th Army; 50,000 Turks killed
30 U-boat sinks three British merchantmen in Irish Sea
31 Tear gas used for first time in war by Germans against Russians at Bolimov

February
3 Russians enter Hungary
4 UK casualties to date total 104,000
18 German blockade of UK sea lanes
26 Clydeside armament workers strike for more pay

March
9 Battle of Grodno; Germany beats Russia

10 Battle of Neuve Chapelle
11 HMS *Bayano* sunk; 200 dead

April
5 France begins offensive on Western Front
22 Germans use mustard gas
Second Battle of Ypres begins (including Battles of Bravenstafel, St Julien, Frezenberg, Bellewaerde and Aubers)
23 Rupert Brooke dies from blood poisoning on way to Dardanelles
26 British, ANZAC and French land in Gallipoli
30 Germany invades Baltic states

May
3 Italy leaves Triple Alliance with Germany and Austria
7 Cunard Line's *Lusitania* sunk by German submarine off Ireland; 1400 dead including 128 Americans
10 First Zeppelin raids on London
13 South Africans capture German South West Africa
16 Second Battle of Artois (Vimy Ridge) begins
23 Italy declares war on Austria
25 Austria bombs Venice
British government forms wartime coalition
Churchill sacked from Admiralty after Gallipoli failure and offers to go to Front as soldier, but stays on as junior minister
Lloyd George confirmed as Minister for Munitions

June
4 Przemsyl falls to Austro-German offensive
8 VC for Flight Sub-lieutenant Reginald Warneford for bombing Zeppelin from 6000 feet (Warneford was later killed in a flying accident)
26 Battle of the Argonne begins

July
2 German submarines sink four British ships off Cornwall
3 German advance into Poland
7 Russia takes Lyublin
20 Russians retreat before German advance on Warsaw
25 Two American merchantmen sunk

August
7 Naval General Service Medal (GSM) instituted
9 Tsar rejects separate peace agreement with Germany
13 British and French attack Turkish fortifications but Gallipoli campaign becomes harder to sustain

19 White Star liner *Arabic* sunk by German submarines; Americans among dead
21 Italy declares war on Turkey
25 British and French advance in Champagne and Artois at standstill
31 Poland partitioned

September
5 Tsar takes command of Russian army
7 TUC opposes conscription
19 Germans take Vilna
22 Bulgaria mobilizes
23 Greece prepares to mobilize
26 Allied autumn offensive on Western Front

October
8 Russia attacks Bulgaria
12 Britain breaks off diplomatic relations with Bulgaria
Nurse Edith Cavell executed by German firing squad
15 US increases army
20 German and Bulgarian armies advance into Serbia

November
4 President Woodrow Wilson announces military planning
11 Churchill resigns and prepares to join army at the front
War Cabinet formed
21 Bosnia under Austro-German control

December
2 Joseph Joffre appointed commander-in-chief of French Army
15 Haig replaces French as commander-in-chief of British forces on Western Front
20 Allies retreat from Gallipoli

1916

January
4 British Home Secretary resigns over government plans for conscription
5 Senate debates European war
13 Miners vote against conscription
14 Austria overruns Montenegro but Balkan state refuses surrender offer
17 Russia starts Turkish offensive
23 British Museum closes for duration of war
27 Labour Party rejects conscription plan
Conscription given Royal Assent (Military Service Bill)

31 US Navy on stand-by for war but America does not join in

February

8 Food riots in Berlin
9 Smuts commands British and South African Alliance in East Africa
18 Germans defeated in Cameroons
21 Government raises extra £420 million war loan
Battle of Verdun begins
23 MPs attempt peace debate in Commons

March

5 12 killed in Zeppelin raids
9 Germany declares war on Portugal
15 Tirpitz resigns
20 Food rationing in Germany
21 Austrians massacre 9000 Serbian civilians
27 Allied Powers conference in Paris
28 Munition strike leaders arrested

April

4 Budget raises income tax
5 Military Medal (MM) introduced
18 America threatens to break off diplomatic relations with Germany
19 Government in trouble over conscription legislation
20 Russia turns down peace offer with Turkey
24 Easter Uprising against British rule in Ireland
25 First ANZAC Day
29 British surrender to Turks in Mesopotamia

May

4 Conscription increased to include all men between the ages of 18 and 41
8 German Meuse offensive
9 Government agrees no conscription in Ireland
15 Sir Roger Casement's trial begins
21 British Summer Time starts
31 Battle of Jutland

June

4 Russia starts Eastern Front offensive
5 Kitchener dies when HMS *Hampshire* hits mine
21 Arab Revolt (Lawrence of Arabia) against Turks
23 Ulster Unionists vote for partition
24 New German offensive at Verdun

July

1 Somme offensive opens with 60,000 British casualties on first day; 21,000 are killed within first hour
6 Lloyd George succeeds late Lord Kitchener as War Secretary
12 Russians push Germans back across Lipa
27 Russians overrun Turks at Erzinjan

August

2 Peace movement strengthens in Germany
3 Sir Roger Casement hanged for treason
French capture Fleury
21 Turkey begins massacre of 500,000 Armenians
27 Protests in Hyde Park against food prices
Romania declares war on Austria-Hungary
Germany declares war on Romania
Hindenberg appointed new German Chief of Staff

September

1 Romania defeats Austria at Battle of Orsova
Bulgaria declares war against Romania
18 Allied offensive in the Balkans
27 Greece declares war on Bulgaria

October

3 VD epidemic among British troops
5 President Wilson says America willing to fight (it is election year)
7 Allied breakthrough on the Somme
24 Second Battle of Verdun
31 350,000 British casualties in August, September and October

November

2 Germans retreat from Verdun
5 Poland declared independent by Germany and Austria
11 Wilson retains US presidency
21 Emperor Franz Josef dies
28 Government figures show 500,000 Allies and 650,000 Germans killed in Battle of the Somme

December

1 Greeks refuse to surrender to Allies
2 Conscription with no employment exemptions for under-26-year-olds
3 French replace Joffre with General Nivelle after Somme failure
7 Lloyd George takes over from Asquith as PM

7 Reports that Germans have deported 1 million Poles to forced labour
15 Verdun offensive casualties: 364,00 Allies and 338,000 Germans
30 Rasputin murdered

1917

January

1 Germans sink Cunard liner *Ivernia*; 153 dead
4 Anglo-German prisoner exchange of over 45s
9 Russian munition workers on strike
14 Provisional Polish parliament
25 Mine sinks HMS *Laurentic*; 350 dead

February

1 Germans say all shipping trading with Allies will be submarine targets
3 American SS *Housatonic* sunk off Sicily
US breaks off diplomatic relations with Germany
25 Cunard liner *Laconia* torpedoed; American casualties
26 Wilson asks Congress for powers to arm US ships

March

10 Riots in Petrograd
12 Tsar suspends Duma, but deputies disobey order
14 French Cabinet resigns
16 Tsar abdicates
18 Three US ships sunk by German submarines
20 British hospital ship *Asturias* torpedoed by Germans.
21 Nicholas II and Tsarina arrested
22 US recognizes Kerensky government in Russia
27 British overrun Turks at Gaza
29 Germany says it does not want war with US

April

6 US declares war on Germany
7 Cuba declares war on Germany
8 Panama declares war on Germany
11 Allied offensive in Arras
12 Bulgarian and Austrians put out peace feelers
16 Lenin returns to Russia
Nivelle offensive begins
17 British hospital ships *Lanfranc* and *Donegal* sunk by Germans
19 The USS *Mongolia* sinks German submarine

May

2 George V calls for people to make sacrifices in war effort
4 French army mutinies
7 British raid on Zeebrugge
15 US draft men between ages of 21 and 30
16 First US naval ships arrive in UK waters
26 German bombing raids kill 76 along south coast of England

June

1 Britain starts protected convoy system to beat U-boat threat
3 Italy claims Albania as protectorate
4 Brazil declares war on Germany
7 Churchill returns to government as Air Board chairman
New British offensive in Flanders
14 First German bombing raid on London; more than 500 casualties
17 US marines land in France
22 King Constantine of Greece abdicates
23 Soviet plans to disband Duma
26 George V changes family name from Saxe-Coburg-Gotha to Windsor; Battenbergs change name to Mountbatten

July

14 German Chancellor, Count Theobald von Bethmann Holweg, resigns
17 Churchill appointed Munitions Minister
25 Mata Hari sentenced to death
26 German advance along Aisne River
31 Third Battle of Ypres (Passchendaele)

August

14 Pope Benedict XV peace plan
17 Pope's plan supported by Kaiser
20 French break through German lines at Verdun
28 Americans reject the Pope's plan

September

9 Britain rejects the Pope's plan
10 Kerensky dismisses Russian army commander, Kornilov
15 Kerensky declares Russian Republic
China offers 300,000 troops to Allies
17 Germany calls for 15-year-olds as volunteers
Germans beat Russians at Riga

October

5 Peru breaks off diplomatic relations with Germany
7 Uruguay breaks off diplomatic relations with Germany
9 US to create black division of black soldiers
12 Admiral von Capelle resigns as German Naval Chief of Staff
15 Mata Hari executed
British government asks for reduction in private motoring
18 German submariners mutiny
27 US troops in battle for first time
29 German naval mutiny at Kiel begins
31 British capture Beersheba from Turks
Italians retreat before German gas attacks and Caporetto front falls

November

6 Canadians capture Passchendaele
7 Kerensky ousted in coup led by Lenin and Trotsky
18 British take Jaffa
26 Lenin offers peace terms to Germans and Austrians
29 Allied Council meets in Paris
Kaiser agrees Russian truce terms

December

1 President Wilson attacks Russian truce proposals
3 Britain refuses to recognize new Russian government
5 Austria willing to negotiate peace
7 US declares war on Austria
9 Finns demand withdrawal of Russian troops
British capture Jerusalem
22 Bolshevik and German peace talks at Brest-Litovsk

1918

January

4 Russia agrees Finnish independence
6 Germans recognize Finland
9 US fourteen-point postwar plan
15 Peace protests in Prague and Budapest
22 British rationing bans meat on two days each week
31 Martial law in Germany following strikes

February

1 Germans bomb Paris; 45 dead
8 Meat rationing in Britain
20 Russo-German armistice collapses

21 Australians take Jericho
27 British hospital ship SS *Gelnart Castle* sunk by U-boat

March
3 Bolsheviks surrender Poland, Lithuania, Riga and part of Byelorussia to Germany and Ardahan, Batum and Kars to Turks
5 Moscow becomes capital of Russia
7 British government need extra £700 million in war loans
9 Conscription age to be raised to 50 and include Irish
13 Tank Week fund-raising produces £138 million
20 Fuel rationing. Theatres and restaurants ordered to close early
26 General Foch appointed commander-in-chief of Allied Forces in France

April
1 Royal Air Force formed from Royal Flying Corps and Royal Naval Air Service
2 Anti-conscription riots in Canada
5–6 British, Japanese and US troops land at Vladivostok
8 Lenin threatens to declare war on Japan
13 Haig says every soldier must fight to the end after German successes at Ypres; 400,000 Allies killed in three weeks
22 Red Baron shot down over Somme
Budget raises taxes
23 British block German U-boat pens at Zeebrugge and Ostende
26 Soviet government agrees diplomatic relations with Germany

May
7 Nicaragua declares war on Germany
10 Mustard gas used at Amiens
29 Germans take Rheims

June
3 Protests over Irish call-up
18 Government asks for further £500 million war loan
19 General rationing
20 Irish conscription cancelled
22 French halt German advance on Paris

July
16 Tsar Nicholas II and his family assassinated at Ekaterinburg
23 Washington conference for 'Big Push' against Germans
29 Germany breaks off diplomatic relations with Turkey
31 Germans retreat across River Marne

August

1 Government asks for extra £700 million war loan

2 Britain and America support White Russian revolution against Russian communists

8 Allied troops push back Germans near Amiens

15 US breaks diplomatic relations with Russia

25 Rioters in Berlin destroy pictures of Kaiser

September

15 UK and US reject Austrian peace offer

24 British take Haifa and Acre from Turks

30 Bulgaria surrenders

October

1 Lawrence and Emir Feisal lead way into Damascus

7 British take Beirut

9 U-boat sinks mailboat SS *Leinster*; 587 dead

15 Czechoslovak Republic established

17 Hungary breaks from Austro-Hungarian Empire

30 Austrian army pulls out of Italy

31 Turkey surrenders
Austria is declared a republic

November

3 Austria signs armistice

6 German High Command orders troops to pull back

9 Kaiser Wilhelm II abdicates

11 Germany surrenders to Marshal Foch

APPENDIX 2

SECOND WORLD WAR DIARY

1939

March

10–16 Germany takes rest of Czech homelands

21 Germany annexes Memel

31 Britain and France guarantee Polish independence

April

7 Italy invades Albania

13 Britain and France guarantee independence to Romania and Greece
Conscription reintroduced

June

Britain, France and USSR start negotiations

August

23 Germany and Russia sign Non-Aggression (Ribbentrop) Pact

24 Britain promises Poland assistance

30 Evacuation starts of 1.5 million British children

31 Tri-service reserves called up
Hitler orders attack on Poland

September

1 Germany invades Poland

3 Britain and France declare war on Germany
Liner *Athenia* torpedoed by U-boat

4 Winston Churchill appointed First Lord of the Admiralty

9 BEF begins crossing to France

17 Soviet armies invade Poland

18 HMS *Courageous* sunk; 500 dead

27 Poland surrenders

October

12 British Expeditionary Force of 158,00 men lands in France

14 HMS *Royal Oak* sunk at Scapa Flow; 800 dead

November

30 USSR attacks Finland

December

17 Battle of River Plate; Germans scuttle *Graf Spee*
Beginning of Battle of the Atlantic

19 Canadian troops arrive in UK

1940

January

1 2 million called up

March

12 Finns surrender

April

9 Germans invade Norway and Denmark

14 Allies retake Narvik

May

10 Churchill becomes prime minister
German troops invade Low Countries
Britain starts internment

14 Dutch surrender

26 Belgians surrender

28 Dunkirk evacuation begins (lasts until 3 June)

June

3 Allies start withdrawal from Norway

4 Dunkirk evacuation completed

7 Norwegian withdrawal complete

10 Italy declares war on Britain and France

14 Germans march into Paris

18 Churchill makes 'Their finest hour' speech
De Gaulle broadcasts to France from London

20 Australian and New Zealander troops arrive in UK

22 French declare armistice with Germany

30 Germans occupy Channel Islands

July

1 Germans invade Channel Islands
3 Royal Navy sinks French fleet in Algeria; 1000 French sailors perish
9 Vichy government set up
10 Battle of Britain begins (lasts until 31 October)
23 Home Guard established

August

25 First bombing raid on London

September

7 Blitz begins (continues for 57 nights)
27 Japan joins German–Italian axis

October

8 Germany invades Romania

November

Hungarian–Romanian–Japanese–Italian–German Pact

December

9 British forces take Sidi Birani

1941

January

22 Australian and British troops capture Tobruk
14 Afrika Korps lands in Tripoli

March

11 Lease Lend Agreement signed with US
Bulgaria joins Axis

April

6 Germany invades Yugoslavia and Greece
17 Yugoslavia surrenders
26 Germans march into Athens

May

10 Commons destroyed by bombing
Rudolf Hess flies to Scotland
20 Germans bomb Crete
24 HMS *Hood* sunk by the *Bismarck*; more than 1300 dead
27 *Bismarck* sunk; 1000 dead

June
1 British and NZ troops evacuate Crete
22 Germans invade USSR

December
7 Japanese attack on Pearl Harbor
8 Britain declares war on Japan
Japanese take Hong Kong

1942

January
26 First US troops arrive in UK

February
15 Singapore falls to Japanese

June
7 Battle of Midway
27 British Eighth Army retreats from Mursa Matruh

July
2 Germans invade northern Caucasus and take Sevastopol

August
6 Montgomery takes command of Eighth Army
19 Raid on Dieppe

September
2 50,000 die in Warsaw ghetto
RAF blanket-bomb Dusseldorf and Bremen

October
24 Battle of El Alamein
26 Hitler purges German High Command

November
8 British and American troops land in North Africa
12 Battle of Guadalcanal
19 Soviet counteroffensive against German invasion starts

1943

January
14–24 Casablanca Conference

31 German surrender at Stalingrad
RAF daylight bombing on Berlin

May
17 Dambusters raid on Möhne and Eder damns

July
10 Allies land in Sicily
24 Eight-day bombing of Hamburg begins
25 Mussolini falls

September
3 Allies invade Italy
8 Italy agrees armistice
10 Germans hold Rome
17 Germans retreat from Salerno

October
13 Italy declares war on Germany

November
6 Soviet armies retake Kiev
28 Teheran Conference

December
24 Eisenhower appointed Supreme Allied Commander
26 *Scharnhorst* sunk

1944

January
22 Anzio landings

March
17 Monte Casino raids
24 Orde Wingate killed in air crash

June
4 Allies enter Rome
6 D-Day; Normandy landings begin
14 V1 (doodle-bug) attacks on southeast England

July
1–22 Bretton Woods Conference
20 Von Stauffenberg attempt on Hitler's life

August

Soviet armies into Poland, Romania and East Prussia
15 Allies land in southern France
21 Dumbarton Oaks Conference (until 9 October)
24 Romanians surrender
25 Allies enter Paris

September

2 Allies enter Brussels
9 V2s launched on London
12 Americans cross into Germany
25 Battle of Arnhem

October

9 Plans for UN announced at Dumbarton Oaks
14 Rommel commits suicide
21 MacArthur back in the Philippines

November

12 RAF sink the *Tirpitz*

December

19 Germans mount fruitless counteroffensive in the Ardennes (until 9 January 1945)

1945

January

17 Soviet troops take Warsaw

February

4–11 Yalta Conference (meeting between Stalin, Roosevelt and Churchill)
14 Destruction of Dresden
23 Battle of Iwo Jima

March

7 Allies cross Rhine

April

12 Roosevelt dies
20 Russians enter Berlin
28 Germans surrender in Italy
Mussolini shot by Italian partisans
30 Hitler commits suicide

May

3 British retake Rangoon
7 German surrender
8 VE Day
23 Himmler commits suicide

June

26 UN established

July

5 Labour wins General Election
16 Potsdam Conference attended by Truman and Stalin and by Churchill and, after election, Attlee

August

6 Atomic bomb dropped on Hiroshima
9 Atomic bomb dropped on Nagasaki
14 Japan surrenders

Index

Abyssinia 185, 188–90
Adams, Gerry 371, 392, 440, 441, 446, 453
Adenauer, Konrad 249, 271, 274, 282, 290
Afghanistan 46, 163, 273, 379, 381–2, 418
Agadir Incident 70–1, 76
agreements, Anglo-Irish (1985) 401, 439–40, 447; Camp David 371; Dayton (1995) 452; Good Friday (1998) 461; Gorbachev-Reagan 410; Helsinki 361–2; Munich (1938) 199–200; Paris Note 1922) 128; Potomac (1954) 268; Suez Canal (1954) 270, 276
agriculture 5, 55, 81, 100, 108, 176, 184–5, 259, 367, 376
aid 332–3, 399, 403, 438, 441, 442; Marshall 240
air raids 200, 209, 211, 222, 229–30; precautions 200–1, 203–4
air travel 23, 59, 151, 154, 158, 204; accidents 288, 403, Lockerbie 411
aircraft, military 95, 183, 187, 190, 196, 200, 229
Albania 24, 77–8, 83, 238–9, 274
Alexander I, of Yugoslavia 184
Algeria 277, 287, 297, 348, 369
alliances 8, 10, 11, 25, 225; Anglo-French (Entente Cordiale) 25–6, 41, 46, 69, 76, 93, 118, 203, 282; Anglo-German 8–12, 76; Anglo-Japanese (1902) 11, 25, 26; Anglo-Russian (1907) 46–7; Franco-Russian 10, 11, 25, 46; Triple (Germany, Italy, Austria-Hungary) 10, 47, 121; Triple Entente (France, Britain, Russia) 47, 91, 92, 225
Amery, Leo 161, 215
Amin, Idi 342, 365, 379
Amory, Derick Heathcoat 286, 289, 295
Amundsen, Roald 71, 158
anarchists 72, 117
Andrew, Prince 407, 434
Andropov, Yuri 392
Anne, Princess 353, 434, 454
Arabs 77, 107, 122, 166, 238, 277, 322–3, 347, 350, 369, 371 *see also individual countries*
Arafat, Yasser 333, 379, 392, 442
Argentina 364, 389–91
Armstrong, Neil 333
Armstrong-Jones (Lord Snowdon) 297, 364
army 27, 45–6, 54, 67, 86, 88, 94, 203, 204; BEF 45, 46, 89, 94, 203, 204, 209; Home Guard 226; Territorial 46, 203, 204
art 49, 98, 198, 270; Pop 305; war artists 98, 233
Ashdown, Paddy 412
Asquith, Herbert Henry 14, 22, 37, 38, 131, 139, 147–51 *passim*, 158; as PM 50–2, 58, 60–4, 68, 69, 75, 76, 89, 93, 102, 109
athletics 154, 270–1; Olympic Games 30, 55, 80, 98, 140, 158, 247, 314, 347
Atlantic Charter 216
atom bombs *see* nuclear weapons
Attlee, Clement 96, 110, 167, 198, 216, 269, 272; as PM 230–55 *passim*
Australia 7–8, 96, 128, 143, 163, 168, 177, 182, 205, 370, 413
Austria 184, 187, 188, 200, 239; -Hungary 10, 53–4, 77–9 *passim*, 83, 88, 89, 94, 115

Baden-Powell, Robert 3, 48
Baekeland, Leo 59
Baird, John Logie 144
Baldwin, Stanley 129, 147, 159, 167, 172, 174, 179, 183, 187, 188; as PM 130–3, 140–59, 185–96 *passim*
Balfour, Arthur James 1–2, 6, 39, 40, 57, 62, 63, 71; as PM 14–37 *passim*, 176; Declaration 106–7, 122, 166, 197
Balkans 24, 53–4, 74, 77–9, 83, 163, 434–6 *see also individual countries*
ballet 59, 175, 199, 301
Baltic States 417, 418
Bangladesh 342, 403, 411
banks 7, 170–2; Barings 452; of England 171–2
Barber, Anthony 337, 339, 350
battles, of Atlantic 209, 219; of Britain 209; of the Bulge 228; El Alamein 217; Passchendaele 103; Somme 100; Stalingrad 217, 219; Tsushima 33; Ypres 103

BBC 133, 140, 144, 148, 152, 202, 275, 301, 304–5, 318, 333, 377
Beatles, The 304, 317
Beaverbrook, Lord 102, 167–8, 312
Beeching, Dr Richard 283, 308
Begin, Menachim 369, 371, 378
Belgium 41–2, 89, 92, 131, 141, 164, 228, 281
Bell, Alexander Graham 99
Benn, Tony 319, 329, 360, 363, 386, 447
Berlin 116, 290, 299; blockade 245–6, 249; East 263; Wall 299, 417, 419
Berry, Albert 80
Bethman-Hollweg, Theobald 83, 90, 91
Bevan, Aneurin 221, 234, 244, 255, 272
Beveridge, Sir William 219–21, 231
Bevin, Ernest 149, 216, 220, 231, 232, 234, 246, 249, 255, 281
Birch, Nigel 283, 285
Birkenhead, Lord 141, 143, 156
Birrell, Augustine 38, 62, 82
Blair, Tony 289, 433, 444–5, 451, 457–8; as PM 458–68 *passim*
Bonar Law, Andrew 71, 75, 80, 85, 102, 109, 128; as PM 129–30
Bondfield, Margaret 159–60
Bosnia 85, 434–6, 441–2, 448, 452, 463
Bowes-Lyon, Lady Elizabeth 133, 192
boxing 55, 266, 297
Brezhnev, Leonid 310, 328, 379, 382, 383, 392, 418; Doctrine 383
Briand, Aristide 156, 161, 164, 239
British summer time 102
Brittan, Leon 400, 404–5
Brown, George 280, 306, 320, 323, 364
Bruton, John 446, 453
BSE 423, 455
budgets 56–8, 94, 98, 170, 241, 295, 350, 355, 411–12, 437; May Committee 170–1
Bulganin, Nikolai 272, 279, 280, 290
Bulgaria 24, 77–9, 83, 94, 128, 234, 274
Burma 241
Bush, George 382, 399, 416, 434, 436, 443, 463
Butler, R.A. 223–4, 259, 260, 271, 278–9, 304, 308, 317
Butlin, Billy 195

Callaghan, James 311, 318–19, 321, 330, 360, 380; as PM 362–73
Cambodia 337
Cameroons 122
Campbell, J.R. 139
Campbell-Bannerman, Sir Henry 4, 14, 36; as PM 37–49 *passim*, 52
Canada 113, 128, 168, 177, 203
Capone, Al 163, 205
Carrington, Lord 307, 316, 354, 374, 378, 379, 390, 422
Carson, Sir Edward 74–5, 85, 102, 123
Carter, Howard 140
Carter, Jimmy 369, 379, 382, 384
Casement, Sir Roger 102
Castle, Barbara 272, 321, 329–30, 360, 361
Castro, Fidel 290, 296, 302
Cawdor, Earl of 28, 52, 62
Ceausescu, Nikolai 419
Chamberlain, Austen 22, 62, 71, 127, 141, 150, 181, 196
Chamberlain, Joseph 4, 8–9, 12, 14, 19–23, 35, 36, 40, 50, 57, 176, 177
Chamberlain, Neville 130, 152, 155, 172, 174, 176, 177, 209, 210; as PM 196–208
Channel Tunnel 404, 444
Chaplin, Charlie 99, 140, 143, 210, 261, 370
Charles, Prince 305, 383, 388, 443, 453, 454, 466
Chernenko, Konstantin 392
Chiang Kai-shek 157, 185
Chichester-Clark, Major James 331, 339
China 72, 161, 253–4, 310, 320, 409–10, 419–20, 459, 463, 464; *Amethyst* incident 249–50; civil war 153, 157, 185, 239
Christie, Agatha 151–2
churches 5–6, Catholic 6, 45, 68, 273, 335; of England 5, 16, 18, 45, 68, 148, 153, 186, 273, 335, 443, 448, 467; Nonconformists 16, 68, 273, 335
Churchill, Clementine 148, 208, 265
Churchill, Winston 22, 29, 35–6, 38, 47, 51, 75, 97, 127–9, 137, 140, 147, 179, 181, 189, 233, 239, 241, 257, 314–15; as Chancellor 141, 142, 152, 156; First Lord of Admiralty 85, 87, 93–4, 96–7, 204; Home Secretary 71–2; PM 208–30, 258–72; War Minister 113
CIS 428–30
Clarke, Kenneth 438
Clemenceau, Georges 117, 118
Clinton, Bill 358, 434, 441, 460–1, 463, 453, 464
cloning 455–6
Collins, Michael 101, 122–3, 126
Commonwealth 125, 168, 251–2, 264, 289, 301, 312, 342, 368, 378, 390, 447; Immigration Act 325
Communist Party of Great Party 194
concentration camps (British) 4, 12, 13; (German) 180, 227, 228
Concorde 311
Conference, Algeciras (1906) 41, 42, 70; Anglo-Irish (1985) 440; Bermuda (1957) 282; Bretton Woods (1944) 225–6; Casablanca (1943) 219; Commonwealth (1971) 342, (1977) 368; constitutional (1910) 62; Disarmament (1932) 181, 183; Dublin (1921) 125; Dumbarton Oaks (1944) 225; Genoa (1922) 127; Geneva

(1954) 272, (1992) 436; G7 (1993) 438; Hague (1929) 160–1; Imperial 20, 131, 168, 177; London (1912) 79, Naval (1930) 164, (1953) 264–5, (1956) 276; Mudania (1922) 128; Paris (1919) 116–18, (1950) 252, (1960) 296, (1973) 351, (1999) 464; peace (1899) 9; Potsdam (1945) 231; San Remo (1920) 122; St Petersburg (1904) 25–6; Washington (1921–2) 161; Yalta (1945) 230
conscription 99, 100, 204, 282, 293
Conservatives 13, 14, 21–2, 29, 35, 58, 62, 71, 97, 127, 130, 139, 175–6, 188, 230, 257, 259, 307–8, 316–17, 359, 393–4, 437, 445, 450; and Europe 339, 437, 445; and sleaze 451
contraception 178; pill 301
Cosgrave, Liam 357
Cousins, Frank 319
Coward, Noel 143, 175, 213, 218
Craig, Sir James 125
Craig, William 331
cricket 55, 133, 143, 182, 266, 295, 305, 370, 388, 448
crime 5, 30, 81, 112, 186, 272–3, 326, 335, 387, 396, 431–2; war 436, 441, 442, 448, 452
Crippen, Hawley Harvey 67
Cripps, Sir Stafford 216, 217, 234, 237, 254
Croatia 434–5
Cromer, Lord 311
Crosland, Anthony 363, 364, 366, 367
Crossman, Richard 323, 341
Cuba 290, 296, 298, 302–3
culture 270, 280, 284–5, 451–2, 457
Curzon, Lord 18, 69, 128, 130, 141
Cyprus 270, 282–3, 286–7, 291, 357
Czechoslovakia 187, 188, 199, 204, 234, 245, 246, 274, 276, 328, 369, 418, 419

Dalton, Hugh 219, 234, 240, 241
Davidson, Archbishop 1, 153
Dawes, Charles G. 137–8, 153
decimalization 338
decolonization 234, 241, 264–5, 283, 294, 297, 311–12
defence policy 6, 24, 26–8, 70, 187, 189, 196, 198, 255–8 *passim*, 268–9, 282, 321, 373–4, 462; civil 201, 269; Committee of Imperial – 27, 69–70
De Gaulle, Charles 211, 219, 239, 287, 297, 301, 303, 308, 324, 328, 332
demobilization 112–13, 232
Deng Xiaoping 410, 419, 420
Denmark 117, 187, 289, 322, 343
Depression, Great 148, 169–70, 177, 185
De Valera, Eamon 101, 122, 125, 197, 283
devaluation 173, 241, 248, 321–2
Devlin, Bernardette 336
devolution 355, 363, 465–6
disarmament 52, 161, 181, 183, 189, 196; CND 286, 300, 396; unilateral 300, 386
disease 12, 38, 82, 101, 199; HIV-AIDS 402–3, 449
divorce 236
DNA 265
Dollfuss, Engelbert 184
Douglas-Home, Sir Alec (Earl of Home) 295, 308, 310 316–17, 337, 340–1; as PM 308, 310
drinking problems 51, 97–8; Licensing Act 51
Dubcek, Alexander 328
Du Cann, Edward 359
Dulles, John Foster 262–3, 277
Dunkirk evacuation 209

earthquakes 43, 133, 205, 411
East–West relations 262-6 *passim*, 268, 272, 274, 290-1, 296, 340-2; summits (Geneva 1955) 272, (Paris 1960) 296, (Reykjavik 1986) 406, (Vienna 1961) 299
economy 6–7, 124, 142, 144, 160, 162, 169–73, 175–7, 184–5, 193–4, 198, 239–41, 248, 255, 259, 273, 283, 295, 299–300, 303–4, 310–11, 318–19, 325–6, 335–6, 350, 355, 361, 363–4, 366, 381, 432, 433, 437; run on pound 170–3, 278, 283, 311, 319, 321, 326, 361, 363–4, 412, 414, 433
Eden, Anthony 96, 187, 189–91, 199, 200, 204, 260, 263, 268, 271; as PM 272–9
education 7, 15–18, 44–5, 81, 108, 136, 152, 169, 186, 223–4, 399; Acts (1902) 15, 18, 19, 40, 81, (1918) 108, 223, (1944) 223–4; Workers Association 17, 81
Edward VII 2–3, 11, 13, 18, 49–50, 52, 58, 60, 64
Edward VIII 191–2, 195
Egypt 10, 41, 166, 237, 245, 254, 256, 257, 260, 269–70, 276–9, 322–3, 346, 352, 369, 371, 388; Suez Canal 122, 237, 254, 257, 259, 270, 276–9
Eichmann, Adolf 301
Einstein, Albert 39
Eisenhower, Dwight D. 219, 261, 263, 265, 268, 271, 277, 278, 282, 284, 290, 296
elections 13, 39, 60, 63, 109, 131, 138, 140, 150, 159, 167, 173–4, 190, 230–1, 251, 257, 272, 288–9, 354, 372, 393, 395, 432, 458; European 445
Elizabeth, Princess 192, 210, 233, 247, 257, 260; Queen 262, 288, 366, 434, 458, 466
Ellis, Ruth 275
Empire 7, 8, 10, 18–20, 22, 40, 65, 164, 168, 234, 241; Imperial Preference 20, 22–3, 65, 176, 177; United Party 167–8
eruptions, volcanic 43, 403
Ethiopian famine 399, 403

Europe 10, 11, 188, 202, 240, 252, 259; federal, pan- 161, 164, 239, 259; policy towards 7, 11, 76, 93, 141, 142, 164, 188, 252, 281; Western Union 246
Europe, Eastern 234, 240, 279, 362, 417–19
European Coal and Steel Community 252, 256, 281
European Common Market/European Union 281; CAP 367, 376; Central Bank 424; Exchange Rate Mechanism 412, 414–15, 424, 432–3, 438; Maastricht Treaty 427; relations with 281–2, 300–1, 308, 324, 339, 343, 349–50, 360–1, 376–7, 381, 385–6, 412–17, 421, 424–5, 427
European Free Trade Association 289, 308, 311, 349
evacuation, of cities 209, 217–18, 223, 232

Fabian Society 110, 395
Falklands 364, 389–91
family allowances 235, 283
Farouk, King 205, 254, 270
Faulkner, Brian 339, 345–6, 356
Feisal II 287
Ferguson, Sarah 407
Festival of Britain 255
films 24, 56, 59, 80, 99, 140, 158, 194, 201, 205, 210, 213, 218, 261, 262, 266, 280, 285, 297, 301, 304, 305, 307, 324, 388, 396, 403
Fisher, Admiral Sir 'Jackie' 27, 28, 97
Fitzgerald, Garret 400–1, 439
Fiume 115–16
floods 87, 240, 266, 422; Thames Barrier 396
Foot, Michael 286, 360, 361, 363, 380, 385, 394
football 80, 133, 266, 288, 318, 336, 358, 379, 403, 426, 448
Ford, Gerald 352, 358
Ford, Henry 23, 83–4, 113, 154; Motor Company 23
France 7, 10, 25, 41, 70, 78, 79, 89, 107, 117, 118, 128, 164, 186, 188, 192, 276–9, 281, 282, 287, 297, 308, 320, 323, 327–8, 332, 348; and Algeria 287, 297; and Germany 117, 118, 124, 131–2, 138, 181, 184, 203, 239, 247, 267, 282, 416; and Indochina 262–3, 267; relations with 25–6, 41, 47, 55, 70–1, 76, 137–8, 141, 181, 203, 256, 282, 301, 308, 323, 324
franchise 7, 64, 76, 108–9, 152, 156, 169, 335
Franco, General 192–3, 200, 205, 320–3
Franz Ferdinand, Archduke 85, 88
Franz Joseph, Emperor 78, 83, 88, 90
French, Field Marshal Sir John 86, 94

Gaddafi, Muammar 322
Gagarin, Yuri 290, 298, 299
Gaitskell, Hugh 254, 272, 277, 288–9, 300, 306
Gallipoli expedition 96–7
Gandhi, Mahatma 47–8, 112, 124, 142, 165–6, 215–17, 237, 241, 245
garden cities 31
George V 60, 62, 63, 71, 134, 156, 161–3, 171, 172, 178, 185, 191, 195
George VI 192, 195, 254, 257, 260
Germany (pre-1945) 7, 11, 28, 41–2, 45, 52–4, 68–71, 78, 79, 83, 89, 93, 116–18, 120–1, 124–5, 131, 141, 142, 145, 153, 164–5, 179–88, 198–230; air force 184, 186–7; army 74, 79, 83, 117, 121, 186, 199; economy 121, 124, 132, 137–8, 165, 179; and Jews 165, 166, 180–1, 187, 197, 199; Navy 24, 25, 28, 52, 69, 74, 83, 117–18, 187; Nazis 120–1, 131, 142, 153, 165, 179–81, 183, 184, 198; rearmament 184, 187–9; relations with 4, 8–12, 25, 28, 69–71, 76–7, 91–3, 117–18, 137, 181–2, 211, First World War 89–111, 469–79, Second 202–3. 209, 211, 215, 217, 219, 228–30, 480–7; and reparations 117, 121, 127, 131, 137–8, 160–1, 188; Rhineland 161, 186; Ruhr 132, 138; Saar 185, 186
Germany, East 234, 249, 261, 263, 266, 274, 279, 290, 299, 417–19 *see also* Berlin
Germany, West/GFR 245–6, 249, 252, 256, 260, 267, 274, 281, 347–8, 416, 435; reunification 249, 267, 272, 416–17, 424
Ghana (Gold Coast) 283
Gibraltar 320, 440
Gibson, Guy 219
Giraud, General Henri 219
Gladstone, Herbert 38, 51, 71
Glenn, John 299
Goddard, Robert H. 151
Goebbels, Josef 184, 187
Goering, Hermann 179, 180, 186, 187, 199
gold standard 142, 145, 173
Goldwater, Barry 313
Gomulka, Wladyslaw 279
Gorbachev, Mikhail 392, 401–2, 406, 416–20 *passim*, 428
Gough, General Hubert 86
Gow, Ian 401, 423
Gowon, Jabuku 320, 332
Greece 77–9 *passim*, 83, 127, 270, 357
Greenwood, Arthur 169, 220, 234
Grey, Sir Edward 37, 38, 51, 53, 61, 62, 69, 70, 75, 76, 79, 89–93 *passim*
Griffiths, James 235
Gromyko, Andrei 280, 341, 368, 401
Gummer, John Selwyn 395, 402

Habash, George 333
Habgood, Archbishop 443
Hague, William 458

Haiti 406
Haldane, Robert Burdon 14, 37, 38, 45–6, 51, 76–7, 134, 135
Halifax (Irwin), Lord 165, 179, 196, 200, 203, 208
Hankey, Sir Maurice 115, 129, 179
Hardie, Keir 48, 52
Harding, Warren 121
Harrington, General 128
Harris, Sir Arthur 217, 228–30
Haughey, Charles 400
Healey, Denis 315, 316, 321, 336, 355, 363, 366, 373, 380
health 82, 101, 126, 151, 152, 155, 157, 185, 207, 220–1; NHS 223–5, 244, charges 255, 299
Heath, Edward 289, 295, 300, 317, 325, 359, 369, 375; as PM 336–55 *passim*
Henderson, Arthur 110, 135, 160–1, 164, 166, 171
Heseltine, Michael 268, 337, 404–5, 422, 424, 426, 427, 445, 450
Hilary, Edmund 182, 266
Himmler, Heinrich 187
Hindenburg, Field Marshal Paul von 142, 179, 184
Hirohito, Emperor 133
Hitler, Adolf 120–1, 131, 133, 140, 142, 153, 165; as Chancellor 177–87 *passim*, 200, 213
Ho Chi Minh 239
Hoare, Sir Samuel 172, 189–91, 196
Hogg, Quintin 176, 308
Holbrooke, Richard 464
Honecker, Erich 419
Hong Kong 237, 365, 399, 420, 459
Hoover, Herbert 177, 382
Hore-Belisha, Leslie 196
housing 135–6, 169, 184, 226, 232, 235–6, 257, 272, 286, 376
Howe, Geoffrey 337, 359, 374, 381, 413–15 *passim*, 421, 422, 425
Huggins, Godfrey 265
Hume, John 439
Hungary 116, 234, 263, 274, 278, 279, 418–19
Hurd, Douglas 413, 426, 439
Hussein, King 287, 468
Hussein, Saddam 383, 428, 443

IBRD *see* World Bank
Iceland 287, 364
India 18, 43, 48, 112, 124, 142–3, 165–6, 190, 215–17, 237, 241–3, 245, 316, 342, 357, 399, 462
Indochina 239, 262–3, 267 *see also individual countries*
industrial relations 113–14, 124, 145–8, 152, 205, 274, 295, 329–30, 353, 380–1; Bill 337, 339 *see also* strikes
industry 7, 66, 113–14, 144–9 *passim*, 155, 185–6, 295; coal 65, 145–9, 167, 185, 215, 226–7, 236, 239, 273, 350, 397–8; construction 136, 184, 236; cotton 54, 66, 124, 144, 185; fishing 81, 364–5; motor 66, 83–4, 113, 273, 384; steel 66, 273
inflation 94, 114, 283, 300, 343–4, 355, 361, 363, 375, 384, 394, 414, 423, 433, 437
Inskip, Sir Thomas Inskip 153
insurance 7, 170; National scheme (1911) 73, 81, 220, 221, (1946) 235, 244
intelligence test 38
interest rates 283, 295, 311, 319, 364, 424, 433
International Monetary Fund 221, 225, 321–2, 361, 364, 366
Iran 256–7, 373, 379, 382–4, 408, 462 *see also* Persia
Iraq 122, 287, 383, 424, 428, 443, 455
Ireland 48, 62–3, 82, 85–6, 89, 91, 101, 120, 122–3, 125–6; Black and Tans in 123; Curragh incident 86; Easter Rising 101– 2; Home Rule 14, 21, 36–7, 60–3, 69, 74–6, 82, 85, 89, 101, 123; IRB/IRA 101, 120, 122–6 *passim,* 205, 207; Nationalists 40, 60, 74, 75, 126 *see also* Irish Free State
Ireland, Northern *see* Ulster
Irish Free State/Eire/Republic 197, 205, 247, 283, 322, 343, 365, 400–1, 441, 446, 461
Isaacs, Sir Rufus 79, 80, 172
Israel 245, 277, 322–3, 347, 352, 365, 392, 462, 301; and Egypt 277, 322, 369, 371; and PLO 442
Issigonis, Alec 291
Italy 7, 10, 77, 89, 115–17, 128, 131, 141, 142, 164, 188–90, 193, 199, 200, 219, 238, 252, 281, 347, 372; and Abyssinia 185, 188–9
Izetbegovic, Alija 448, 452

Japan 7, 8, 11, 25, 26, 33–5, 48, 133, 164, 179, 183, 185, 231, 399; Second World War 203, 213, 214, 231–2
Jay, Douglas 361; Peter 368
Jenkins, Clive 386
Jenkins, Roy 322, 330, 335–6, 361, 363, 365, 367, 380, 384–6
Jerusalem 107, 197, 237, 239, 322, 369
Jews 24, 34, 48, 52, 106–7, 122, 165, 166, 180–1, 187, 197, 199, 237–8, 365 *see also* Israel; Zionism
Jinnah, Muhammad Ali 216, 237, 241, 245
John Paul II, Pope 372, 383, 388
Johnson, Lyndon Baines 309, 313, 315–16, 323, 327
Jordan/Transjordan 122, 287, 322
Joseph, Keith 337, 374
Joynson-Hicks, Sir William 153
Jung, Carl Gustav 80

Kádár, János 279, 419
Kamenev, Leon 137, 151, 210
Kapp, Wolfgang von 121
Karadzic, Radovan 436, 442, 448
Kashmir 316
Kellogg-Briand Pact 156
Kemal, Mustafa 127–8
Kennan, George F. 246–7
Kennedy, Edward 333; John F. 296, 298, 299, 302–3, 308–9; Robert 309, 327
Kenya 260, 261, 325, 464
Kerensky, Alexander 105, 111
Kesselring, Field Marshal 228
Keynes, John Maynard 121, 124, 142, 162, 167, 170, 182, 194, 221, 225
Khomeini, Ayatollah 373, 379, 384
Khrushchev, Nikita 262, 275, 279, 280, 290, 296, 299, 302–3, 310, 418
King, Martin Luther 309, 327
Kinnock, Neil 395, 432
Kitchener, Lord 4, 13, 94, 97
Kohl, Helmut 417, 434
Korea 11, 25, 26, 34, 48, 252–3, 256, 259, 260, 262, 462
Kosovo 78, 435, 452–3, 463–5
Kosygin, Alexei 310
Knox-Johnston, Robert 333
Kuwait 424, 428

Labour Party 39, 44, 60, 99, 109–10, 114, 126, 130, 131, 134–5, 138–9, 152, 159, 168, 171, 172, 174, 188, 192, 198, 208, 227, 230, 289, 300, 306, 380, 384–6, 394–5, 398, 433–4, 444–5, 451, 457–8; Clause Four 110, 135, 234, 289, 300, 306, 398, 451; and Europe 339, 360, 385–6, 437; ILP 7, 15, 134, 174; Militant Tendency 380; and trade unions 353–5, 364
Lamont, Norman 433, 437, 438
Lane, Elizabeth 317
Lang, Archbishop Cosmo 153, 195
Lansbury, George 134–5, 174
Lansdowne, Lord 9–10, 25, 62–3, 68–9, 466
Laos 296, 298
Laurence, Timothy 434
Laval, Pierre 190–1
Lawrence, Ruth 403
Lawson, Nigel 393, 404, 411–16 *passim*, 421, 422
League of Nations 115, 117, 118, 120–2 *passim*, 150, 153, 161, 164, 181, 184, 186–92 *passim*, 224
Lebanon 122, 287, 347, 365, 392–3, 403, 407–8
Leeson, Nick 452
Lenin, V.I. 23, 74, 104, 111, 120, 132, 137
Lennon, John 383
Levien, Max 116
Levin, Bernard 317
Lewinsky, Monica 460, 464
Liberals 13–14, 29, 36–8, 40–6, 50–2, 61, 109, 126, 131, 139, 140, 149–51, 159, 167, 169, 176, 204, 303, 317, 354–5, 368–9, 412; Lib–Lab pact 369
Libya 332, 369, 399
Lie, Trygve 238
literature 39, 48, 55, 84, 95, 96, 99, 133, 140, 143, 158, 163, 178, 191, 192, 198, 210, 213, 250, 285, 297, 301
Livingstone, Ken 392
Lloyd, Selwyn 277, 278, 289, 295, 299–300, 304
Lloyd George, David 6, 13, 16, 29, 38, 42, 51–2, 56, 58, 62, 70, 73, 80, 85, 90–2, 94, 97, 126–9, 139–41 *passim*, 148, 149, 151, 159, 162, 171, 219; as PM 102, 109, 114–15, 118, 123–4, 126
local government 16, 375, 423, 451; reform 155–6
lock-outs 65–6, 146
London 12, 23, 30, 31, 38, 42, 112, 143, 168–9, 209, 211, 288, 392, 410
Lords, House of 40, 44–5, 51, 56–8, 61–4, 68–9, 109, 386, 459, 466
Lubbock, Eric 303
Lutyens, Sir Edwin 201, 227
Lynn, Vera 214

MacArthur, General Douglas 222, 253, 254, 256
MacDonald, Malcolm 189, 196; Ramsay 130, 134, 138, 195, 198, as PM 134–9, 159–89
Macedonia 24, 54, 77–8, 83, 435, 453
Macleod, Iain 289, 308, 337
Macmillan, Harold 96, 268, 272, 277, 278, 281, 407; as PM 281–307
Major, John 415, 422, 423; as PM 426–58
majority, age of 335
Makarios, Archbishop 282, 287, 291
Malawi (Nyasaland) 264, 312
Malaya 257, 260, 283
Malenkov, Georgi 262, 264, 268, 275, 290
Mallory, George Leigh 182, 266
Manchuria 25, 26, 33, 34
Mandela, Nelson 422, 447–8
Mao Zedong 185, 249, 320, 365
Marconi, Guglielmo 12, 59; Company scandal 79–80
Margaret, Princess 275, 297, 364
Markievicz, Countess 109
Marples, Ernest 289, 308
Marshall, George C. 240, 246
Marten, Neil 361
McCarthy, Joseph 263
McGregor, Ian 397
medicine 16, 39, 67, 87, 126, 143, 154, 222, 265, 326, 329, 333, 449; abortion 326; insulin 126, 143, 265; penicillin 154, 222

Menzies, Robert 205, 264, 277
Middle East 106–7, 166, 237–8, 287, 346–7, 352, 379, 392, 424 *see also individual countries*
Milosevic, Slobodan 436, 441, 448, 452, 463–5 *passim*
Mitchell, Senator George 453, 461
Mitterrand, Francois 328, 404
Molotov, Vyacheslav 248, 290
Moltke, Helmuth von 83, 91
monarchy 8, 32–3, 443, 454–5, 459, 466–7
Monnet, Jean 252
Montenegro 77–9 *passim*
Montgomery, Field Marshal 204, 217, 219, 222, 228
Morant, Robert 15–16, 45
Moro, Aldo 372
Morocco 41, 42, 70
Morrison, Herbert 215, 234, 255, 272
Mosley, Sir Oswald 167
Mossadeq, Mohammed 256–7
motor cars 23, 30, 38, 66, 83–4, 113, 157, 178, 193, 273, 291, 396; accidents 38, 157, 273; speed records 154, 158, 182
motorways 288, 289, 291, 308
Mountbatten, Lord 241–3, 245, 260, 277, 377, 458
MPs, payment of 73
Mubarak, Hosni 388
Mudania Convention (1922) 128–9
Mugabe, Robert 320, 378
music 80, 84, 96, 98, 140, 154, 163, 175, 178, 191, 205, 214, 227, 270, 285, 288, 294, 301, 305, 348, 388
Mussolini, Benito 117, 131, 140, 142, 151, 184, 189, 200
mutinies 112–13; Black Sea 33–4; Invergordon 172–3; Petrograd 105; Vladivostok 34

Nagy, Imre 263, 279
Nasser, Gamal Abdel 270, 276–9 *passim*, 287, 322–3
National Government 168, 171–86
nationalization 110, 114, 131, 227, 239–40, 244, 248, 365, 386
NATO 47, 118, 189, 246, 248, 249, 259, 267, 272, 274, 281, 282, 308, 320, 352, 383, 416, 434, 441, 463–5
Navy 9, 10, 27–8, 45, 52, 87, 93, 143, 161, 165, 196, 209
Neave, Airey 259, 377
Nehru, Jawaharlal 216, 237, 241, 243, 245
Netherlands 164, 281
New Zealand 128, 168, 322, 360, 390
Nicholas II 9, 11, 24, 32–3, 47, 52, 89, 90, 103–5 *passim*, 111
Nigeria 320; Biafra war 322–3
Nightingale, Florence 64
Nixon, Richard 296, 337, 347, 351, 358
Noel Baker, Philip 161
Normandy landing 219, 222, 445
Norway 208, 214, 246, 289, 343
Nott, John 374, 389, 390
nuclear power 379, 406–7; weapons 27, 231–2, 245, 248, 256, 259, 265, 268–9, 274, 282, 284, 287, 297, 303, 373–4, 402, 406, 410, 422, 462; Polaris 303, 308, 373–4; SDI 395–6, 402, 406; tests 269, 297, 310, 357, 462, ban 287, 310, 462

Obote, Milton 342
oil 256–7, 276, 278, 323, 350, 352–3, 365; North Sea 361
O'Neill, Terence 330, 331
opera 73, 98, 202, 370
Owen, David 367, 380, 384–6, 435–6, 442, 448
Oxfam 222

Paget, General Sir Arthur 86
Paisley, Reverend Ian 446, 453
Pakistan 237, 245, 316, 342, 462
Palestine 24, 106, 107, 122, 166, 197, 205, 237–8, 245; Palestinians 322, 333, 347, 442; PLO 333, 392, 442
Palme, Olaf 406
Panama Canal 84
Pankhurst, Christabel 23, 39, 55, 56; Emmeline 23, 76, 82, 87, 156; Sylvia 82, 87
Parker Bowles, Camilla 443, 454
Parkinson, Cecil 394, 395
Parliament Act (1910) 61–3, 68–9, 169
Parnell, Charles Stewart 74
pay 65, 148, 172–3, 205, 336, 355; equal 100, 205, 226; restraint 300, 344, 350, 355, 361, 366–7, 373
Pearson, Lester 264, 318
Peary, Robert E. 59
Persia 46–7, 53
Philip, Prince 233, 257, 260, 458–9
Philippines 406
Phillips, Mark 353
Piccard, Auguste 174
Poincaré, Raymond 92, 117, 132
Poland 117, 145, 184, 188, 202, 228, 234, 274, 279, 383, 418, 419
police 30, 114, 286, 375, 387; in N. Ireland 331, 332
Pompidou, Georges 328, 349
population 31, 81, 144, 178, 272, 335, 431
postal services 30
Powell, Enoch 283, 285, 299, 308, 325, 361
Powers, Gary 296
press 4, 57, 73, 102, 135, 139, 151, 167, 168, 179, 200–1, 234, 304, 325, 344–5
Prior, James 337, 359, 439

privatization 375, 399, 431
Profumo, John 306, 307
protectionism 130–1, 140, 176
public works 159, 162, 167, 177–8, 194

Quisling, Vidkun 214

Rabin, Yitzhak 442, 453
racing, car 133, 154, 288; horse 98, 266, 271, 370, 396
racism 286, 324–5, 364, 365
RADAR 189–90
radio 16, 31, 43, 59, 67, 79, 113, 133, 144, 178, 201, 213–14, 258, 275, 304–5, 377
RAF 187, 190, 196, 209, 228–30
Rahman, Sheikh Mujibur 342
railways 30, 66, 84, 194, 244, 284, 308; accidents 411
rationing, clothing 233, 248; coal 124; food 108, 114, 204–5, 207, 232, 236, 239, 244, 248, 259, 270; petrol 219, 353
Reagan, Ronald 382, 388, 392, 395–6, 399, 402, 406, 408, 416
rearmament 6, 183, 187, 188, 198, 200, 257–8
Redmond, John 61, 74
Redwood, John 450
Reith, John 144, 152
religion 5–6, 16, 18, 45, 68, 153, 224, 273, 335
reparations 117, 121, 127, 131, 137–8, 160–1, 188; Dawes Plan 138; Young Plan 160
Reuter, Admiral von 117–18
Reynolds, Albert 440–1, 446
Rhodesia 264–5, 312–13, 316, 319–20, 364, 367, 378
Ribbentrop, Joachim von 183
Ridley, Nicholas 389, 391
riots 48, 72, 327–8, 331, 365, 387–8, 403, 423, 455; in Ulster 336, 339, 387
Roberts, Lord 27, 70
Robinson, Peter 447
Rodgers, William 380, 384–6
Röhm, Ernst 184
Romania 77, 94, 234, 274, 419
Rommel, Erwin, 211, 217, 219, 222
Roosevelt, F.D. 177–8, 194, 216, 217, 230; Theodore 33, 106
Rosebery, Lord 36, 37
Rugova, Ibrahim 464
Rundstedt, Field Marshal von 228
Russia 10, 11, 24–6 *passim*, 32–5, 43, 48, 52–4, 78, 79, 83, 88, 89, 92, 94, 103–5, 111, 127; civil war 111, 120; Jews om 24, 34, 48, 52; relations with 26, 46–7, 111; revolution 35, 103–5, 111, 134
Rutherford, Ernest 55, 118, 227

Sadat, Anwar 346, 369, 371, 379, 388
sailing 297, 333, 342, 449
Salisbury, Lord 6, 7, 10, 12–14 *passim*, 21
Samuel, Herbert 79, 146, 171, 172
Sands, Bobby 386–7
Saudi Arabia 153, 353, 383
Scargill, Arthur 398
Schmidt, Helmut 373
Schuman, Robert 252, 281
Scotland 68, 100, 194, 317, 355, 363, 431, 465
Scott, Robert Falcon 24, 71, 80, 84
SDP 380, 384–6
Serbia 24, 54, 77–9 *passim*, 83, 88, 89, 94, 435, 436, 441, 442, 448, 453, 463–5
Seychelles 368
Shackleton, Ernest 24
Sharon, Ariel 278
Shaw, G.B. 110, 143
Shepard, Alan 299
Shinwell, Emmanuel 221, 234, 240
shipping 8, 48, 202, 207, 215, 228; *Herald of Free Enterprise* 410; *Titanic* 73; warships 8, 9, 28, 45, 52, 80, 87, 196, 202, 214–15
Short, Nigel 370
Sidney Street siege 71–2
Silkin, Lewis 235
Simon, Sir John 99, 165, 186, 196, 203
Simpson, Wallis 191–2, 195, 407
Sinclair, Clive 370
Singapore 143, 214, 237
Smith, Adam 19, 21
Smith, Ian 310, 312, 313, 316, 319–20, 364, 367, 378
Smith, John 432, 444, 447
smoking 157
Smuts, Jan 13, 47, 125
Snowden, Philip 134, 160, 170–2 *passim*, 174, 177
social security 21–2, 31, 50–2, 56–7, 73, 81, 155, 220–2, 234, 235
Solzhenitsyn, Alexander 358, 449
South Africa 4, 13, 47–9, 168, 294–5, 443, 447–8
Soviet Union 132–3, 151, 157, 193, 197, 202, 210, 239, 240, 248, 252, 253, 261, 262, 267, 274, 277, 279, 284, 290, 296, 298–9, 323, 328, 340–1, 346–7, 383, 395, 438; and Cuba 296, 302–3; and Eastern Europe 234, 263, 279, 328, 362, 383; and Germany 200, 217, 219, 267 *see also* Berlin; reform in 401–2, 417–18, 428–30 *passim*; relations with 137–40, 142, 161, 187, 261, 263–6 *passim*, 274–5, 340–1, 402; space programme 284, 290, 298–9, 396
Spaak, Paul 238
Spain 41, 133, 192, 199, 200, 320, 348; civil war 192–3, 200, 205
Spencer, Lady Diana 383, 388; Princess of Wales 393, 434, 443, 453, 454, 456–7

Spring, Dick 446
Stalin, Joseph 74, 104, 132–3, 137, 142, 151, 157, 210, 231, 234, 240, 247, 262, 280
Steel, David 317, 365
Stevenson, Adlai 261
stock exchange crash 157, 162, 408–9
Stoltenberg, Thorvald 442
Stolypin, Pyotr 48, 72, 104
Stonehouse, John 364
Stopes, Marie 110–11
Stresemann, Gustav 156, 161
strikes 65–6, 72, 74, 81, 87, 97, 100, 112–14, 124, 130, 136–7, 185, 186, 227, 248, 274, 296, 337, 339, 343, 350, 353, 357, 373, 381; General 146–9; miners' 65, 74, 87, 97, 146, 226–7, 343, 353–4, 397–8, 400
Sudan 166, 238, 254, 269
suffragettes *see* women
Summerskill, Dr Shirley 217–18
Sun Yat-sen, Dr 72
Switzerland 202, 289
Syria 107, 122, 322, 347, 352, 369

Tanganyika/Tanzania 122, 464
tariffs 20, 22–3, 36, 40, 57, 63, 130–1, 175, 176
taxation 57–8, 88, 94, 98, 142, 152, 172, 193, 197, 198, 221, 286, 311, 366, 376, 381, 411–12; poll 422–3, 427
Tebbit, Norman 394, 404–5
telephone 87, 99, 185, 199
television 144, 202, 275, 280, 293, 304, 318, 353, 377, 396, 412
tennis 98, 358, 396, 403
Tenzing, Sherpa 182, 266
Tereshkova, Valentina 396
terrorism 238, 261, 272, 282–3, 291, 340, 347–8, 356–7, 365, 372, 377–8, 382, 387, 399, 403, 439–41 *passim*, 453, 463; Prevention of Act (1974) 356, 446
test tube baby 333
Thailand 239
Thant, U 320, 323
Thatcher, Margaret 337, 359, 360, 450, 458; as PM 374–426, 439, 440
theatre 24, 31, 48, 98, 99, 143, 152, 163, 175, 191, 201, 213, 227, 261–2, 280, 285, 286, 297, 305, 348, 365, 384, 388, 410
Theresa, Mother 456
Thomas, James 113, 114, 149, 162–3, 167, 172
Thorneycroft, Peter 283, 285, 394, 412
Thorpe, Jeremy 304, 355, 364
three-day week 350, 353
Tisdall, Sarah 399
Tito, Marshal 234, 245, 434
Toller, Ernst 117
towns, new 235
Townsend, Peter 275
trade 7, 19, 65, 144–5, 169–70, 175–6, 273, 295, 299, 335–6, 437; free 19–23, 28–9, 36–7, 40, 63, 130–1, 137, 140, 175–6; GATT 226
trade unions 7, 15, 65–6, 72, 81, 100, 113, 114, 124, 145–9, 152, 185–6, 204, 329–30, 336, 337, 339, 350, 353–5, 364, 366, 375, 386, 397–8; TUC 15, 99, 114, 145–9 *passim*, 171, 204, 350, 354, 366
treaties, Anglo-Irish (1921) 123, 125–6; Jeddah (1927) 153; Locarno (1925) 141, 196; London (1839) 89, 92, (1913) 83, naval (1930) 166; Maastricht (1991) 427, 437, 438, 445; Middle East (1979) 379; Nanking (1842) 459; NATO (1949) 47, 249; Pacific (1929) 161; Rome (1957) 281; SALT (1979) 379, 382; test ban 287; Versailles (1919) 115, 117–18, 120, 121, 131, 186–8 *passim*; Washington naval (1929) 161, 164
Trevelyan, Charles 136, 169
Trotsky, Leon 104, 132, 137, 142, 151, 157, 210
Truman, Harry S. 230, 238, 249, 256, 259
Tudjman, Franjo 452
Turkey 24, 53–4, 77–8, 83, 94, 96, 106, 115–16, 127–8, 303, 357

Uganda 24, 342, 365
Ulster 74, 82, 85–6, 125–6, 139, 247–8, 283, 330–2, 337, 339–40, 344–6, 356–7, 364, 365, 371, 377–8, 386–7, 400–1, 409, 438–41, 445–7, 451, 453, 455, 461; Bloody Sunday 344–5; IRA 283, 331, 337, 339–40, 345, 347, 348, 356–7, 366, 377, 387, 391–2, 399, 409, 439–41, 445, 447, 453, 455, 461, decommissioning 447, 453, 461; Sinn Fein 377, 400, 438–41, 446, 453, 461; Unionists 74–5, 85–6, 125, 331, 345–6, 356–7, 401, 440, 447, 461
Umberto II 238
unemployment 54, 65, 81, 112, 124, 130, 136, 144, 155, 159–60, 167, 171, 172, 186, 188, 194, 220, 255, 283, 335, 336, 339, 343, 361, 363, 365, 381, 423, 431, 451; benefits 124, 130, 170–2 *passim*, 188; Jarrow march 194
United Nations 222, 225, 238–9, 245, 253, 264, 278, 322, 323, 390, 391, 427–8, 435–6, 441, 442, 453; UNPROFOR 435
United States 7, 33, 93, 94, 132, 156, 162, 165, 177–8, 201, 225, 240, 248, 249, 296, 327, 337–8, 460–1; bases in Britain 282, 286, 296, 373–4, 396, 398–9, 402; and Communism 240, 246–7, 256, 262–3; and Cuba 90, 296, 298, 302–3; and Europe 240, 246, 249, 252, 282, 308, 416; and Germany 118, 416, First World War 105–6, Second 203, 213; and Iraq 443; and

Ireland 377, 446, 453; and Israel 323, 352, 369; and League of Nations 120, 121, 224; and Middle East 276–9, 287, 369, 383, 392–3; and Soviet Union 246–7, 290, 299, 302–3, 395, 406; and Vietnam 313, 315–16, 326–7, 337, 347, 351; Irangate 408; Jewish lobby 238, 323; relations with 161, 164, 212–13, 217, 238–40 *passim*, 246, 252, 253, 256, 259, 261, 276–9, 282, 303, 308, 321, 351, 368, 391, 402, 416, 446; space programme 284, 290, 299, 337–8, 370, 396, 407; Watergate 347, 351–2, 358
universities 17–118, 45; vote 156, 169, 244

Vance, Cyrus 435–6, 442
Vansittart, Sir Robert 197
Victoria, Queen 1–2
Vietnam 296, 313, 315–16, 320, 326–7, 337, 347, 351
Villa, Pancho 133
Visnier, Kurt 116

wages 87, 114, 145–9 *passim*, 171, 194, 295, 299–300, 336, 343–4, 350, 355, 364, 366–7; minimum 74, 87, 427 *see also* pay
Waite, Terry 407–8
Wales 16, 65, 72, 194, 201, 226, 355, 363, 465–6
Walesa, Lech 383, 396
Wallis, Barnes 219
Walters, Alan 414, 415
war 26–7, 94–5, 284; Arab-Israeli 245, 322–3, 352–3; Balkan 24, 74, 77–9 *passim*, 83; Biafra 322–3; Boer 3–6, 13, 264; Bosnia 441; 'cod' 287, 364; Falklands 390–1; Gulf 383, 427–8; Indochina 239, 262–3, 267; Indo-Pakistan 316; Iran–Iraq 383; Korean 252–4, 256, 259, 262; Kosovo 463; Lebanon 365, 403; Pakistan 342; Russo-Japanese 26–7, 33–4, 103; Spanish Civil 192–3; Vietnam 313, 315–16, 320, 326–7, 337, 347, 351; World, First 85, 89, 91–111, 181, 182, 264 469–79, Second 202–3, 209, 211, 214–15, 217, 219, 222, 227–30 264, 480–6
Warsaw Pact 267, 272, 274, 328
weather 38, 74, 87, 207, 239–40, 251, 364, 365, 408, 422
Webb, Sydney and Beatrice 110
Welensky, Roy 265
Wells, H.G. 101, 181, 201
West, Frederick and Rosemary 448
West Indies, bases 212–13; immigrants 273–4
Westland affair 404–6, 421, 422
Wheatley, James 135–6
White, Harry Dexter 225
Whitehouse, Mary 318
Whitelaw, William 345–6, 359, 374, 422
Wilberforce, Judge Lord 343
Wilhelm II 1, 8–11 *passim*, 33, 41, 52, 83, 88–90 *passim*, 116
Wilkinson, Ellen 234
William, Prince 393, 466
Williams, Shirley 361, 380, 384–6
Williams, Tom 234
Willoughby de Broke, Lord 69, 85
Wilson, Edward 24, 84
Wilson, Harold 255, 306; as PM 310–36 *passim*, 341, 355–63 *passim*
Wilson, Sir Henry 86, 123
Wilson, Woodrow 80, 106, 115, 118, 121, 224
women 151, 159, 217; education 17–18; employment 99, 100, 113, 226; ordination 448; suffrage 23, 39, 42–4, 55, 64–5, 76, 82, 87, 108–9, 152, 156
Woodward, Admiral Sandy 391
work camps 160
World Bank 225, 276, 326
Wright, Peter 413

Yeltsin, Boris 402, 428, 434, 438, 464
Yemen 77
Young, Owen 160, 165
Yugoslavia 163, 184, 234, 434–6

Zahedi, General 257
Zaire 371–2
Zambia (N. Rhodesia) 264, 312
Zapata, Emiliano 72
Zec, Philip 215, 233
Zeppelin, Count von 59
Zetland, Marquess of 215
Zinoviev, Grigori 132, 137, 139, 140, 151, 210
Zionism 24, 107, 122, 166, 197, 238, 239
Zog, King 238

Acknowledgements

BBC Worldwide would like to thank the following for permission to reproduce copyright material. While every effort has been made to trace and acknowledge all copyright holders, we would like to apologize should there have been any errors or omissions.

Pages 29, 51, 58, 63, 147, 183, 273, 300, 315, 332, 425 Parlimentary copyright material is reproduced with the permission of the Controller of Her Majesty's Stationery Office on behalf of Parliament; pages 29, 208, 233, 257 Reproduced with permission of Curtis Brown Ltd, London, on behalf of the Estate of Sir Winston S. Churchill. Copyright the Estate of Sir Winston S. Churchill; page 43 G.K. Chesterton March 1907 (*The Illustrated London News*); page 179 Leader from *The Times* 17 February 1933. Copyright Times Newspapers Limited 1933; page 193 H. Thornton Rutter 1936 (*The Illustrated London News*); page 201 Turnover from *The Times* 10 January 1938. Copyright Times Newspapers Limited 1938; page 209 *Women and Children Last* by Hilda Marchant, 1941 (Victor Gollancz); pages 211, 212, 229, 260 *Fringes of Power* by John Colville, 1985 (Hodder & Stoughton Publishers); page 280 Review of *Look Back in Anger* by Alan Pryce-Jones, *The Times* 26 May 1956. Copyright Times Newspapers Limited 1956; page 305 Obituary of Marilyn Monroe, *The Times* 6 August 1962. Copyright Times Newspapers Limited 1962; page 315 *Denis Healey: The Time of My Life* by Denis Healey, 1989. Reproduced by permission of Penguin Books Ltd; page 321 *The Castle Diaries 1964–1976* by Barbara Castle, 1984 (Weidenfeld & Nicolson); page 330 *A Life at the Centre* by Roy Jenkins, 1991 (Macmillan Publishers Ltd); page 346 *The Whitelaw Memoirs* by William Whitelaw, 1989. Reproduced by permission of the Estate of Lord Whitelaw.